Sticky Dilly Buns

VOLUME 1
OMNIBUS

STORY/PENCILS/LETTERS
Gisèle Lagacé

INKS
M. Victoria Robado (Shouri)
Gisèle Lagacé
Cassandra Wedeking
Saiful Remy "Eisu" Mokhtar

CHAPTER BREAK ILLUSTRATIONS
CH.1-4 **M. Victoria Robado (Shouri)**
CH.5-13 **Gisèle Lagacé**

SERIES EDITOR
T Campbell

FRONT/BACK COVER COLORS
Pete Pantazis

Follow us online at:
ma3comic.com

CONTENTS

AUTHOR'S MESSAGE

Thank you so much for picking up this collection. STICKY DILLY BUNS came about from my desire to explore more of Dillon, a character from my other series, MÉNAGE À 3. He and Amber had moved in together and their lives had drifted a bit from the others, so I had a cast of two ready-made for a spinoff. And then came Ruby. I had no idea how important the introduction of Amber's sister would be, but Ruby moving in basically made the series what it is, and her scenes with Dillon practically wrote themselves. It ended up being a short series but one that I love deeply, and that I'm very proud of. I hope you enjoy it as much as I had fun making it.

--GISÈLE

Howdy, Neighbor

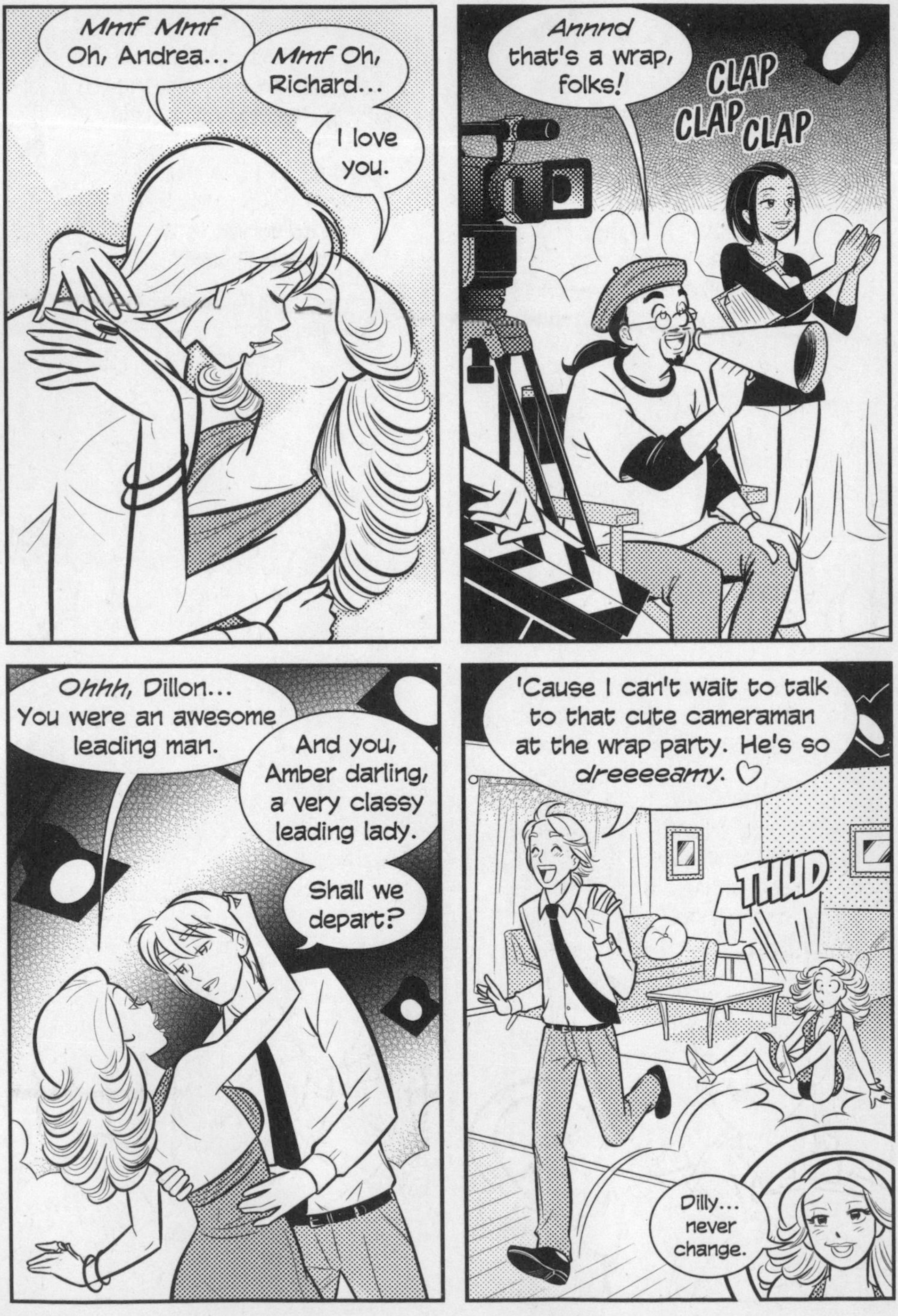
Mmf Mmf
Oh, Andrea...
Mmf Oh, Richard...
I love you.
Annnd that's a wrap, folks!
CLAP CLAP CLAP
Ohhh, Dillon... You were an awesome leading man.
And you, Amber darling, a very classy leading lady.
Shall we depart?
'Cause I can't wait to talk to that cute cameraman at the wrap party. He's so dreeeeamy. ♡
THUD
Dilly... never change.

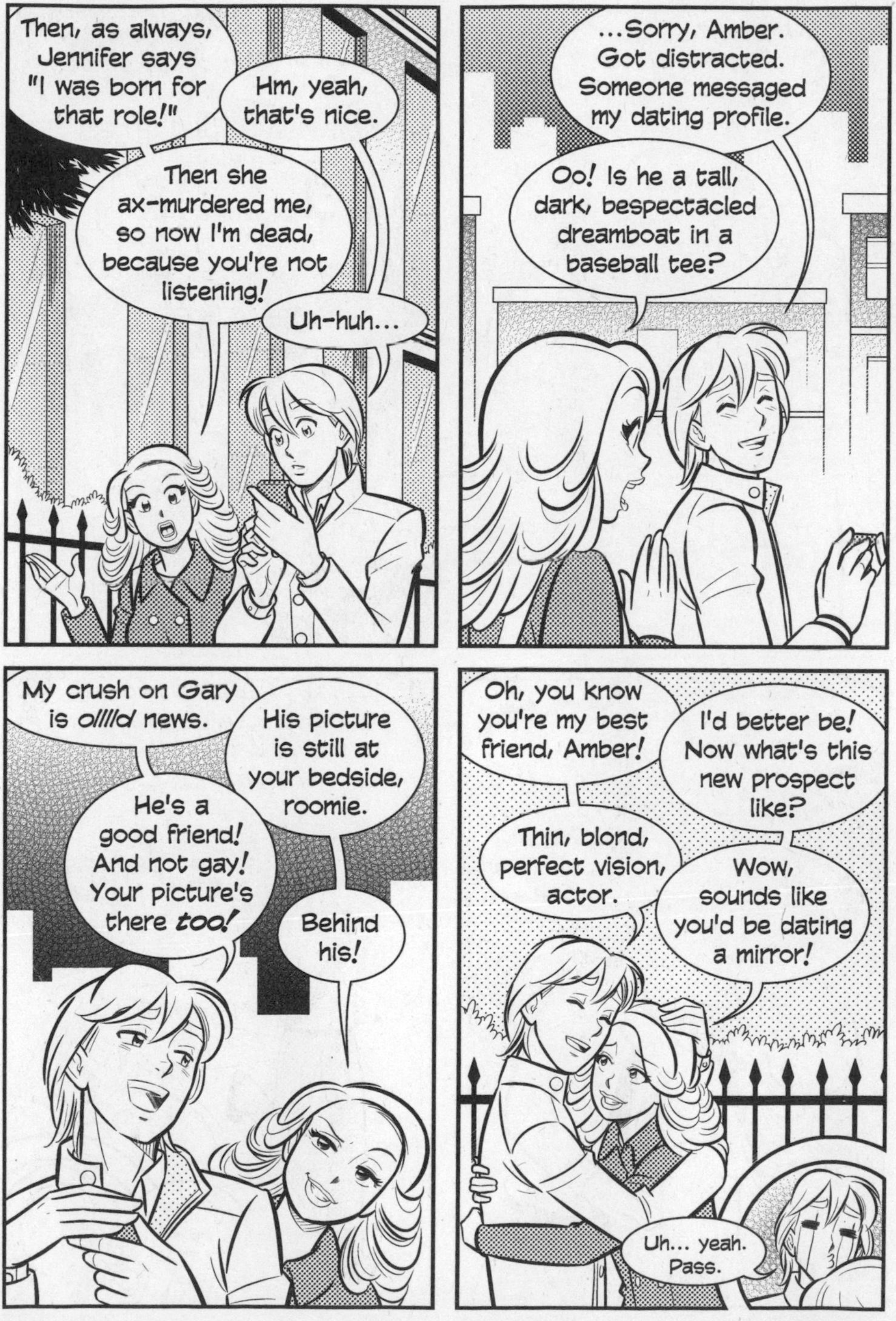
Then, as always, Jennifer says "I was born for that role!"
Hm, yeah, that's nice.
Then she ax-murdered me, so now I'm dead, because you're not listening!
Uh-huh...
...Sorry, Amber. Got distracted. Someone messaged my dating profile.
Oo! Is he a tall, dark, bespectacled dreamboat in a baseball tee?
My crush on Gary is *olllld* news.
His picture is still at your bedside, roomie.
He's a good friend! And not gay! Your picture's there ***too!***
Behind his!
Oh, you know you're my best friend, Amber!
I'd better be! Now what's this new prospect like?
Thin, blond, perfect vision, actor.
Wow, sounds like you'd be dating a mirror!
Uh... yeah. Pass.

Going to the dépanneur.* Need anything, Amber?

Let me see...

Oh, hi, there... Moving in?

Yup. Hello, new neighbor!

Books!

*French for convenience store. It's Montreal, folks!

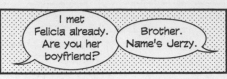

I met Felicia already. Are you her boyfriend?

Brother. Name's Jerzy.

Nice to meet you, Jerzy. I'm--

Tampons! One box!

Girlfriend?

Roommate.

And hurry up, Dilly-poo. I want my full body massage. ♡♡

Roommate. Right... I better let you go.

It's... not what you think! I enjoy giving massages! I... I could give you one too!

May take you up on that...

Dilly-poo.

8

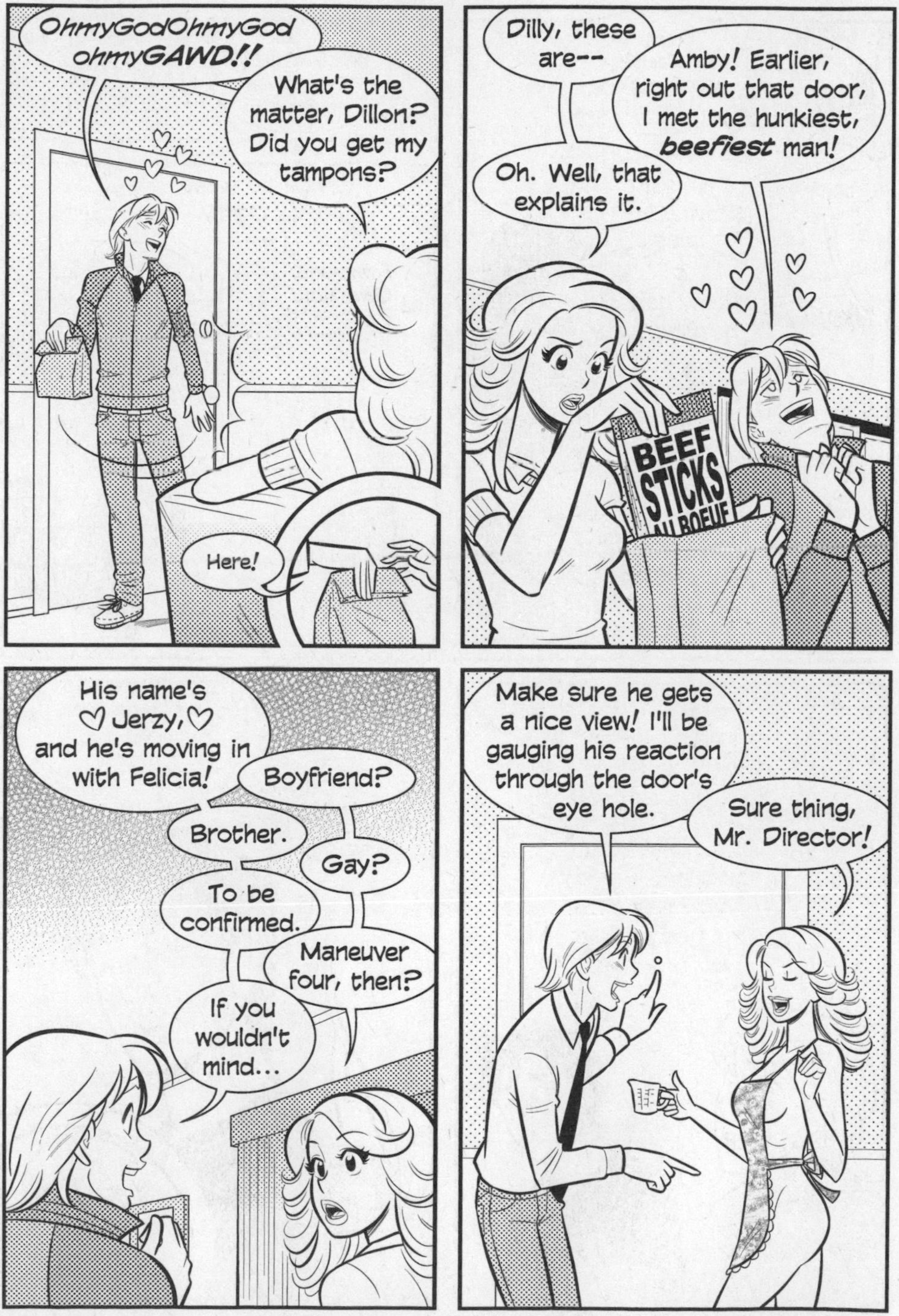
OhmyGodOhmyGod ohmyGAWD!!
What's the matter, Dillon? Did you get my tampons?
Here!
Dilly, these are--
Amby! Earlier, right out that door, I met the hunkiest, beefiest man!
Oh. Well, that explains it.
BEEF STICKS
His name's ♡ Jerzy, ♡ and he's moving in with Felicia!
Boyfriend?
Brother.
Gay?
To be confirmed.
Maneuver four, then?
If you wouldn't mind...
Make sure he gets a nice view! I'll be gauging his reaction through the door's eye hole.
Sure thing, Mr. Director!

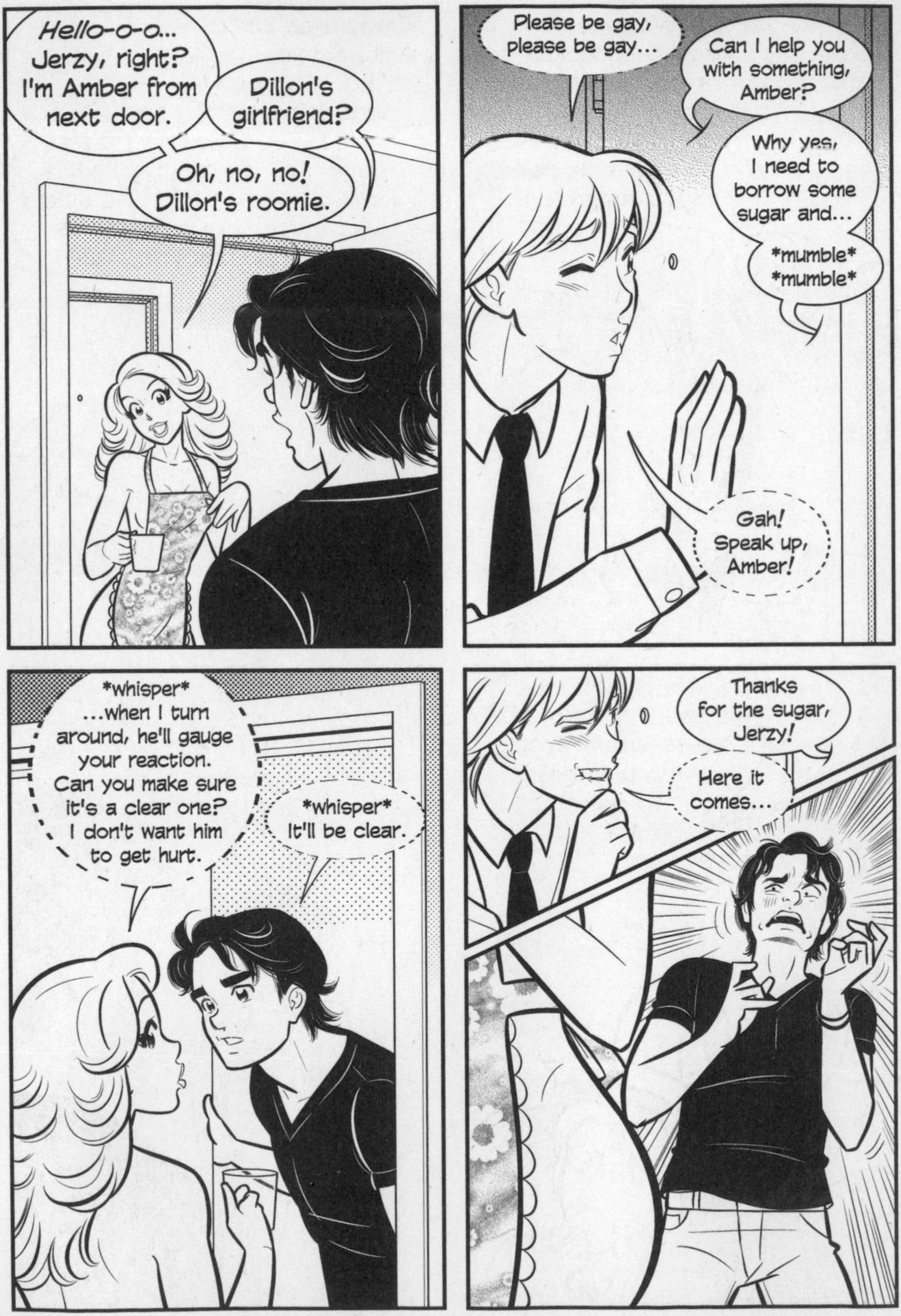
Hello-o-o... Jerzy, right? I'm Amber from next door.
Dillon's girlfriend?
Oh, no, no! Dillon's roomie.
Please be gay, please be gay...
Can I help you with something, Amber?
Why yes, I need to borrow some sugar and...
mumble *mumble*
Gah! Speak up, Amber!
whisper ...when I turn around, he'll gauge your reaction. Can you make sure it's a clear one? I don't want him to get hurt.
whisper It'll be clear.
Thanks for the sugar, Jerzy!
Here it comes...

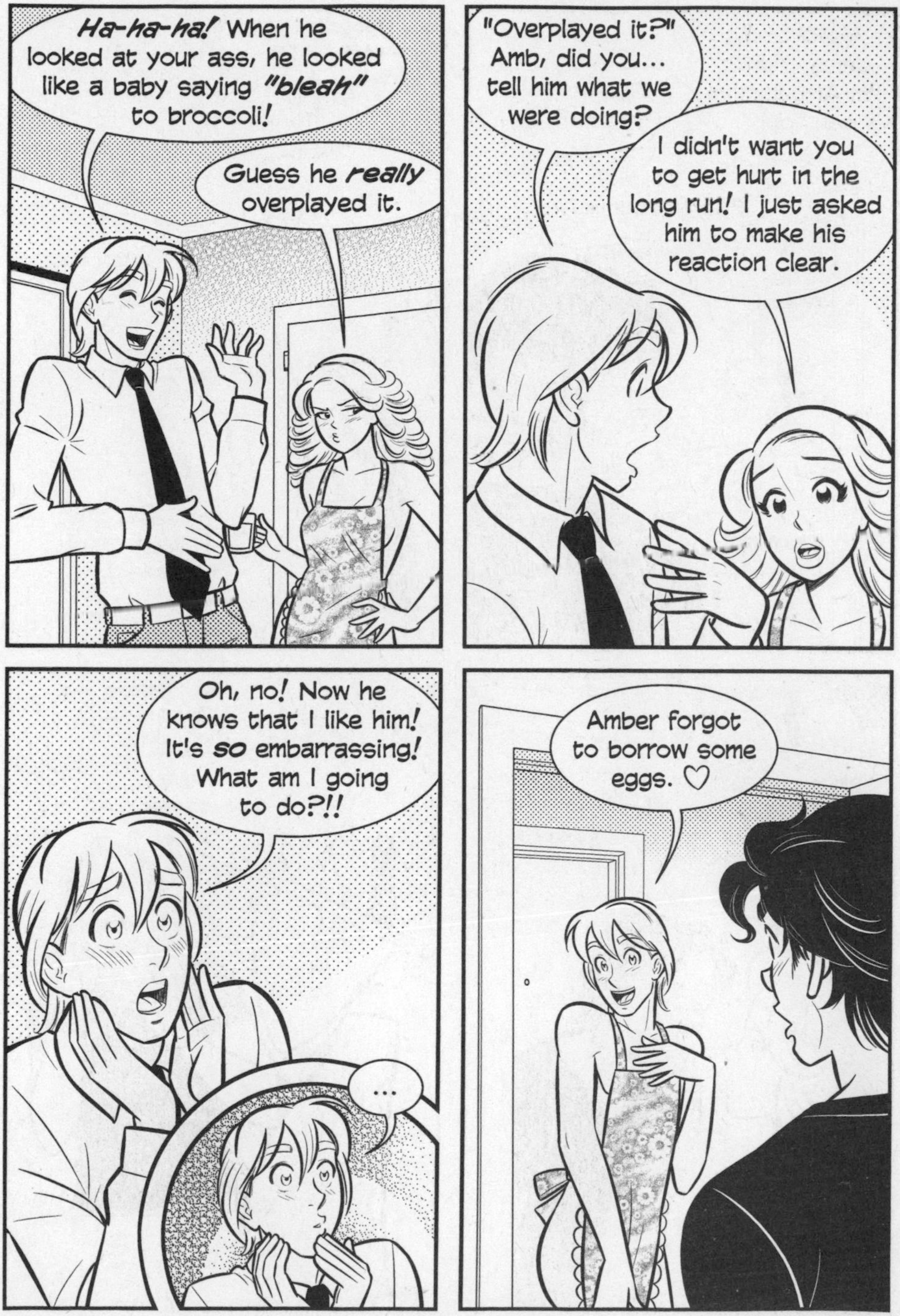
Ha-ha-ha! When he looked at your ass, he looked like a baby saying "bleah" to broccoli!
Guess he really overplayed it.
"Overplayed it?" Amb, did you... tell him what we were doing?
I didn't want you to get hurt in the long run! I just asked him to make his reaction clear.
Oh, no! Now he knows that I like him! It's so embarrassing! What am I going to do?!!
...
Amber forgot to borrow some eggs. ♡

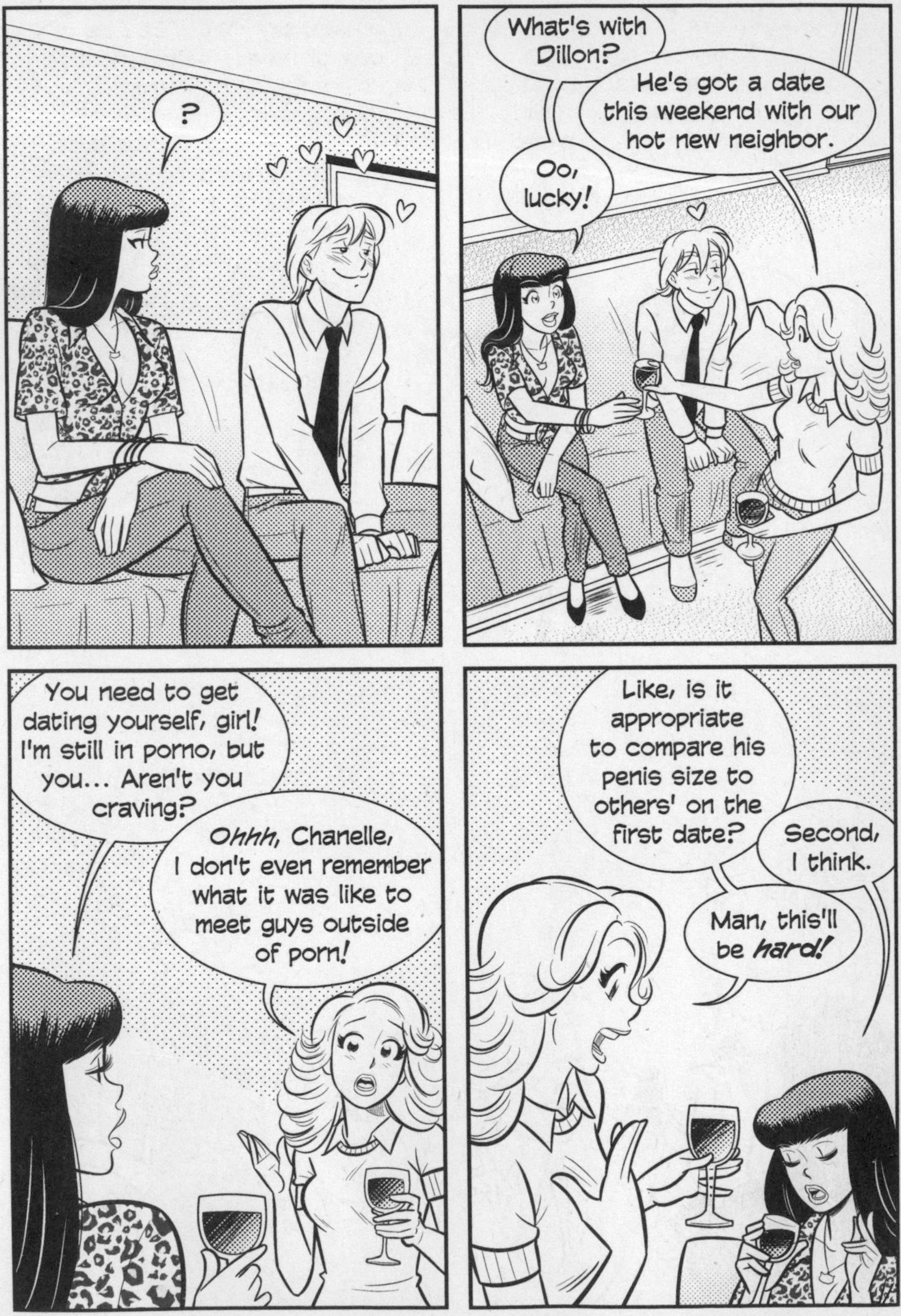
?
What's with Dillon?
He's got a date this weekend with our hot new neighbor.
Oo, lucky!
You need to get dating yourself, girl! I'm still in porno, but you... Aren't you craving?
Ohhh, Chanelle, I don't even remember what it was like to meet guys outside of porn!
Like, is it appropriate to compare his penis size to others' on the first date?
Second, I think.
Man, this'll be ***hard!***

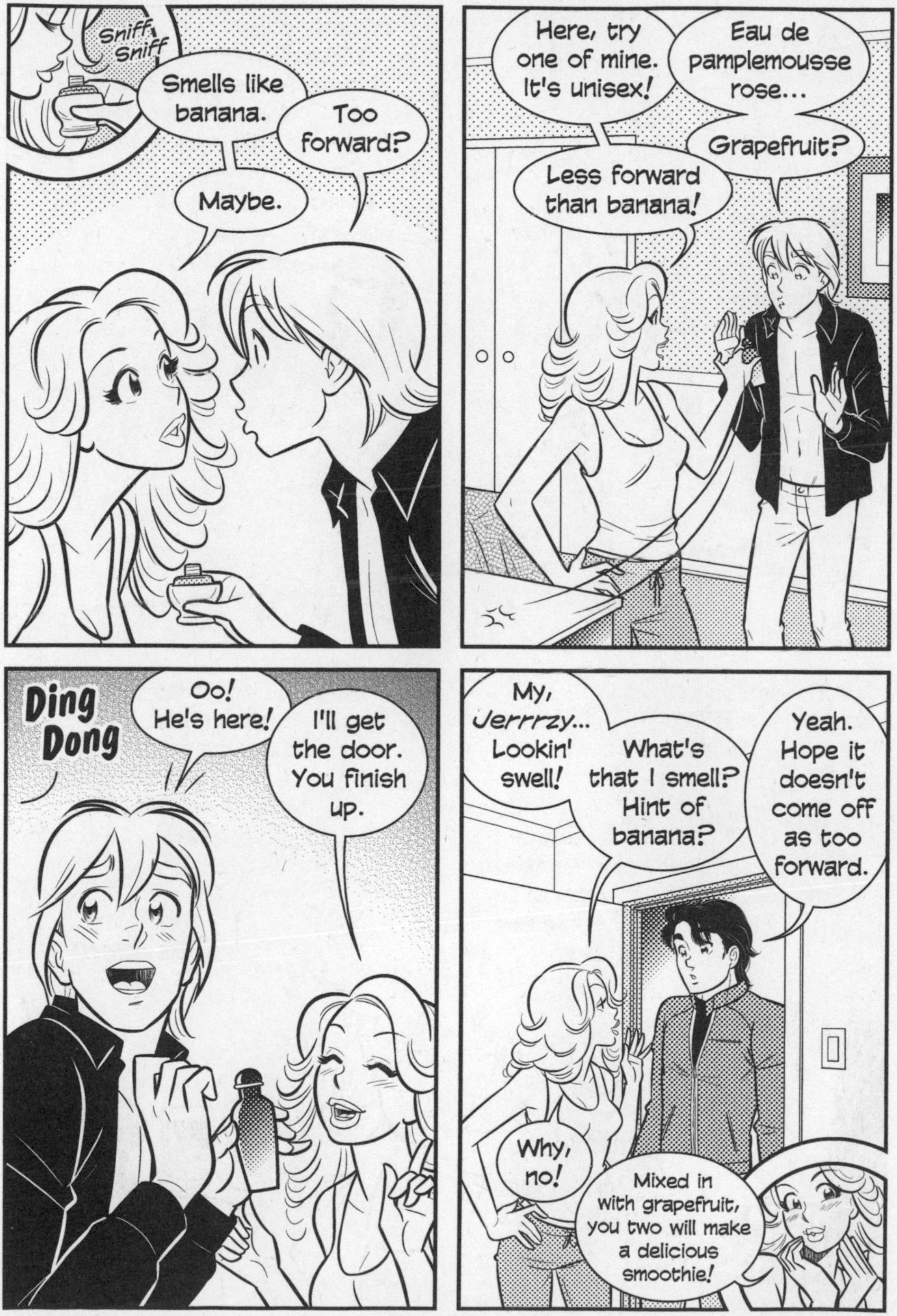
Sniff Sniff
Smells like banana.
Too forward?
Maybe.
Here, try one of mine. It's unisex!
Eau de pamplemousse rose...
Grapefruit?
Less forward than banana!
Ding Dong
Oo! He's here!
I'll get the door. You finish up.
My, Jerrrzy... Lookin' swell!
What's that I smell? Hint of banana?
Yeah. Hope it doesn't come off as too forward.
Why, no!
Mixed in with grapefruit, you two will make a delicious smoothie!

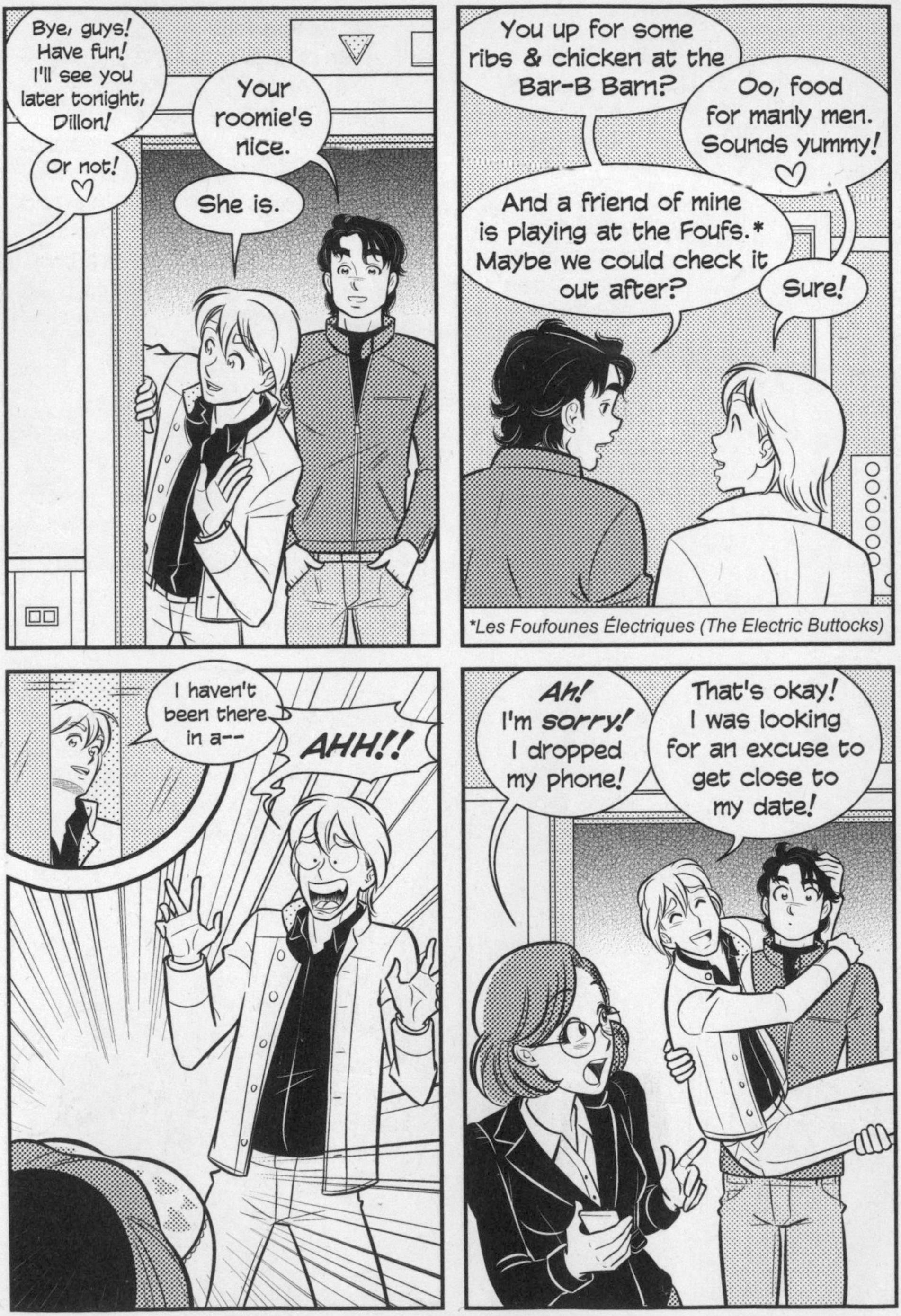
Bye, guys! Have fun! I'll see you later tonight, Dillon!
Or not! ♡
Your roomie's nice.
She is.
You up for some ribs & chicken at the Bar-B Barn?
Oo, food for manly men. Sounds yummy! ♡
And a friend of mine is playing at the Foufs.* Maybe we could check it out after?
Sure!
*Les Foufounes Électriques (The Electric Buttocks)
I haven't been there in a--
AHH!!
Ah! I'm sorry! I dropped my phone!
That's okay! I was looking for an excuse to get close to my date!

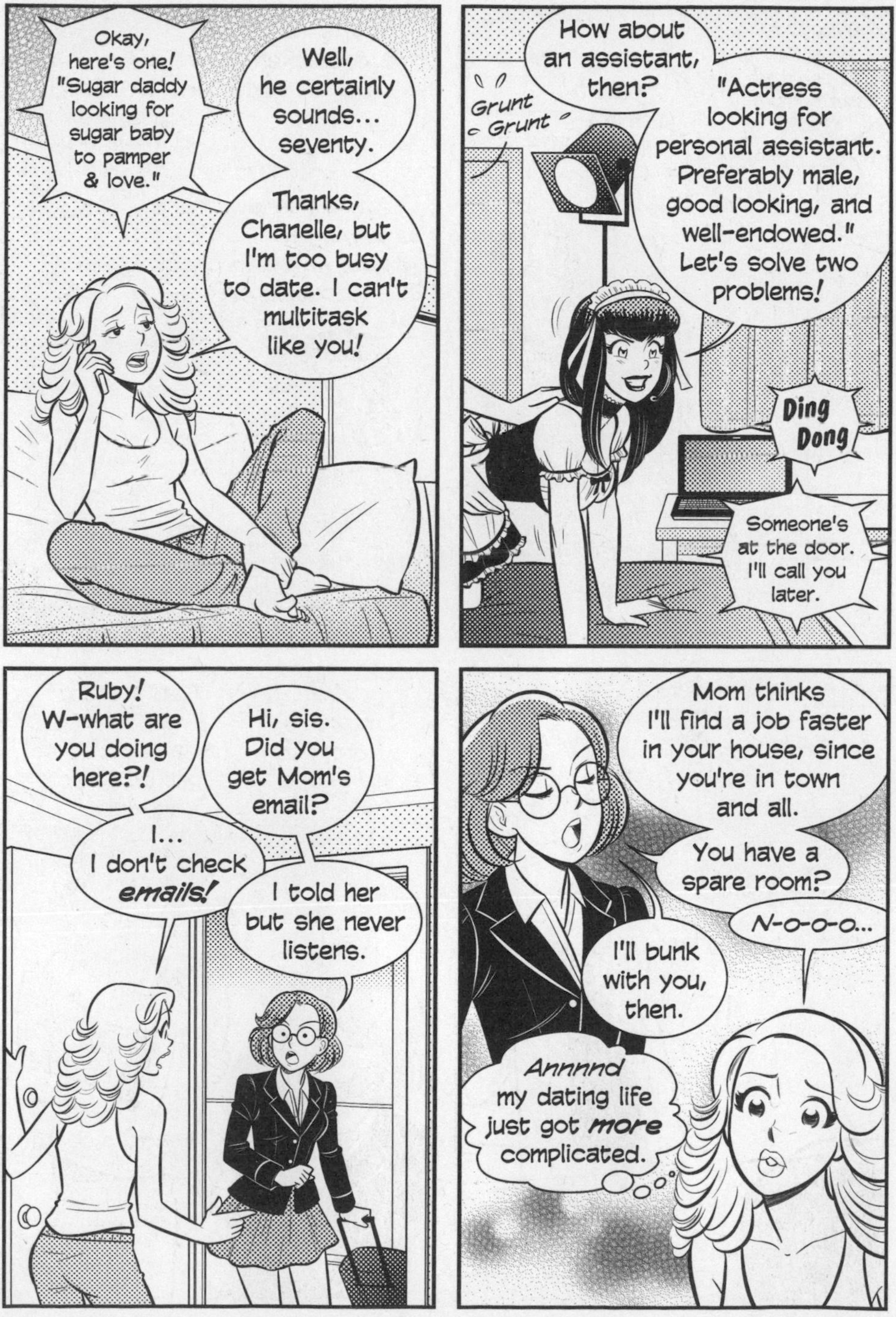

Okay, here's one! "Sugar daddy looking for sugar baby to pamper & love."
Well, he certainly sounds... seventy.
Thanks, Chanelle, but I'm too busy to date. I can't multitask like you!
How about an assistant, then?
Grunt Grunt
"Actress looking for personal assistant. Preferably male, good looking, and well-endowed." Let's solve two problems!
Ding Dong
Someone's at the door. I'll call you later.
Ruby! W-what are you doing here?!
Hi, sis. Did you get Mom's email?
I... I don't check *emails!*
I told her but she never listens.
Mom thinks I'll find a job faster in your house, since you're in town and all.
You have a spare room?
N-o-o-o...
I'll bunk with you, then.
Annnnd my dating life just got *more* complicated.

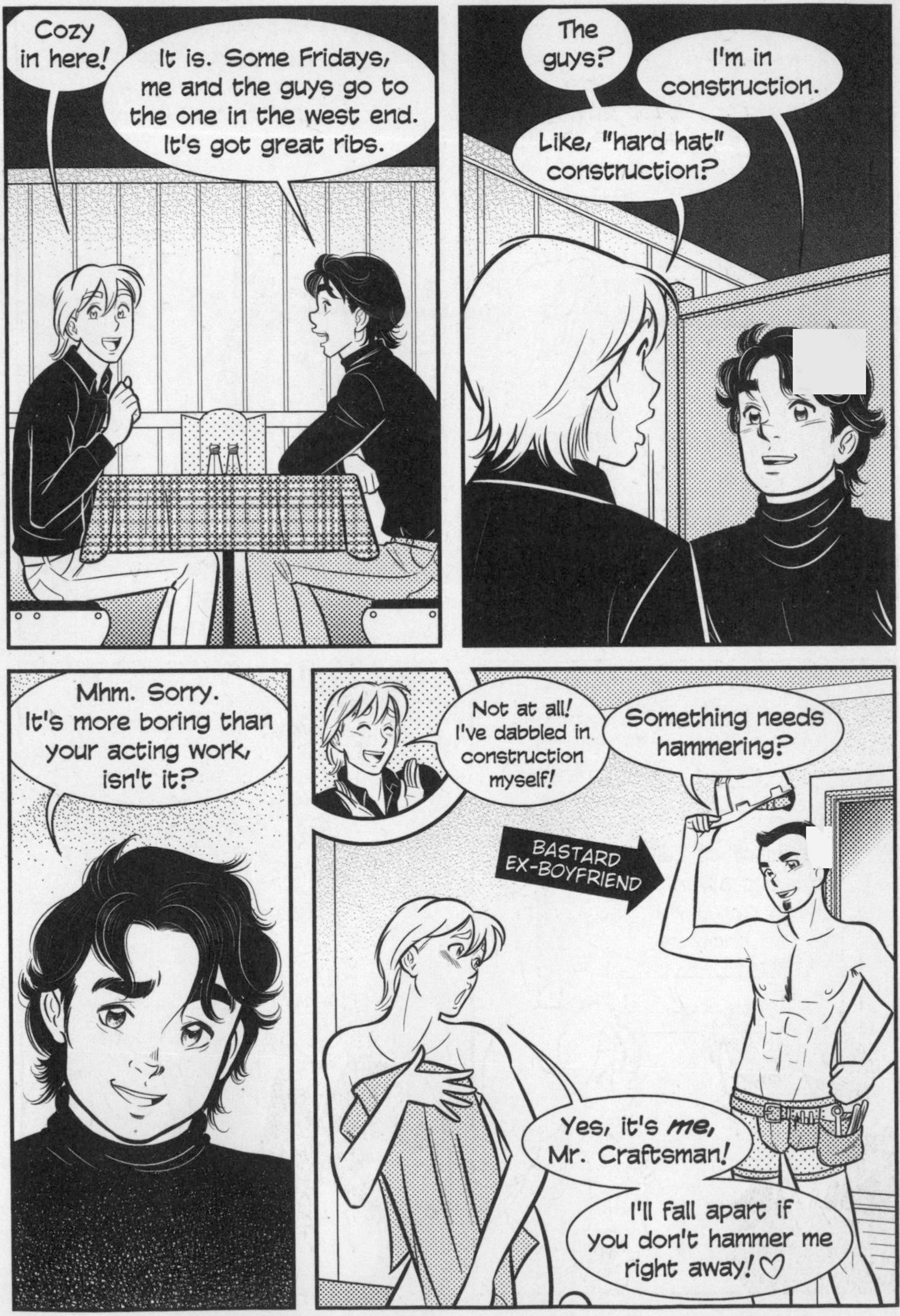

Cozy in here!
It is. Some Fridays, me and the guys go to the one in the west end. It's got great ribs.
The guys?
I'm in construction.
Like, "hard hat" construction?
Mhm. Sorry. It's more boring than your acting work, isn't it?
Not at all! I've dabbled in construction myself!
Something needs hammering?
BASTARD EX-BOYFRIEND
Yes, it's *me*, Mr. Craftsman!
I'll fall apart if you don't hammer me right away! ♡

So how's Mom & Dad's favorite daughter doing?

Ruby! Stop saying I'm Mom & Dad's favorite!

But you are! So long as I keep quiet about your porny past.

Though they'd probably forgive you. As they always do.

Sayyy! If you're looking for a job, that means you're done with school, right?

University, Amber. I got my B.B.A.

Grrrreat! Let's toast!

Uhhh, what's a B.B...

Bachelor of Business Administration, Amber! How could you not know--

BZZZZ

What's that...?

That's *my* B.O.B.!

B.O...?

Battery Operated Boyfriend.

Bzzz

Shall we toast?

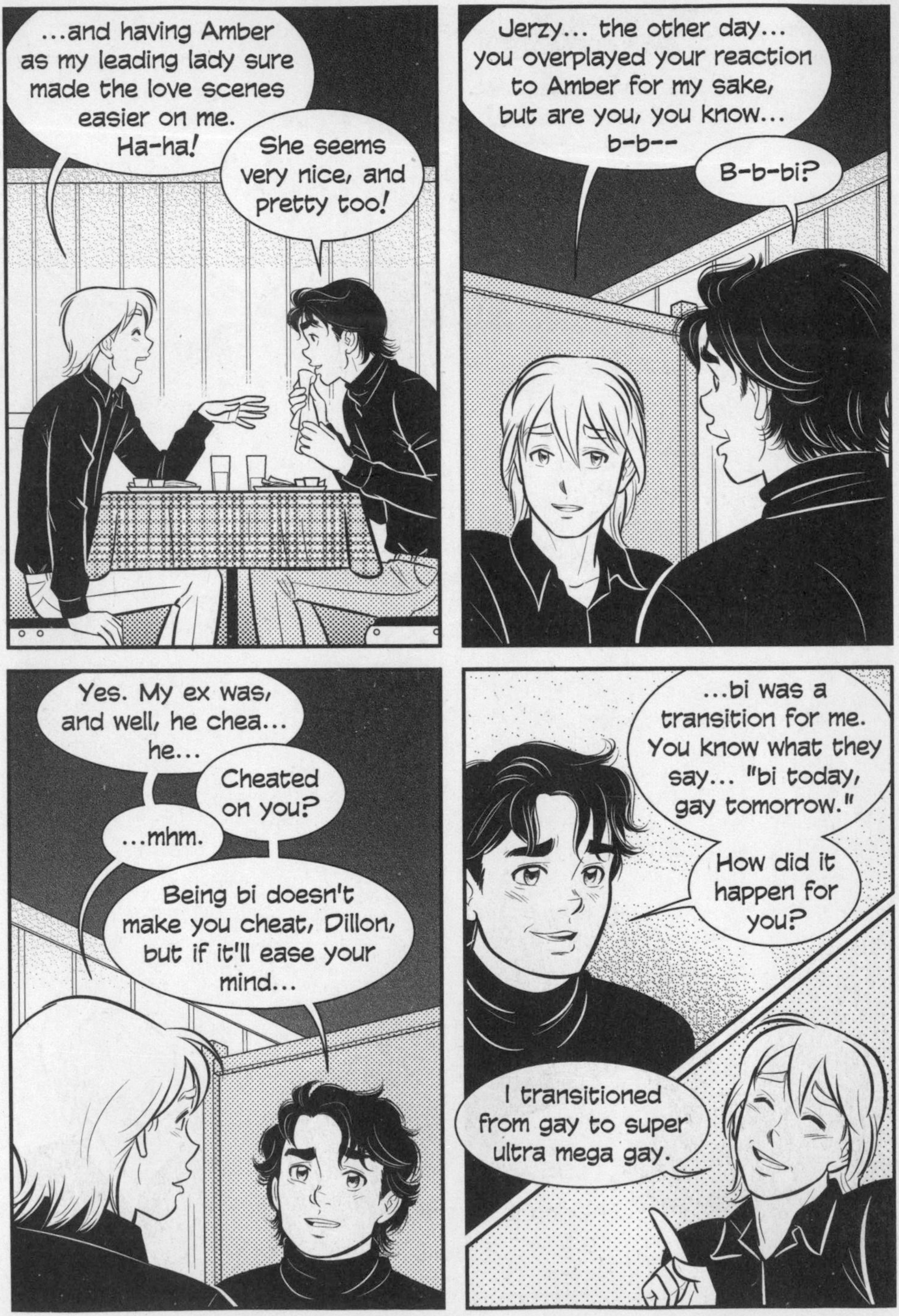
...and having Amber as my leading lady sure made the love scenes easier on me. Ha-ha!
She seems very nice, and pretty too!
Jerzy... the other day... you overplayed your reaction to Amber for my sake, but are you, you know... b-b--
B-b-bi?
Yes. My ex was, and well, he chea... he...
Cheated on you?
...mhm.
Being bi doesn't make you cheat, Dillon, but if it'll ease your mind...
...bi was a transition for me. You know what they say... "bi today, gay tomorrow."
How did it happen for you?
I transitioned from gay to super ultra mega gay.

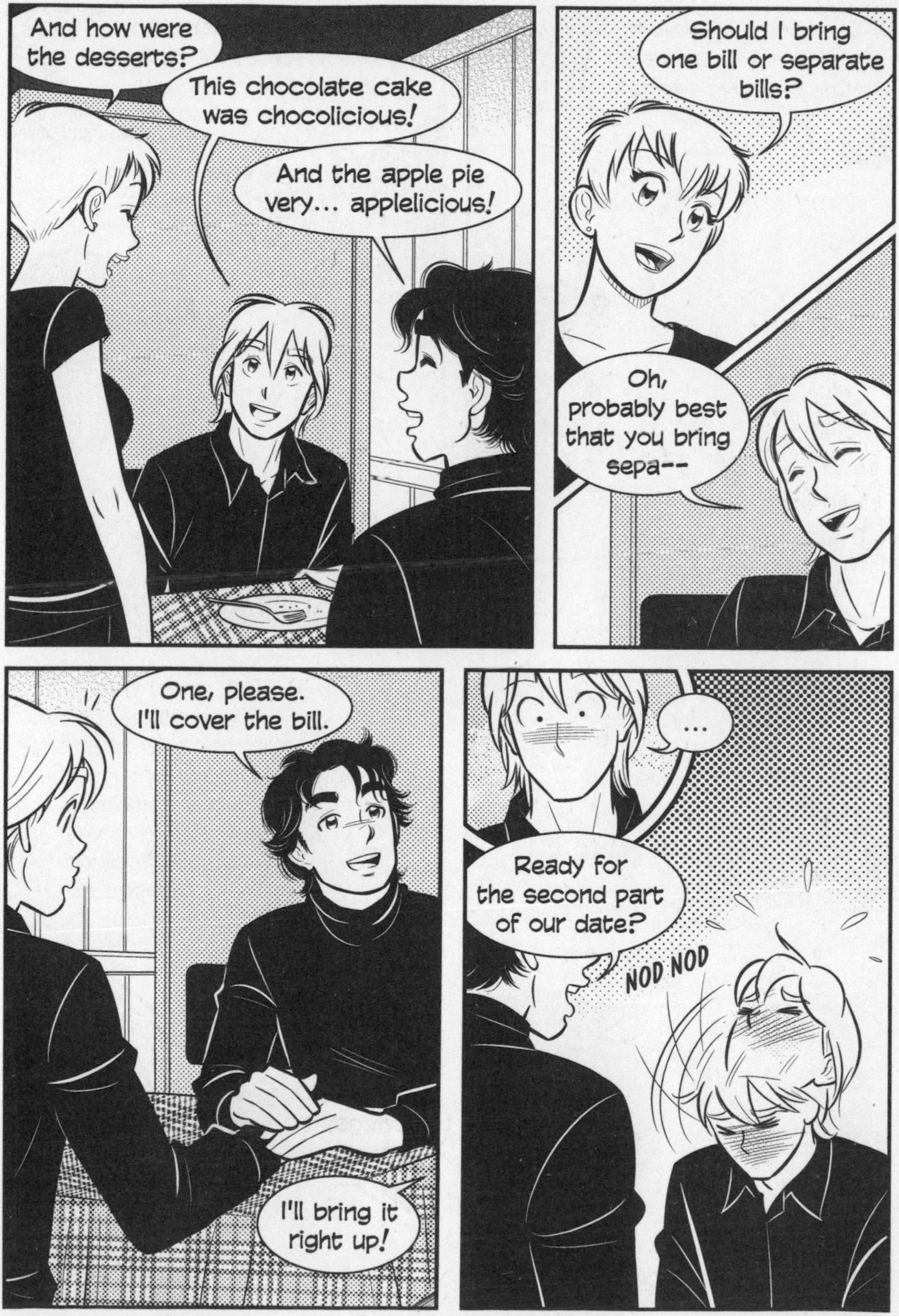
And how were the desserts?
This chocolate cake was chocolicious!
And the apple pie very... applelicious!
Should I bring one bill or separate bills?
Oh, probably best that you bring sepa--
One, please. I'll cover the bill.
I'll bring it right up!
...
Ready for the second part of our date?
NOD NOD

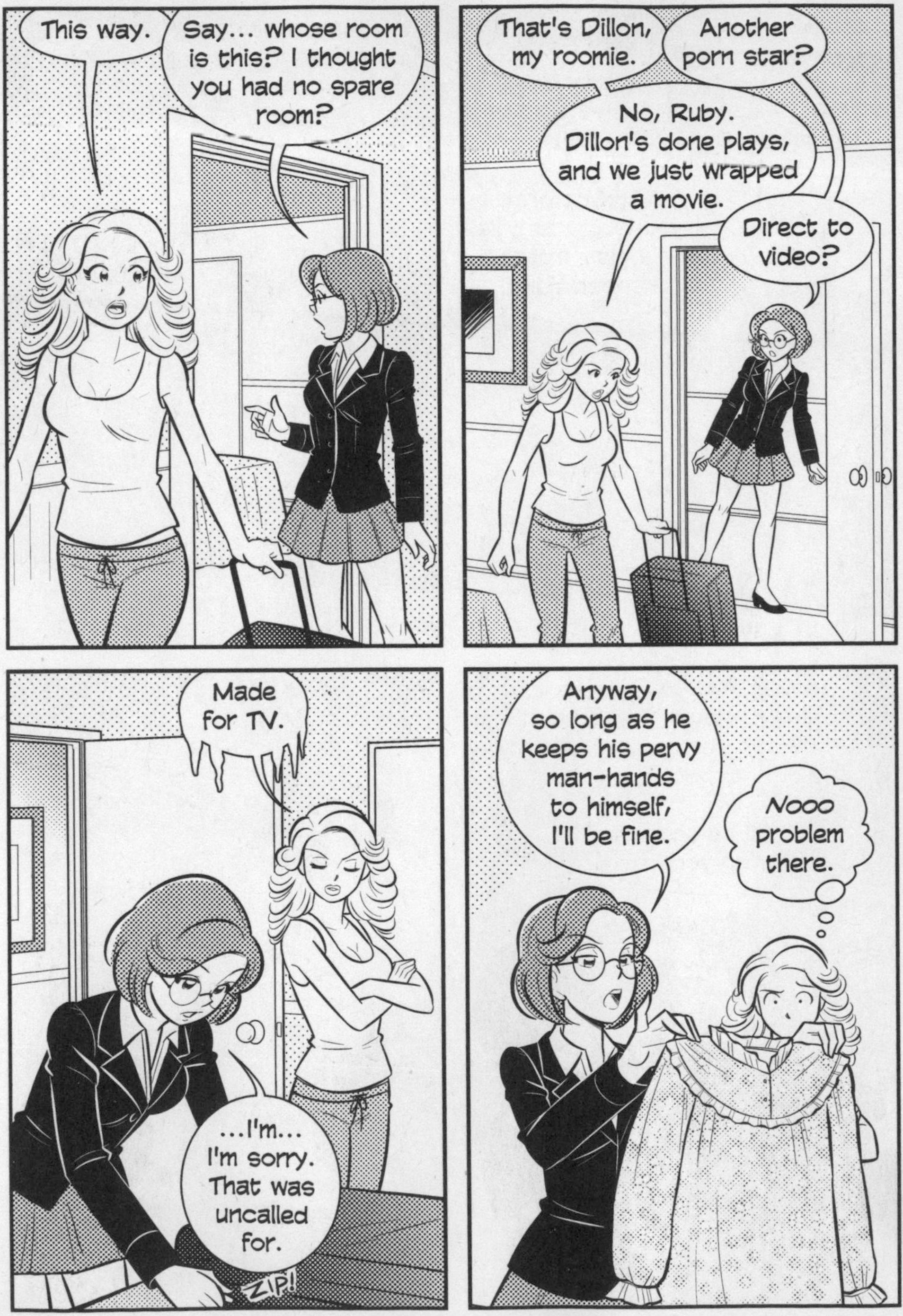
This way.
Say... whose room is this? I thought you had no spare room?
That's Dillon, my roomie.
Another porn star?
No, Ruby. Dillon's done plays, and we just wrapped a movie.
Direct to video?
Made for TV.
...I'm... I'm sorry. That was uncalled for.
ZIP!
Anyway, so long as he keeps his pervy man-hands to himself, I'll be fine.
Nooo problem there.

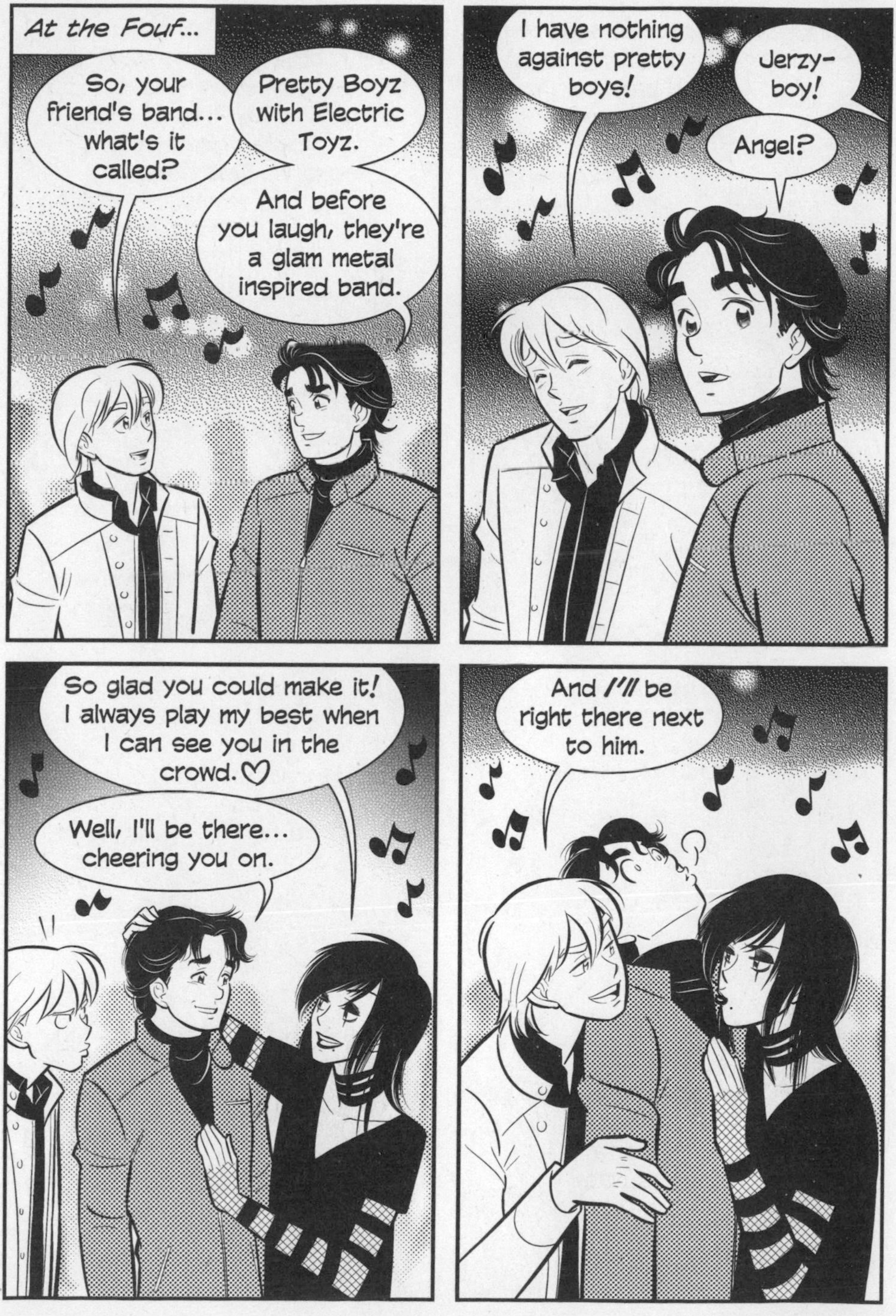
At the Fouf...
So, your friend's band... what's it called?
Pretty Boyz with Electric Toyz.
And before you laugh, they're a glam metal inspired band.
I have nothing against pretty boys!
Jerzy-boy!
Angel?
So glad you could make it! I always play my best when I can see you in the crowd. ♡
Well, I'll be there... cheering you on.
And *I'll* be right there next to him.

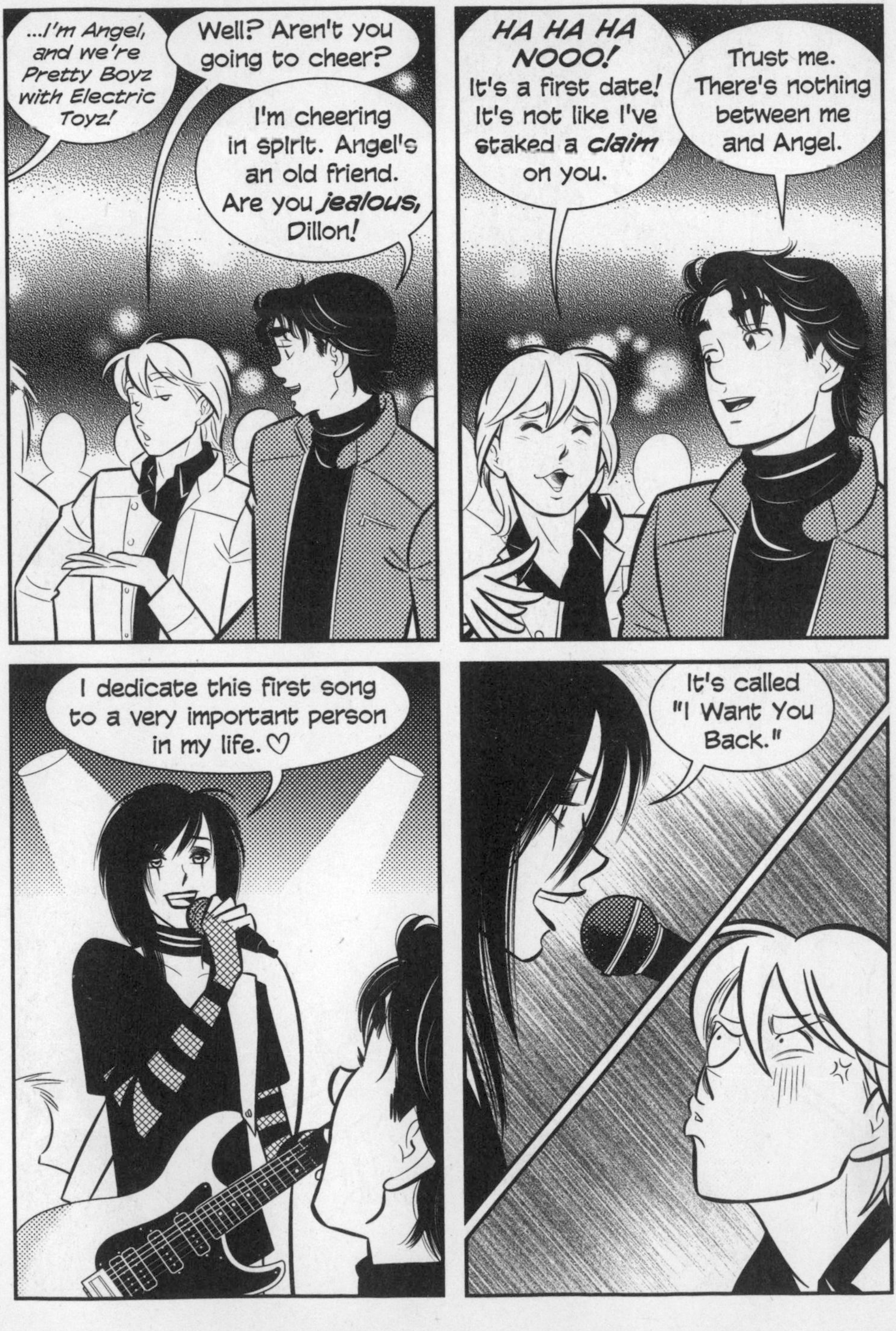
...I'm Angel, and we're Pretty Boyz with Electric Toyz!
Well? Aren't you going to cheer?
I'm cheering in spirit. Angel's an old friend. Are you *jealous,* Dillon!
HA HA HA NOOO! It's a first date! It's not like I've staked a *claim* on you.
Trust me. There's nothing between me and Angel.
I dedicate this first song to a very important person in my life. ♡
It's called "I Want You Back."

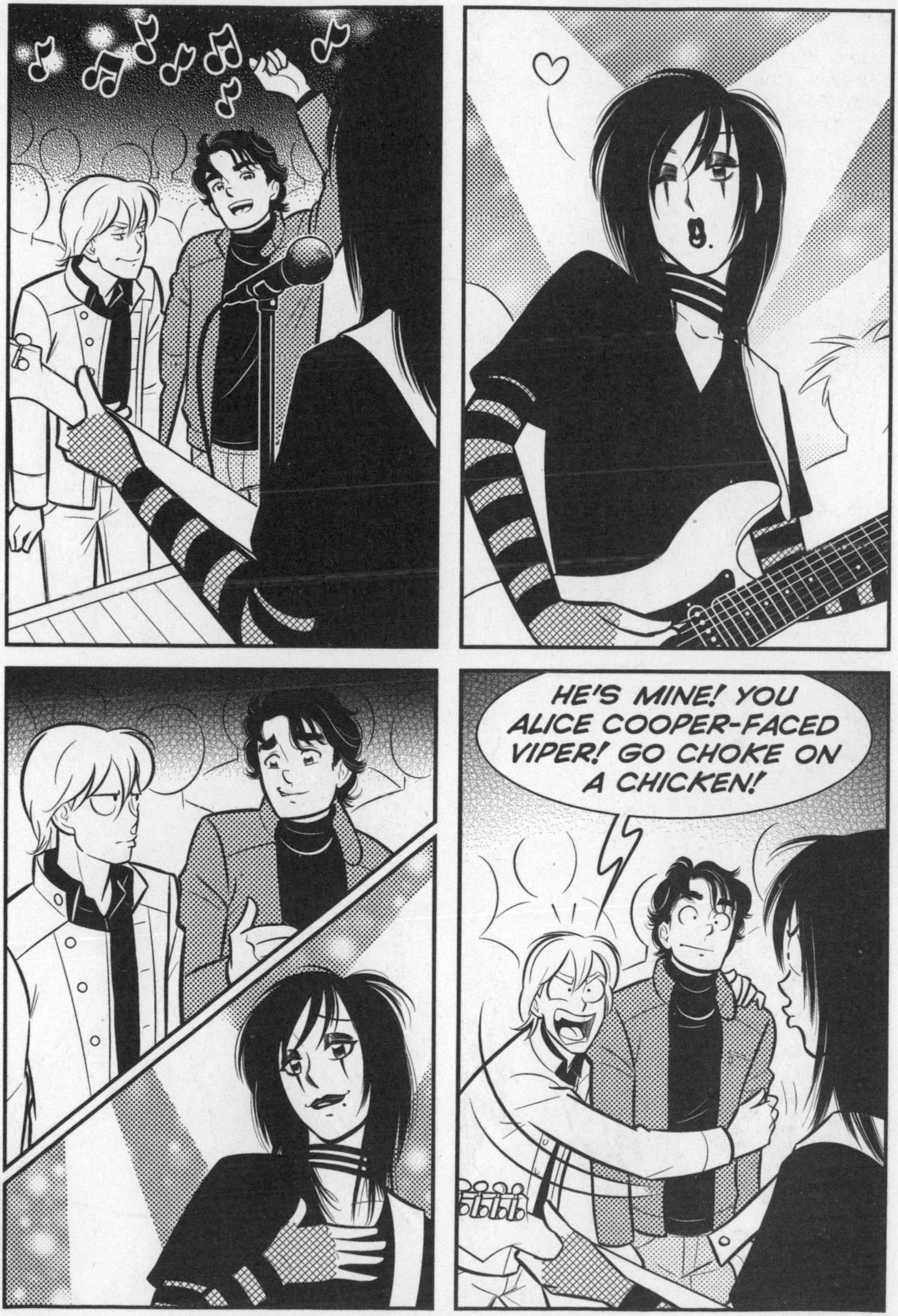
HE'S MINE! YOU ALICE COOPER-FACED VIPER! GO CHOKE ON A CHICKEN!

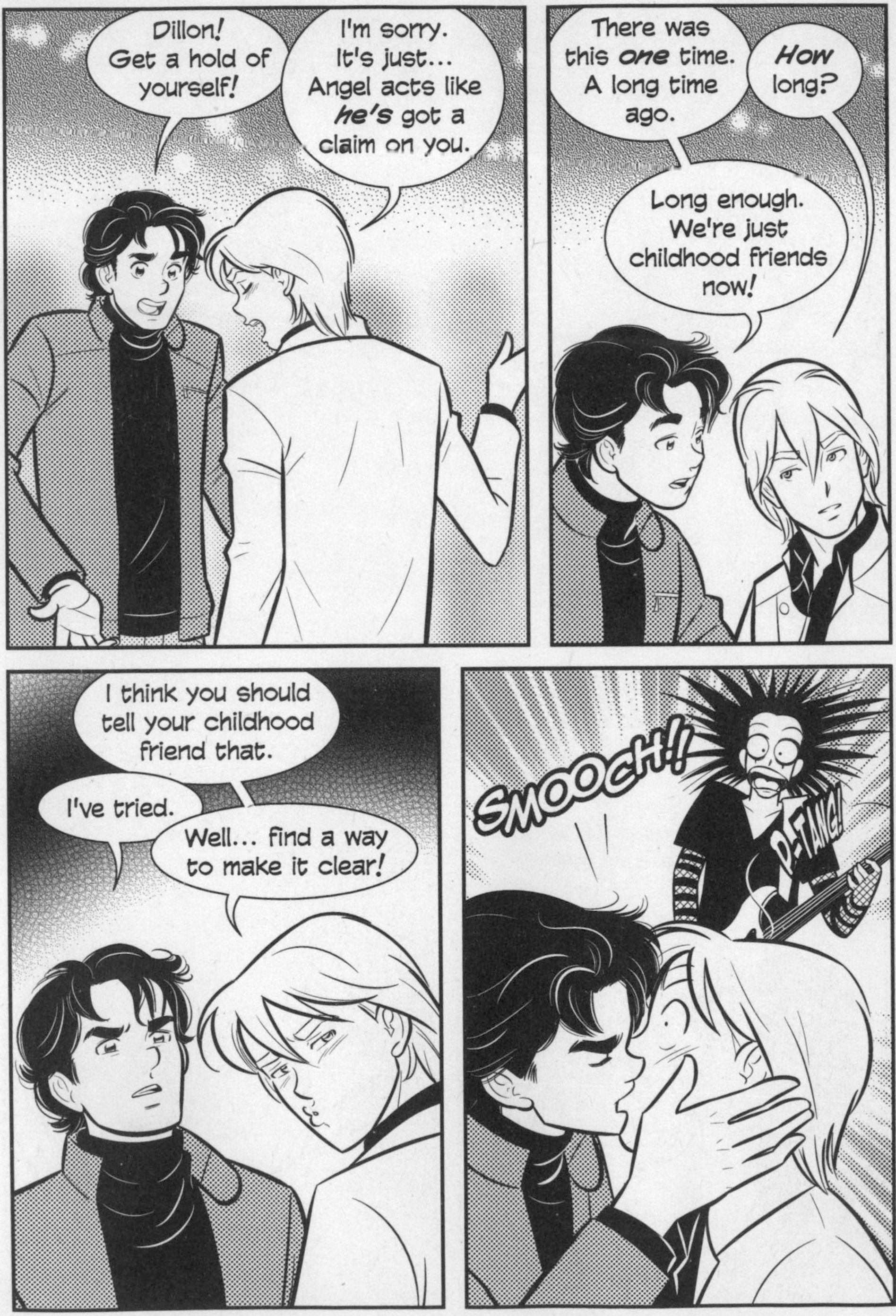
Dillon! Get a hold of yourself!
I'm sorry. It's just... Angel acts like *he's* got a claim on you.
There was this *one* time. A long time ago.
How long?
Long enough. We're just childhood friends now!
I think you should tell your childhood friend that.
I've tried.
Well... find a way to make it clear!
SMOOCH!!
D-TANG!

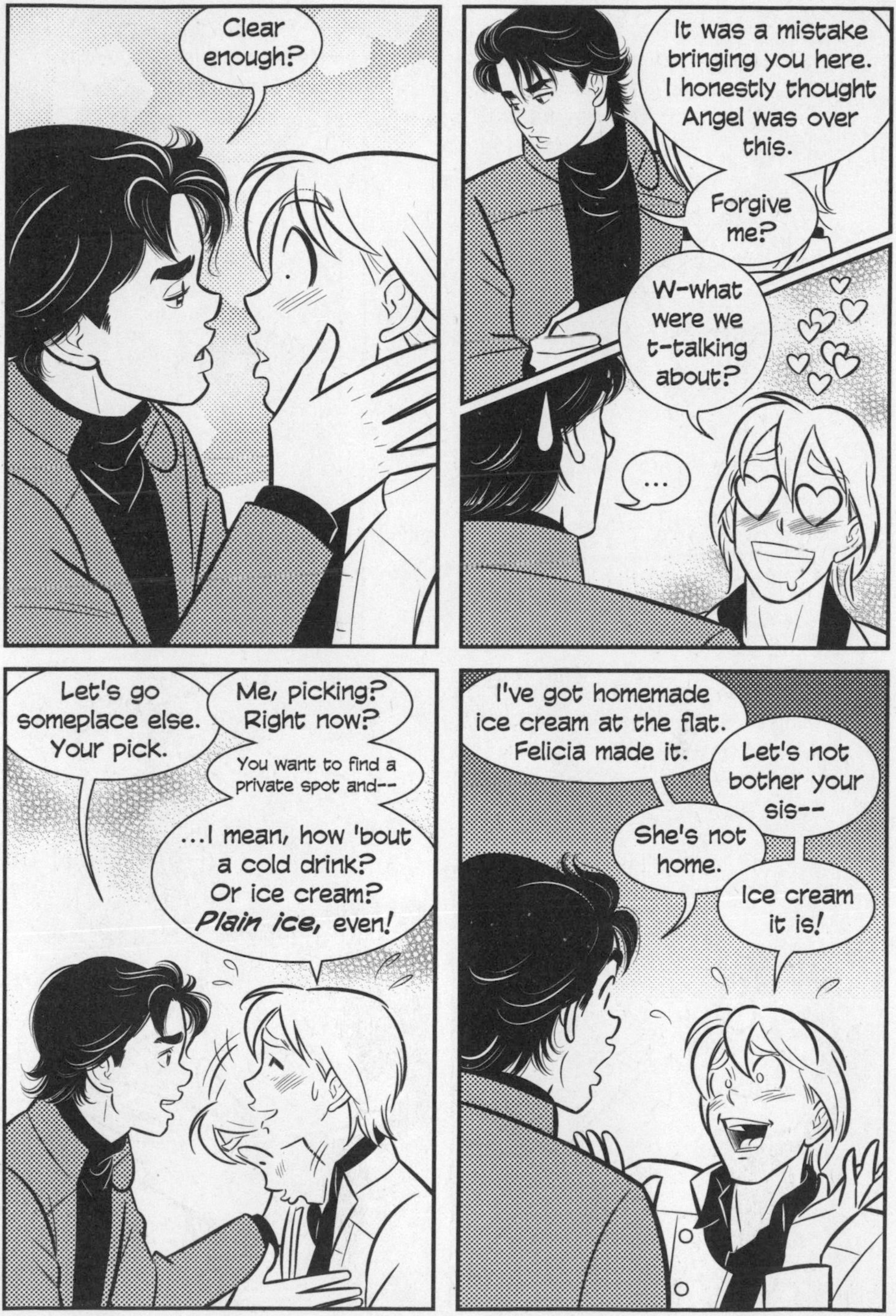
Clear enough?
It was a mistake bringing you here. I honestly thought Angel was over this.
Forgive me?
W-what were we t-talking about?
...
Let's go someplace else. Your pick.
Me, picking? Right now?
You want to find a private spot and--
...I mean, how 'bout a cold drink? Or ice cream? *Plain ice,* even!
I've got homemade ice cream at the flat. Felicia made it.
Let's not bother your sis--
She's not home.
Ice cream it is!

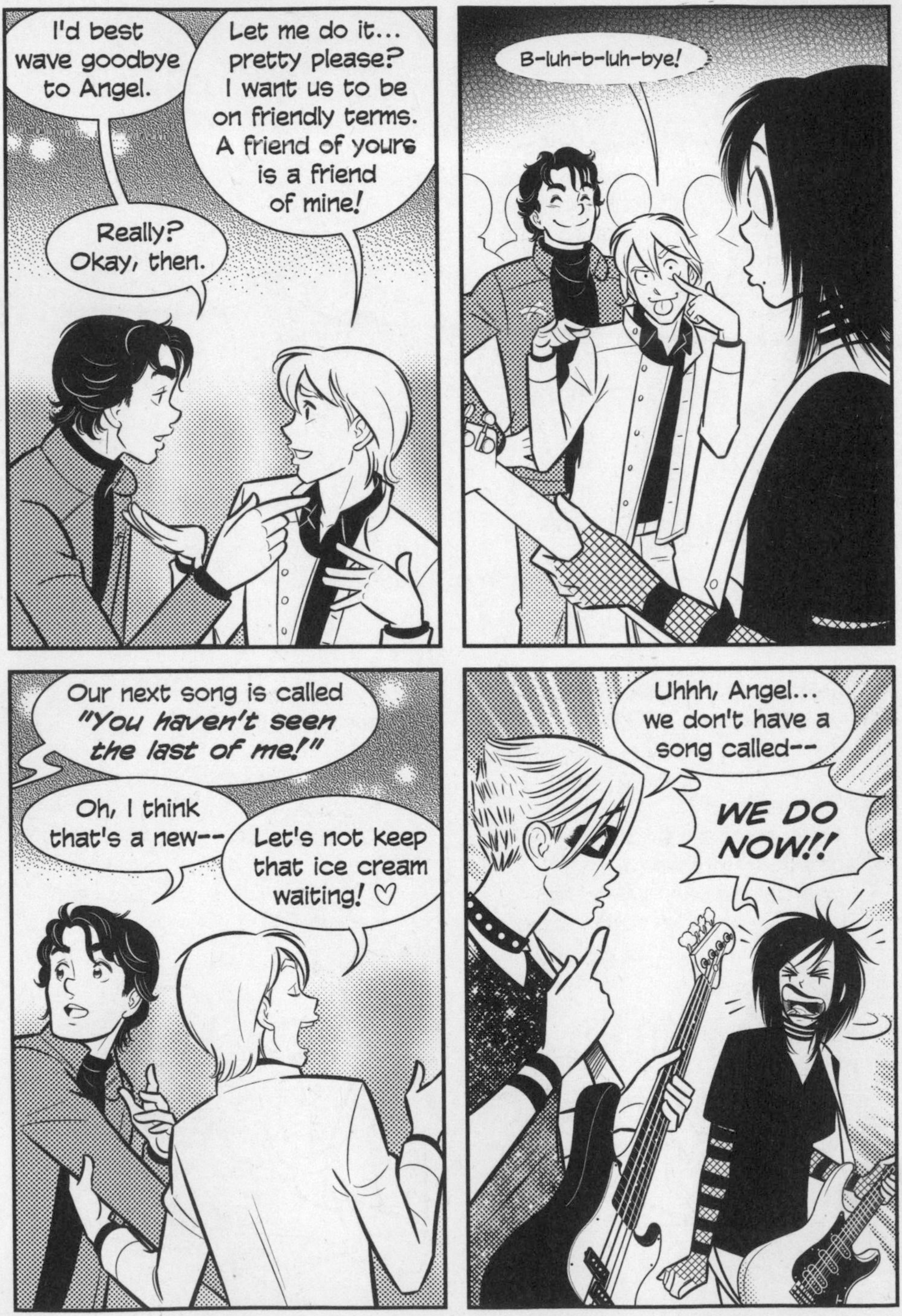
I'd best wave goodbye to Angel.
Let me do it... pretty please? I want us to be on friendly terms. A friend of yours is a friend of mine!
Really? Okay, then.
B-luh-b-luh-bye!
Our next song is called *"You haven't seen the last of me!"*
Oh, I think that's a new--
Let's not keep that ice cream waiting! ♡
Uhhh, Angel... we don't have a song called--
WE DO NOW!!

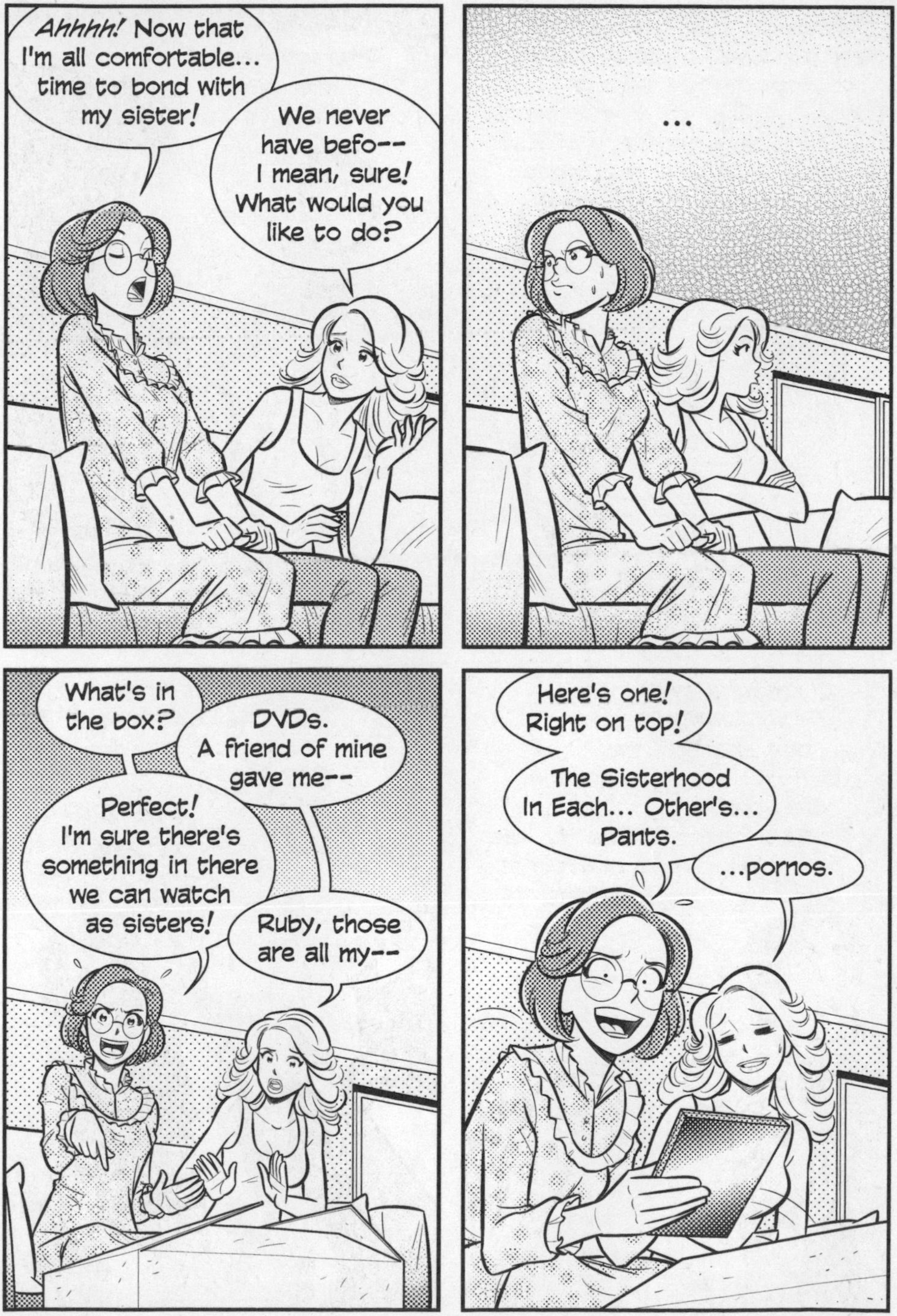

Ahhhh! Now that I'm all comfortable... time to bond with my sister!
We never have befo-- I mean, sure! What would you like to do?
...
What's in the box?
DVDs. A friend of mine gave me--
Perfect! I'm sure there's something in there we can watch as sisters!
Ruby, those are all my--
Here's one! Right on top!
The Sisterhood In Each... Other's... Pants.
...pornos.

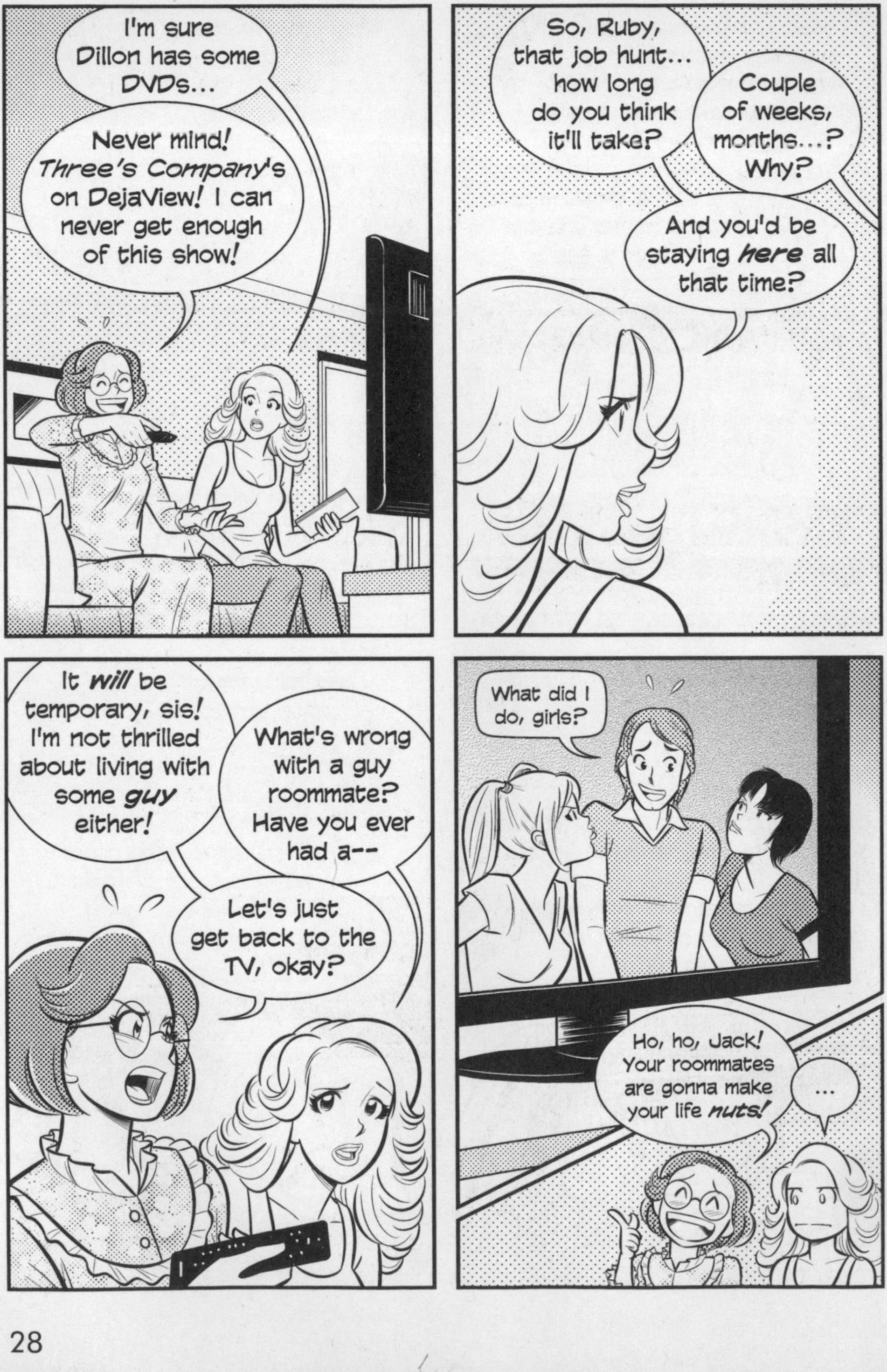
I'm sure Dillon has some DVDs...
Never mind! *Three's Company*'s on DejaView! I can never get enough of this show!
So, Ruby, that job hunt... how long do you think it'll take?
Couple of weeks, months...? Why?
And you'd be staying ***here*** all that time?
It ***will*** be temporary, sis! I'm not thrilled about living with some ***guy*** either!
What's wrong with a guy roommate? Have you ever had a--
Let's just get back to the TV, okay?
What did I do, girls?
Ho, ho, Jack! Your roommates are gonna make your life ***nuts!***
...

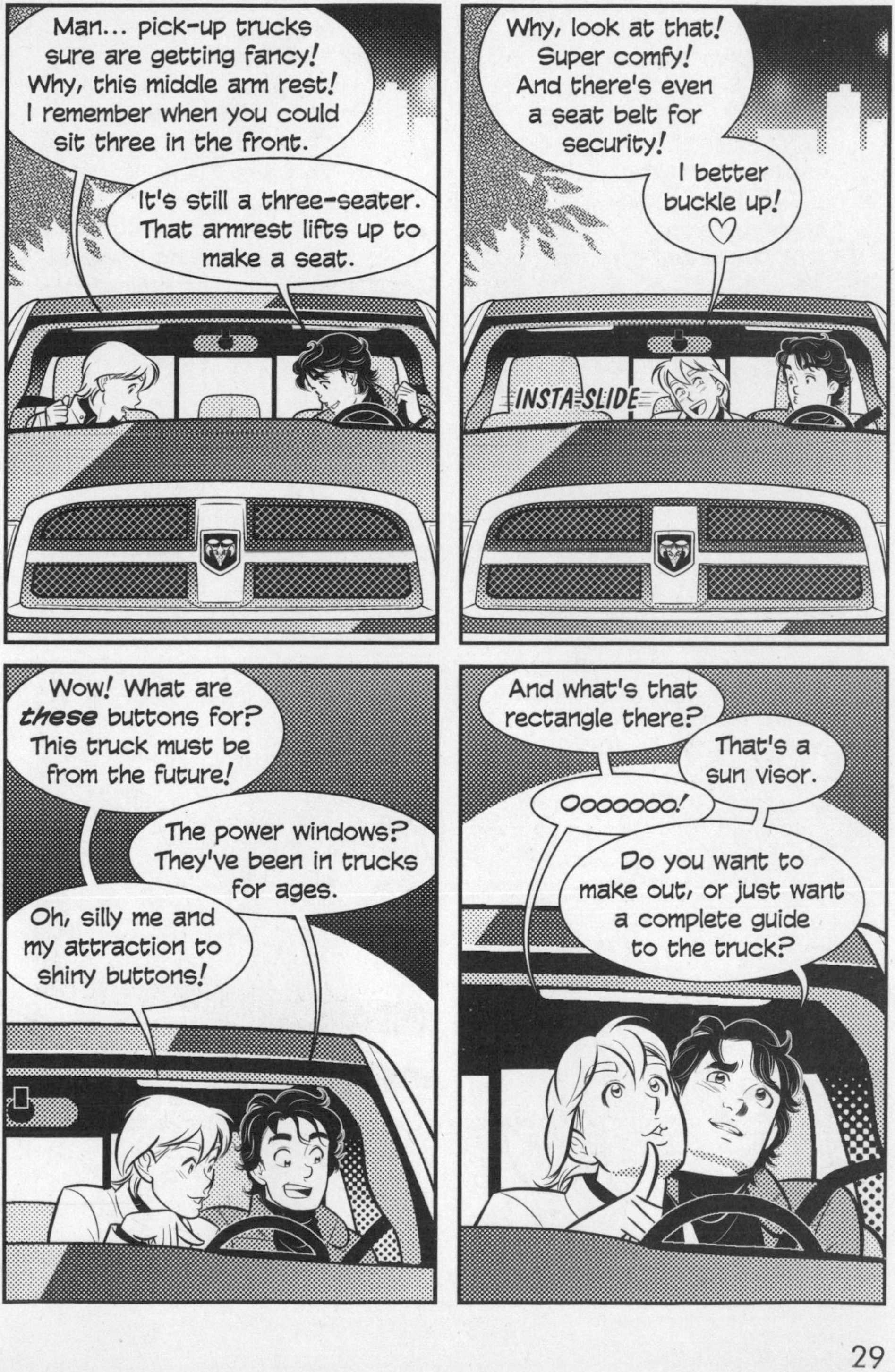
Man... pick-up trucks sure are getting fancy! Why, this middle arm rest! I remember when you could sit three in the front.
It's still a three-seater. That armrest lifts up to make a seat.
Why, look at that! Super comfy! And there's even a seat belt for security!
INSTA-SLIDE
I better buckle up! ♡
Wow! What are *these* buttons for? This truck must be from the future!
The power windows? They've been in trucks for ages.
Oh, silly me and my attraction to shiny buttons!
And what's that rectangle there?
That's a sun visor.
Ooooooo!
Do you want to make out, or just want a complete guide to the truck?

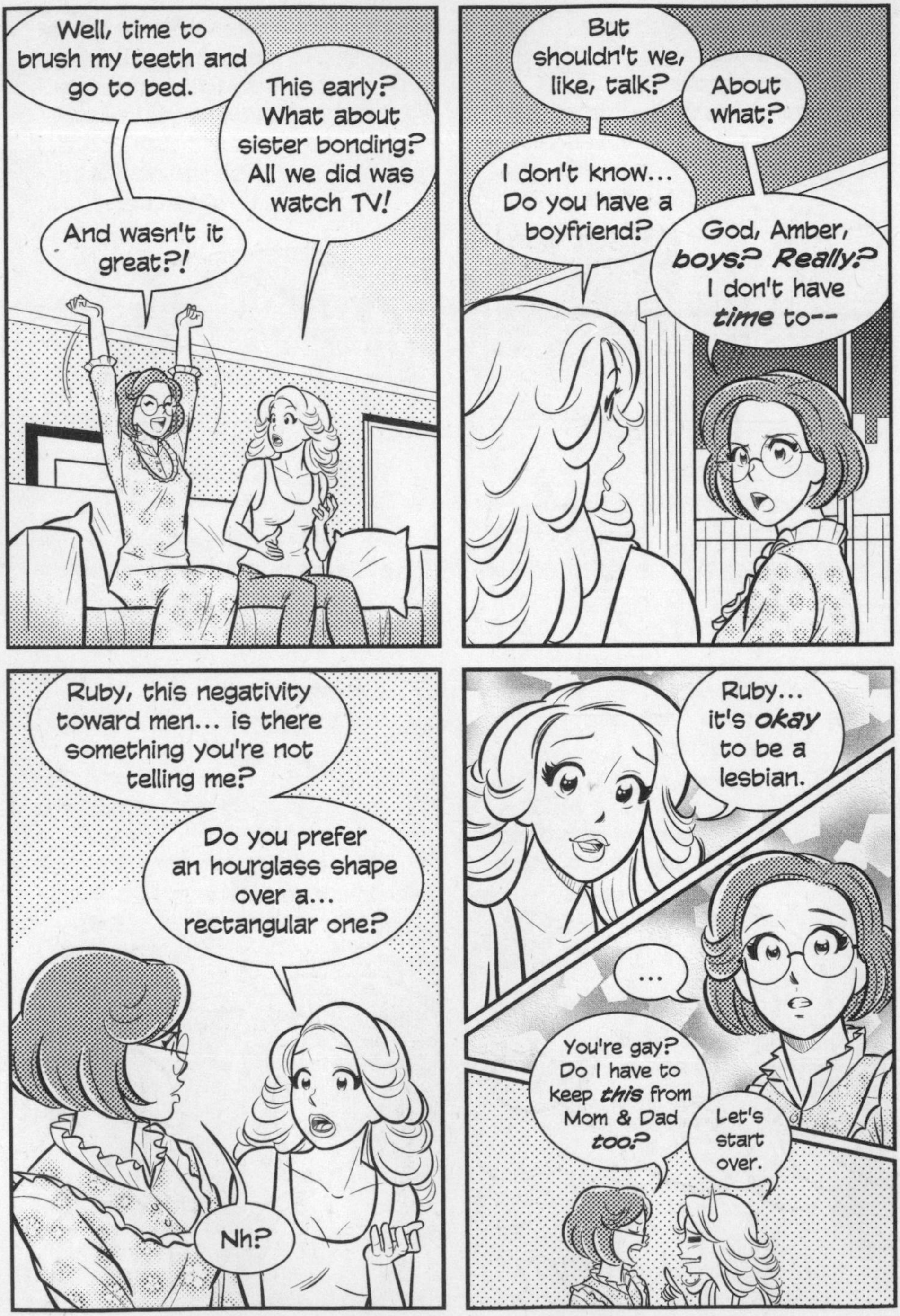

Well, time to brush my teeth and go to bed.
This early? What about sister bonding? All we did was watch TV!
And wasn't it great?!
But shouldn't we, like, talk?
About what?
I don't know... Do you have a boyfriend?
God, Amber, ***boys? Really?*** I don't have ***time*** to--
Ruby, this negativity toward men... is there something you're not telling me?
Do you prefer an hourglass shape over a... rectangular one?
Nh?
Ruby... it's ***okay*** to be a lesbian.
...
You're gay? Do I have to keep ***this*** from Mom & Dad ***too?***
Let's start over.

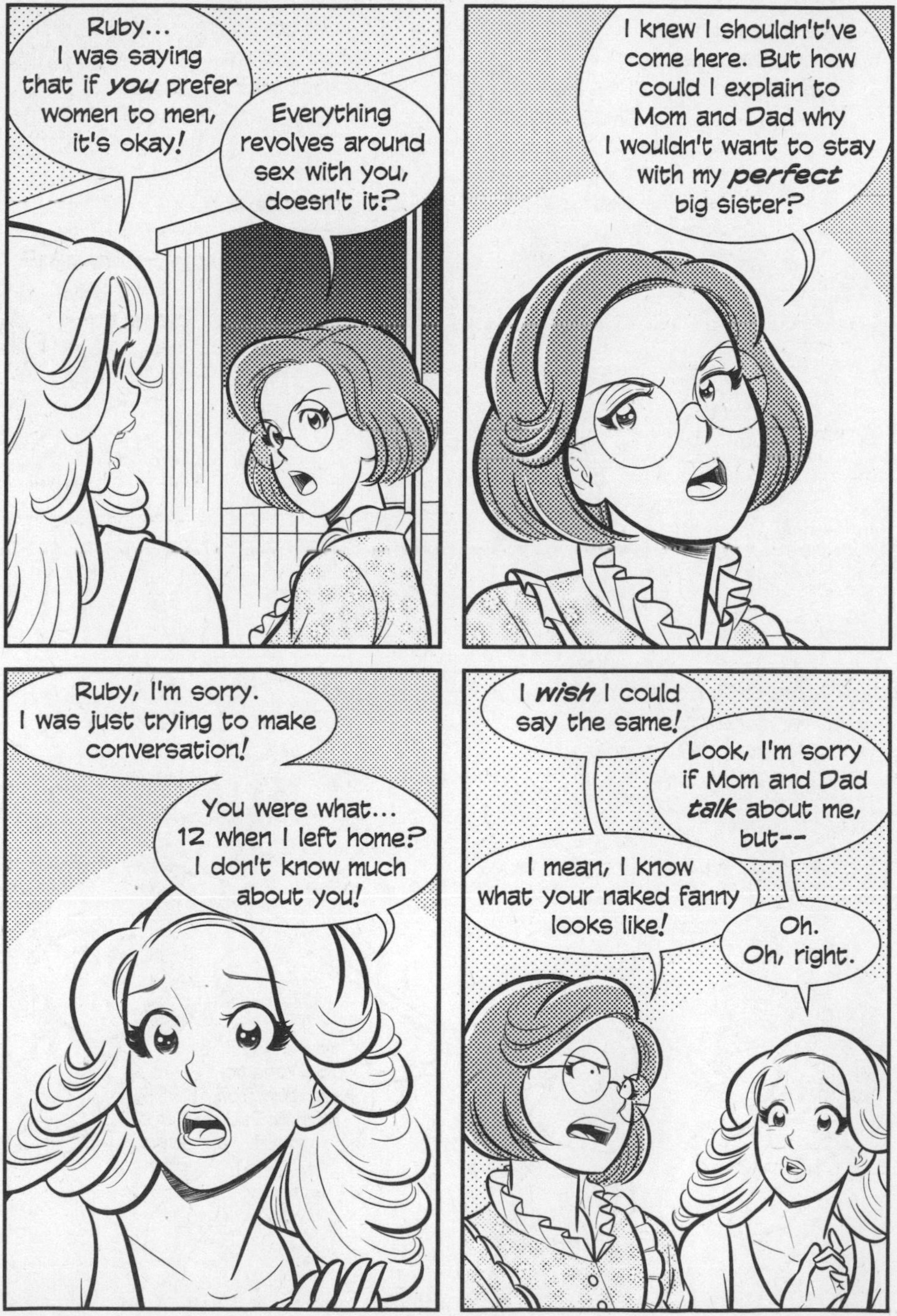

Ruby... I was saying that if *you* prefer women to men, it's okay!
Everything revolves around sex with you, doesn't it?
I knew I shouldn't've come here. But how could I explain to Mom and Dad why I wouldn't want to stay with my *perfect* big sister?
Ruby, I'm sorry. I was just trying to make conversation!
You were what... 12 when I left home? I don't know much about you!
I *wish* I could say the same!
Look, I'm sorry if Mom and Dad *talk* about me, but--
I mean, I know what your naked fanny looks like!
Oh. Oh, right.

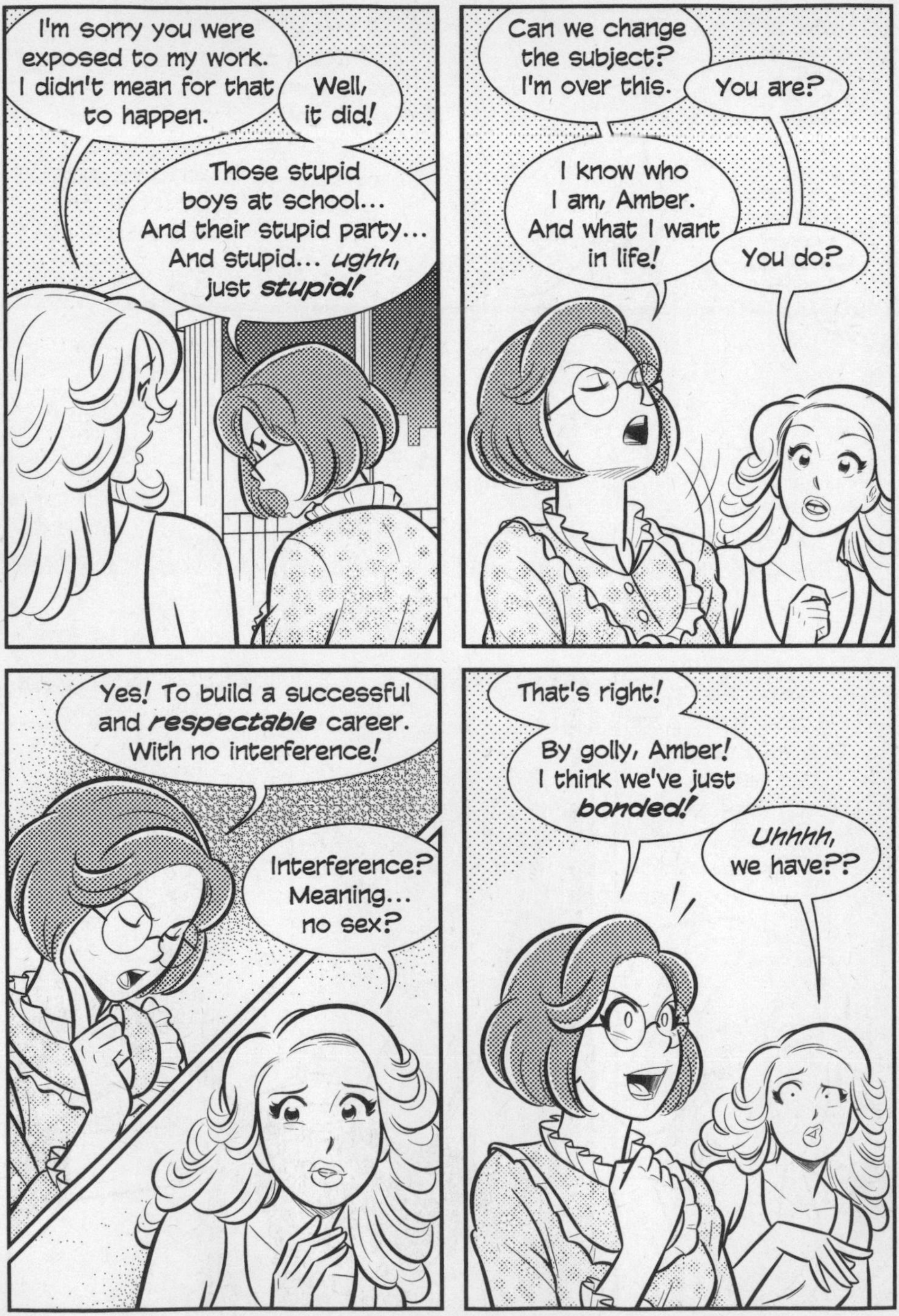
I'm sorry you were exposed to my work. I didn't mean for that to happen.
Well, it did!
Those stupid boys at school... And their stupid party... And stupid... *ughh,* just ***stupid!***
Can we change the subject? I'm over this.
You are?
I know who I am, Amber. And what I want in life!
You do?
Yes! To build a successful and ***respectable*** career. With no interference!
Interference? Meaning... no sex?
That's right!
By golly, Amber! I think we've just ***bonded!***
Uhhhh, we have??

Ew! Someone left a tube of toothpaste on the counter!

It oozed white paste everywhere! Gooey! Blech! *Yuck!*

...Living with Ruby won't be easy.

I should call Dillon to let him know we've got a new roomie.

Then again, it would be rude to interrupt him on his date.

...

Bah, it's a first date. They're probably just talking about likes and dislikes.

Oo! Yes! I like that! ♡♡

33

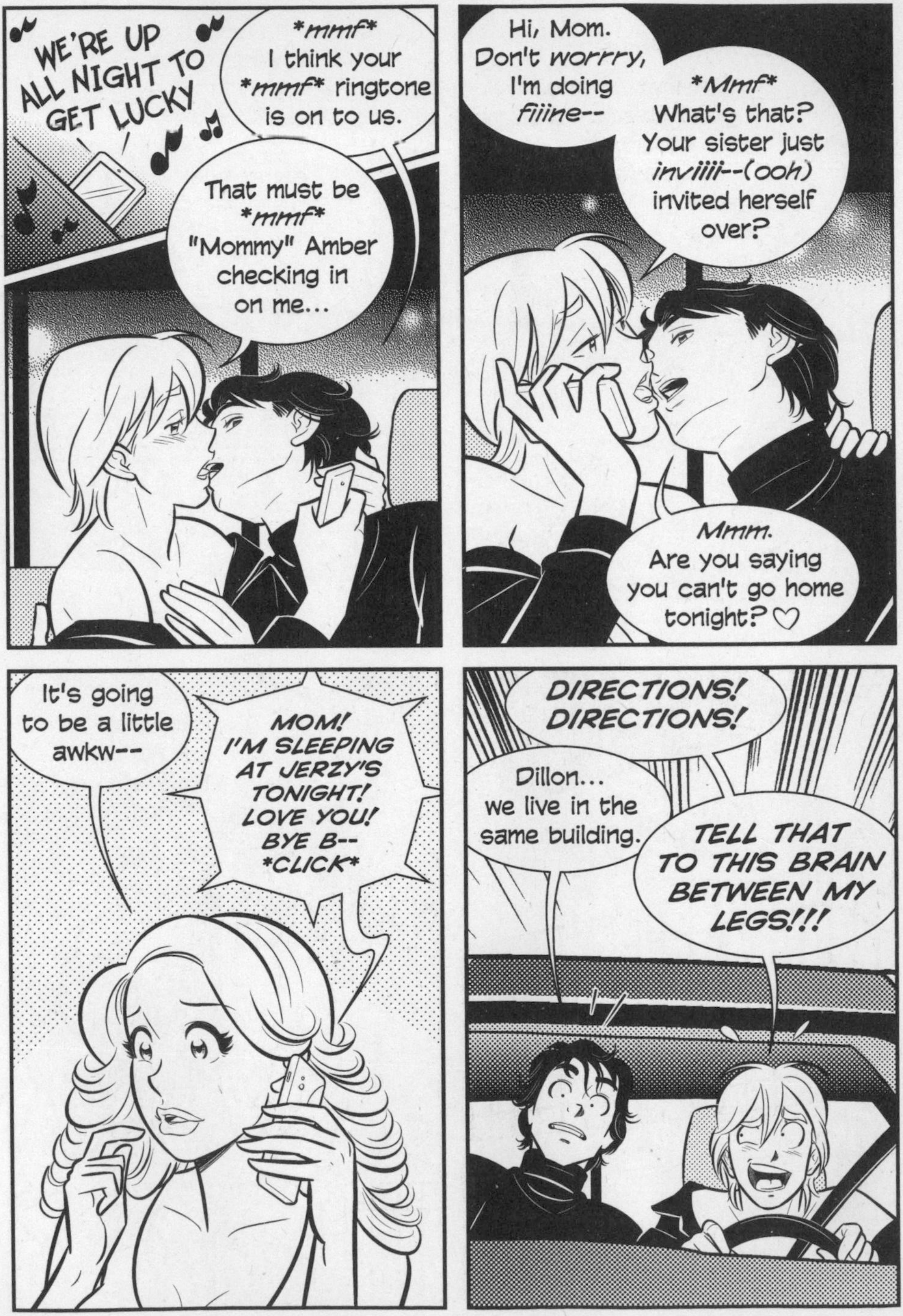
WE'RE UP ALL NIGHT TO GET LUCKY
mmf I think your *mmf* ringtone is on to us.
That must be *mmf* "Mommy" Amber checking in on me...
Hi, Mom. Don't worrry, I'm doing fiiine--
Mmf What's that? Your sister just inviiii--(ooh) invited herself over?
Mmm. Are you saying you can't go home tonight? ♡
It's going to be a little awkw--
MOM! I'M SLEEPING AT JERZY'S TONIGHT! LOVE YOU! BYE B-- *CLICK*
DIRECTIONS! DIRECTIONS!
Dillon... we live in the same building.
TELL THAT TO THIS BRAIN BETWEEN MY LEGS!!!

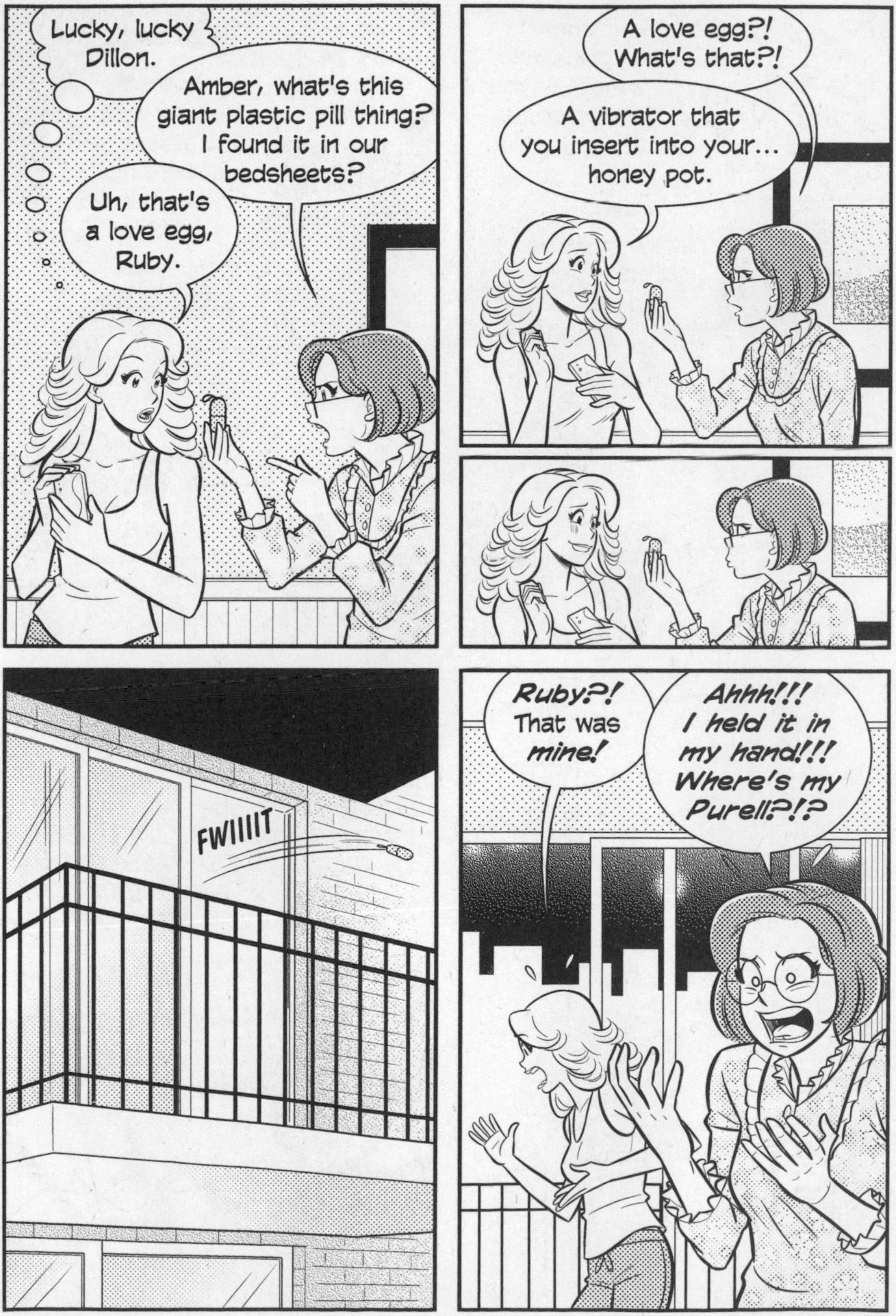
Lucky, lucky Dillon.
Amber, what's this giant plastic pill thing? I found it in our bedsheets?
Uh, that's a love egg, Ruby.
A love egg?! What's that?!
A vibrator that you insert into your... honey pot.
FWIIIIT
Ruby?! That was mine!
Ahhh!!! I held it in my hand!!! Where's my Purell?!?

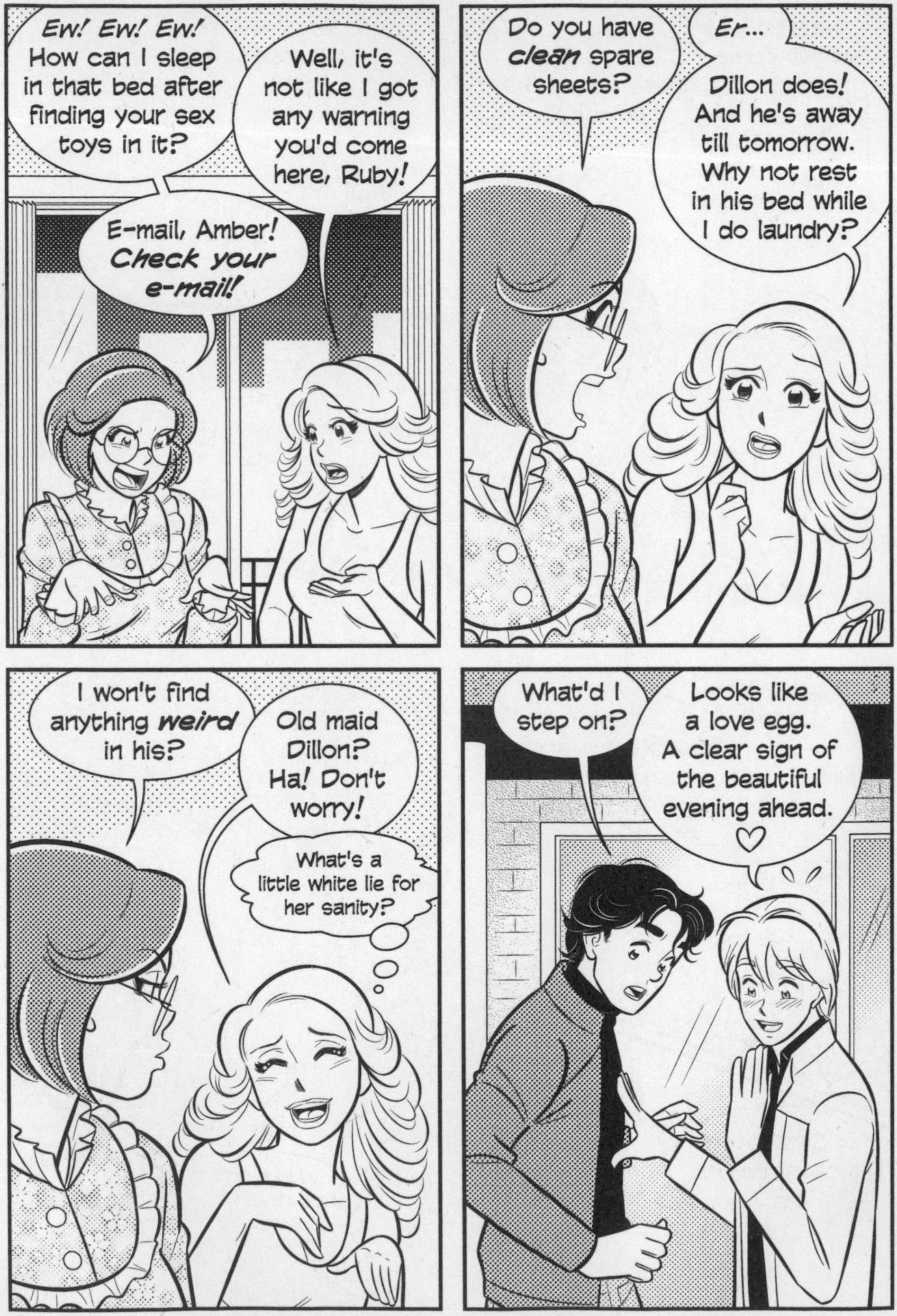
Ew! Ew! Ew! How can I sleep in that bed after finding your sex toys in it?
Well, it's not like I got any warning you'd come here, Ruby!
E-mail, Amber! Check your e-mail!
Do you have clean spare sheets?
Er...
Dillon does! And he's away till tomorrow. Why not rest in his bed while I do laundry?
I won't find anything weird in his?
Old maid Dillon? Ha! Don't worry!
What's a little white lie for her sanity?
What'd I step on?
Looks like a love egg. A clear sign of the beautiful evening ahead. ♡

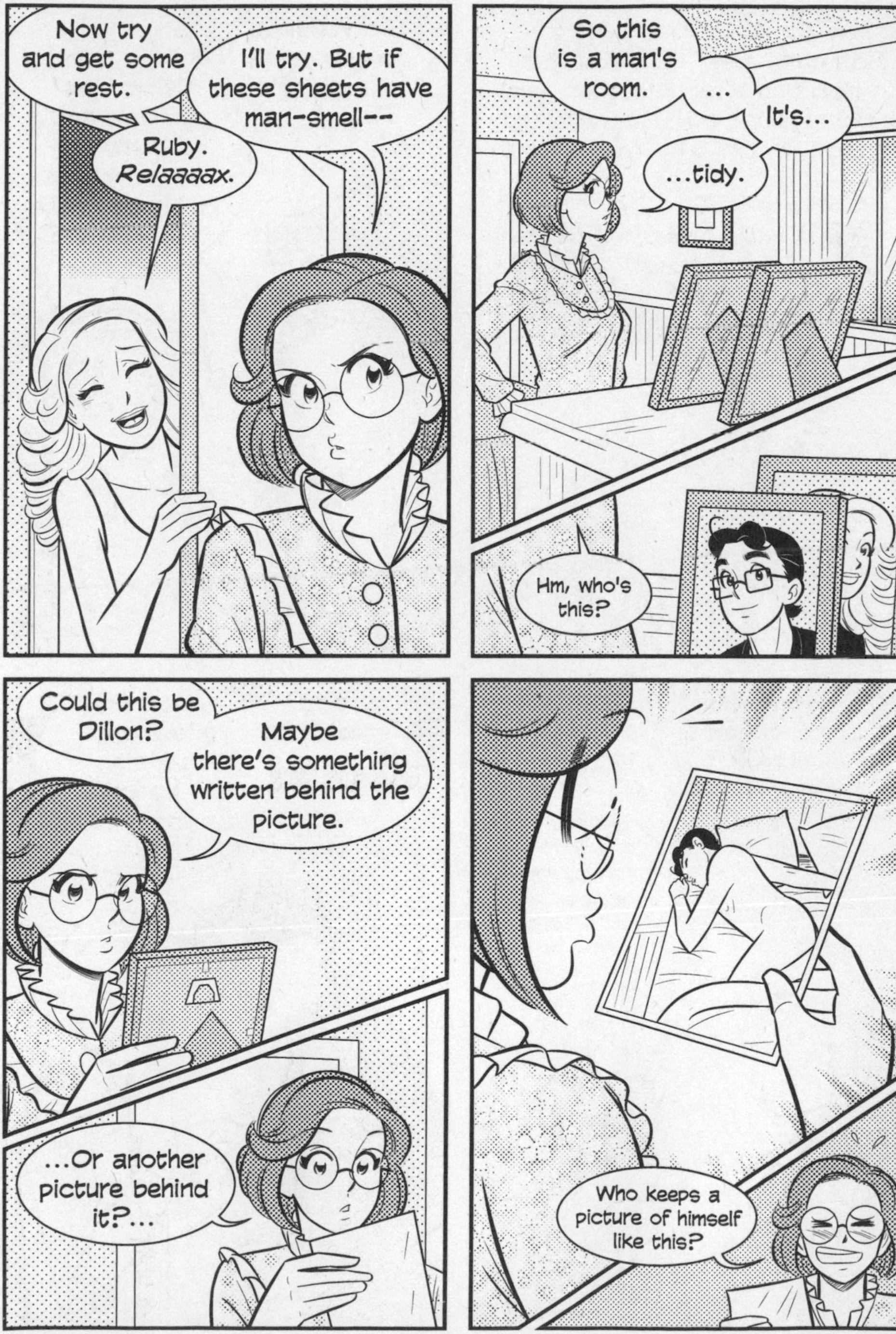

Now try and get some rest.
I'll try. But if these sheets have man-smell--
Ruby. *Relaaaax.*
So this is a man's room.
...
It's...
...tidy.
Hm, who's this?
Could this be Dillon?
Maybe there's something written behind the picture.
...Or another picture behind it?...
Who keeps a picture of himself like this?

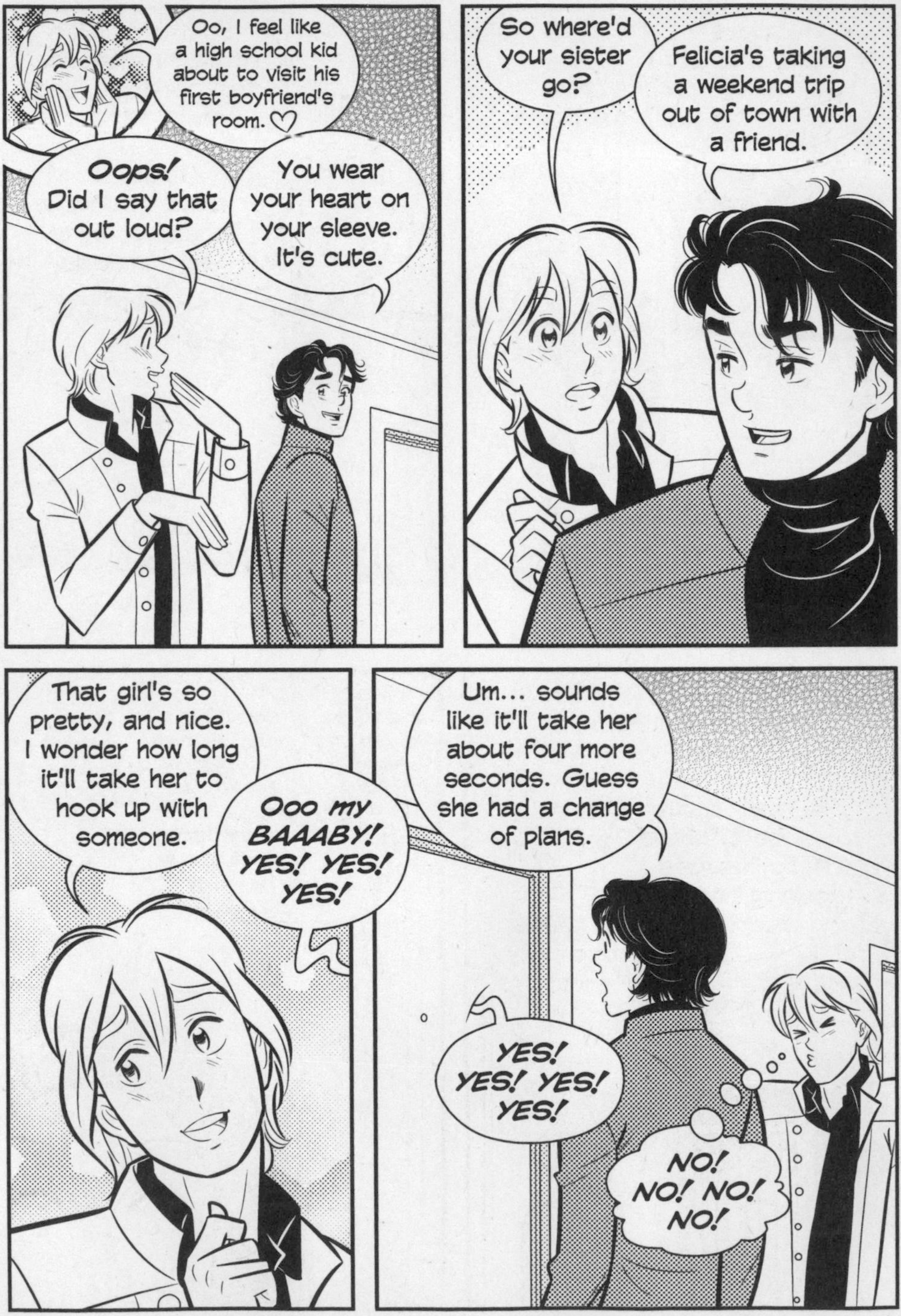
Oo, I feel like a high school kid about to visit his first boyfriend's room. ♡
Oops! Did I say that out loud?
You wear your heart on your sleeve. It's cute.
So where'd your sister go?
Felicia's taking a weekend trip out of town with a friend.
That girl's so pretty, and nice. I wonder how long it'll take her to hook up with someone.
Ooo my BAAABY! YES! YES! YES!
Um... sounds like it'll take her about four more seconds. Guess she had a change of plans.
YES! YES! YES! YES!
NO! NO! NO! NO!

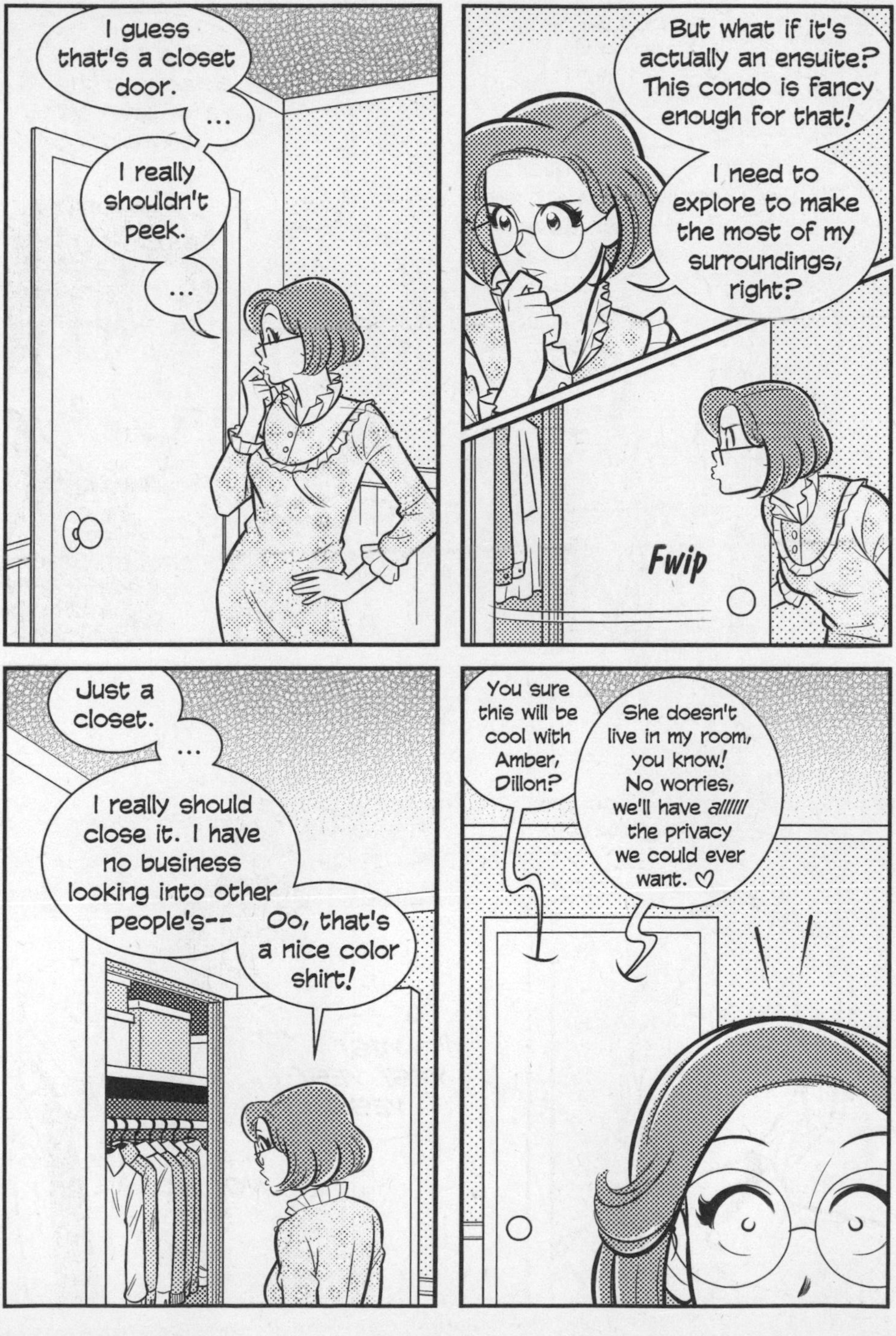
I guess that's a closet door.
...
I really shouldn't peek.
...
But what if it's actually an ensuite? This condo is fancy enough for that!
I need to explore to make the most of my surroundings, right?
Fwip
Just a closet.
...
I really should close it. I have no business looking into other people's--
Oo, that's a nice color shirt!
You sure this will be cool with Amber, Dillon?
She doesn't live in my room, you know! No worries, we'll have *allllll* the privacy we could ever want. ♡

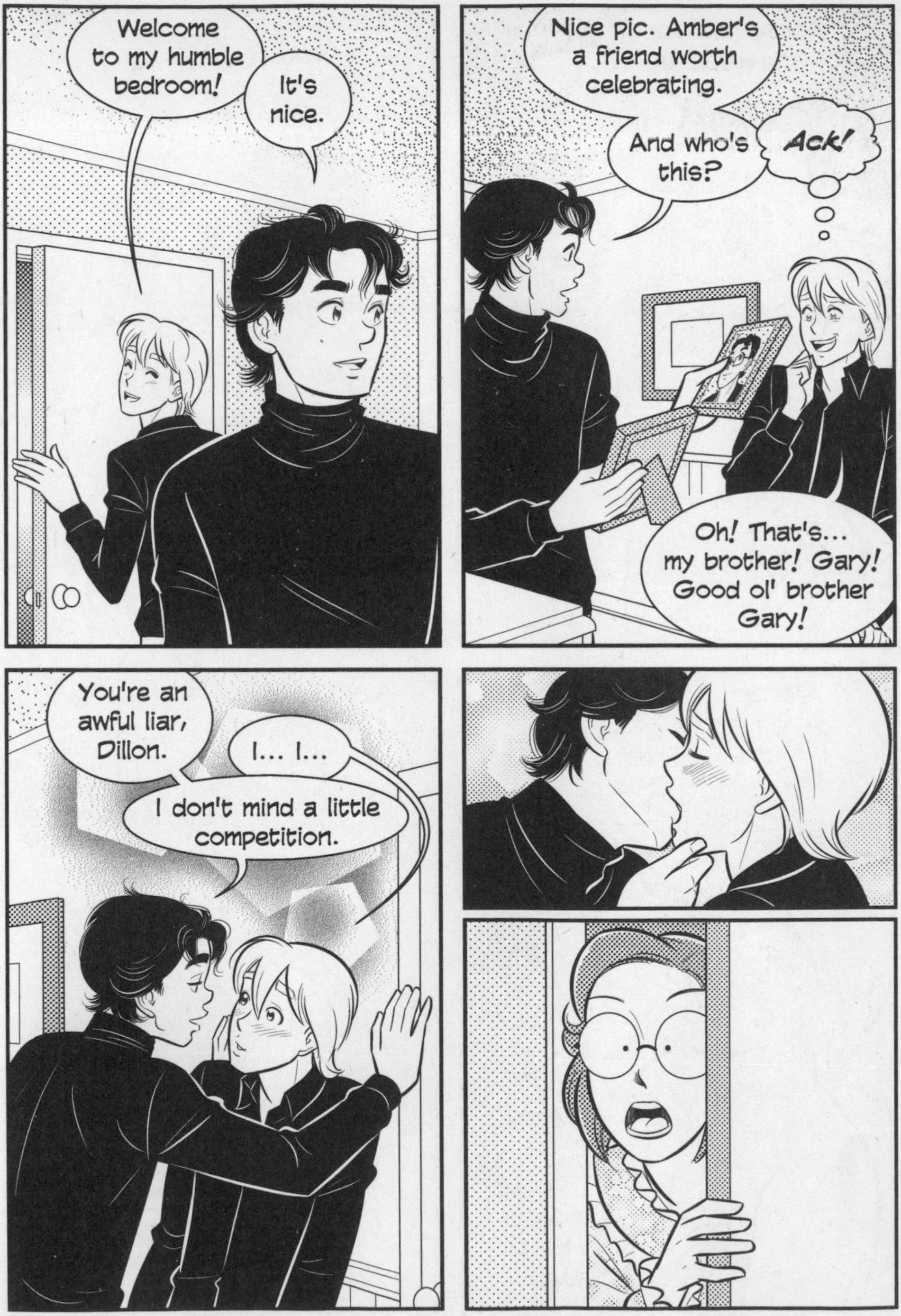
Welcome to my humble bedroom!
It's nice.
Nice pic. Amber's a friend worth celebrating.
And who's this?
Ack!
Oh! That's... my brother! Gary! Good ol' brother Gary!
You're an awful liar, Dillon.
I... I...
I don't mind a little competition.

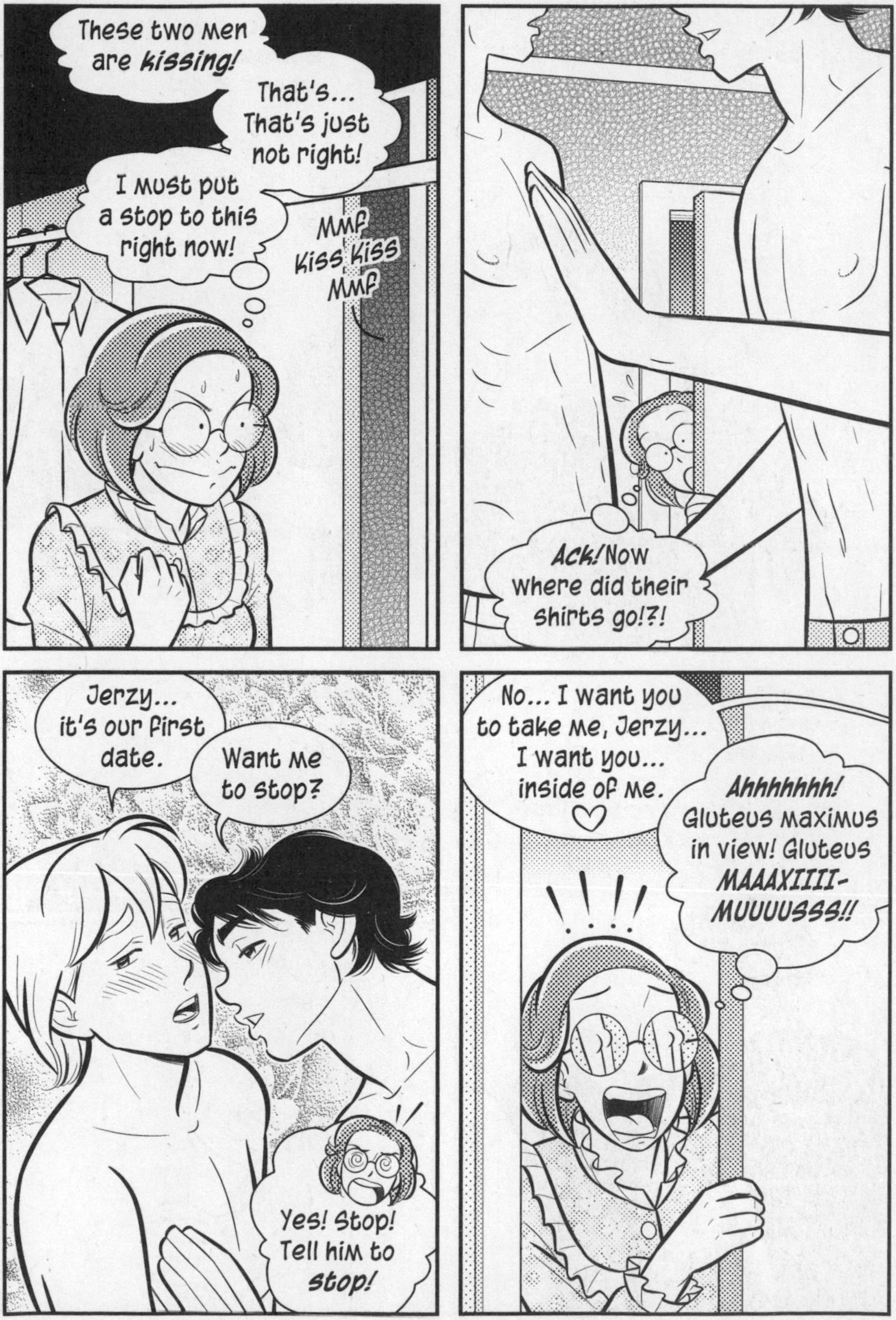
These two men are *kissing!*
That's... That's just not right!
I must put a stop to this right now!
Mmf Kiss Kiss Mmf
Ack! Now where did their shirts go!?!
Jerzy... it's our first date.
Want me to stop?
Yes! Stop! Tell him to *stop!*
No... I want you to take me, Jerzy... I want you... inside of me.
Ahhhhhhh! Gluteus maximus in view! Gluteus *MAAAXIIII-MUUUUSSS!!*

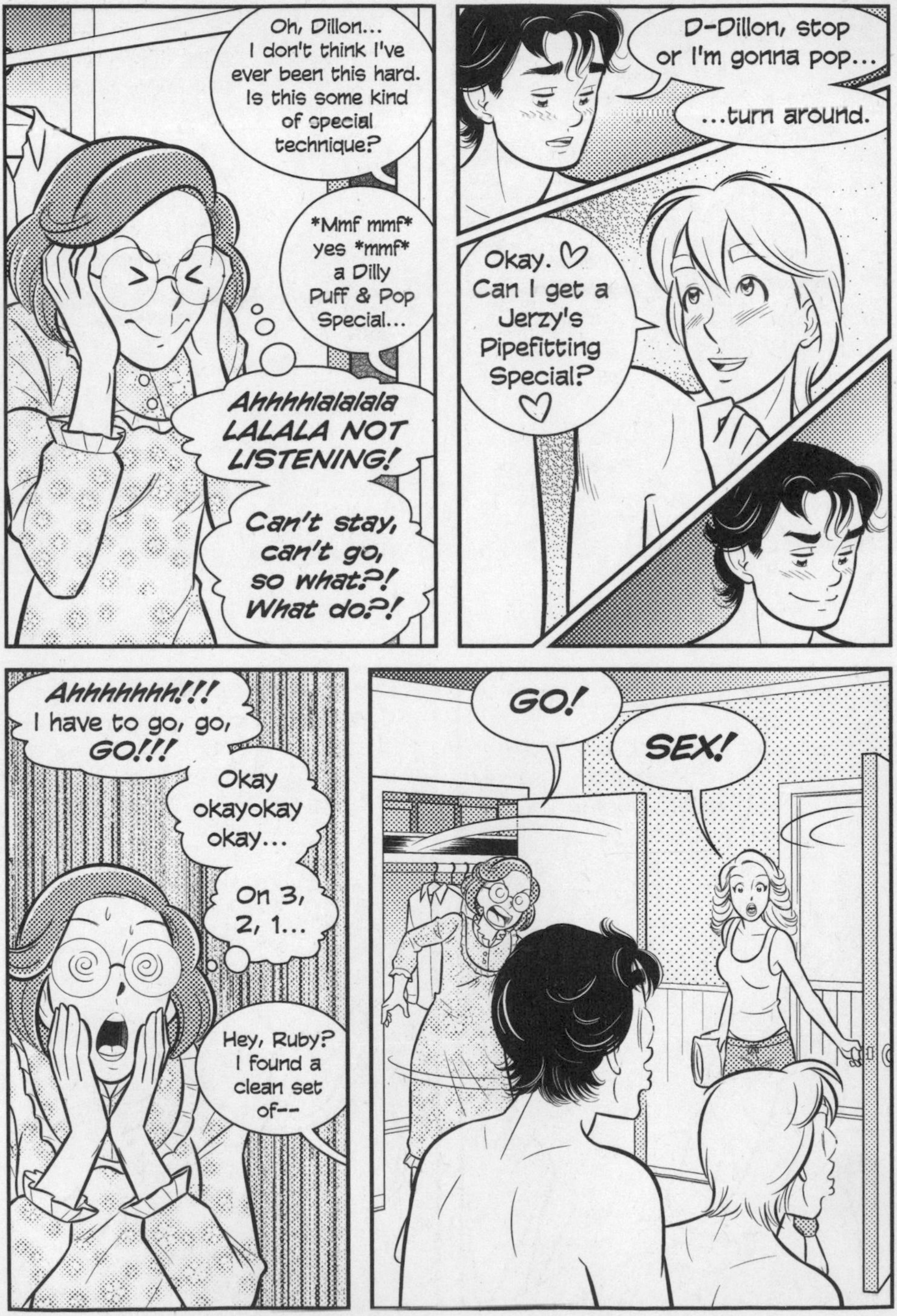

Oh, Dillon... I don't think I've ever been this hard. Is this some kind of special technique?
Mmf mmf yes *mmf* a Dilly Puff & Pop Special...
Ahhhlalalala LALALA NOT LISTENING!
Can't stay, can't go, so what?! What do?!
D-Dillon, stop or I'm gonna pop...
...turn around.
Okay. ♡ Can I get a Jerzy's Pipefitting Special? ♡
Ahhhhhhh!!! I have to go, go, GO!!!
Okay okayokay okay...
On 3, 2, 1...
Hey, Ruby? I found a clean set of--
GO!
SEX!

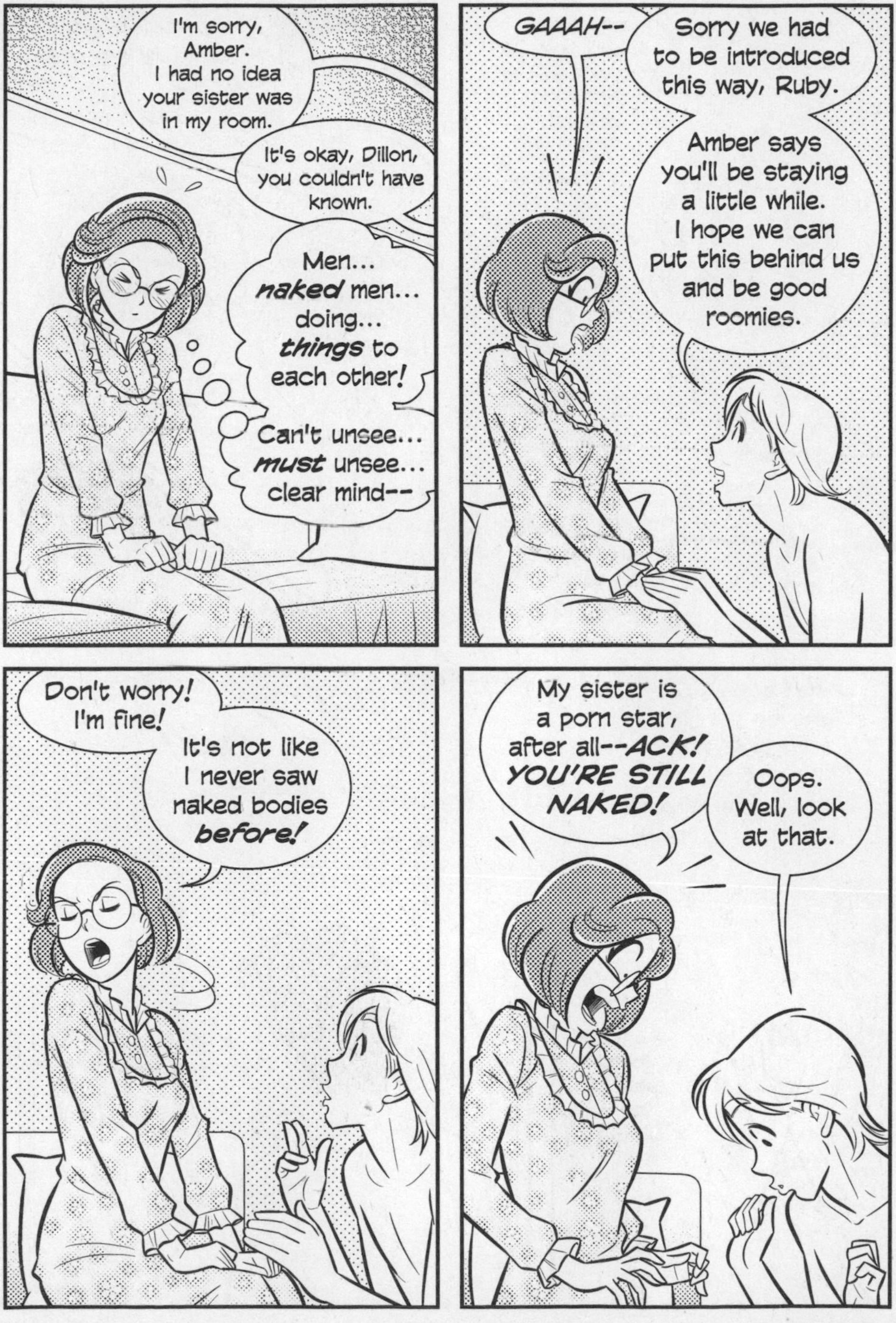
I'm sorry, Amber. I had no idea your sister was in my room.
It's okay, Dillon, you couldn't have known.
Men... *naked* men... doing... *things* to each other!
Can't unsee... *must* unsee... clear mind--
GAAAH--
Sorry we had to be introduced this way, Ruby.
Amber says you'll be staying a little while. I hope we can put this behind us and be good roomies.
Don't worry! I'm fine!
It's not like I never saw naked bodies *before!*
My sister is a porn star, after all--*ACK! YOU'RE STILL NAKED!*
Oops. Well, look at that.

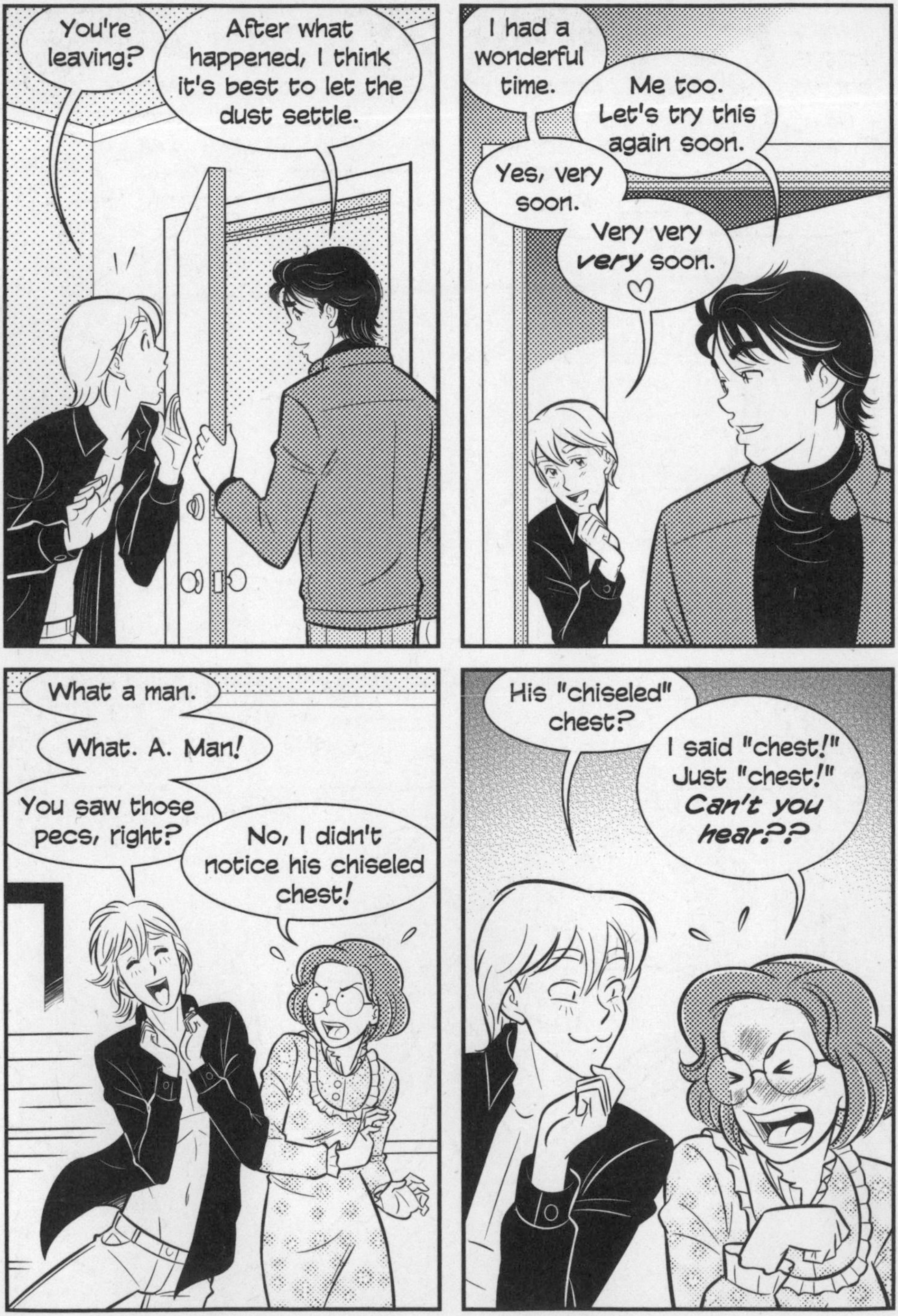
You're leaving?
After what happened, I think it's best to let the dust settle.
I had a wonderful time.
Me too. Let's try this again soon.
Yes, very soon.
Very very *very* soon. ♡
What a man.
What. A. Man!
You saw those pecs, right?
No, I didn't notice his chiseled chest!
His "chiseled" chest?
I said "chest!" Just "chest!" *Can't you hear??*

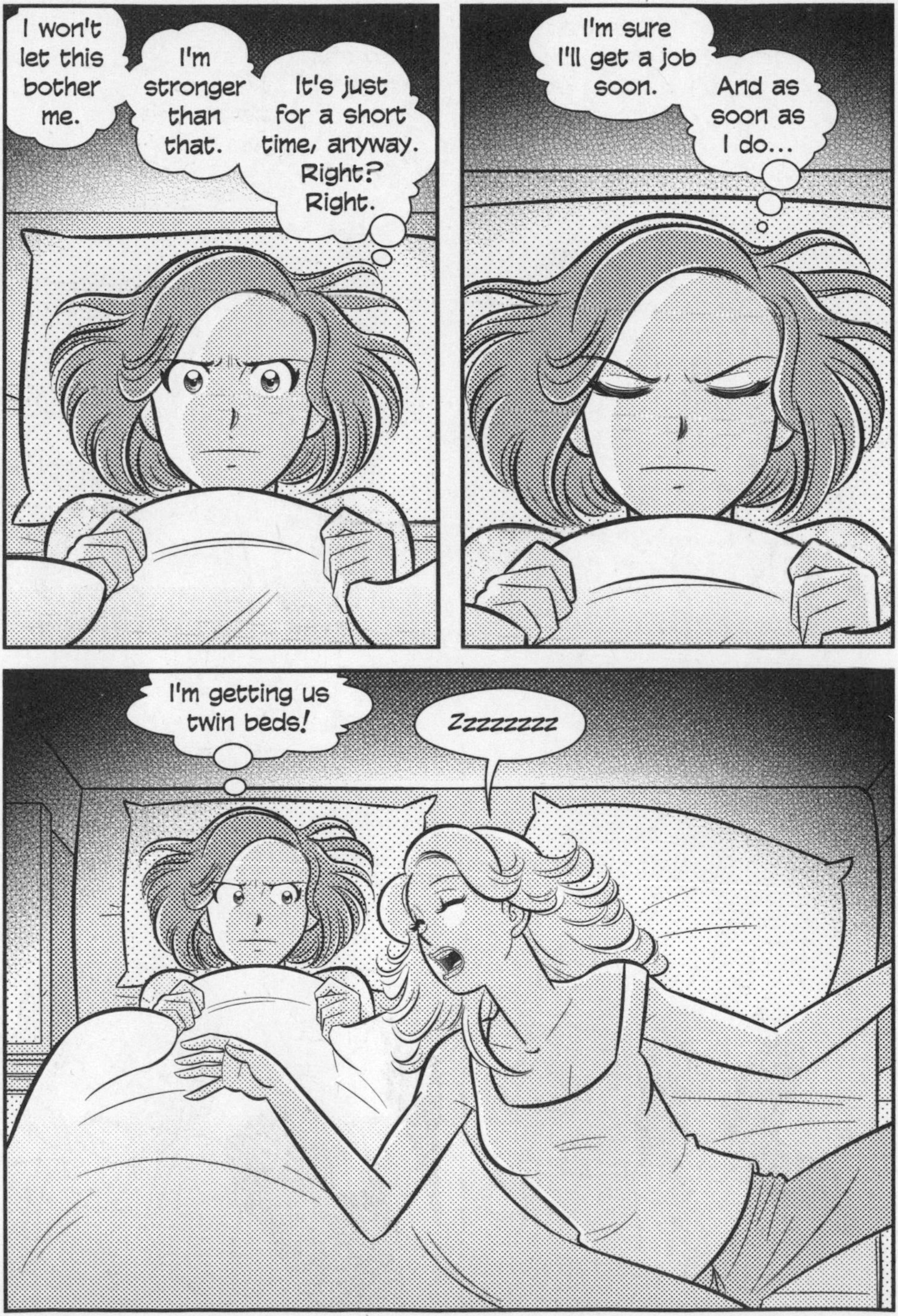
I won't let this bother me.
I'm stronger than that.
It's just for a short time, anyway. Right? Right.
I'm sure I'll get a job soon.
And as soon as I do...
I'm getting us twin beds!
Zzzzzzzz

Self-Marketing for Young Graduates

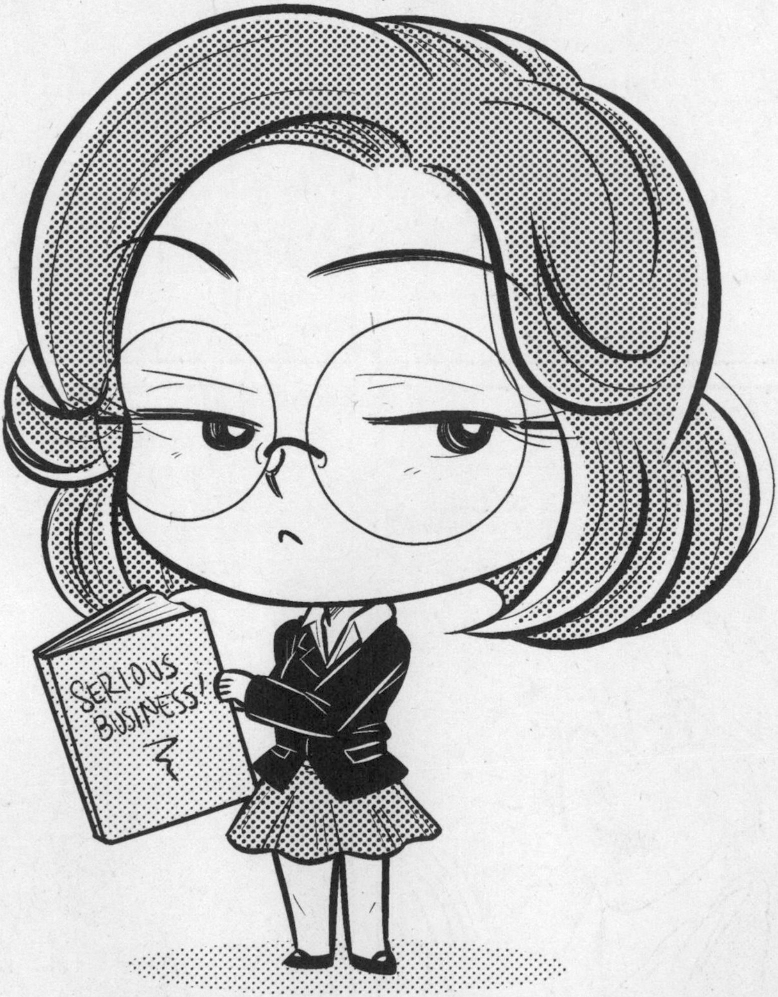
SERIOUS BUSINESS!

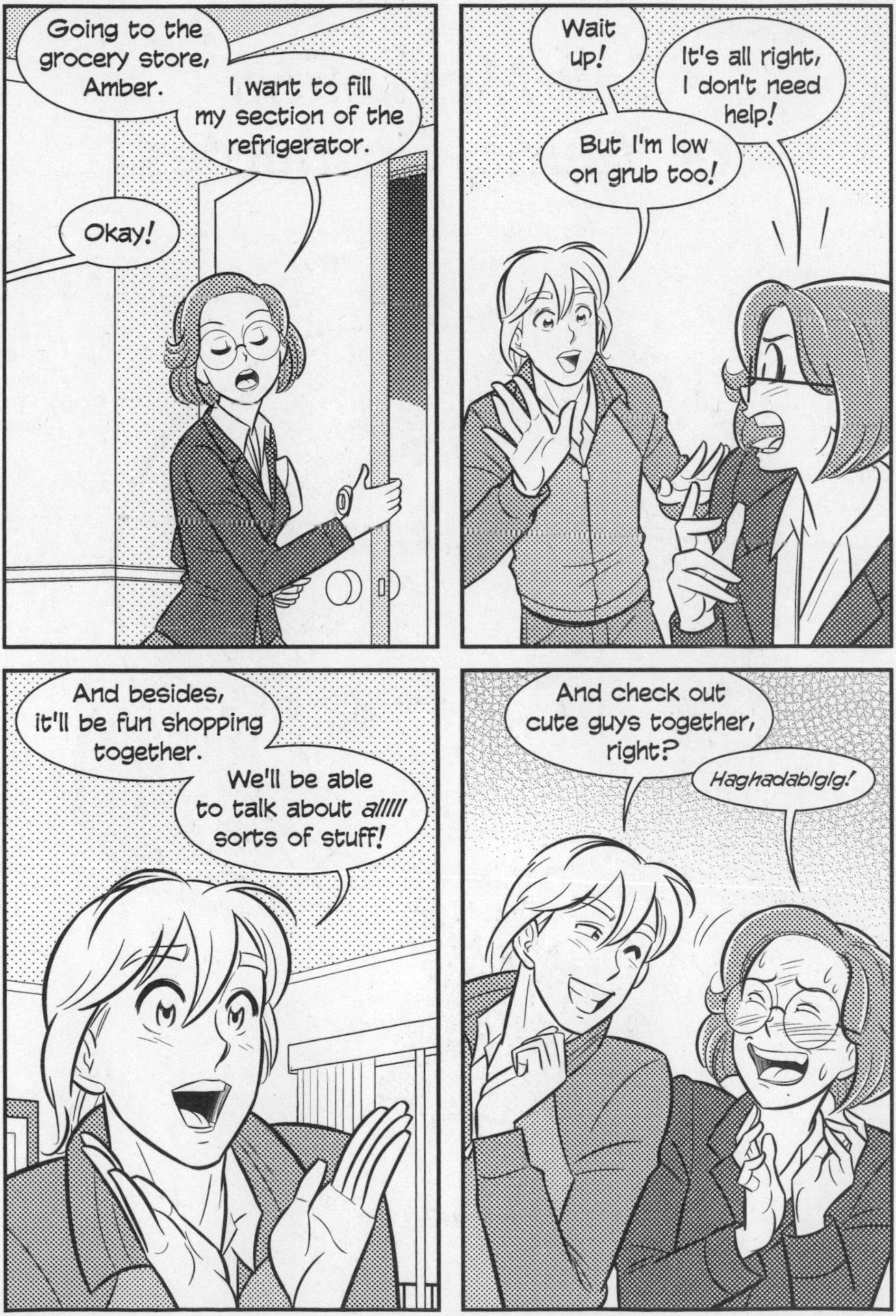
Going to the grocery store, Amber.
I want to fill my section of the refrigerator.
Okay!
Wait up!
It's all right, I don't need help!
But I'm low on grub too!
And besides, it'll be fun shopping together.
We'll be able to talk about *allll* sorts of stuff!
And check out cute guys together, right?
Haghadablglg!

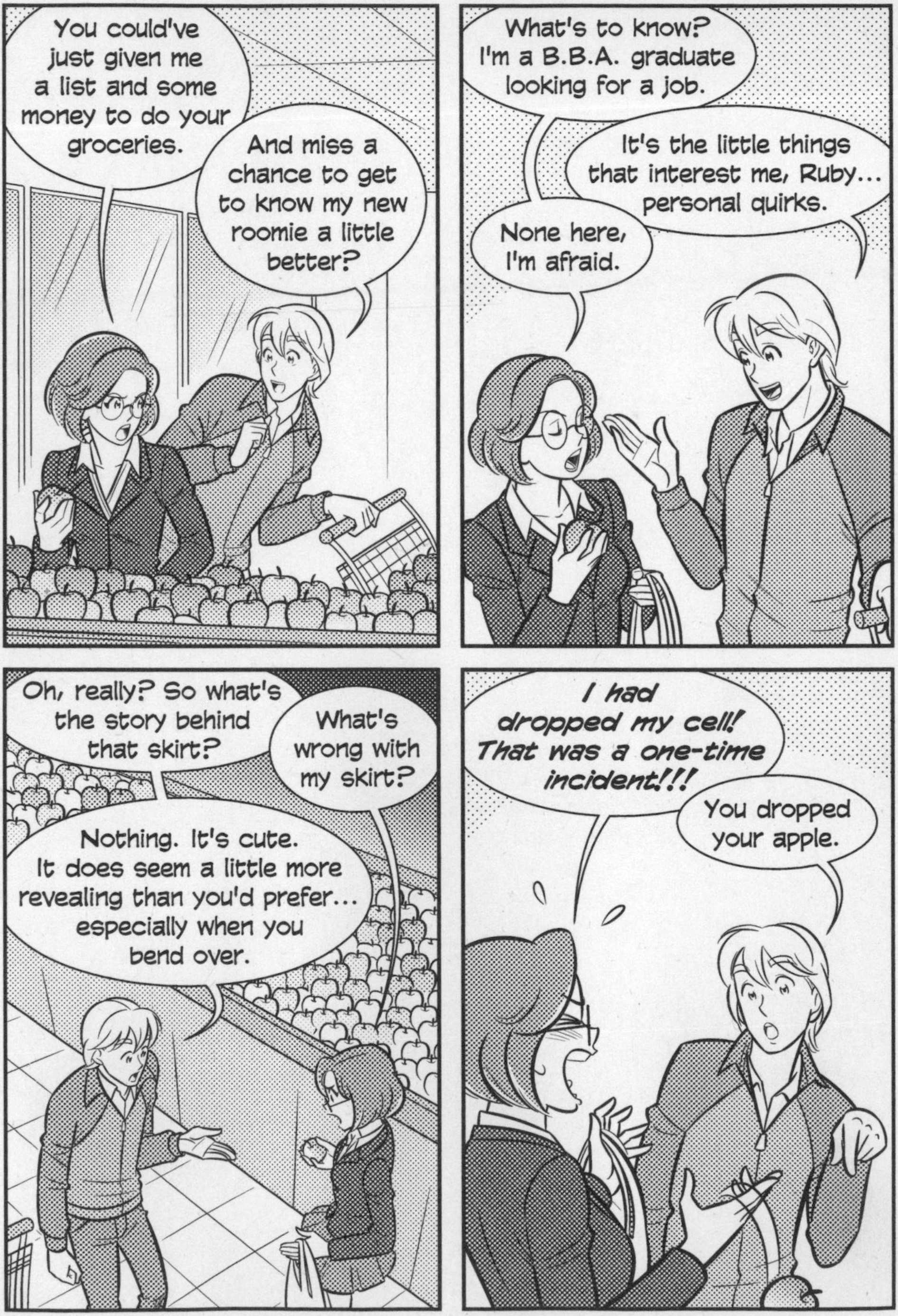
You could've just given me a list and some money to do your groceries.
And miss a chance to get to know my new roomie a little better?
What's to know? I'm a B.B.A. graduate looking for a job.
It's the little things that interest me, Ruby... personal quirks.
None here, I'm afraid.
Oh, really? So what's the story behind that skirt?
What's wrong with my skirt?
Nothing. It's cute. It does seem a little more revealing than you'd prefer... especially when you bend over.
I had dropped my cell! That was a one-time incident!!!
You dropped your apple.

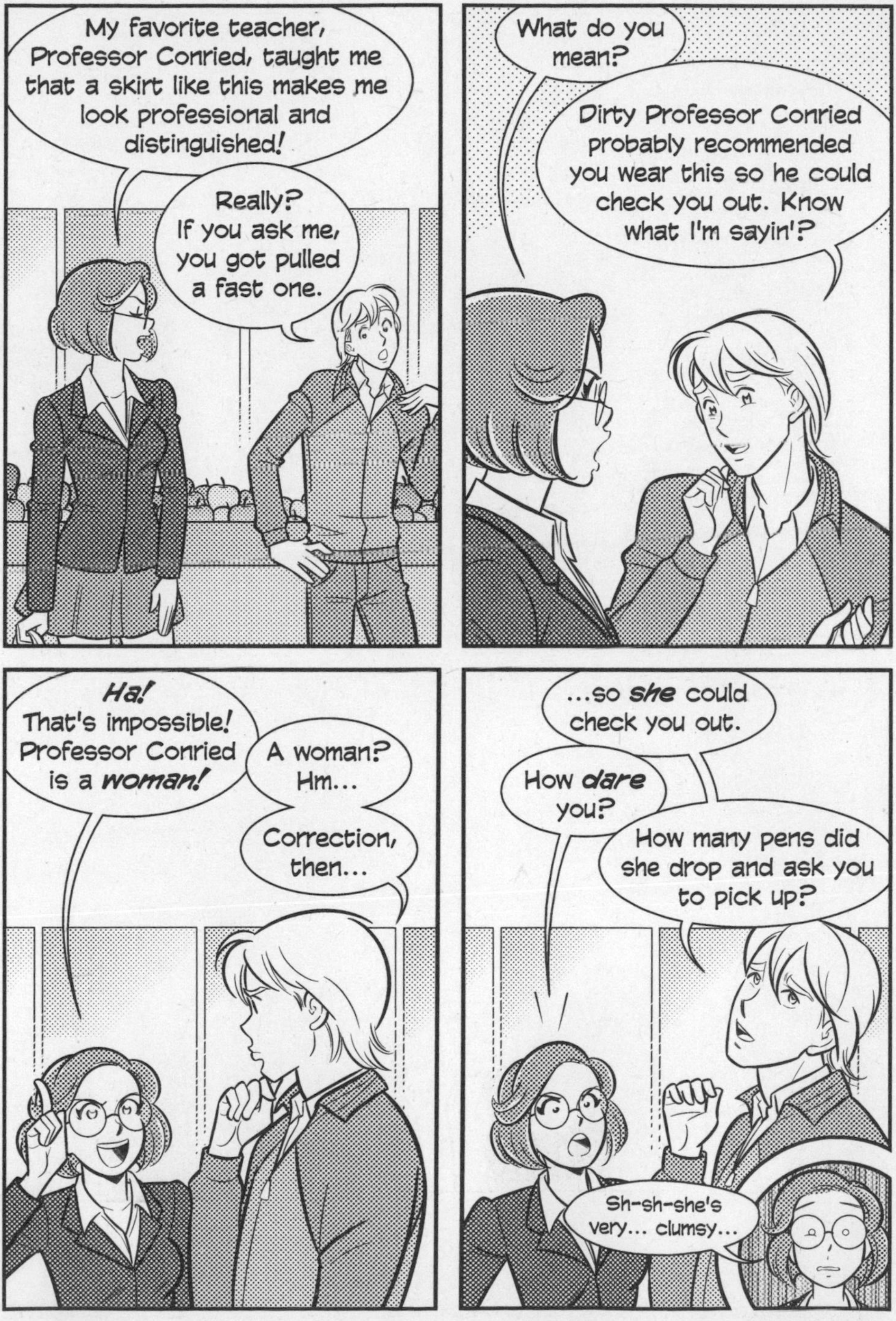
My favorite teacher, Professor Conried, taught me that a skirt like this makes me look professional and distinguished!
Really? If you ask me, you got pulled a fast one.
What do you mean?
Dirty Professor Conried probably recommended you wear this so he could check you out. Know what I'm sayin'?
Ha! That's impossible! Professor Conried is a *woman!*
A woman? Hm...
Correction, then...
...so *she* could check you out.
How *dare* you?
How many pens did she drop and ask you to pick up?
Sh-sh-she's very... clumsy...

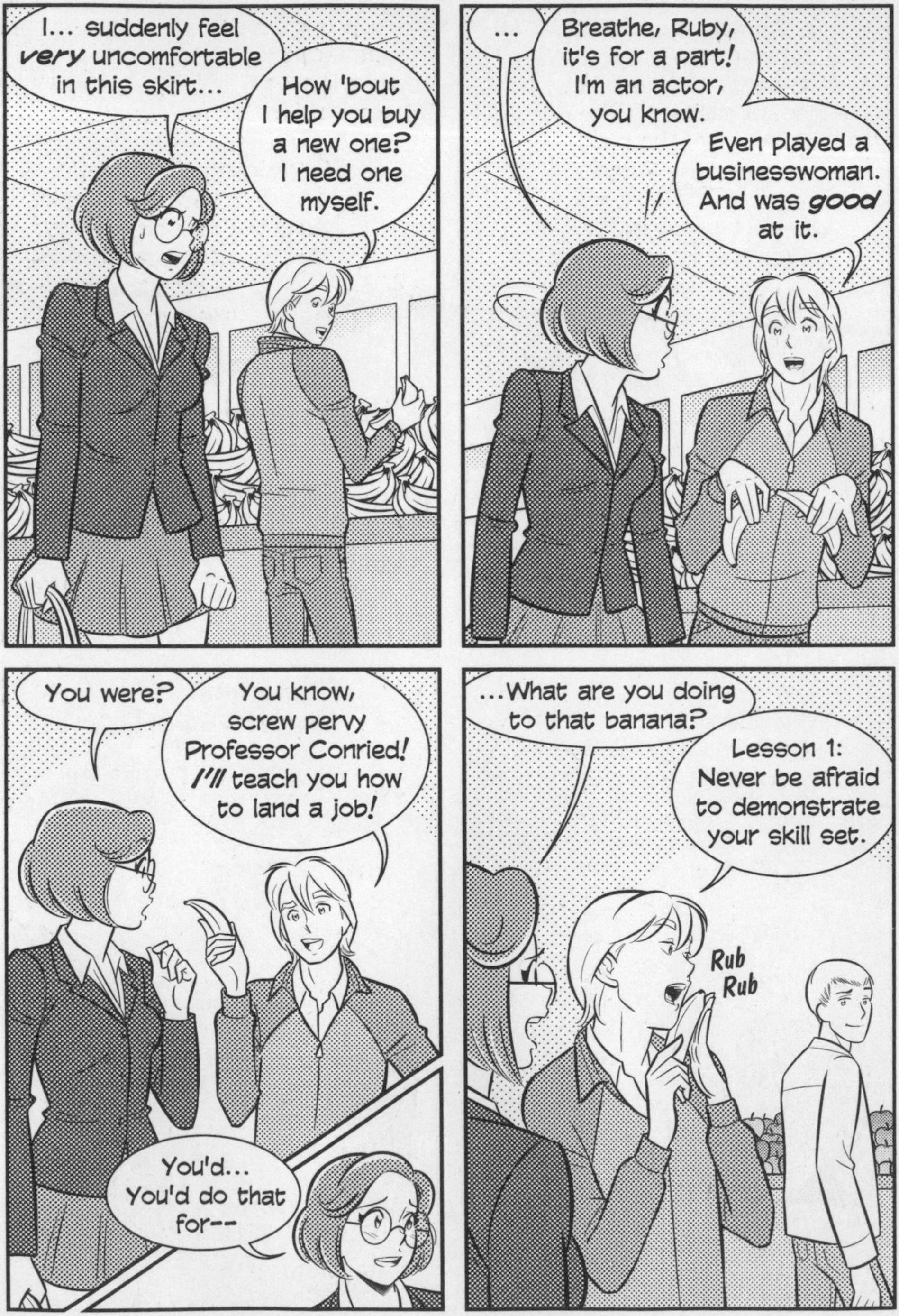
I... suddenly feel *very* uncomfortable in this skirt...
How 'bout I help you buy a new one? I need one myself.
...
Breathe, Ruby, it's for a part! I'm an actor, you know.
Even played a businesswoman. And was *good* at it.
!!
You were?
You know, screw pervy Professor Conried! *I'll* teach you how to land a job!
You'd... You'd do that for--
...What are you doing to that banana?
Lesson 1: Never be afraid to demonstrate your skill set.
Rub Rub

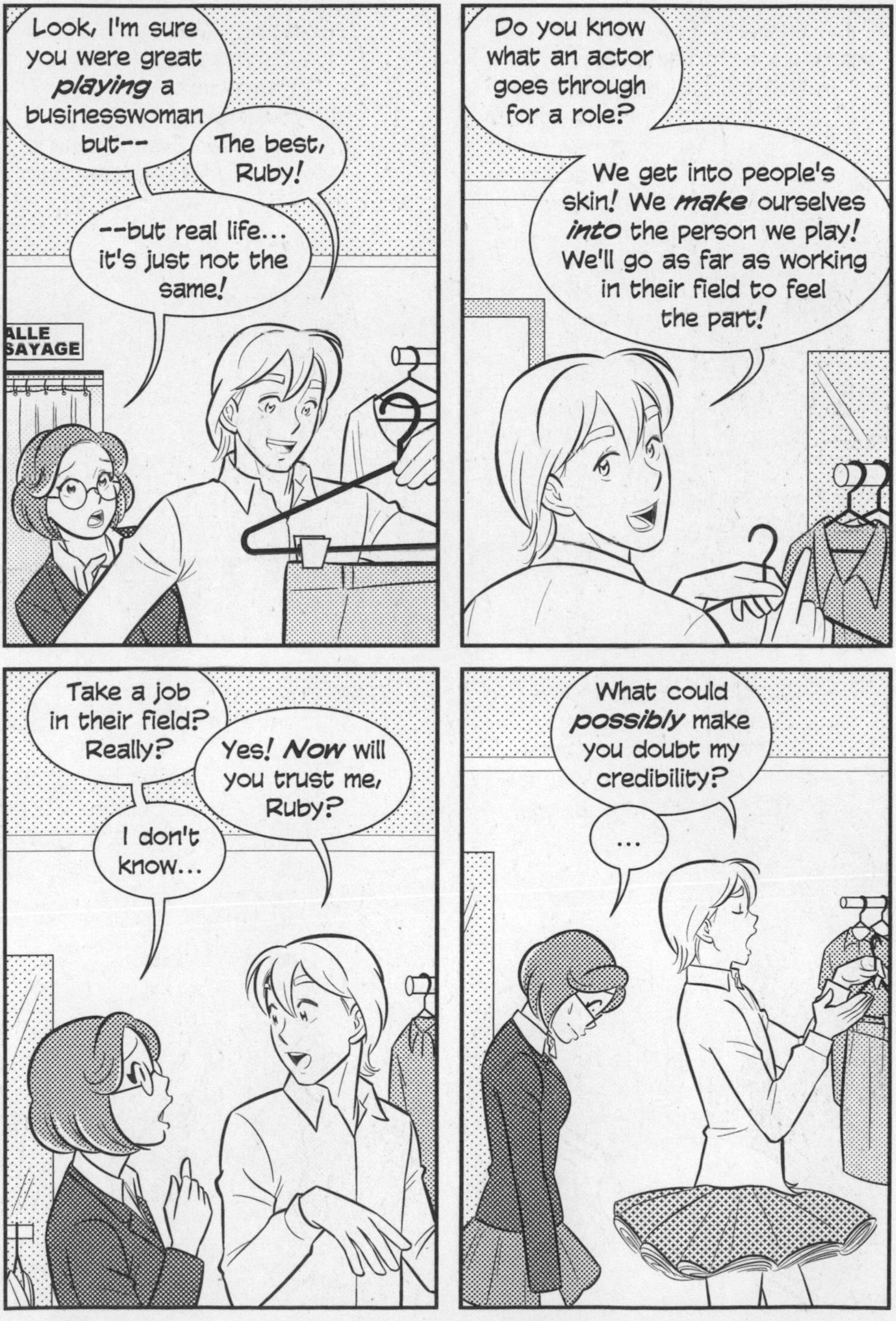
Look, I'm sure you were great *playing* a businesswoman but--
The best, Ruby!
--but real life... it's just not the same!
ALLE SAYAGE
Do you know what an actor goes through for a role?
We get into people's skin! We *make* ourselves *into* the person we play! We'll go as far as working in their field to feel the part!
Take a job in their field? Really?
Yes! *Now* will you trust me, Ruby?
I don't know...
What could *possibly* make you doubt my credibility?
...

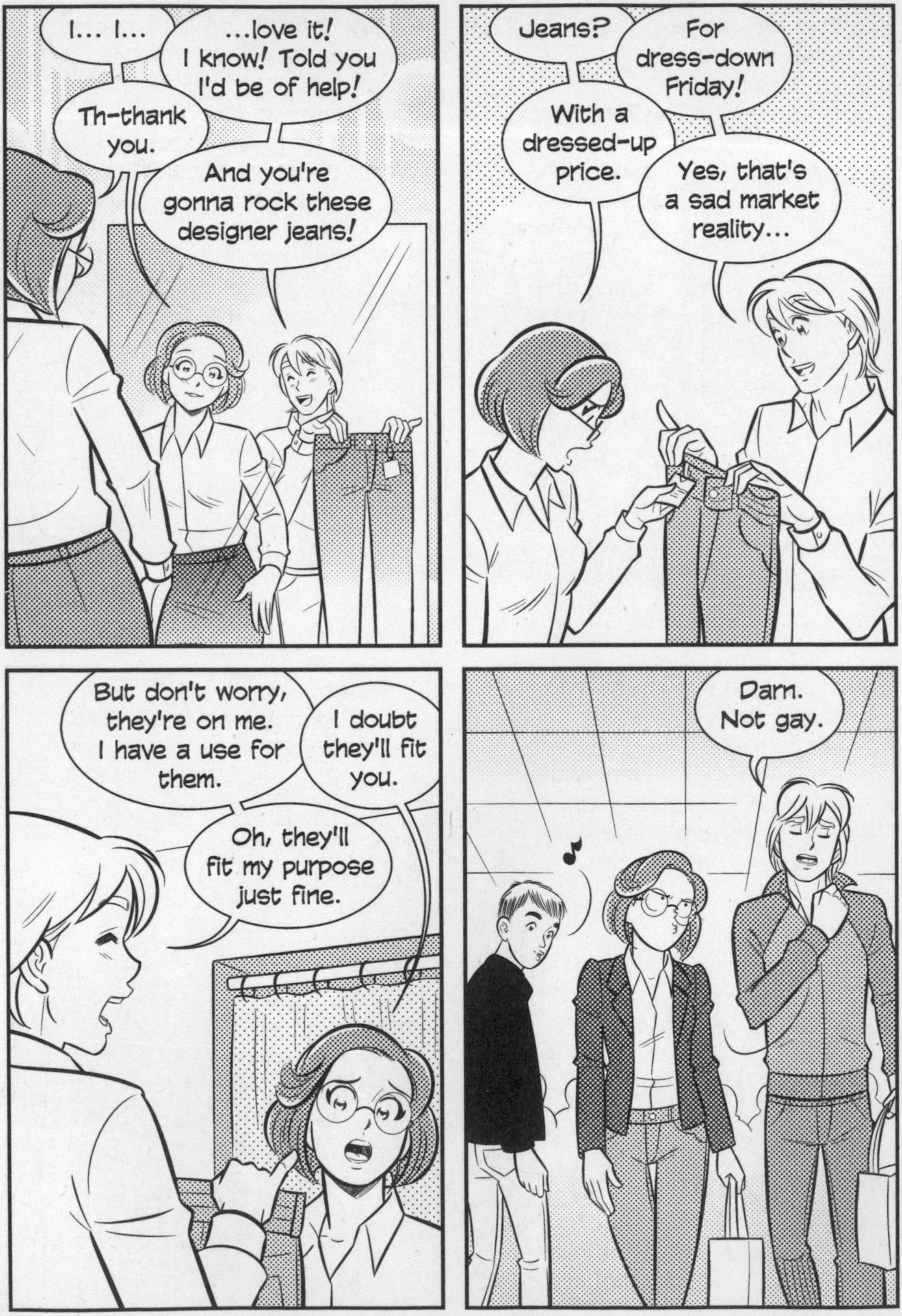
I... I...
...love it! I know! Told you I'd be of help!
Th-thank you.
And you're gonna rock these designer jeans!
Jeans?
For dress-down Friday!
With a dressed-up price.
Yes, that's a sad market reality...
But don't worry, they're on me. I have a use for them.
I doubt they'll fit you.
Oh, they'll fit my purpose just fine.
Darn. Not gay.

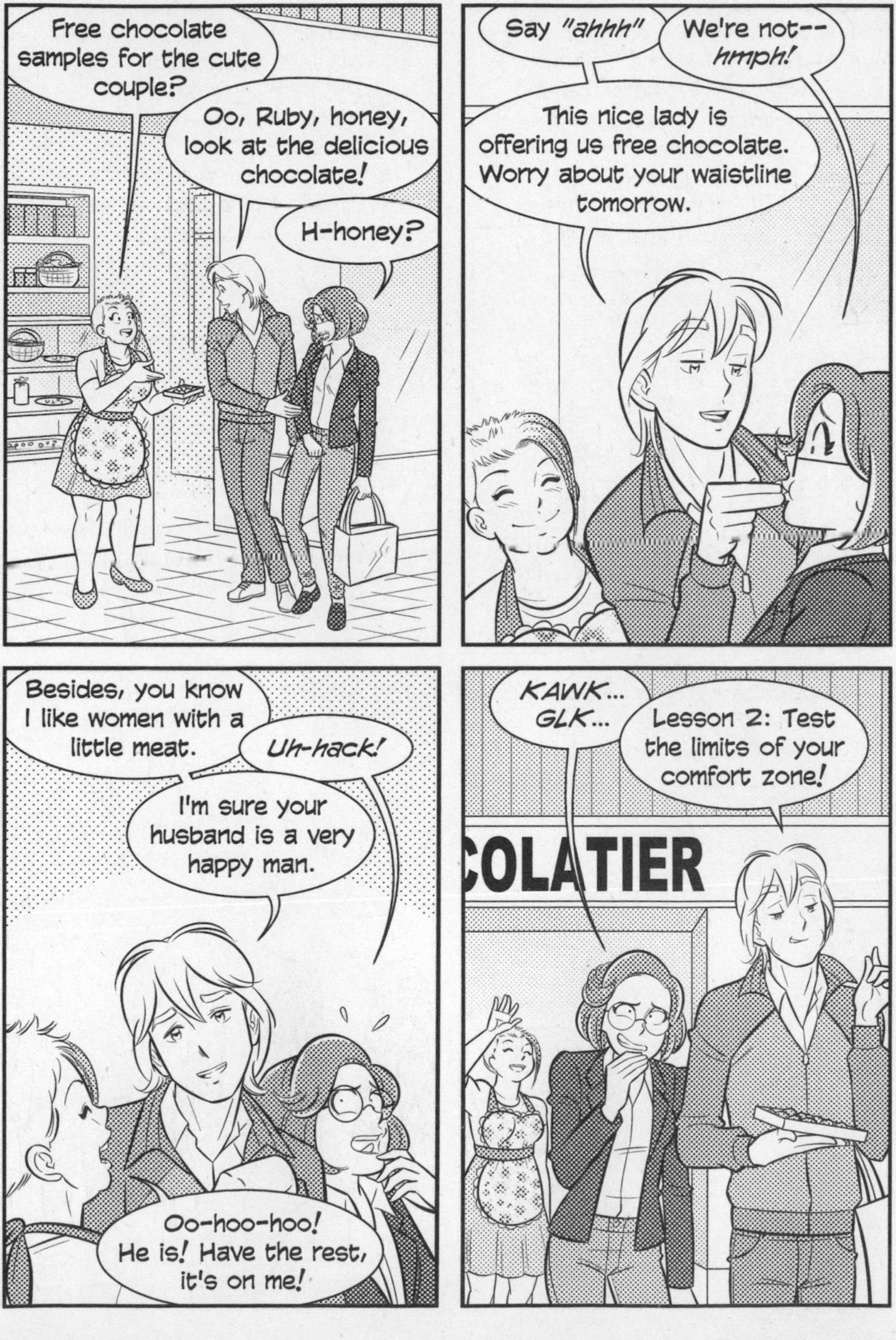
Free chocolate samples for the cute couple?
Oo, Ruby, honey, look at the delicious chocolate!
H-honey?
Say "ahhh"
We're not-- hmph!
This nice lady is offering us free chocolate. Worry about your waistline tomorrow.
Besides, you know I like women with a little meat.
Uh-hack!
I'm sure your husband is a very happy man.
Oo-hoo-hoo! He is! Have the rest, it's on me!
KAWK... GLK...
Lesson 2: Test the limits of your comfort zone!
COLATIER

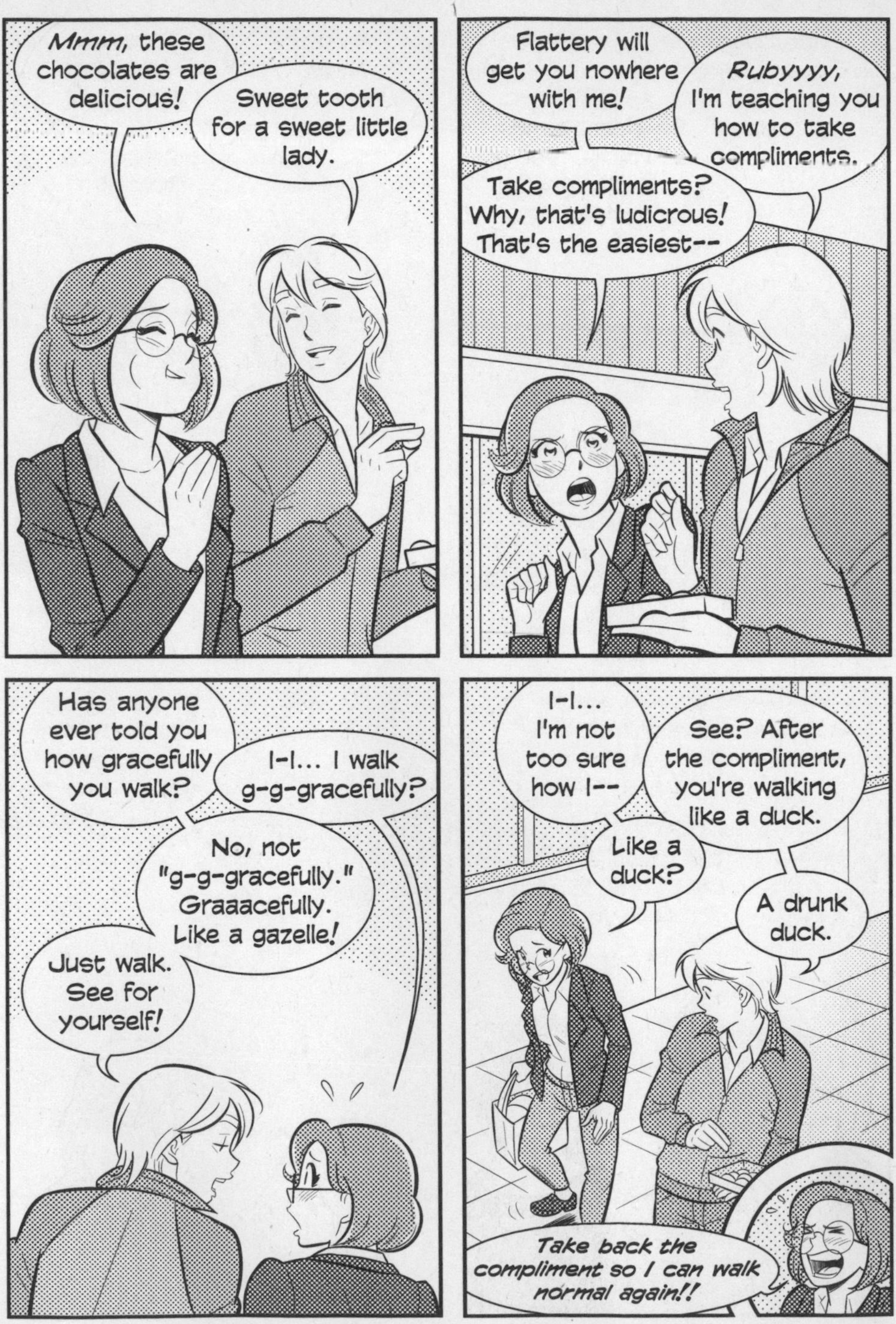

Mmm, these chocolates are delicious!
Sweet tooth for a sweet little lady.
Flattery will get you nowhere with me!
Rubyyyy, I'm teaching you how to take compliments.
Take compliments? Why, that's ludicrous! That's the easiest--
Has anyone ever told you how gracefully you walk?
I-I... I walk g-g-gracefully?
No, not "g-g-gracefully." Graaacefully. Like a gazelle!
Just walk. See for yourself!
I-I... I'm not too sure how I--
See? After the compliment, you're walking like a duck.
Like a duck?
A drunk duck.
Take back the compliment so I can walk normal again!!

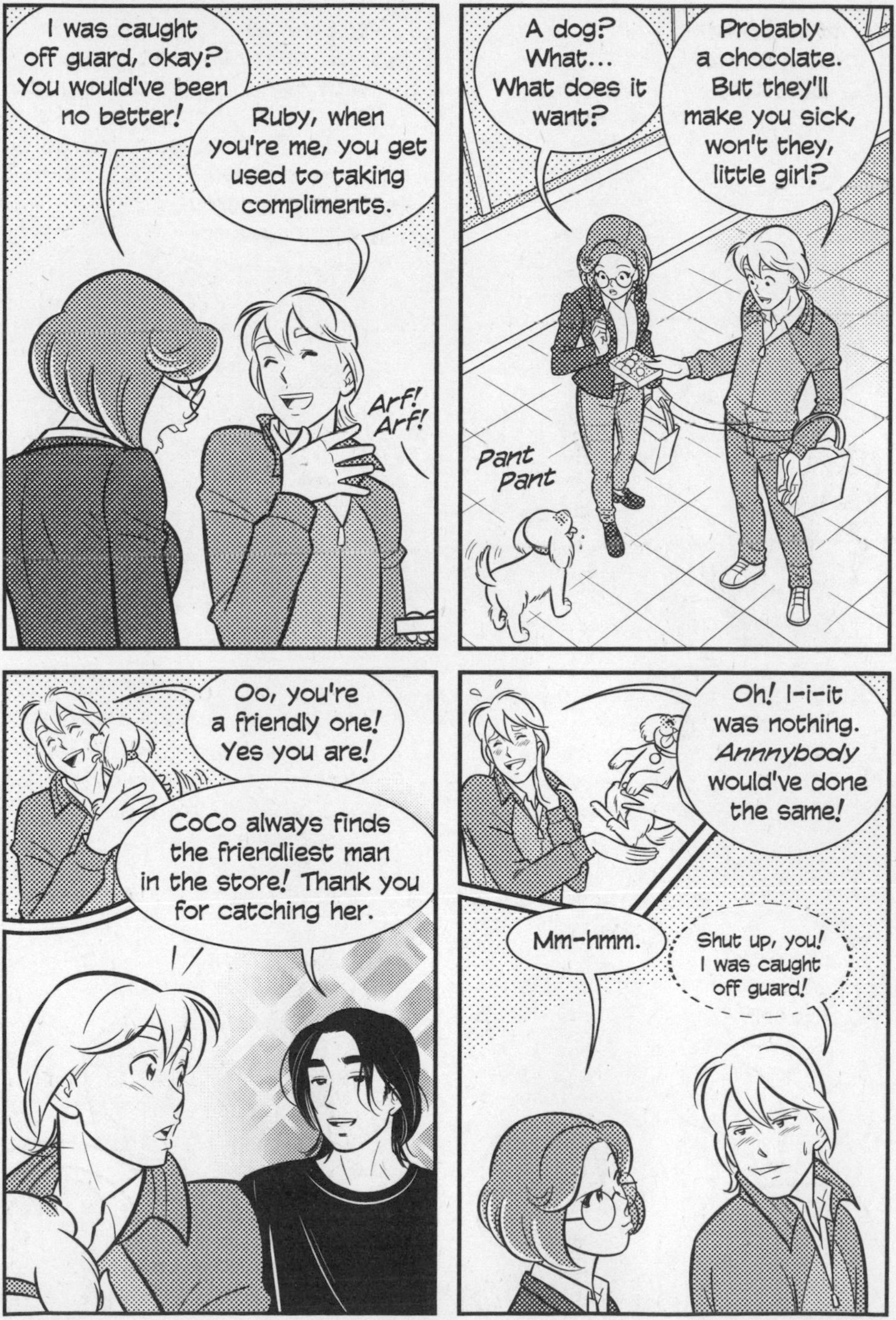
I was caught off guard, okay? You would've been no better!
Ruby, when you're me, you get used to taking compliments.
Arf! Arf!
A dog? What... What does it want?
Probably a chocolate. But they'll make you sick, won't they, little girl?
Pant Pant
Oo, you're a friendly one! Yes you are!
CoCo always finds the friendliest man in the store! Thank you for catching her.
Oh! I-i-it was nothing. *Annnybody* would've done the same!
Mm-hmm.
Shut up, you! I was caught off guard!

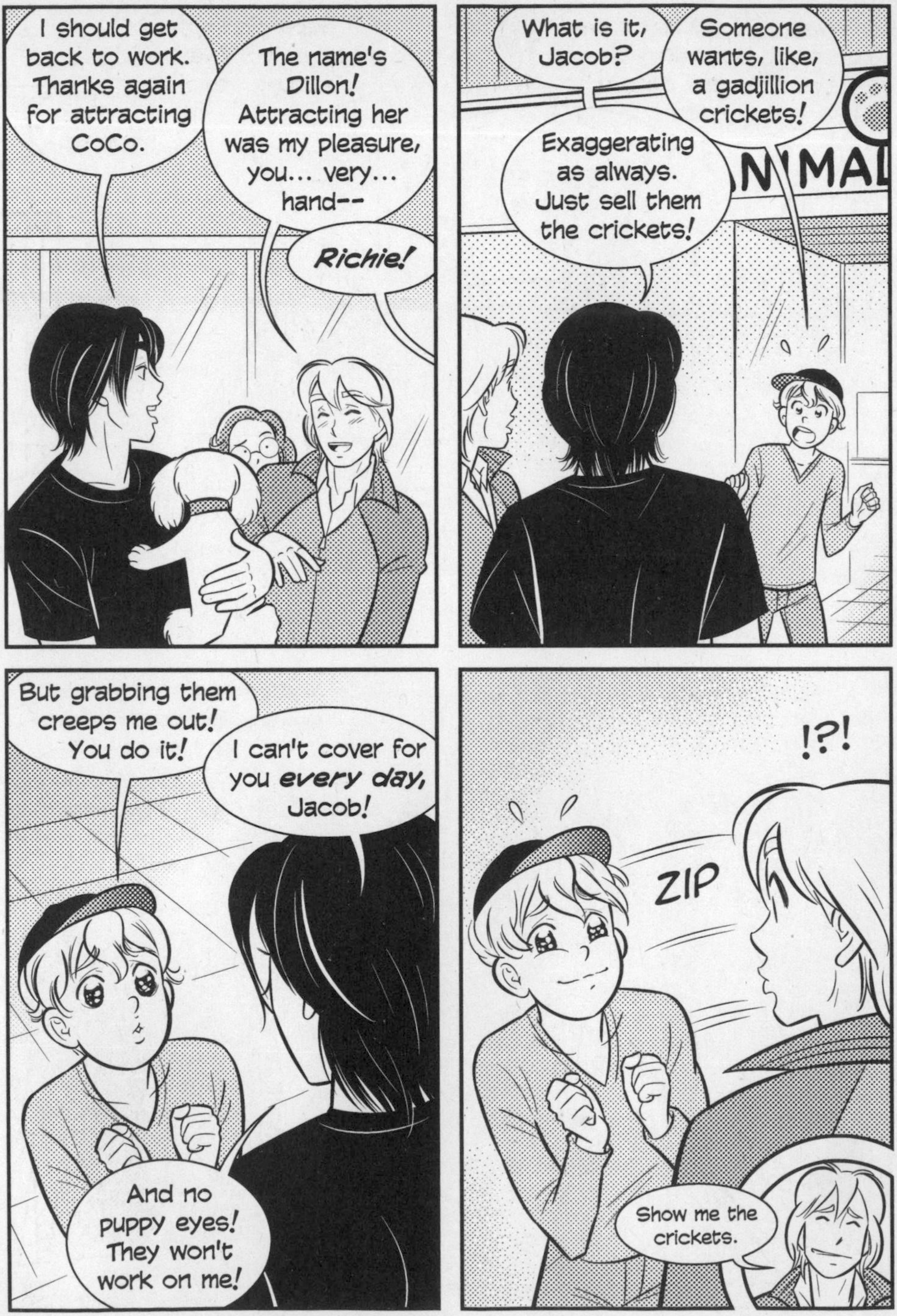
I should get back to work. Thanks again for attracting CoCo.
The name's Dillon! Attracting her was my pleasure, you... very... hand--
Richie!
What is it, Jacob?
Someone wants, like, a gadjillion crickets!
Exaggerating as always. Just sell them the crickets!
ANIMAL
But grabbing them creeps me out! You do it!
I can't cover for you every day, Jacob!
And no puppy eyes! They won't work on me!
!?!
ZIP
Show me the crickets.

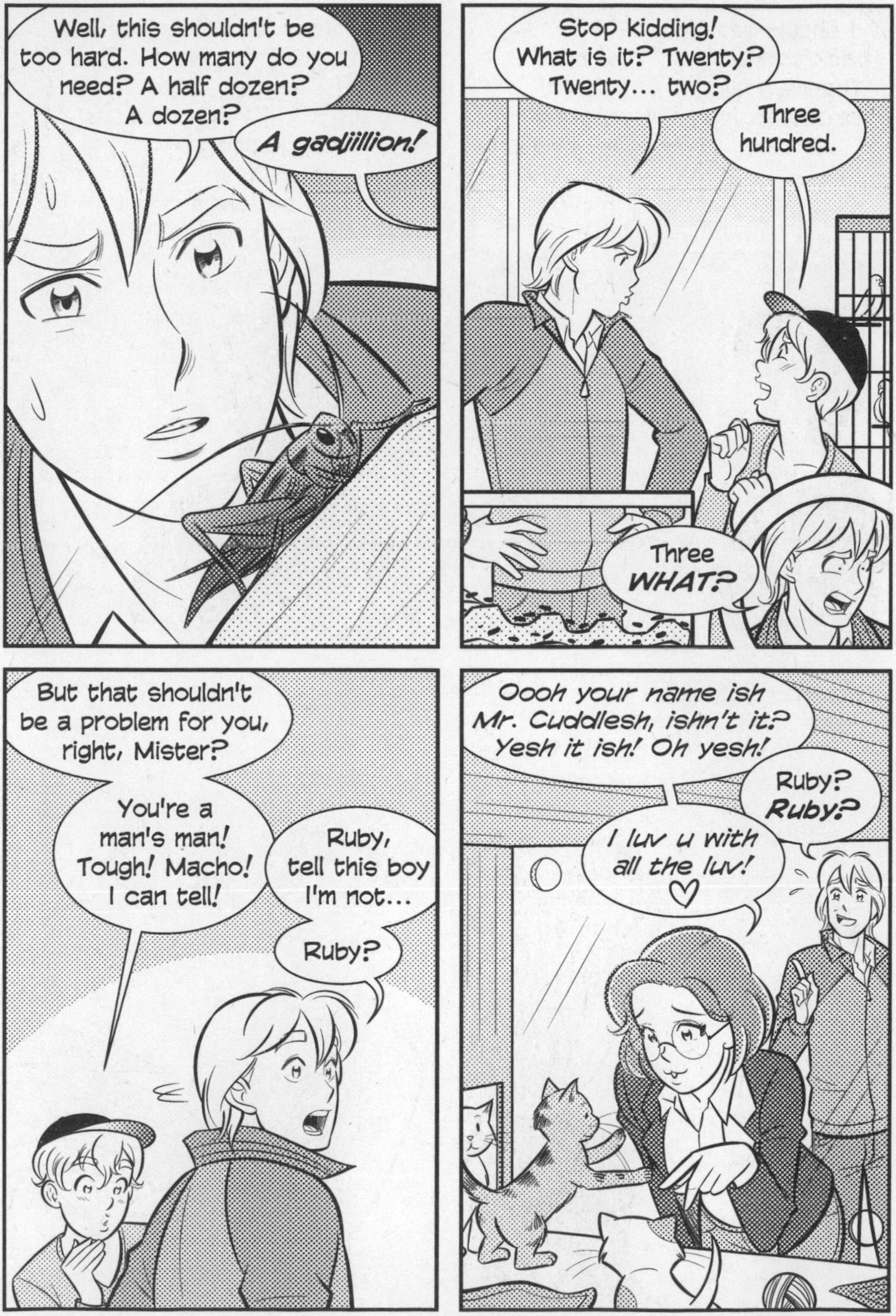
Well, this shouldn't be too hard. How many do you need? A half dozen? A dozen?
A gadjillion!
Stop kidding! What is it? Twenty? Twenty... two?
Three hundred.
Three WHAT?
But that shouldn't be a problem for you, right, Mister?
You're a man's man! Tough! Macho! I can tell!
Ruby, tell this boy I'm not...
Ruby?
Oooh your name ish Mr. Cuddlesh, ishn't it? Yesh it ish! Oh yesh!
Ruby? Ruby?
I luv u with all the luv! ♥

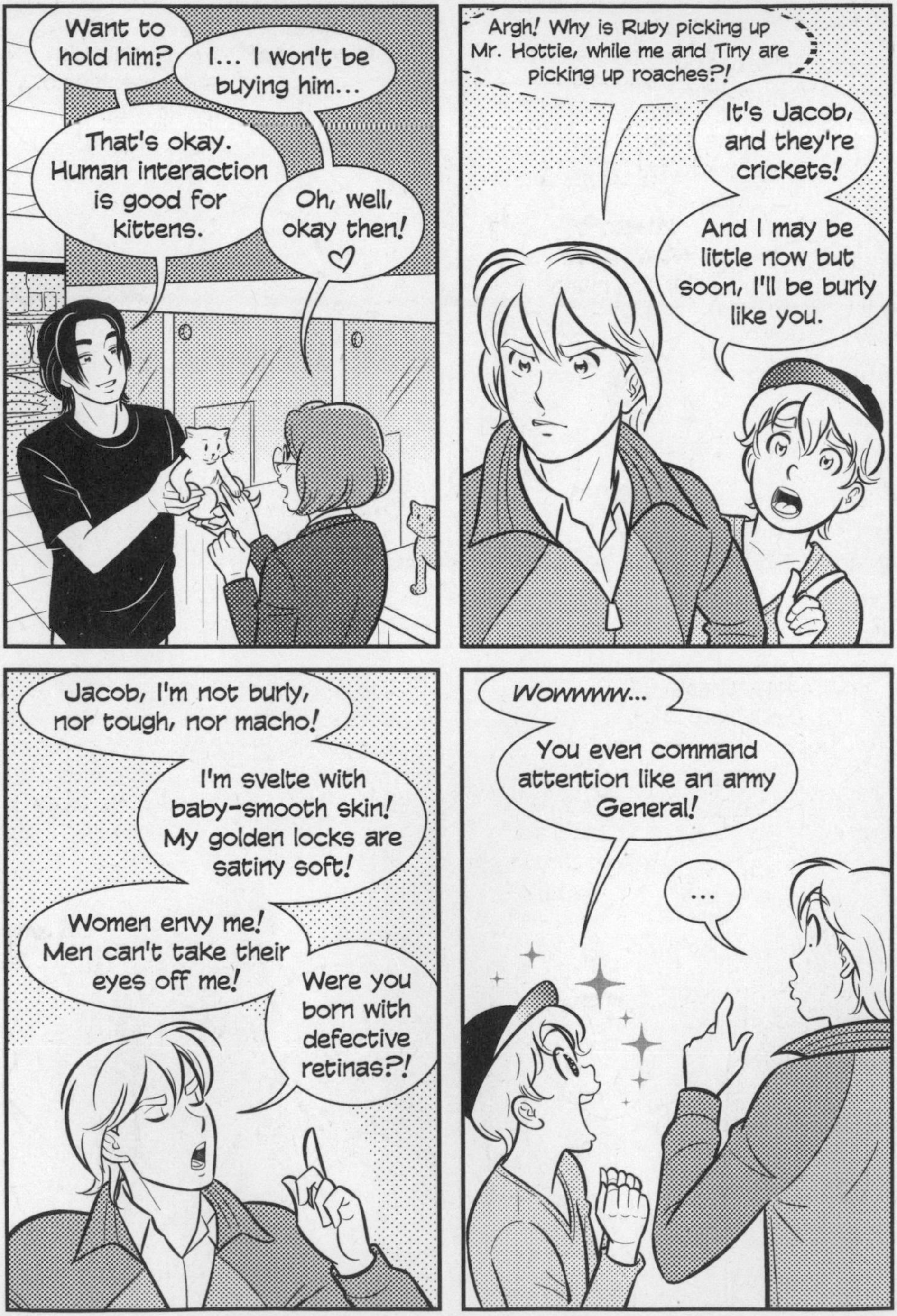

Want to hold him?
I... I won't be buying him...
That's okay. Human interaction is good for kittens.
Oh, well, okay then! ♡
Argh! Why is Ruby picking up Mr. Hottie, while me and Tiny are picking up roaches?!
It's Jacob, and they're crickets!
And I may be little now but soon, I'll be burly like you.
Jacob, I'm not burly, nor tough, nor macho!
I'm svelte with baby-smooth skin! My golden locks are satiny soft!
Women envy me! Men can't take their eyes off me!
Were you born with defective retinas?!
Wowwww...
You even command attention like an army General!
...

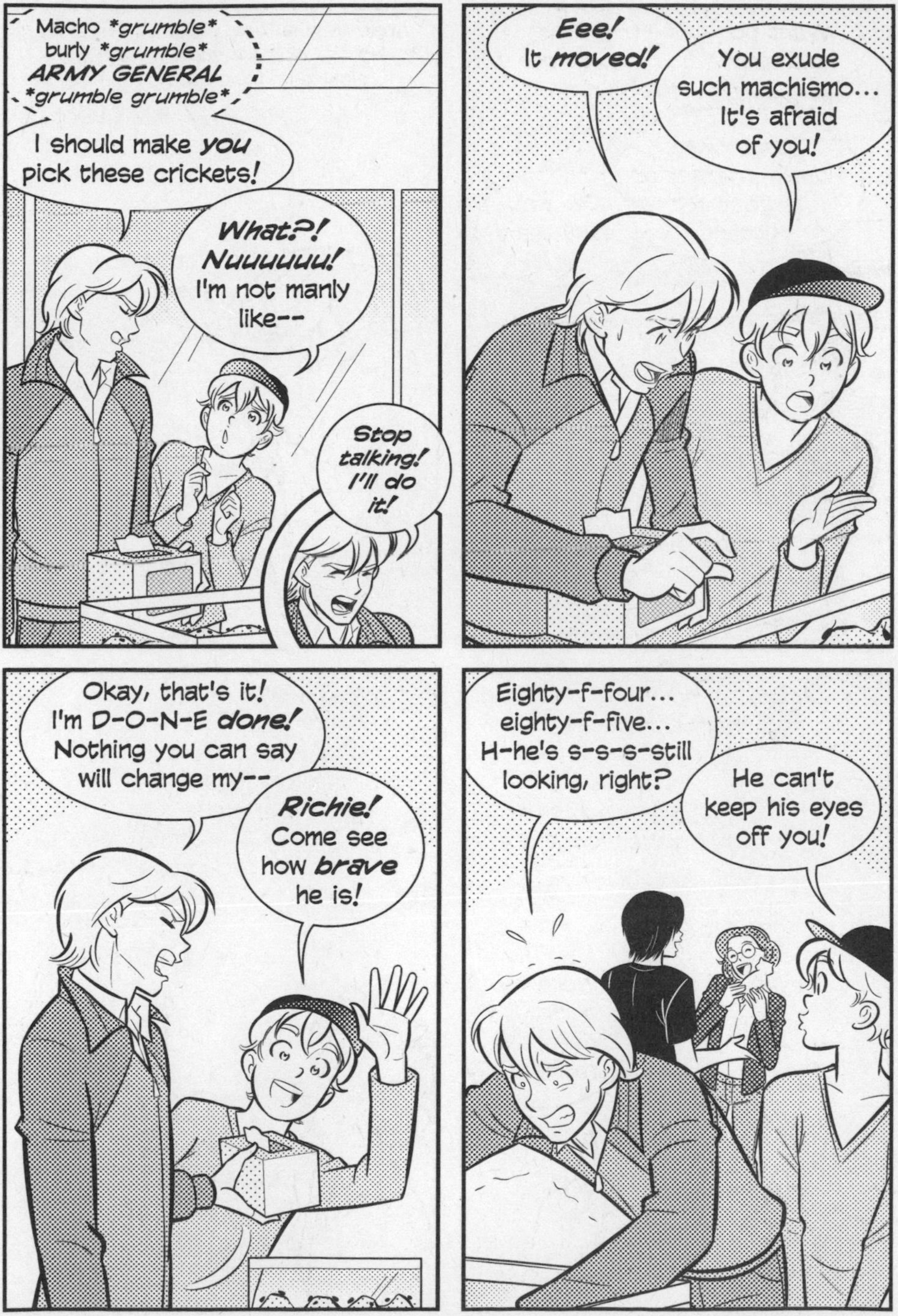
Macho *grumble* burly *grumble* ARMY GENERAL *grumble grumble*
I should make you pick these crickets!
What?! Nuuuuuu! I'm not manly like--
Stop talking! I'll do it!
Eee! It moved!
You exude such machismo... It's afraid of you!
Okay, that's it! I'm D-O-N-E done! Nothing you can say will change my--
Richie! Come see how brave he is!
Eighty-f-four... eighty-f-five... H-he's s-s-s-still looking, right?
He can't keep his eyes off you!

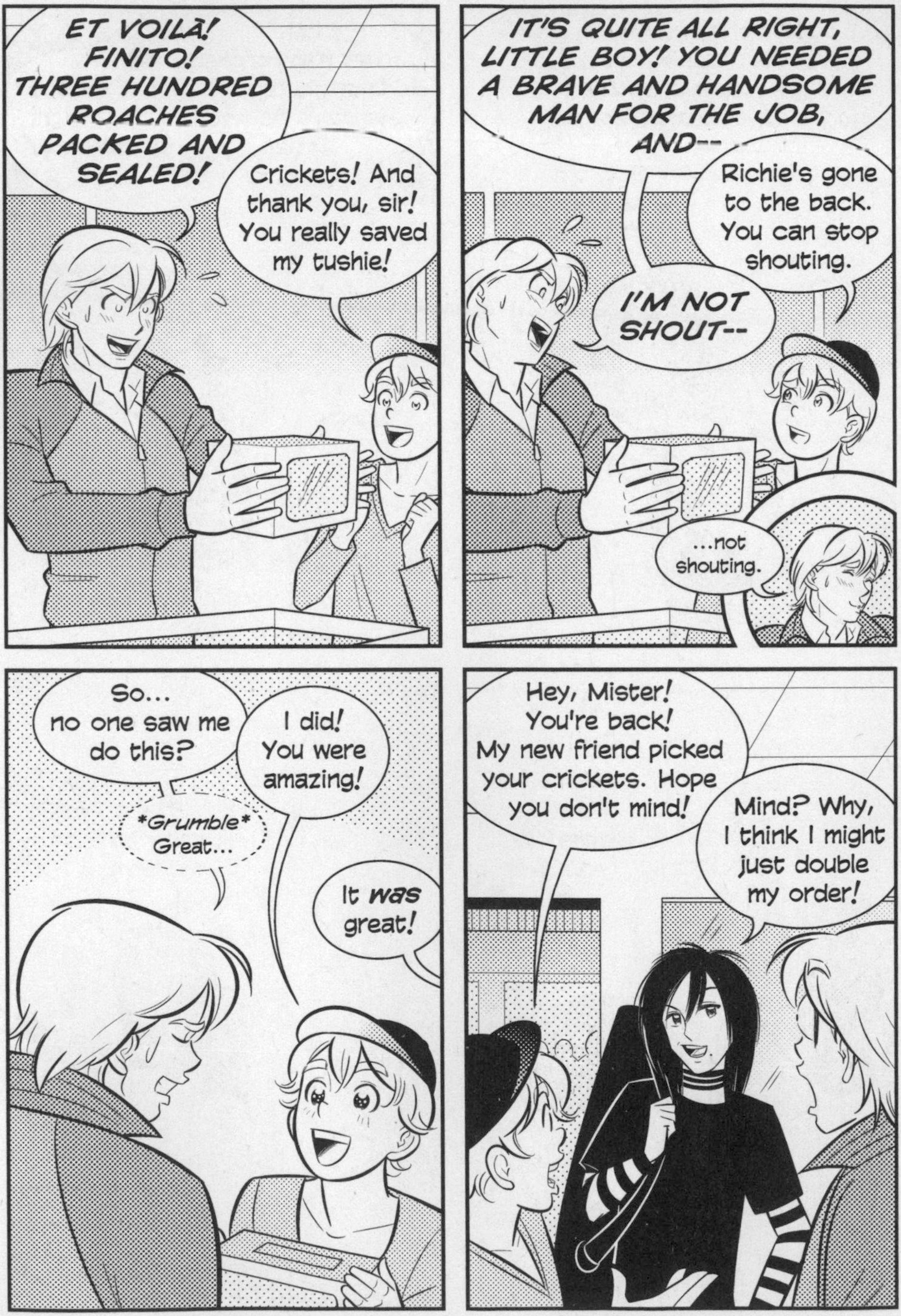
ET VOILÀ! FINITO! THREE HUNDRED ROACHES PACKED AND SEALED!
Crickets! And thank you, sir! You really saved my tushie!
IT'S QUITE ALL RIGHT, LITTLE BOY! YOU NEEDED A BRAVE AND HANDSOME MAN FOR THE JOB, AND--
Richie's gone to the back. You can stop shouting.
I'M NOT SHOUT--
...not shouting.
So... no one saw me do this?
I did! You were amazing!
Grumble Great...
It *was* great!
Hey, Mister! You're back! My new friend picked your crickets. Hope you don't mind!
Mind? Why, I think I might just double my order!

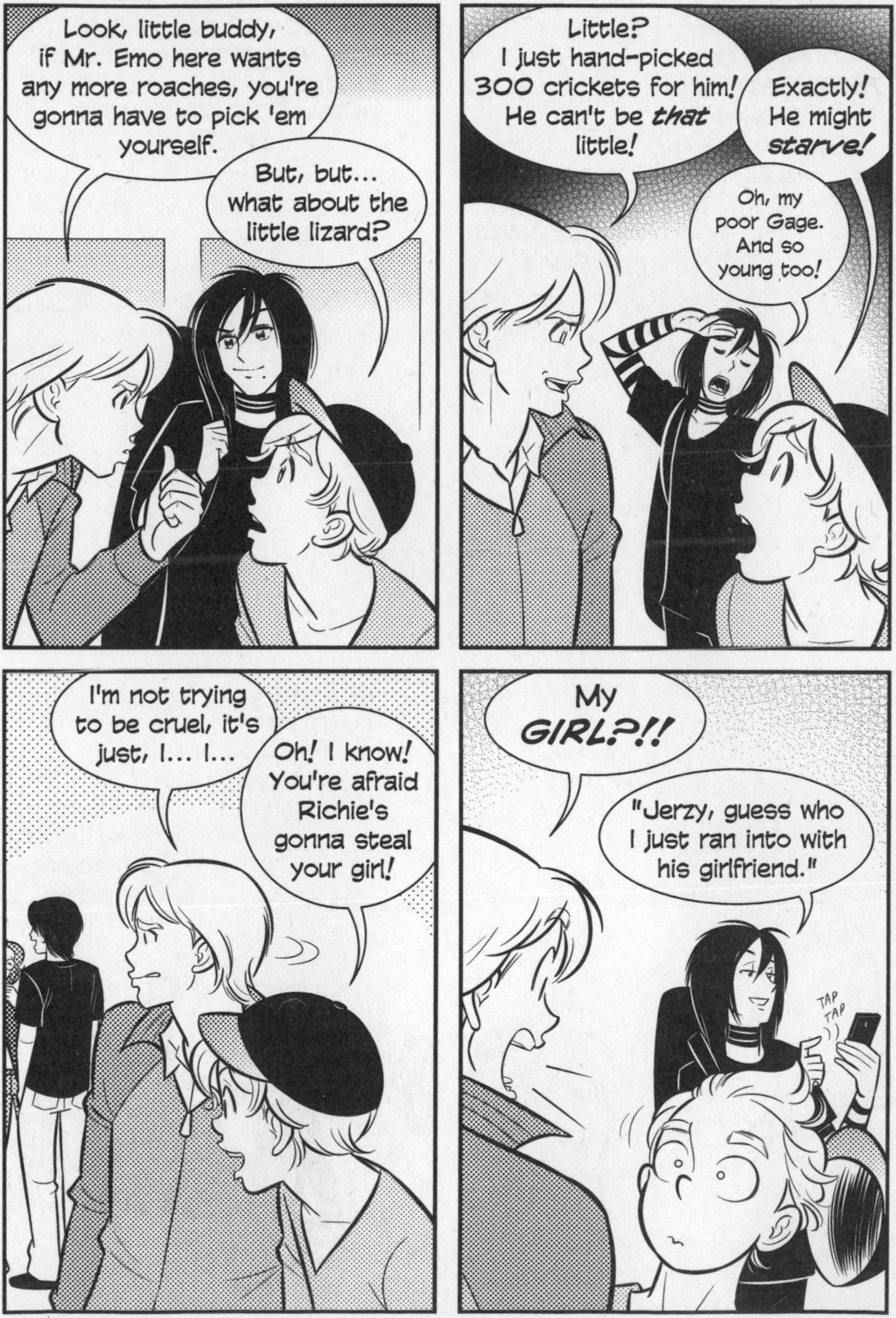
Look, little buddy, if Mr. Emo here wants any more roaches, you're gonna have to pick 'em yourself.
But, but... what about the little lizard?
Little? I just hand-picked 300 crickets for him! He can't be *that* little!
Exactly! He might *starve!*
Oh, my poor Gage. And so young too!
I'm not trying to be cruel, it's just, I... I...
Oh! I know! You're afraid Richie's gonna steal your girl!
My *GIRL?!!*
"Jerzy, guess who I just ran into with his girlfriend."
TAP TAP

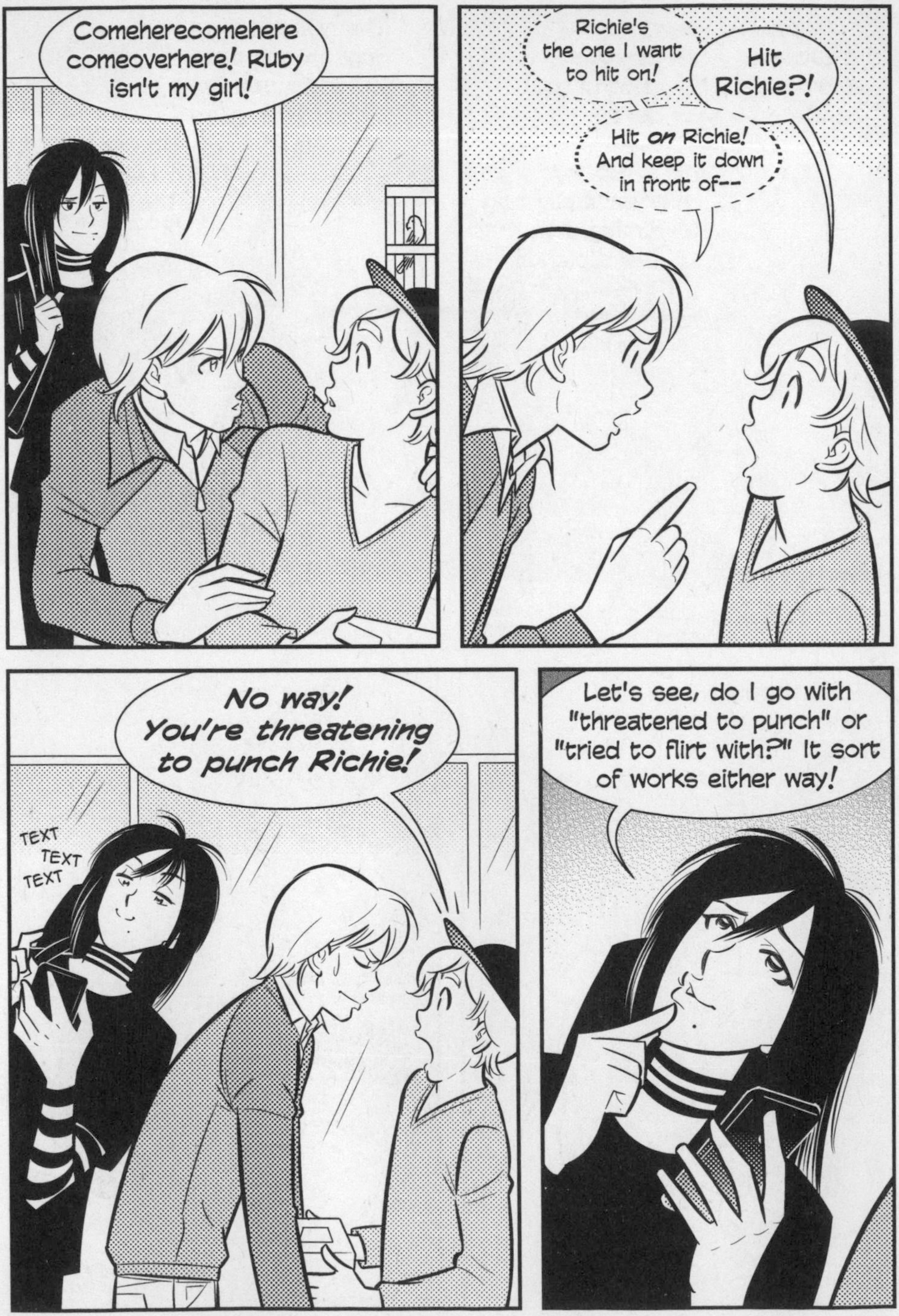
Comeherecomehere comeoverhere! Ruby isn't my girl!
Richie's the one I want to hit on!
Hit Richie?!
Hit *on* Richie! And keep it down in front of--
No way! You're threatening to punch Richie!
TEXT TEXT TEXT
Let's see, do I go with "threatened to punch" or "tried to flirt with?" It sort of works either way!

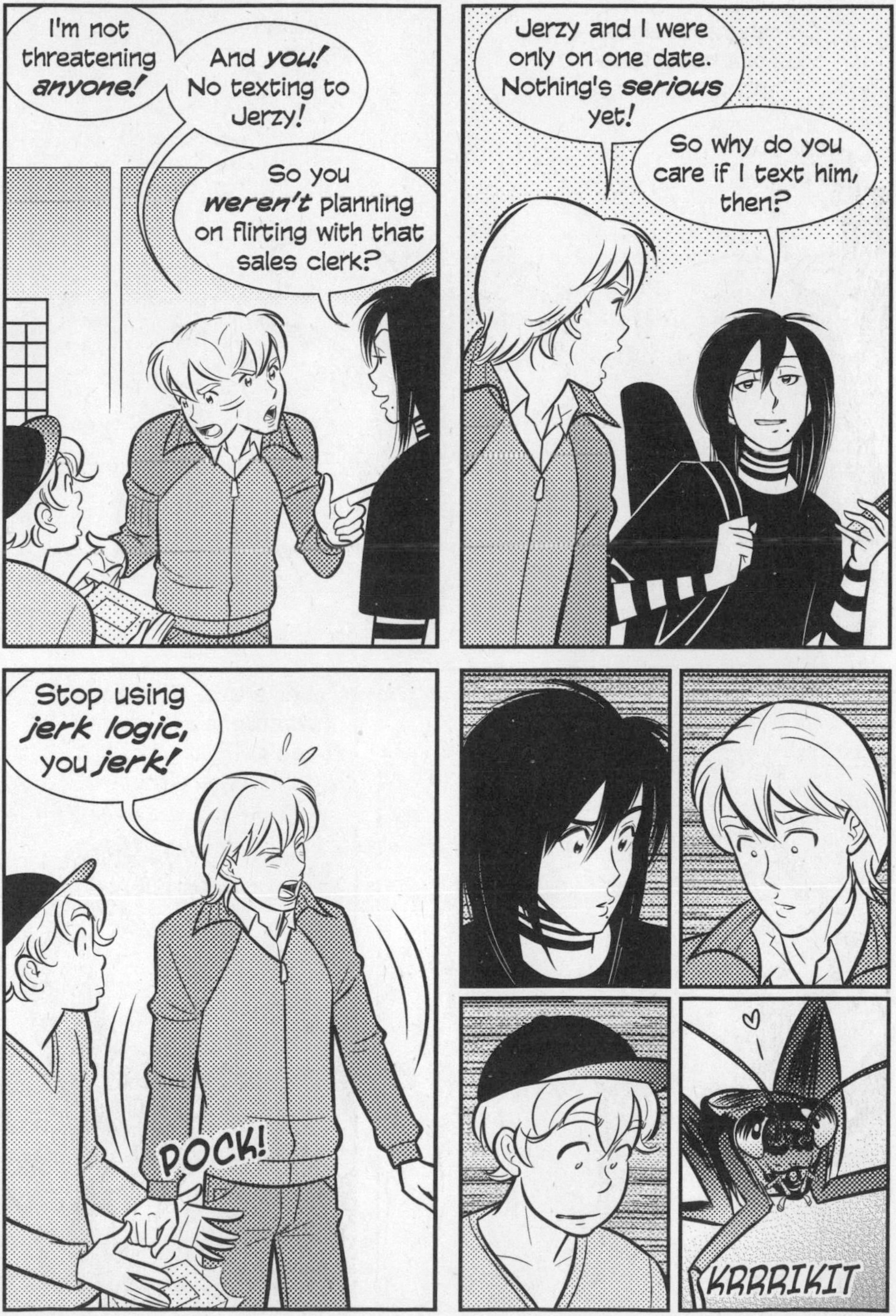
I'm not threatening *anyone!*
And *you!* No texting to Jerzy!
So you *weren't* planning on flirting with that sales clerk?
Jerzy and I were only on one date. Nothing's *serious* yet!
So why do you care if I text him, then?
Stop using *jerk logic,* you *jerk!*
POCK!
KRRRIKIT

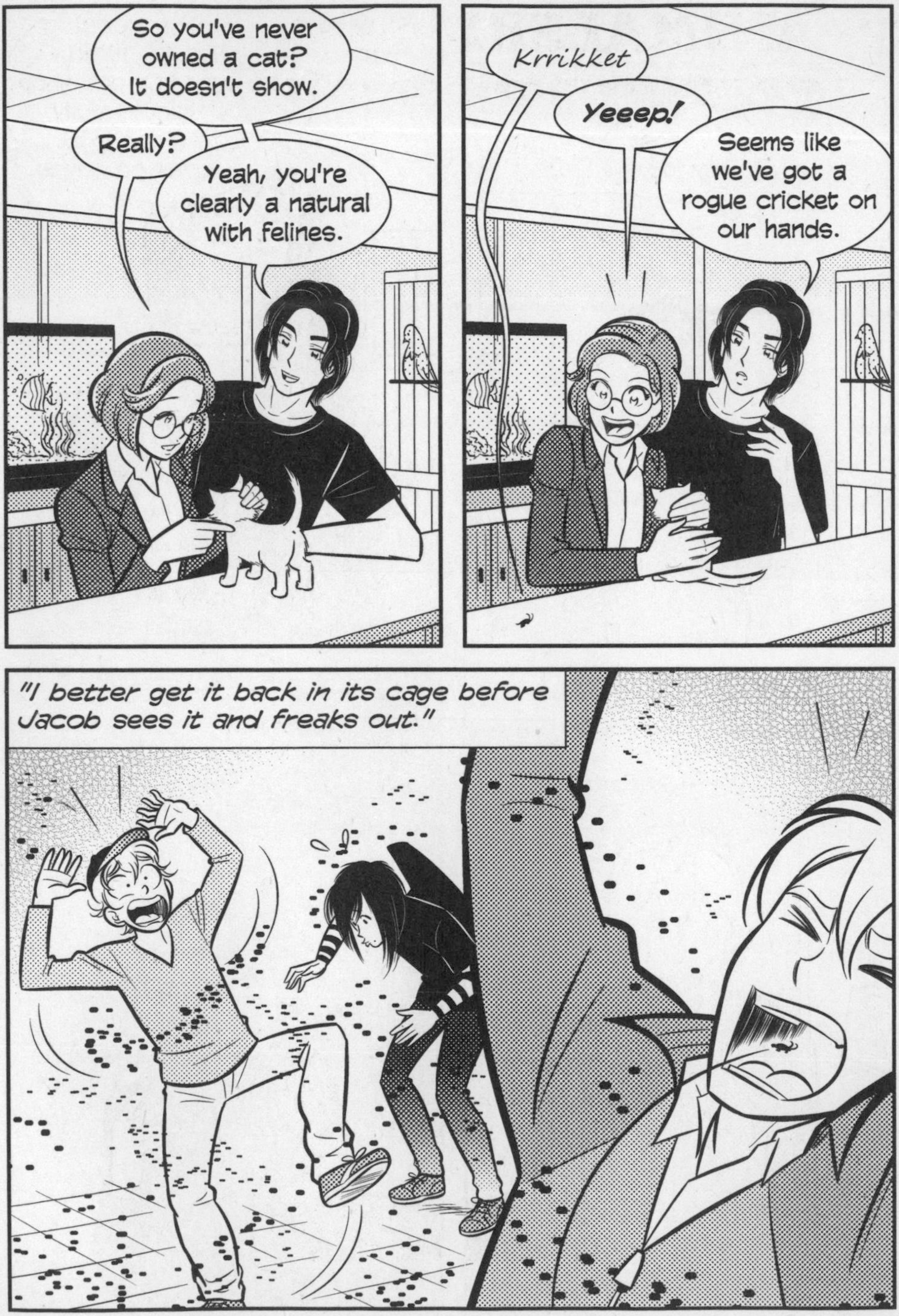

So you've never owned a cat? It doesn't show.
Really?
Yeah, you're clearly a natural with felines.
Krrikket
Yeeep!
Seems like we've got a rogue cricket on our hands.
"I better get it back in its cage before Jacob sees it and freaks out."

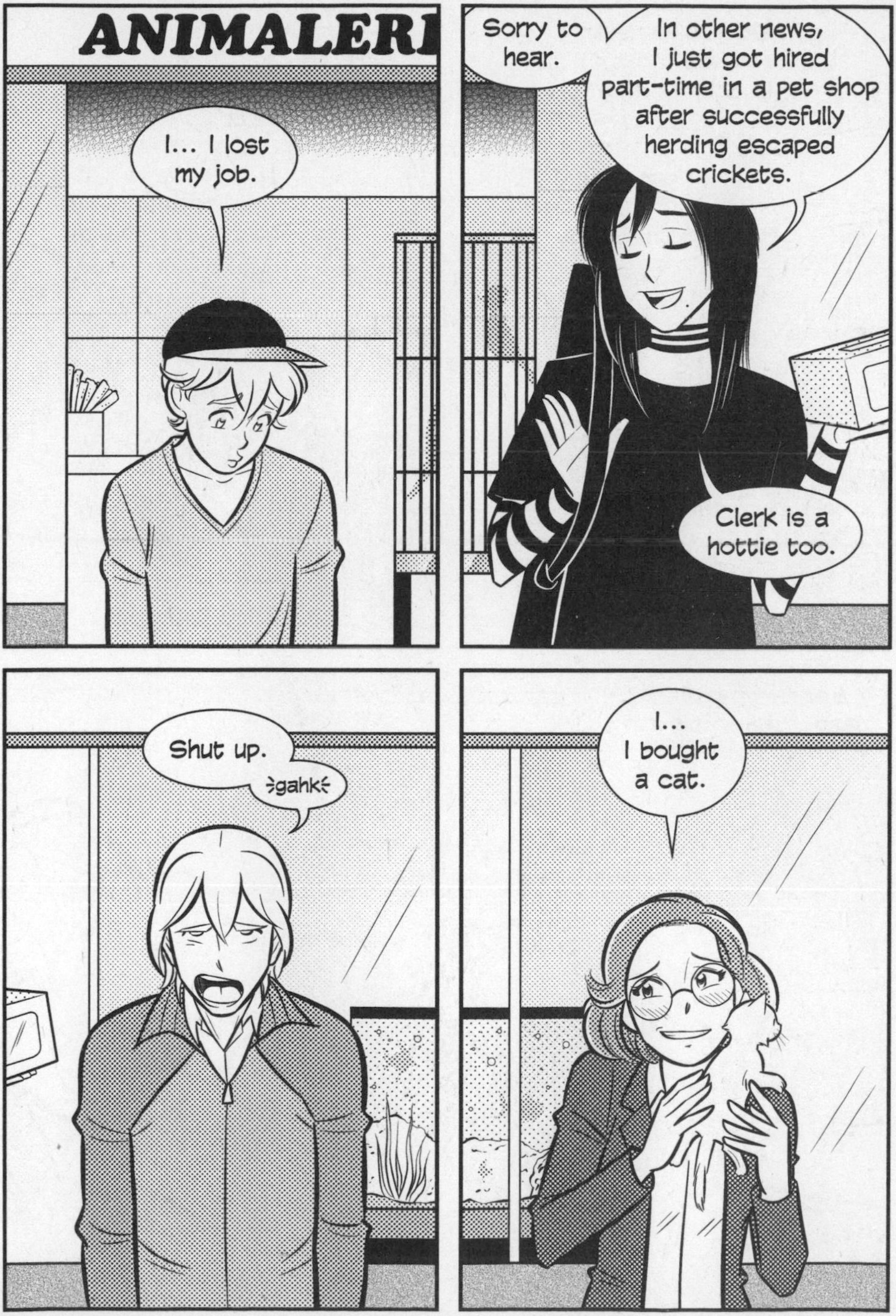
ANIMALERI
I... I lost my job.
Sorry to hear.
In other news, I just got hired part-time in a pet shop after successfully herding escaped crickets.
Clerk is a hottie too.
Shut up.
gahk
I... I bought a cat.

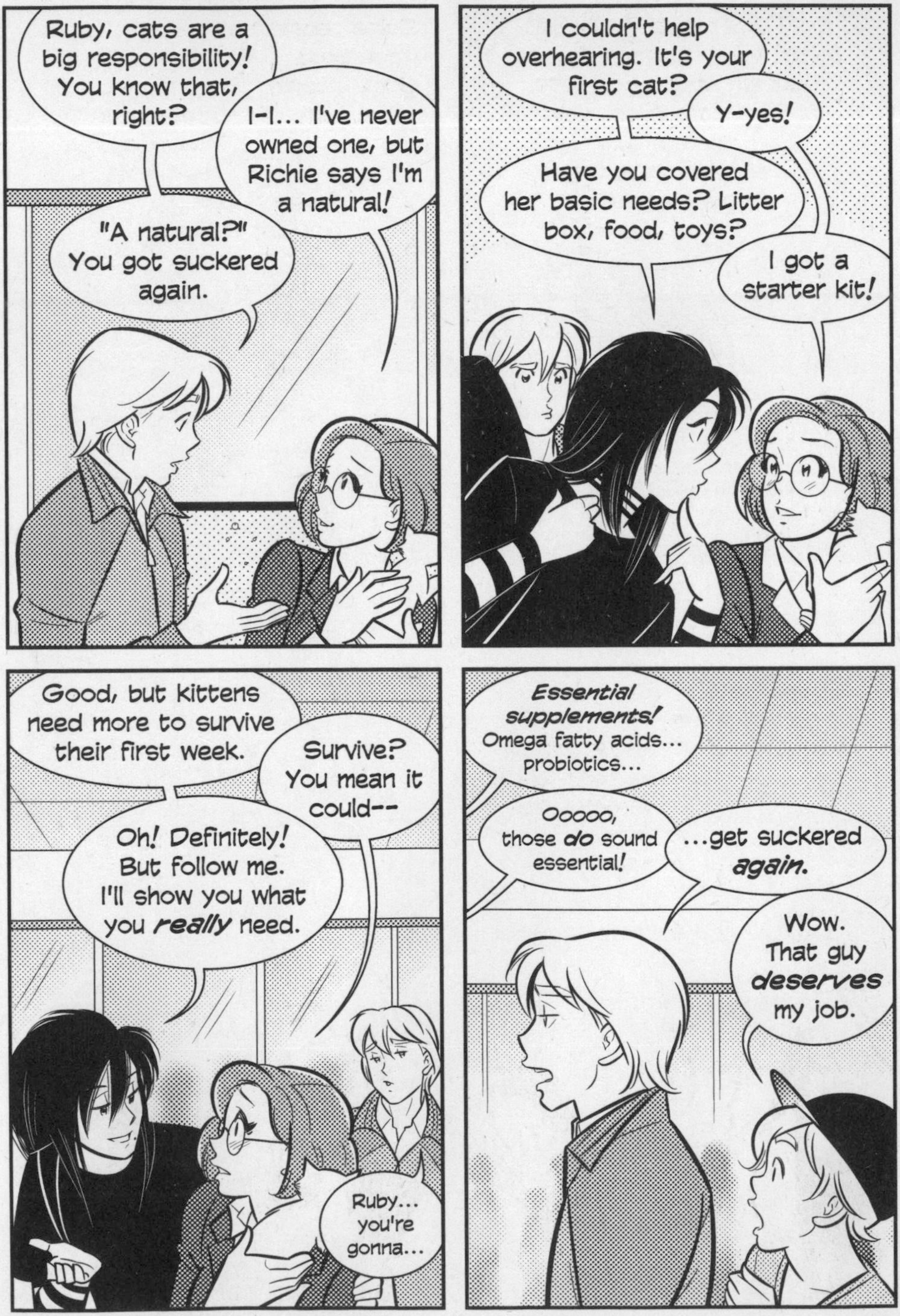
Ruby, cats are a big responsibility! You know that, right?
I-I... I've never owned one, but Richie says I'm a natural!
"A natural?" You got suckered again.
I couldn't help overhearing. It's your first cat?
Y-yes!
Have you covered her basic needs? Litter box, food, toys?
I got a starter kit!
Good, but kittens need more to survive their first week.
Survive? You mean it could--
Oh! Definitely! But follow me. I'll show you what you *really* need.
Ruby... you're gonna...
Essential supplements! Omega fatty acids... probiotics...
Ooooo, those *do* sound essential!
...get suckered ***again.***
Wow. That guy ***deserves*** my job.

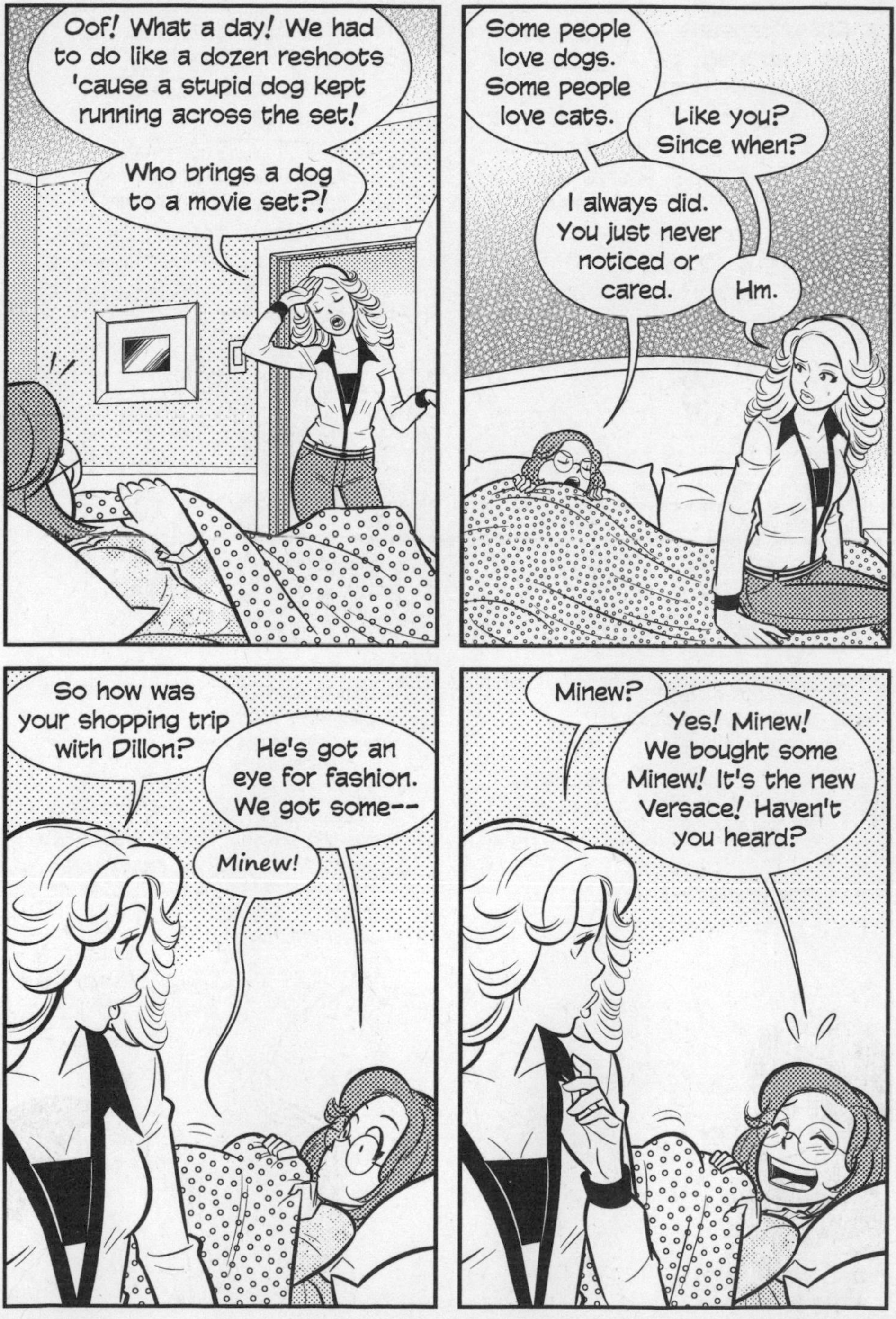
Oof! What a day! We had to do like a dozen reshoots 'cause a stupid dog kept running across the set!
Who brings a dog to a movie set?!
Some people love dogs. Some people love cats.
Like you? Since when?
I always did. You just never noticed or cared.
Hm.
So how was your shopping trip with Dillon?
He's got an eye for fashion. We got some--
Minew!
Minew?
Yes! Minew! We bought some Minew! It's the new Versace! Haven't you heard?

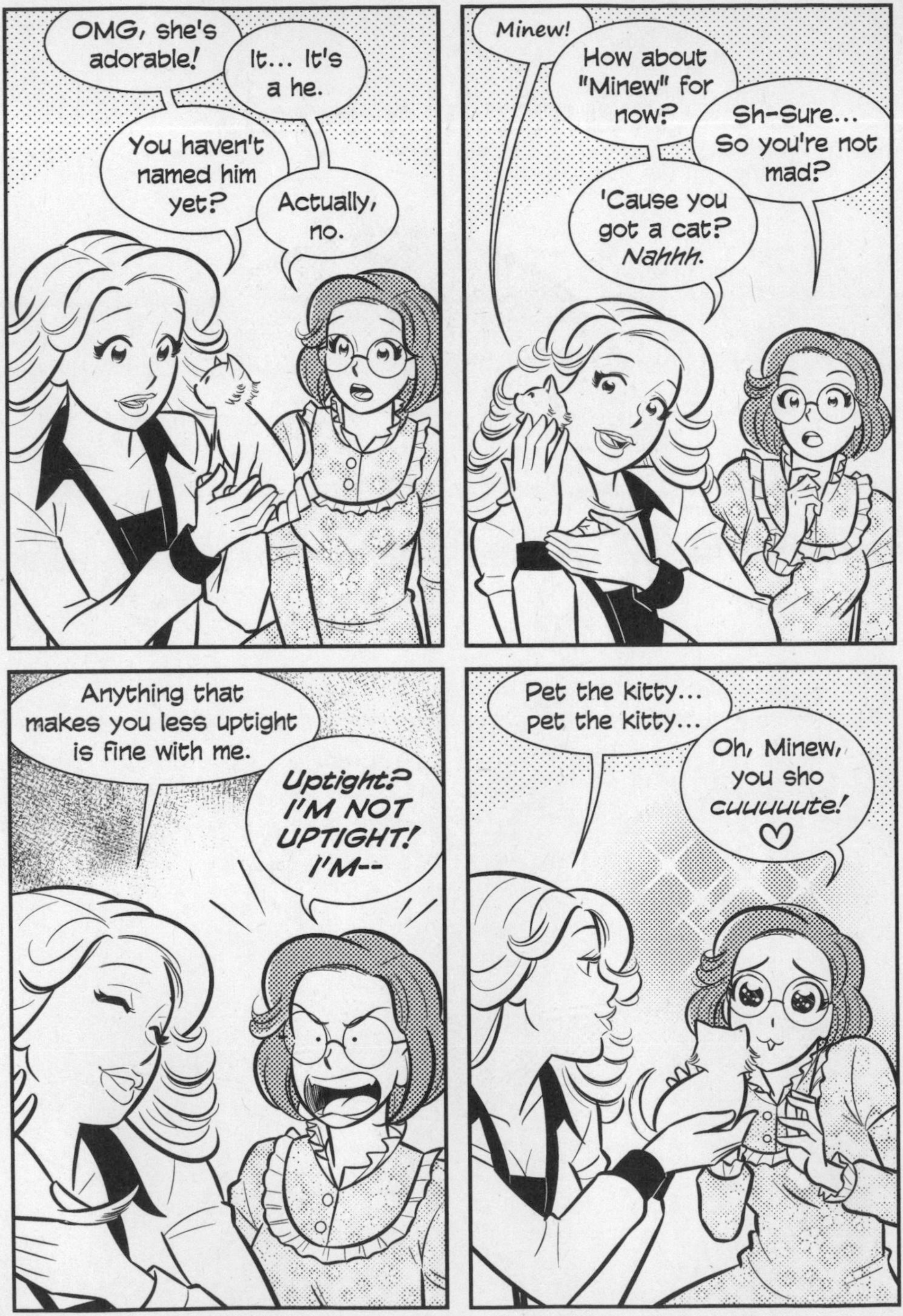
OMG, she's adorable!
It... It's a he.
You haven't named him yet?
Actually, no.
Minew!
How about "Minew" for now?
Sh-Sure... So you're not mad?
'Cause you got a cat? *Nahhh.*
Anything that makes you less uptight is fine with me.
Uptight? I'M NOT UPTIGHT! I'M--
Pet the kitty... pet the kitty...
Oh, Minew, you sho *cuuuuute!* ♡

Swimming Fools

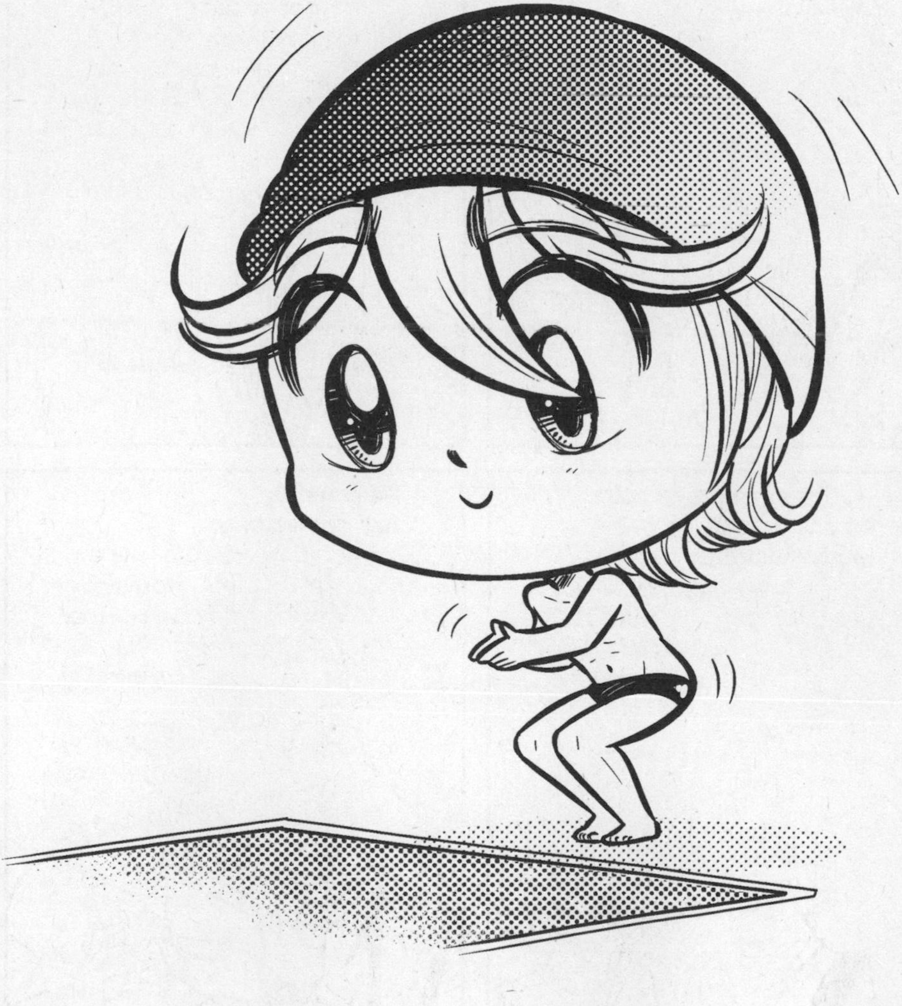

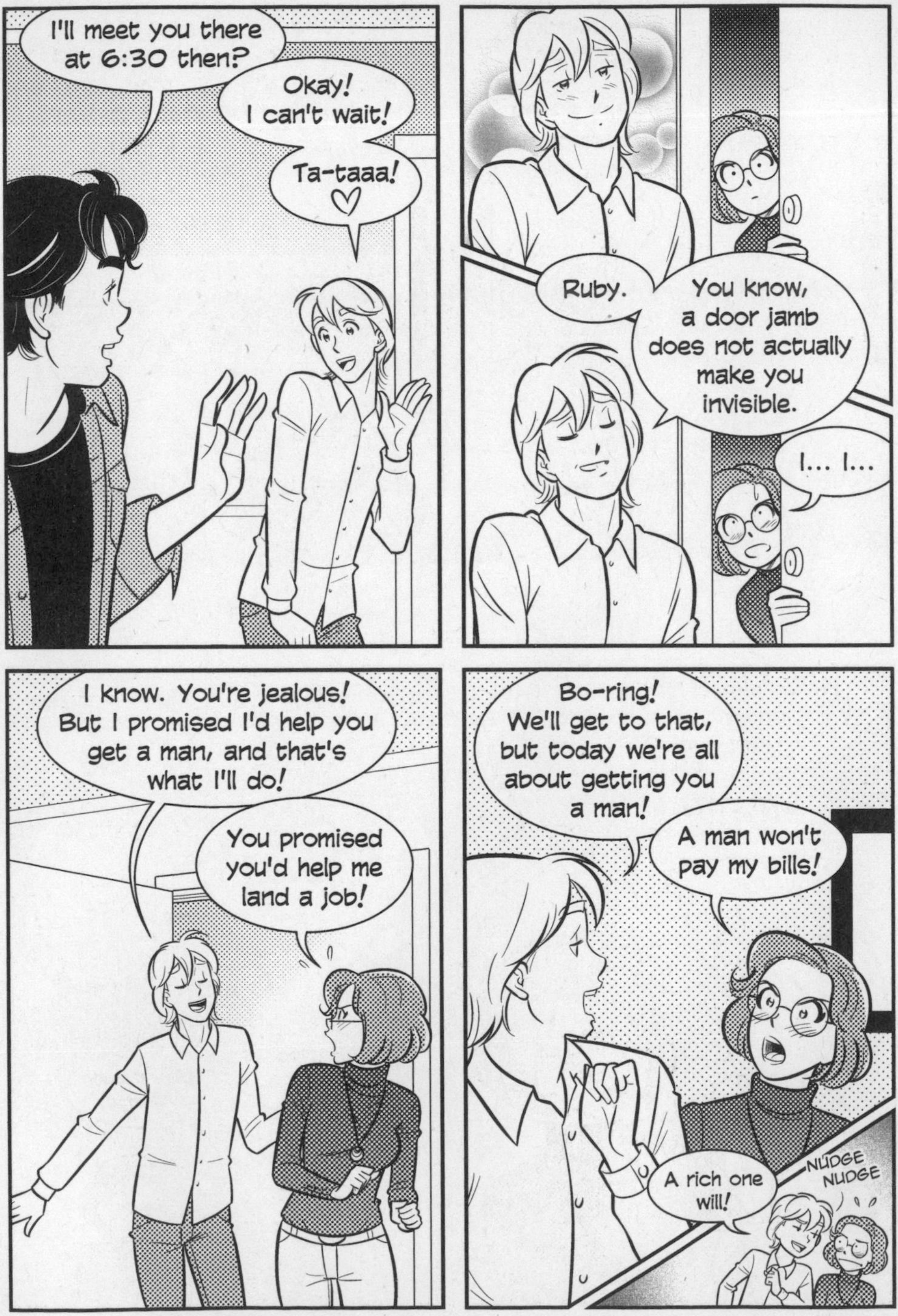
I'll meet you there at 6:30 then?
Okay! I can't wait!
Ta-taaa! ♡
Ruby.
You know, a door jamb does not actually make you invisible.
I... I...
I know. You're jealous! But I promised I'd help you get a man, and that's what I'll do!
You promised you'd help me land a job!
Bo-ring! We'll get to that, but today we're all about getting you a man!
A man won't pay my bills!
A rich one will!
NUDGE NUDGE

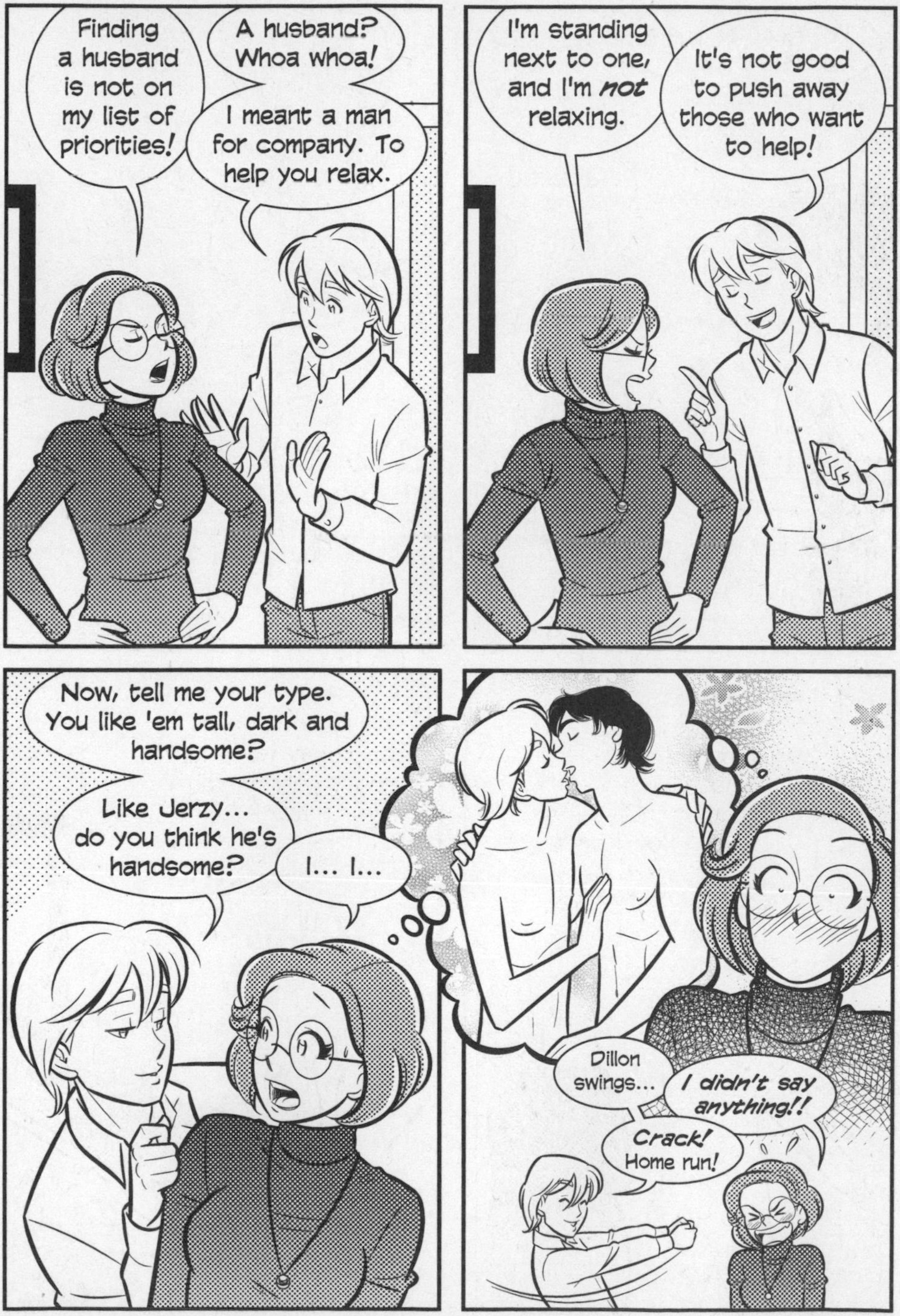
Finding a husband is not on my list of priorities!
A husband? Whoa whoa!
I meant a man for company. To help you relax.
I'm standing next to one, and I'm *not* relaxing.
It's not good to push away those who want to help!
Now, tell me your type. You like 'em tall, dark and handsome?
Like Jerzy... do you think he's handsome?
I... I...
Dillon swings...
I didn't say anything!!
Crack! Home run!

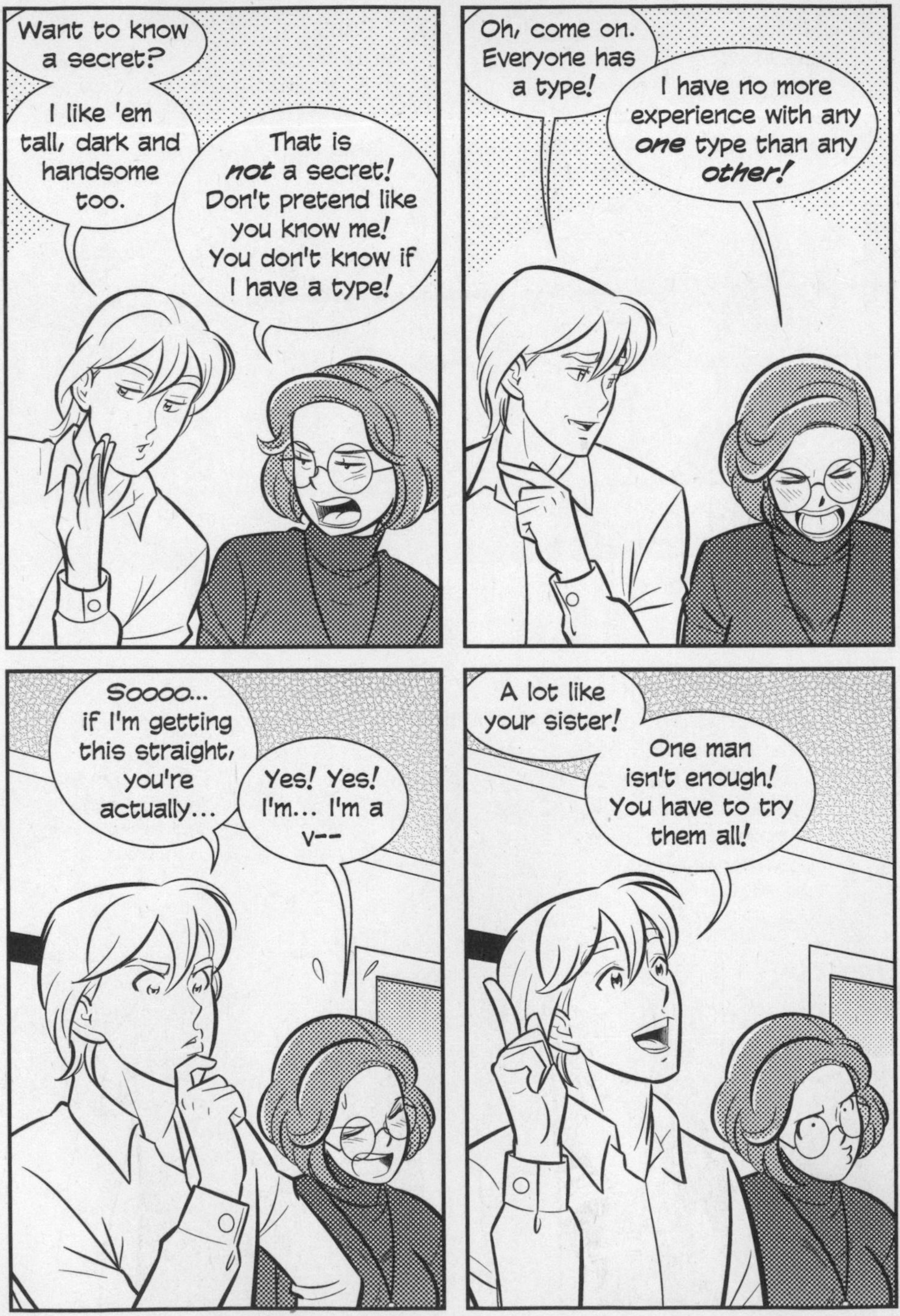
Want to know a secret?
I like 'em tall, dark and handsome too.
That is *not* a secret! Don't pretend like you know me! You don't know if I have a type!
Oh, come on. Everyone has a type!
I have no more experience with any *one* type than any *other!*
Soooo... if I'm getting this straight, you're actually...
Yes! Yes! I'm... I'm a v--
A lot like your sister!
One man isn't enough! You have to try them all!

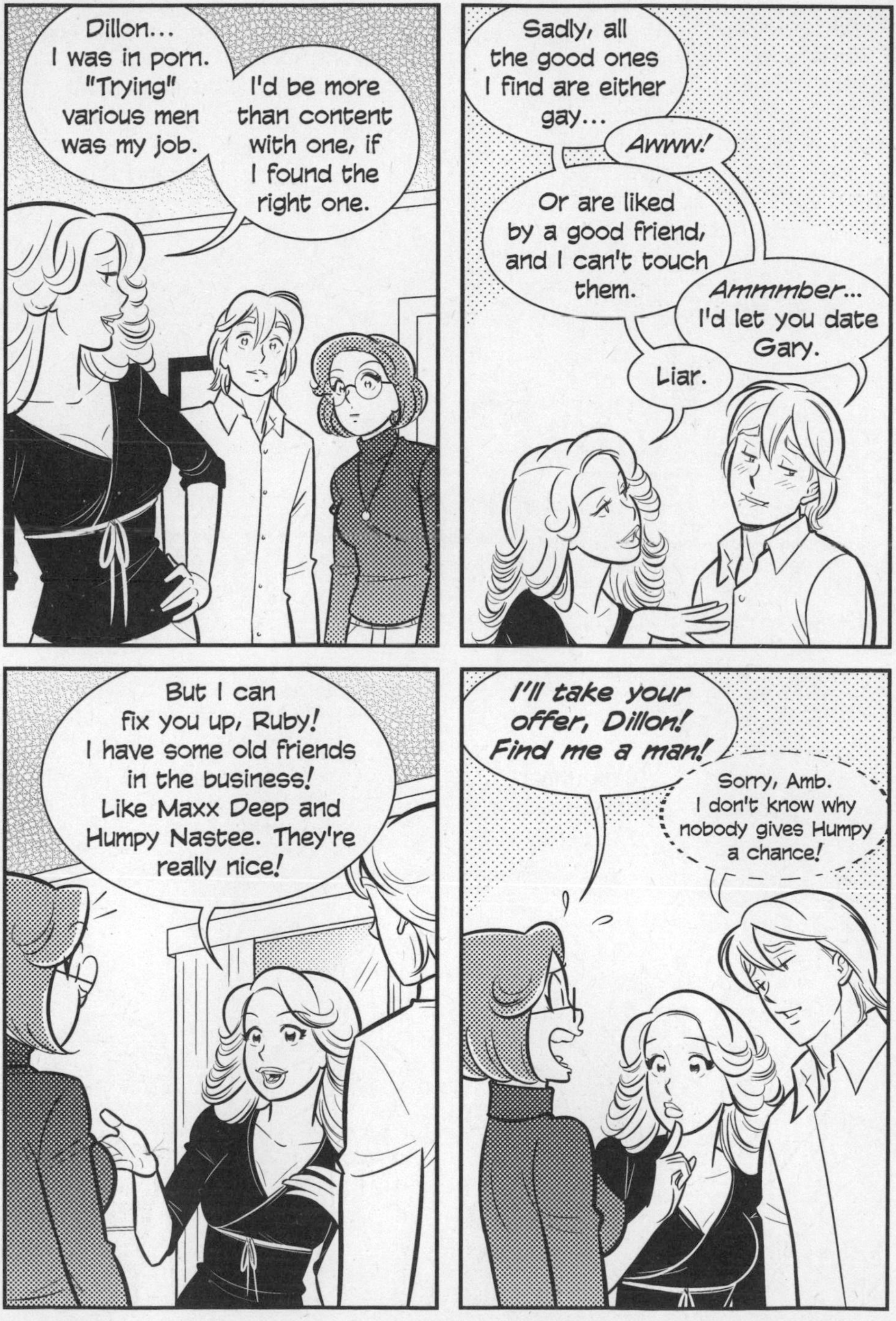
Dillon... I was in porn. "Trying" various men was my job.
I'd be more than content with one, if I found the right one.
Sadly, all the good ones I find are either gay...
Awww!
Or are liked by a good friend, and I can't touch them.
Ammmber... I'd let you date Gary.
Liar.
But I can fix you up, Ruby! I have some old friends in the business! Like Maxx Deep and Humpy Nastee. They're really nice!
I'll take your offer, Dillon! Find me a man!
Sorry, Amb. I don't know why nobody gives Humpy a chance!

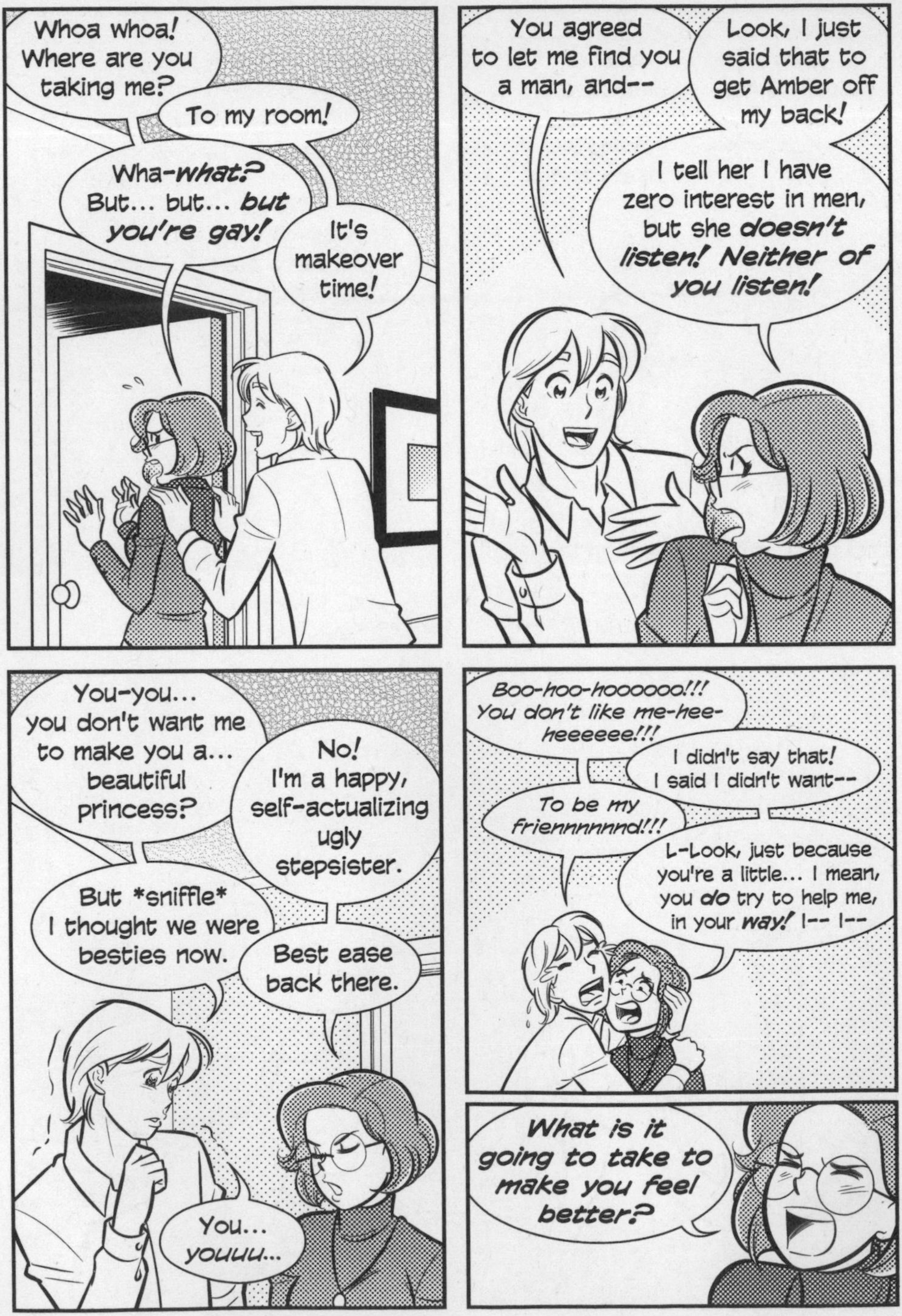
Whoa whoa! Where are you taking me?
To my room!
Wha-*what?* But... but... *but you're gay!*
It's makeover time!
You agreed to let me find you a man, and--
Look, I just said that to get Amber off my back!
I tell her I have zero interest in men, but she *doesn't listen! Neither of you listen!*
You-you... you don't want me to make you a... beautiful princess?
No! I'm a happy, self-actualizing ugly stepsister.
But *sniffle* I thought we were besties now.
Best ease back there.
You... *youuu...*
Boo-hoo-hoooooo!!! You don't like me-hee-heeeeee!!!
I didn't say that! I said I didn't want--
To be my friennnnnnd!!!
L-Look, just because you're a little... I mean, you *do* try to help me, in your *way!* I-- I--
What is it going to take to make you feel better?

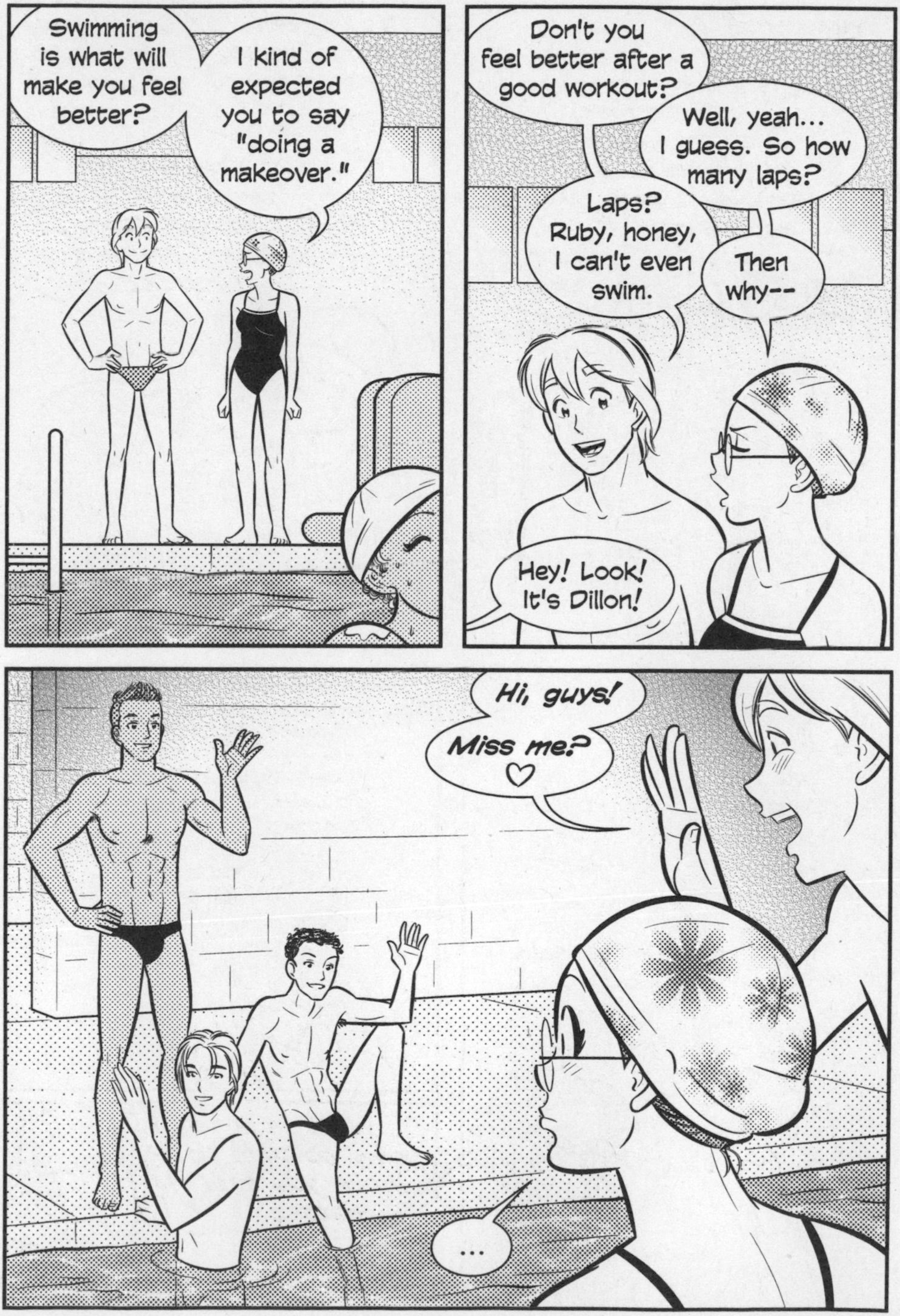
Swimming is what will make you feel better?
I kind of expected you to say "doing a makeover."
Don't you feel better after a good workout?
Well, yeah... I guess. So how many laps?
Laps? Ruby, honey, I can't even swim.
Then why--
Hey! Look! It's Dillon!
Hi, guys!
Miss me? ♡
...

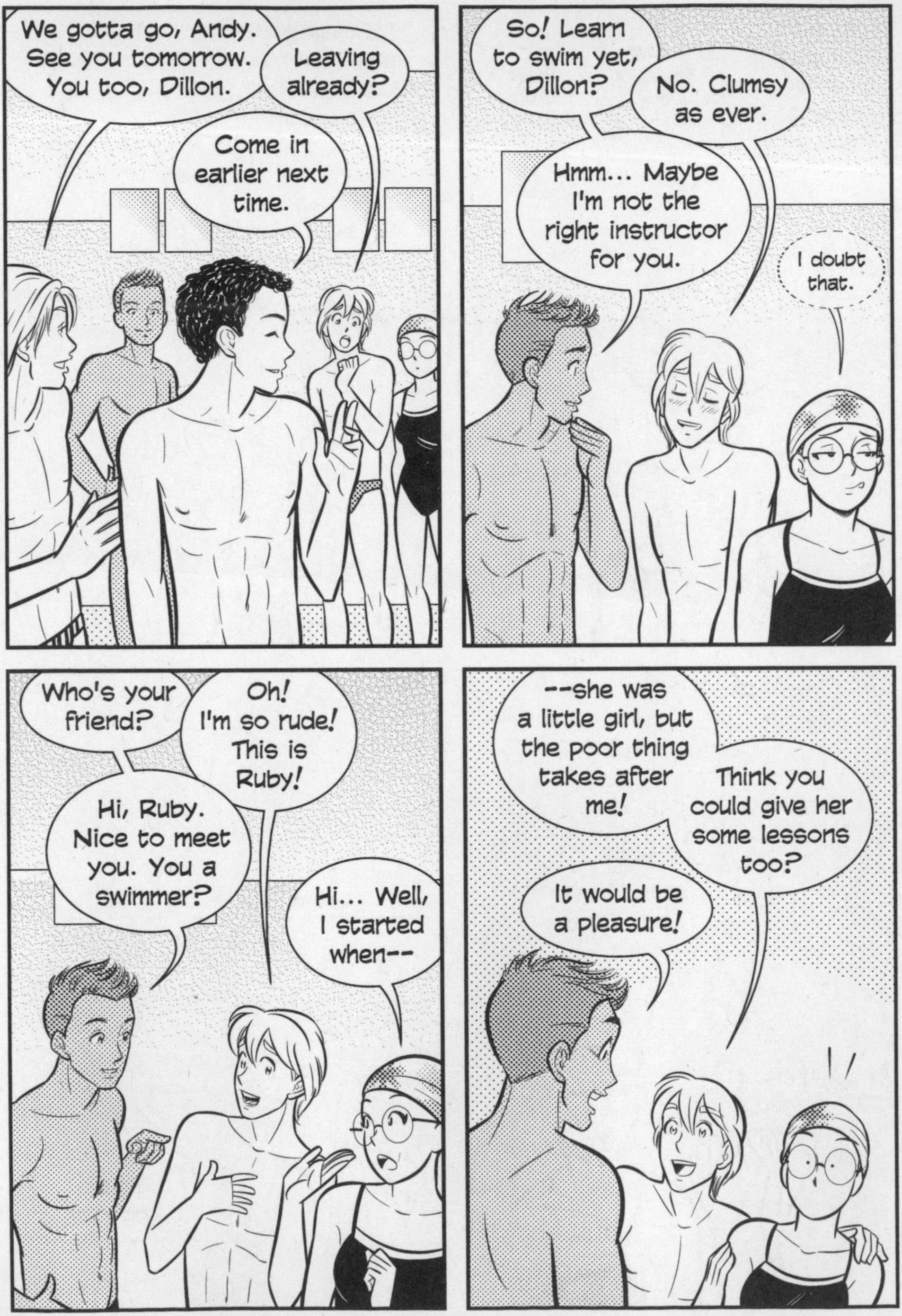
We gotta go, Andy. See you tomorrow. You too, Dillon.
Leaving already?
Come in earlier next time.
So! Learn to swim yet, Dillon?
No. Clumsy as ever.
Hmm... Maybe I'm not the right instructor for you.
I doubt that.
Who's your friend?
Oh! I'm so rude! This is Ruby!
Hi, Ruby. Nice to meet you. You a swimmer?
Hi... Well, I started when--
--she was a little girl, but the poor thing takes after me!
Think you could give her some lessons too?
It would be a pleasure!

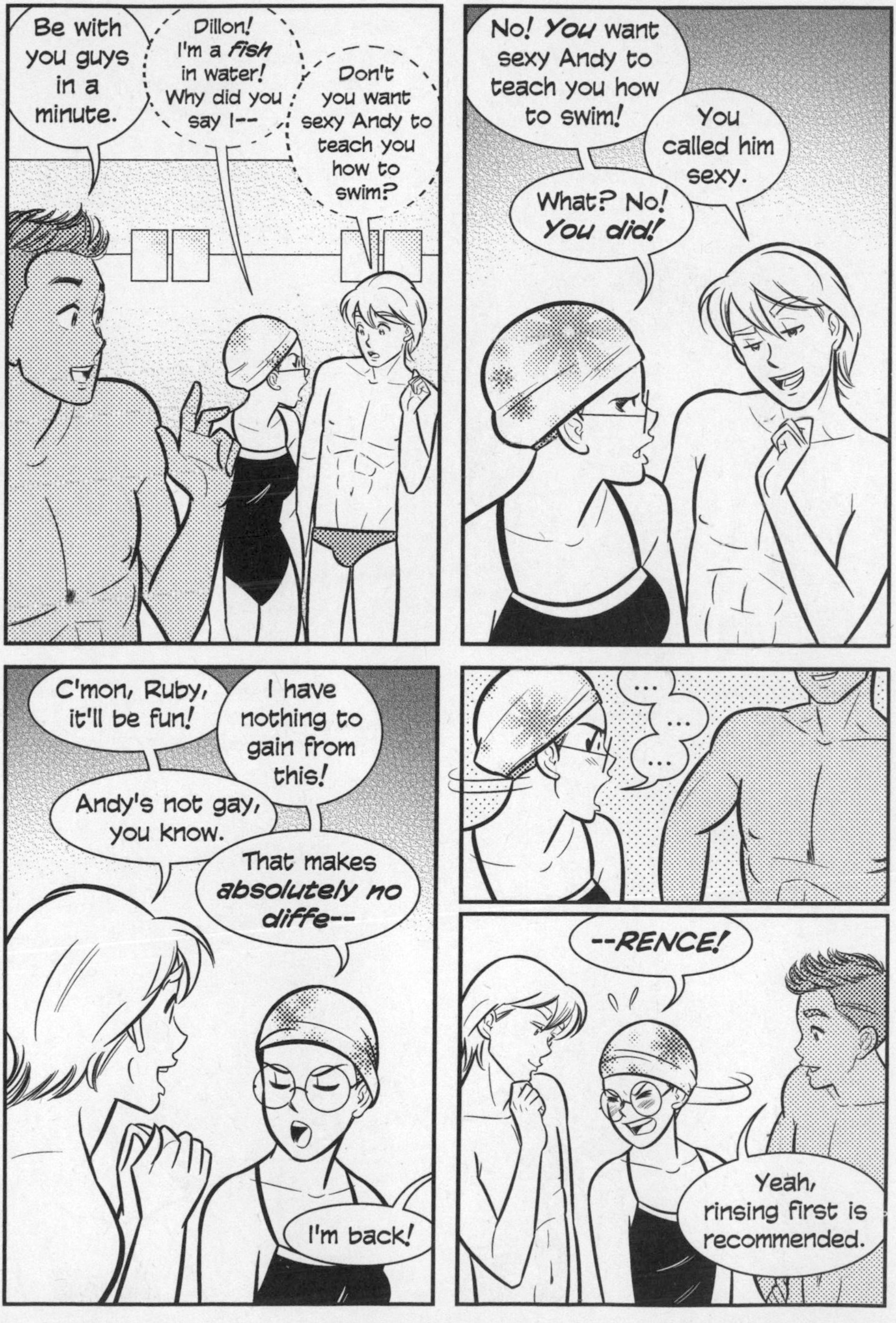
Be with you guys in a minute.
Dillon! I'm a *fish* in water! Why did you say I--
Don't you want sexy Andy to teach you how to swim?
No! *You* want sexy Andy to teach you how to swim!
You called him sexy.
What? No! *You did!*
C'mon, Ruby, it'll be fun!
I have nothing to gain from this!
Andy's not gay, you know.
That makes *absolutely no diffe--*
I'm back!
...
...
...
--RENCE!
Yeah, rinsing first is recommended.

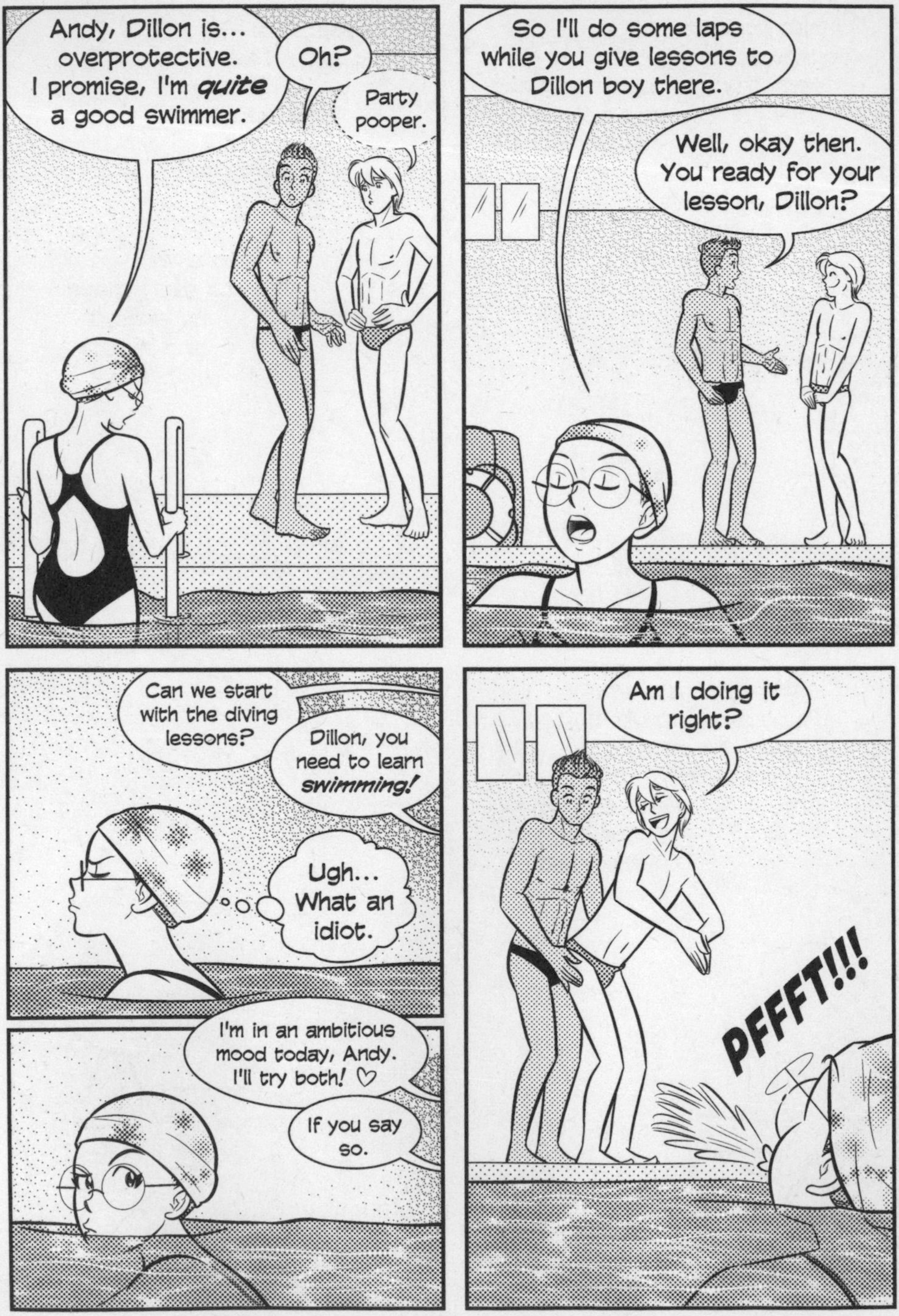
Andy, Dillon is... overprotective. I promise, I'm *quite* a good swimmer.
Oh?
Party pooper.
So I'll do some laps while you give lessons to Dillon boy there.
Well, okay then. You ready for your lesson, Dillon?
Can we start with the diving lessons?
Dillon, you need to learn *swimming!*
Ugh... What an idiot.
I'm in an ambitious mood today, Andy. I'll try both! ♡
If you say so.
Am I doing it right?
PFFFT!!!

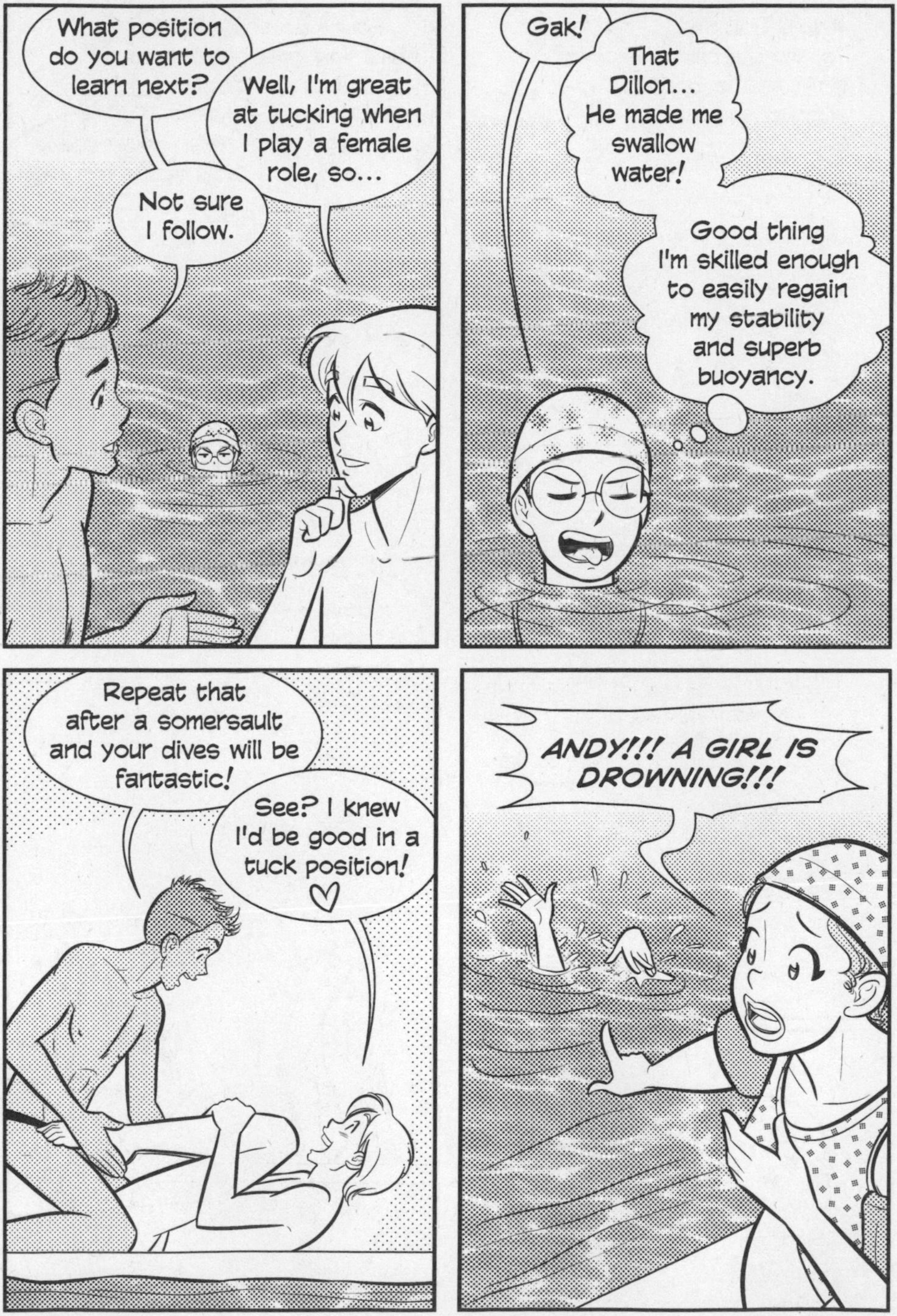
What position do you want to learn next?
Well, I'm great at tucking when I play a female role, so...
Not sure I follow.
Gak!
That Dillon... He made me swallow water!
Good thing I'm skilled enough to easily regain my stability and superb buoyancy.
Repeat that after a somersault and your dives will be fantastic!
See? I knew I'd be good in a tuck position! ♡
ANDY!!! A GIRL IS DROWNING!!!

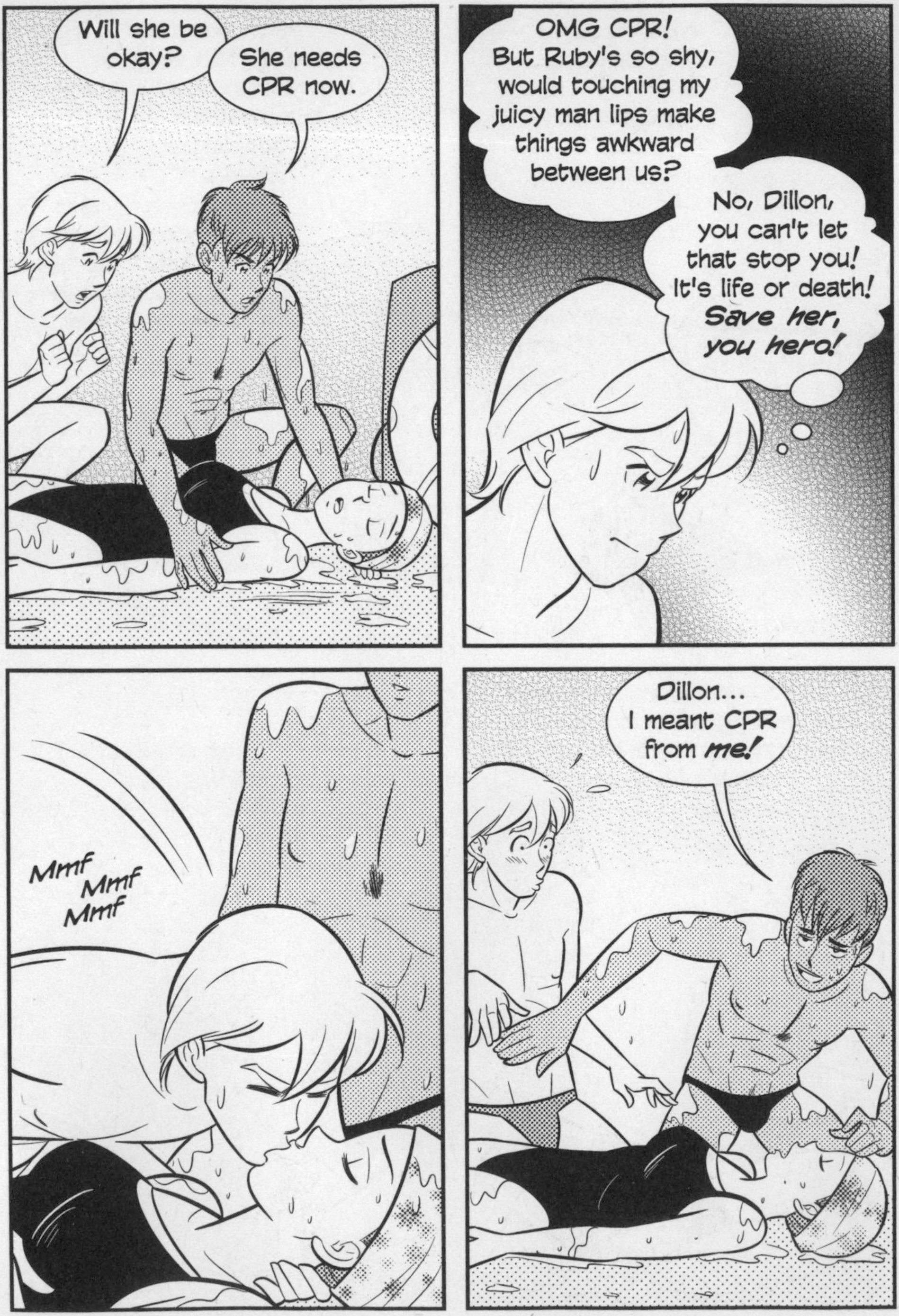
Will she be okay?
She needs CPR now.
OMG CPR! But Ruby's so shy, would touching my juicy man lips make things awkward between us?
No, Dillon, you can't let that stop you! It's life or death! *Save her, you hero!*
Mmf Mmf Mmf
Dillon... I meant CPR from *me!*

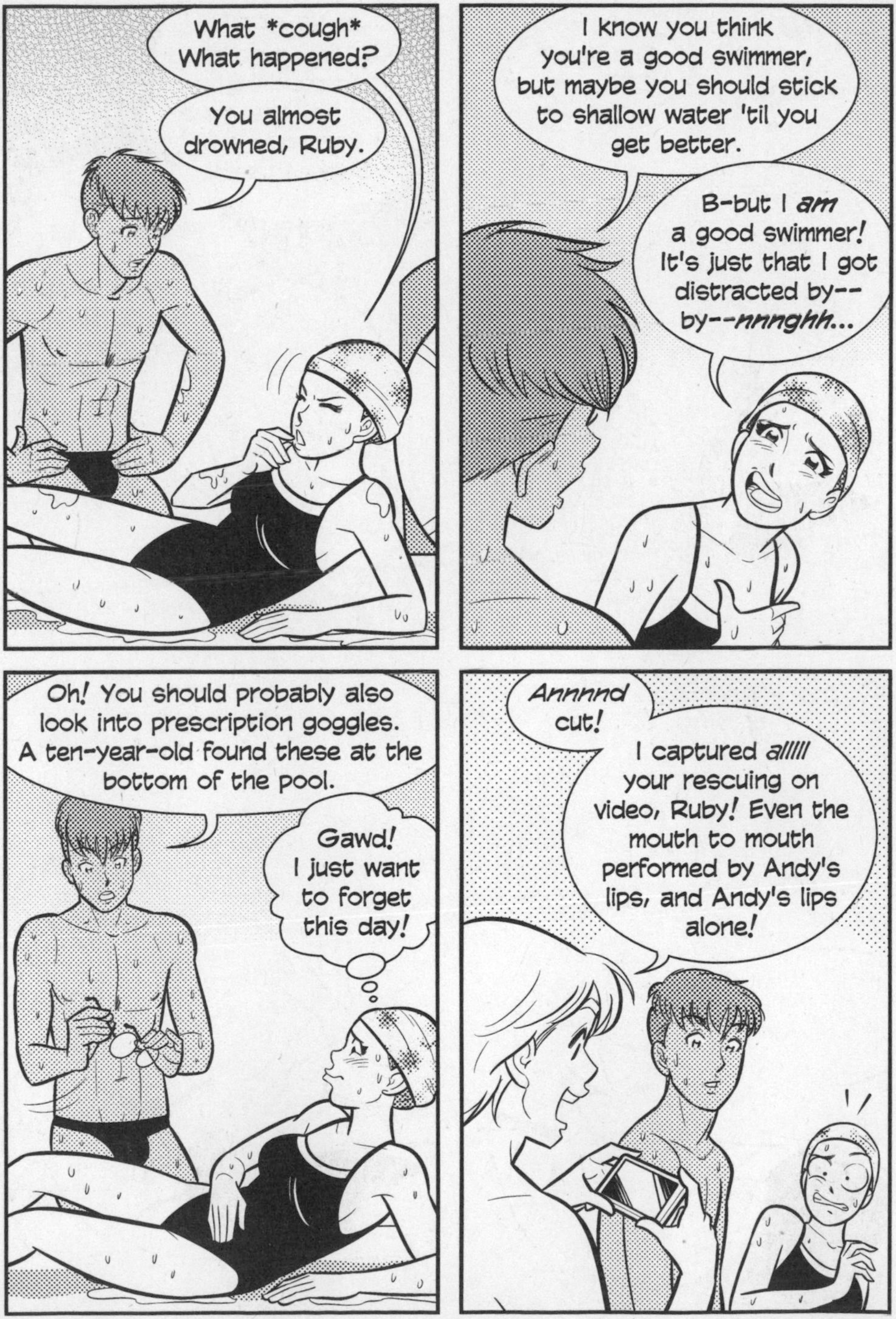
What *cough* What happened?
You almost drowned, Ruby.
I know you think you're a good swimmer, but maybe you should stick to shallow water 'til you get better.
B-but I *am* a good swimmer! It's just that I got distracted by-- by--*nnnghh*...
Oh! You should probably also look into prescription goggles. A ten-year-old found these at the bottom of the pool.
Gawd! I just want to forget this day!
Annnnd cut!
I captured *alllll* your rescuing on video, Ruby! Even the mouth to mouth performed by Andy's lips, and Andy's lips alone!

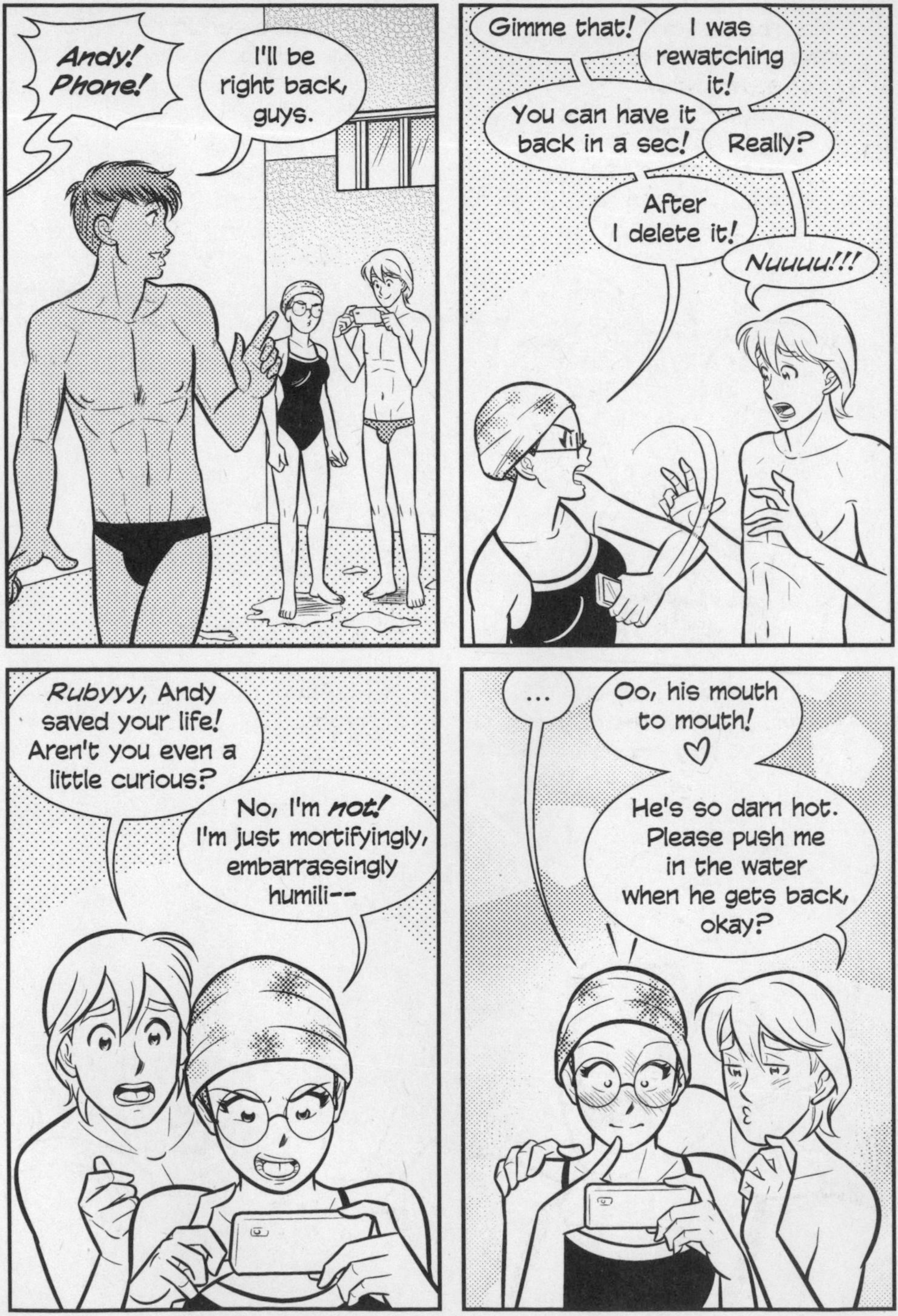
Andy! Phone!
I'll be right back, guys.
Gimme that!
I was rewatching it!
You can have it back in a sec!
Really?
After I delete it!
Nuuuu!!!
Rubyyy, Andy saved your life! Aren't you even a little curious?
No, I'm not! I'm just mortifyingly, embarrassingly humili--
...
Oo, his mouth to mouth!
He's so darn hot. Please push me in the water when he gets back, okay?

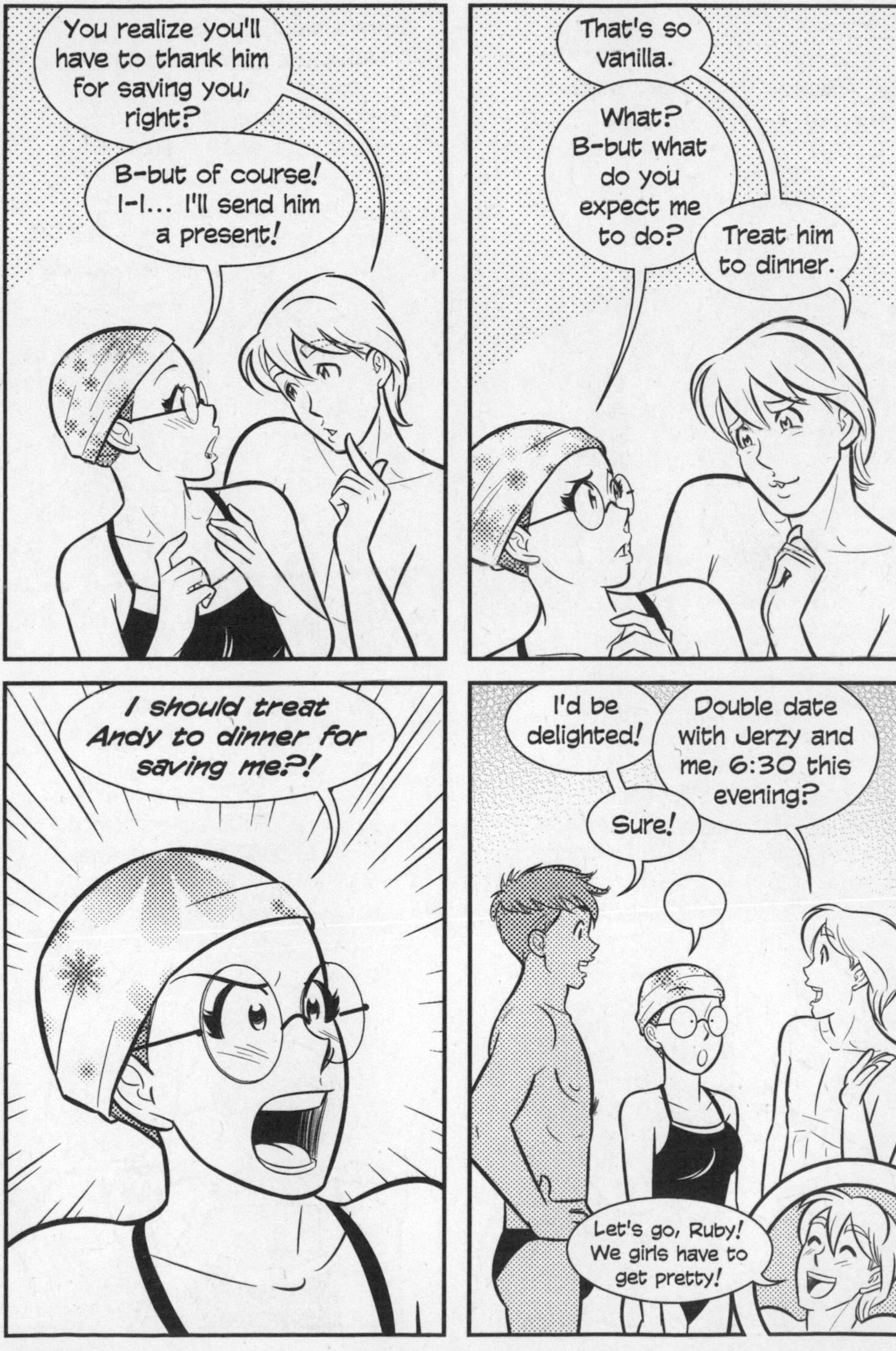
You realize you'll have to thank him for saving you, right?
B-but of course! I-I... I'll send him a present!
That's so vanilla.
What? B-but what do you expect me to do?
Treat him to dinner.
I should treat Andy to dinner for saving me?!
I'd be delighted!
Double date with Jerzy and me, 6:30 this evening?
Sure!
Let's go, Ruby! We girls have to get pretty!

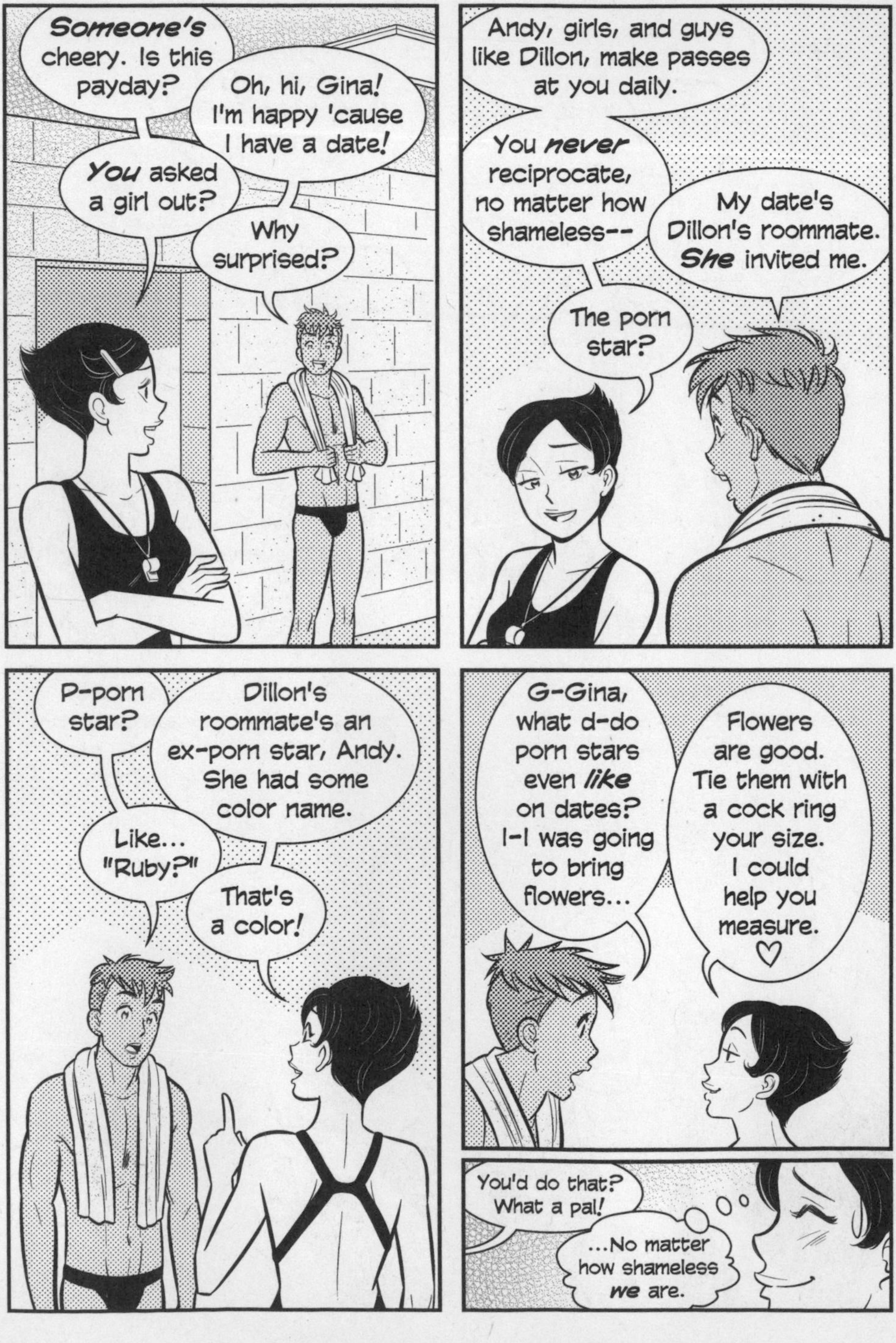
Someone's cheery. Is this payday?
Oh, hi, Gina! I'm happy 'cause I have a date!
You asked a girl out?
Why surprised?
Andy, girls, and guys like Dillon, make passes at you daily.
You never reciprocate, no matter how shameless--
My date's Dillon's roommate. She invited me.
The porn star?
P-porn star?
Dillon's roommate's an ex-porn star, Andy. She had some color name.
Like... "Ruby?"
That's a color!
G-Gina, what d-do porn stars even like on dates? I-I was going to bring flowers...
Flowers are good. Tie them with a cock ring your size. I could help you measure. ♡
You'd do that? What a pal!
...No matter how shameless we are.

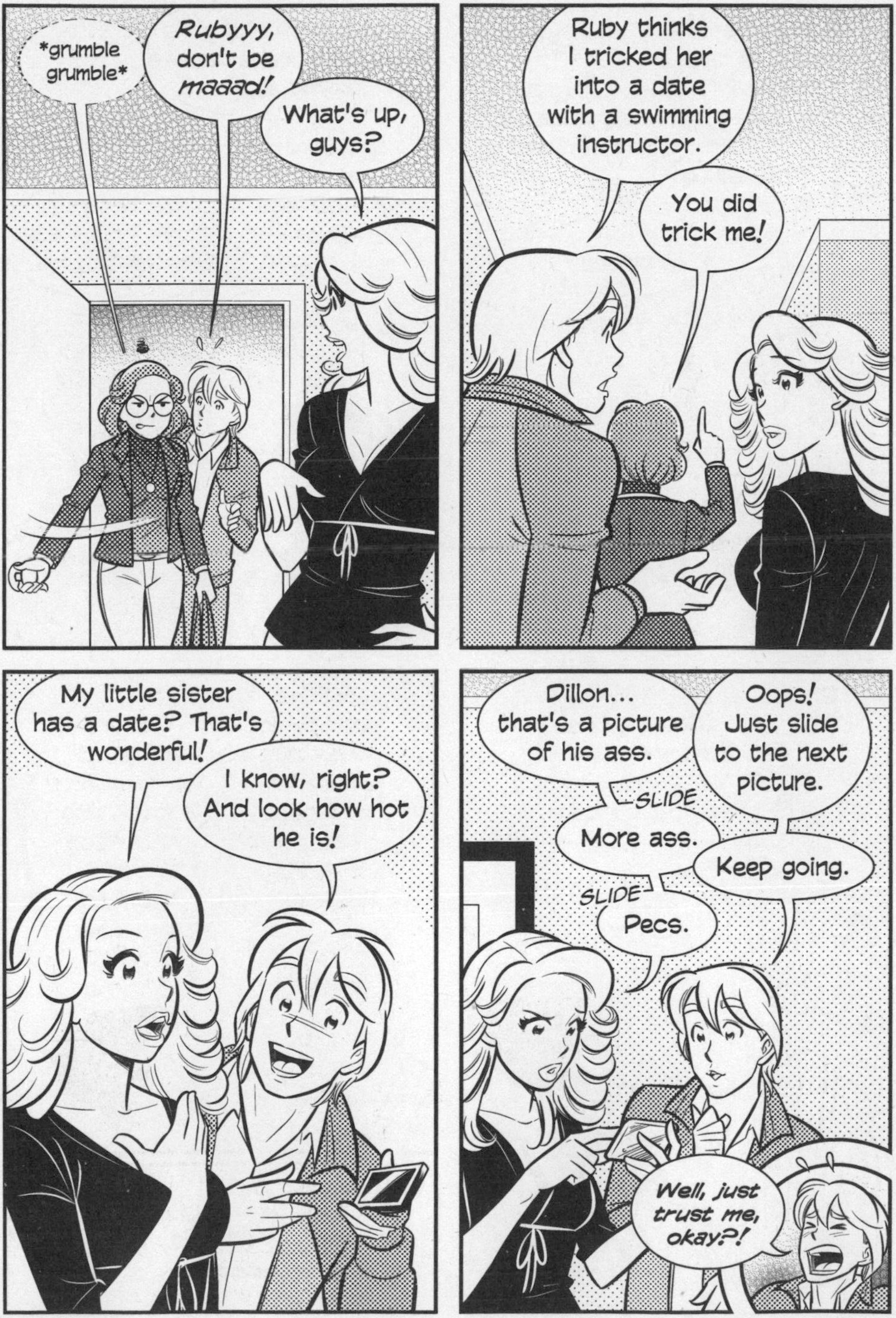
grumble grumble
Rubyyy, don't be maaad!
What's up, guys?
Ruby thinks I tricked her into a date with a swimming instructor.
You did trick me!
My little sister has a date? That's wonderful!
I know, right? And look how hot he is!
Dillon... that's a picture of his ass.
Oops! Just slide to the next picture.
SLIDE
More ass.
Keep going.
SLIDE
Pecs.
Well, just trust me, okay?!

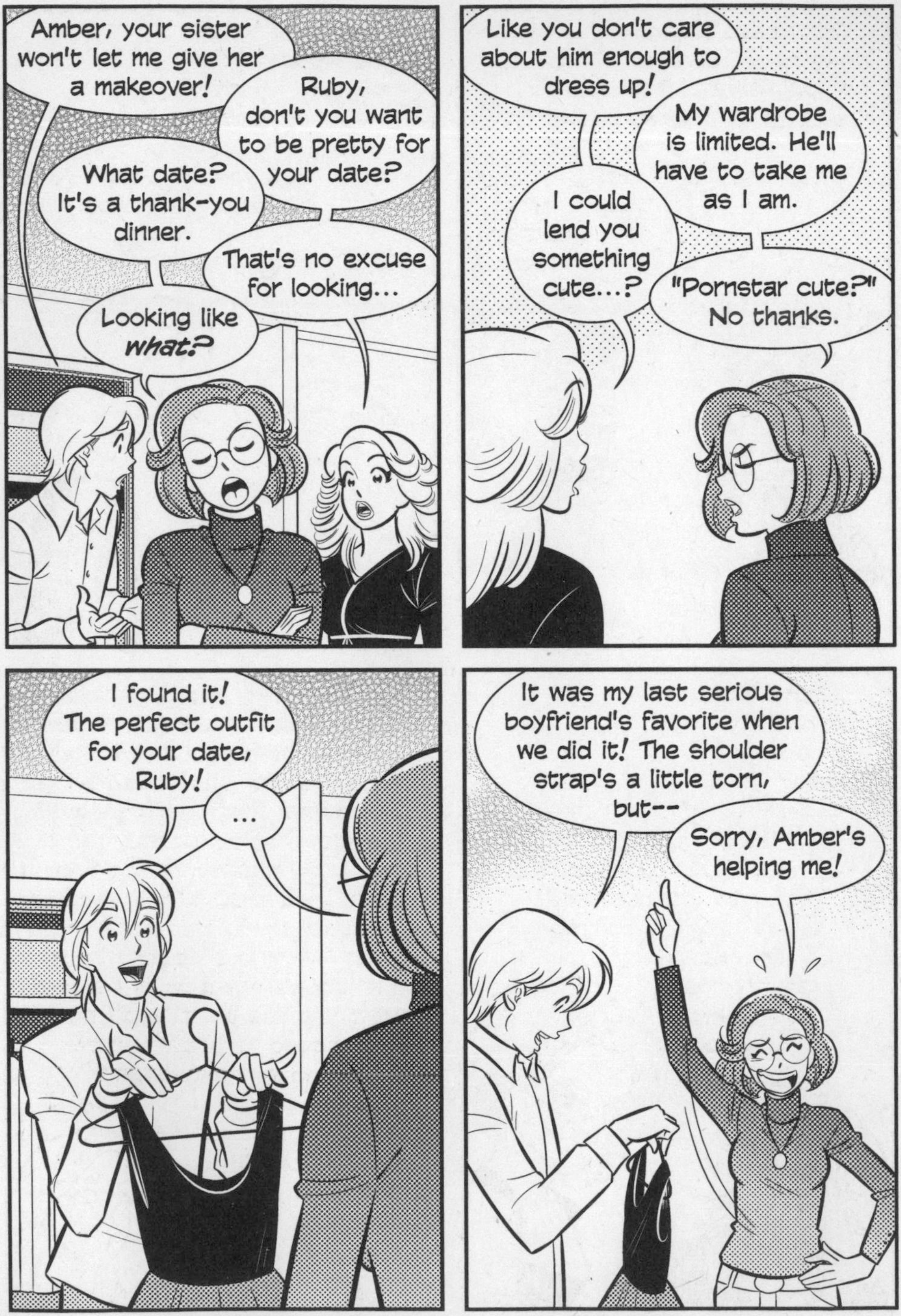
Amber, your sister won't let me give her a makeover!
Ruby, don't you want to be pretty for your date?
What date? It's a thank-you dinner.
That's no excuse for looking...
Looking like *what?*
Like you don't care about him enough to dress up!
My wardrobe is limited. He'll have to take me as I am.
I could lend you something cute...?
"Pornstar cute?" No thanks.
I found it! The perfect outfit for your date, Ruby!
...
It was my last serious boyfriend's favorite when we did it! The shoulder strap's a little torn, but--
Sorry, Amber's helping me!

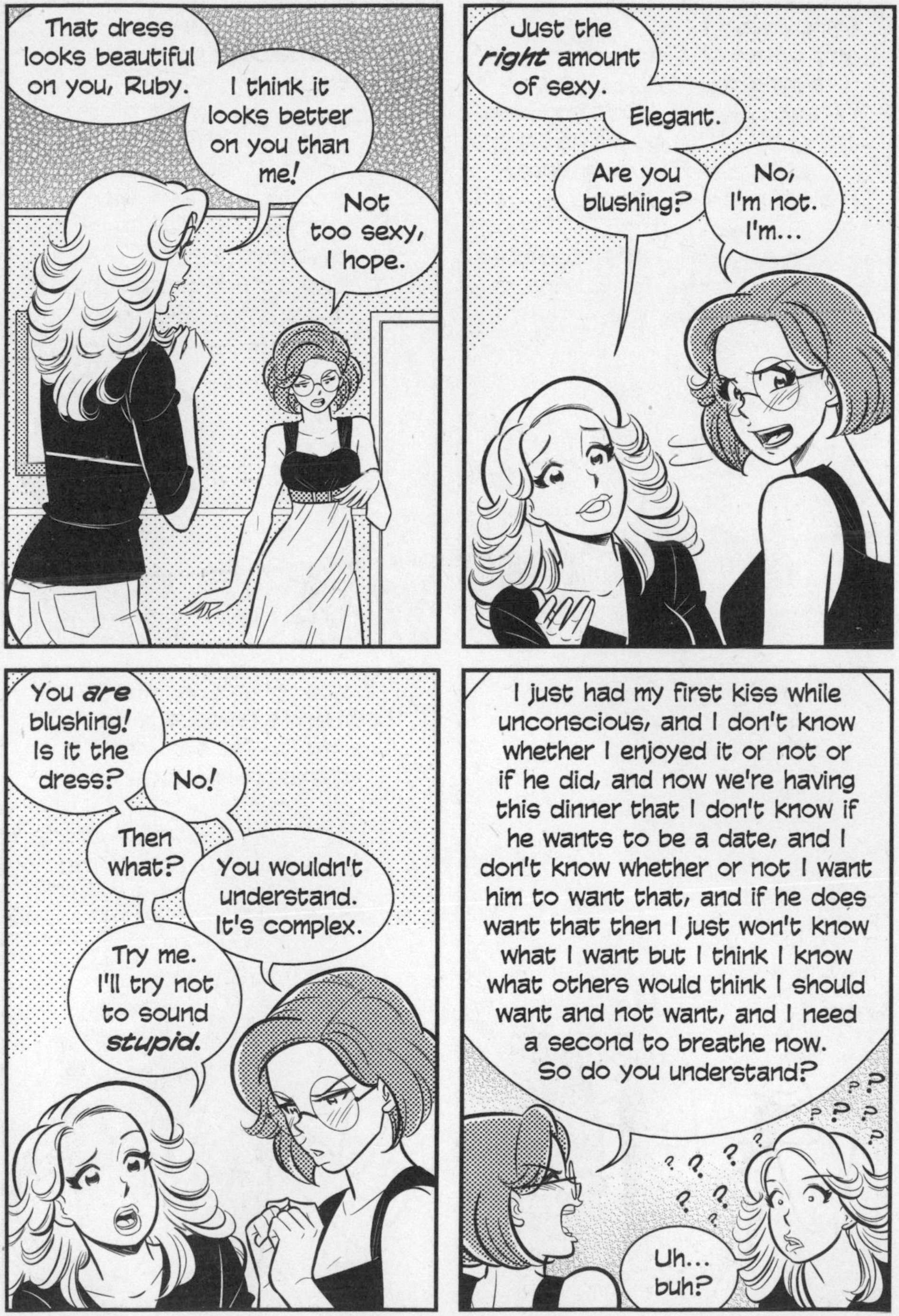
That dress looks beautiful on you, Ruby.
I think it looks better on you than me!
Not too sexy, I hope.
Just the *right* amount of sexy.
Elegant.
Are you blushing?
No, I'm not. I'm...
You *are* blushing! Is it the dress?
No!
Then what?
You wouldn't understand. It's complex.
Try me. I'll try not to sound *stupid*.
I just had my first kiss while unconscious, and I don't know whether I enjoyed it or not or if he did, and now we're having this dinner that I don't know if he wants to be a date, and I don't know whether or not I want him to want that, and if he does want that then I just won't know what I want but I think I know what others would think I should want and not want, and I need a second to breathe now. So do you understand?
Uh... buh?

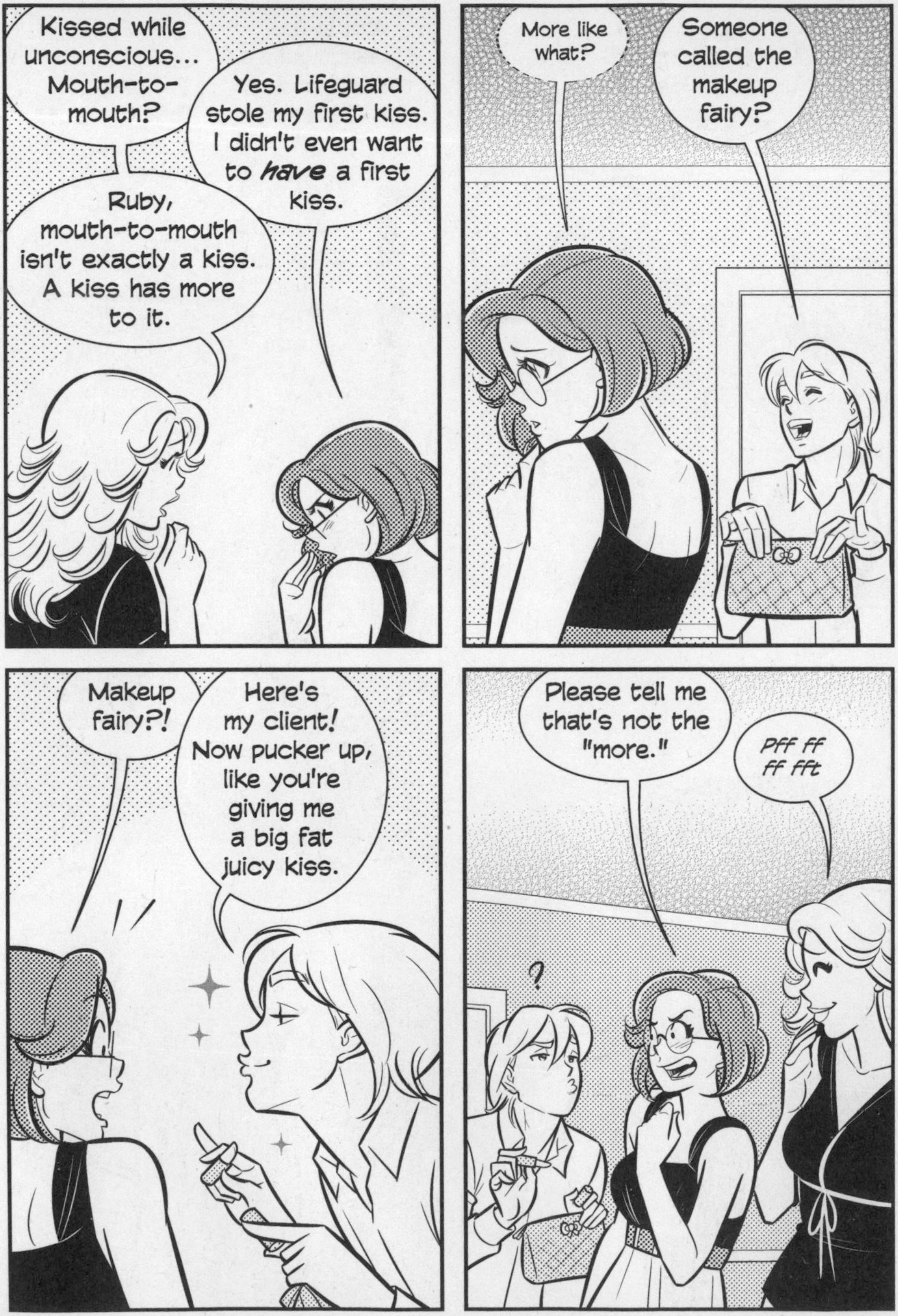

Kissed while unconscious... Mouth-to-mouth?
Yes. Lifeguard stole my first kiss. I didn't even want to *have* a first kiss.
Ruby, mouth-to-mouth isn't exactly a kiss. A kiss has more to it.
More like what?
Someone called the makeup fairy?
Makeup fairy?!
Here's my client! Now pucker up, like you're giving me a big fat juicy kiss.
Please tell me that's not the "more."
Pff ff ff fft
?

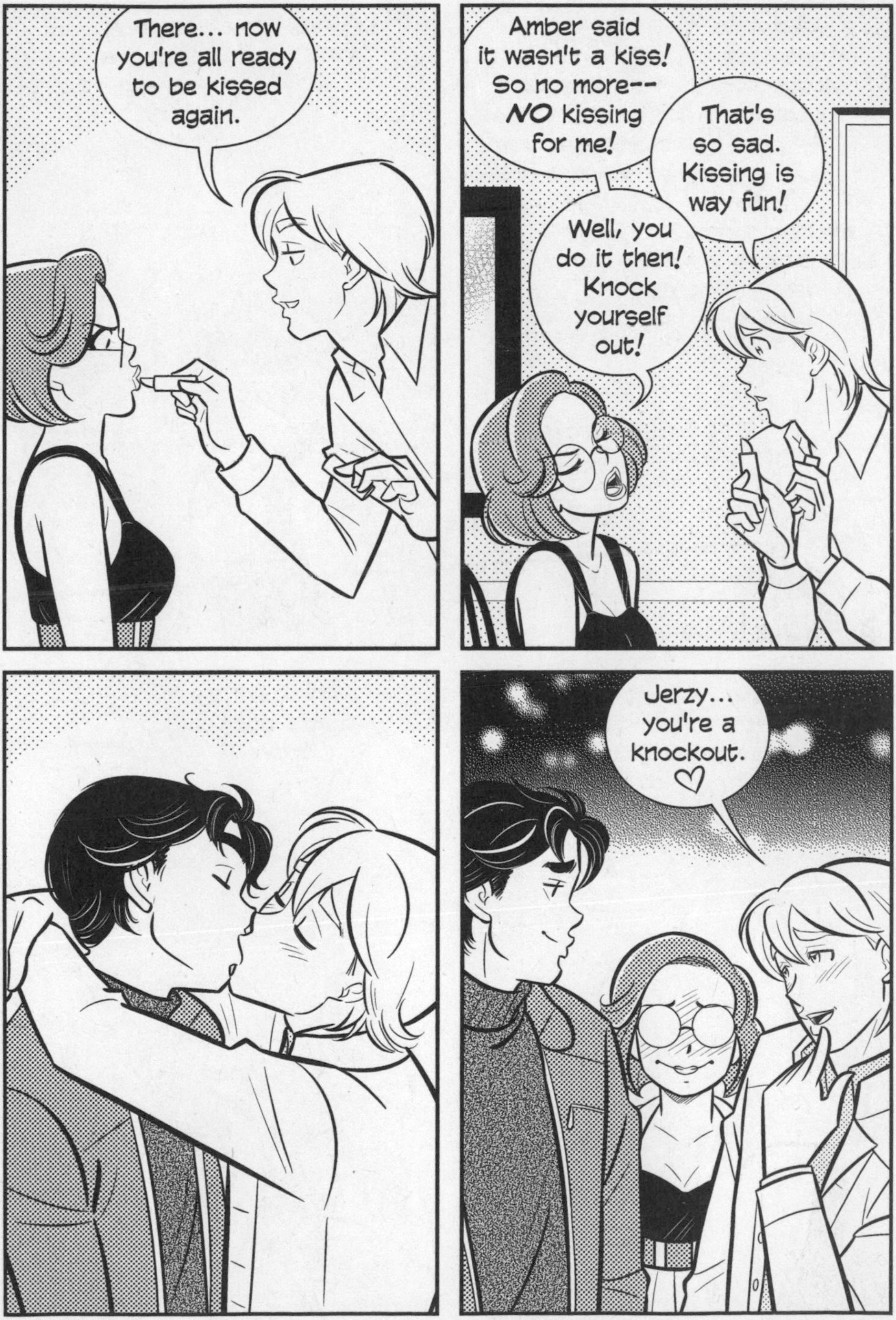
There... now you're all ready to be kissed again.
Amber said it wasn't a kiss! So no more-- NO kissing for me!
That's so sad. Kissing is way fun!
Well, you do it then! Knock yourself out!
Jerzy... you're a knockout. ♡

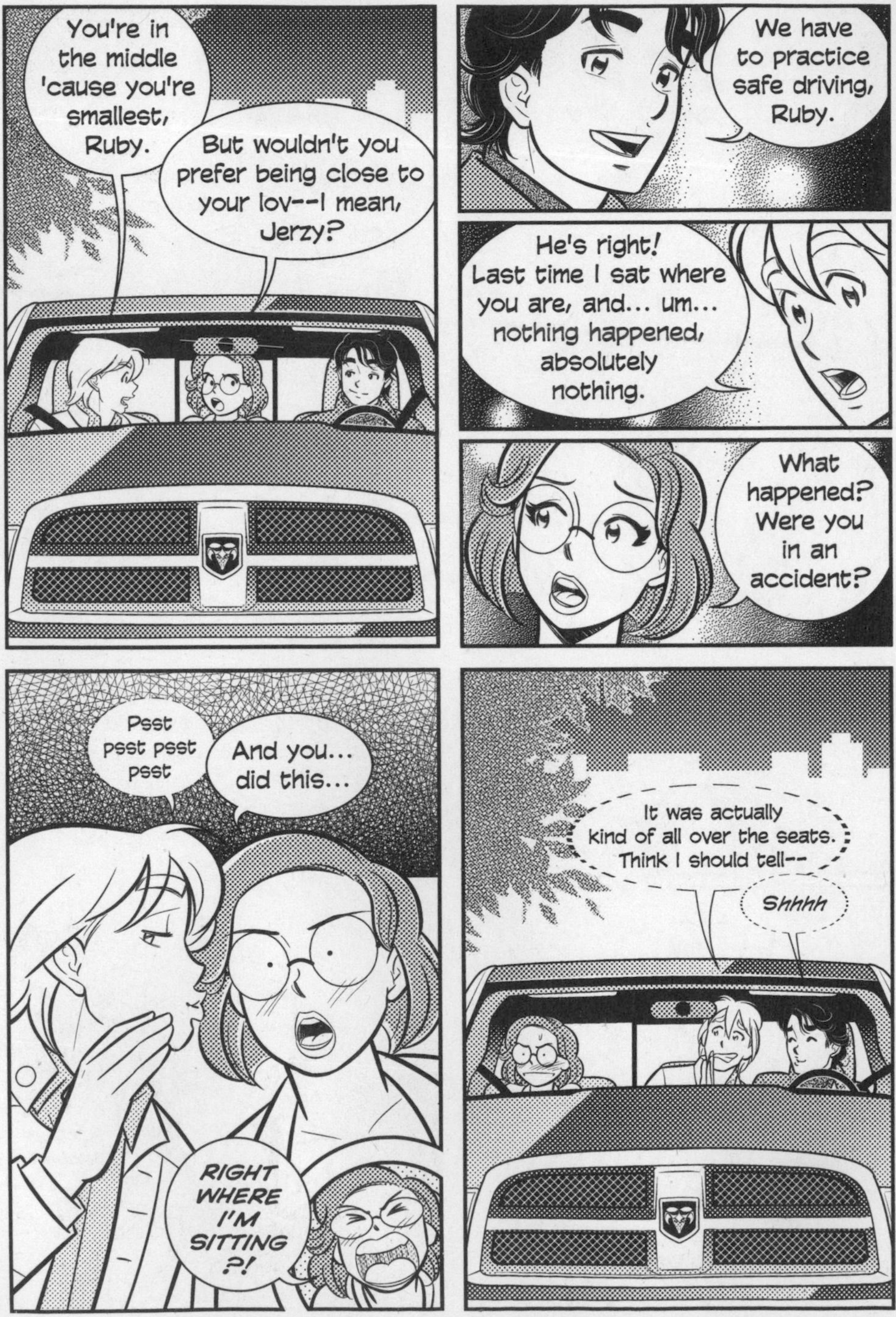
You're in the middle 'cause you're smallest, Ruby.
But wouldn't you prefer being close to your lov--I mean, Jerzy?
We have to practice safe driving, Ruby.
He's right! Last time I sat where you are, and... um... nothing happened, absolutely nothing.
What happened? Were you in an accident?
Psst psst psst psst
And you... did this...
RIGHT WHERE I'M SITTING ?!
It was actually kind of all over the seats. Think I should tell--
Shhhh

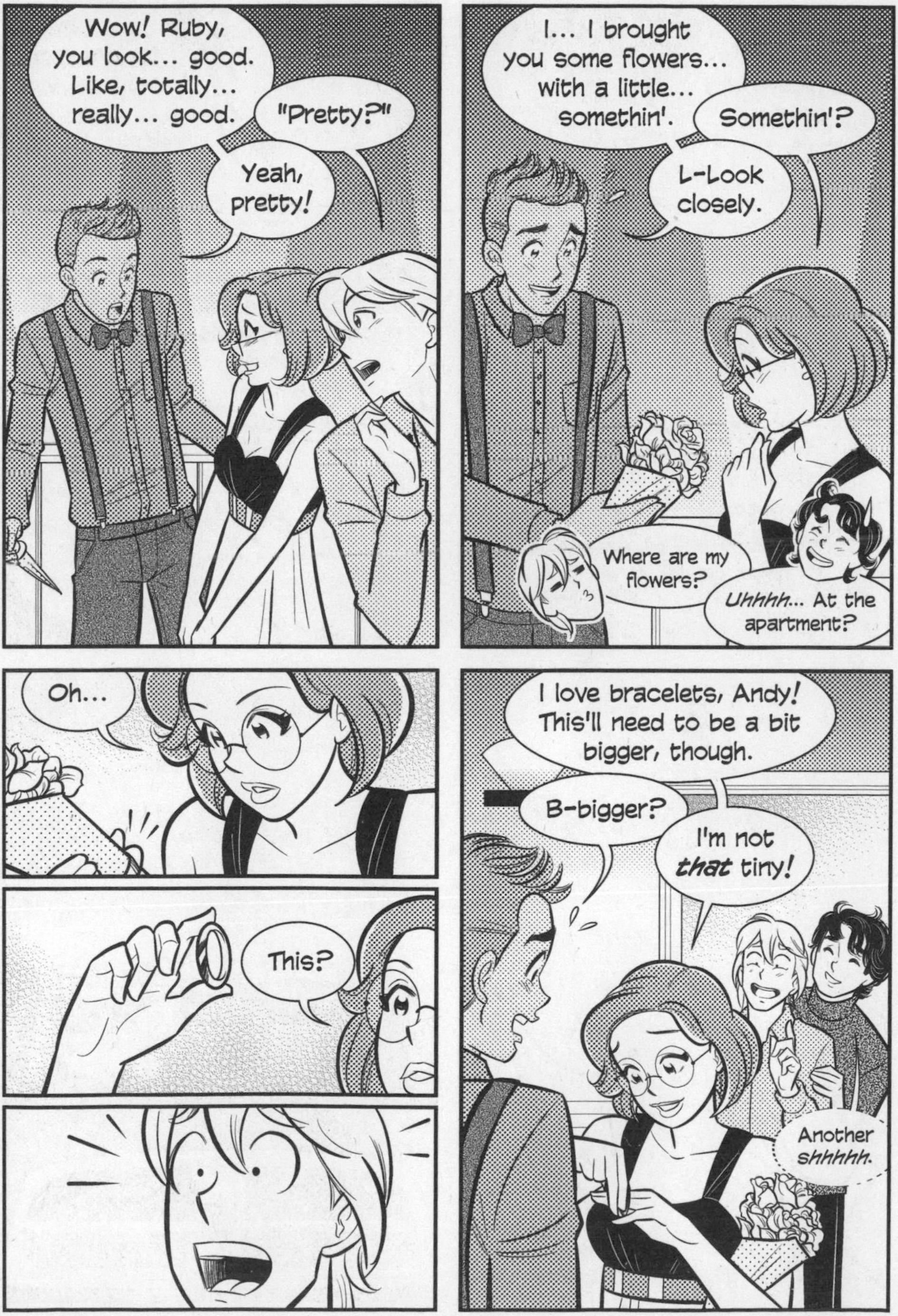

Wow! Ruby, you look... good. Like, totally... really... good.
"Pretty?"
Yeah, pretty!
I... I brought you some flowers... with a little... somethin'.
Somethin'?
L-Look closely.
Where are my flowers?
Uhhhh... At the apartment?
Oh...
This?
I love bracelets, Andy! This'll need to be a bit bigger, though.
B-bigger?
I'm not ***that*** tiny!
Another *shhhhh.*

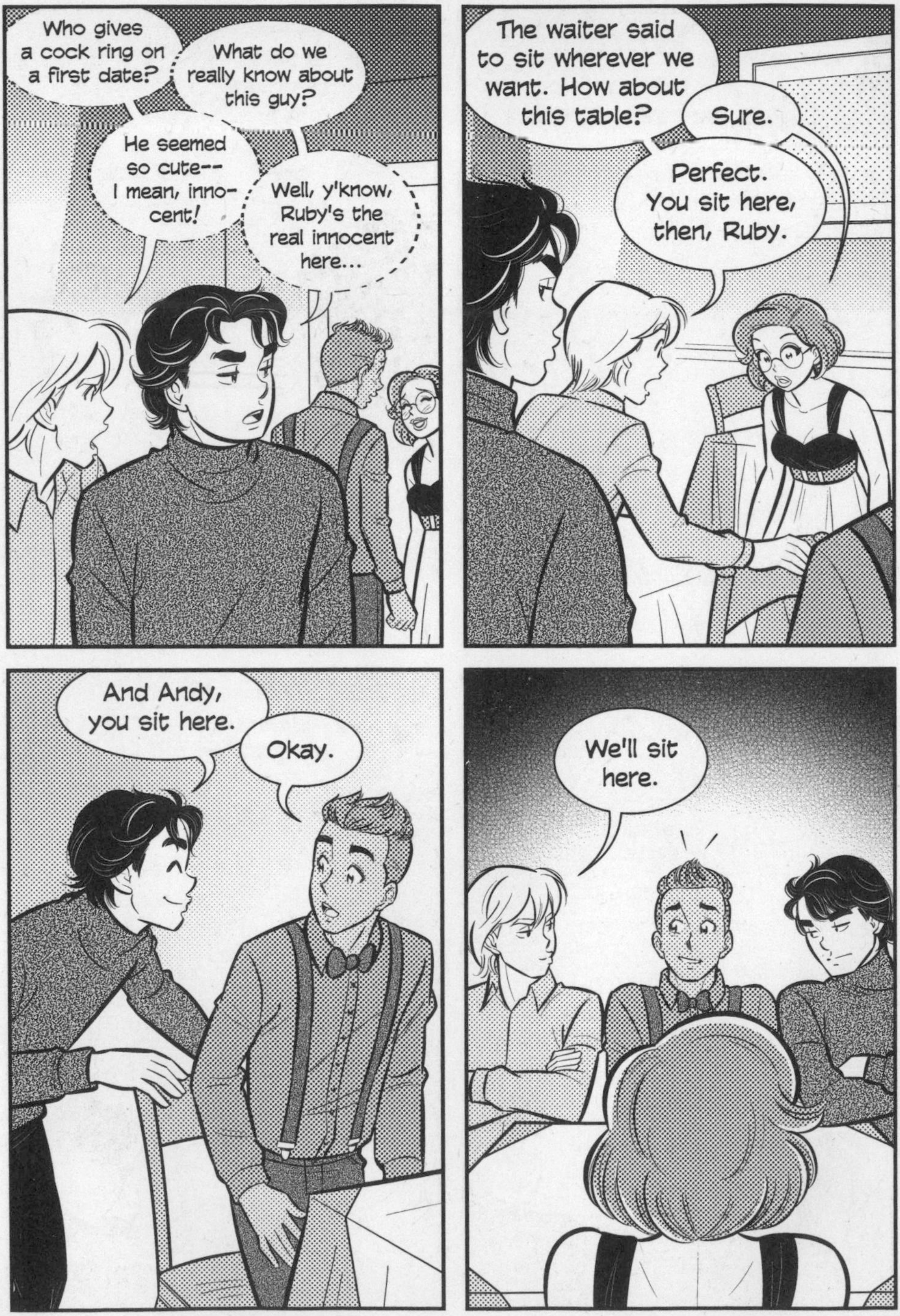

Who gives a cock ring on a first date?
What do we really know about this guy?
He seemed so cute-- I mean, inno-cent!
Well, y'know, Ruby's the real innocent here...
The waiter said to sit wherever we want. How about this table?
Sure.
Perfect. You sit here, then, Ruby.
And Andy, you sit here.
Okay.
We'll sit here.

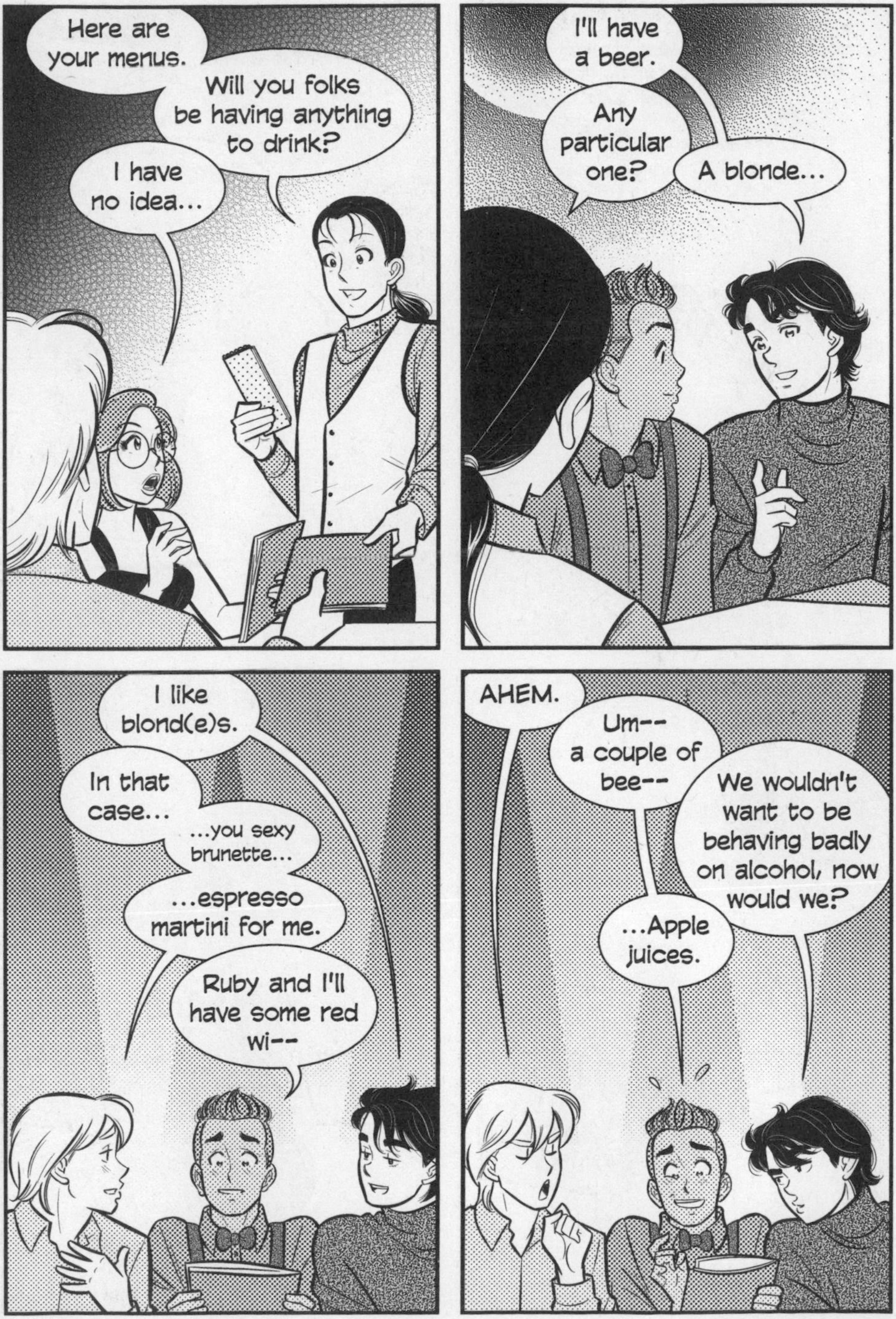
Here are your menus.
Will you folks be having anything to drink?
I have no idea...
I'll have a beer.
Any particular one?
A blonde...
I like blond(e)s.
In that case...
...you sexy brunette...
...espresso martini for me.
Ruby and I'll have some red wi--
AHEM.
Um-- a couple of bee--
We wouldn't want to be behaving badly on alcohol, now would we?
...Apple juices.

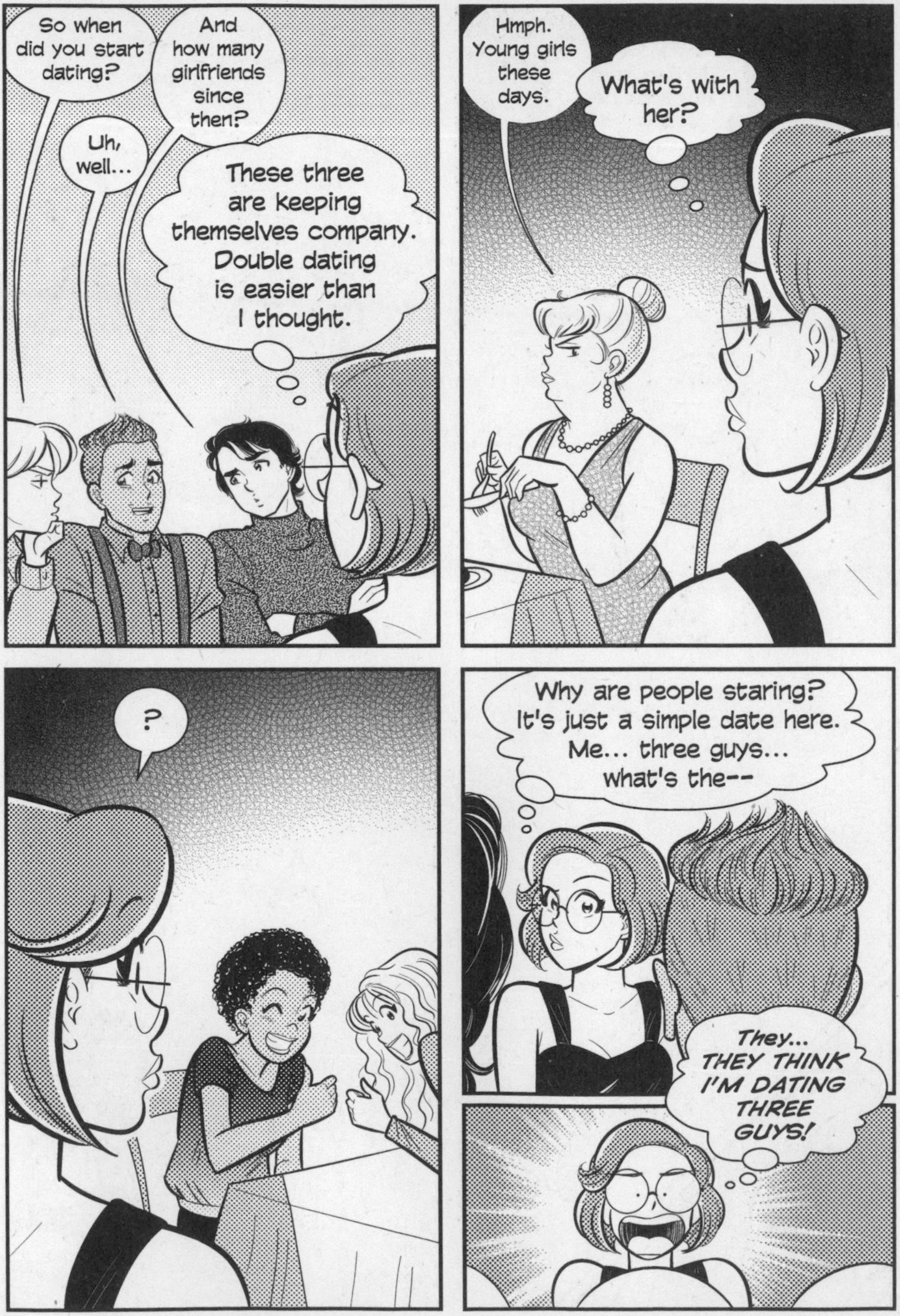
So when did you start dating?
And how many girlfriends since then?
Uh, well...
These three are keeping themselves company. Double dating is easier than I thought.
Hmph. Young girls these days.
What's with her?
?
Why are people staring? It's just a simple date here. Me... three guys... what's the--
They... THEY THINK I'M DATING THREE GUYS!

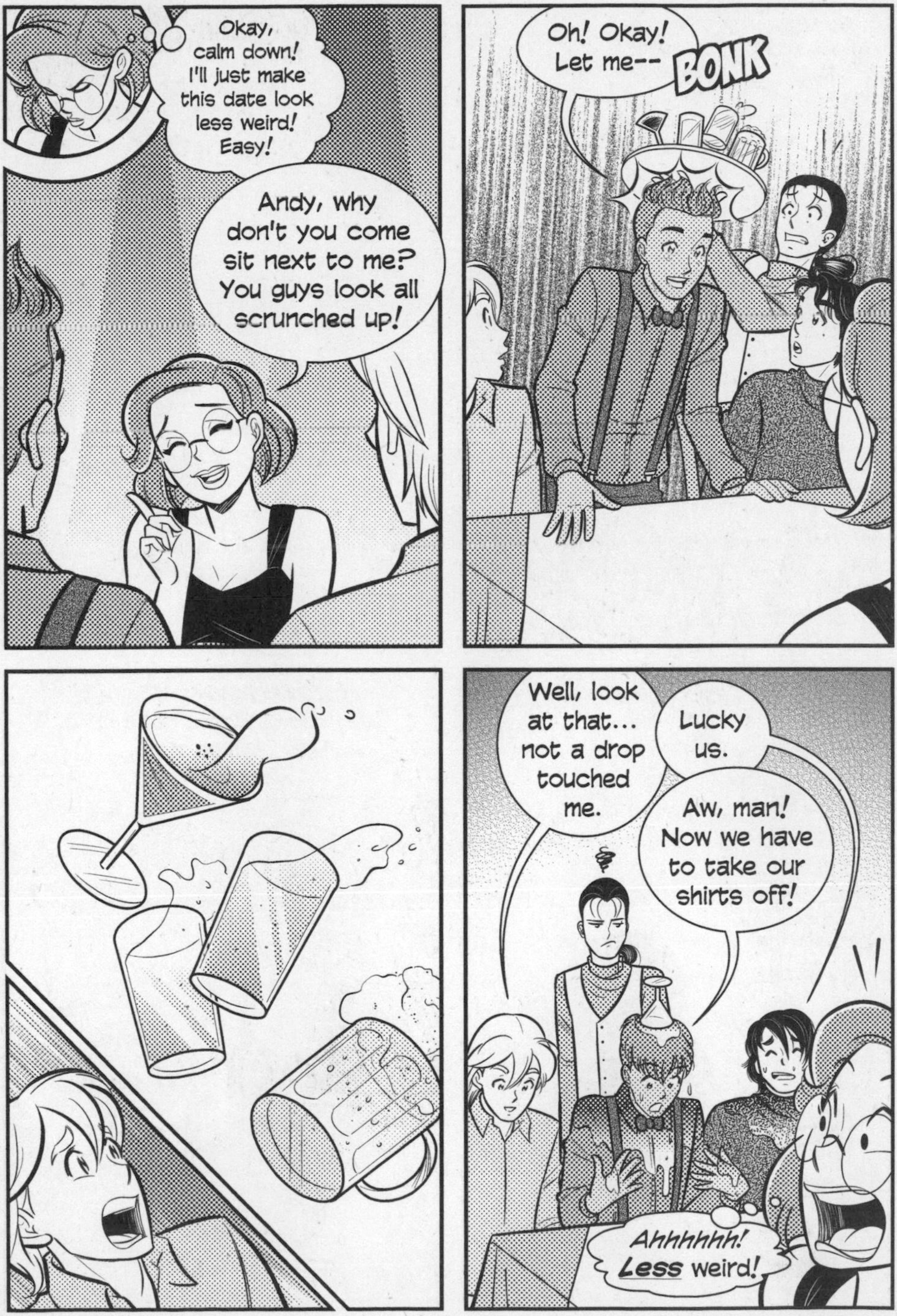
Okay, calm down! I'll just make this date look less weird! Easy!
Andy, why don't you come sit next to me? You guys look all scrunched up!
Oh! Okay! Let me--
BONK
Well, look at that... not a drop touched me.
Lucky us.
Aw, man! Now we have to take our shirts off!
Ahhhhhh! Less weird!

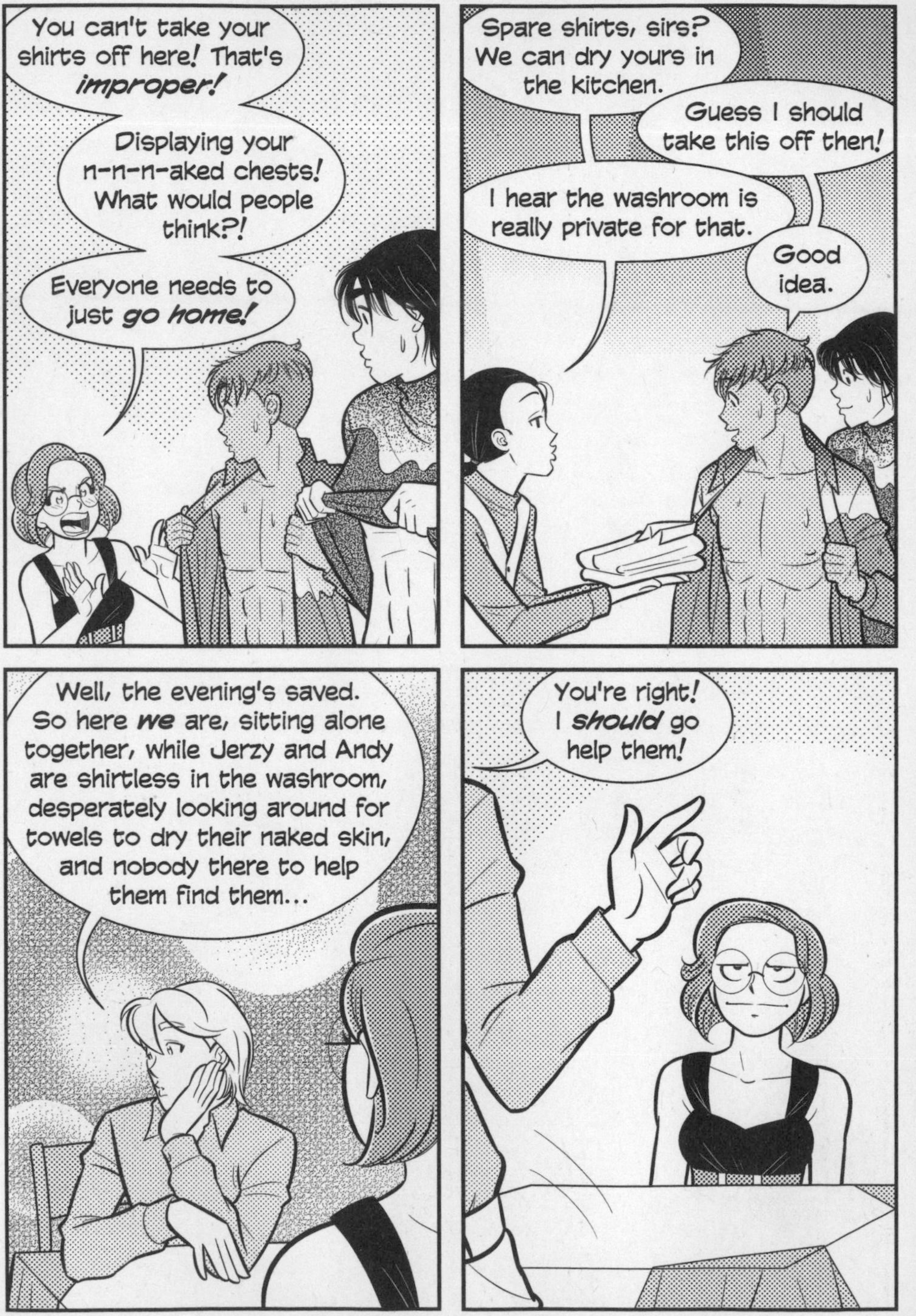
You can't take your shirts off here! That's *improper!*
Displaying your n-n-n-aked chests! What would people think?!
Everyone needs to just *go home!*
Spare shirts, sirs? We can dry yours in the kitchen.
Guess I should take this off then!
I hear the washroom is really private for that.
Good idea.
Well, the evening's saved. So here *we* are, sitting alone together, while Jerzy and Andy are shirtless in the washroom, desperately looking around for towels to dry their naked skin, and nobody there to help them find them...
You're right! I *should* go help them!

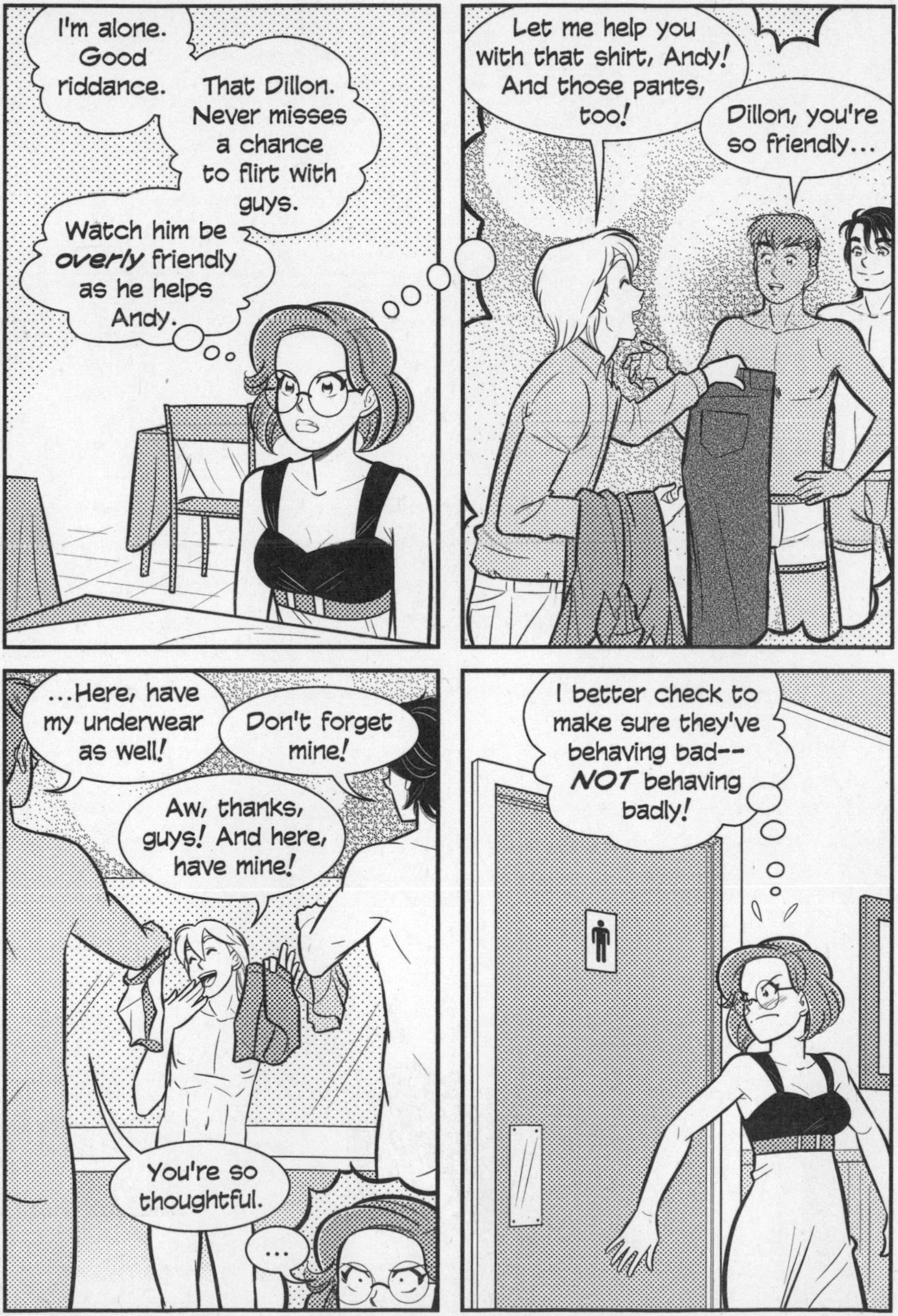

I'm alone. Good riddance.
That Dillon. Never misses a chance to flirt with guys.
Watch him be *overly* friendly as he helps Andy.
Let me help you with that shirt, Andy! And those pants, too!
Dillon, you're so friendly...
...Here, have my underwear as well!
Don't forget mine!
Aw, thanks, guys! And here, have mine!
You're so thoughtful.
...
I better check to make sure they've behaving bad-- *NOT* behaving badly!

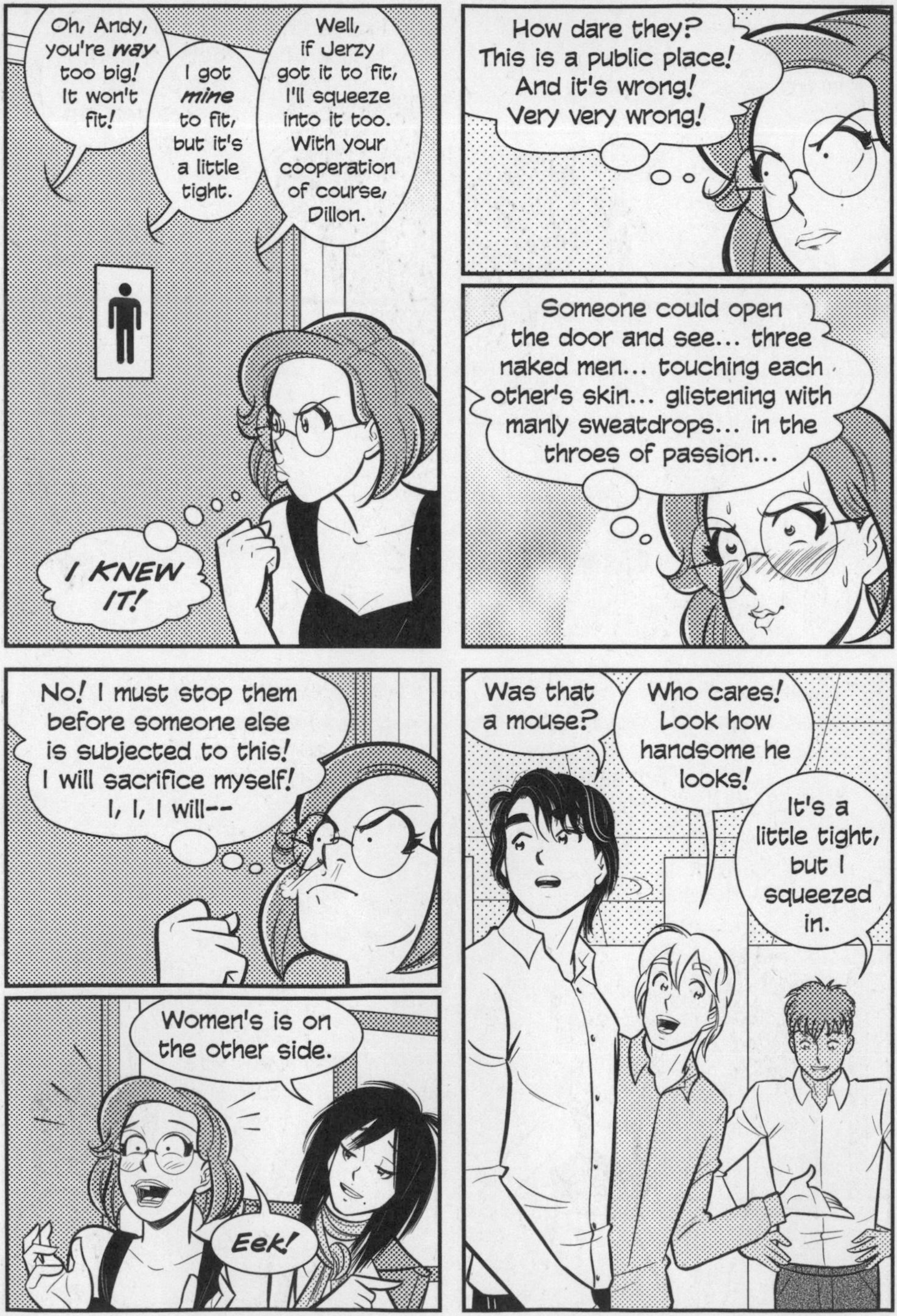
Oh, Andy, you're *way* too big! It won't fit!
I got *mine* to fit, but it's a little tight.
Well, if Jerzy got it to fit, I'll squeeze into it too. With your cooperation of course, Dillon.
I KNEW IT!
How dare they? This is a public place! And it's wrong! Very very wrong!
Someone could open the door and see... three naked men... touching each other's skin... glistening with manly sweatdrops... in the throes of passion...
No! I must stop them before someone else is subjected to this! I will sacrifice myself! I, I, I will--
Women's is on the other side.
Eek!
Was that a mouse?
Who cares! Look how handsome he looks!
It's a little tight, but I squeezed in.

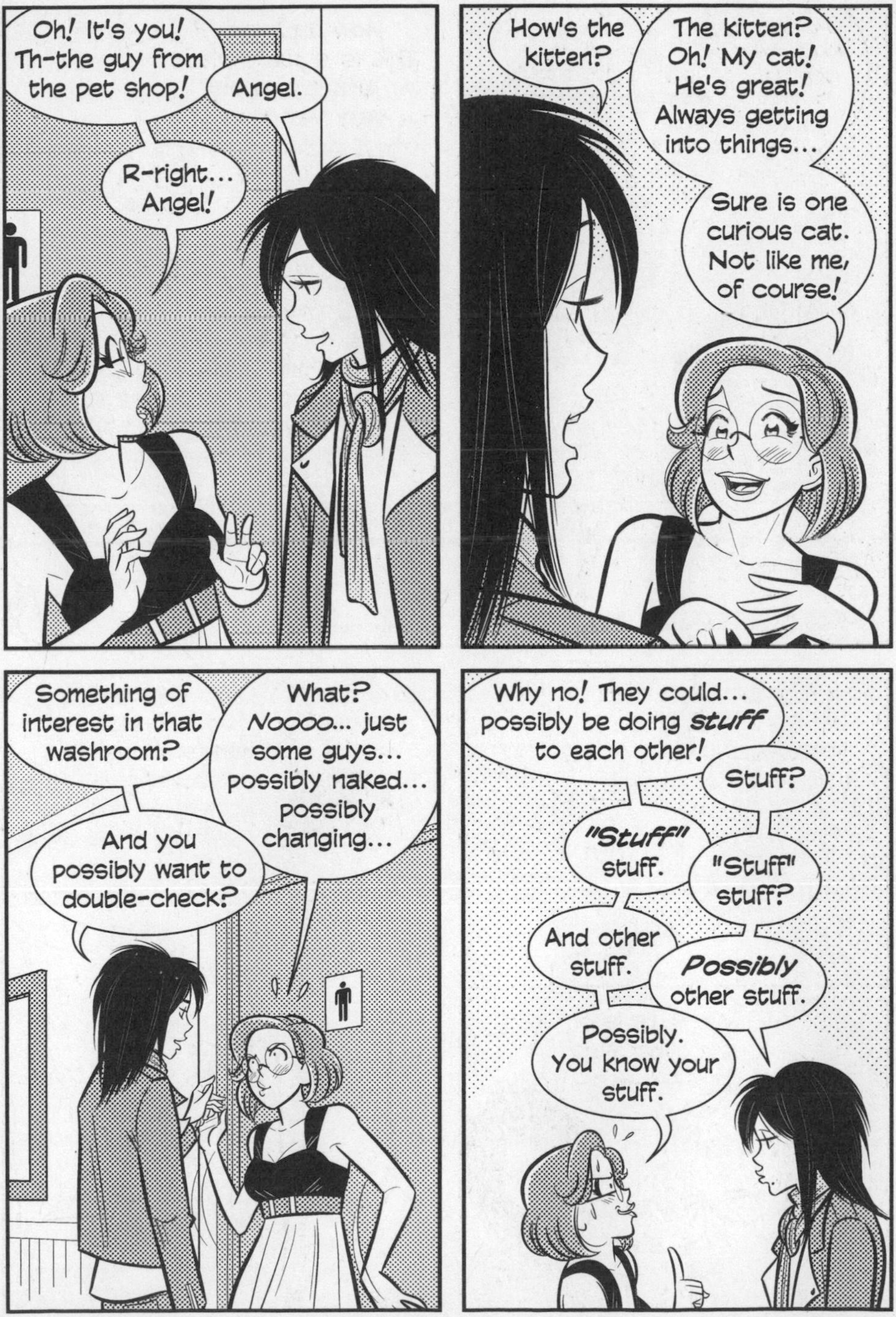

Oh! It's you! Th-the guy from the pet shop!
Angel.
R-right... Angel!
How's the kitten?
The kitten? Oh! My cat! He's great! Always getting into things...
Sure is one curious cat. Not like me, of course!
Something of interest in that washroom?
What? *Noooo*... just some guys... possibly naked... possibly changing...
And you possibly want to double-check?
Why no! They could... possibly be doing ***stuff*** to each other!
Stuff?
"Stuff" stuff.
"Stuff" stuff?
And other stuff.
Possibly other stuff.
Possibly. You know your stuff.

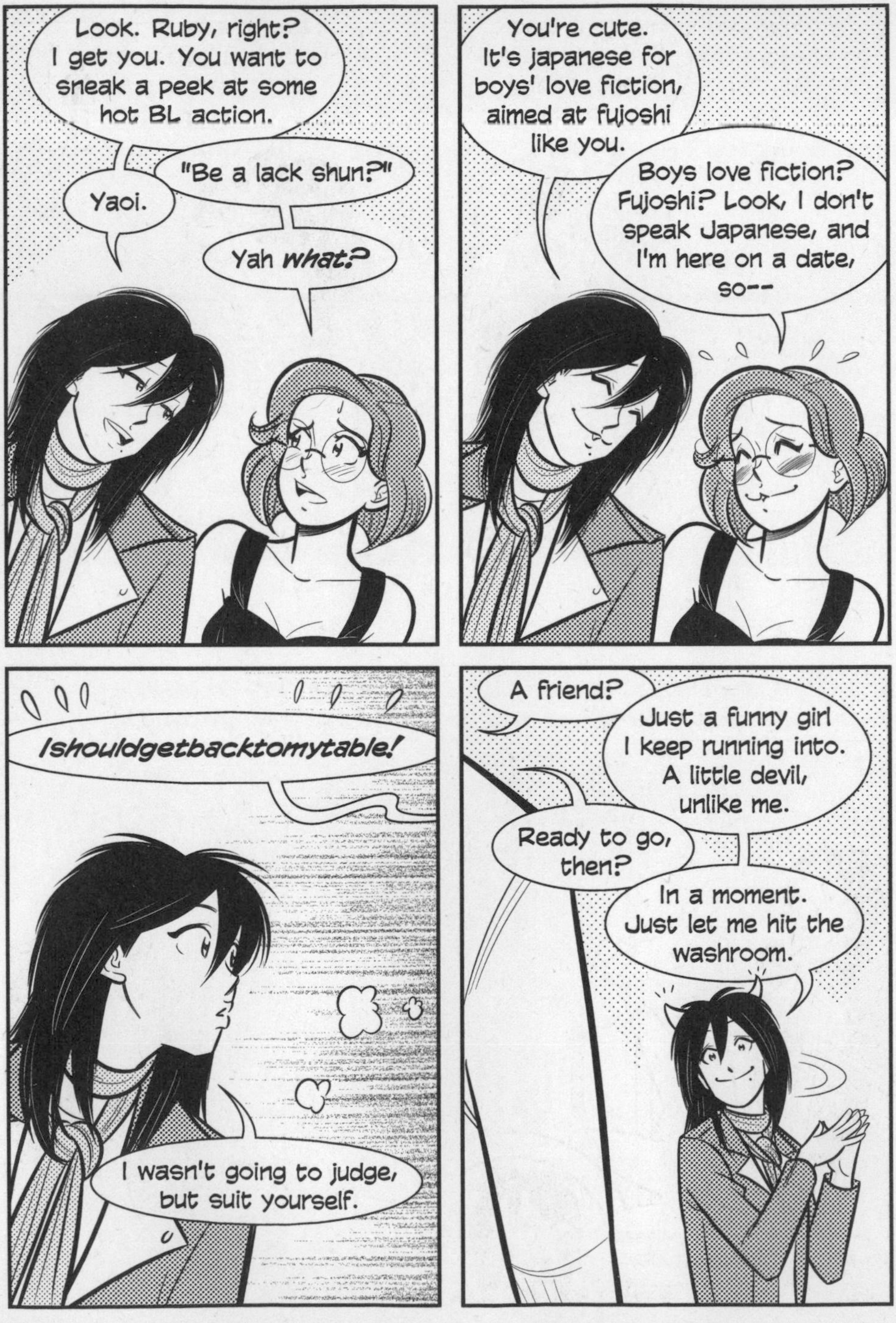
Look. Ruby, right? I get you. You want to sneak a peek at some hot BL action.
"Be a lack shun?"
Yaoi.
Yah *what?*
You're cute. It's japanese for boys' love fiction, aimed at fujoshi like you.
Boys love fiction? Fujoshi? Look, I don't speak Japanese, and I'm here on a date, so--
Ishouldgetbacktomytable!
I wasn't going to judge, but suit yourself.
A friend?
Just a funny girl I keep running into. A little devil, unlike me.
Ready to go, then?
In a moment. Just let me hit the washroom.

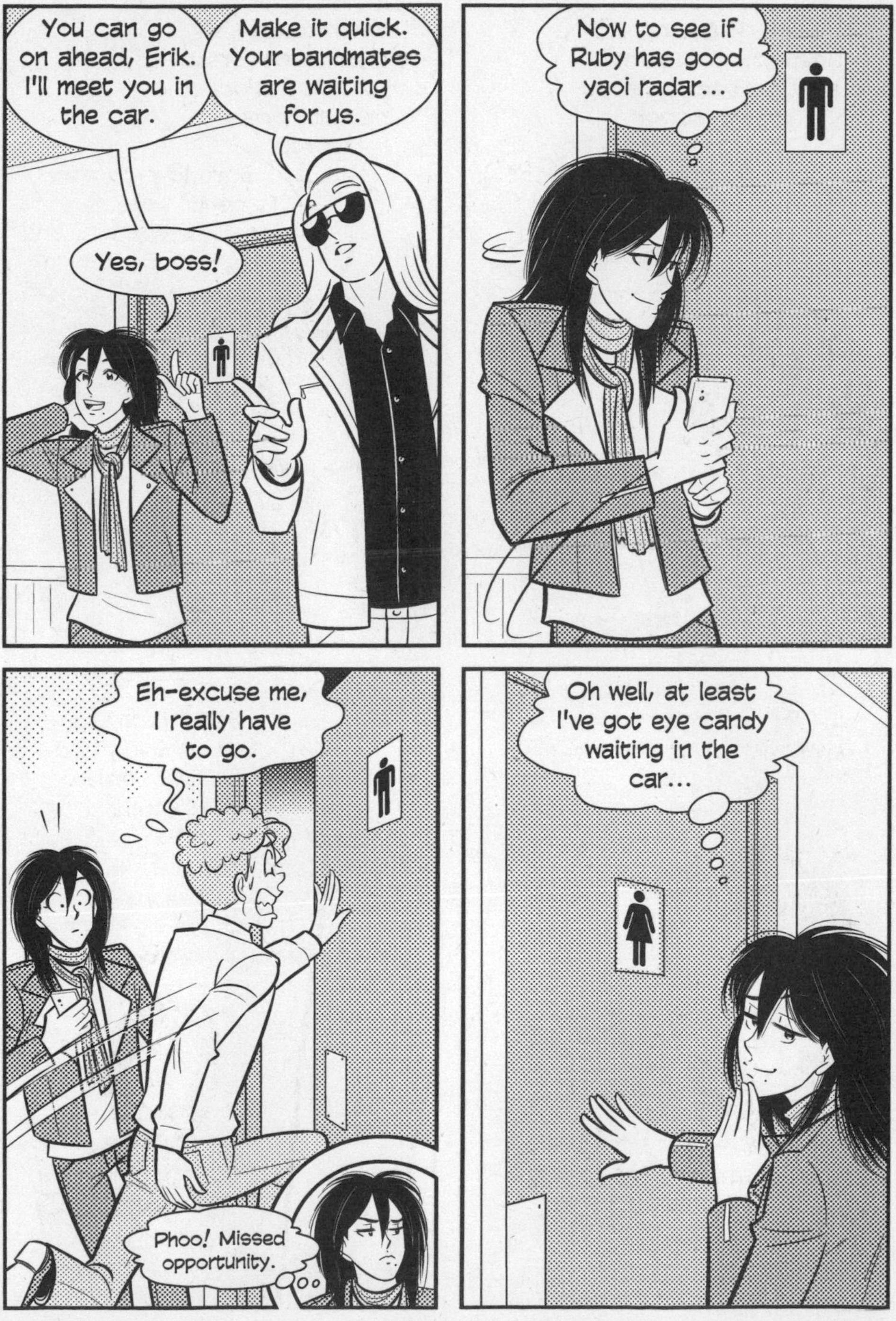
You can go on ahead, Erik. I'll meet you in the car.
Make it quick. Your bandmates are waiting for us.
Yes, boss!
Now to see if Ruby has good yaoi radar...
Eh-excuse me, I really have to go.
Phoo! Missed opportunity.
Oh well, at least I've got eye candy waiting in the car...

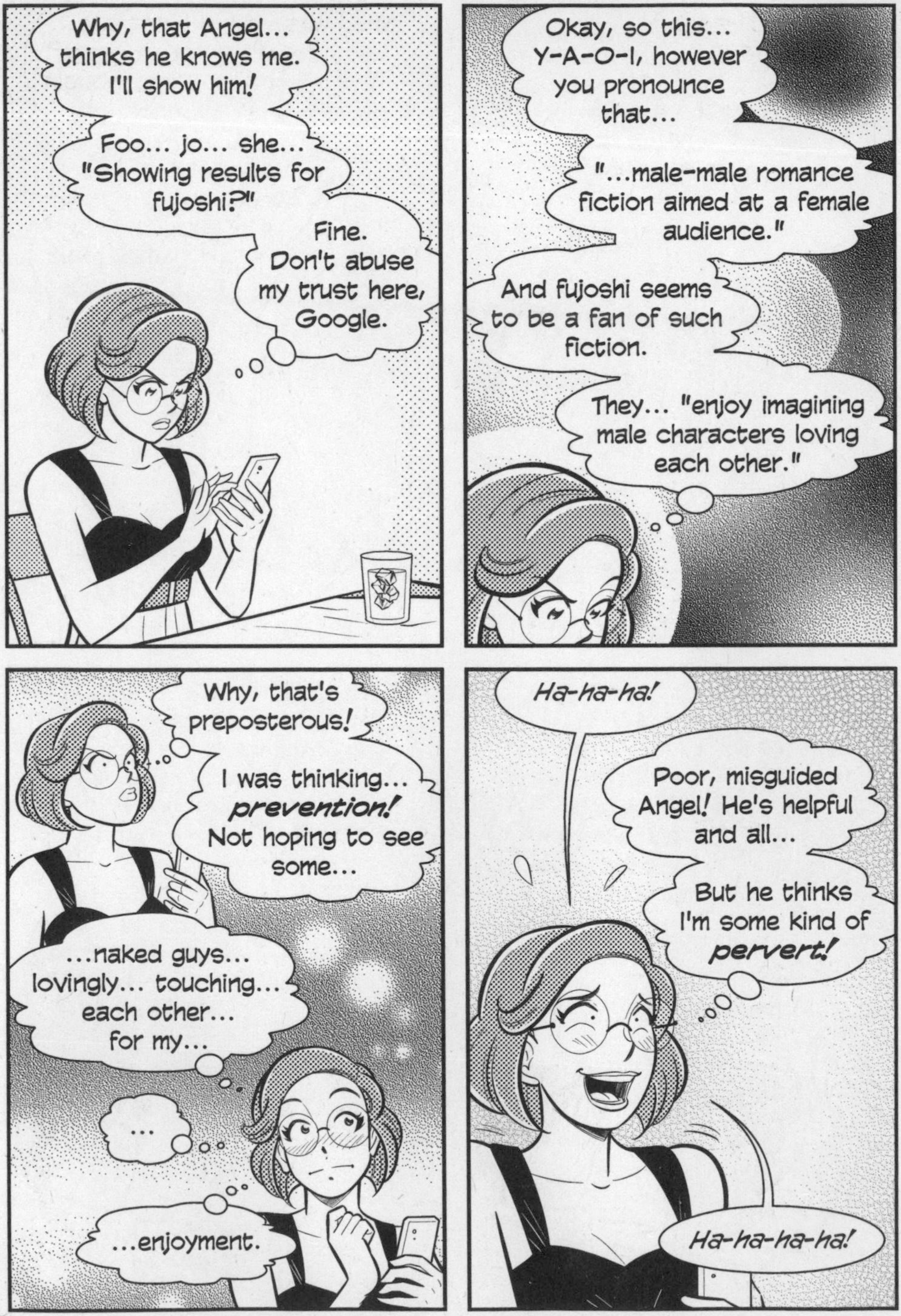
Why, that Angel... thinks he knows me. I'll show him!
Foo... jo... she... "Showing results for fujoshi?"
Fine. Don't abuse my trust here, Google.
Okay, so this... Y-A-O-I, however you pronounce that...
"...male-male romance fiction aimed at a female audience."
And fujoshi seems to be a fan of such fiction.
They... "enjoy imagining male characters loving each other."
Why, that's preposterous!
I was thinking... *prevention!* Not hoping to see some...
...naked guys... lovingly... touching... each other... for my...
...
...enjoyment.
Ha-ha-ha!
Poor, misguided Angel! He's helpful and all...
But he thinks I'm some kind of *pervert!*
Ha-ha-ha-ha!

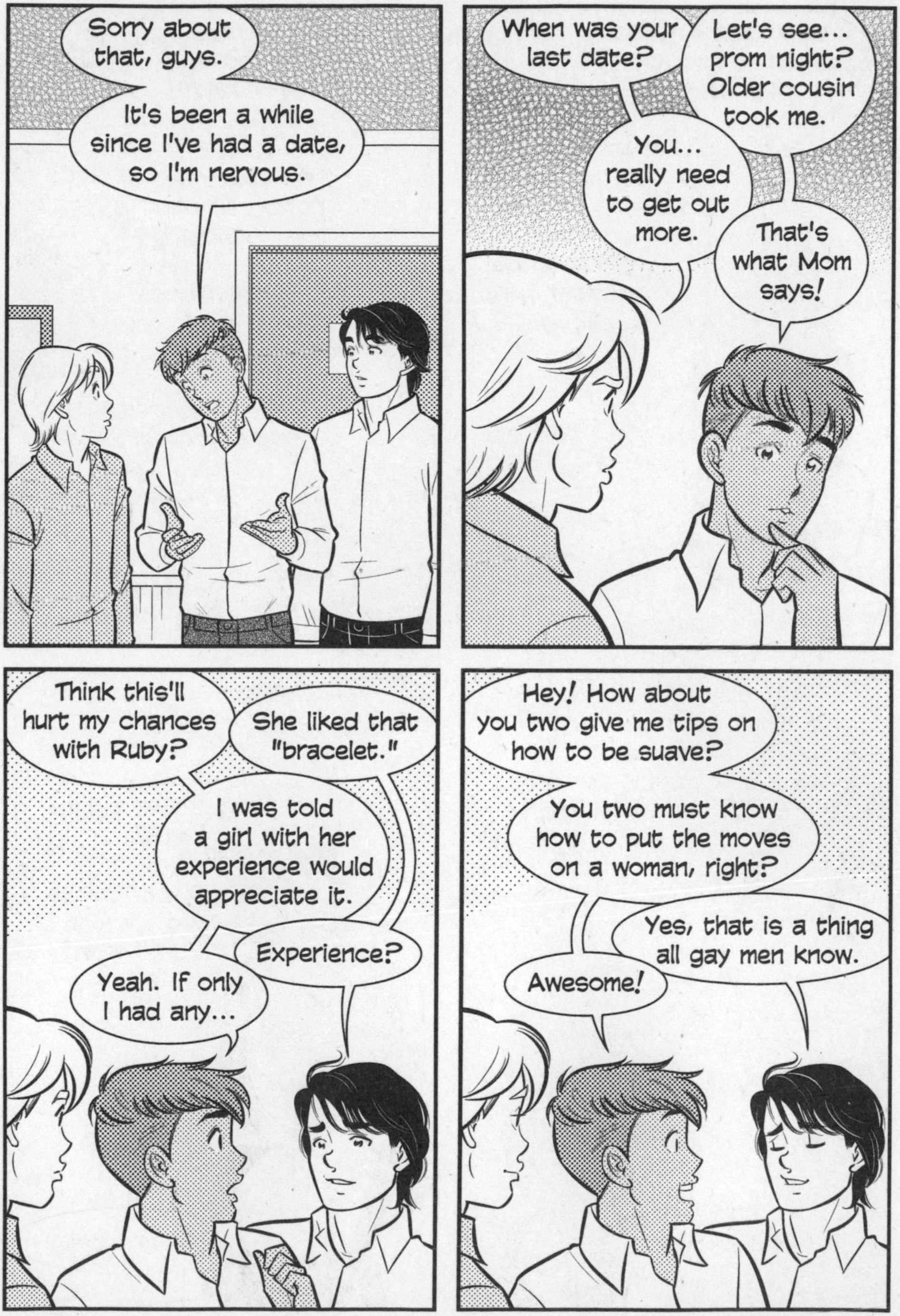
Sorry about that, guys.
It's been a while since I've had a date, so I'm nervous.
When was your last date?
Let's see... prom night? Older cousin took me.
You... really need to get out more.
That's what Mom says!
Think this'll hurt my chances with Ruby?
She liked that "bracelet."
I was told a girl with her experience would appreciate it.
Experience?
Yeah. If only I had any...
Hey! How about you two give me tips on how to be suave?
You two must know how to put the moves on a woman, right?
Yes, that is a thing all gay men know.
Awesome!

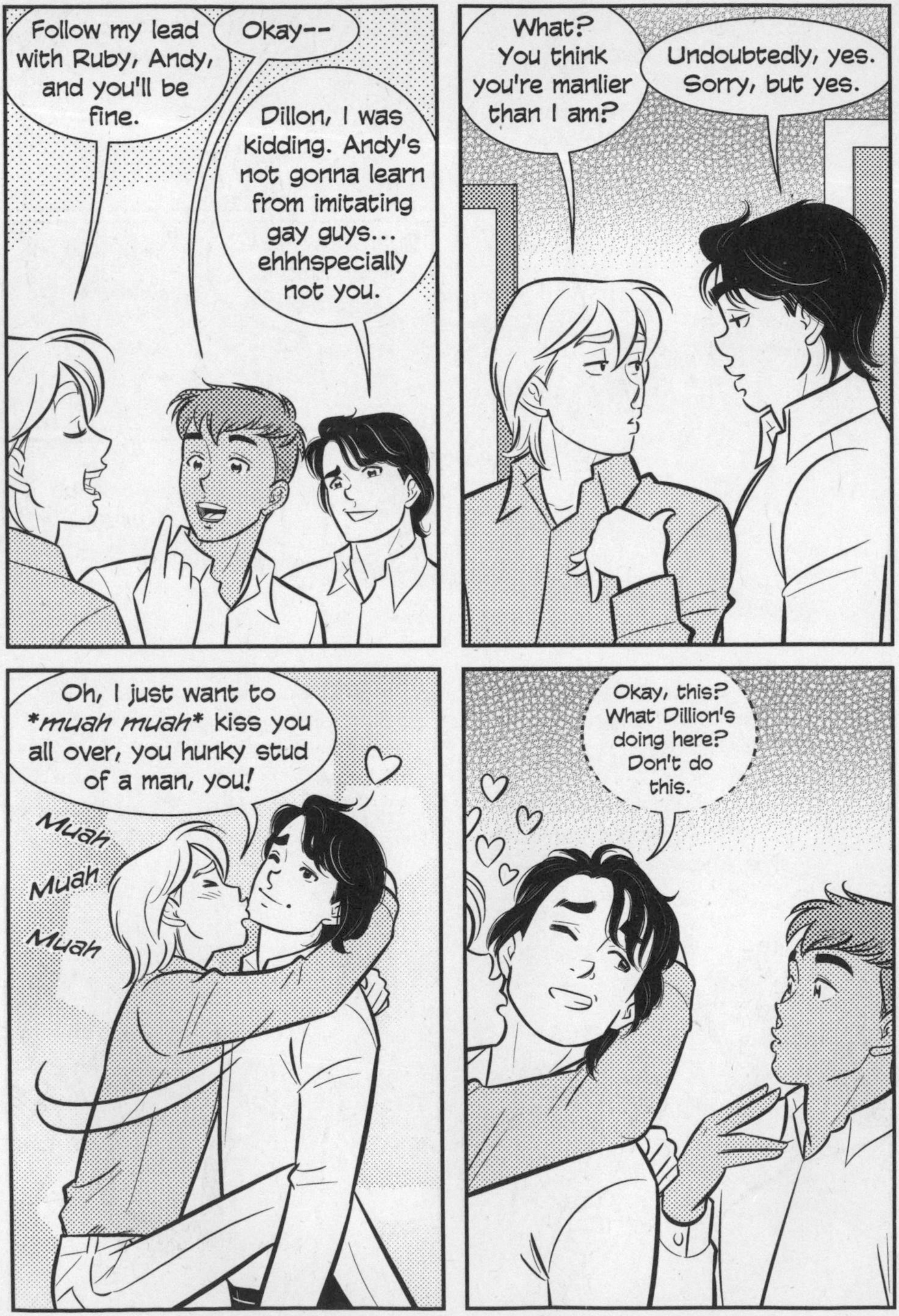
Follow my lead with Ruby, Andy, and you'll be fine.
Okay--
Dillon, I was kidding. Andy's not gonna learn from imitating gay guys... ehhhspecially not you.
What? You think you're manlier than I am?
Undoubtedly, yes. Sorry, but yes.
Oh, I just want to *muah muah* kiss you all over, you hunky stud of a man, you!
Muah
Muah
Muah
Okay, this? What Dillion's doing here? Don't do this.

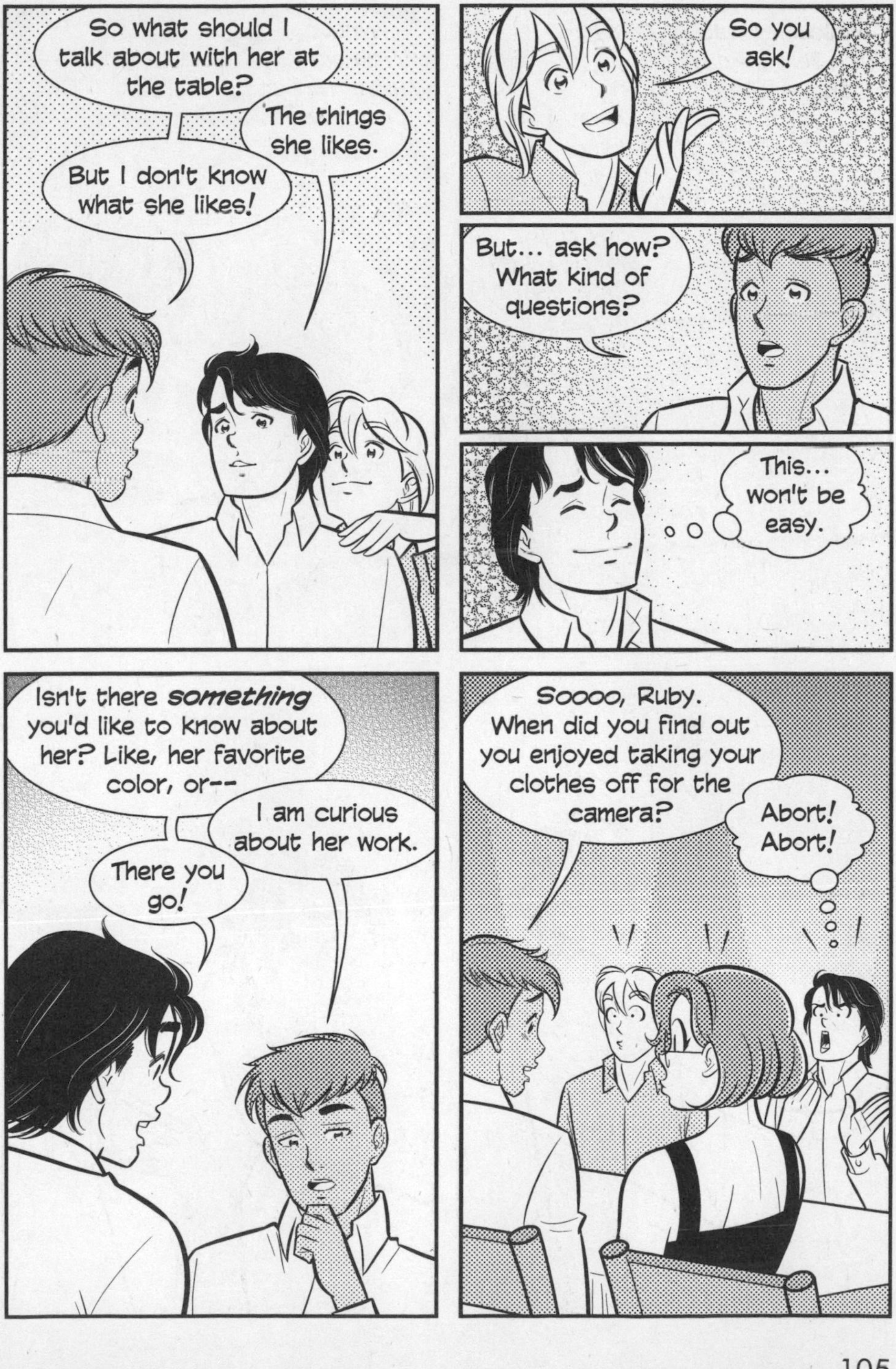
So what should I talk about with her at the table?
The things she likes.
But I don't know what she likes!
So you ask!
But... ask how? What kind of questions?
This... won't be easy.
Isn't there *something* you'd like to know about her? Like, her favorite color, or--
I am curious about her work.
There you go!
Soooo, Ruby. When did you find out you enjoyed taking your clothes off for the camera?
Abort! Abort!

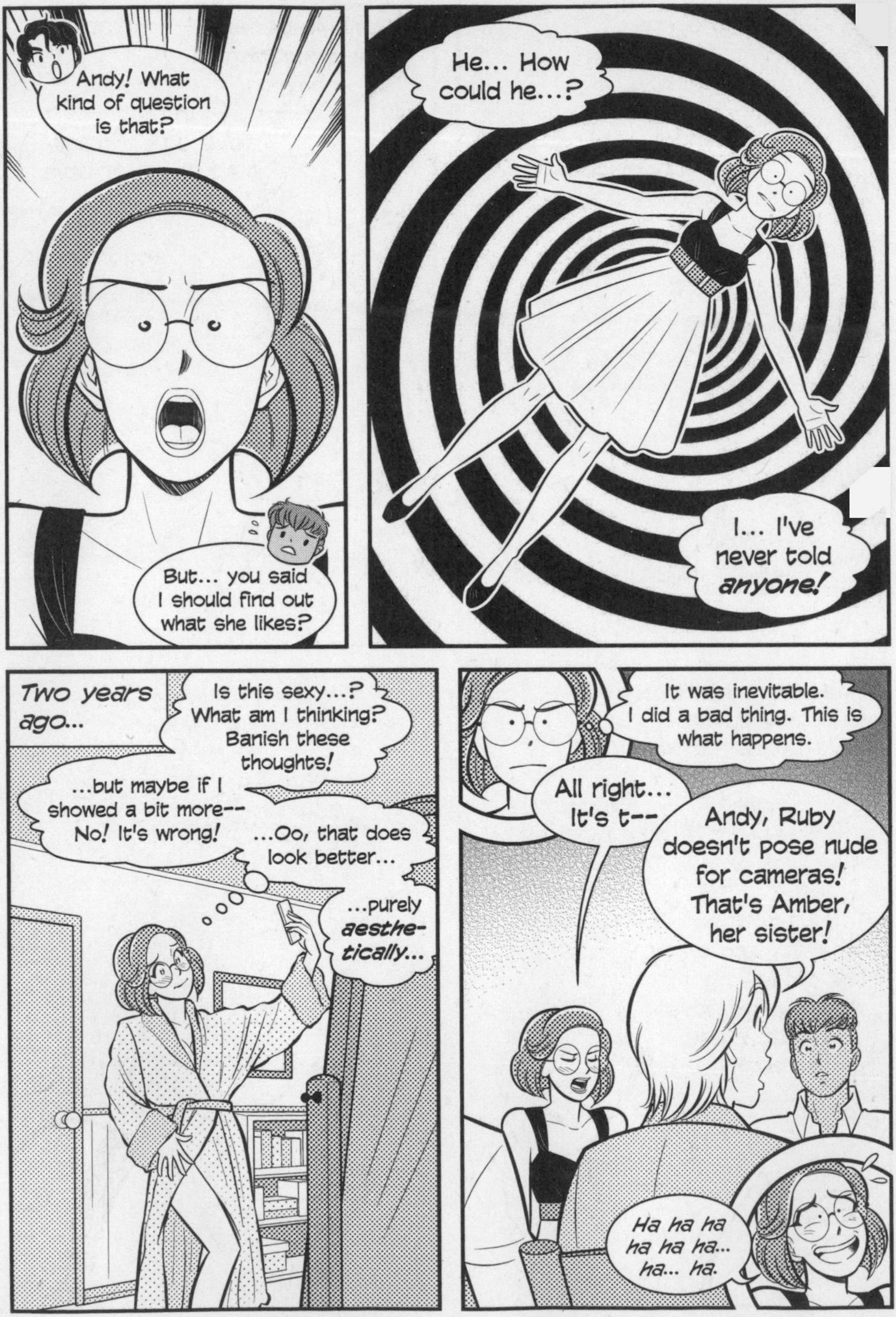

Andy! What kind of question is that?
But... you said I should find out what she likes?
He... How could he...?
I... I've never told *anyone!*
Two years ago...
Is this sexy...? What am I thinking? Banish these thoughts!
...but maybe if I showed a bit more-- No! It's wrong!
...Oo, that does look better...
...purely *aesthetically...*
It was inevitable. I did a bad thing. This is what happens.
All right... It's t--
Andy, Ruby doesn't pose nude for cameras! That's Amber, her sister!
Ha ha ha ha ha ha... ha... ha.

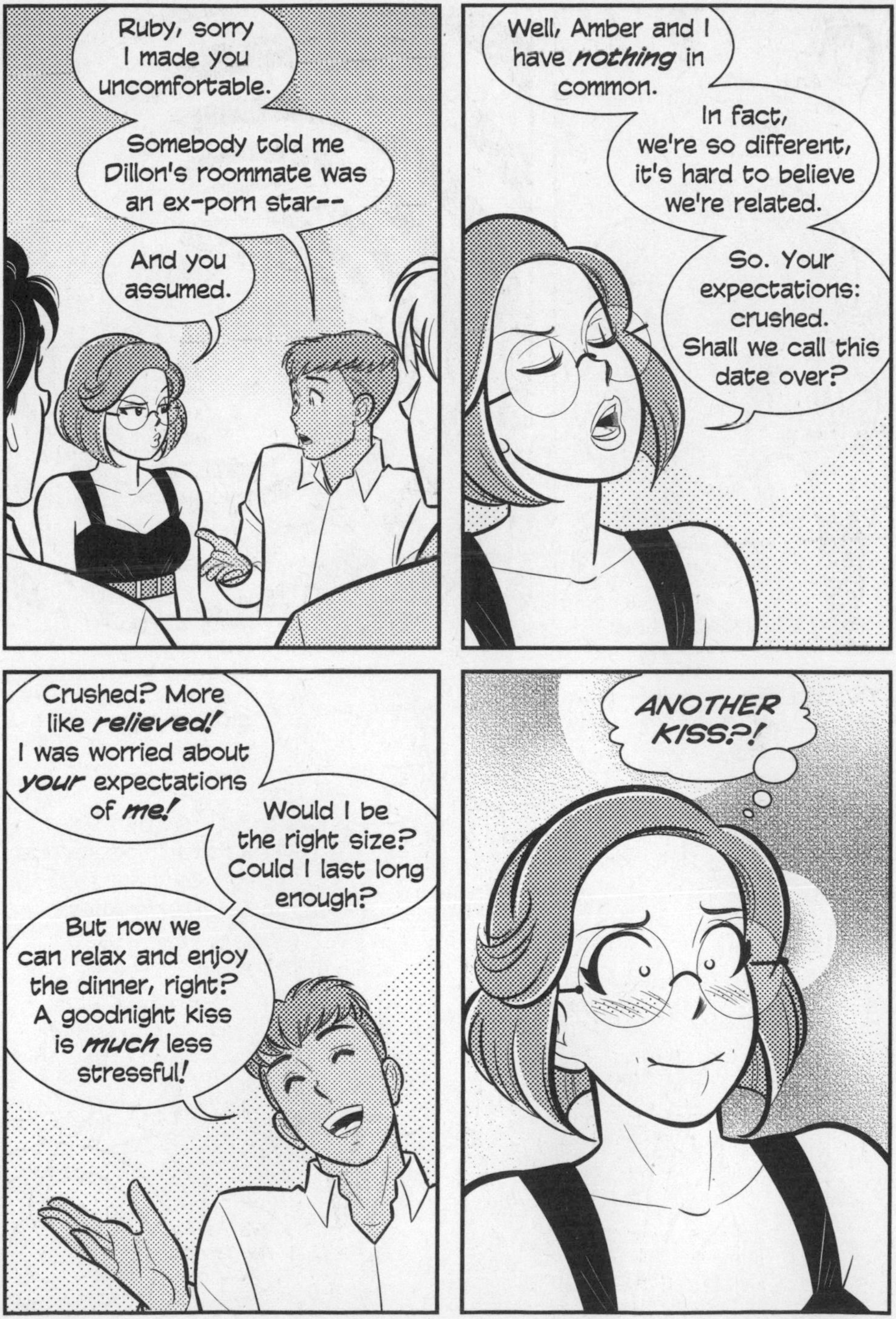
Ruby, sorry I made you uncomfortable.
Somebody told me Dillon's roommate was an ex-porn star--
And you assumed.
Well, Amber and I have *nothing* in common.
In fact, we're so different, it's hard to believe we're related.
So. Your expectations: crushed. Shall we call this date over?
Crushed? More like *relieved!* I was worried about *your* expectations of *me!*
Would I be the right size? Could I last long enough?
But now we can relax and enjoy the dinner, right? A goodnight kiss is *much* less stressful!
ANOTHER KISS?!

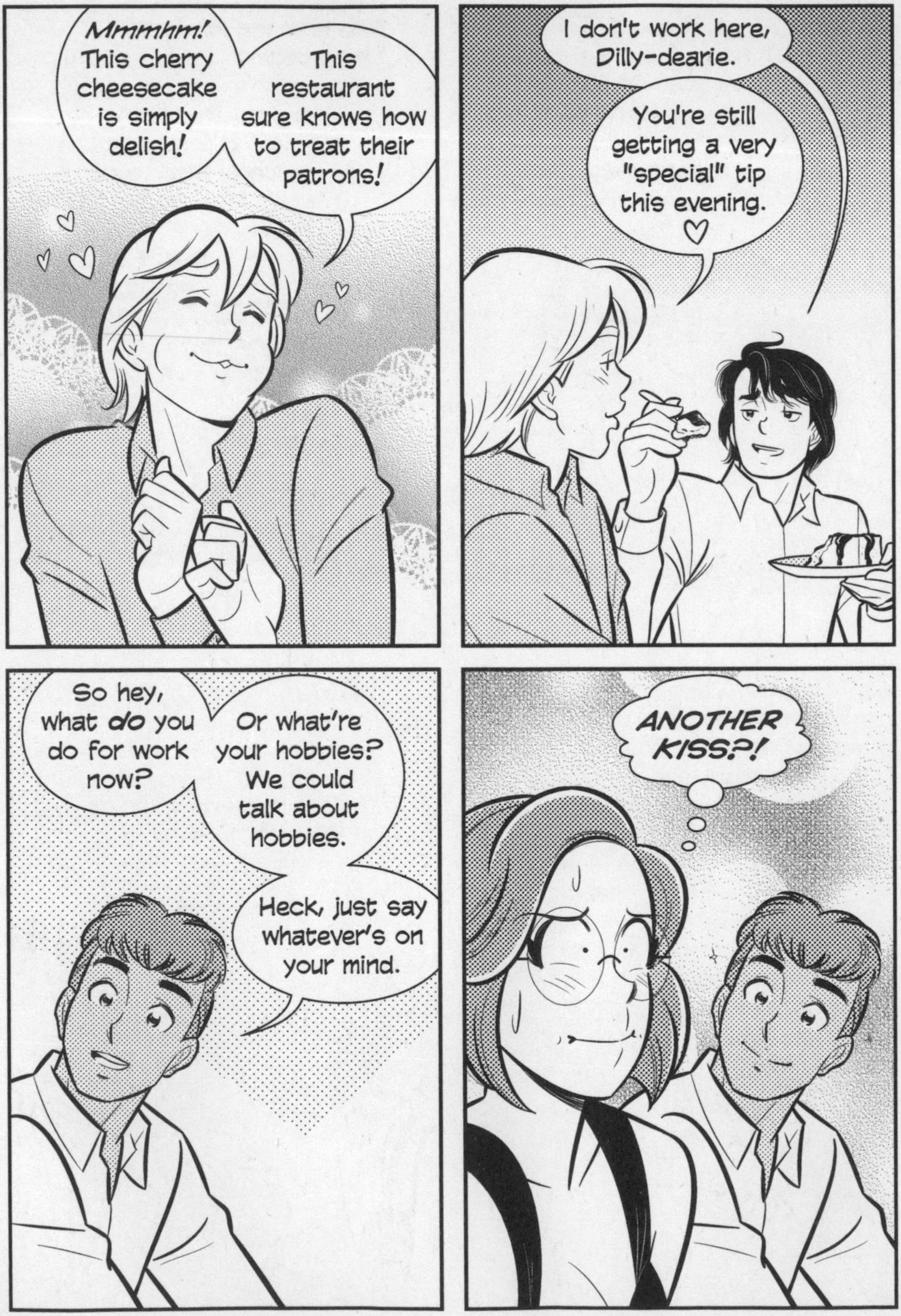

Mmmhm! This cherry cheesecake is simply delish!
This restaurant sure knows how to treat their patrons!
I don't work here, Dilly-dearie.
You're still getting a very "special" tip this evening. ♡
So hey, what *do* you do for work now?
Or what're your hobbies? We could talk about hobbies.
Heck, just say whatever's on your mind.
ANOTHER KISS?!

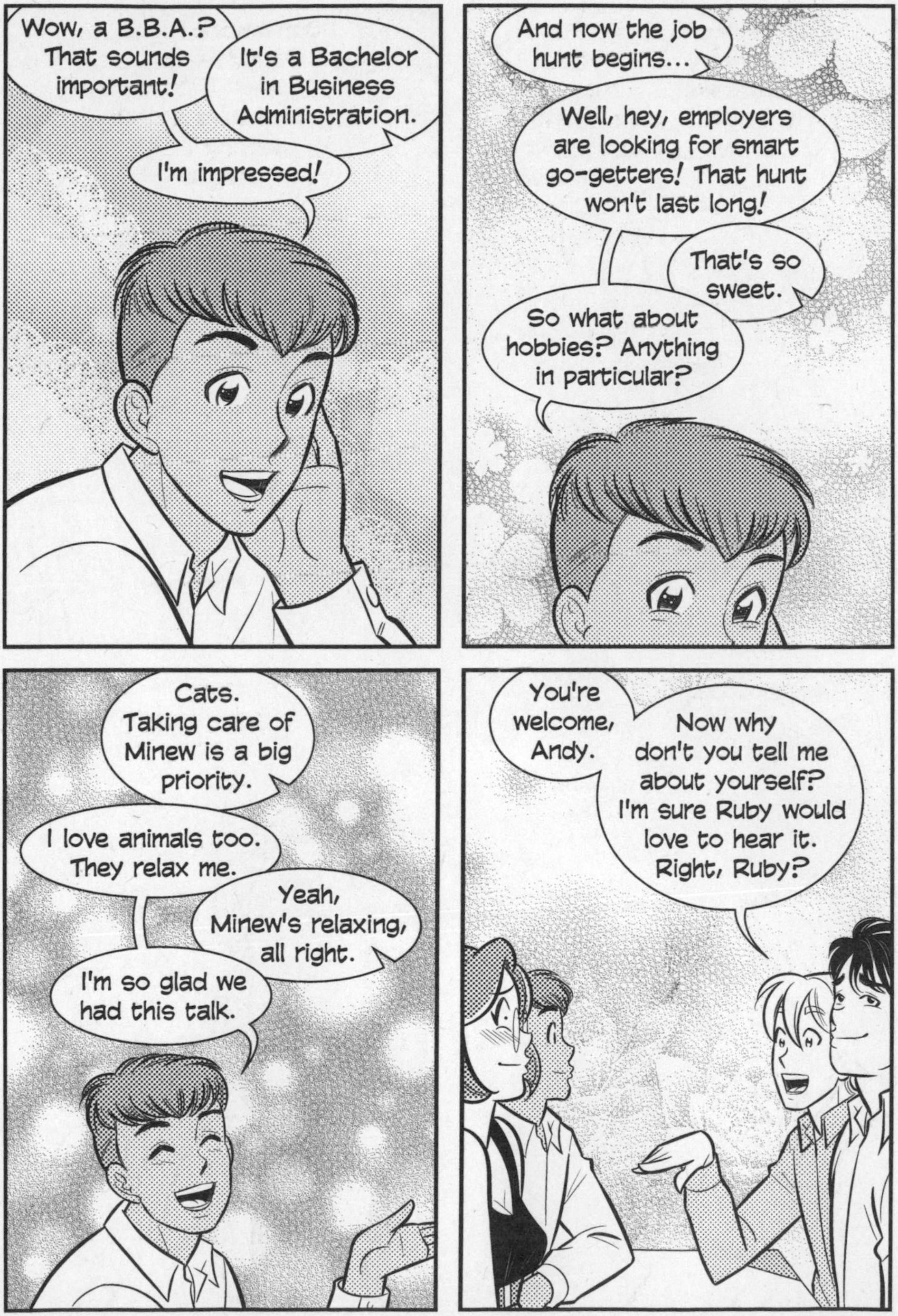
Wow, a B.B.A.? That sounds important!
It's a Bachelor in Business Administration.
I'm impressed!
And now the job hunt begins...
Well, hey, employers are looking for smart go-getters! That hunt won't last long!
That's so sweet.
So what about hobbies? Anything in particular?
Cats. Taking care of Minew is a big priority.
I love animals too. They relax me.
Yeah, Minew's relaxing, all right.
I'm so glad we had this talk.
You're welcome, Andy.
Now why don't you tell me about yourself? I'm sure Ruby would love to hear it. Right, Ruby?

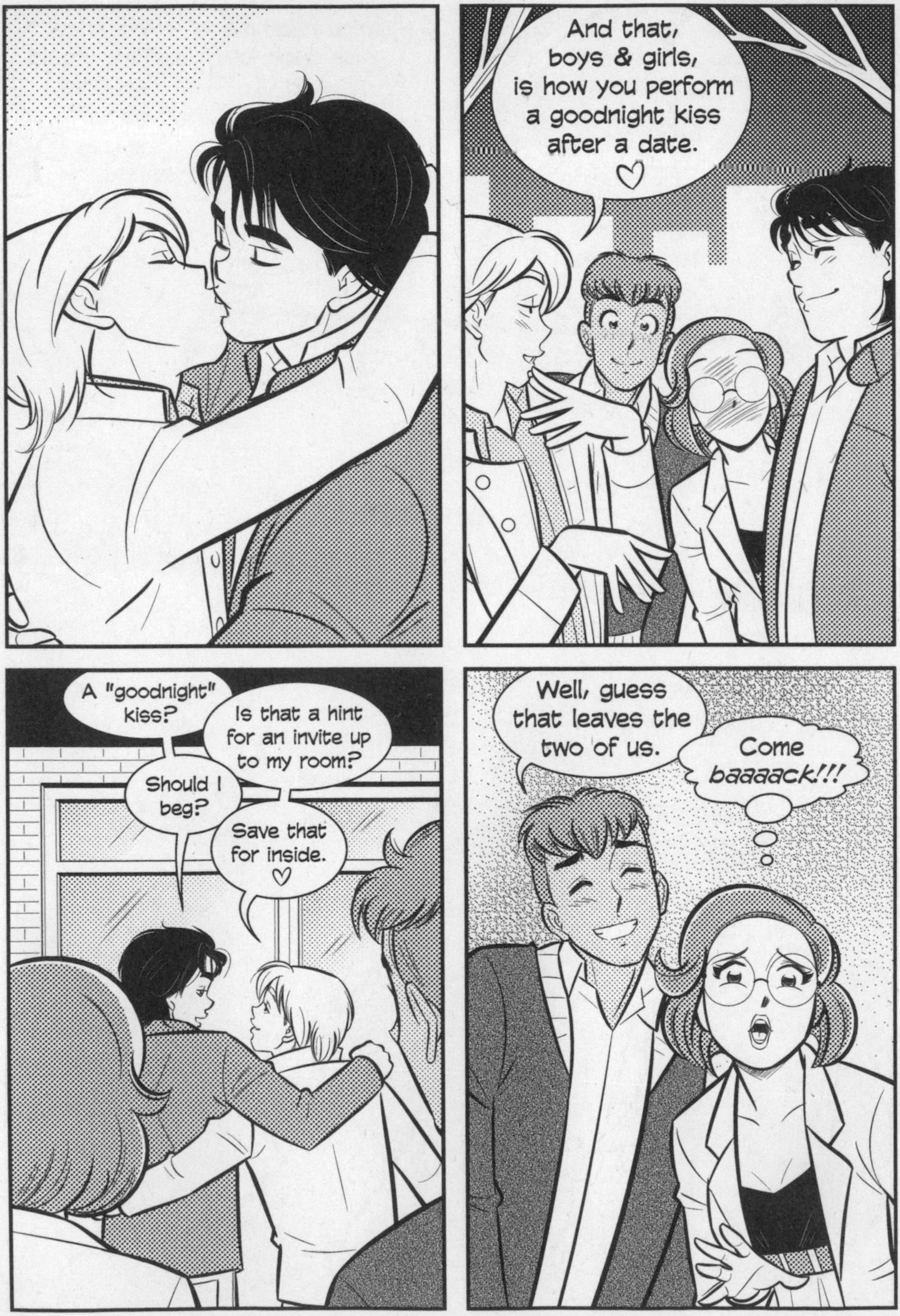
And that, boys & girls, is how you perform a goodnight kiss after a date. ♡
A "goodnight" kiss?
Should I beg?
Is that a hint for an invite up to my room?
Save that for inside. ♡
Well, guess that leaves the two of us.
Come *baaaack!!!*

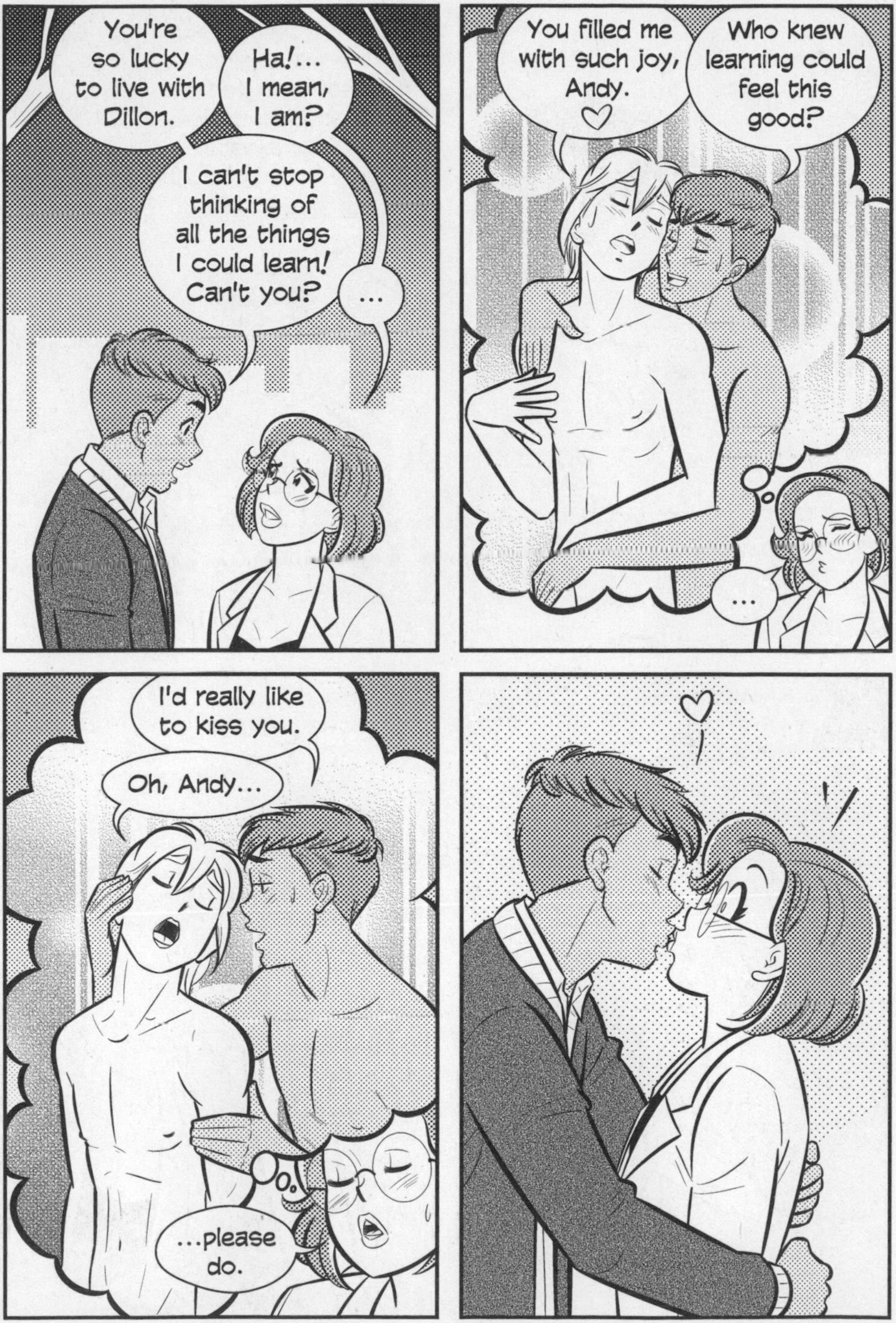
You're so lucky to live with Dillon.
Ha!... I mean, I am?
I can't stop thinking of all the things I could learn! Can't you?
...
You filled me with such joy, Andy.
Who knew learning could feel this good?
...
I'd really like to kiss you.
Oh, Andy...
...please do.

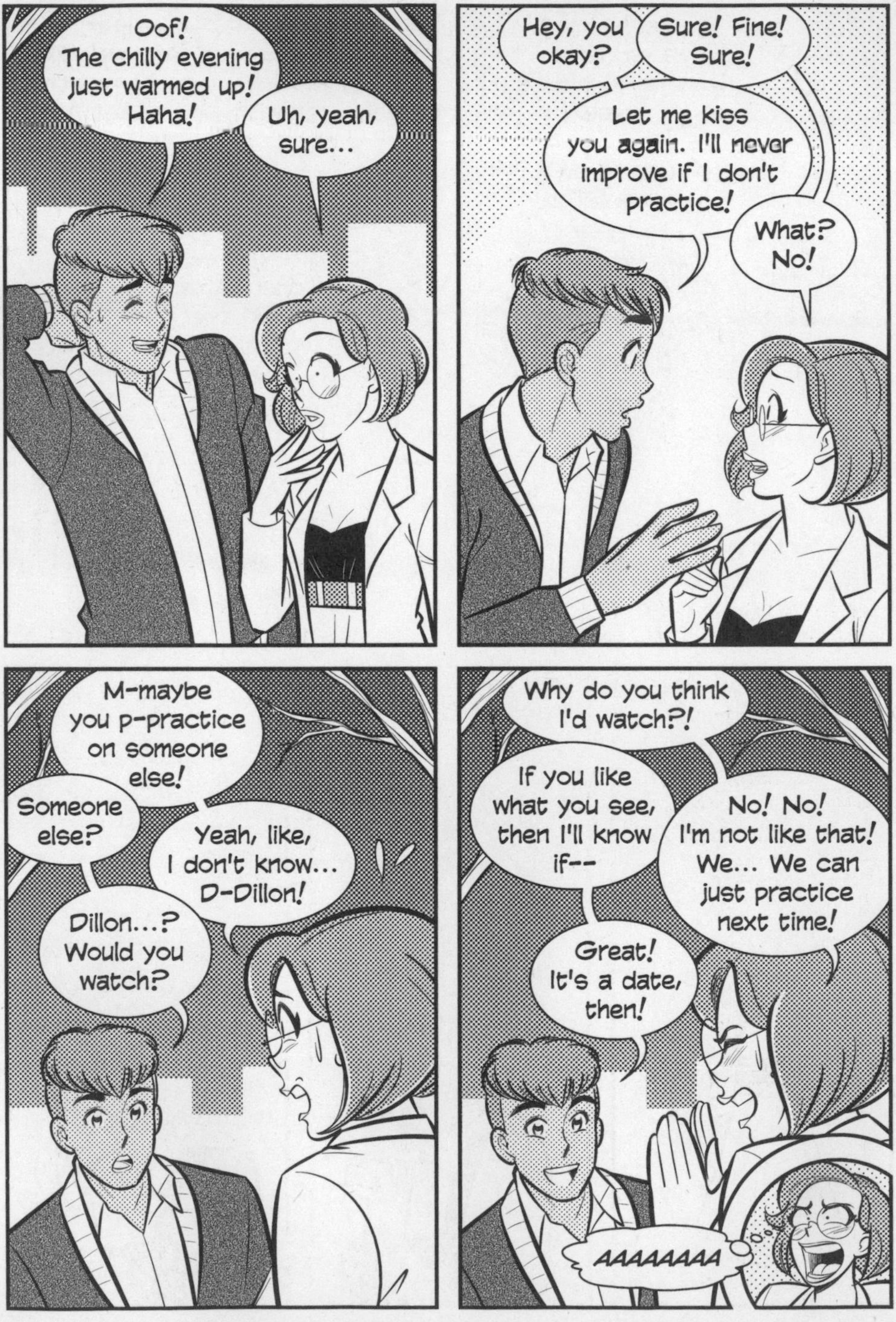
Oof!
The chilly evening just warmed up! Haha!
Uh, yeah, sure...
Hey, you okay?
Sure! Fine! Sure!
Let me kiss you again. I'll never improve if I don't practice!
What? No!
M-maybe you p-practice on someone else!
Someone else?
Yeah, like, I don't know... D-Dillon!
Dillon...? Would you watch?
Why do you think I'd watch?!
If you like what you see, then I'll know if--
No! No! I'm not like that! We... We can just practice next time!
Great! It's a date, then!
AAAAAAAA

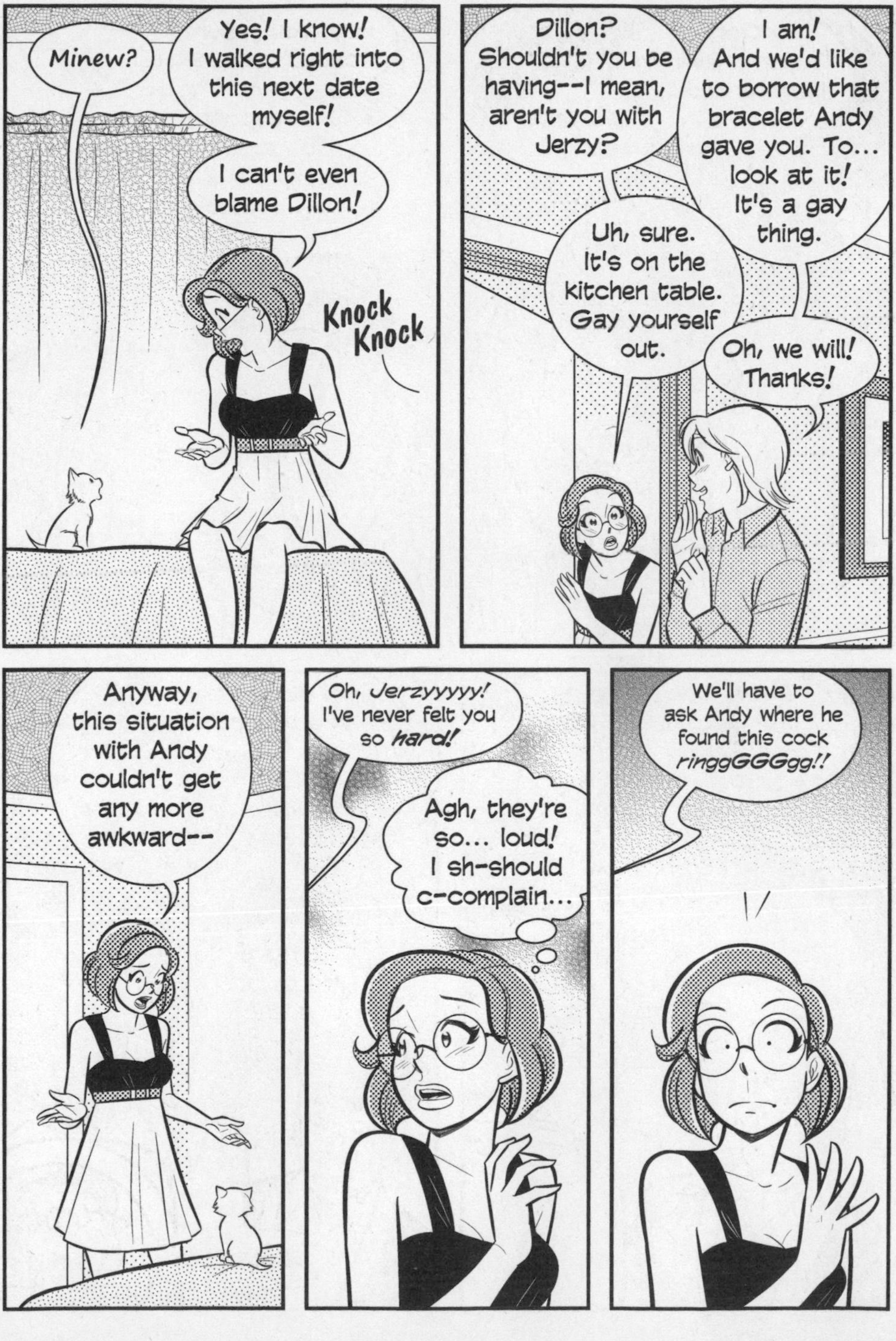
Minew?
Yes! I know! I walked right into this next date myself!
I can't even blame Dillon!
Knock Knock
Dillon? Shouldn't you be having--I mean, aren't you with Jerzy?
I am! And we'd like to borrow that bracelet Andy gave you. To... look at it! It's a gay thing.
Uh, sure. It's on the kitchen table. Gay yourself out.
Oh, we will! Thanks!
Anyway, this situation with Andy couldn't get any more awkward--
Oh, Jerzyyyyy! I've never felt you so *hard!*
Agh, they're so... loud! I sh-should c-complain...
We'll have to ask Andy where he found this cock *ringgGGGgg!!*

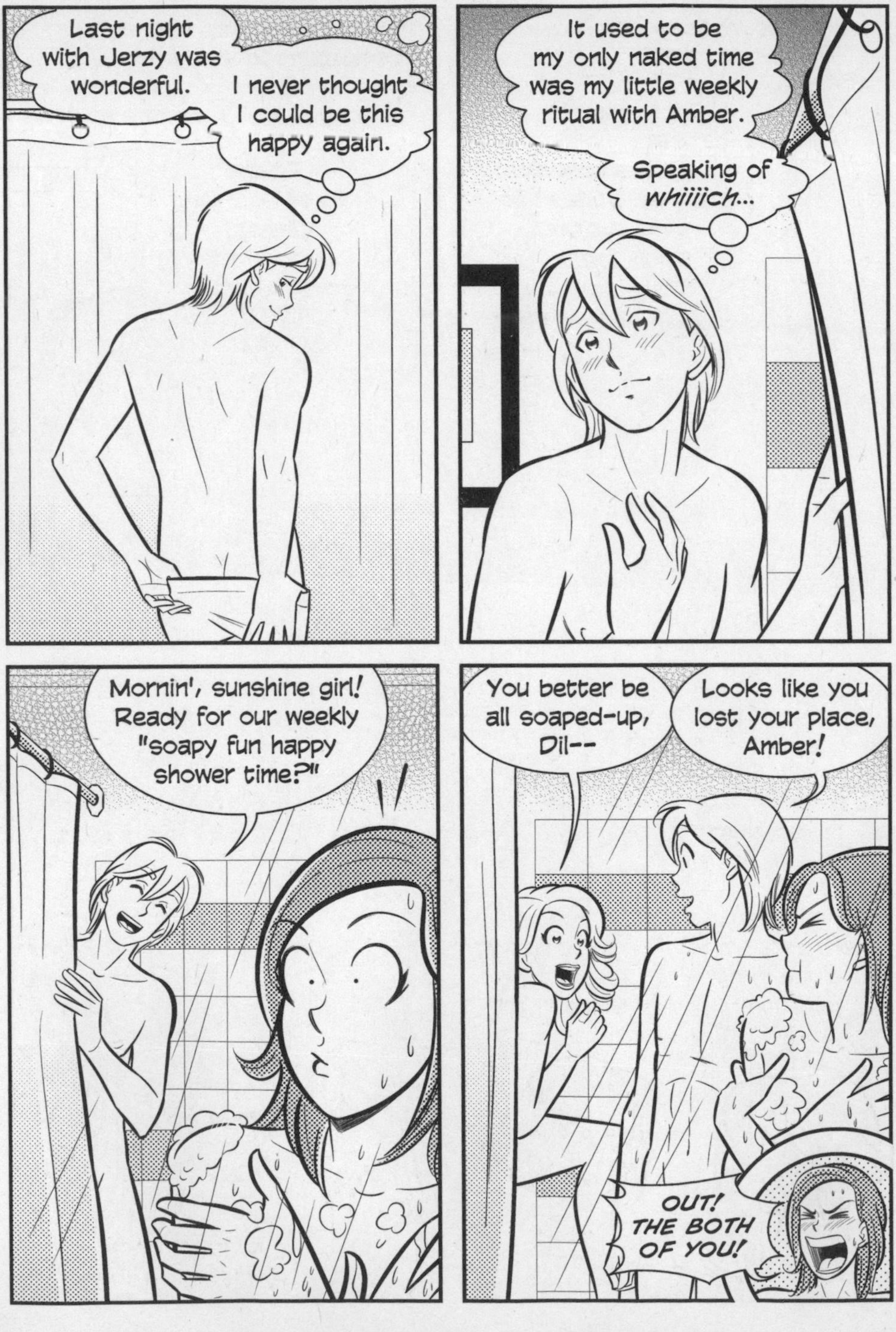
Last night with Jerzy was wonderful.
I never thought I could be this happy again.
It used to be my only naked time was my little weekly ritual with Amber.
Speaking of *whiiiich*...
Mornin', sunshine girl! Ready for our weekly "soapy fun happy shower time?"
You better be all soaped-up, Dil--
Looks like you lost your place, Amber!
OUT! THE BOTH OF YOU!

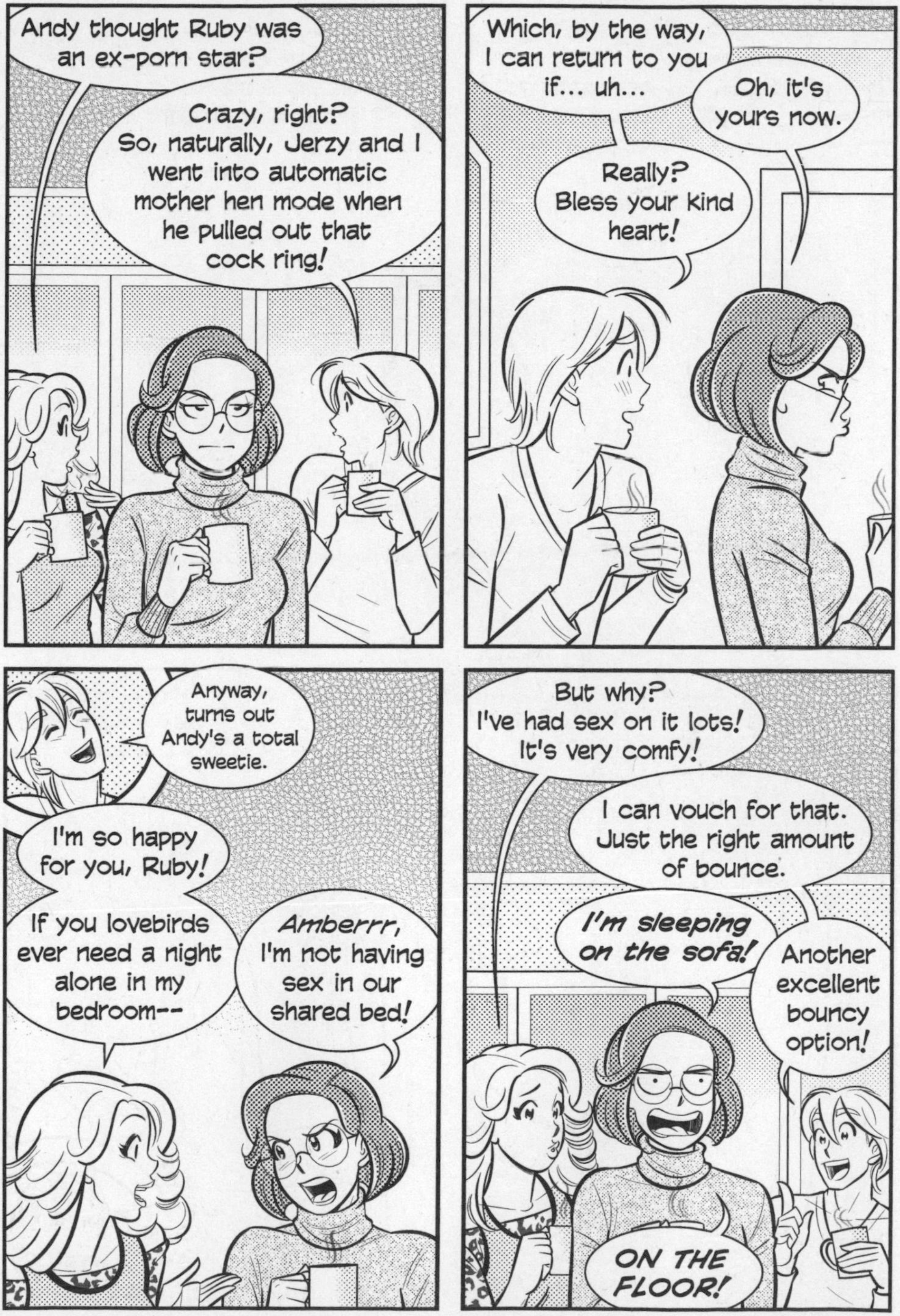

Andy thought Ruby was an ex-porn star?
Crazy, right? So, naturally, Jerzy and I went into automatic mother hen mode when he pulled out that cock ring!
Which, by the way, I can return to you if... uh...
Oh, it's yours now.
Really? Bless your kind heart!
Anyway, turns out Andy's a total sweetie.
I'm so happy for you, Ruby!
If you lovebirds ever need a night alone in my bedroom--
Amberrr, I'm not having sex in our shared bed!
But why? I've had sex on it lots! It's very comfy!
I can vouch for that. Just the right amount of bounce.
I'm sleeping on the sofa!
Another excellent bouncy option!
ON THE FLOOR!

Fault-Finding Mission

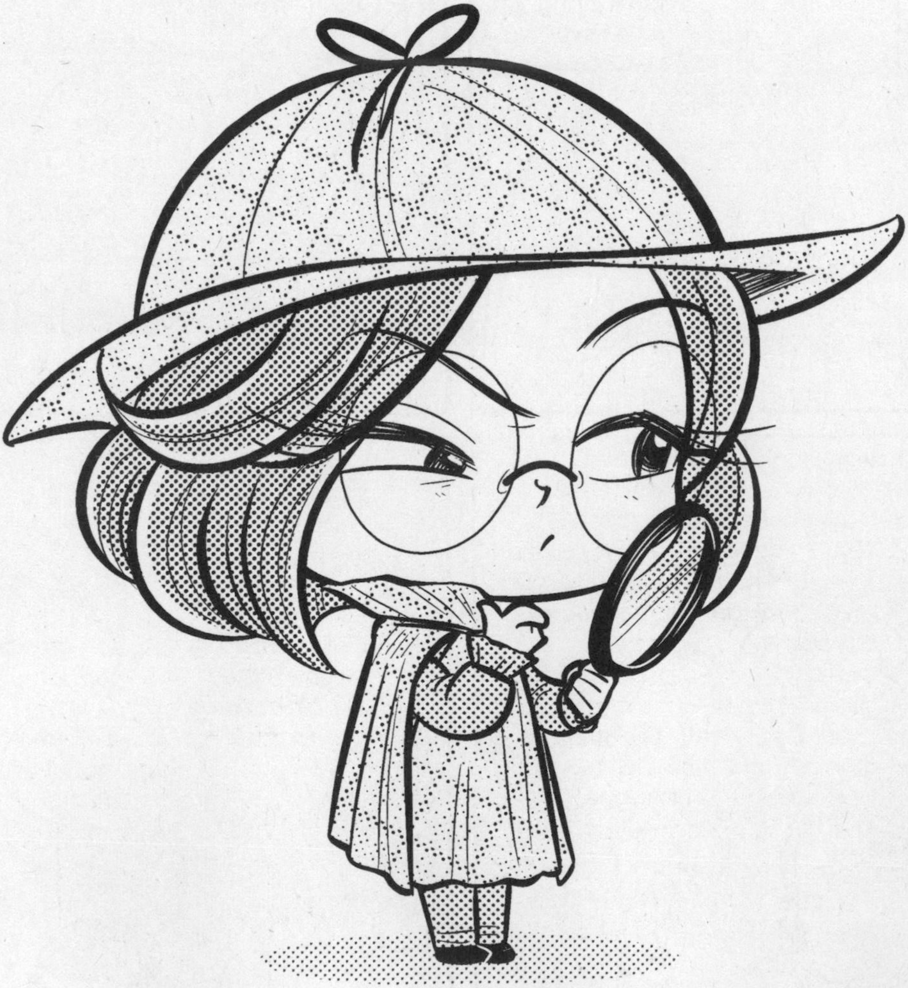

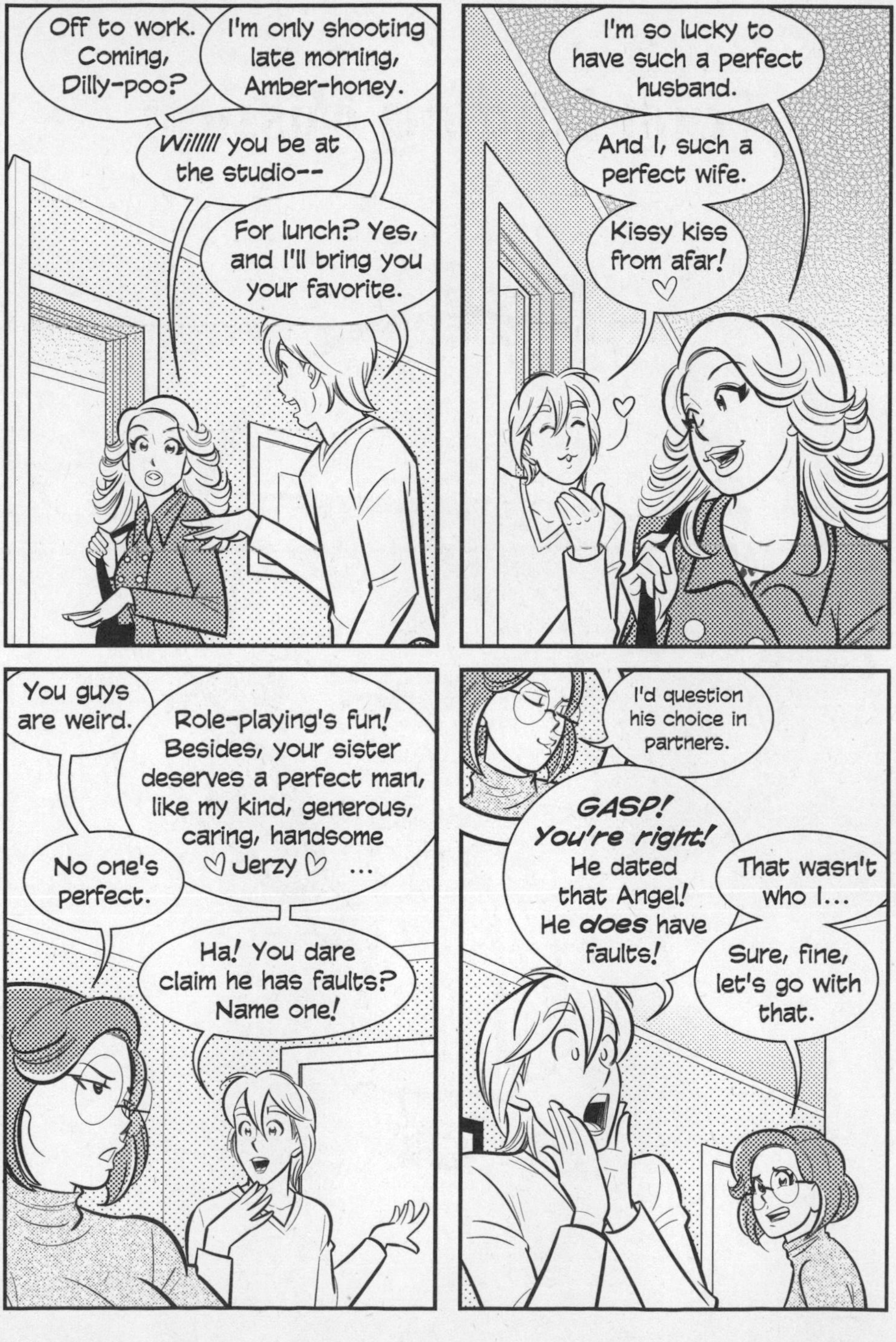
Off to work. Coming, Dilly-poo?
I'm only shooting late morning, Amber-honey.
Willlll you be at the studio--
For lunch? Yes, and I'll bring you your favorite.
I'm so lucky to have such a perfect husband.
And I, such a perfect wife.
Kissy kiss from afar! ♡
You guys are weird.
Role-playing's fun! Besides, your sister deserves a perfect man, like my kind, generous, caring, handsome ♡ Jerzy ♡ ...
No one's perfect.
Ha! You dare claim he has faults? Name one!
I'd question his choice in partners.
GASP! You're right! He dated that Angel! He *does* have faults!
That wasn't who I...
Sure, fine, let's go with that.

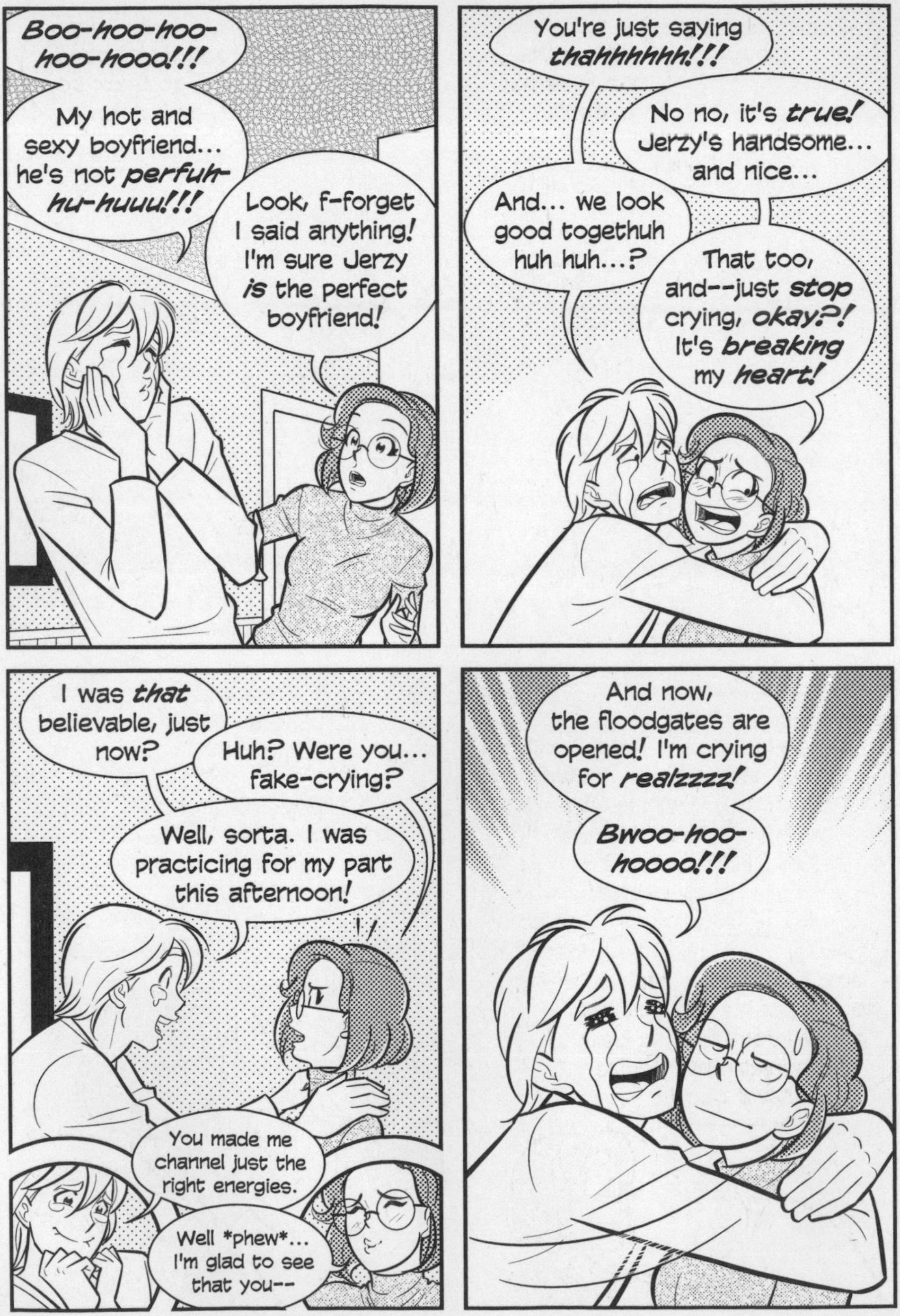

Boo-hoo-hoo-hoo-hooo!!!
My hot and sexy boyfriend... he's not perfuh-hu-huuu!!!
Look, f-forget I said anything! I'm sure Jerzy is the perfect boyfriend!
You're just saying thahhhhhh!!!
No no, it's true! Jerzy's handsome... and nice...
And... we look good togethuh huh huh...?
That too, and--just stop crying, okay?! It's breaking my heart!
I was that believable, just now?
Huh? Were you... fake-crying?
Well, sorta. I was practicing for my part this afternoon!
You made me channel just the right energies.
Well *phew*... I'm glad to see that you--
And now, the floodgates are opened! I'm crying for realzzzz!
Bwoo-hoo-hoooo!!!

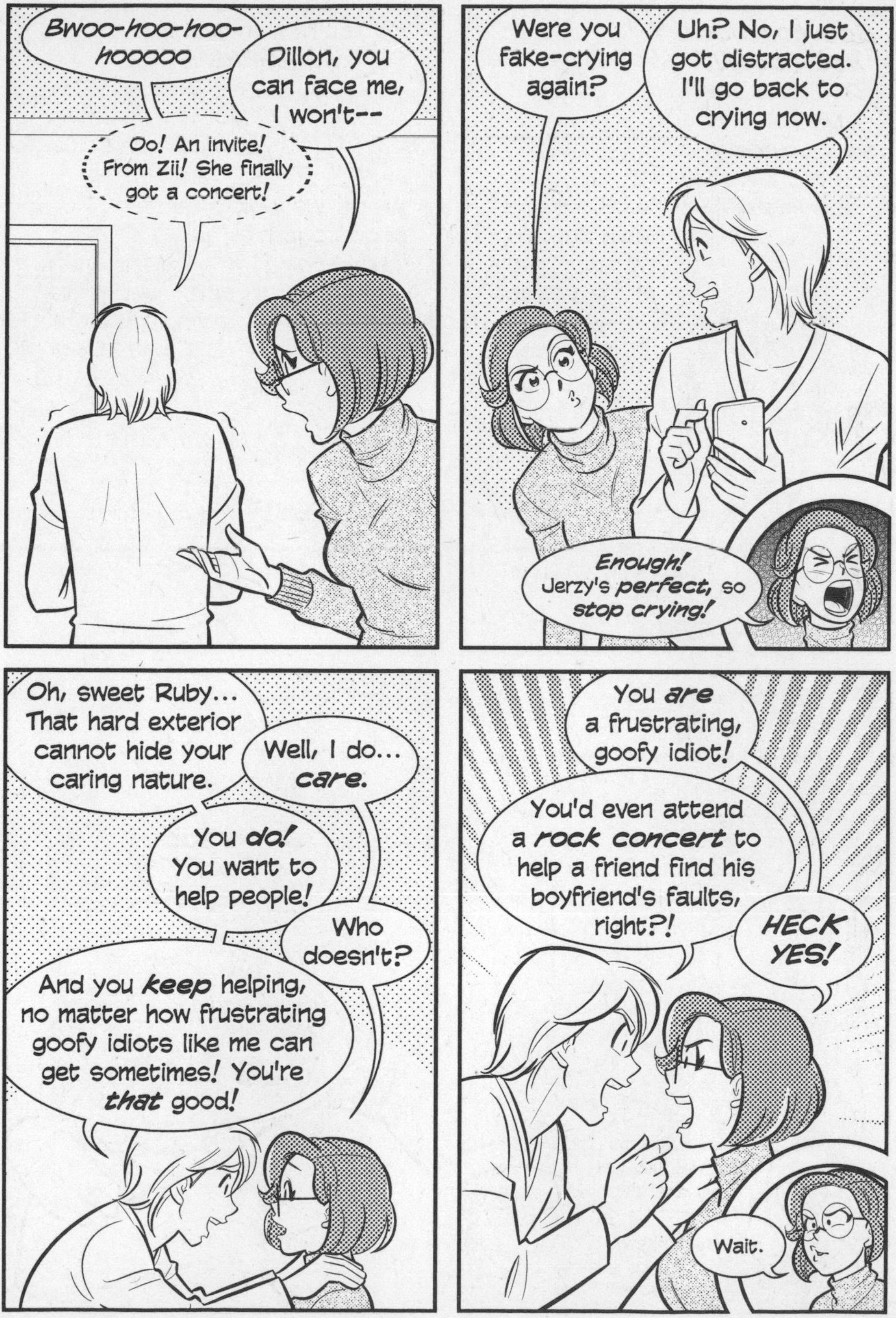

Bwoo-hoo-hoo-hooooo
Dillon, you can face me, I won't--
Oo! An invite! From Zii! She finally got a concert!
Were you fake-crying again?
Uh? No, I just got distracted. I'll go back to crying now.
Enough! Jerzy's perfect, so stop crying!
Oh, sweet Ruby... That hard exterior cannot hide your caring nature.
Well, I do... care.
You do! You want to help people!
Who doesn't?
And you keep helping, no matter how frustrating goofy idiots like me can get sometimes! You're that good!
You are a frustrating, goofy idiot!
You'd even attend a rock concert to help a friend find his boyfriend's faults, right?!
HECK YES!
Wait.

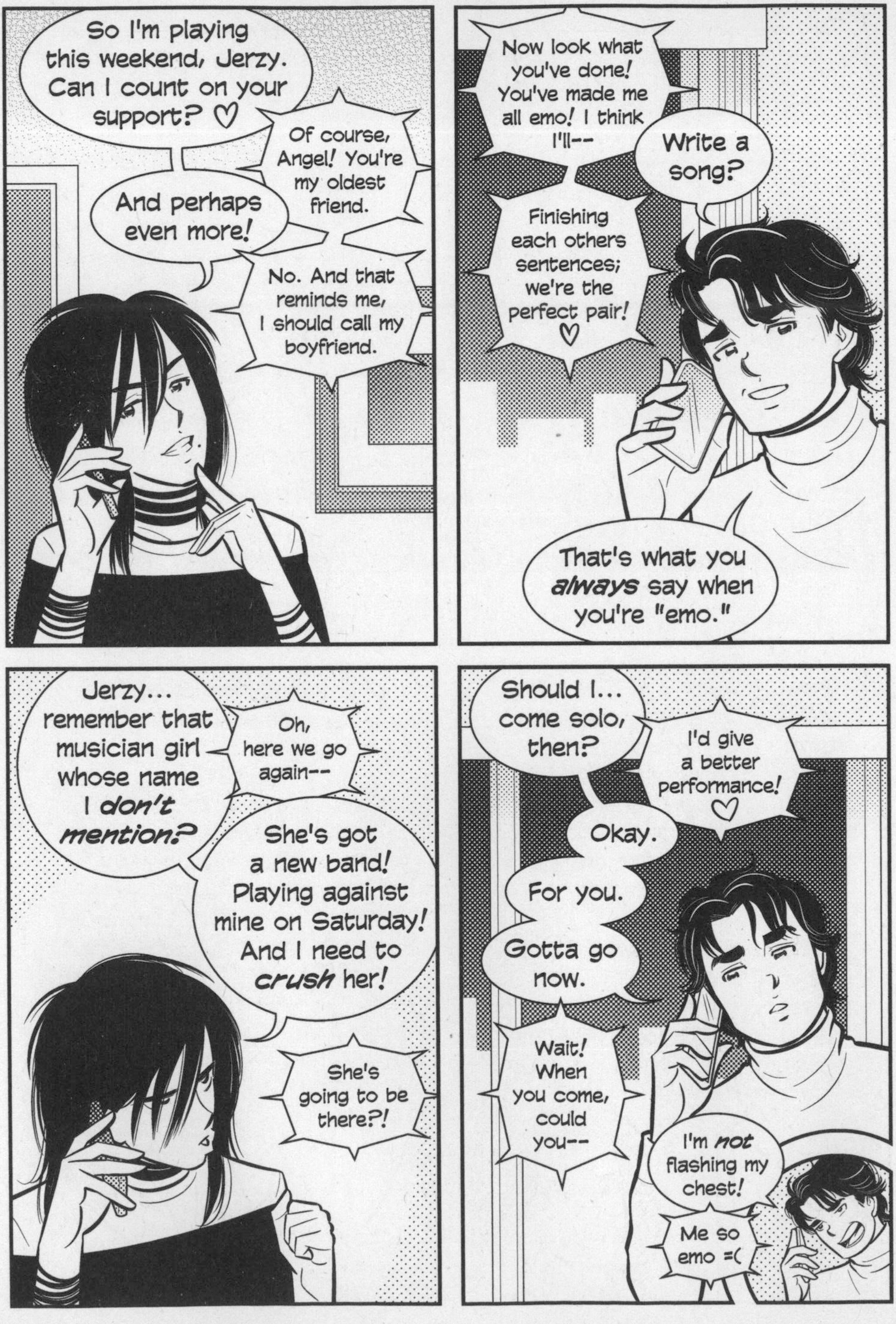
So I'm playing this weekend, Jerzy. Can I count on your support? ♡
Of course, Angel! You're my oldest friend.
And perhaps even more!
No. And that reminds me, I should call my boyfriend.
Now look what you've done! You've made me all emo! I think I'll--
Write a song?
Finishing each others sentences; we're the perfect pair! ♡
That's what you *always* say when you're "emo."
Jerzy... remember that musician girl whose name I *don't mention?*
Oh, here we go again--
She's got a new band! Playing against mine on Saturday! And I need to *crush* her!
She's going to be there?!
Should I... come solo, then?
I'd give a better performance! ♡
Okay.
For you.
Gotta go now.
Wait! When you come, could you--
I'm *not* flashing my chest!
Me so emo =(

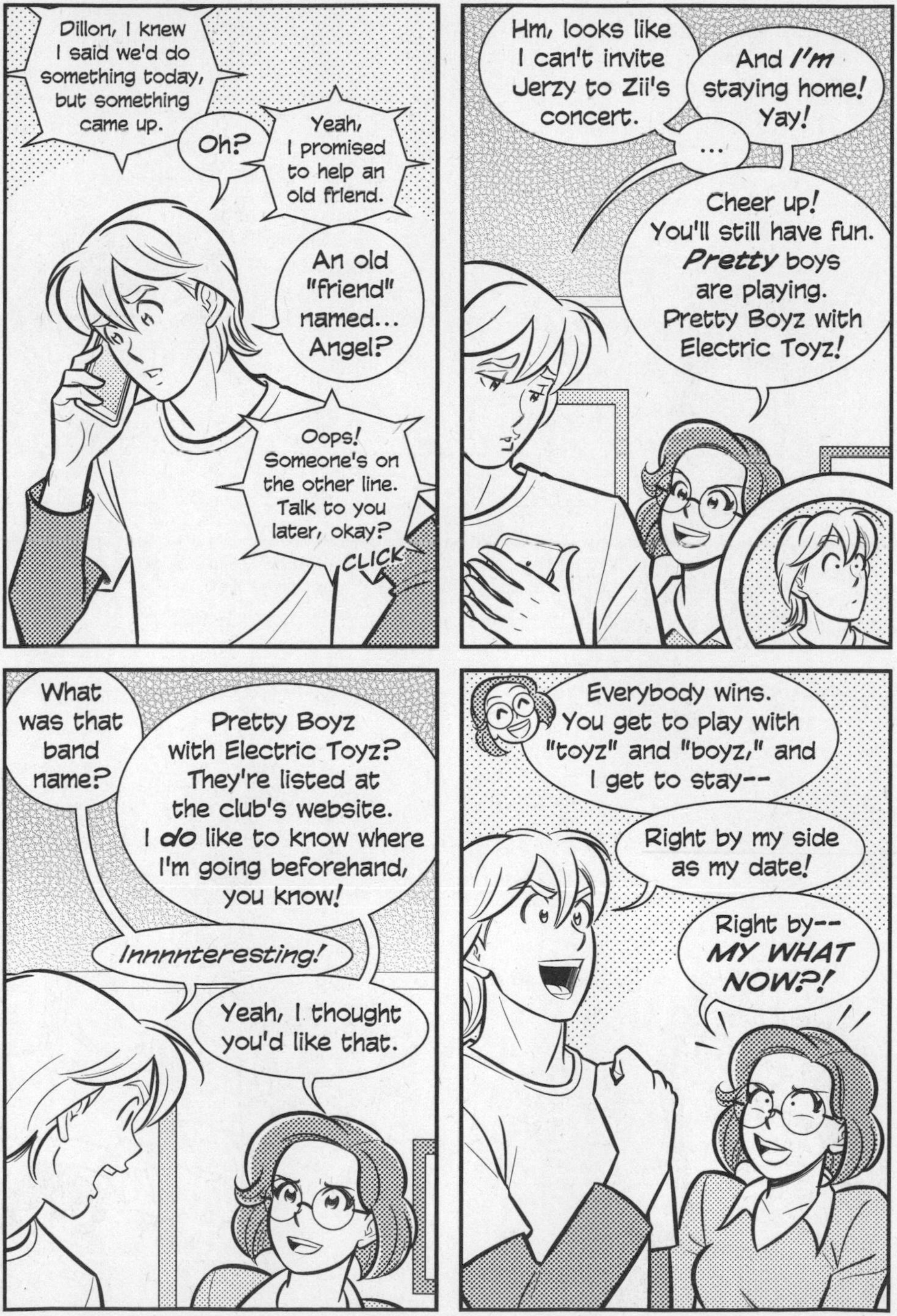
Dillon, I knew I said we'd do something today, but something came up.
Oh?
Yeah, I promised to help an old friend.
An old "friend" named... Angel?
Oops! Someone's on the other line. Talk to you later, okay?
CLICK
Hm, looks like I can't invite Jerzy to Zii's concert.
And *I'm* staying home! Yay!
...
Cheer up! You'll still have fun. *Pretty* boys are playing. Pretty Boyz with Electric Toyz!
What was that band name?
Pretty Boyz with Electric Toyz? They're listed at the club's website. I *do* like to know where I'm going beforehand, you know!
Innnteresting!
Yeah, I thought you'd like that.
Everybody wins. You get to play with "toyz" and "boyz," and I get to stay--
Right by my side as my date!
Right by-- ***MY WHAT NOW?!***

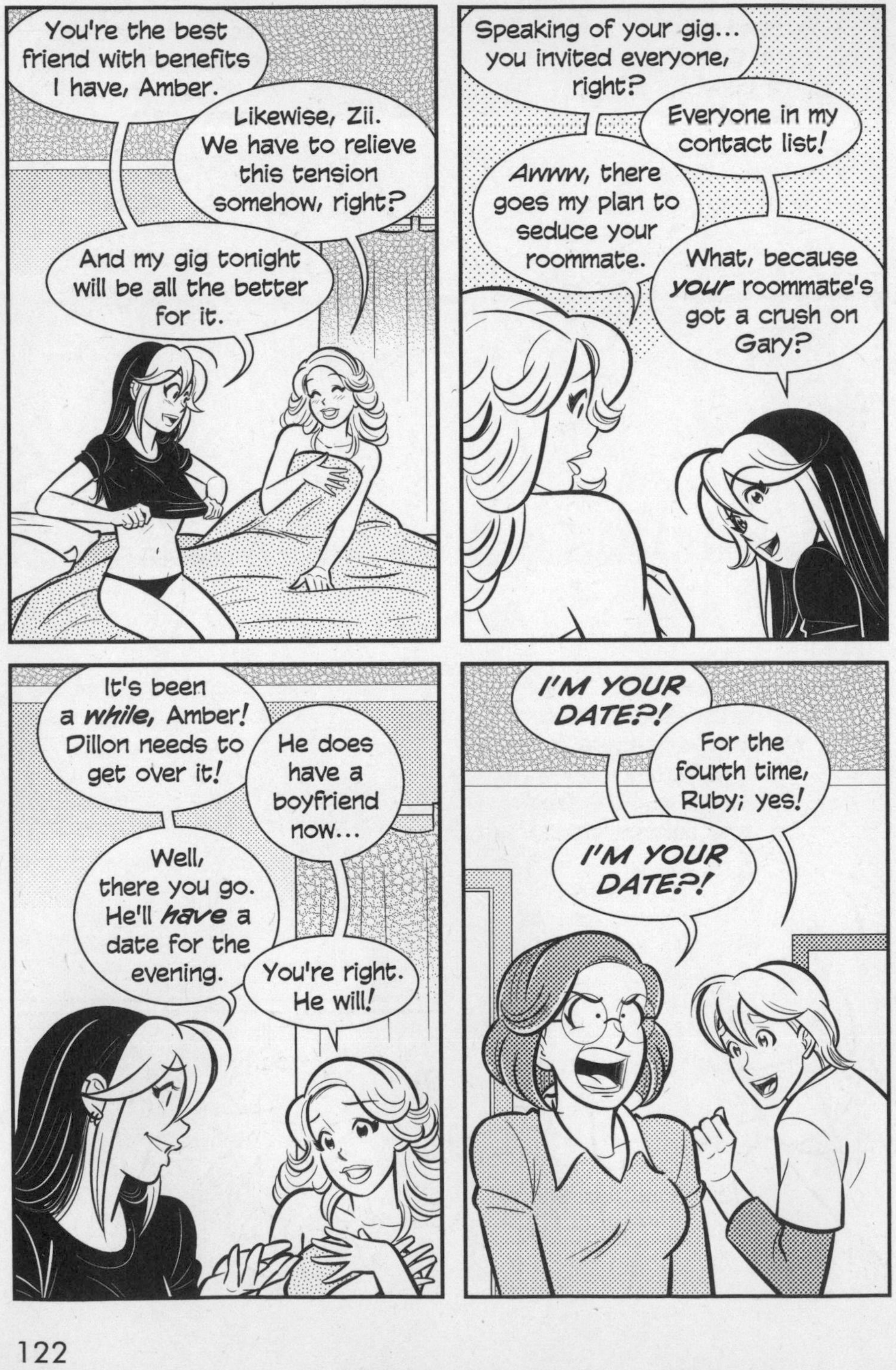
You're the best friend with benefits I have, Amber.
Likewise, Zii. We have to relieve this tension somehow, right?
And my gig tonight will be all the better for it.
Speaking of your gig... you invited everyone, right?
Everyone in my contact list!
Awww, there goes my plan to seduce your roommate.
What, because *your* roommate's got a crush on Gary?
It's been a *while,* Amber! Dillon needs to get over it!
He does have a boyfriend now...
Well, there you go. He'll *have* a date for the evening.
You're right. He will!
I'M YOUR DATE?!
For the fourth time, Ruby; yes!
I'M YOUR DATE?!

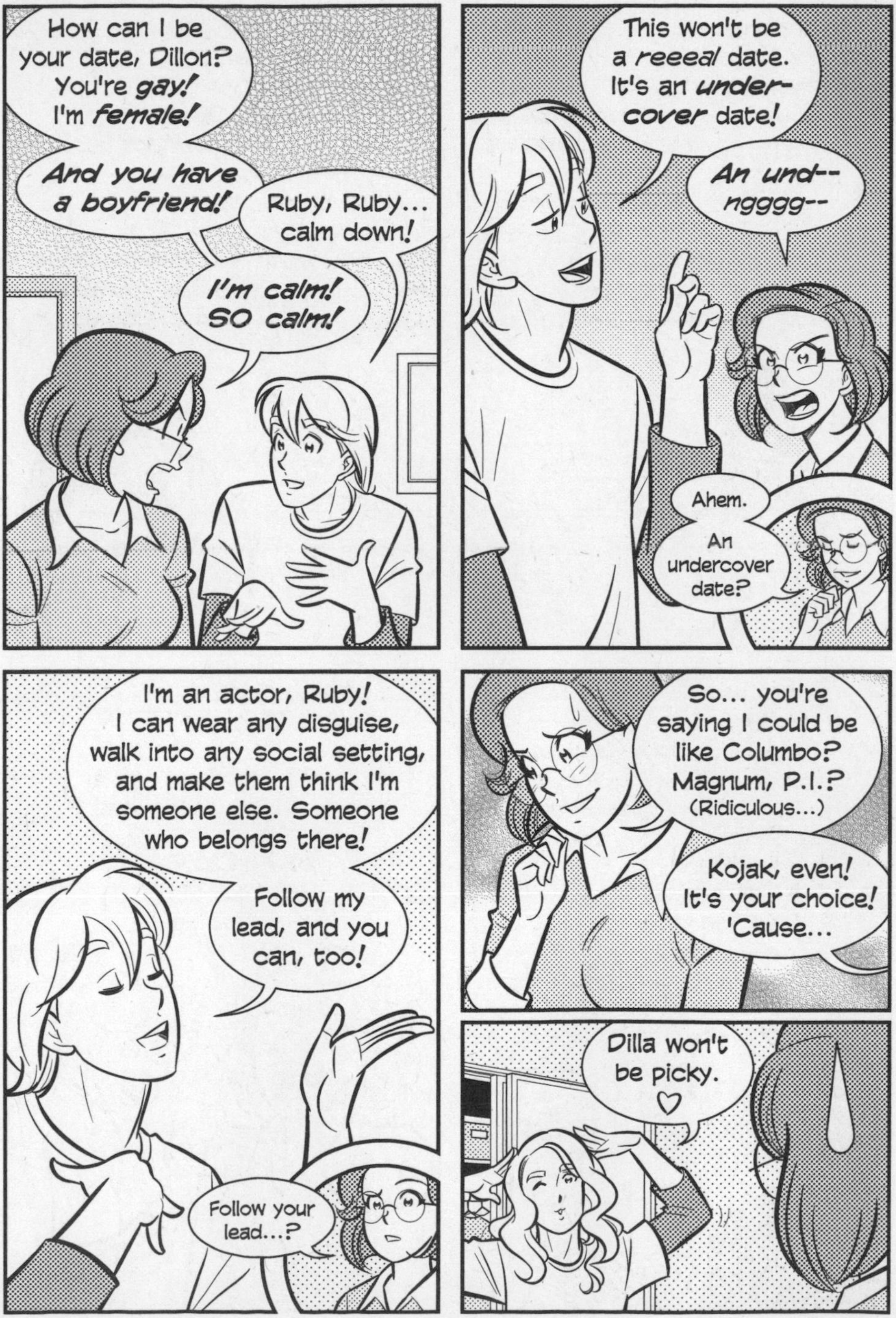
How can I be your date, Dillon? You're *gay!* I'm *female!*
And you have a boyfriend!
Ruby, Ruby... calm down!
I'm calm! SO calm!
This won't be a *reeeal* date. It's an *under-cover* date!
An und-- ngggg--
Ahem.
An undercover date?
I'm an actor, Ruby! I can wear any disguise, walk into any social setting, and make them think I'm someone else. Someone who belongs there!
Follow my lead, and you can, too!
Follow your lead...?
So... you're saying I could be like Columbo? Magnum, P.I.? (Ridiculous...)
Kojak, even! It's your choice! 'Cause...
Dilla won't be picky. ♡

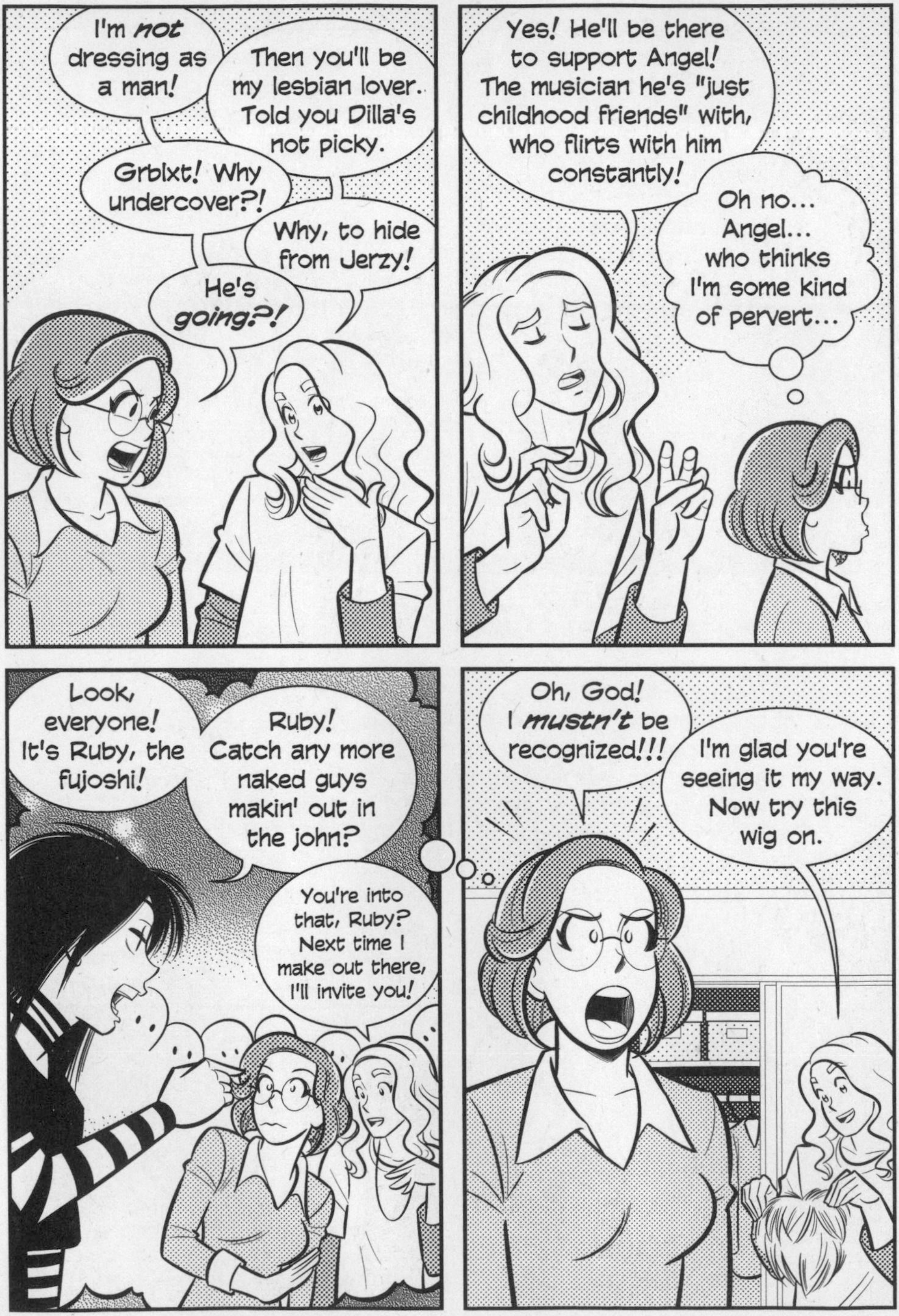
I'm *not* dressing as a man!
Then you'll be my lesbian lover. Told you Dilla's not picky.
Grblxt! Why undercover?!
Why, to hide from Jerzy!
He's *going?!*
Yes! He'll be there to support Angel! The musician he's "just childhood friends" with, who flirts with him constantly!
Oh no... Angel... who thinks I'm some kind of pervert...
Look, everyone! It's Ruby, the fujoshi!
Ruby! Catch any more naked guys makin' out in the john?
You're into that, Ruby? Next time I make out there, I'll invite you!
Oh, God! I *mustn't* be recognized!!!
I'm glad you're seeing it my way. Now try this wig on.

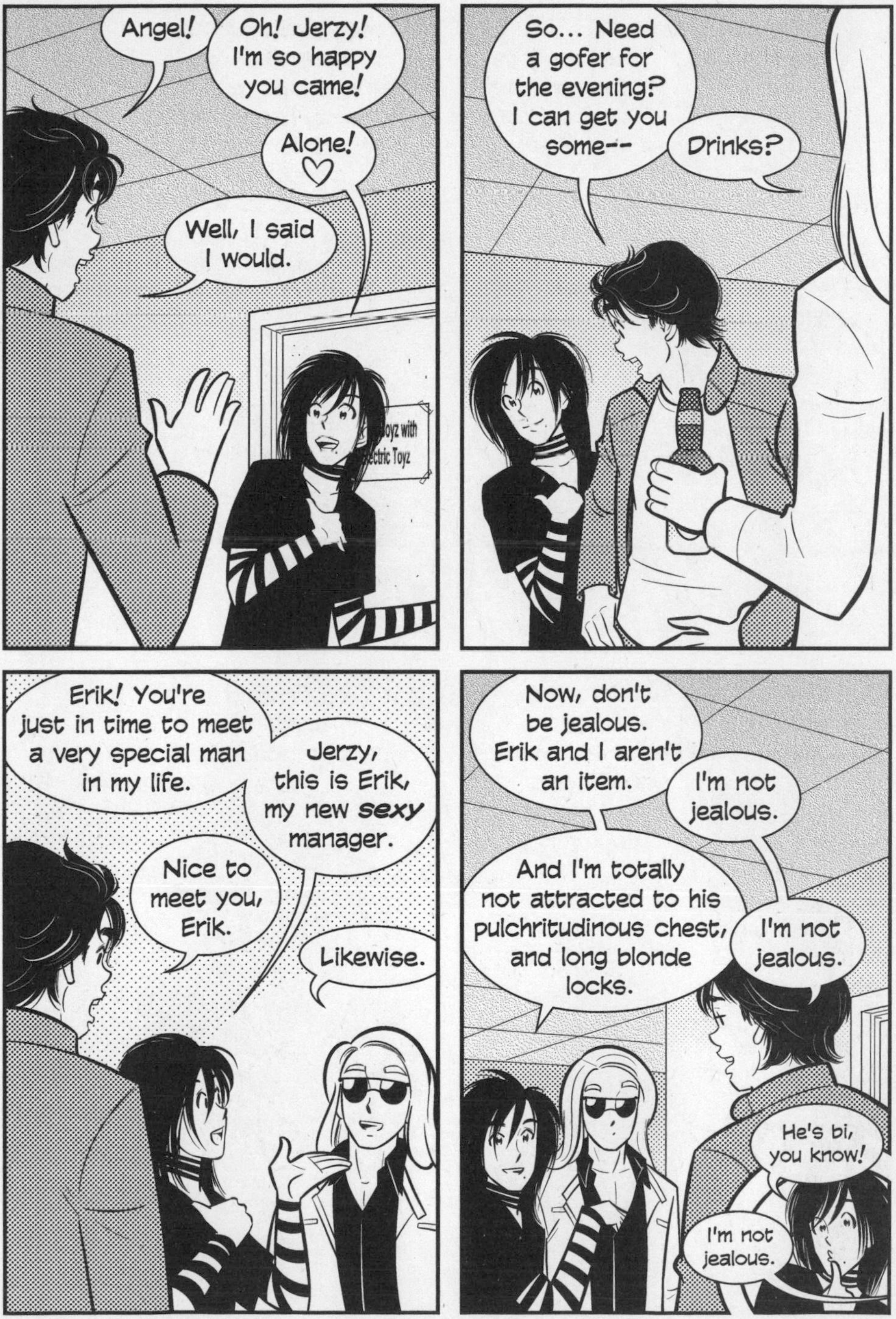
Angel!
Oh! Jerzy! I'm so happy you came!
Alone! ♡
Well, I said I would.
So... Need a gofer for the evening? I can get you some--
Drinks?
Erik! You're just in time to meet a very special man in my life.
Jerzy, this is Erik, my new *sexy* manager.
Nice to meet you, Erik.
Likewise.
Now, don't be jealous. Erik and I aren't an item.
I'm not jealous.
And I'm totally not attracted to his pulchritudinous chest, and long blonde locks.
I'm not jealous.
He's bi, you know!
I'm not jealous.

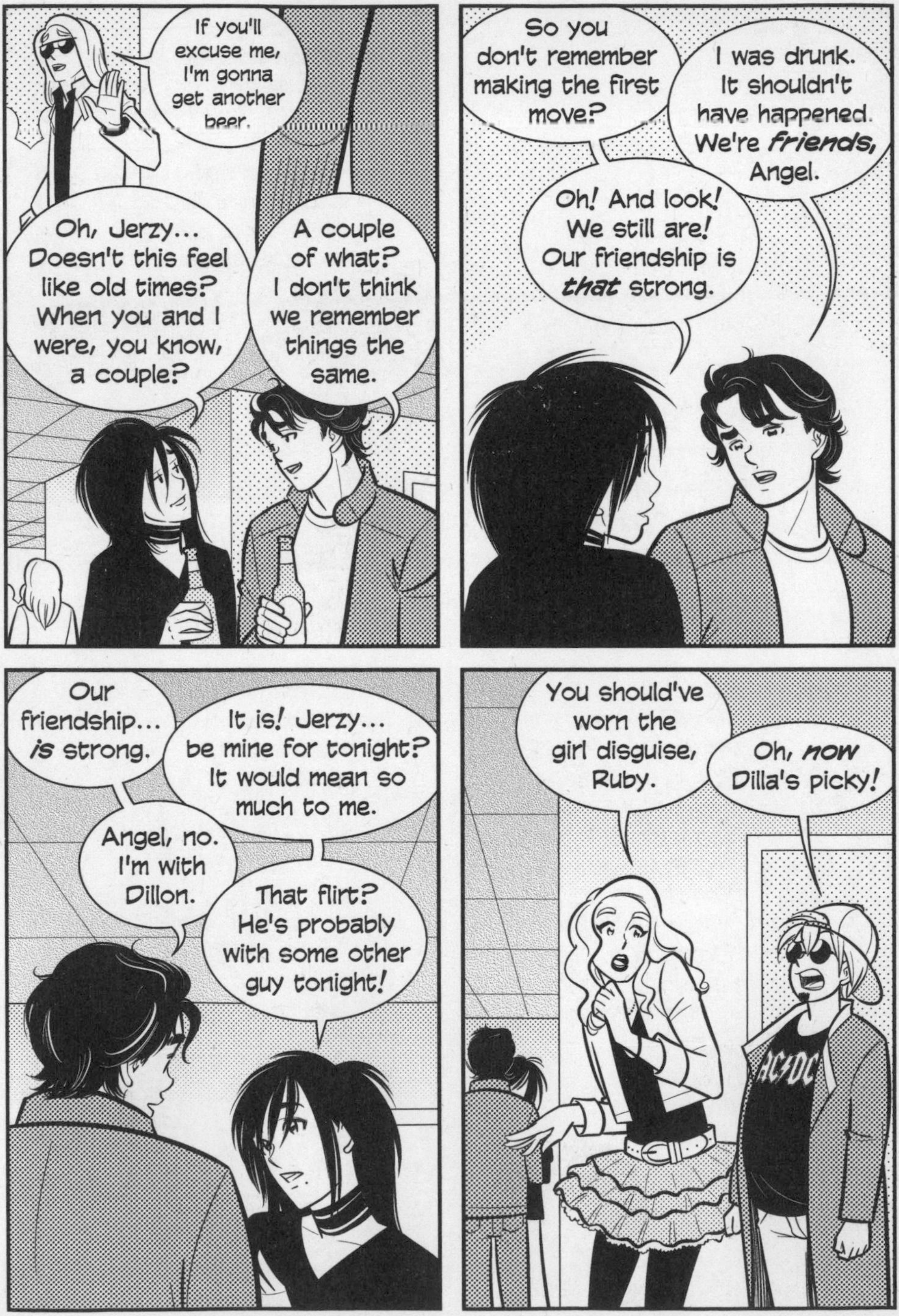
If you'll excuse me, I'm gonna get another beer.
Oh, Jerzy... Doesn't this feel like old times? When you and I were, you know, a couple?
A couple of what? I don't think we remember things the same.
So you don't remember making the first move?
I was drunk. It shouldn't have happened. We're *friends,* Angel.
Oh! And look! We still are! Our friendship is *that* strong.
Our friendship... *is* strong.
It is! Jerzy... be mine for tonight? It would mean so much to me.
Angel, no. I'm with Dillon.
That flirt? He's probably with some other guy tonight!
You should've worn the girl disguise, Ruby.
Oh, *now* Dilla's picky!
AC/DC

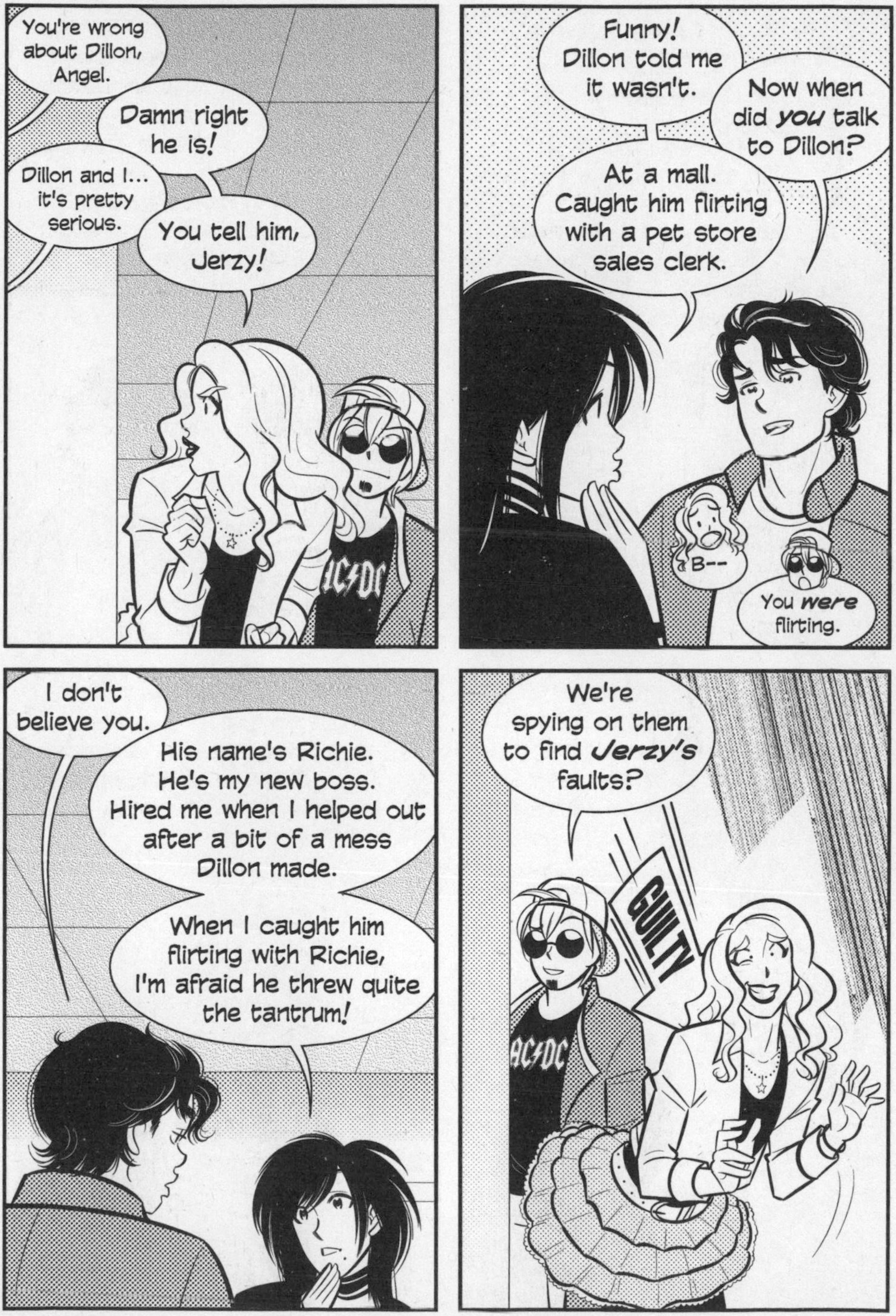
You're wrong about Dillon, Angel.
Damn right he is!
Dillon and I... it's pretty serious.
You tell him, Jerzy!
Funny! Dillon told me it wasn't.
Now when did *you* talk to Dillon?
At a mall. Caught him flirting with a pet store sales clerk.
B--
You *were* flirting.
I don't believe you.
His name's Richie. He's my new boss. Hired me when I helped out after a bit of a mess Dillon made.
When I caught him flirting with Richie, I'm afraid he threw quite the tantrum!
We're spying on them to find *Jerzy's* faults?
GUILTY

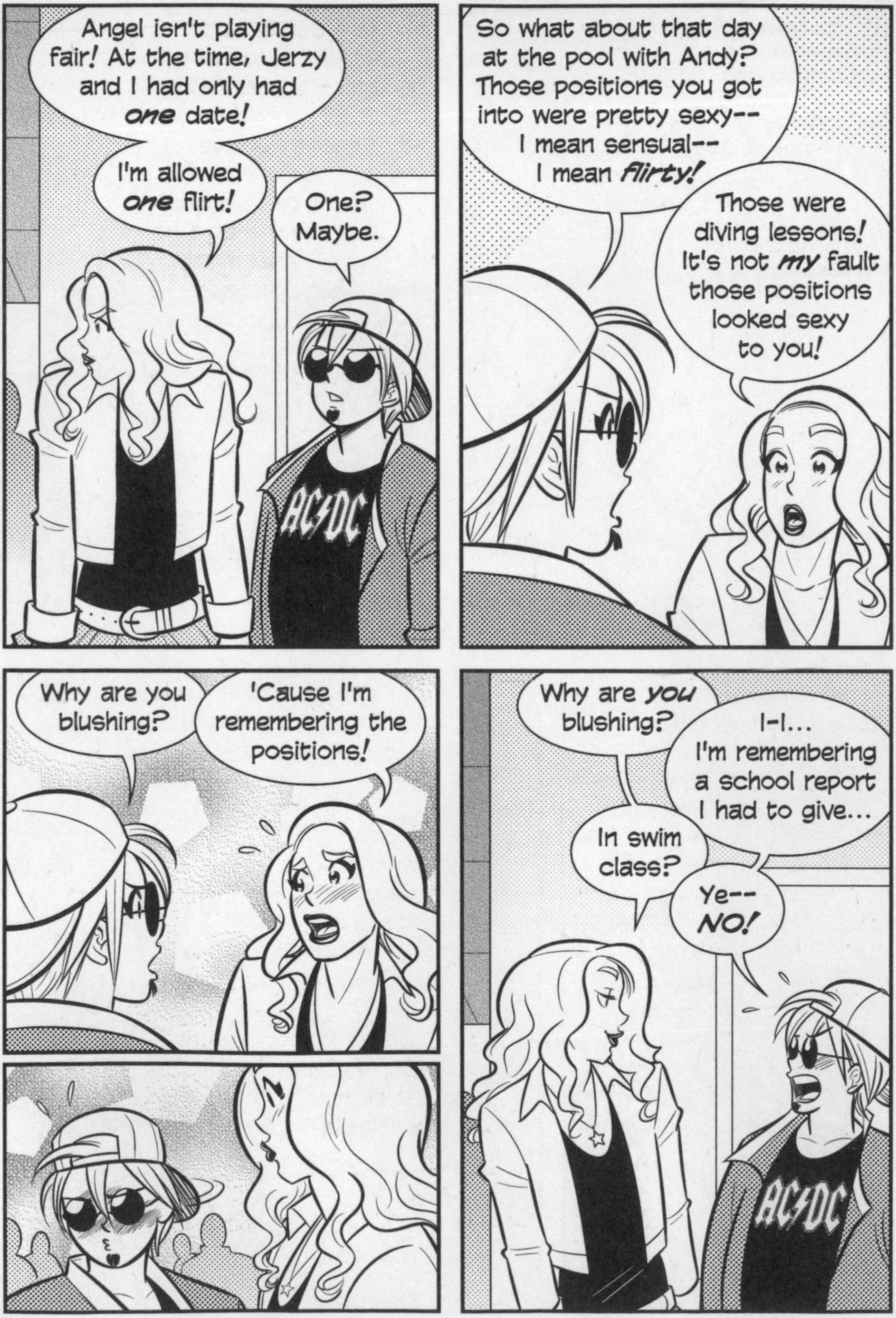
Angel isn't playing fair! At the time, Jerzy and I had only had one date!
I'm allowed one flirt!
One? Maybe.
So what about that day at the pool with Andy? Those positions you got into were pretty sexy-- I mean sensual-- I mean flirty!
Those were diving lessons! It's not my fault those positions looked sexy to you!
Why are you blushing?
'Cause I'm remembering the positions!
Why are you blushing?
I-I... I'm remembering a school report I had to give...
In swim class?
Ye-- NO!
AC/DC
AC/DC

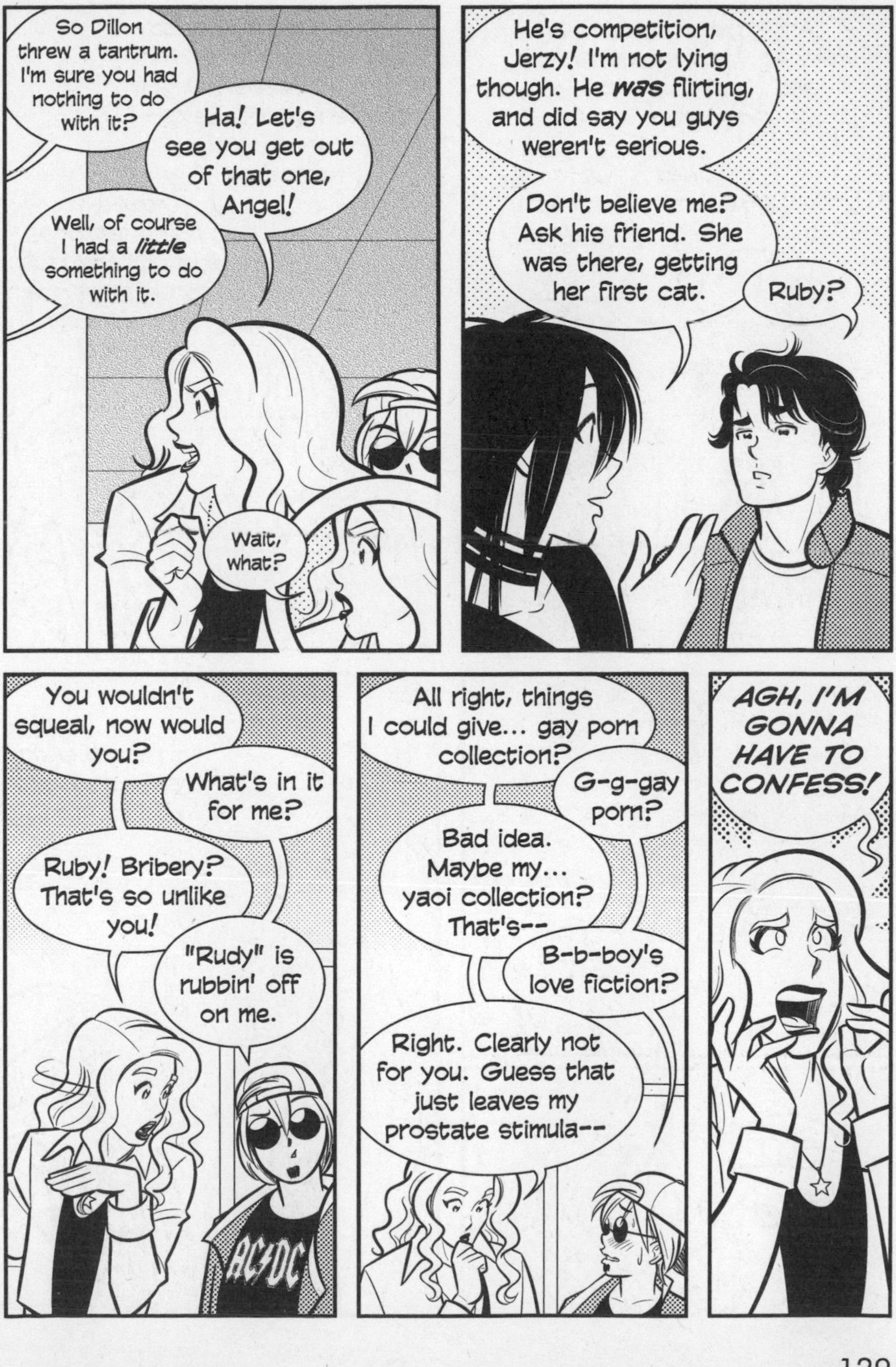

So Dillon threw a tantrum. I'm sure you had nothing to do with it?
Ha! Let's see you get out of that one, Angel!
Well, of course I had a *little* something to do with it.
Wait, what?
He's competition, Jerzy! I'm not lying though. He *was* flirting, and did say you guys weren't serious.
Don't believe me? Ask his friend. She was there, getting her first cat.
Ruby?
You wouldn't squeal, now would you?
What's in it for me?
Ruby! Bribery? That's so unlike you!
"Rudy" is rubbin' off on me.
AC/DC
All right, things I could give... gay porn collection?
G-g-gay porn?
Bad idea. Maybe my... yaoi collection? That's--
B-b-boy's love fiction?
Right. Clearly not for you. Guess that just leaves my prostate stimula--
AGH, I'M GONNA HAVE TO CONFESS!

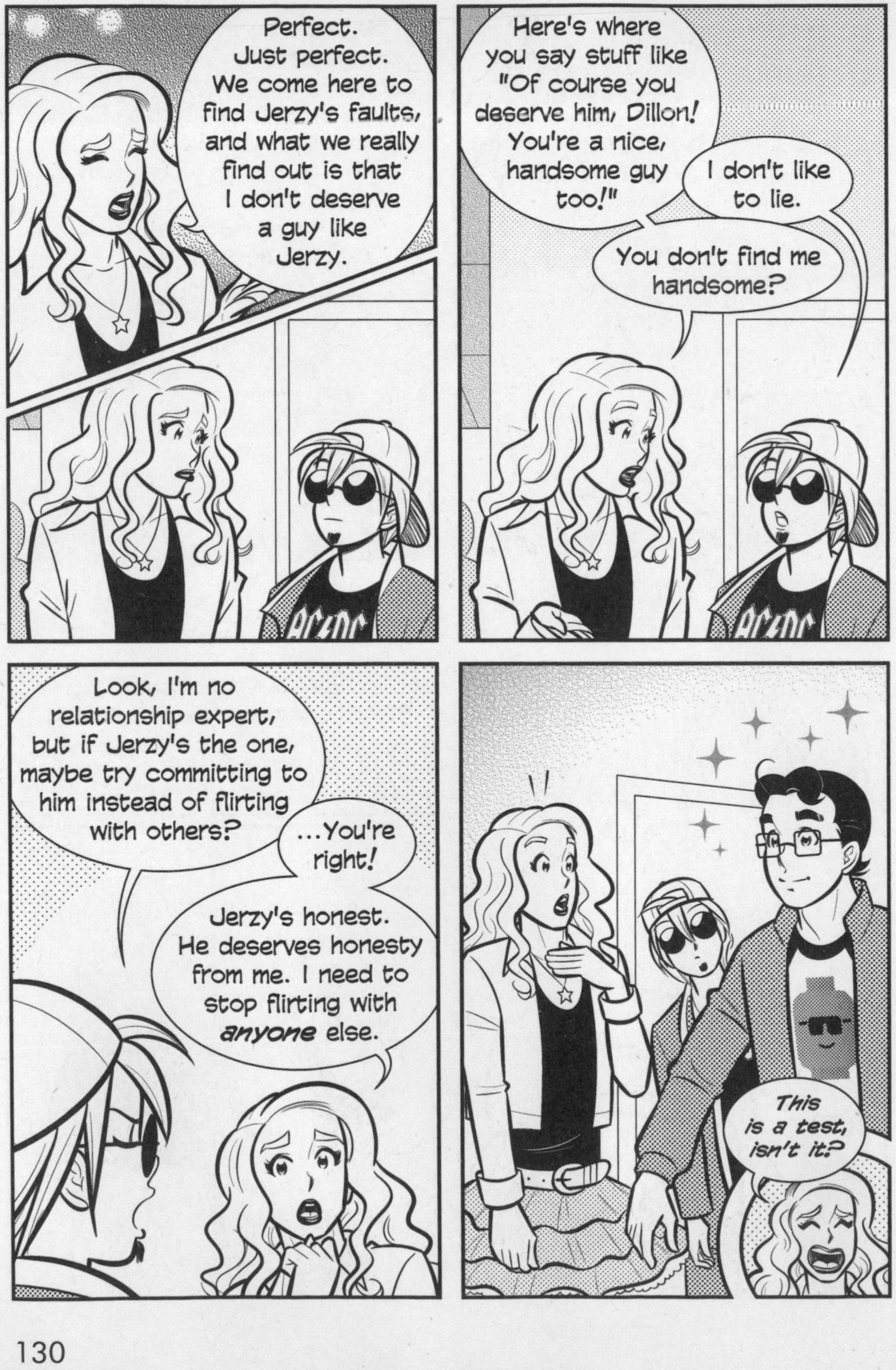
Perfect. Just perfect. We come here to find Jerzy's faults, and what we really find out is that I don't deserve a guy like Jerzy.
Here's where you say stuff like "Of course you deserve him, Dillon! You're a nice, handsome guy too!"
I don't like to lie.
You don't find me handsome?
Look, I'm no relationship expert, but if Jerzy's the one, maybe try committing to him instead of flirting with others?
...You're right!
Jerzy's honest. He deserves honesty from me. I need to stop flirting with *anyone* else.
This is a test, isn't it?

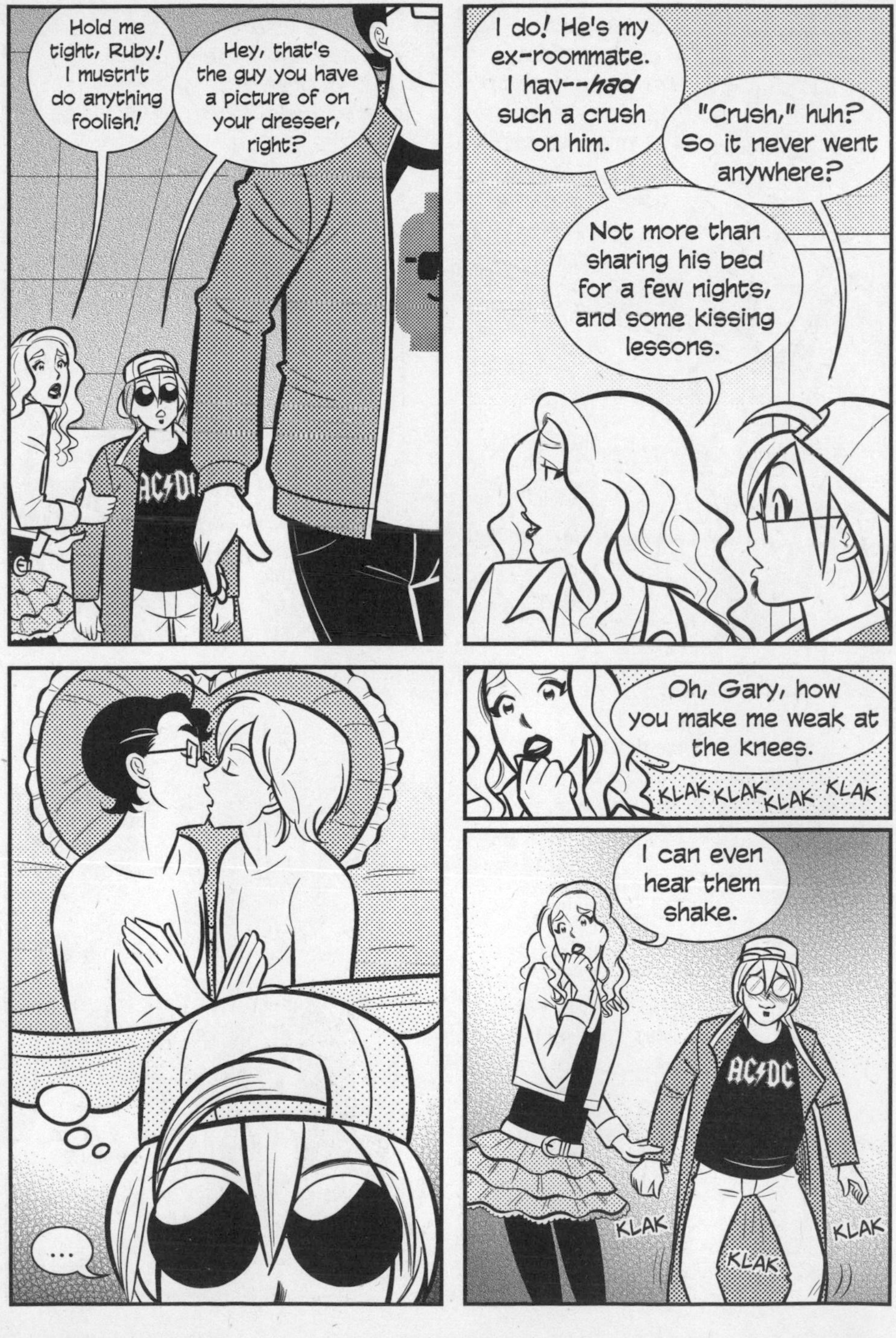
Hold me tight, Ruby! I mustn't do anything foolish!
Hey, that's the guy you have a picture of on your dresser, right?
AC/DC
I do! He's my ex-roommate. I hav--*had* such a crush on him.
"Crush," huh? So it never went anywhere?
Not more than sharing his bed for a few nights, and some kissing lessons.
...
Oh, Gary, how you make me weak at the knees.
KLAK KLAK KLAK KLAK
I can even hear them shake.
AC/DC
KLAK
KLAK
KLAK

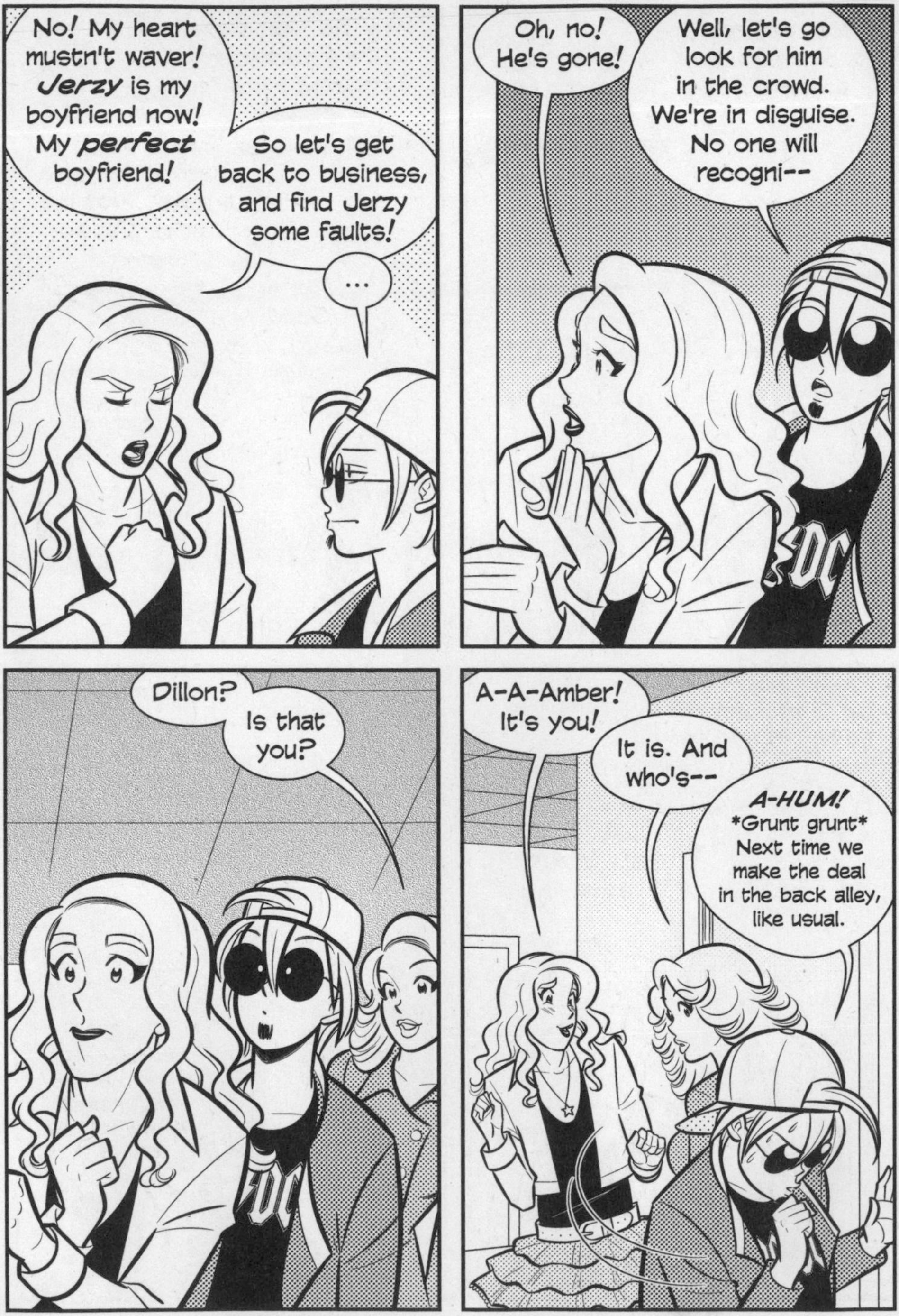
No! My heart mustn't waver! *Jerzy* is my boyfriend now! My *perfect* boyfriend!
So let's get back to business, and find Jerzy some faults!
...
Oh, no! He's gone!
Well, let's go look for him in the crowd. We're in disguise. No one will recogni--
Dillon?
Is that you?
A-A-Amber! It's you!
It is. And who's--
A-HUM! *Grunt grunt* Next time we make the deal in the back alley, like usual.

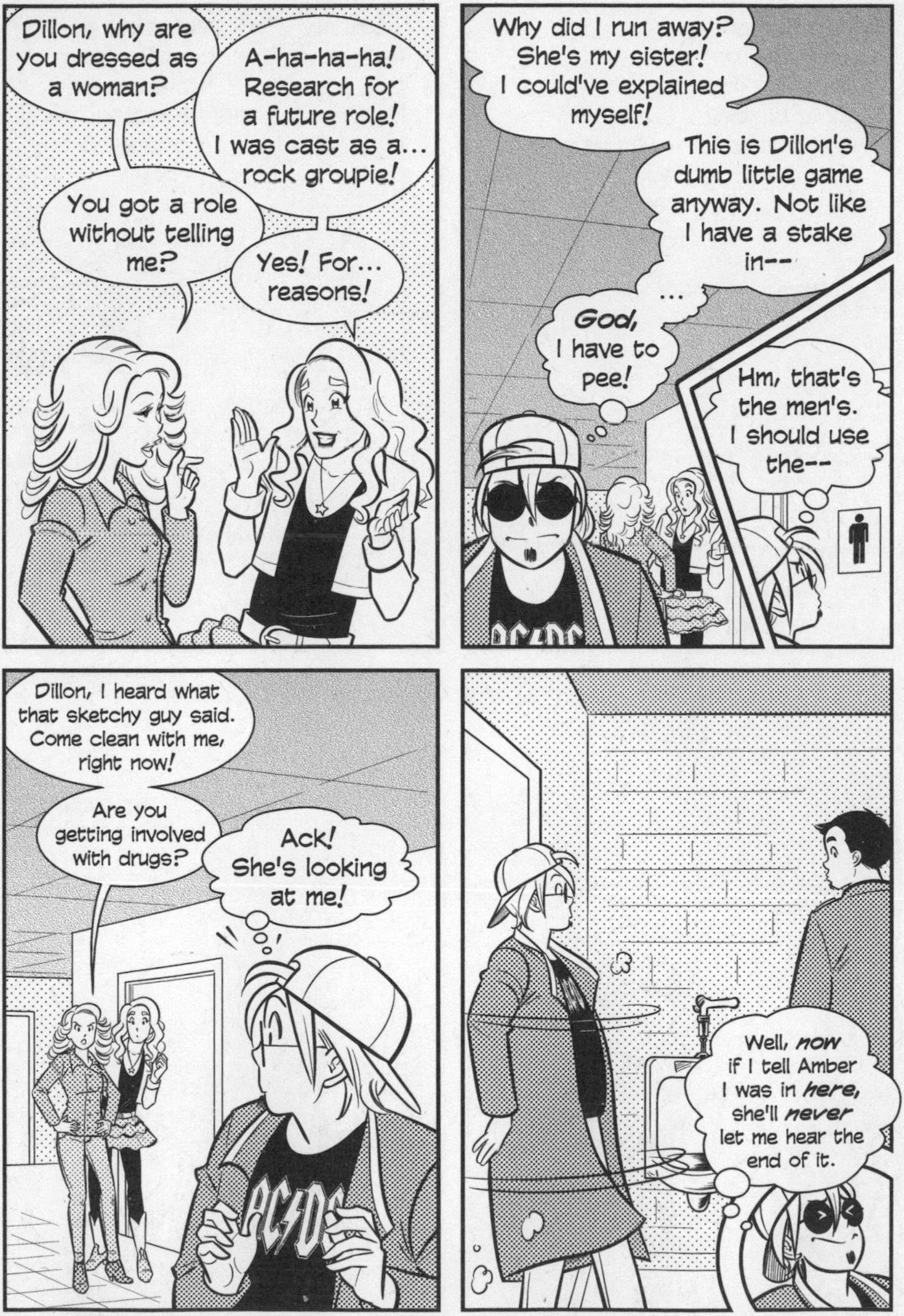
Dillon, why are you dressed as a woman?
A-ha-ha-ha! Research for a future role! I was cast as a... rock groupie!
You got a role without telling me?
Yes! For... reasons!
Why did I run away? She's my sister! I could've explained myself!
This is Dillon's dumb little game anyway. Not like I have a stake in--
...
God, I have to pee!
Hm, that's the men's. I should use the--
Dillon, I heard what that sketchy guy said. Come clean with me, right now!
Are you getting involved with drugs?
Ack! She's looking at me!
Well, *now* if I tell Amber I was in *here,* she'll *never* let me hear the end of it.

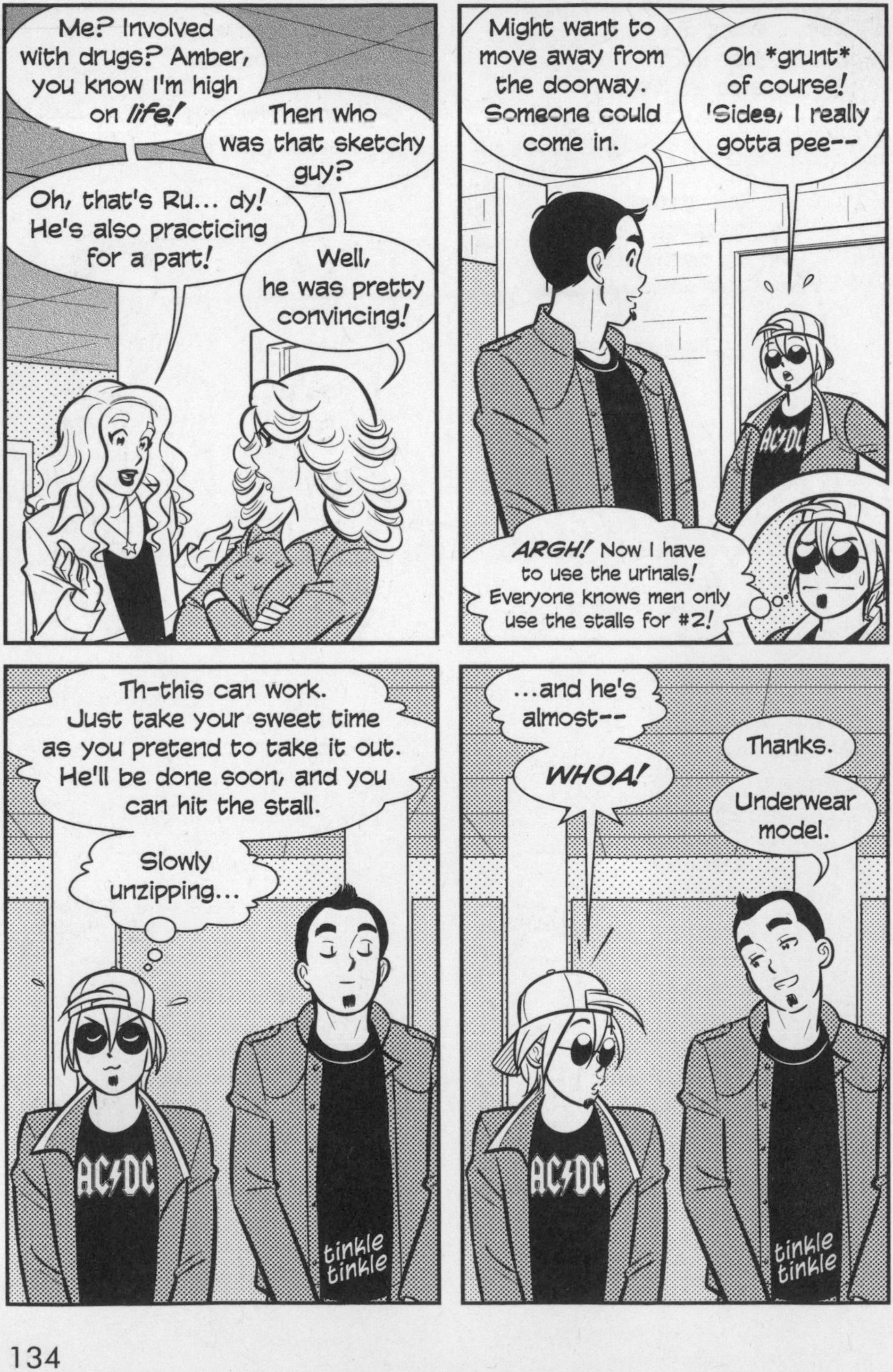
Me? Involved with drugs? Amber, you know I'm high on *life!*
Then who was that sketchy guy?
Oh, that's Ru... dy! He's also practicing for a part!
Well, he was pretty convincing!
Might want to move away from the doorway. Someone could come in.
Oh *grunt* of course! 'Sides, I really gotta pee--
ARGH! Now I have to use the urinals! Everyone knows men only use the stalls for #2!
Th-this can work. Just take your sweet time as you pretend to take it out. He'll be done soon, and you can hit the stall.
Slowly unzipping...
tinkle tinkle
...and he's almost--
WHOA!
Thanks.
Underwear model.
tinkle tinkle

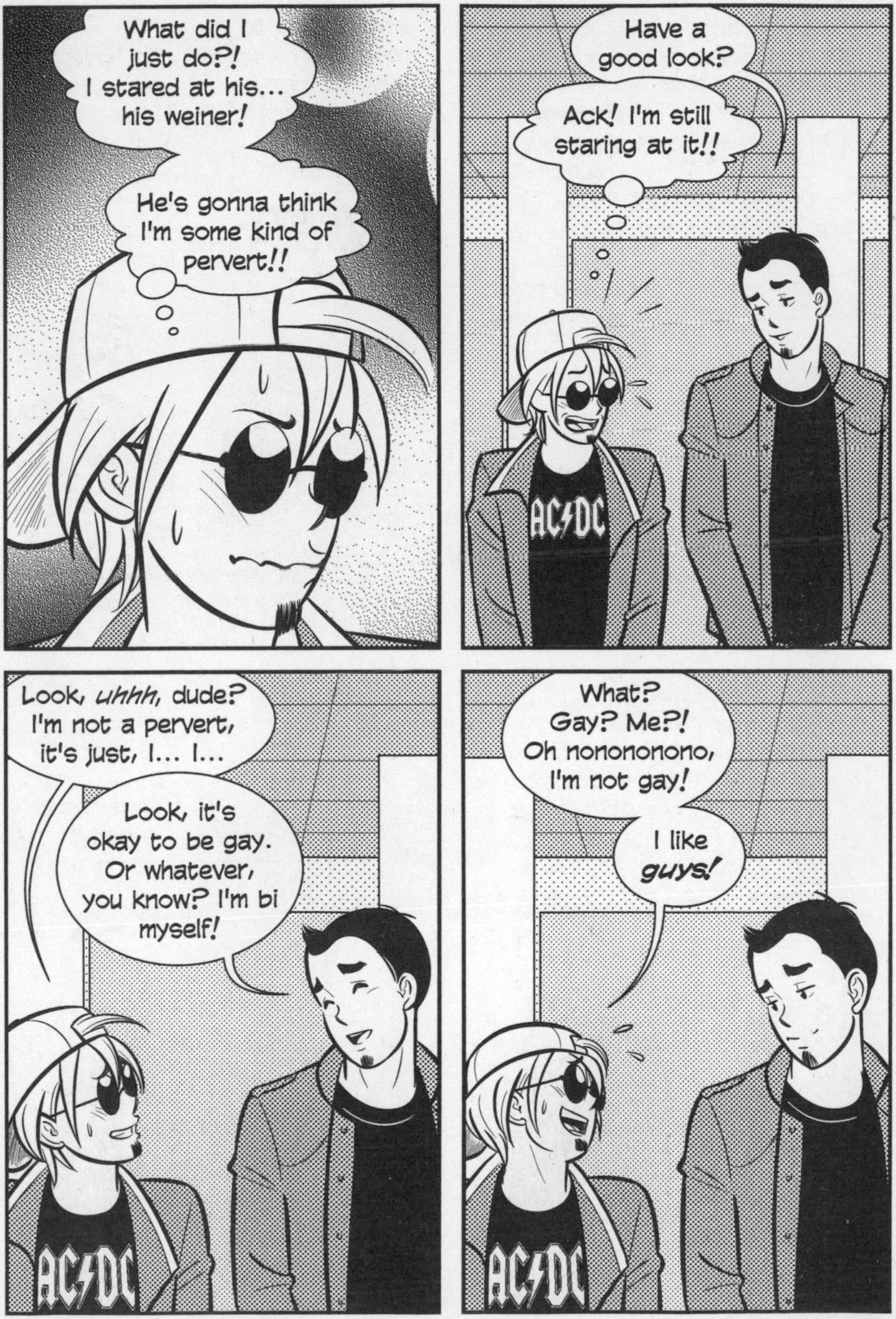
What did I just do?! I stared at his... his weiner!
He's gonna think I'm some kind of pervert!!
Have a good look?
Ack! I'm still staring at it!!
AC/DC
Look, *uhhh*, dude? I'm not a pervert, it's just, I... I...
Look, it's okay to be gay. Or whatever, you know? I'm bi myself!
AC/DC
What? Gay? Me?! Oh nonononono, I'm not gay!
I like ***guys!***
AC/DC

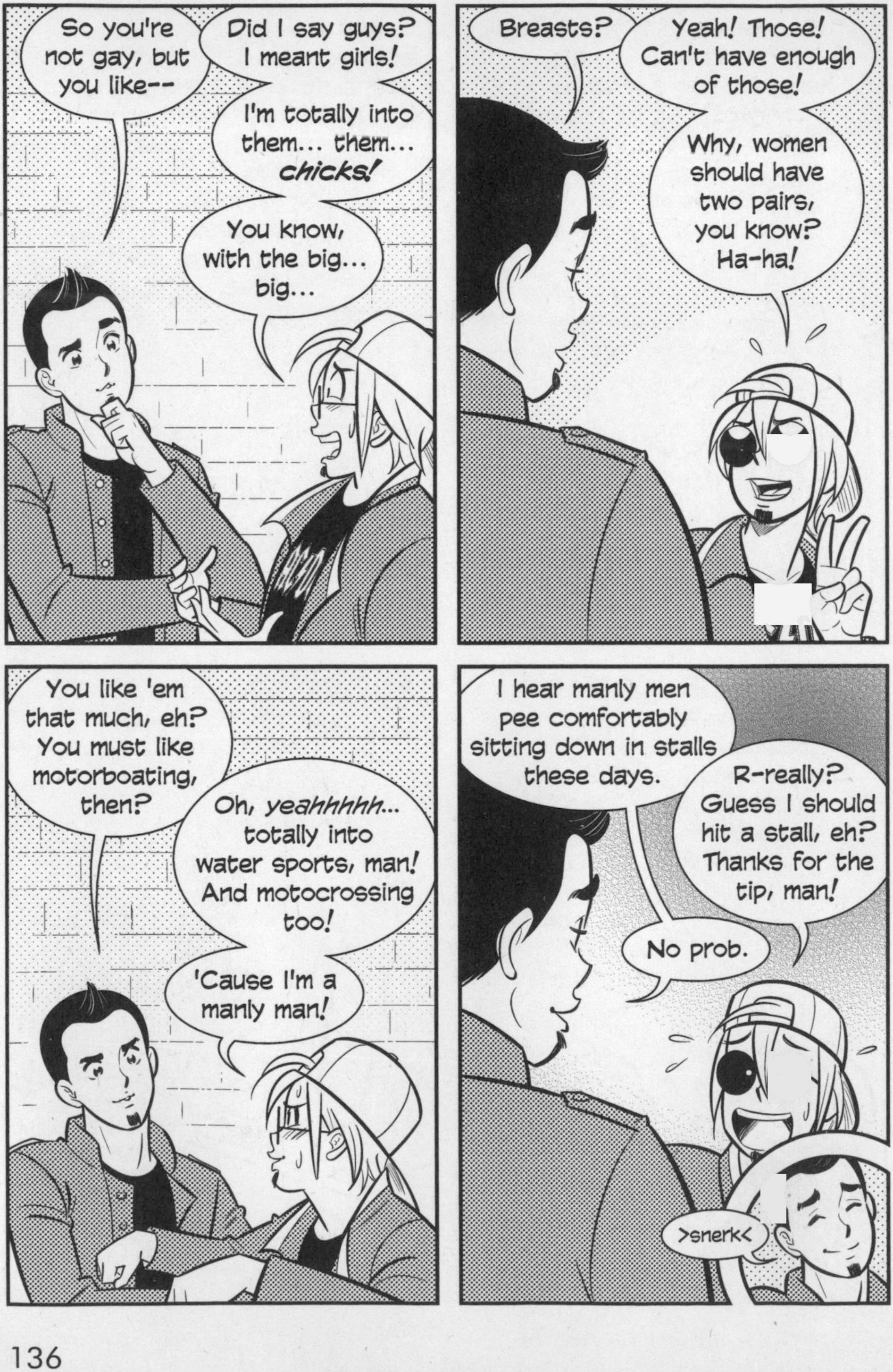
So you're not gay, but you like--
Did I say guys? I meant girls!
I'm totally into them... them... *chicks!*
You know, with the big... big...
Breasts?
Yeah! Those! Can't have enough of those!
Why, women should have two pairs, you know? Ha-ha!
You like 'em that much, eh? You must like motorboating, then?
Oh, *yeahhhhh*... totally into water sports, man! And motocrossing too!
'Cause I'm a manly man!
I hear manly men pee comfortably sitting down in stalls these days.
R-really? Guess I should hit a stall, eh? Thanks for the tip, man!
No prob.
>snerk<

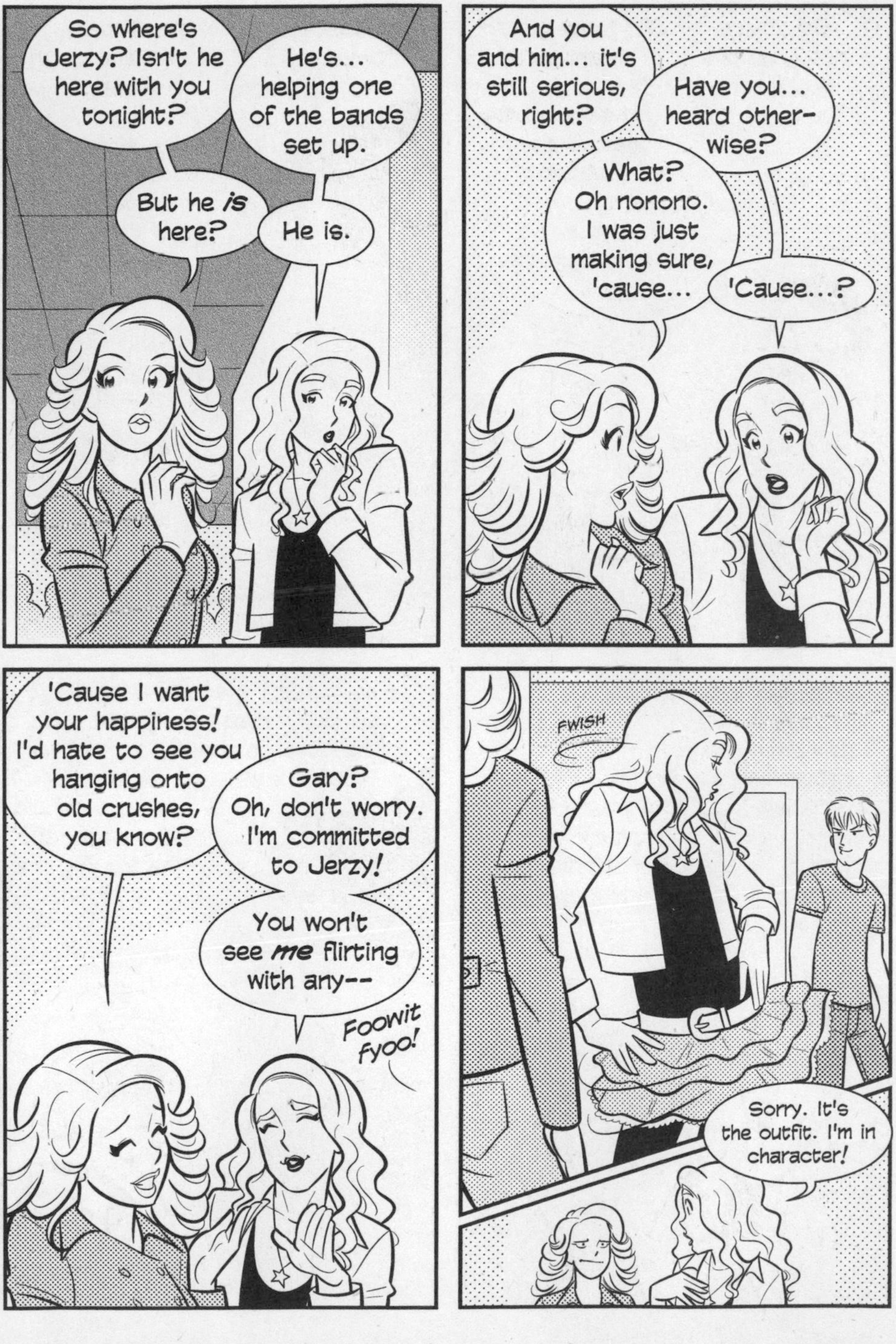
So where's Jerzy? Isn't he here with you tonight?
He's... helping one of the bands set up.
But he *is* here?
He is.
And you and him... it's still serious, right?
Have you... heard other-wise?
What? Oh nonono. I was just making sure, 'cause...
'Cause...?
'Cause I want your happiness! I'd hate to see you hanging onto old crushes, you know?
Gary? Oh, don't worry. I'm committed to Jerzy!
You won't see *me* flirting with any--
Foowit fyoo!
FWISH
Sorry. It's the outfit. I'm in character!

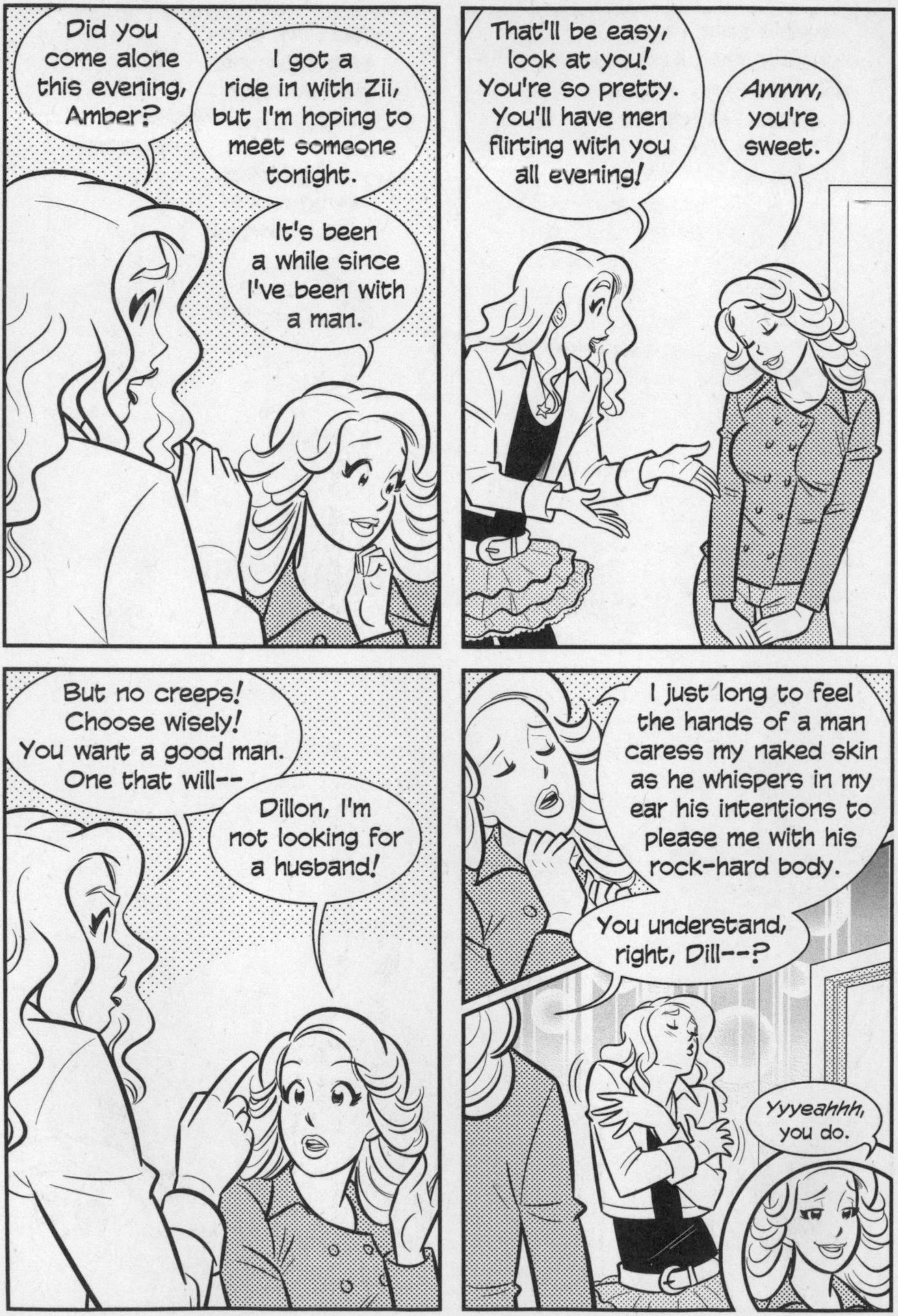
Did you come alone this evening, Amber?
I got a ride in with Zii, but I'm hoping to meet someone tonight.
It's been a while since I've been with a man.
That'll be easy, look at you! You're so pretty. You'll have men flirting with you all evening!
Awww, you're sweet.
But no creeps! Choose wisely! You want a good man. One that will--
Dillon, I'm not looking for a husband!
I just long to feel the hands of a man caress my naked skin as he whispers in my ear his intentions to please me with his rock-hard body.
You understand, right, Dill--?
Yyyeahhh, you do.

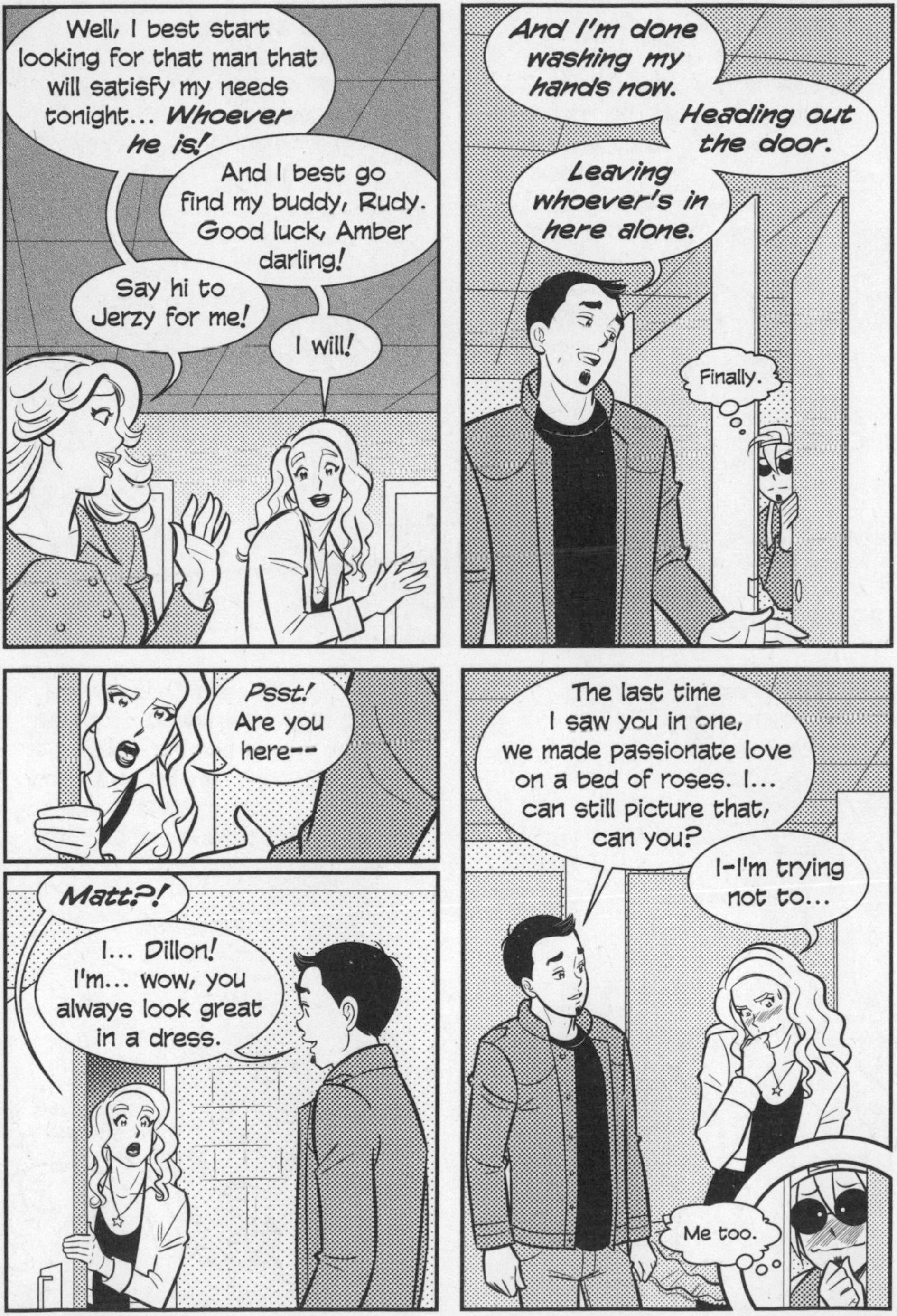

Well, I best start looking for that man that will satisfy my needs tonight... *Whoever he is!*
And I best go find my buddy, Rudy. Good luck, Amber darling!
Say hi to Jerzy for me!
I will!
And I'm done washing my hands now.
Heading out the door.
Leaving whoever's in here alone.
Finally.
Psst! Are you here--
Matt?!
I... Dillon! I'm... wow, you always look great in a dress.
The last time I saw you in one, we made passionate love on a bed of roses. I... can still picture that, can you?
I-I'm trying not to...
Me too.

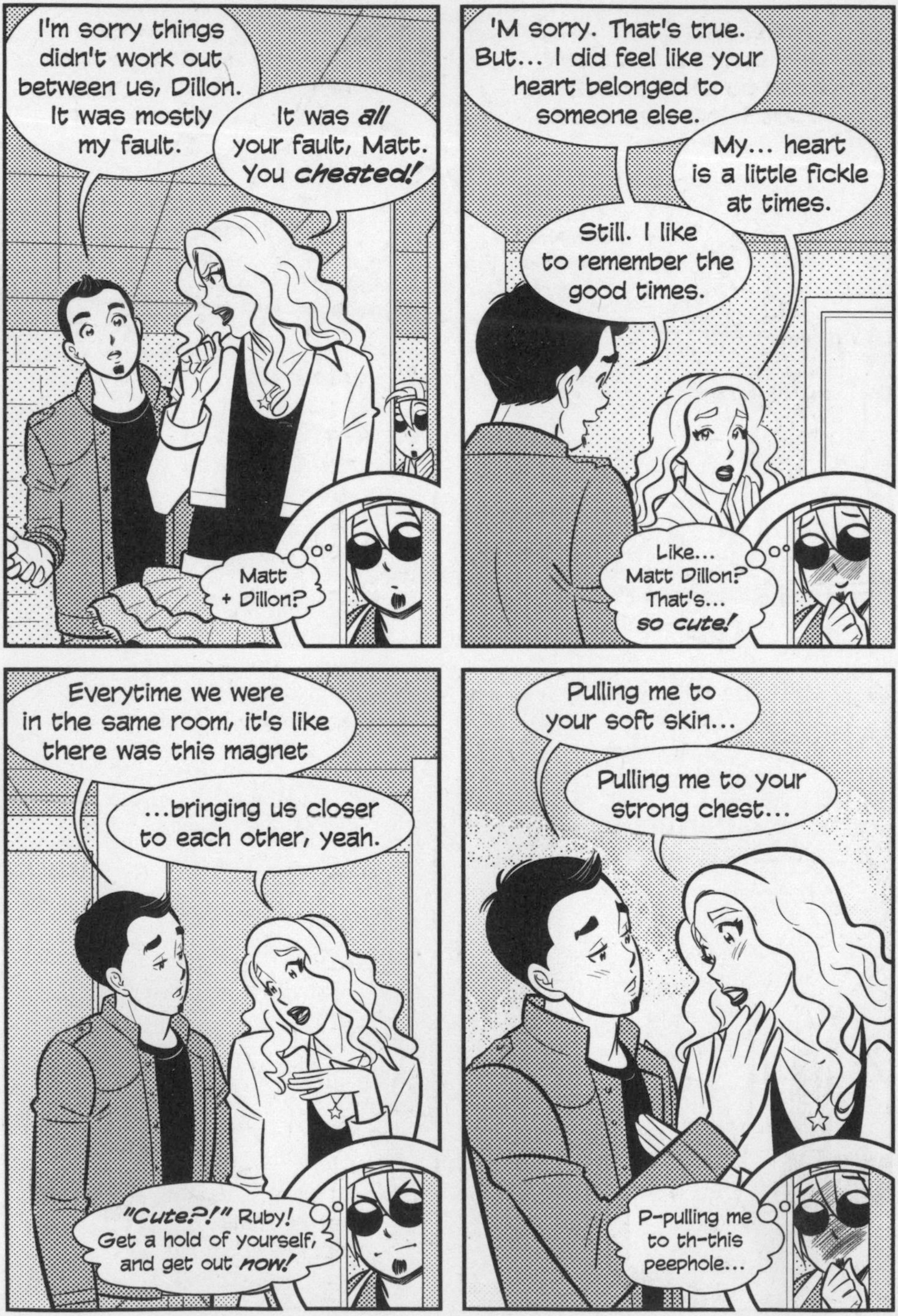
I'm sorry things didn't work out between us, Dillon. It was mostly my fault.
It was *all* your fault, Matt. You ***cheated!***
Matt + Dillon?
'M sorry. That's true. But... I did feel like your heart belonged to someone else.
My... heart is a little fickle at times.
Still. I like to remember the good times.
Like... Matt Dillon? That's... ***so cute!***
Everytime we were in the same room, it's like there was this magnet
...bringing us closer to each other, yeah.
"Cute?!" Ruby! Get a hold of yourself, and get out ***now!***
Pulling me to your soft skin...
Pulling me to your strong chest...
P-pulling me to th-this peephole...

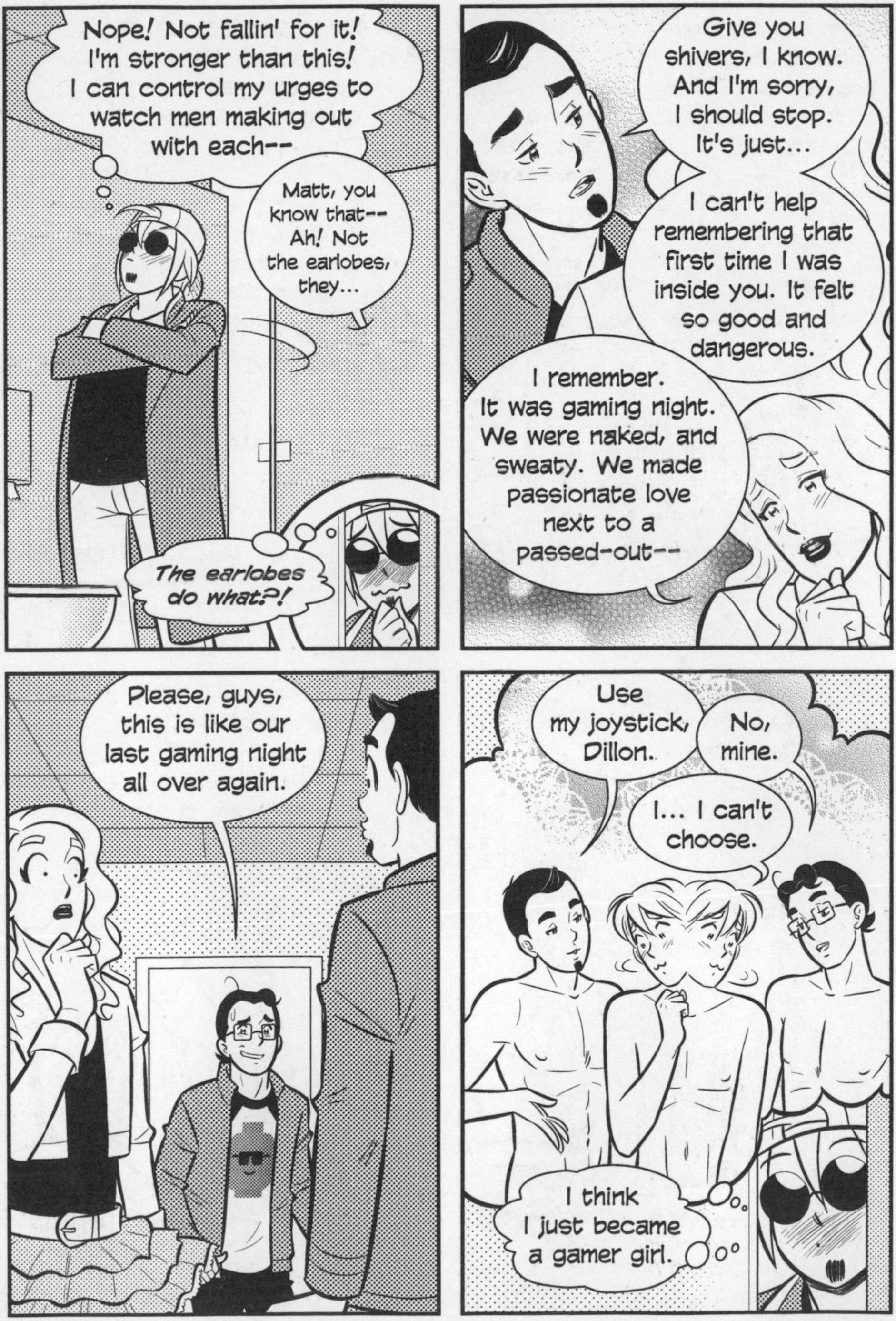
Nope! Not fallin' for it! I'm stronger than this! I can control my urges to watch men making out with each--
Matt, you know that-- Ah! Not the earlobes, they...
The earlobes do what?!
Give you shivers, I know. And I'm sorry, I should stop. It's just...
I can't help remembering that first time I was inside you. It felt so good and dangerous.
I remember. It was gaming night. We were naked, and sweaty. We made passionate love next to a passed-out--
Please, guys, this is like our last gaming night all over again.
Use my joystick, Dillon.
No, mine.
I... I can't choose.
I think I just became a gamer girl.

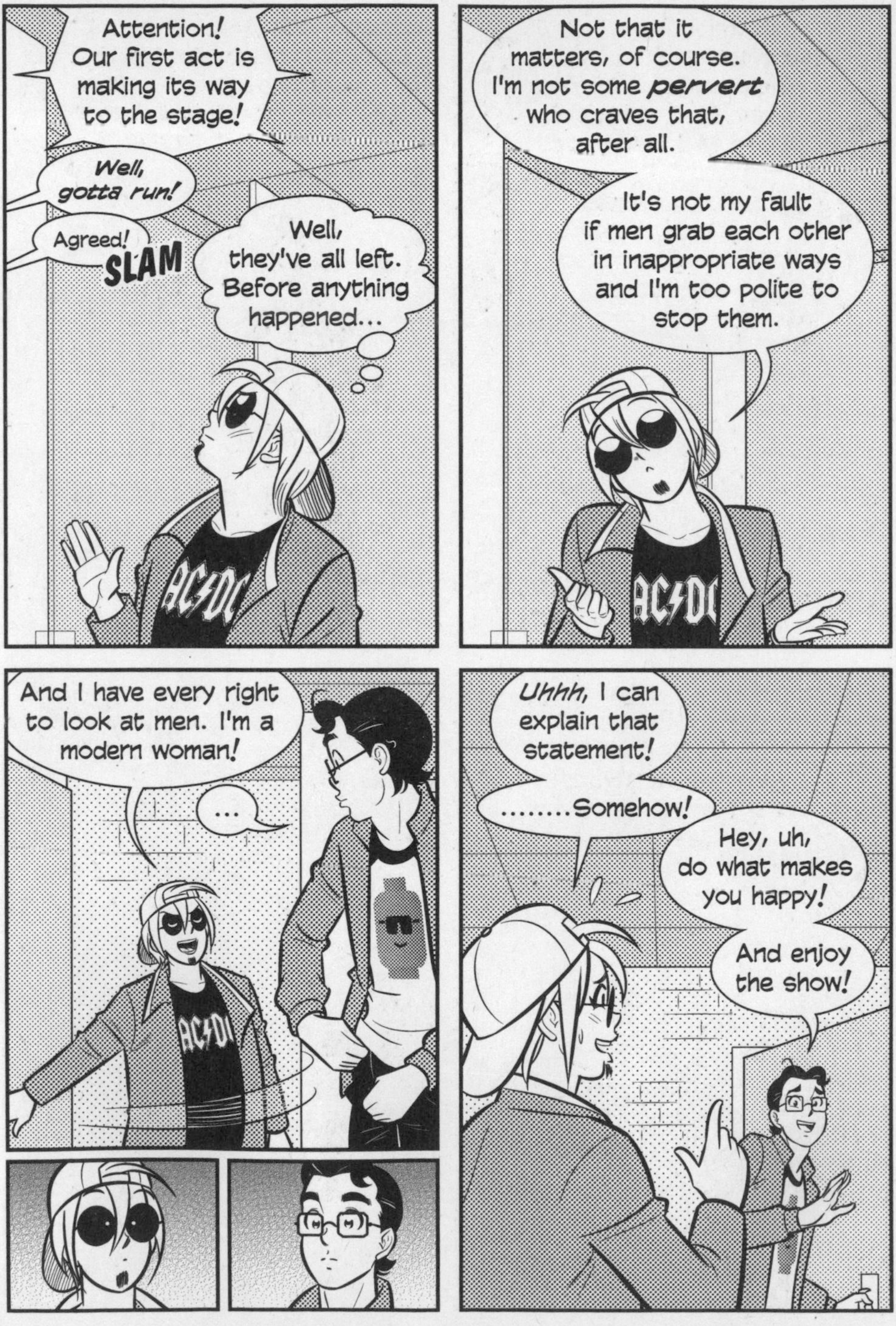
Attention! Our first act is making its way to the stage!
Well, gotta run!
Agreed!
SLAM
Well, they've all left. Before anything happened...
Not that it matters, of course. I'm not some *pervert* who craves that, after all.
It's not my fault if men grab each other in inappropriate ways and I'm too polite to stop them.
And I have every right to look at men. I'm a modern woman!
...
Uhhh, I can explain that statement!
........Somehow!
Hey, uh, do what makes you happy!
And enjoy the show!

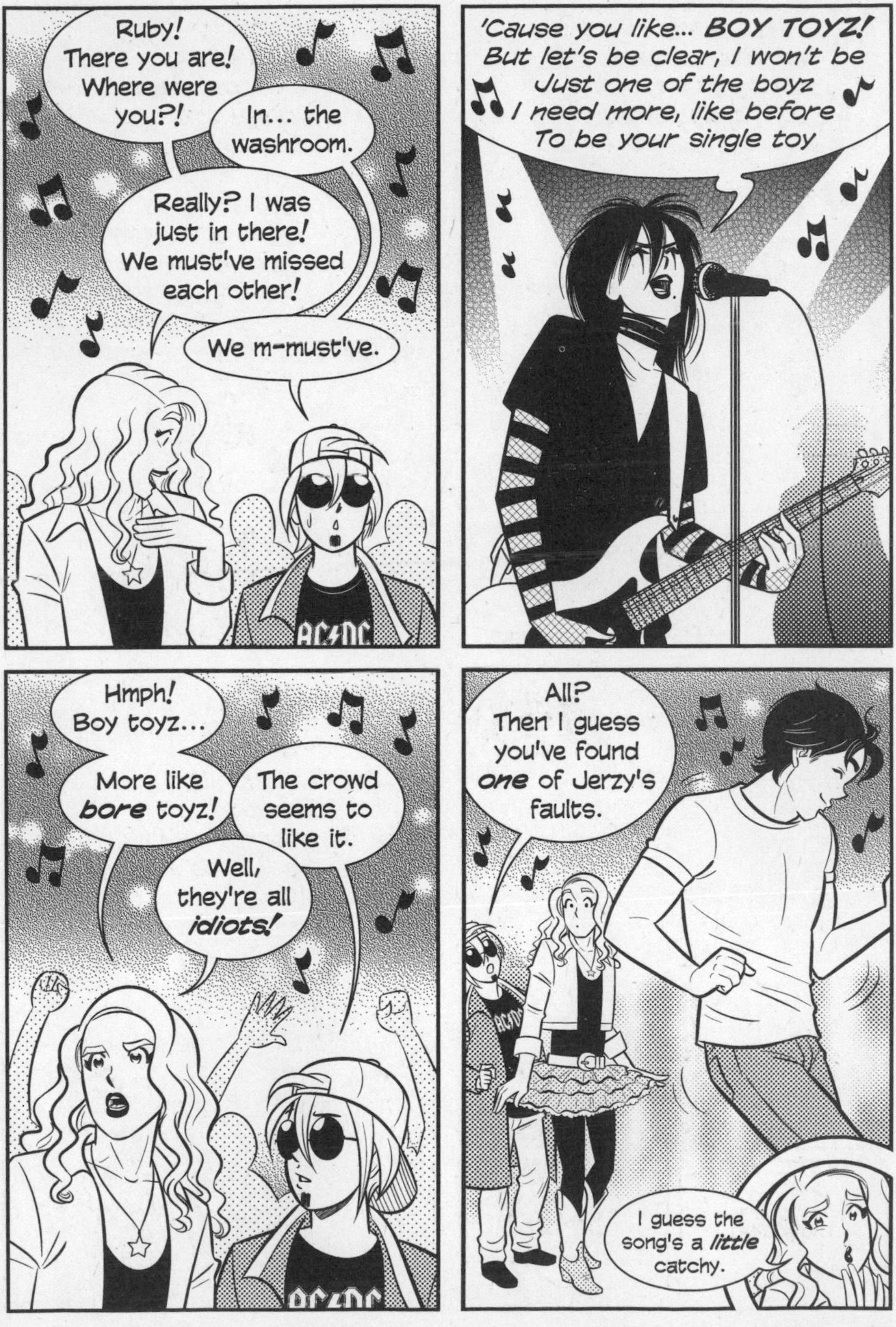
Ruby! There you are! Where were you?!
In... the washroom.
Really? I was just in there! We must've missed each other!
We m-must've.
'Cause you like... BOY TOYZ! But let's be clear, I won't be Just one of the boyz I need more, like before To be your single toy
AC/DC
Hmph! Boy toyz...
More like *bore* toyz!
The crowd seems to like it.
Well, they're all *idiots!*
AC/DC
All? Then I guess you've found *one* of Jerzy's faults.
I guess the song's a *little* catchy.

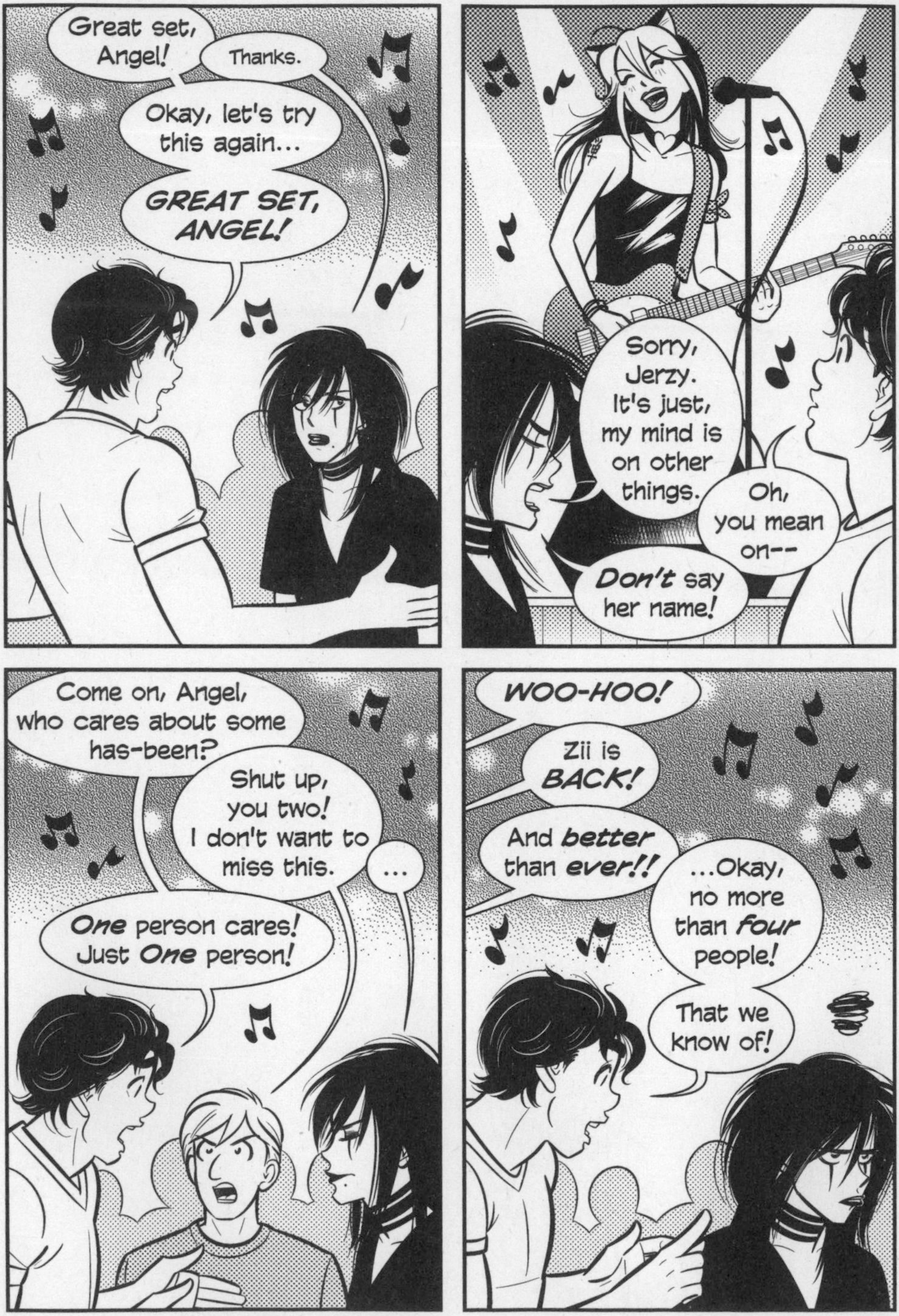
Great set, Angel!
Thanks.
Okay, let's try this again...
GREAT SET, ANGEL!
Sorry, Jerzy. It's just, my mind is on other things.
Oh, you mean on--
Don't say her name!
Come on, Angel, who cares about some has-been?
Shut up, you two! I don't want to miss this.
...
One person cares! Just One person!
WOO-HOO!
Zii is BACK!
And better than ever!!
...Okay, no more than four people!
That we know of!

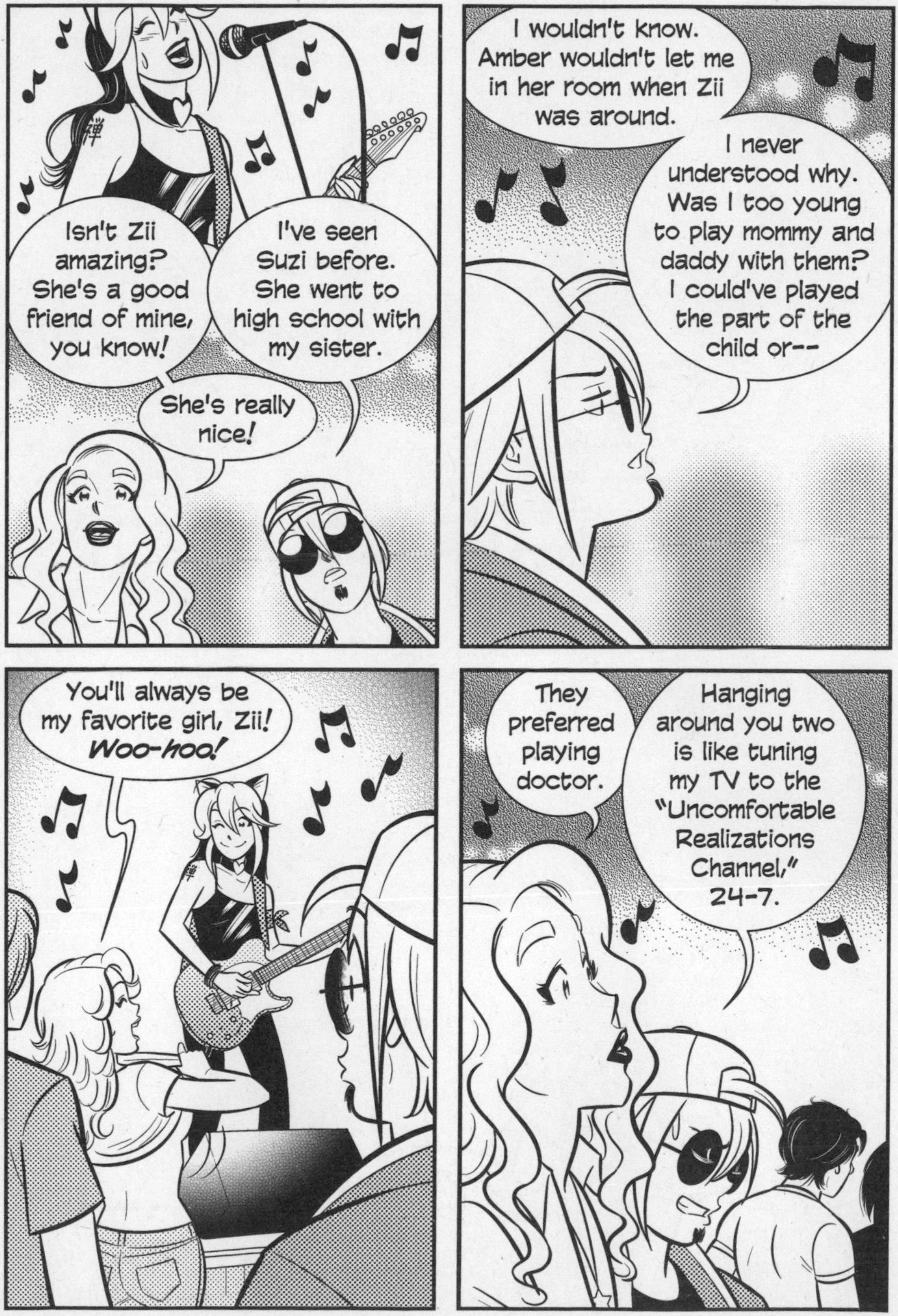
Isn't Zii amazing? She's a good friend of mine, you know!
I've seen Suzi before. She went to high school with my sister.
She's really nice!
I wouldn't know. Amber wouldn't let me in her room when Zii was around.
I never understood why. Was I too young to play mommy and daddy with them? I could've played the part of the child or--
You'll always be my favorite girl, Zii! *Woo-hoo!*
They preferred playing doctor.
Hanging around you two is like tuning my TV to the "Uncomfortable Realizations Channel," 24-7.

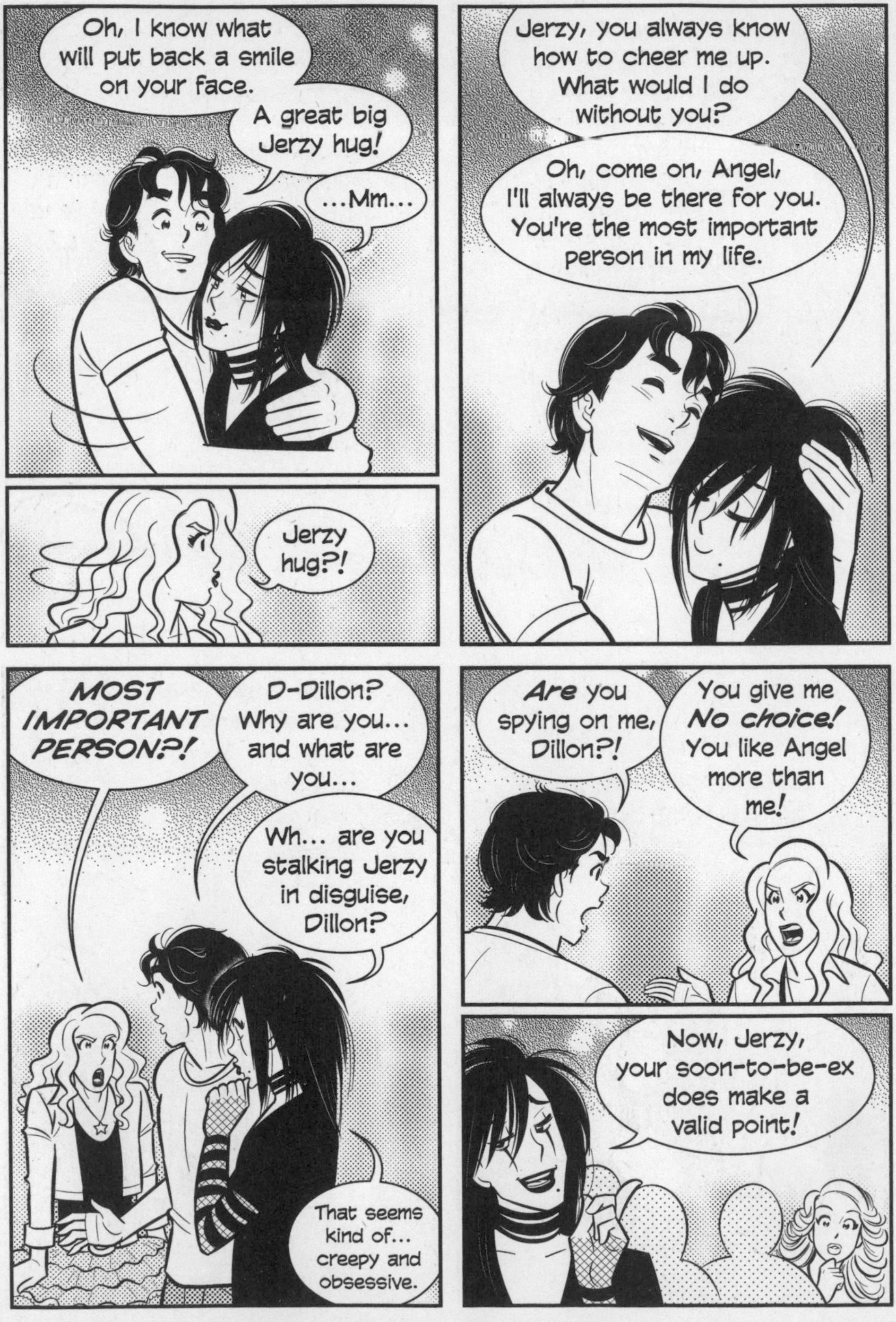

Oh, I know what will put back a smile on your face.
A great big Jerzy hug!
...Mm...
Jerzy hug?!
Jerzy, you always know how to cheer me up. What would I do without you?
Oh, come on, Angel, I'll always be there for you. You're the most important person in my life.
MOST IMPORTANT PERSON?!
D-Dillon? Why are you... and what are you...
Wh... are you stalking Jerzy in disguise, Dillon?
That seems kind of... creepy and obsessive.
Are you spying on me, Dillon?!
You give me *No choice!* You like Angel more than me!
Now, Jerzy, your soon-to-be-ex does make a valid point!

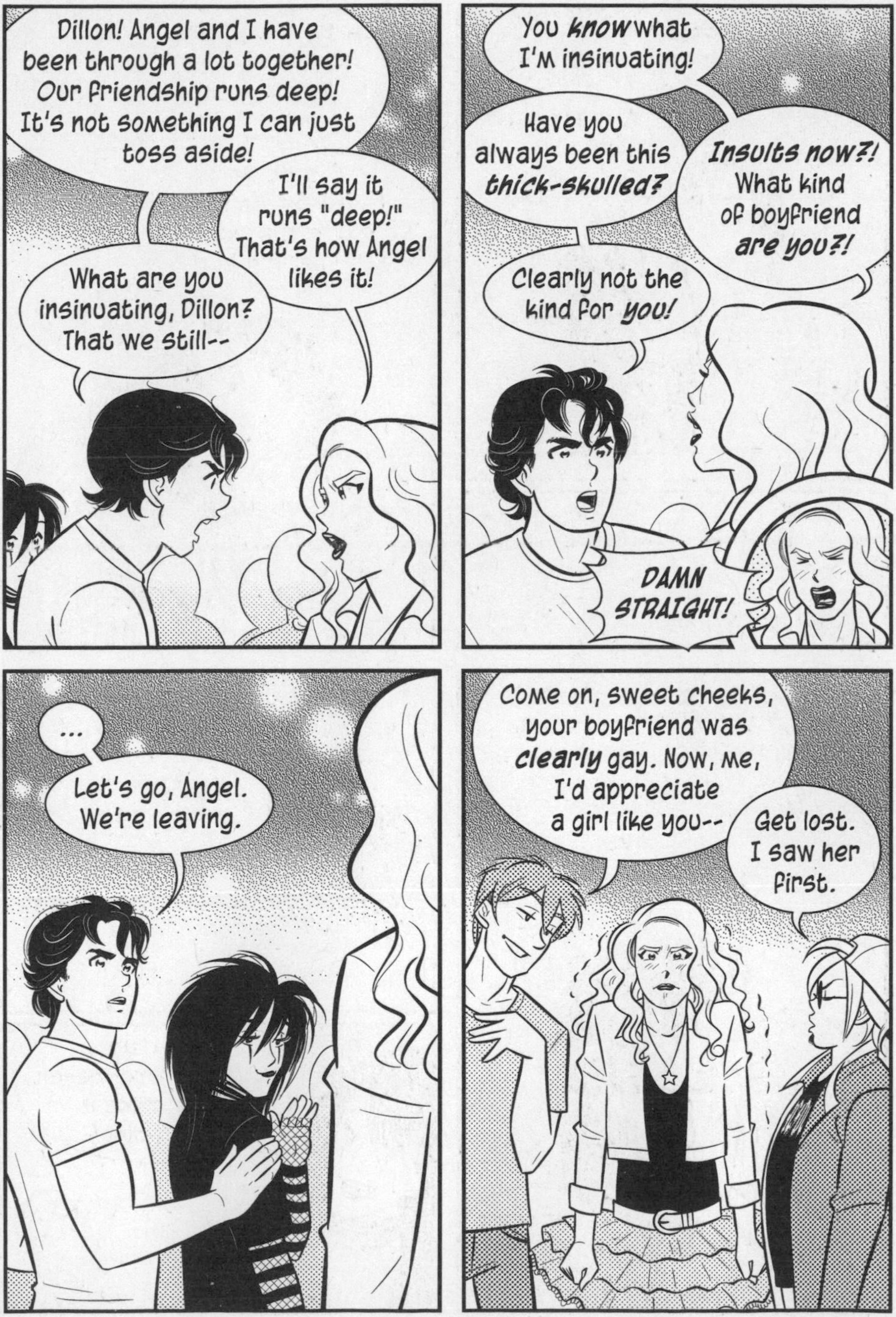
Dillon! Angel and I have been through a lot together! Our friendship runs deep! It's not something I can just toss aside!
What are you insinuating, Dillon? That we still--
I'll say it runs "deep!" That's how Angel likes it!
You *know* what I'm insinuating!
Have you always been this *thick-skulled?*
Insults now?! What kind of boyfriend *are you?!*
Clearly not the kind for *you!*
DAMN STRAIGHT!
...
Let's go, Angel. We're leaving.
Come on, sweet cheeks, your boyfriend was *clearly* gay. Now, me, I'd appreciate a girl like you--
Get lost. I saw her first.

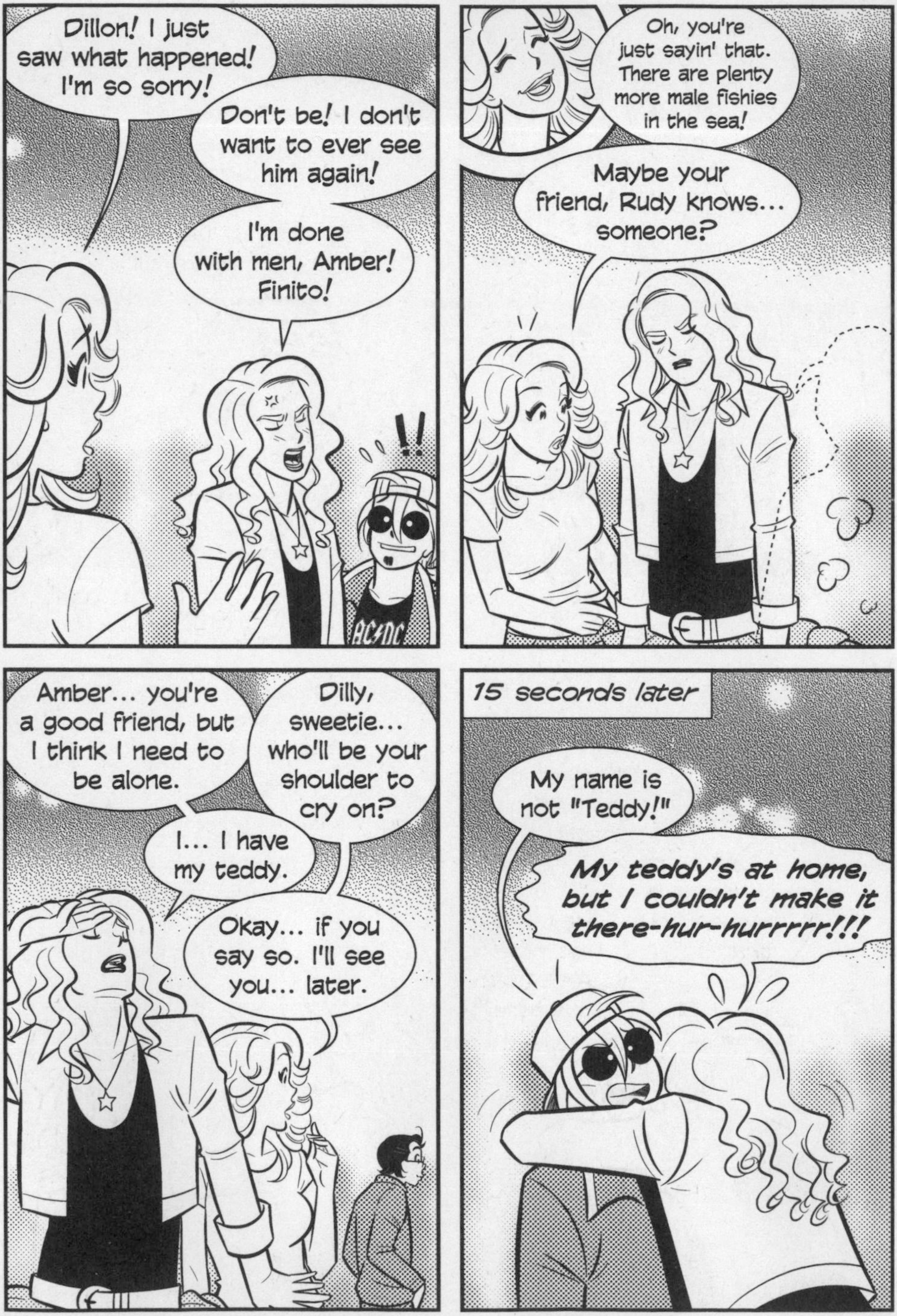
Dillon! I just saw what happened! I'm so sorry!
Don't be! I don't want to ever see him again!
I'm done with men, Amber! Finito!
!!
AC/DC
Oh, you're just sayin' that. There are plenty more male fishies in the sea!
Maybe your friend, Rudy knows... someone?
Amber... you're a good friend, but I think I need to be alone.
Dilly, sweetie... who'll be your shoulder to cry on?
I... I have my teddy.
Okay... if you say so. I'll see you... later.
15 seconds later
My name is not "Teddy!"
My teddy's at home, but I couldn't make it there-hur-hurrrrr!!!

That's it! *Sniffle* Enough crying for selfish men! Who needs 'em!
I'll die an old cat lady!
Siiiiiigh
Look, you heard Amber.
There are plenty of male fishies in the sea! Male fishies that will think only of *your* needs, and never think a *moment* about theirs!
AC/DC
Oo-hoo-Rudyyyyyy... if only you were that man!
Now now, you're making a scene again...
I'd take you to the gym to sweat off that belly.
Hey, let's go now! Anywhere but here!
Rudy...? Thank you for giving me faith in men.
I've never felt gayer in my life, and it's all because of you.
...

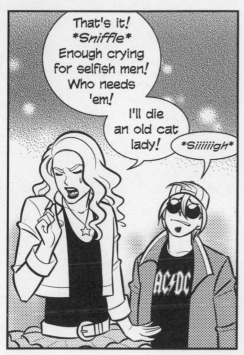

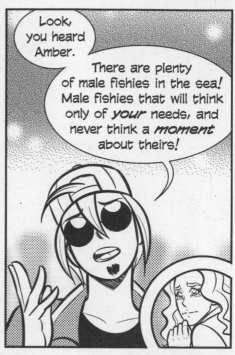

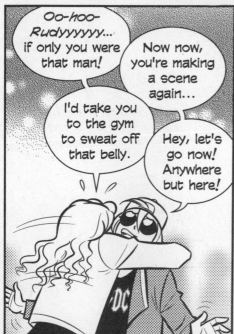

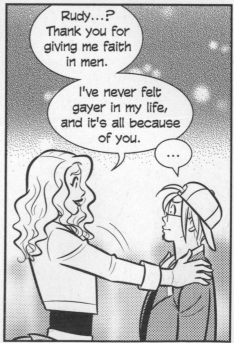

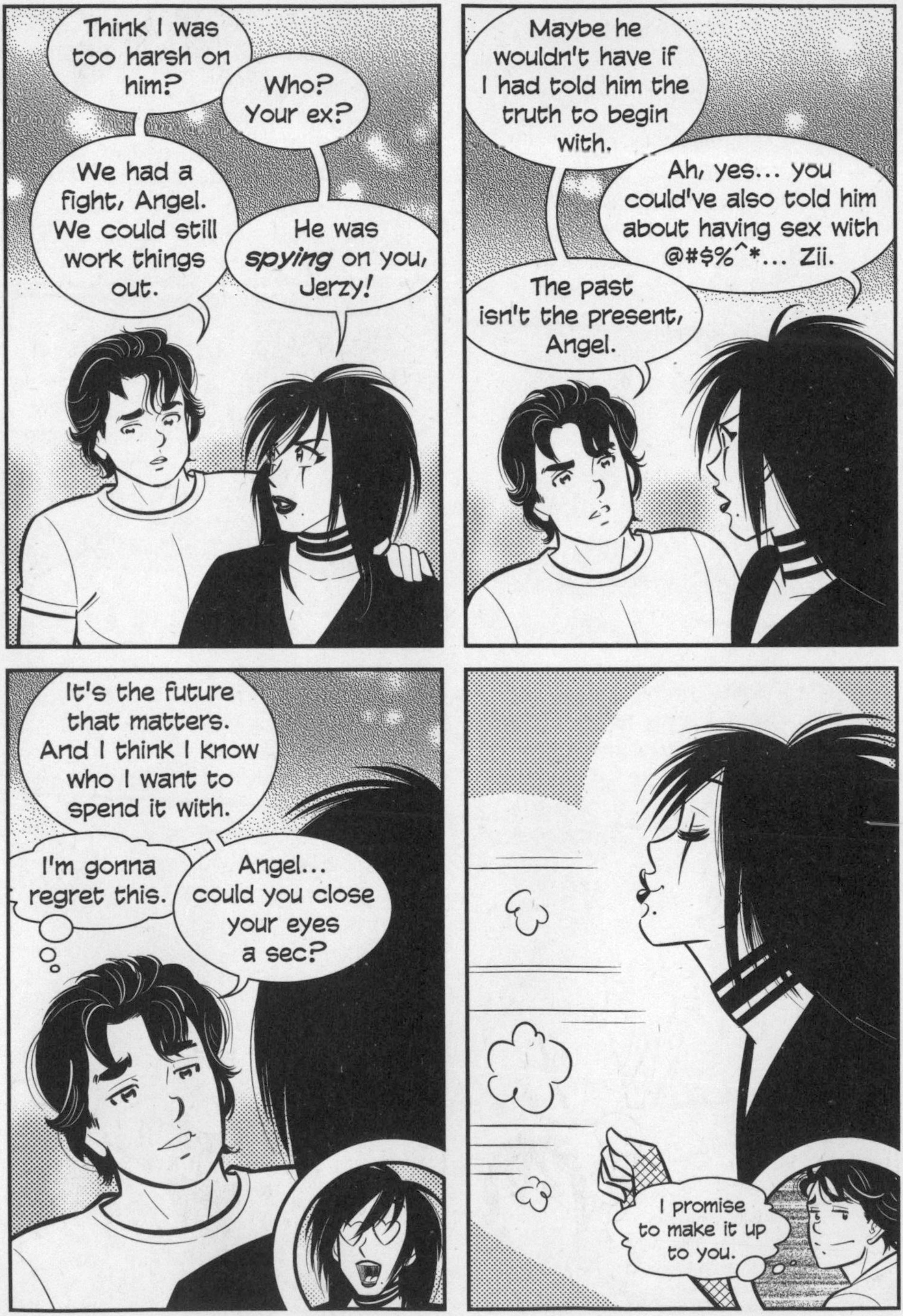
Think I was too harsh on him?
Who? Your ex?
We had a fight, Angel. We could still work things out.
He was *spying* on you, Jerzy!
Maybe he wouldn't have if I had told him the truth to begin with.
Ah, yes... you could've also told him about having sex with @#$%^*... Zii.
The past isn't the present, Angel.
It's the future that matters. And I think I know who I want to spend it with.
I'm gonna regret this.
Angel... could you close your eyes a sec?
I promise to make it up to you.

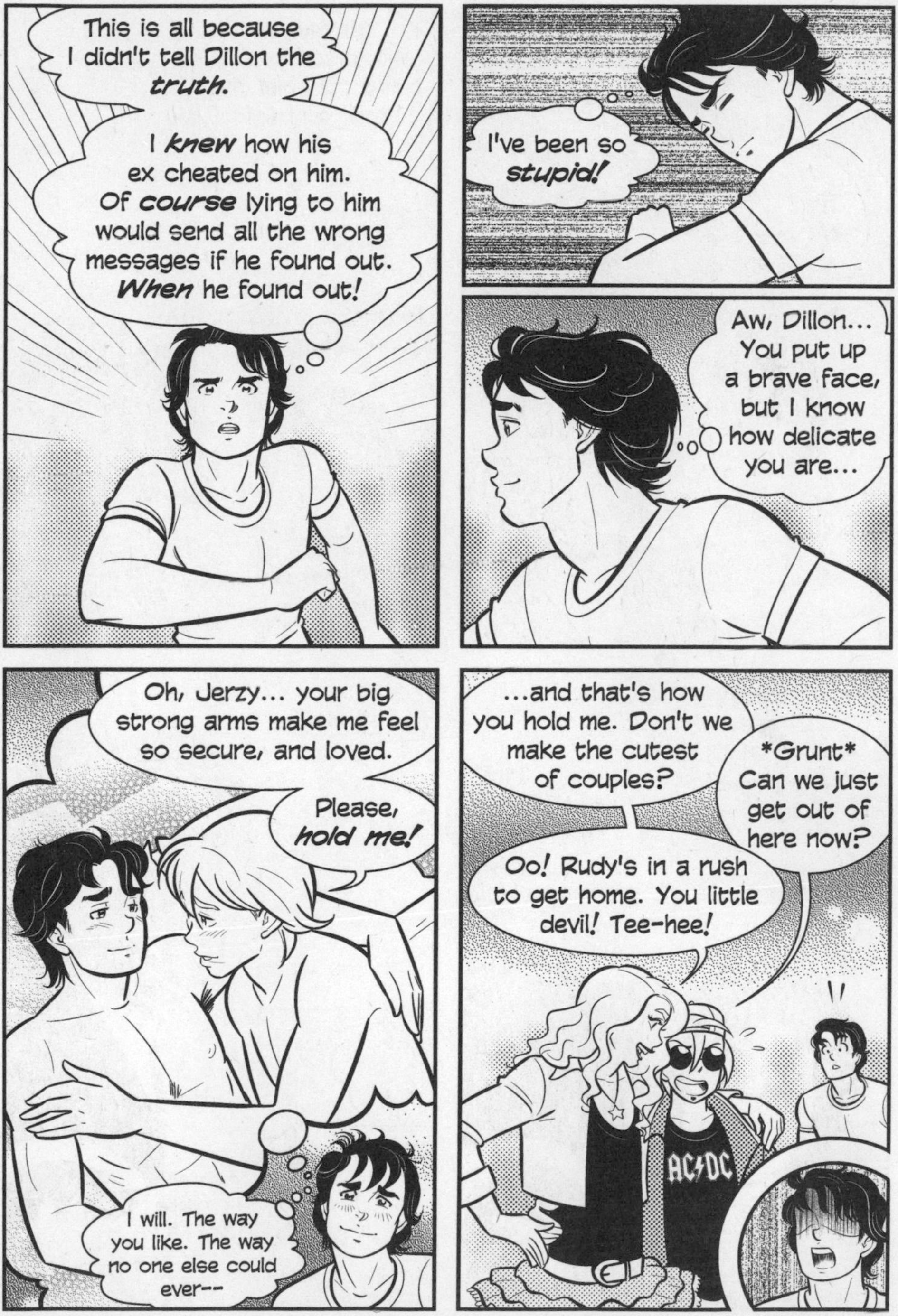
This is all because I didn't tell Dillon the *truth.*
I *knew* how his ex cheated on him. Of *course* lying to him would send all the wrong messages if he found out. *When* he found out!
I've been so *stupid!*
Aw, Dillon... You put up a brave face, but I know how delicate you are...
Oh, Jerzy... your big strong arms make me feel so secure, and loved.
Please, *hold me!*
I will. The way you like. The way no one else could ever--
...and that's how you hold me. Don't we make the cutest of couples?
Grunt Can we just get out of here now?
Oo! Rudy's in a rush to get home. You little devil! Tee-hee!
AC/DC

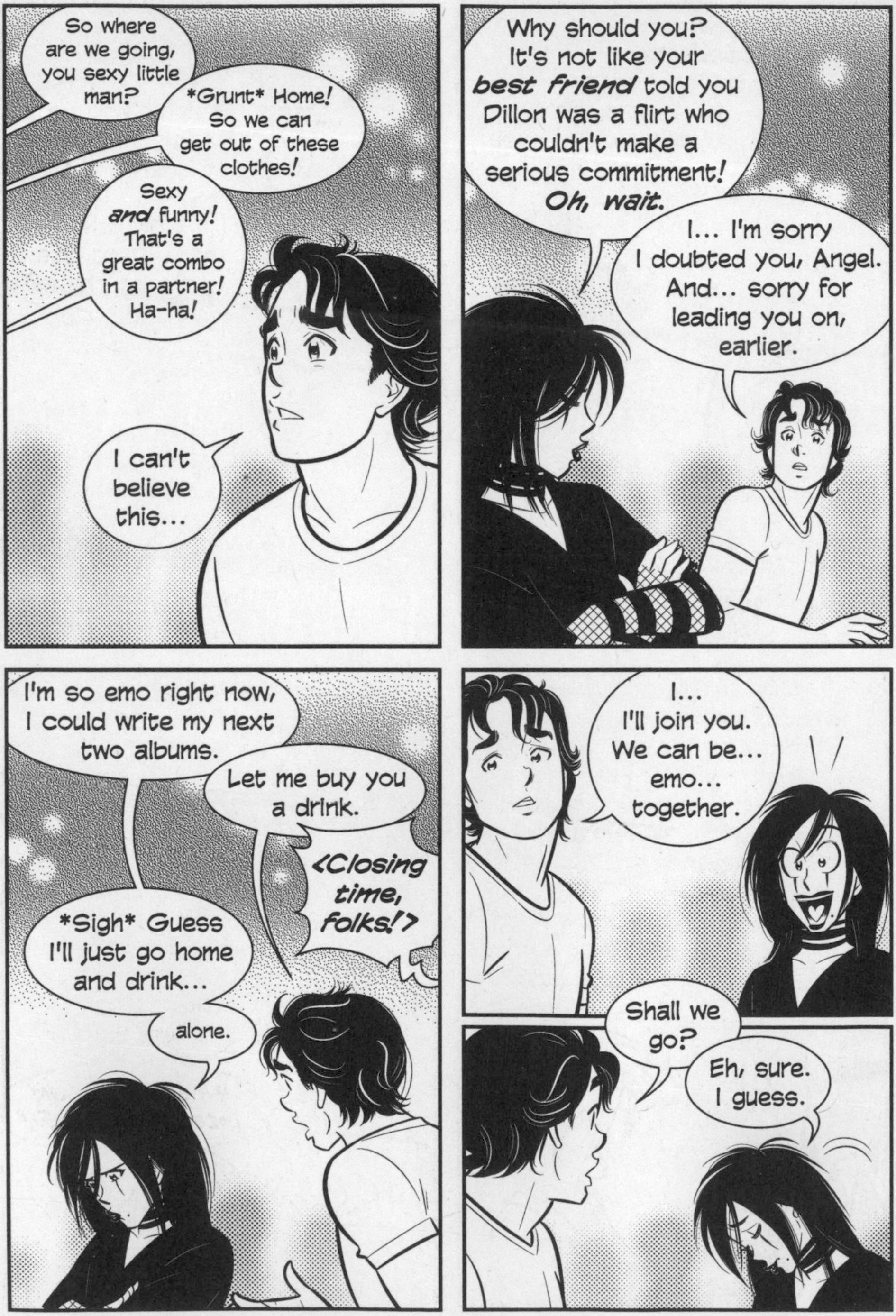
So where are we going, you sexy little man?
Grunt Home! So we can get out of these clothes!
Sexy and funny! That's a great combo in a partner! Ha-ha!
I can't believe this...
Why should you? It's not like your best friend told you Dillon was a flirt who couldn't make a serious commitment! Oh, wait.
I... I'm sorry I doubted you, Angel. And... sorry for leading you on, earlier.
I'm so emo right now, I could write my next two albums.
Let me buy you a drink.
<Closing time, folks!>
Sigh Guess I'll just go home and drink...
alone.
I... I'll join you. We can be... emo... together.
Shall we go?
Eh, sure. I guess.

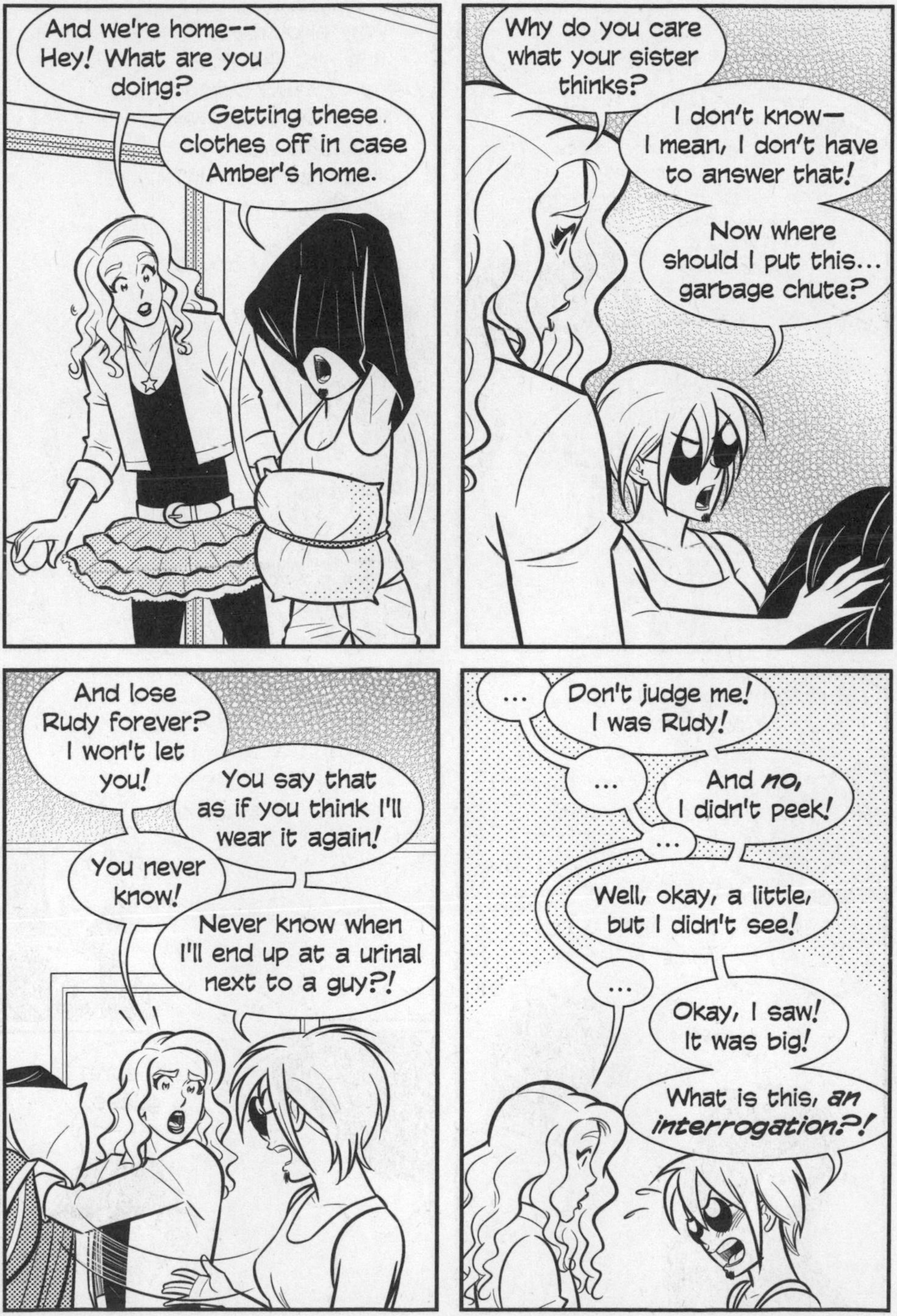
And we're home-- Hey! What are you doing?
Getting these clothes off in case Amber's home.
Why do you care what your sister thinks?
I don't know— I mean, I don't have to answer that!
Now where should I put this... garbage chute?
And lose Rudy forever? I won't let you!
You say that as if you think I'll wear it again!
You never know!
Never know when I'll end up at a urinal next to a guy?!
...
Don't judge me! I was Rudy!
...
And *no*, I didn't peek!
...
Well, okay, a little, but I didn't see!
...
Okay, I saw! It was big!
What is this, ***an interrogation?!***

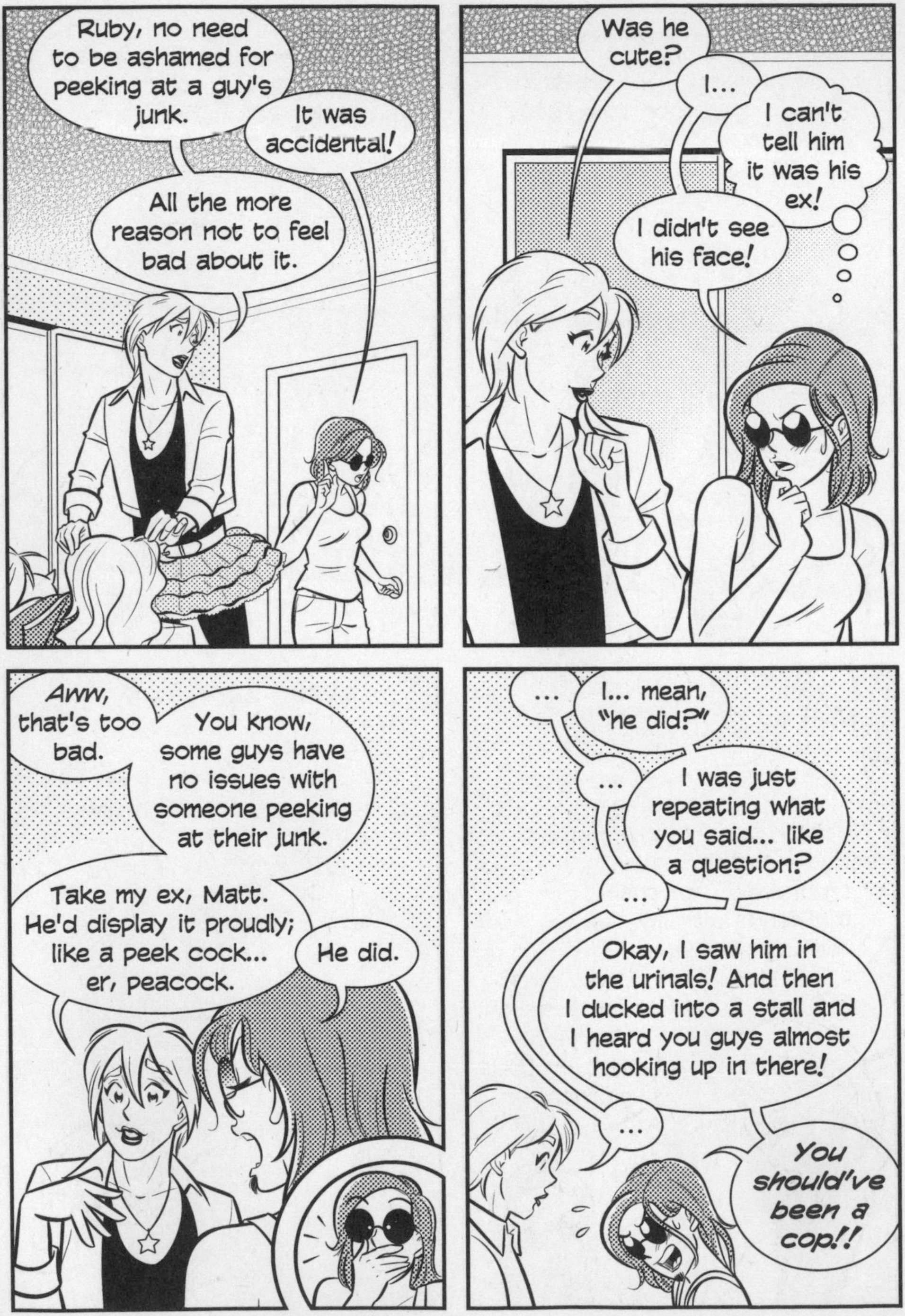
Ruby, no need to be ashamed for peeking at a guy's junk.
It was accidental!
All the more reason not to feel bad about it.
Was he cute?
I...
I can't tell him it was his ex!
I didn't see his face!
Aww, that's too bad.
You know, some guys have no issues with someone peeking at their junk.
Take my ex, Matt. He'd display it proudly; like a peek cock... er, peacock.
He did.
...
I... mean, "he did?"
...
I was just repeating what you said... like a question?
...
Okay, I saw him in the urinals! And then I ducked into a stall and I heard you guys almost hooking up in there!
...
You should've been a cop!!

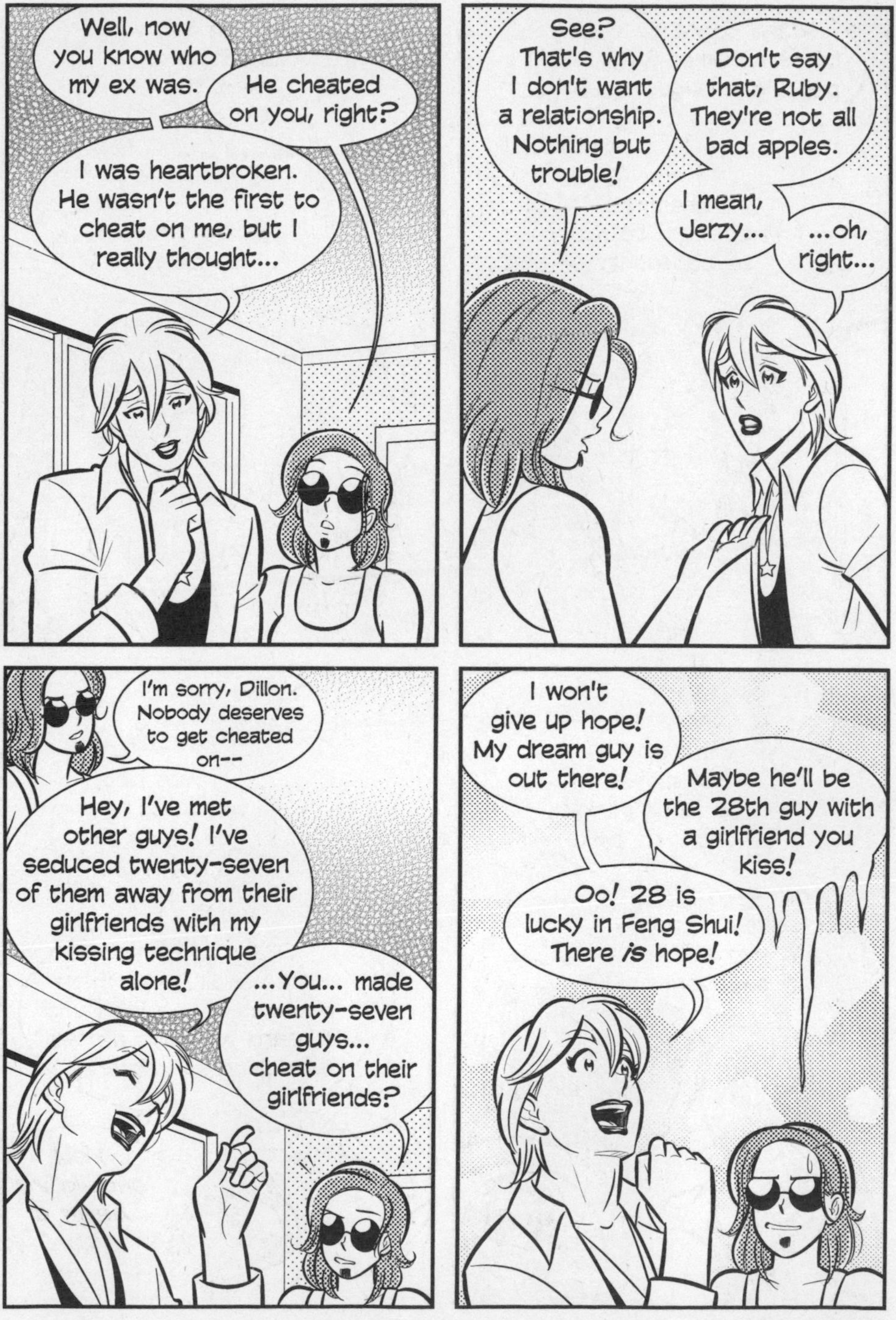
Well, now you know who my ex was.
He cheated on you, right?
I was heartbroken. He wasn't the first to cheat on me, but I really thought...
See? That's why I don't want a relationship. Nothing but trouble!
Don't say that, Ruby. They're not all bad apples.
I mean, Jerzy...
...oh, right...
I'm sorry, Dillon. Nobody deserves to get cheated on--
Hey, I've met other guys! I've seduced twenty-seven of them away from their girlfriends with my kissing technique alone!
...You... made twenty-seven guys... cheat on their girlfriends?
I won't give up hope! My dream guy is out there!
Maybe he'll be the 28th guy with a girlfriend you kiss!
Oo! 28 is lucky in Feng Shui! There *is* hope!

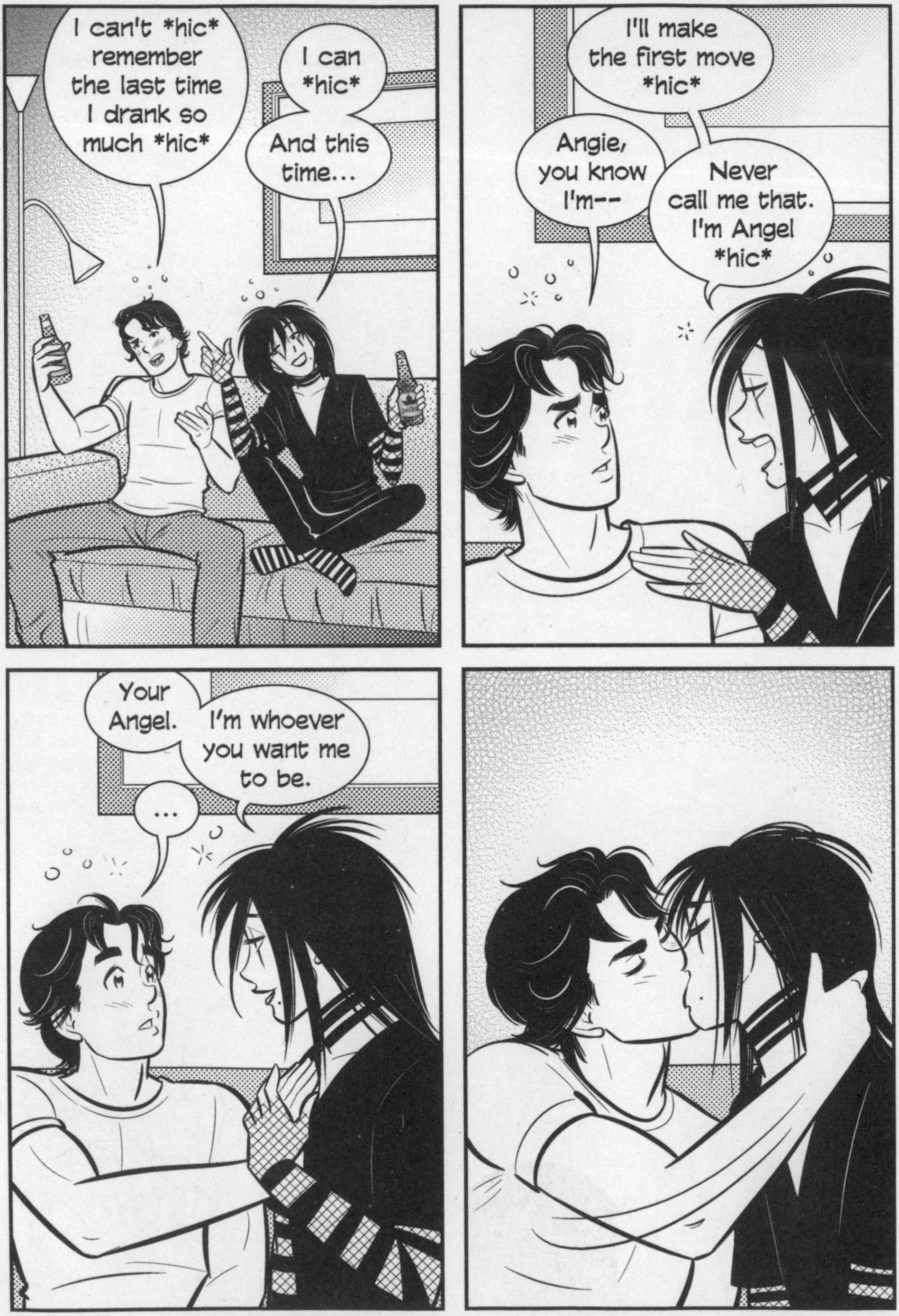
I can't *hic* remember the last time I drank so much *hic*
I can *hic*
And this time...
I'll make the first move *hic*
Angie, you know I'm--
Never call me that. I'm Angel *hic*
Your Angel.
I'm whoever you want me to be.
...

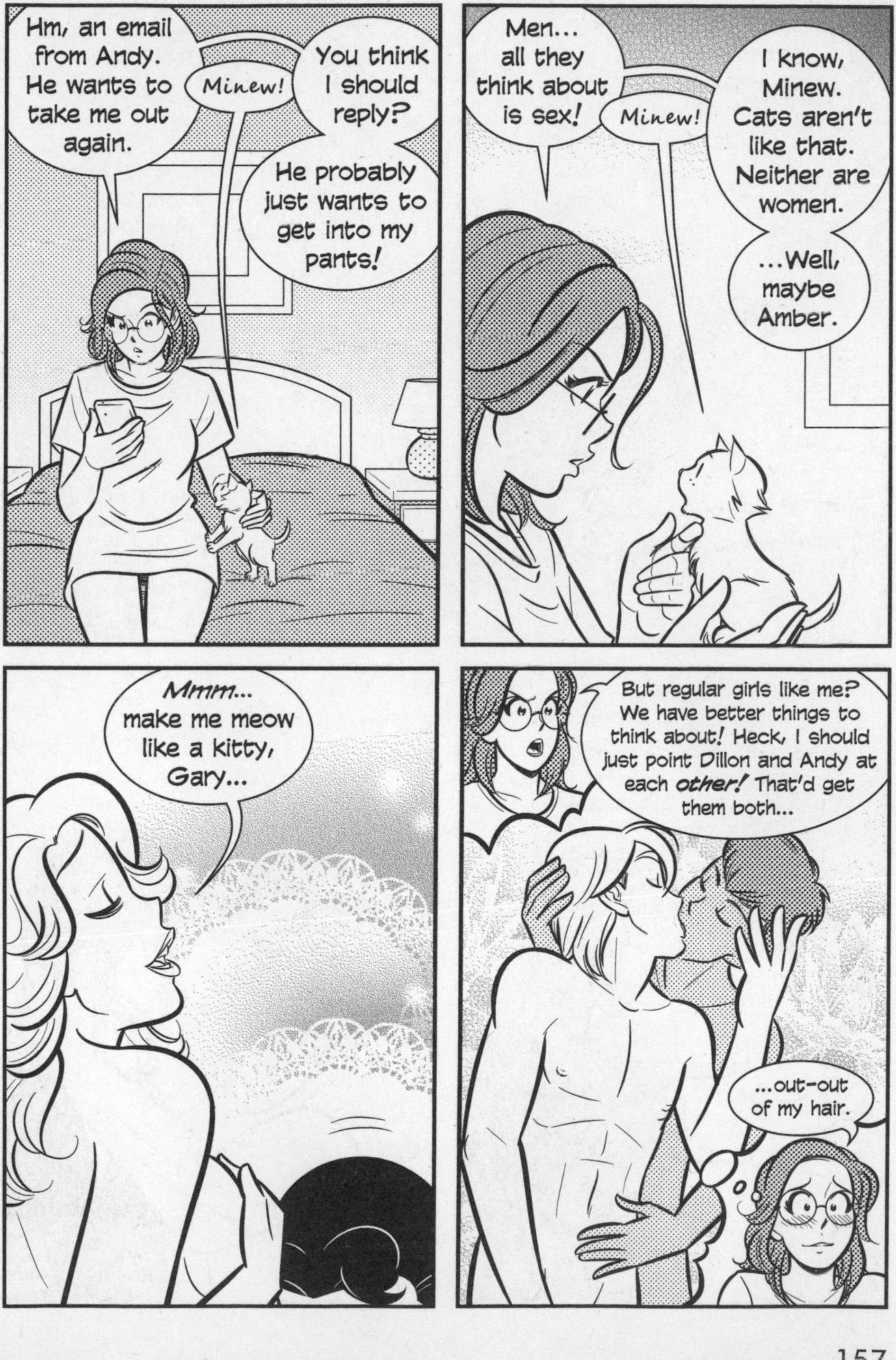
Hm, an email from Andy. He wants to take me out again.
Minew!
You think I should reply?
He probably just wants to get into my pants!
Men... all they think about is sex!
Minew!
I know, Minew. Cats aren't like that. Neither are women.
...Well, maybe Amber.
Mmm... make me meow like a kitty, Gary...
But regular girls like me? We have better things to think about! Heck, I should just point Dillon and Andy at each *other!* That'd get them both...
...out-out of my hair.

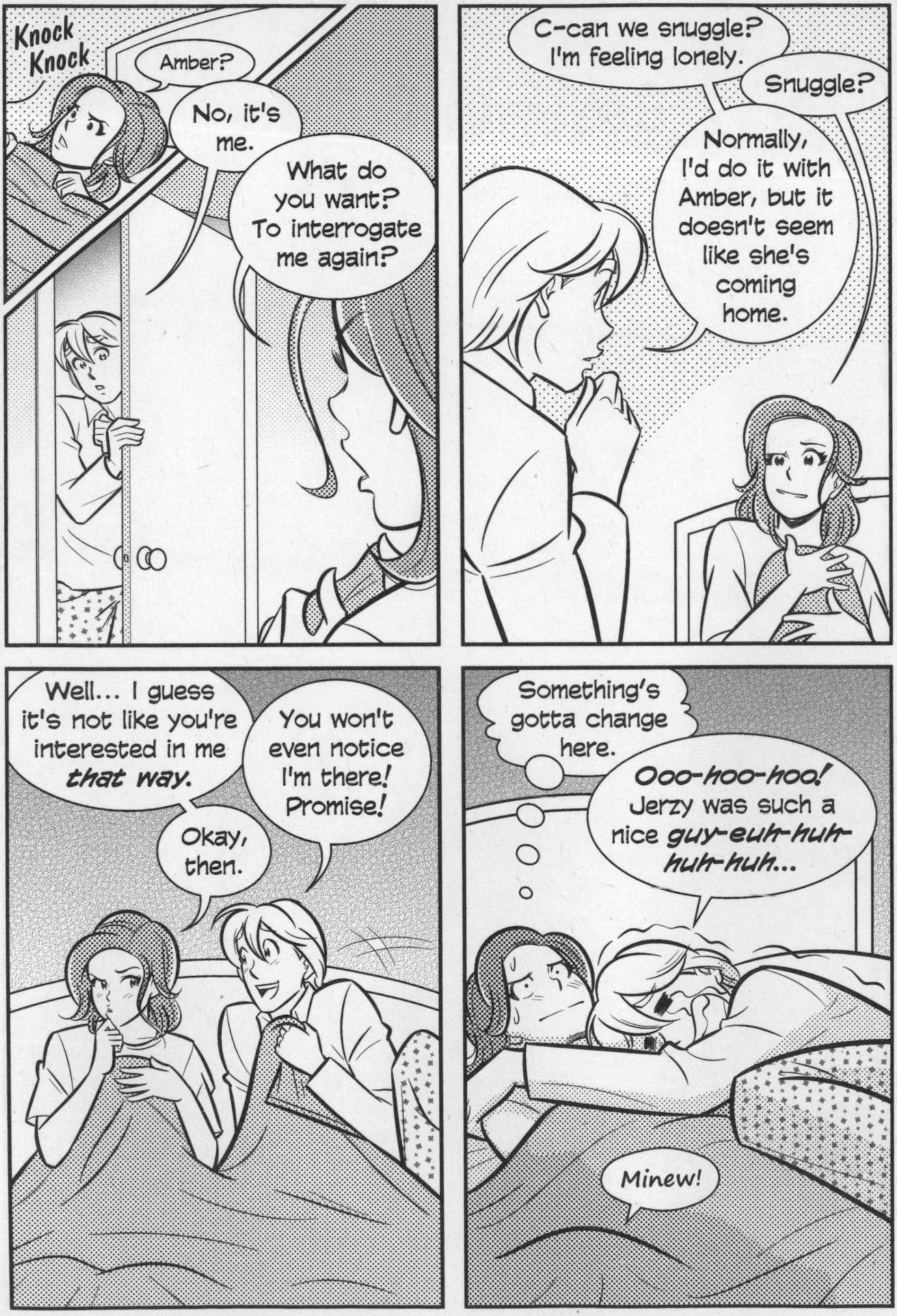
Knock Knock
Amber?
No, it's me.
What do you want? To interrogate me again?
C-can we snuggle? I'm feeling lonely.
Snuggle?
Normally, I'd do it with Amber, but it doesn't seem like she's coming home.
Well... I guess it's not like you're interested in me *that way.*
You won't even notice I'm there! Promise!
Okay, then.
Something's gotta change here.
Ooo-hoo-hoo! Jerzy was such a nice *guy-euh-huh-huh-huh...*
Minew!

Resume-Builder

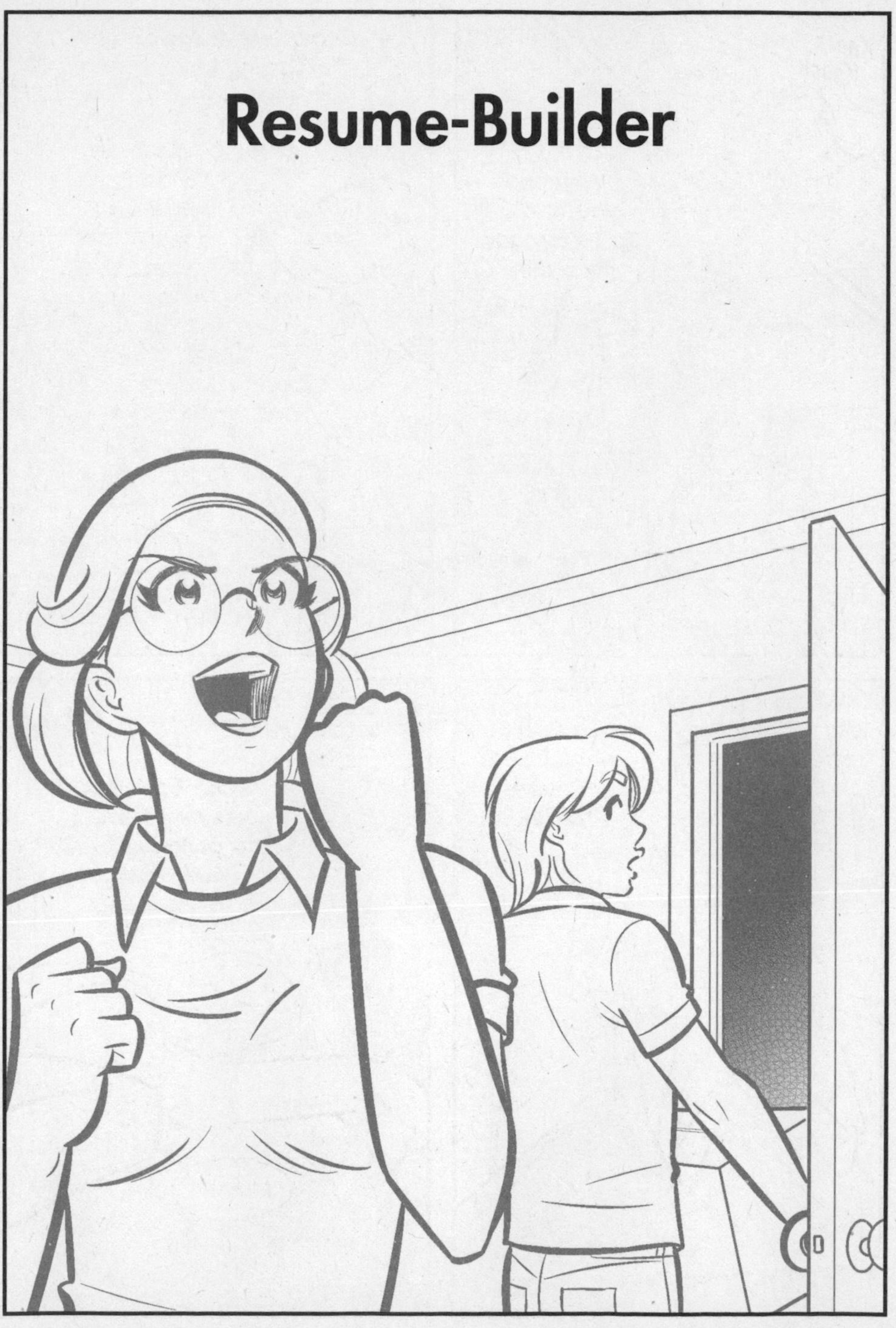

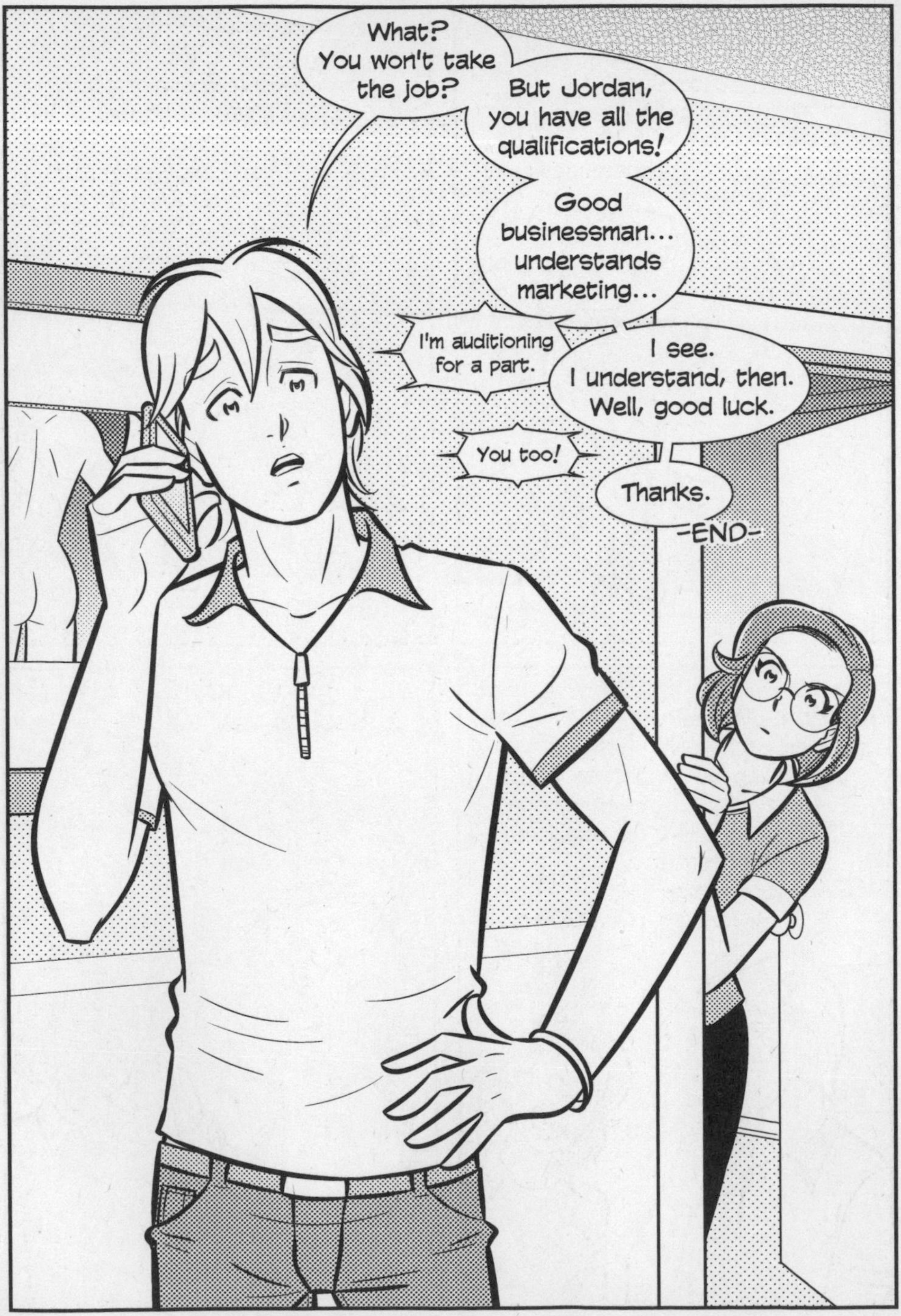
What? You won't take the job?
But Jordan, you have all the qualifications!
Good businessman... understands marketing...
I'm auditioning for a part.
I see. I understand, then. Well, good luck.
You too!
Thanks.
-END-

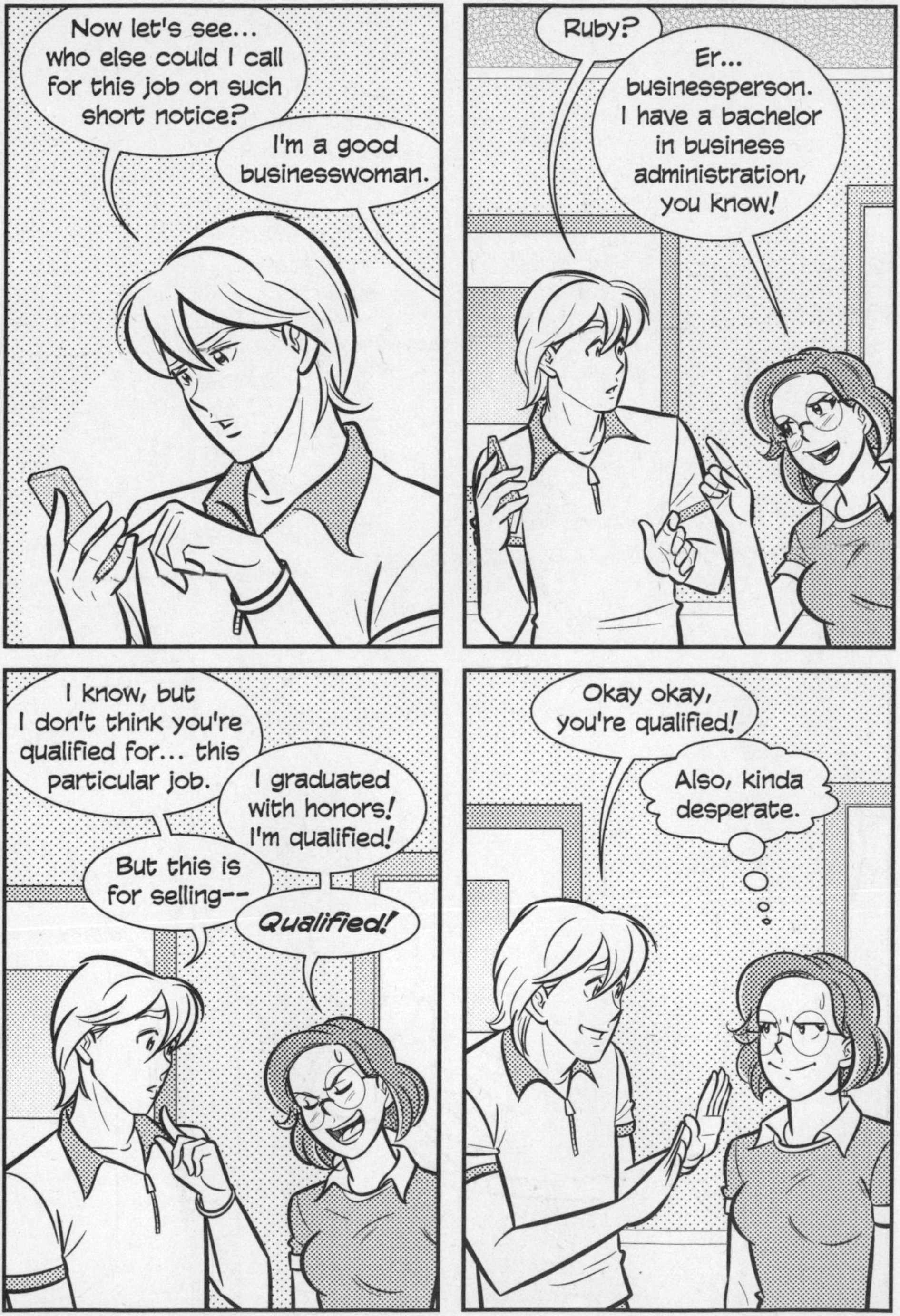
Now let's see... who else could I call for this job on such short notice?
I'm a good businesswoman.
Ruby?
Er... businessperson. I have a bachelor in business administration, you know!
I know, but I don't think you're qualified for... this particular job.
I graduated with honors! I'm qualified!
But this is for selling--
Qualified!
Okay okay, you're qualified!
Also, kinda desperate.

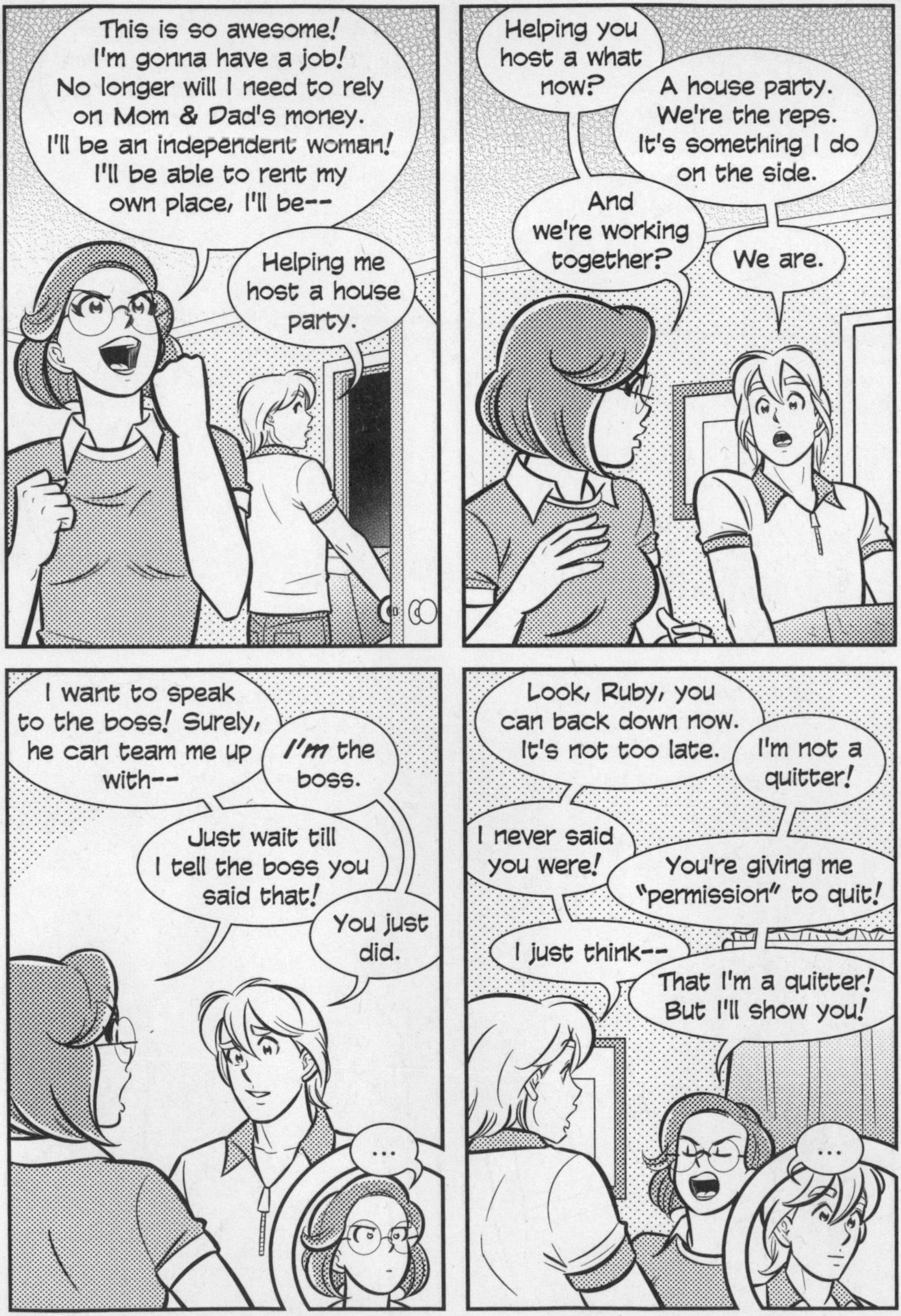
This is so awesome! I'm gonna have a job! No longer will I need to rely on Mom & Dad's money. I'll be an independent woman! I'll be able to rent my own place, I'll be--
Helping me host a house party.
Helping you host a what now?
A house party. We're the reps. It's something I do on the side.
And we're working together?
We are.
I want to speak to the boss! Surely, he can team me up with--
I'm the boss.
Just wait till I tell the boss you said that!
You just did.
...
Look, Ruby, you can back down now. It's not too late.
I'm not a quitter!
I never said you were!
You're giving me "permission" to quit!
I just think--
That I'm a quitter! But I'll show you!
...

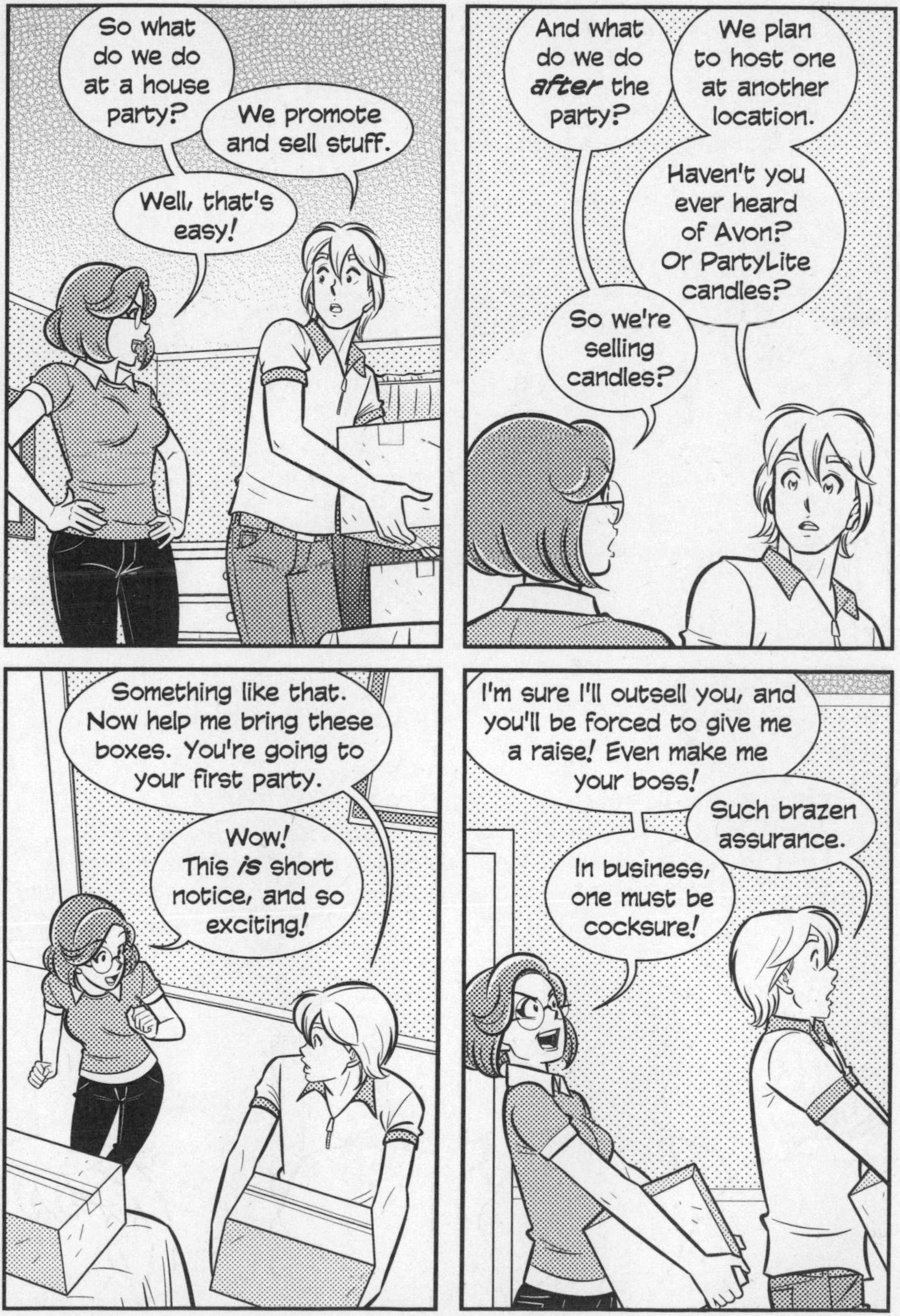
So what do we do at a house party?
We promote and sell stuff.
Well, that's easy!
And what do we do *after* the party?
We plan to host one at another location.
Haven't you ever heard of Avon? Or PartyLite candles?
So we're selling candles?
Something like that. Now help me bring these boxes. You're going to your first party.
Wow! This *is* short notice, and so exciting!
I'm sure I'll outsell you, and you'll be forced to give me a raise! Even make me your boss!
Such brazen assurance.
In business, one must be cocksure!

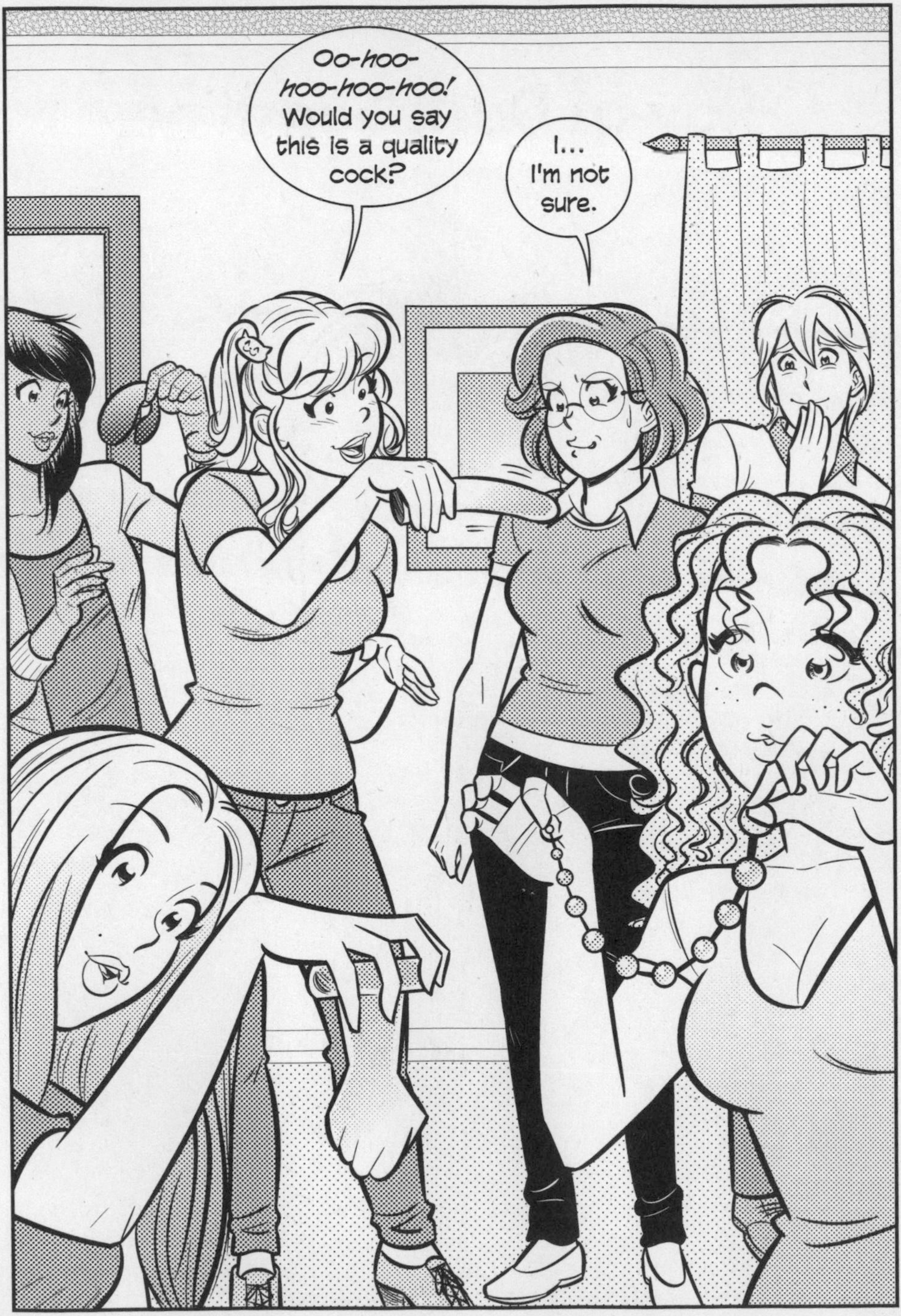
Oo-hoo-hoo-hoo-hoo! Would you say this is a quality cock?
I... I'm not sure.

Ray of Dark Sunshine

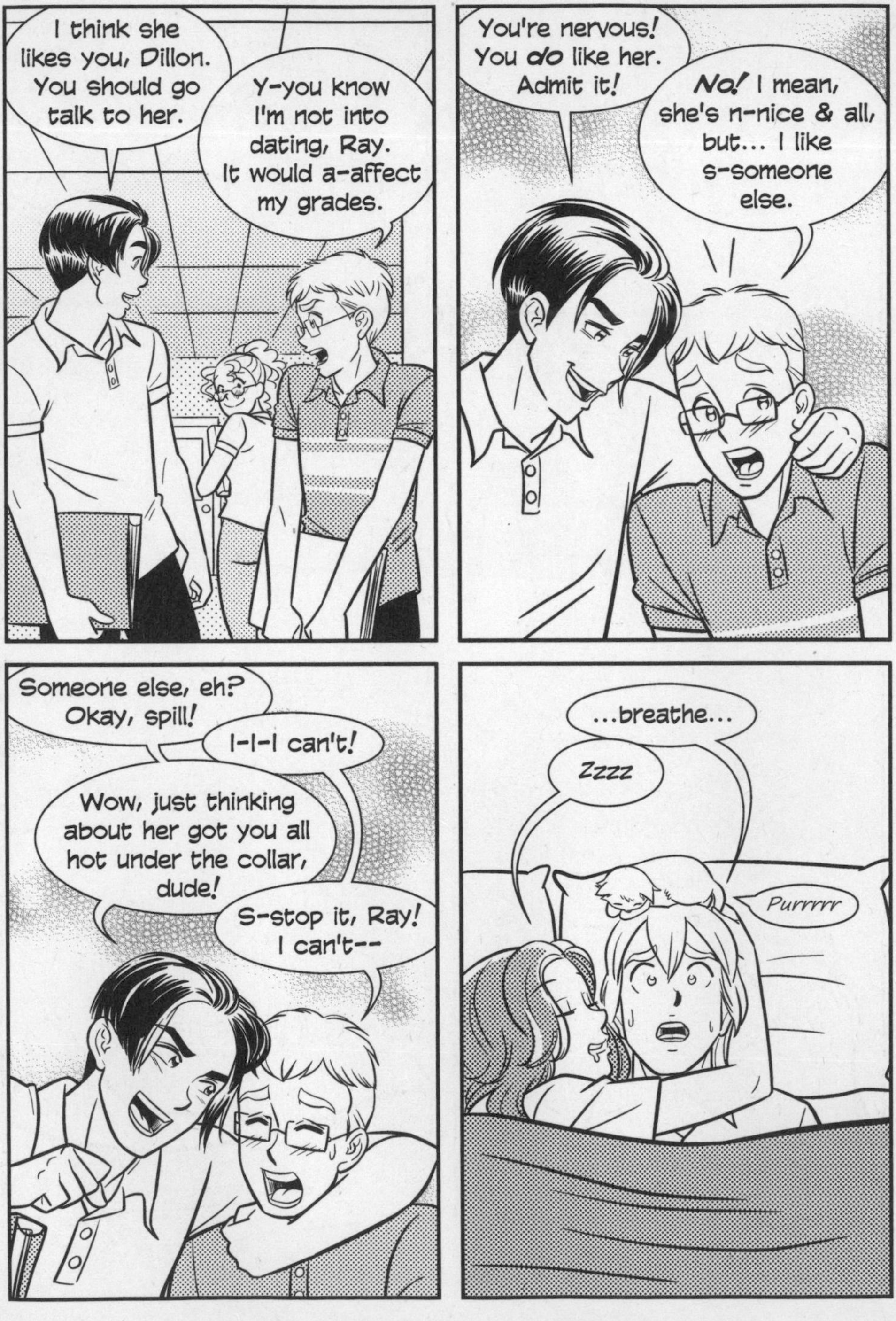
I think she likes you, Dillon. You should go talk to her.
Y-you know I'm not into dating, Ray. It would a-affect my grades.
You're nervous! You *do* like her. Admit it!
No! I mean, she's n-nice & all, but... I like s-someone else.
Someone else, eh? Okay, spill!
I-I-I can't!
Wow, just thinking about her got you all hot under the collar, dude!
S-stop it, Ray! I can't--
...breathe...
Zzzz
Purrrrr

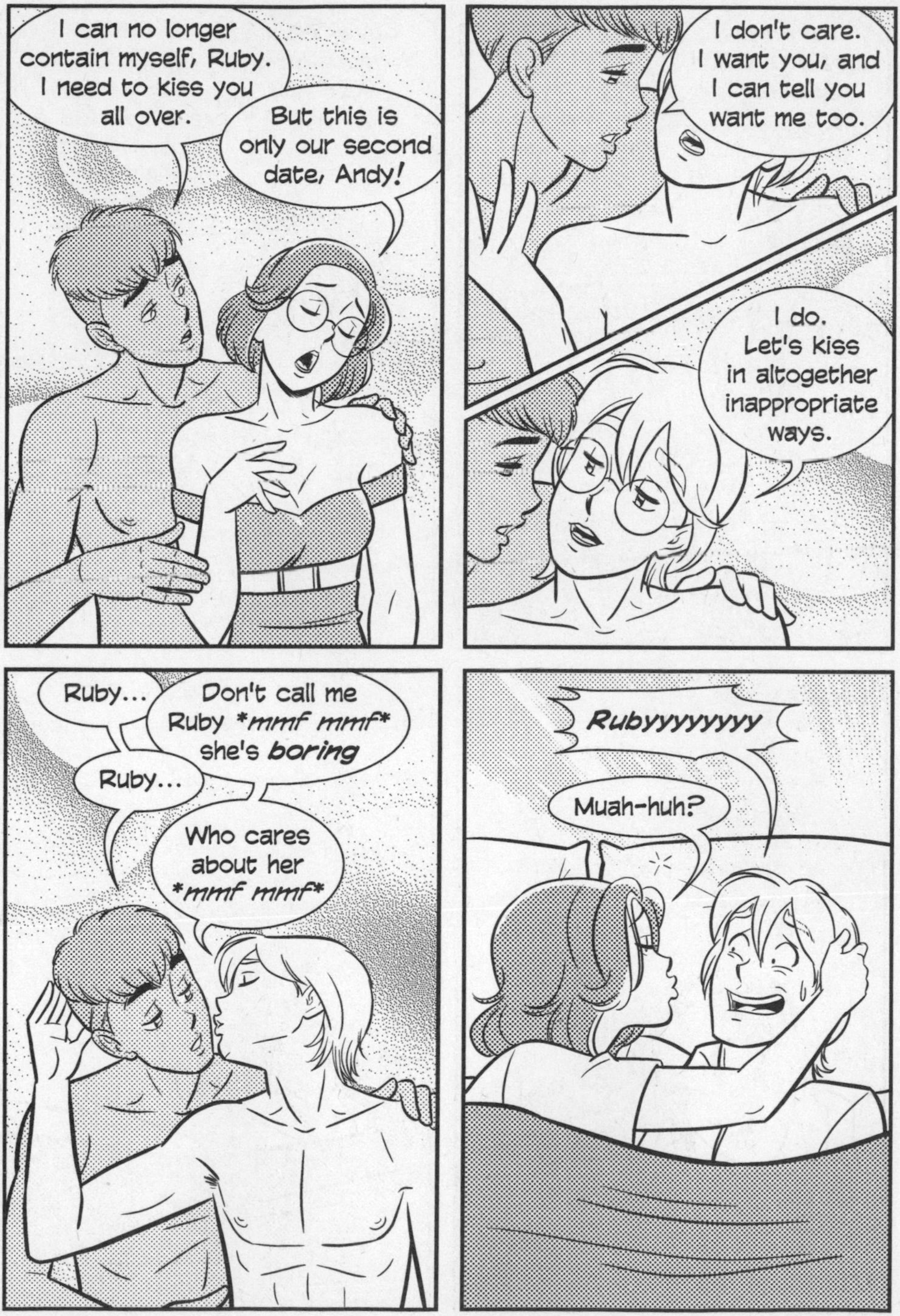
I can no longer contain myself, Ruby. I need to kiss you all over.
But this is only our second date, Andy!
I don't care. I want you, and I can tell you want me too.
I do. Let's kiss in altogether inappropriate ways.
Ruby...
Don't call me Ruby *mmf mmf* she's boring
Ruby...
Who cares about her *mmf mmf*
Rubyyyyyyyy
Muah-huh?

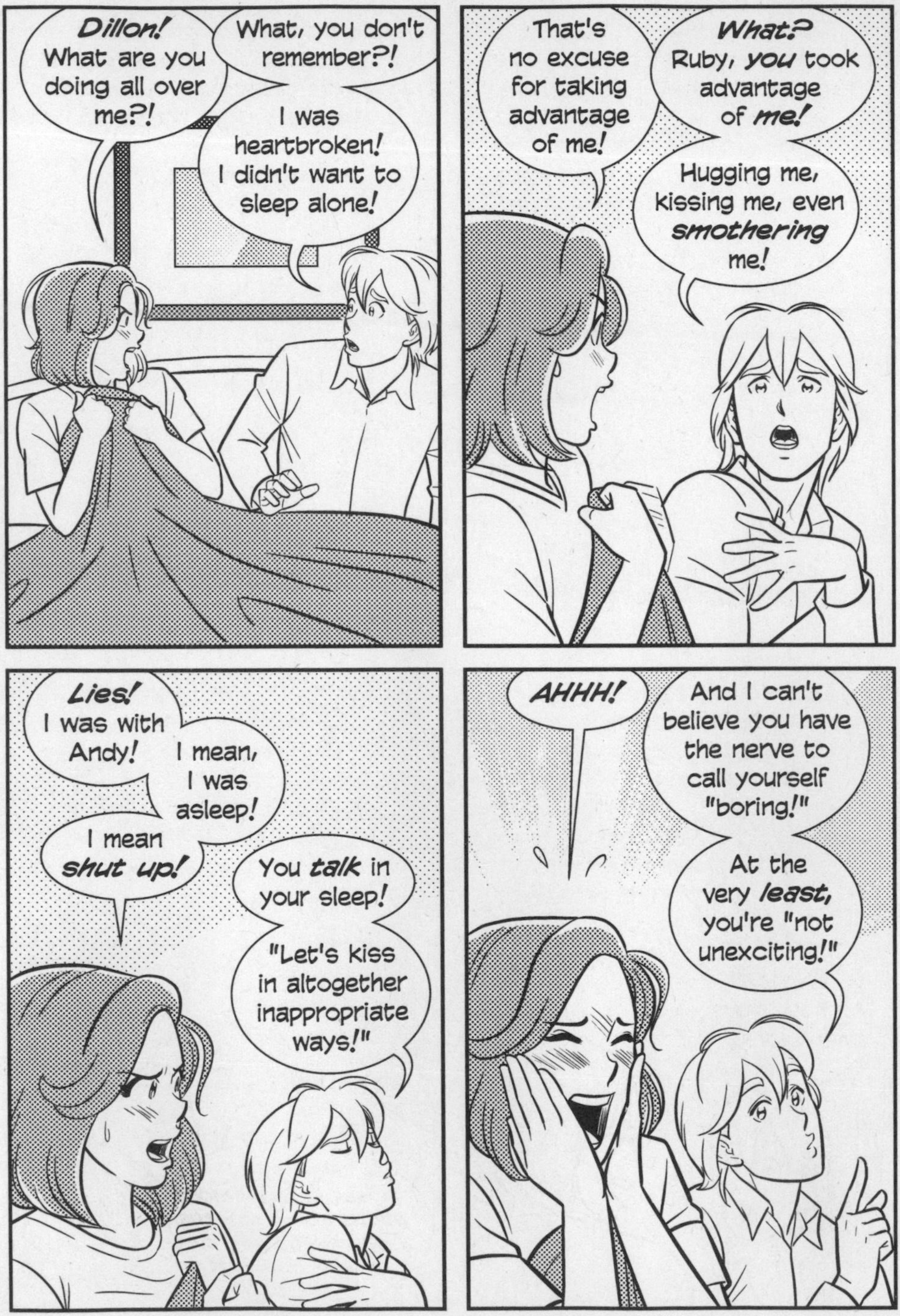
Dillon! What are you doing all over me?!
What, you don't remember?!
I was heartbroken! I didn't want to sleep alone!
That's no excuse for taking advantage of me!
What? Ruby, *you* took advantage of *me!*
Hugging me, kissing me, even *smothering* me!
Lies! I was with Andy!
I mean, I was asleep!
I mean *shut up!*
You *talk* in your sleep!
"Let's kiss in altogether inappropriate ways!"
AHHH!
And I can't believe you have the nerve to call yourself "boring!"
At the very *least,* you're "not unexciting!"

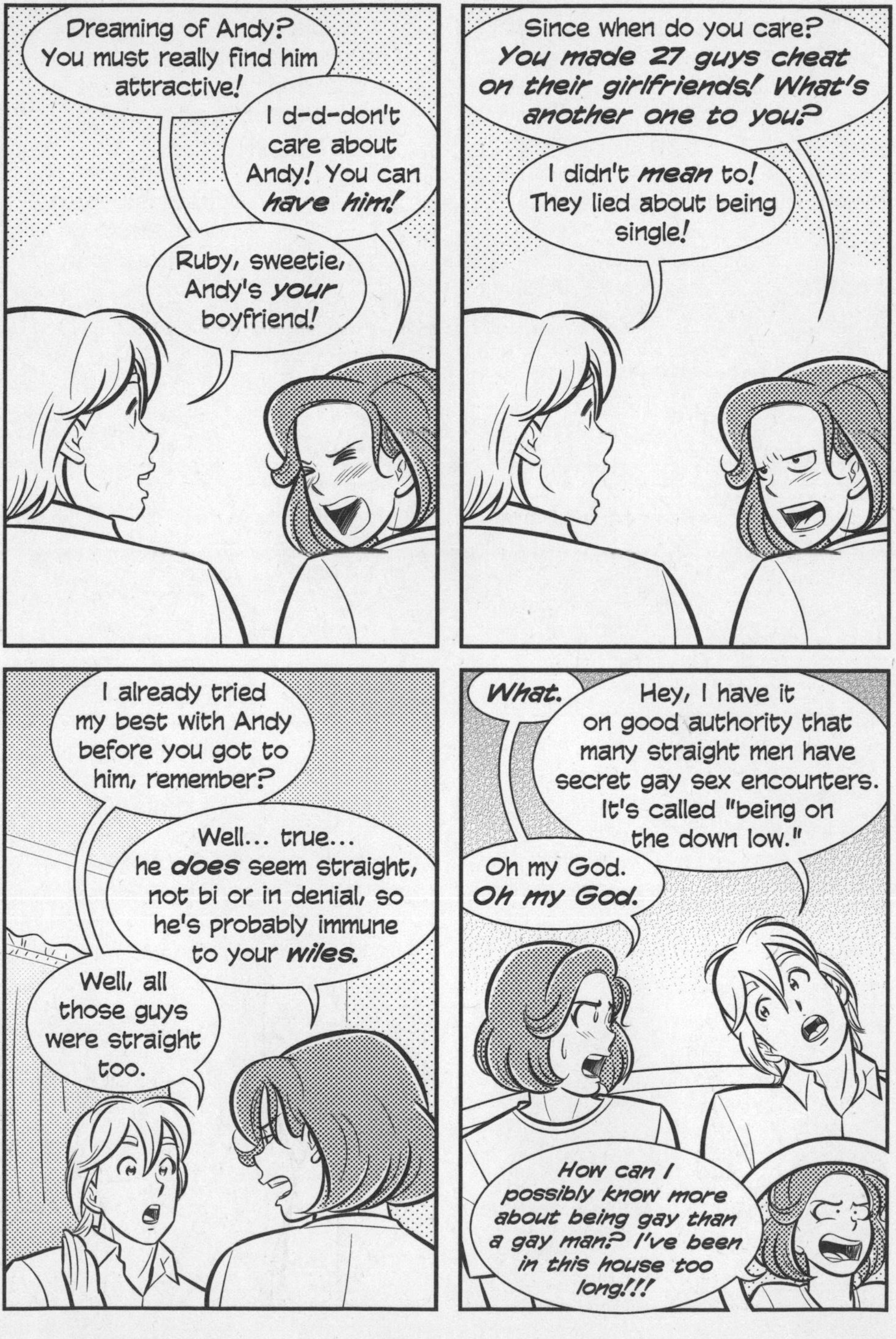
Dreaming of Andy? You must really find him attractive!
I d-d-don't care about Andy! You can *have him!*
Ruby, sweetie, Andy's *your* boyfriend!
Since when do you care? *You made 27 guys cheat on their girlfriends! What's another one to you?*
I didn't *mean* to! They lied about being single!
I already tried my best with Andy before you got to him, remember?
Well... true... he *does* seem straight, not bi or in denial, so he's probably immune to your *wiles.*
Well, all those guys were straight too.
What.
Hey, I have it on good authority that many straight men have secret gay sex encounters. It's called "being on the down low."
Oh my God. *Oh my God.*
How can I possibly know more about being gay than a gay man? I've been in this house too long!!!

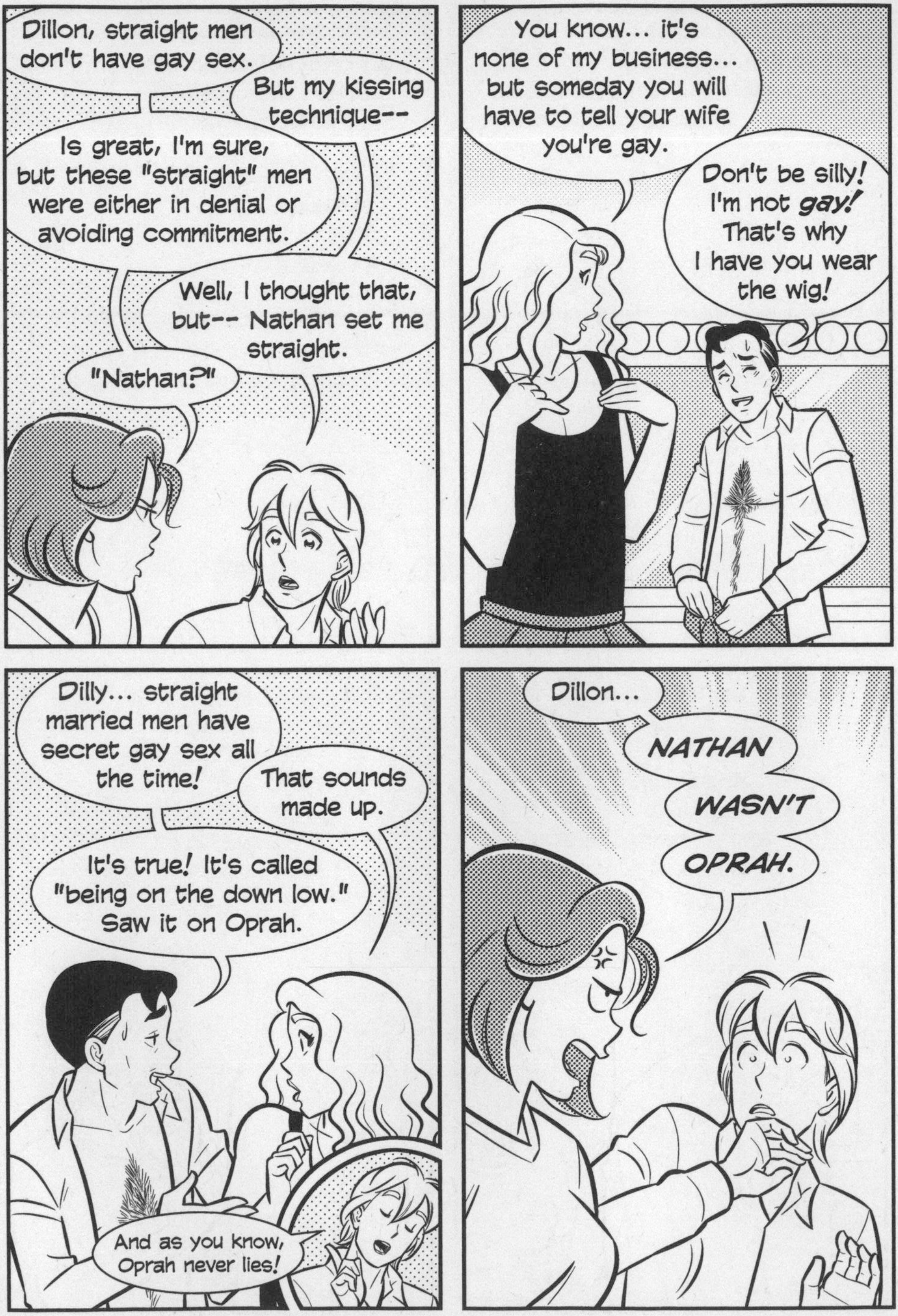
Dillon, straight men don't have gay sex.
But my kissing technique--
Is great, I'm sure, but these "straight" men were either in denial or avoiding commitment.
Well, I thought that, but-- Nathan set me straight.
"Nathan?"
You know... it's none of my business... but someday you will have to tell your wife you're gay.
Don't be silly! I'm not gay! That's why I have you wear the wig!
Dilly... straight married men have secret gay sex all the time!
That sounds made up.
It's true! It's called "being on the down low." Saw it on Oprah.
And as you know, Oprah never lies!
Dillon...
NATHAN
WASN'T
OPRAH.

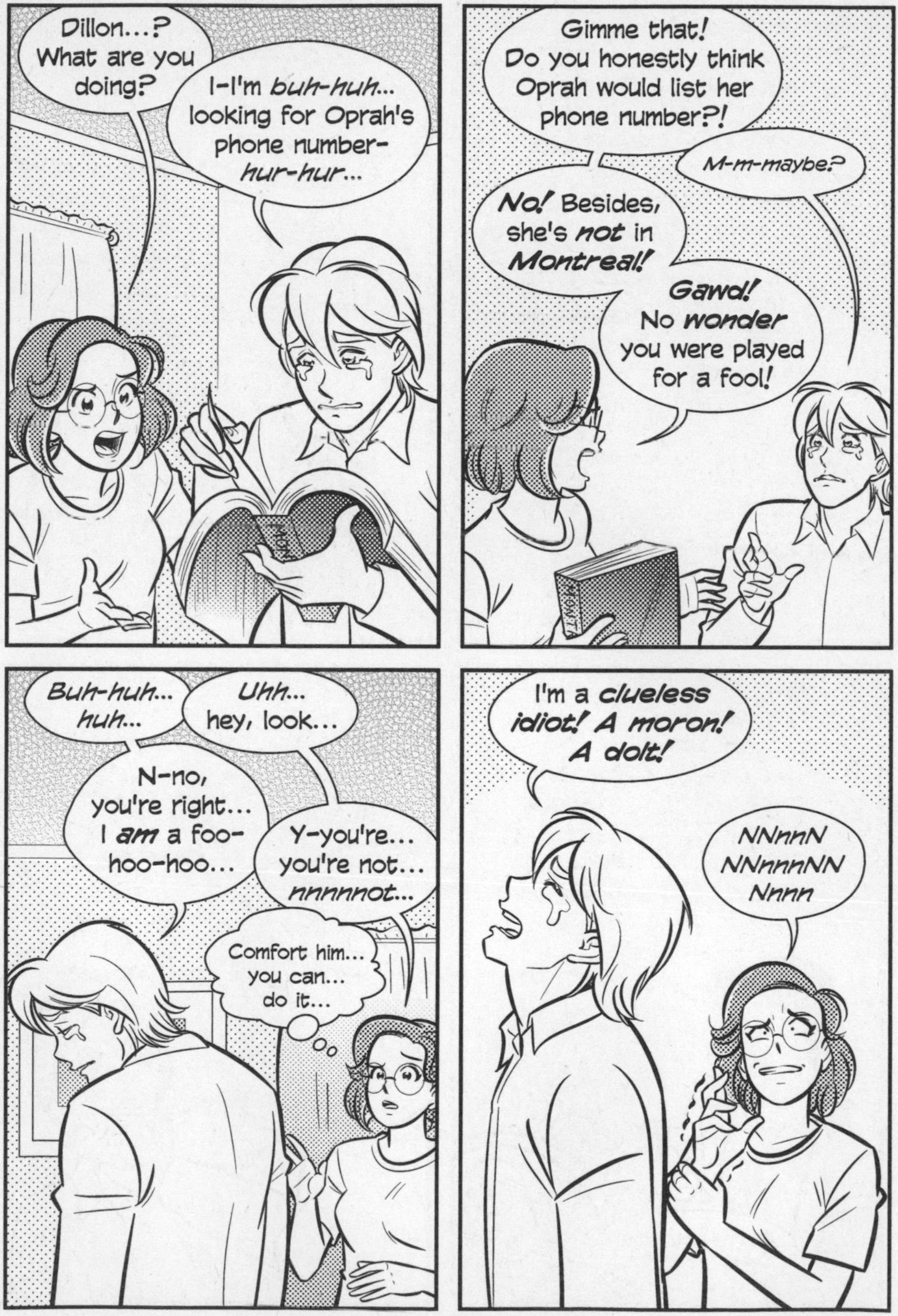
Dillon...? What are you doing?
I-I'm buh-huh... looking for Oprah's phone number-hur-hur...
Gimme that! Do you honestly think Oprah would list her phone number?!
M-m-maybe?
No! Besides, she's not in Montreal!
Gawd! No wonder you were played for a fool!
Buh-huh... huh...
Uhh... hey, look...
N-no, you're right... I am a foo-hoo-hoo...
Y-you're... you're not... nnnnnot...
Comfort him... you can... do it...
I'm a clueless idiot! A moron! A dolt!
NNnnN NNnnnNN Nnnn

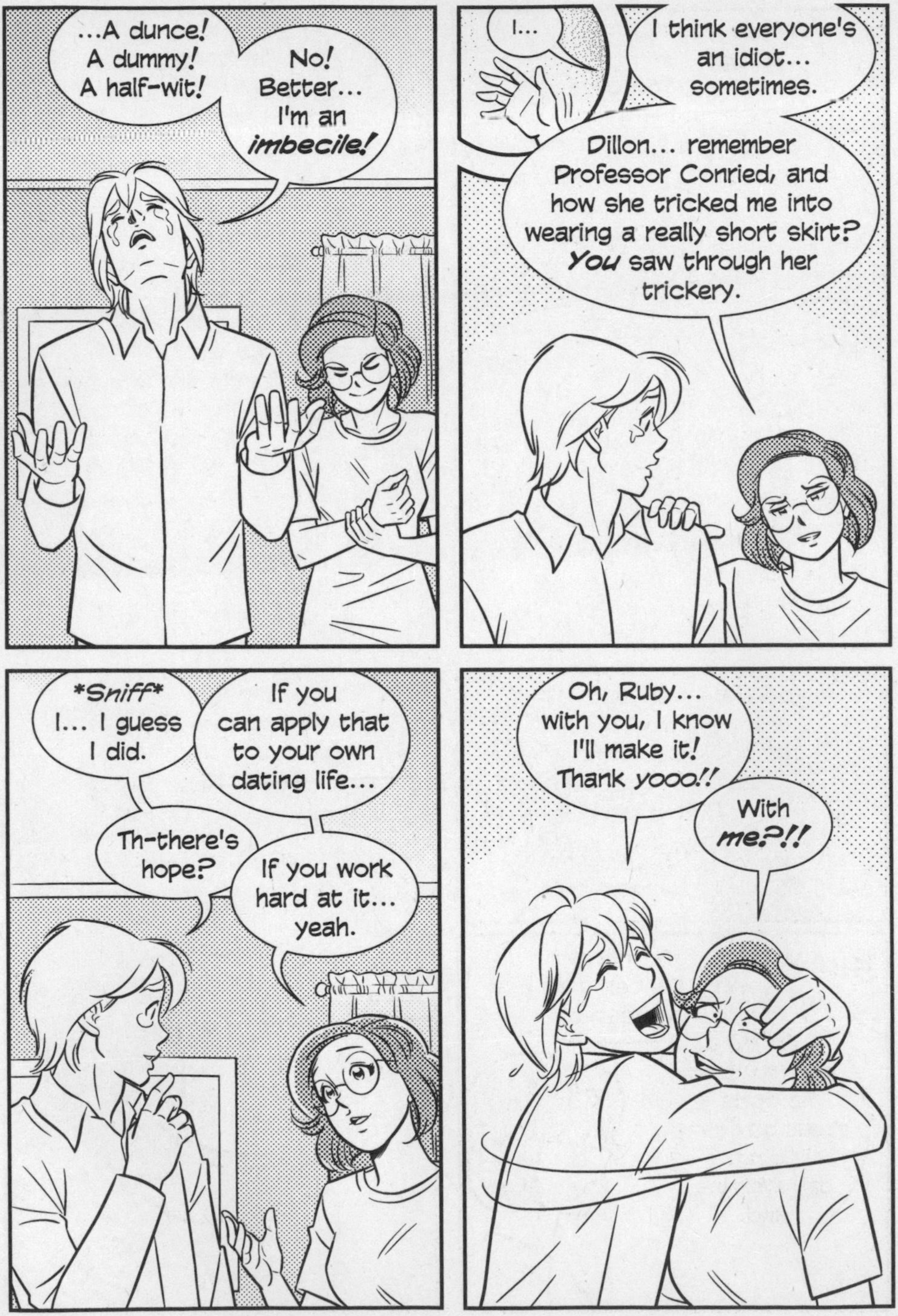
...A dunce! A dummy! A half-wit!
No! Better... I'm an *imbecile!*
I...
I think everyone's an idiot... sometimes.
Dillon... remember Professor Conried, and how she tricked me into wearing a really short skirt? ***You*** saw through her trickery.
Sniff I... I guess I did.
If you can apply that to your own dating life...
Th-there's hope?
If you work hard at it... yeah.
Oh, Ruby... with you, I know I'll make it! Thank *yooo!!*
With ***me?!!***

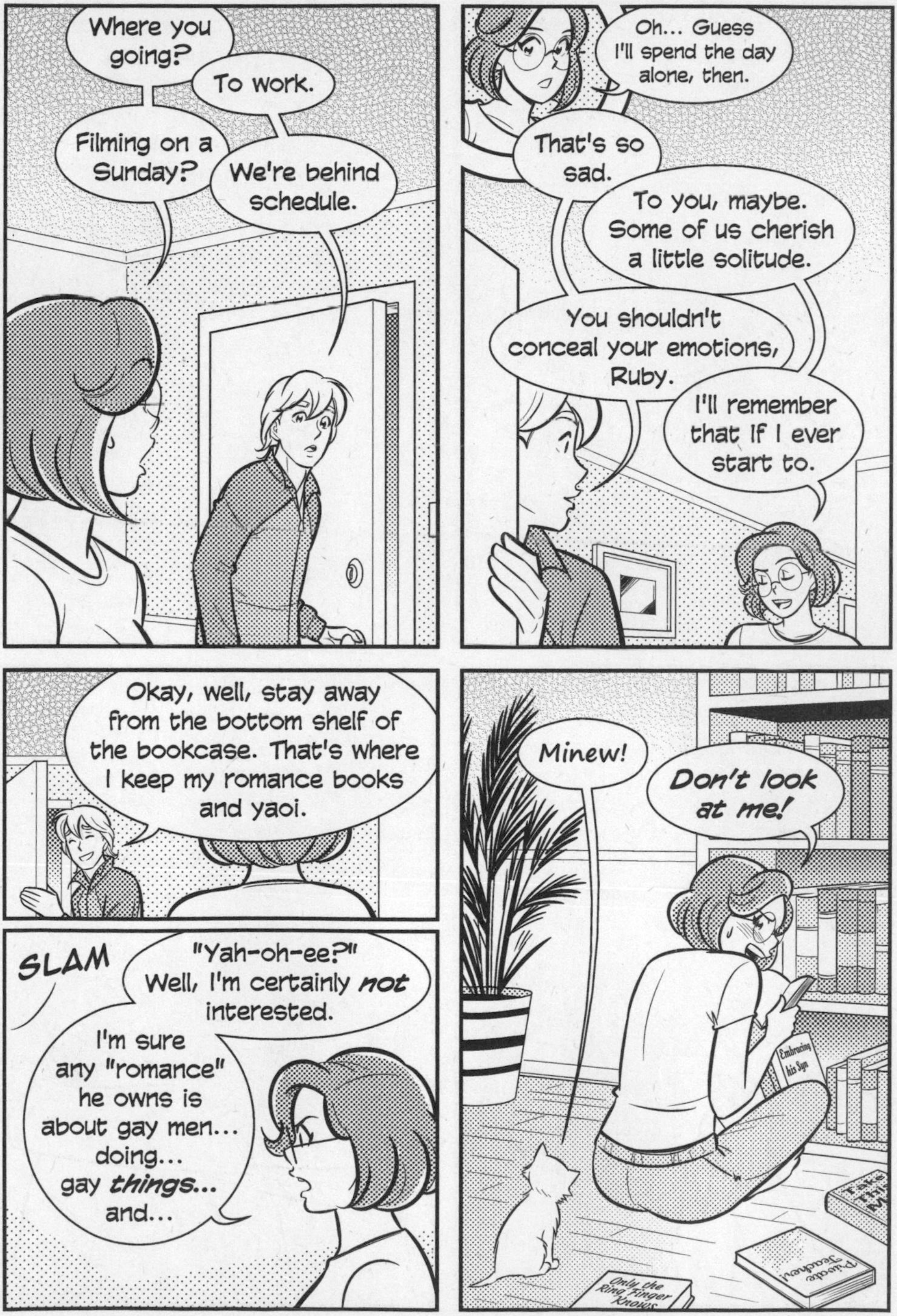
Where you going?
To work.
Filming on a Sunday?
We're behind schedule.
Oh... Guess I'll spend the day alone, then.
That's so sad.
To you, maybe. Some of us cherish a little solitude.
You shouldn't conceal your emotions, Ruby.
I'll remember that if I ever start to.
Okay, well, stay away from the bottom shelf of the bookcase. That's where I keep my romance books and yaoi.
SLAM
"Yah-oh-ee?" Well, I'm certainly *not* interested.
I'm sure any "romance" he owns is about gay men... doing... gay *things*... and...
Minew!
Don't look at me!

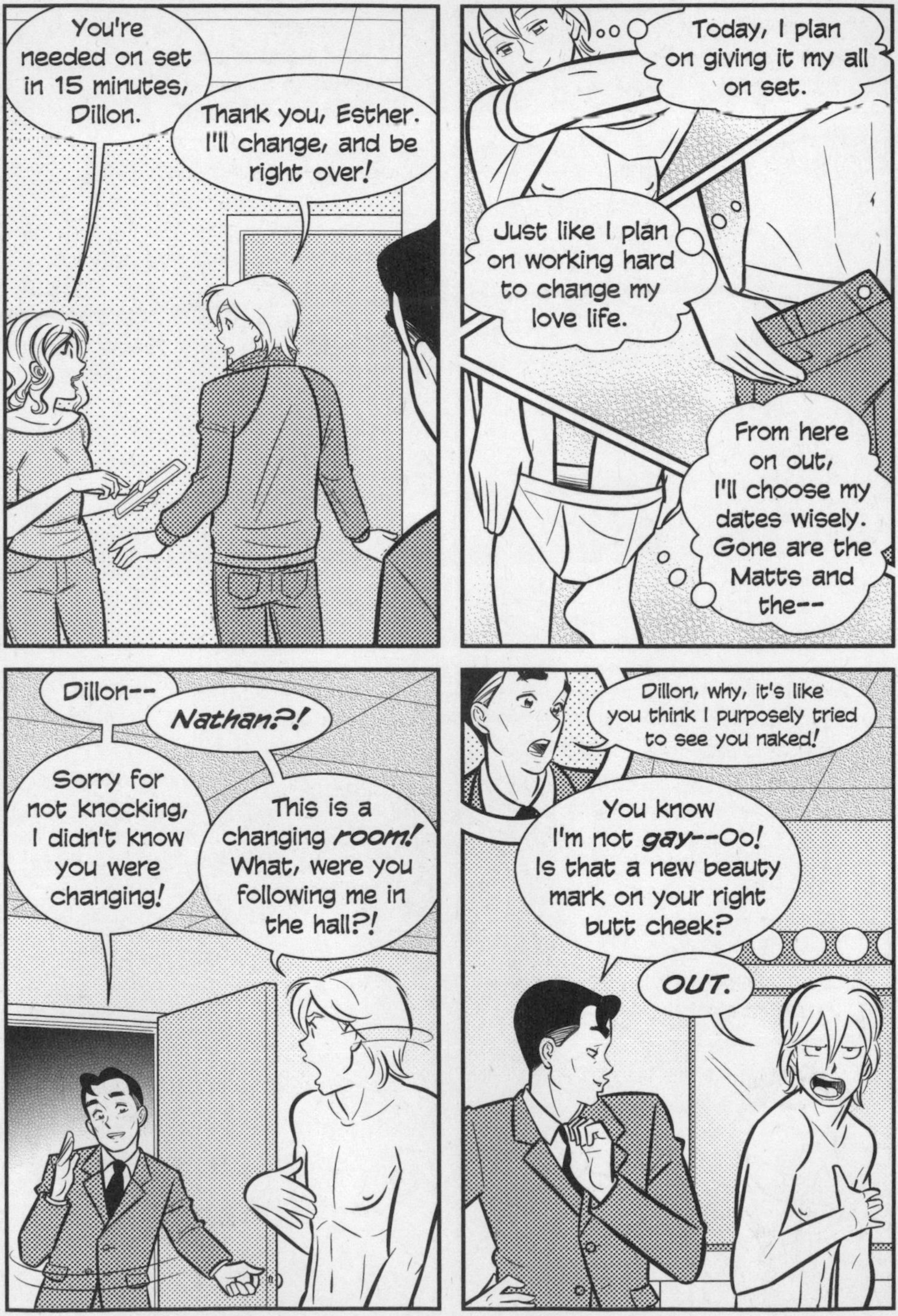
You're needed on set in 15 minutes, Dillon.
Thank you, Esther. I'll change, and be right over!
Today, I plan on giving it my all on set.
Just like I plan on working hard to change my love life.
From here on out, I'll choose my dates wisely. Gone are the Matts and the--
Dillon--
Nathan?!
Sorry for not knocking, I didn't know you were changing!
This is a changing room! What, were you following me in the hall?!
Dillon, why, it's like you think I purposely tried to see you naked!
You know I'm not gay--Oo! Is that a new beauty mark on your right butt cheek?
OUT.

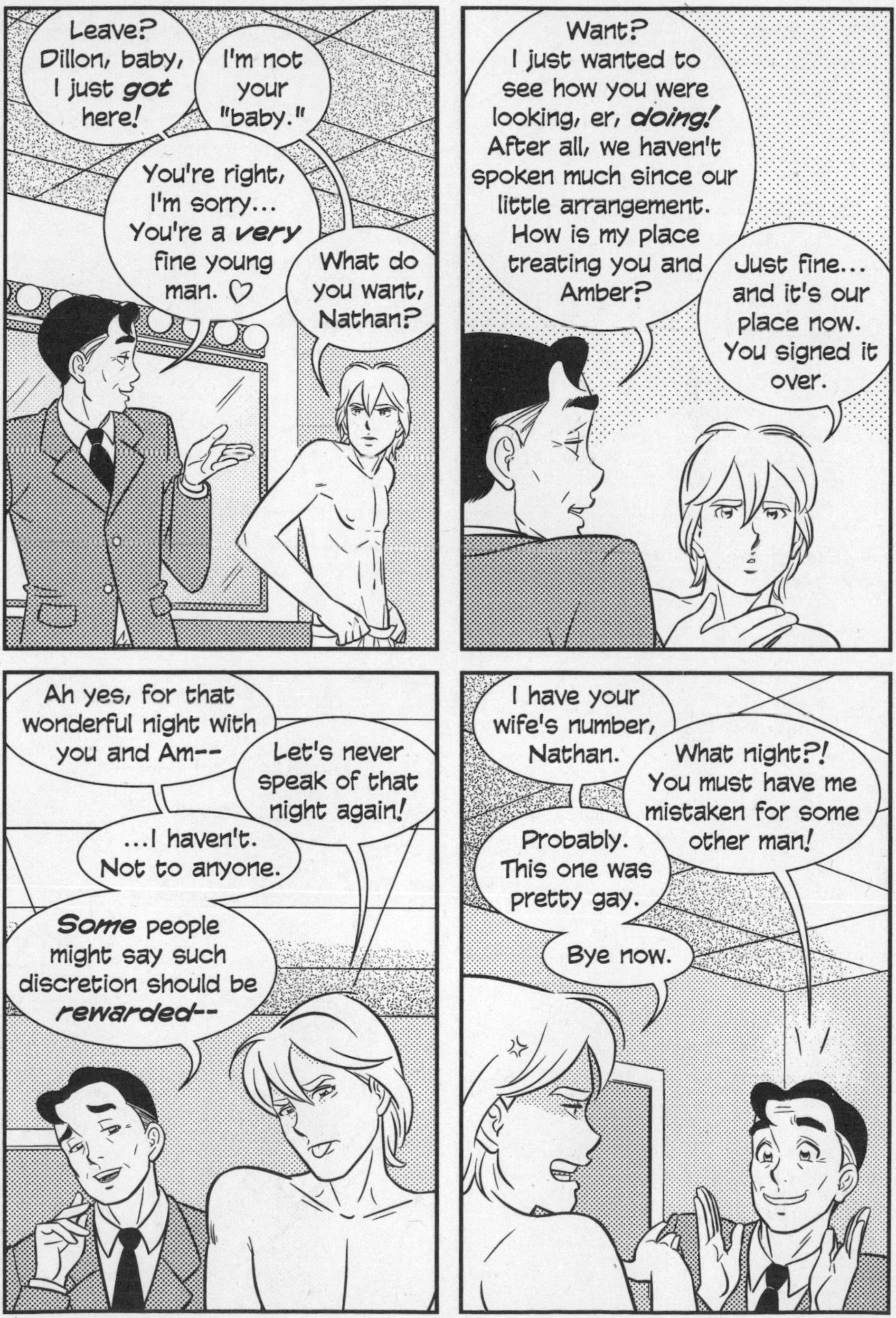
Leave? Dillon, baby, I just *got* here!
I'm not your "baby."
You're right, I'm sorry... You're a *very* fine young man. ♡
What do you want, Nathan?
Want? I just wanted to see how you were looking, er, *doing!* After all, we haven't spoken much since our little arrangement. How is my place treating you and Amber?
Just fine... and it's our place now. You signed it over.
Ah yes, for that wonderful night with you and Am--
Let's never speak of that night again!
...I haven't. Not to anyone.
Some people might say such discretion should be *rewarded*--
I have your wife's number, Nathan.
What night?! You must have me mistaken for some other man!
Probably. This one was pretty gay.
Bye now.

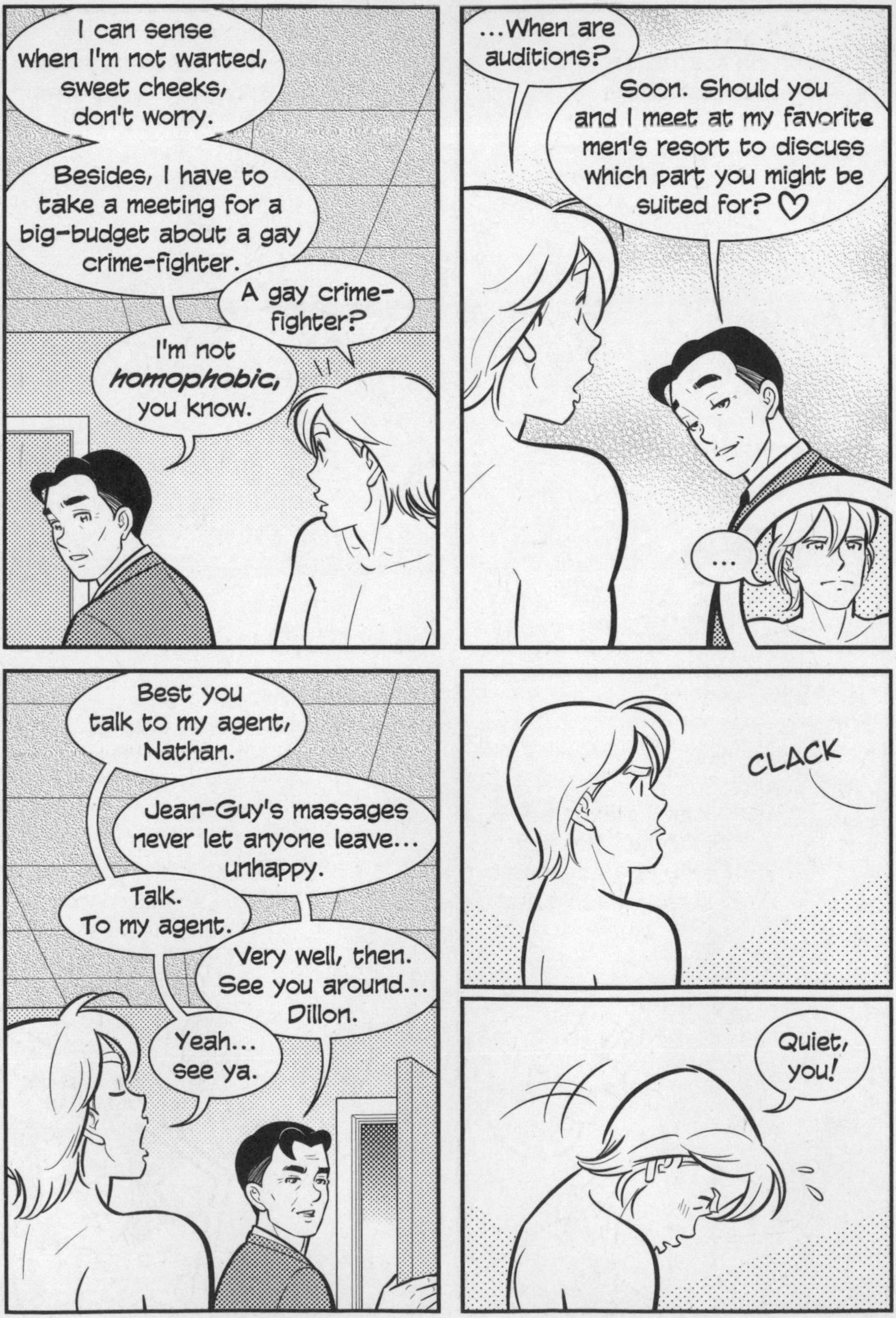

I can sense when I'm not wanted, sweet cheeks, don't worry.
Besides, I have to take a meeting for a big-budget about a gay crime-fighter.
A gay crime-fighter?
I'm not *homophobic,* you know.
...When are auditions?
Soon. Should you and I meet at my favorite men's resort to discuss which part you might be suited for? ♡
...
Best you talk to my agent, Nathan.
Jean-Guy's massages never let anyone leave... unhappy.
Talk. To my agent.
Very well, then. See you around... Dillon.
Yeah... see ya.
CLACK
Quiet, you!

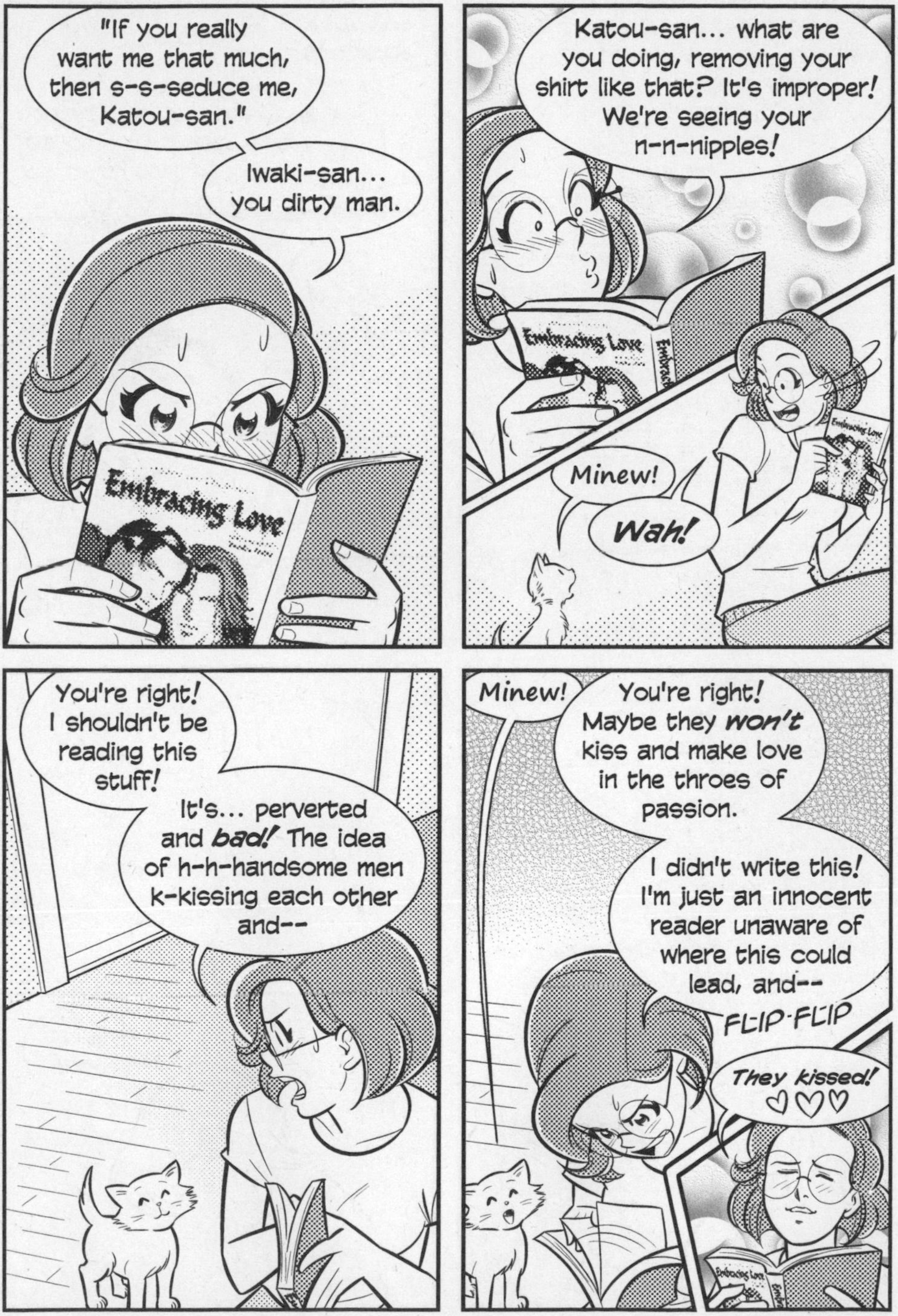
"If you really want me that much, then s-s-seduce me, Katou-san."
Iwaki-san... you dirty man.
Embracing Love
Katou-san... what are you doing, removing your shirt like that? It's improper! We're seeing your n-n-nipples!
Embracing Love
Embracing Love
Minew!
Wah!
You're right! I shouldn't be reading this stuff!
It's... perverted and bad! The idea of h-h-handsome men k-kissing each other and--
Minew!
You're right! Maybe they won't kiss and make love in the throes of passion.
I didn't write this! I'm just an innocent reader unaware of where this could lead, and--
FLIP FLIP
They kissed! ♡♡♡
Embracing Love

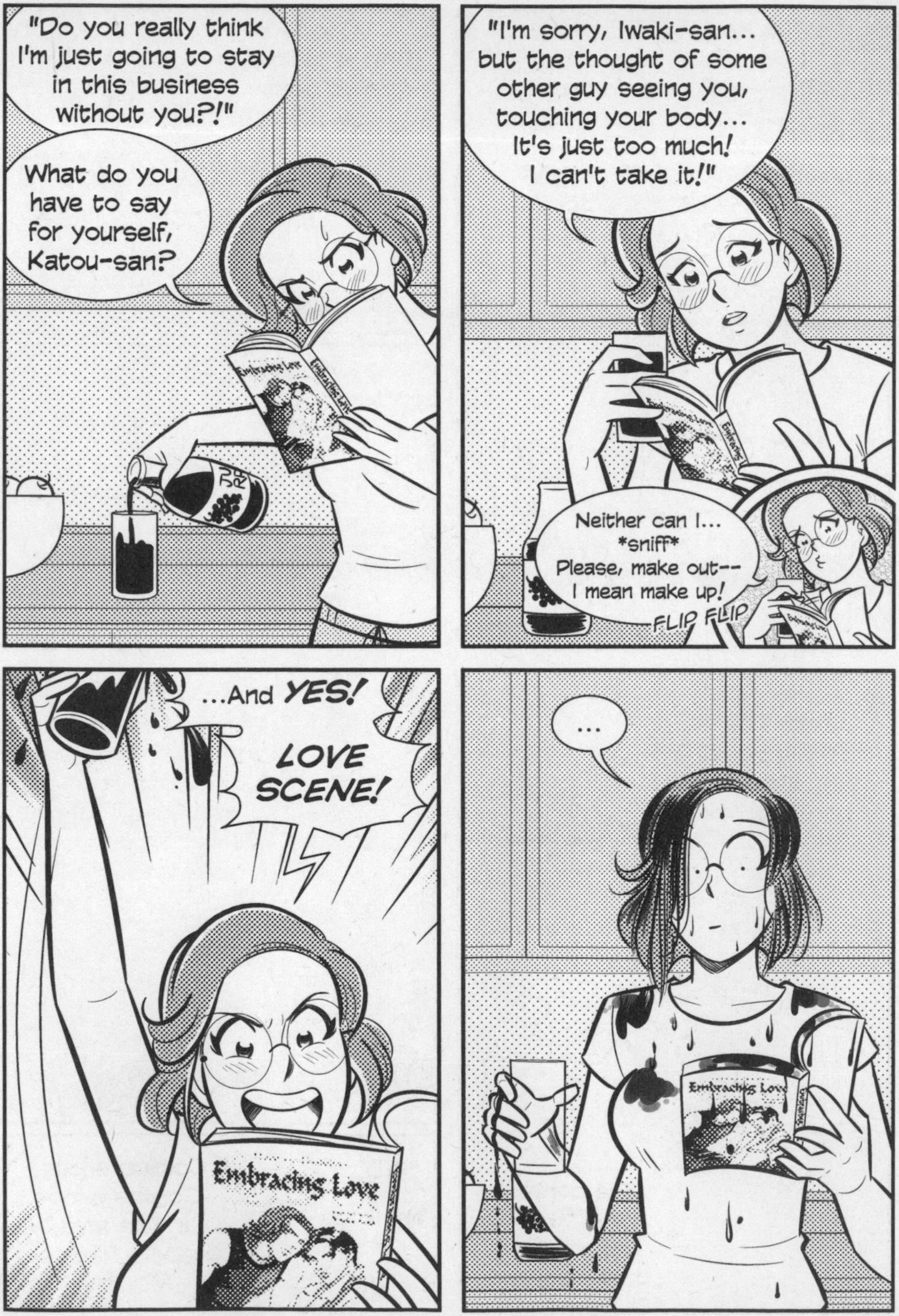
"Do you really think I'm just going to stay in this business without you?!"
What do you have to say for yourself, Katou-san?
Embracing Love
"I'm sorry, Iwaki-san... but the thought of some other guy seeing you, touching your body... It's just too much! I can't take it!"
Neither can I... *sniff* Please, make out-- I mean make up!
FLIP FLIP
...And YES!
LOVE SCENE!
Embracing Love
...
Embracing Love

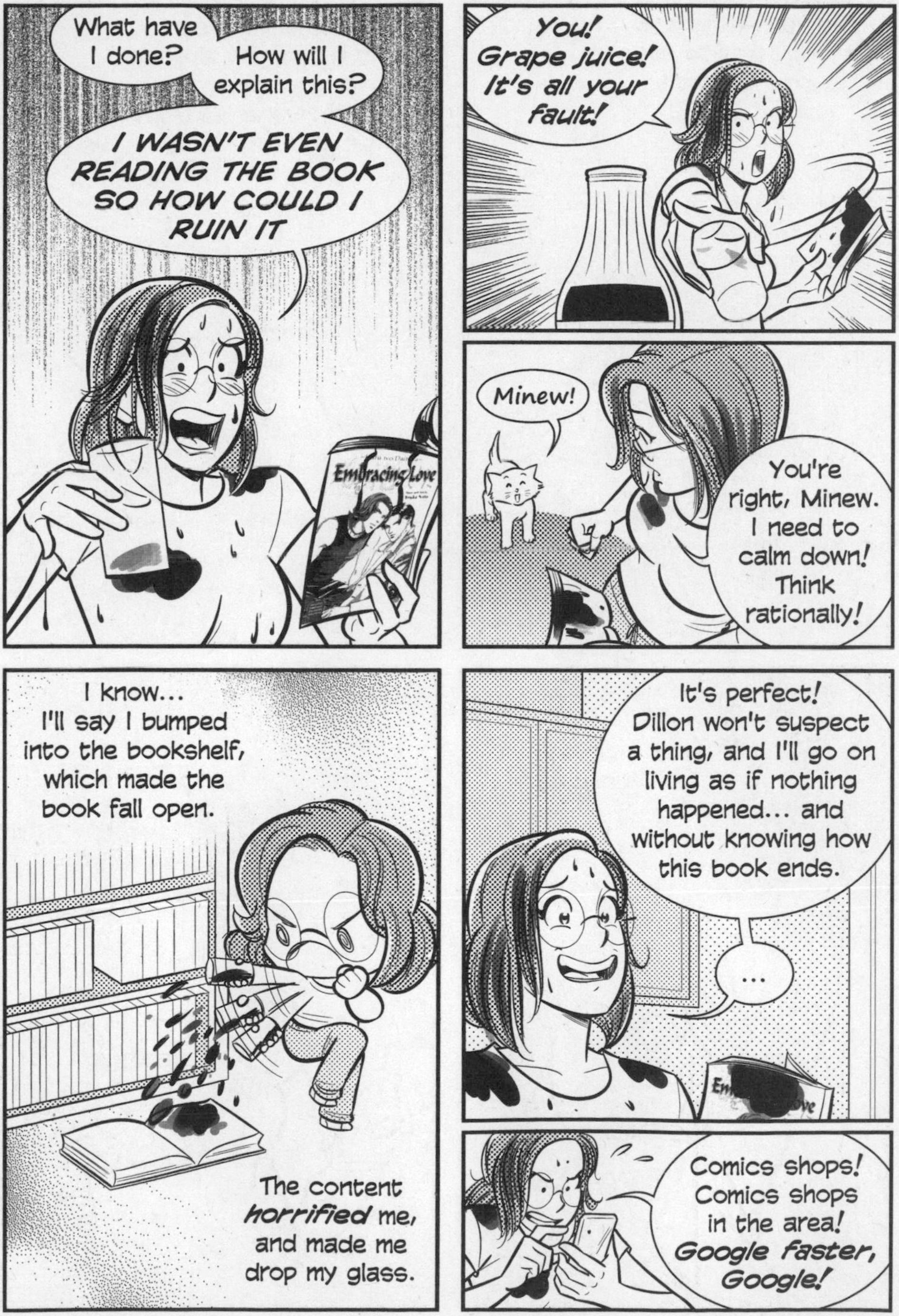
What have I done?
How will I explain this?
I WASN'T EVEN READING THE BOOK SO HOW COULD I RUIN IT
Embracing Love
You! Grape juice! It's all your fault!
Minew!
You're right, Minew. I need to calm down! Think rationally!
I know... I'll say I bumped into the bookshelf, which made the book fall open.
The content *horrified* me, and made me drop my glass.
It's perfect! Dillon won't suspect a thing, and I'll go on living as if nothing happened... and without knowing how this book ends.
...
Comics shops! Comics shops in the area! Google faster, Google!

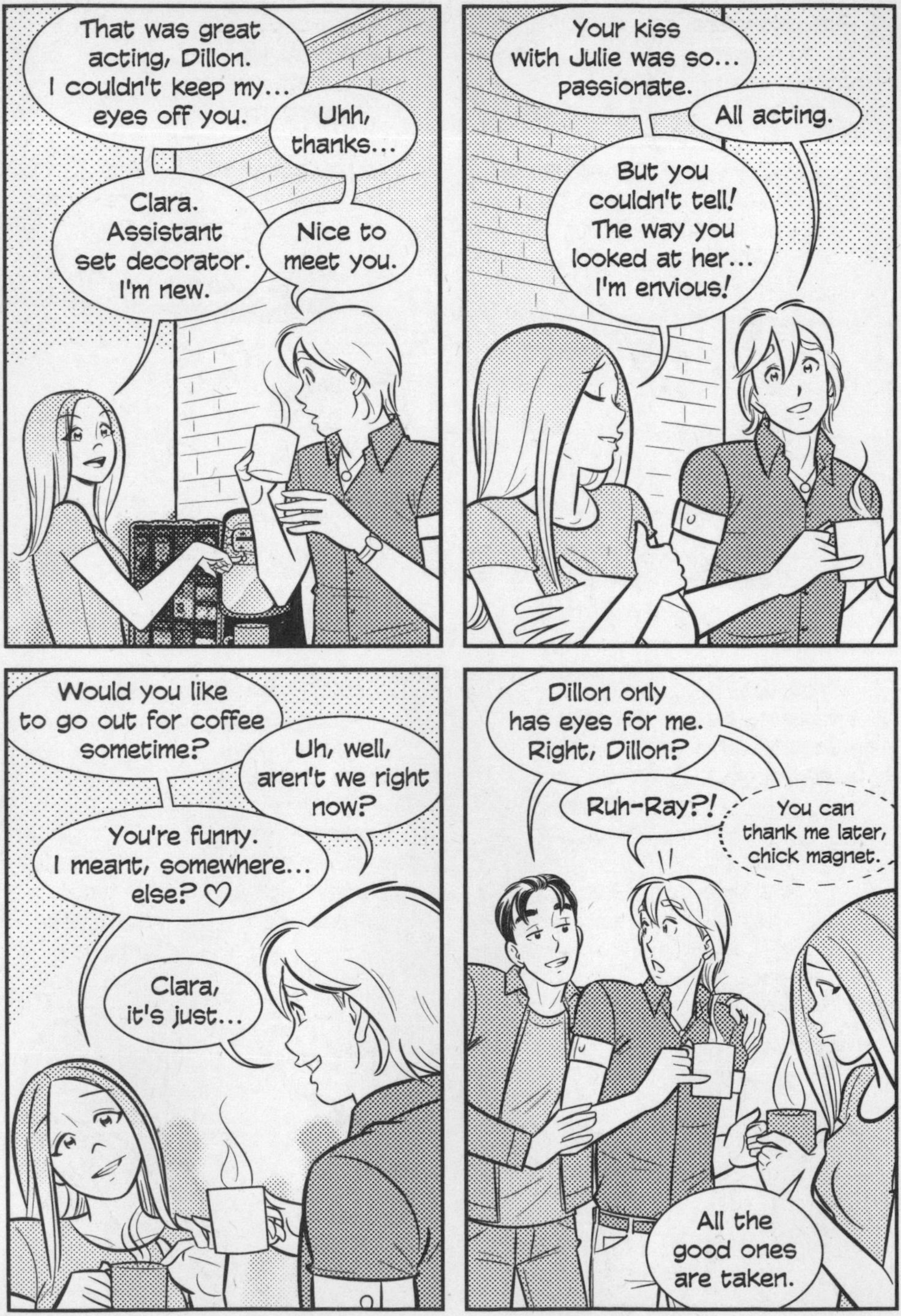
That was great acting, Dillon. I couldn't keep my... eyes off you.
Uhh, thanks...
Clara. Assistant set decorator. I'm new.
Nice to meet you.
Your kiss with Julie was so... passionate.
All acting.
But you couldn't tell! The way you looked at her... I'm envious!
Would you like to go out for coffee sometime?
Uh, well, aren't we right now?
You're funny. I meant, somewhere... else? ♡
Clara, it's just...
Dillon only has eyes for me. Right, Dillon?
Ruh-Ray?!
You can thank me later, chick magnet.
All the good ones are taken.

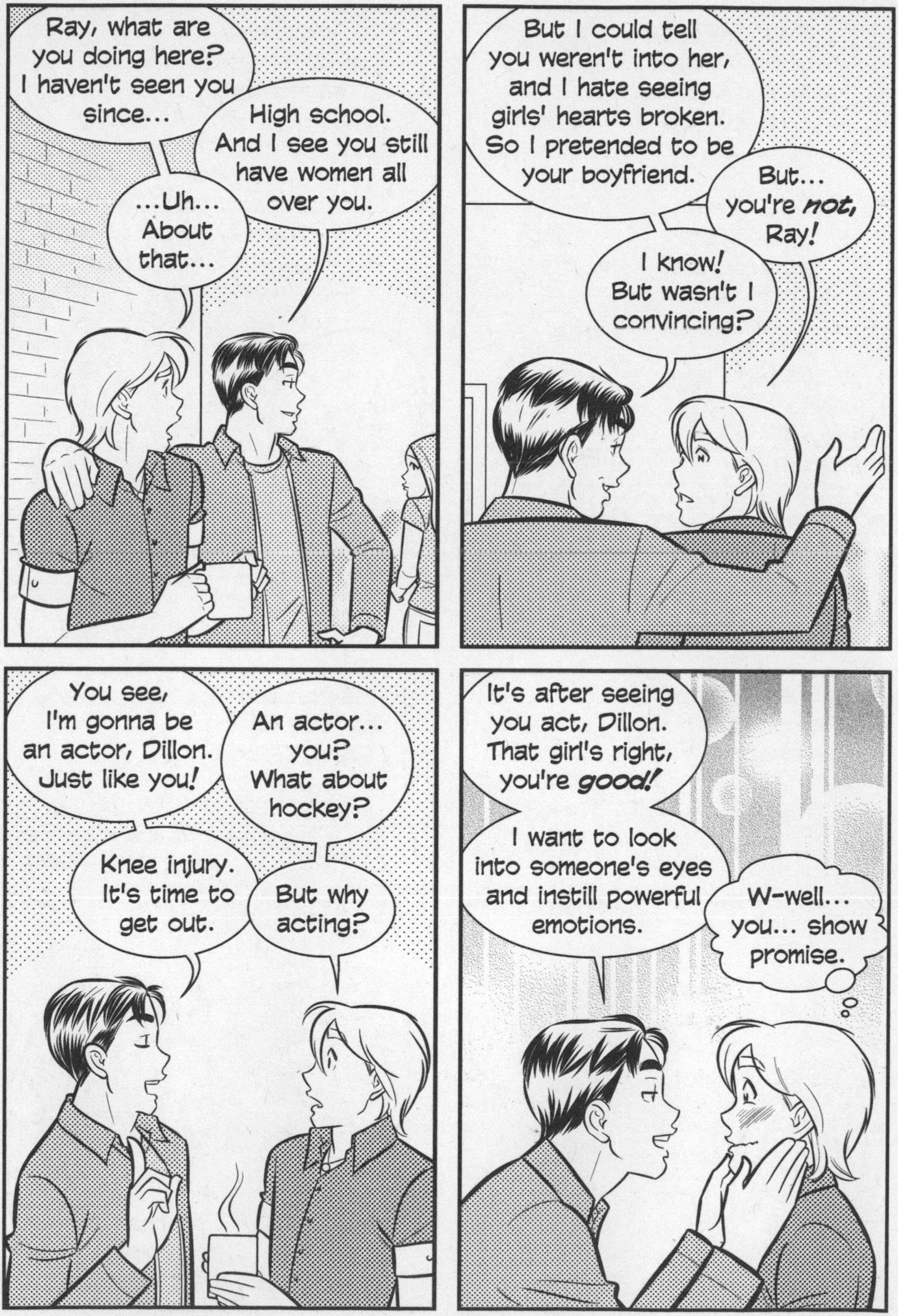
Ray, what are you doing here? I haven't seen you since...
High school. And I see you still have women all over you.
...Uh... About that...
But I could tell you weren't into her, and I hate seeing girls' hearts broken. So I pretended to be your boyfriend.
But... you're *not*, Ray!
I know! But wasn't I convincing?
You see, I'm gonna be an actor, Dillon. Just like you!
An actor... you? What about hockey?
Knee injury. It's time to get out.
But why acting?
It's after seeing you act, Dillon. That girl's right, you're *good!*
I want to look into someone's eyes and instill powerful emotions.
W-well... you... show promise.

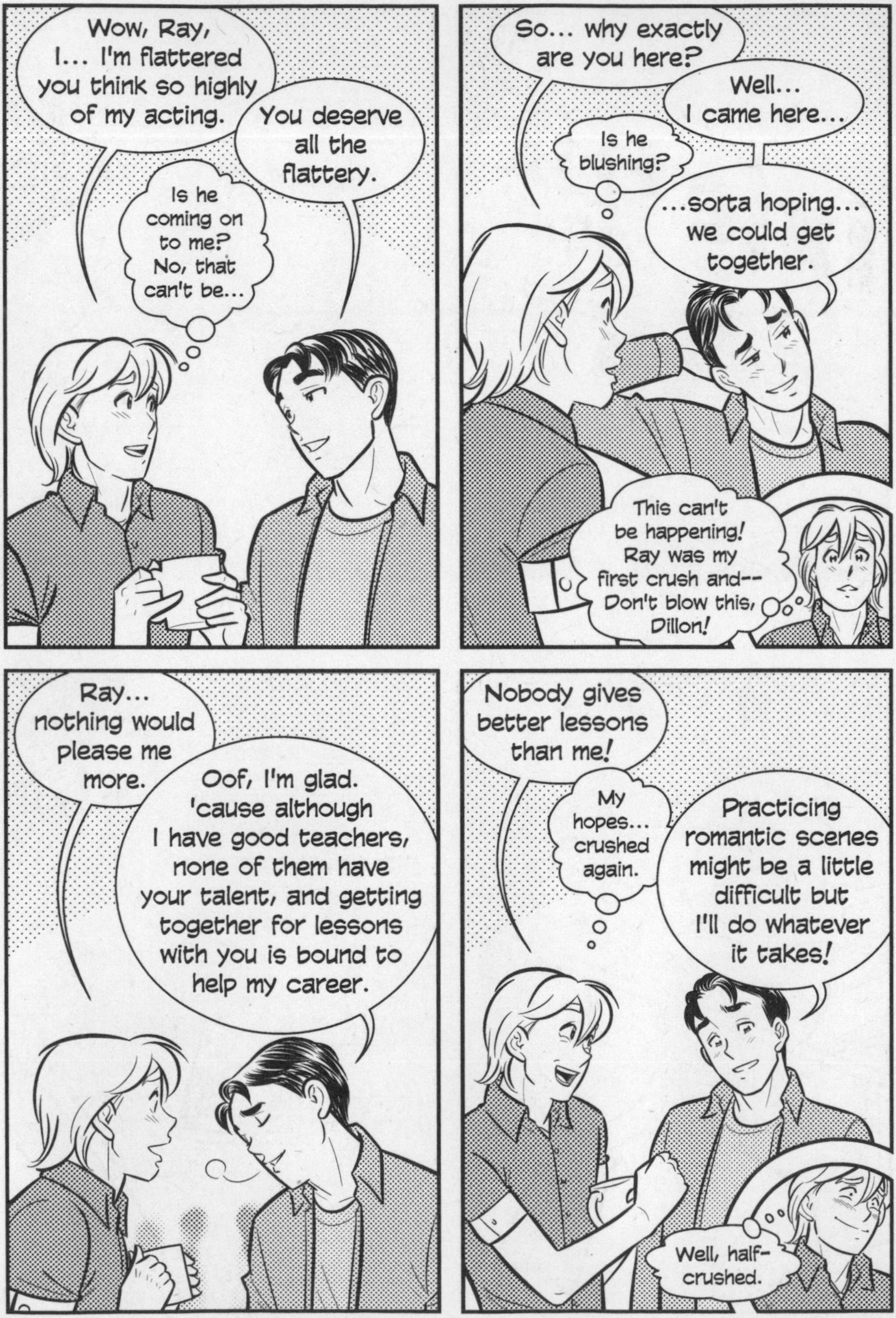

Wow, Ray, I... I'm flattered you think so highly of my acting.
Is he coming on to me? No, that can't be...
You deserve all the flattery.
So... why exactly are you here?
Well... I came here...
Is he blushing?
...sorta hoping... we could get together.
This can't be happening! Ray was my first crush and-- Don't blow this, Dillon!
Ray... nothing would please me more.
Oof, I'm glad. 'cause although I have good teachers, none of them have your talent, and getting together for lessons with you is bound to help my career.
Nobody gives better lessons than me!
My hopes... crushed again.
Practicing romantic scenes might be a little difficult but I'll do whatever it takes!
Well, half-crushed.

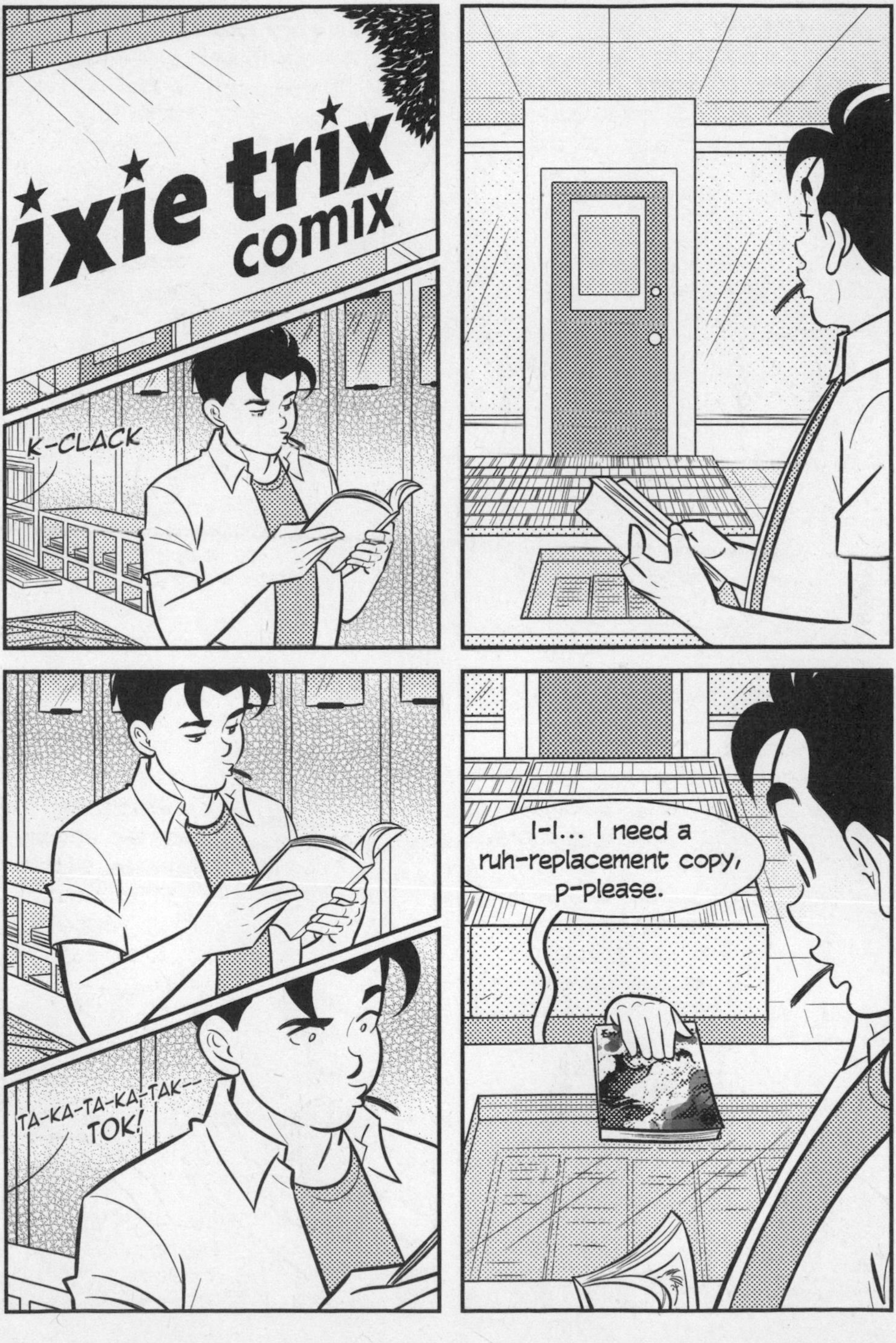
ixie trix comix
K-CLACK
TA-KA-TA-KA-TAK--
TOK!
I-I... I need a ruh-replacement copy, p-please.

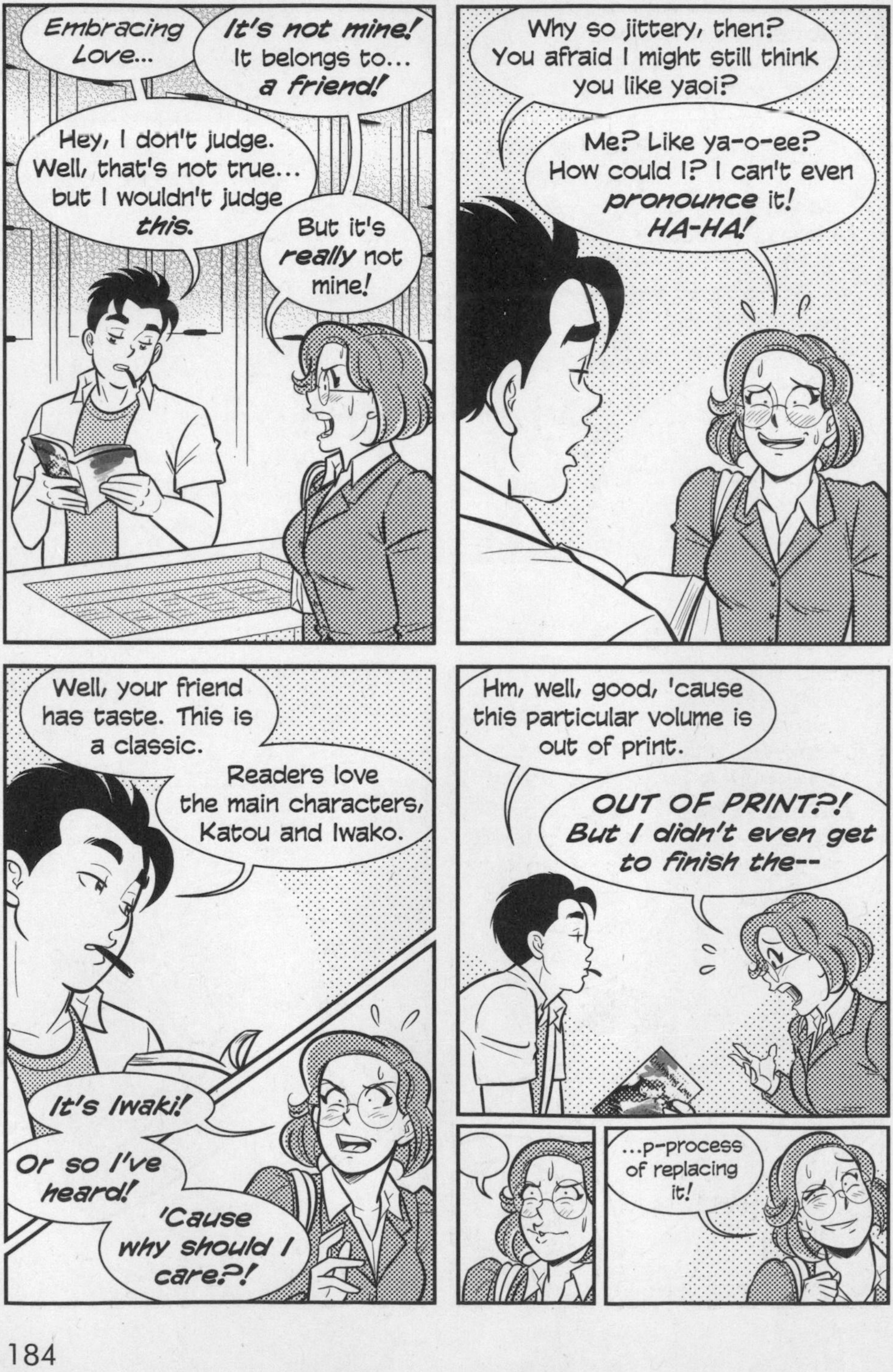
Embracing Love...
It's not mine! It belongs to... a friend!
Hey, I don't judge. Well, that's not true... but I wouldn't judge this.
But it's really not mine!
Why so jittery, then? You afraid I might still think you like yaoi?
Me? Like ya-o-ee? How could I? I can't even pronounce it! HA-HA!
Well, your friend has taste. This is a classic.
Readers love the main characters, Katou and Iwako.
It's Iwaki!
Or so I've heard!
'Cause why should I care?!
Hm, well, good, 'cause this particular volume is out of print.
OUT OF PRINT?! But I didn't even get to finish the--
...p-process of replacing it!

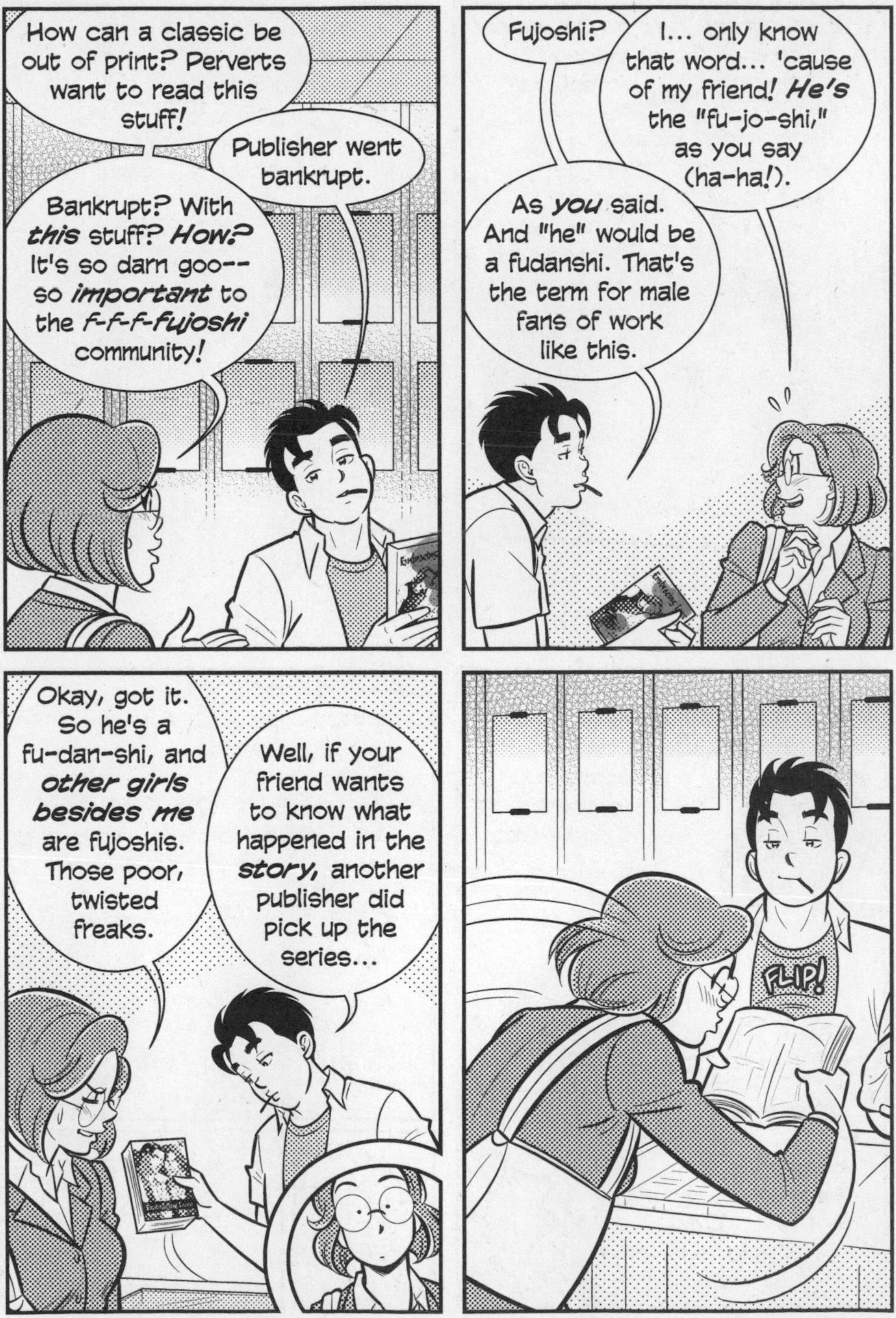
How can a classic be out of print? Perverts want to read this stuff!
Publisher went bankrupt.
Bankrupt? With this stuff? How? It's so darn goo-- so important to the f-f-f-fujoshi community!
Fujoshi?
I... only know that word... 'cause of my friend! He's the "fu-jo-shi," as you say (ha-ha!).
As you said. And "he" would be a fudanshi. That's the term for male fans of work like this.
Okay, got it. So he's a fu-dan-shi, and other girls besides me are fujoshis. Those poor, twisted freaks.
Well, if your friend wants to know what happened in the story, another publisher did pick up the series...
FLIP!

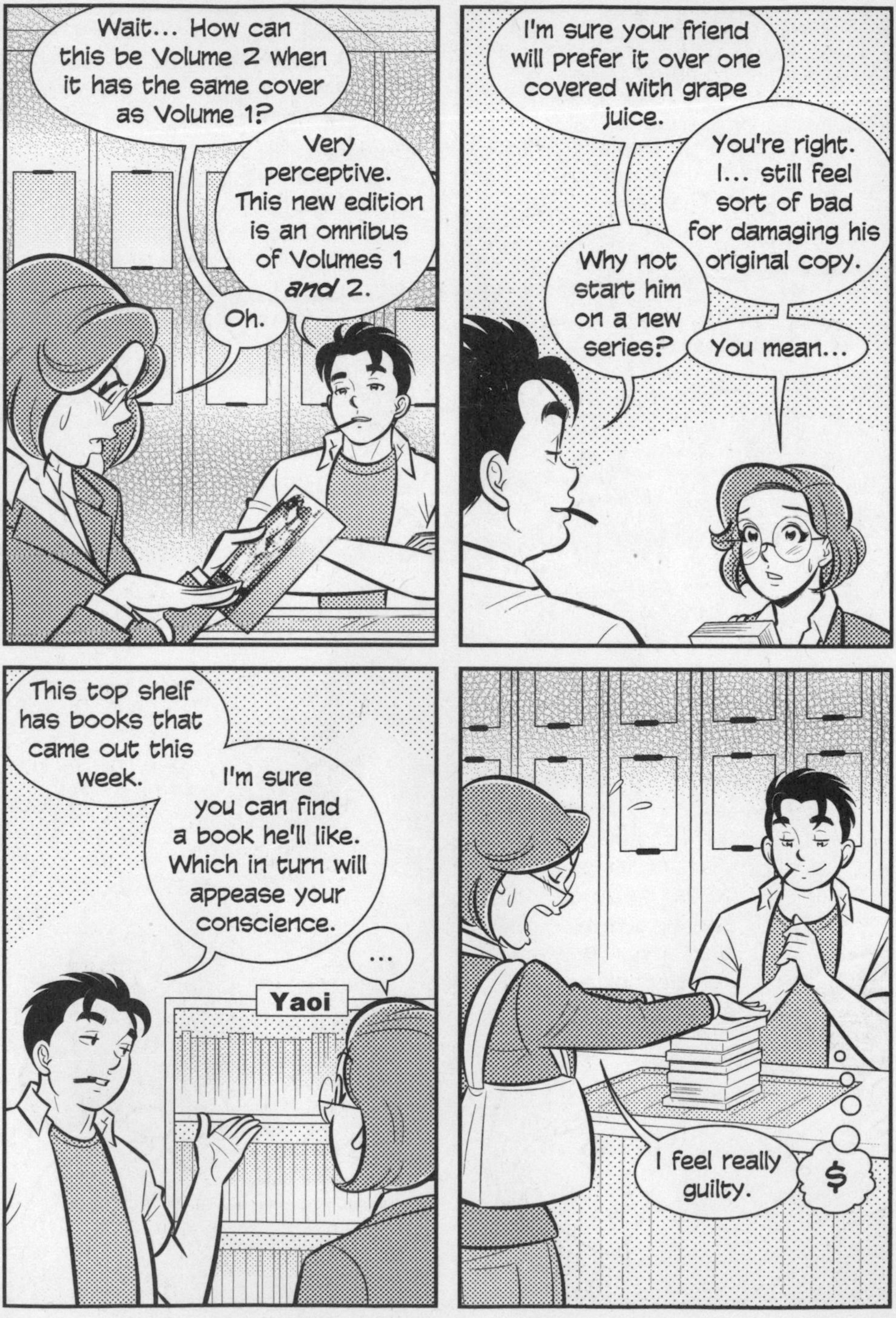
Wait... How can this be Volume 2 when it has the same cover as Volume 1?
Very perceptive. This new edition is an omnibus of Volumes 1 *and* 2.
Oh.
I'm sure your friend will prefer it over one covered with grape juice.
You're right. I... still feel sort of bad for damaging his original copy.
Why not start him on a new series?
You mean...
This top shelf has books that came out this week.
I'm sure you can find a book he'll like. Which in turn will appease your conscience.
...
Yaoi
I feel really guilty.
$

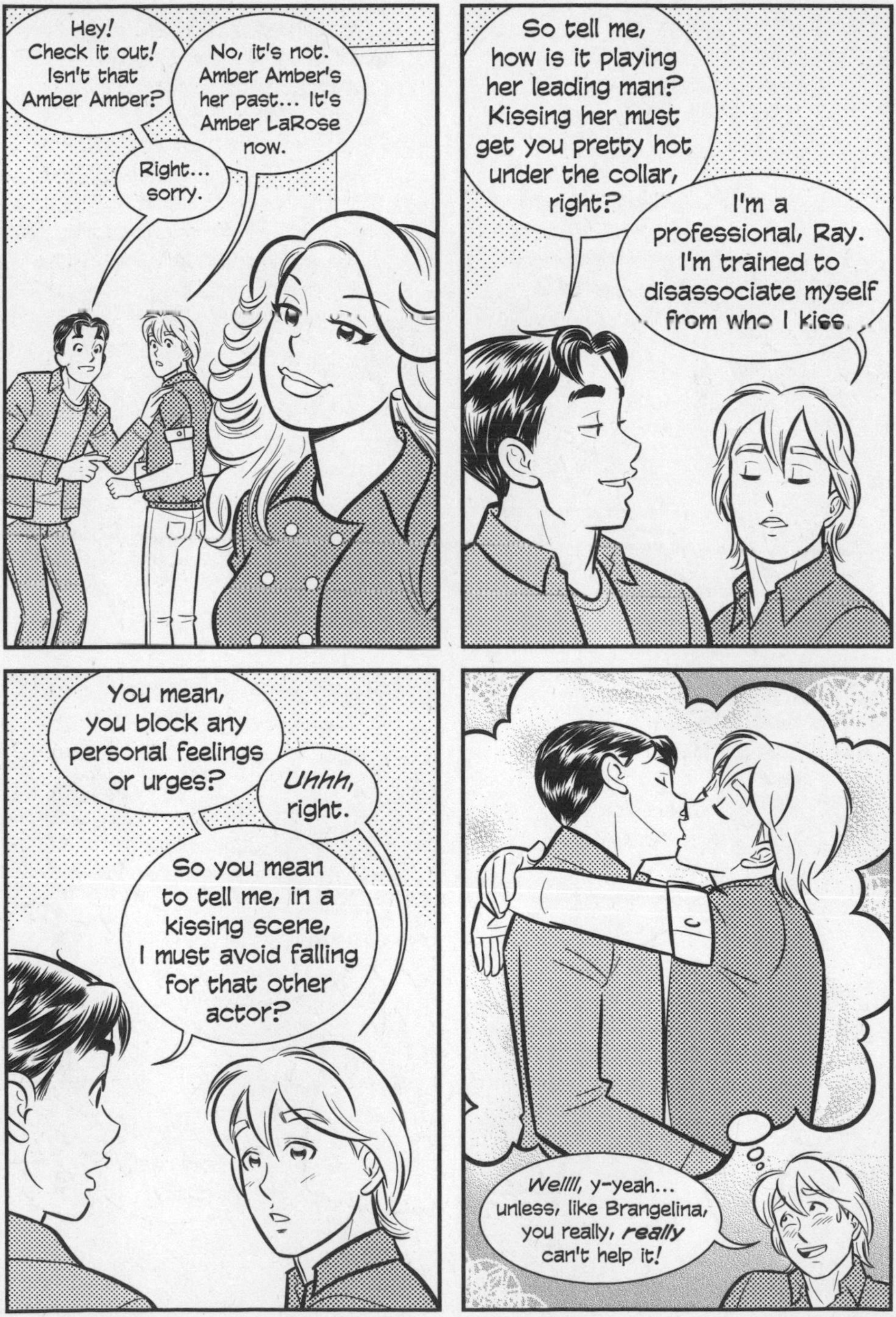
Hey! Check it out! Isn't that Amber Amber?
No, it's not. Amber Amber's her past... It's Amber LaRose now.
Right... sorry.
So tell me, how is it playing her leading man? Kissing her must get you pretty hot under the collar, right?
I'm a professional, Ray. I'm trained to disassociate myself from who I kiss...
You mean, you block any personal feelings or urges?
Uhhh, right.
So you mean to tell me, in a kissing scene, I must avoid falling for that other actor?
Wellll, y-yeah... unless, like Brangelina, you really, ***really*** can't help it!

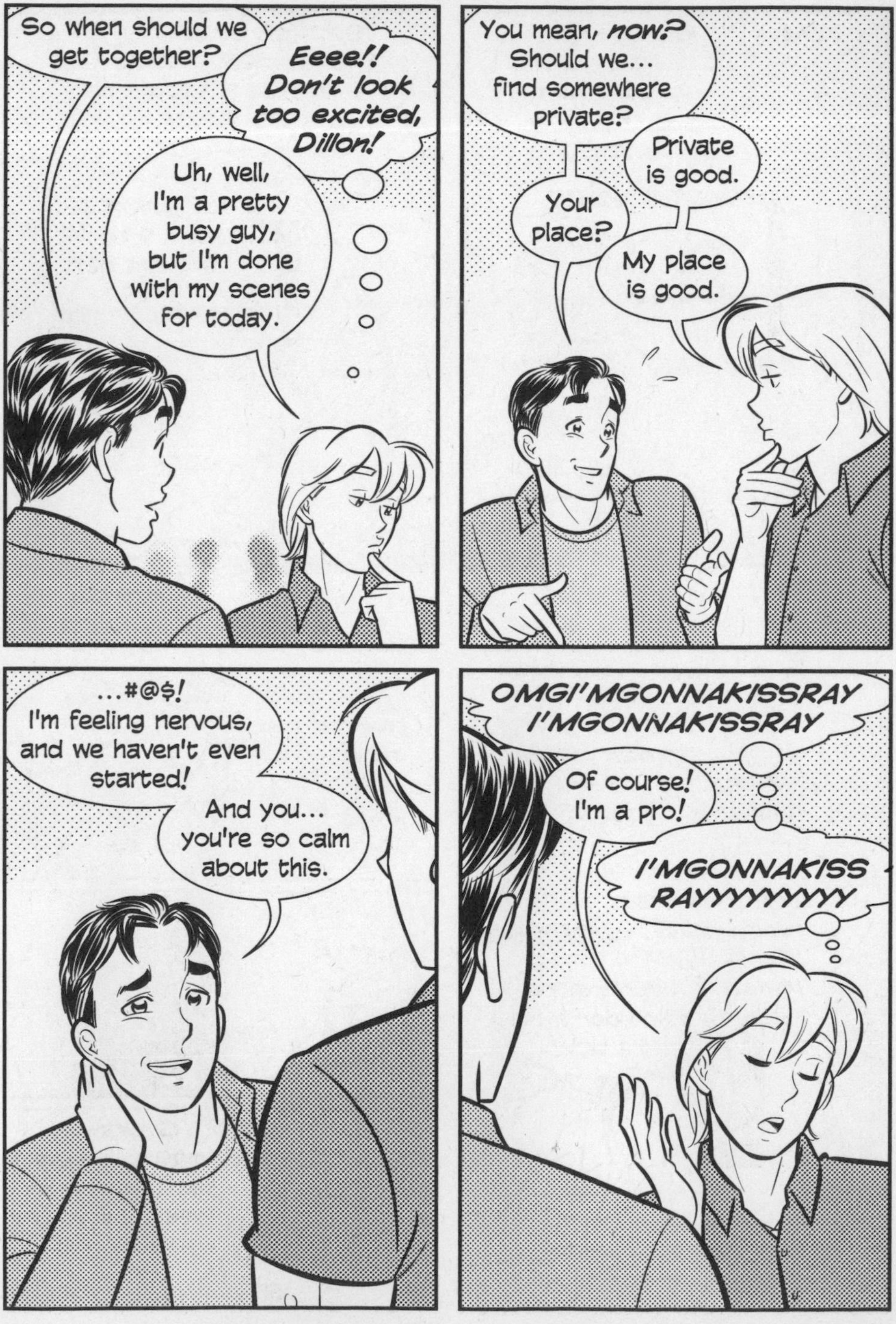
So when should we get together?
Eeee!! Don't look too excited, Dillon!
Uh, well, I'm a pretty busy guy, but I'm done with my scenes for today.
You mean, now? Should we... find somewhere private?
Private is good.
Your place?
My place is good.
...#@$! I'm feeling nervous, and we haven't even started!
And you... you're so calm about this.
OMGI'MGONNAKISSRAY I'MGONNAKISSRAY
Of course! I'm a pro!
I'MGONNAKISS RAYYYYYYYYY

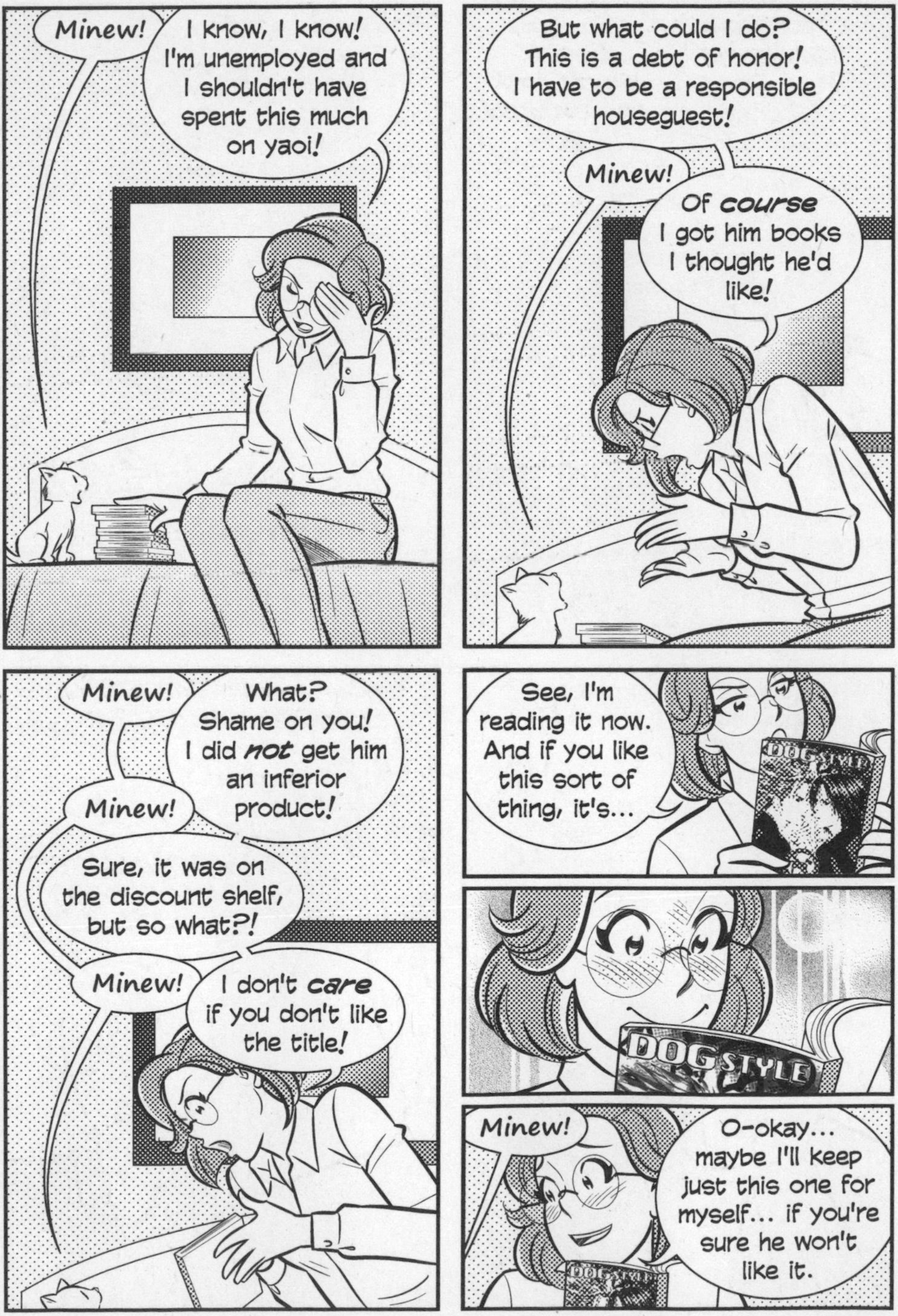
Minew!
I know, I know! I'm unemployed and I shouldn't have spent this much on yaoi!
But what could I do? This is a debt of honor! I have to be a responsible houseguest!
Minew!
Of course I got him books I thought he'd like!
Minew!
What? Shame on you! I did not get him an inferior product!
Minew!
Sure, it was on the discount shelf, but so what?!
Minew!
I don't care if you don't like the title!
See, I'm reading it now. And if you like this sort of thing, it's...
DOG STYLE
Minew!
O-okay... maybe I'll keep just this one for myself... if you're sure he won't like it.

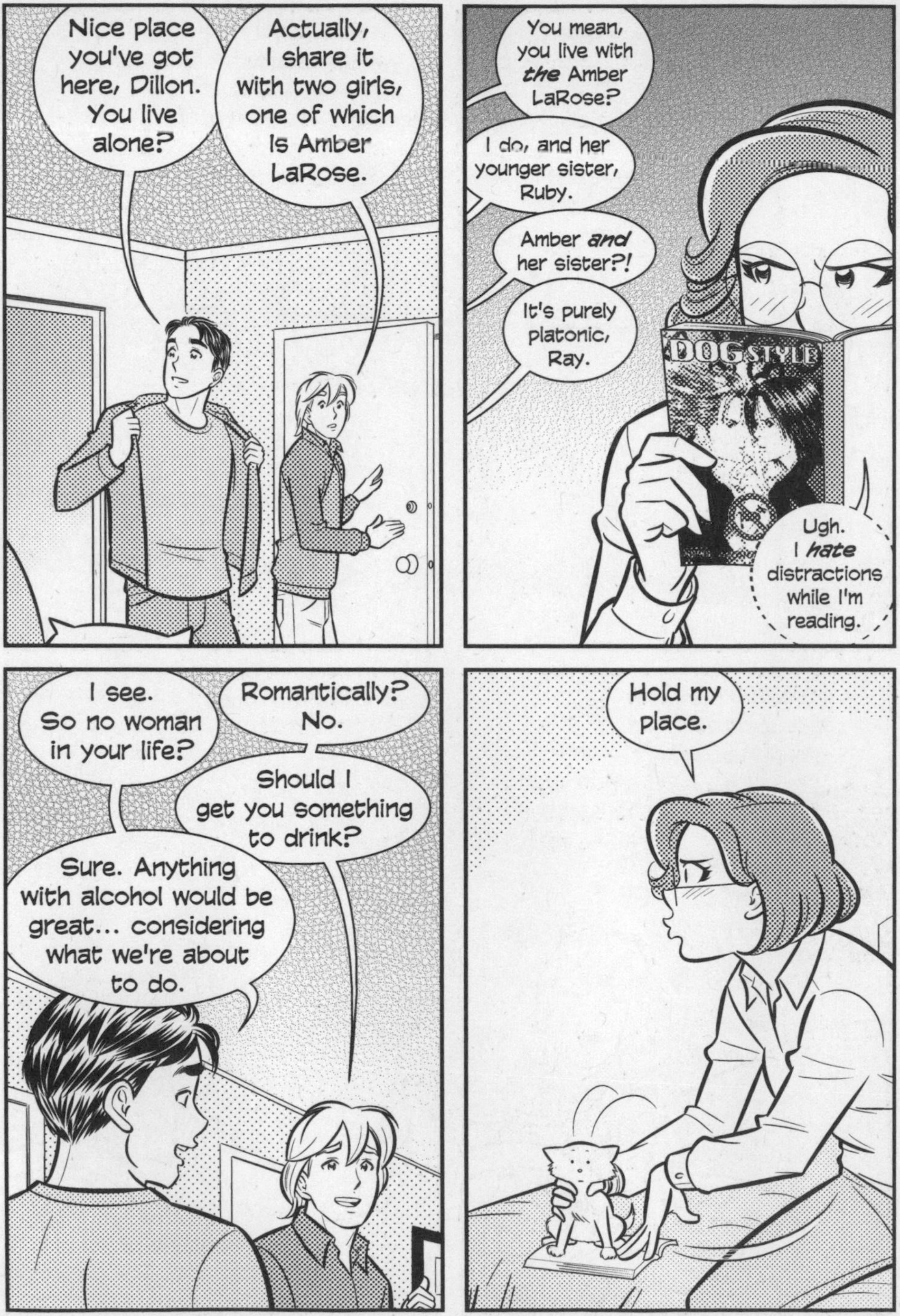
Nice place you've got here, Dillon. You live alone?
Actually, I share it with two girls, one of which is Amber LaRose.
You mean, you live with *the* Amber LaRose?
I do, and her younger sister, Ruby.
Amber *and* her sister?!
It's purely platonic, Ray.
DOG STYLE
Ugh. I *hate* distractions while I'm reading.
I see. So no woman in your life?
Romantically? No.
Should I get you something to drink?
Sure. Anything with alcohol would be great... considering what we're about to do.
Hold my place.

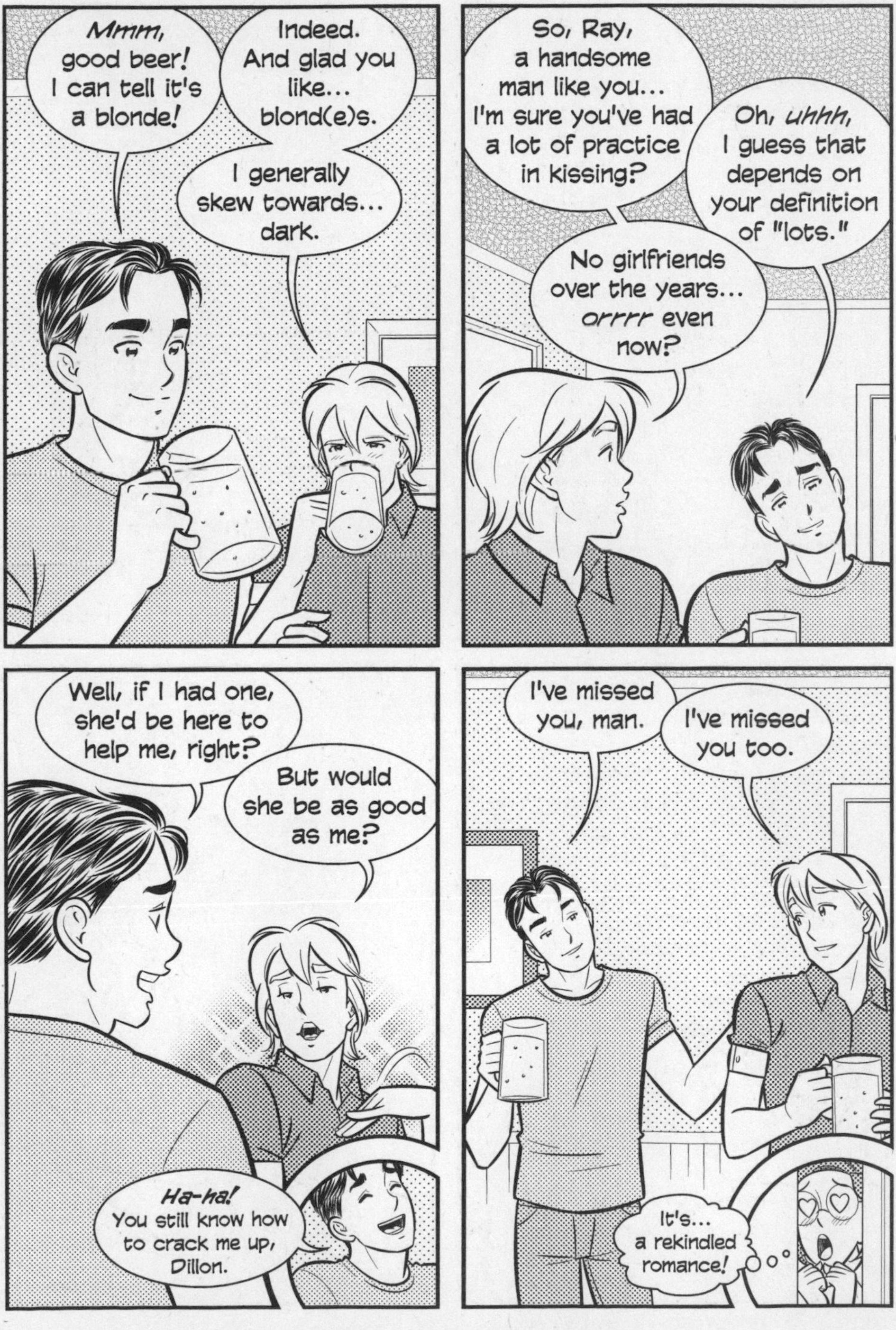
Mmm, good beer! I can tell it's a blonde!
Indeed. And glad you like... blond(e)s.
I generally skew towards... dark.
So, Ray, a handsome man like you... I'm sure you've had a lot of practice in kissing?
No girlfriends over the years... orrrr even now?
Oh, uhhh, I guess that depends on your definition of "lots."
Well, if I had one, she'd be here to help me, right?
But would she be as good as me?
Ha-ha! You still know how to crack me up, Dillon.
I've missed you, man.
I've missed you too.
It's... a rekindled romance!

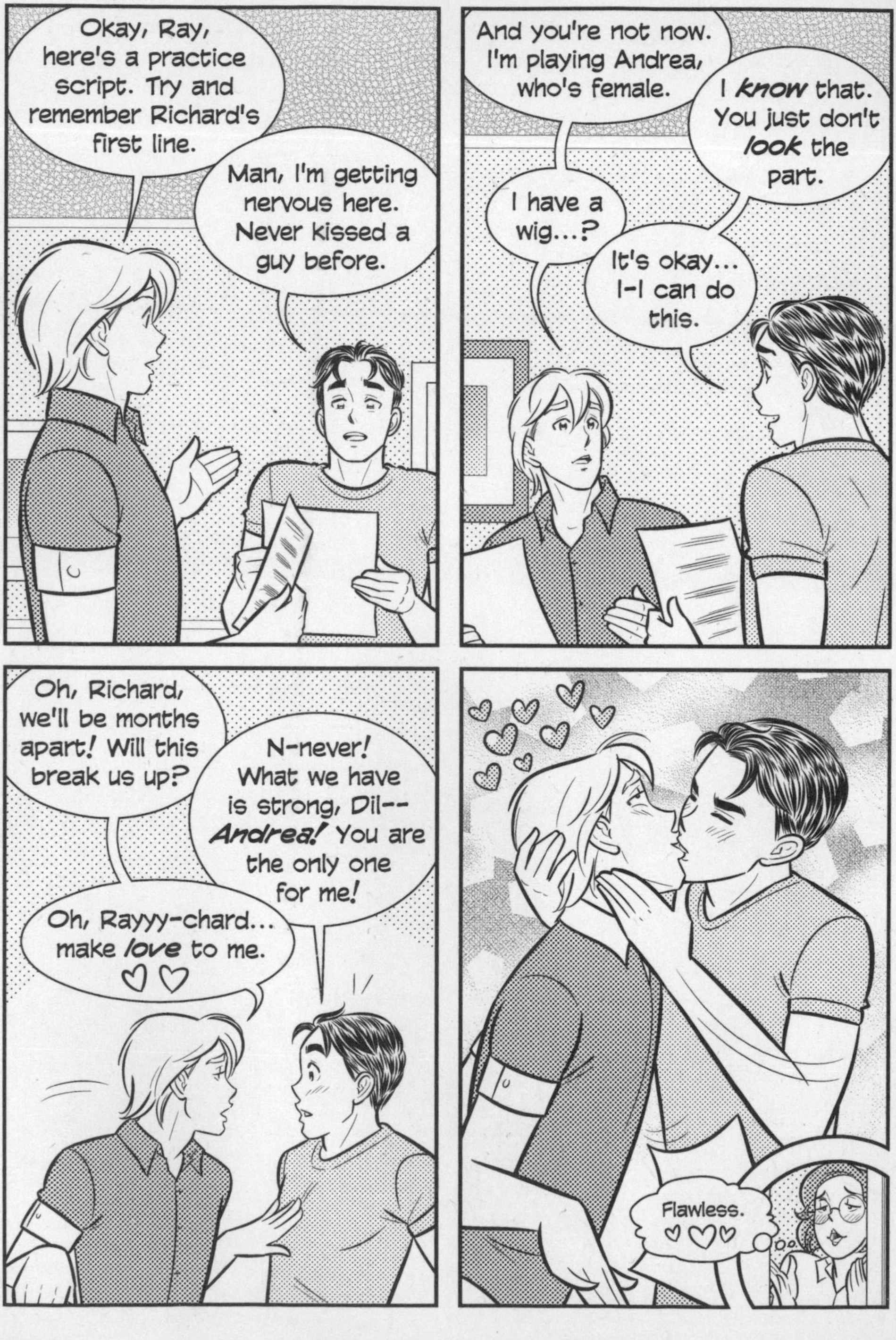
Okay, Ray, here's a practice script. Try and remember Richard's first line.
Man, I'm getting nervous here. Never kissed a guy before.
And you're not now. I'm playing Andrea, who's female.
I *know* that. You just don't *look* the part.
I have a wig...?
It's okay... I-I can do this.
Oh, Richard, we'll be months apart! Will this break us up?
N-never! What we have is strong, Dil-- *Andrea!* You are the only one for me!
Oh, Rayyy-chard... make *love* to me. ♡♡
Flawless. ♡♡♡

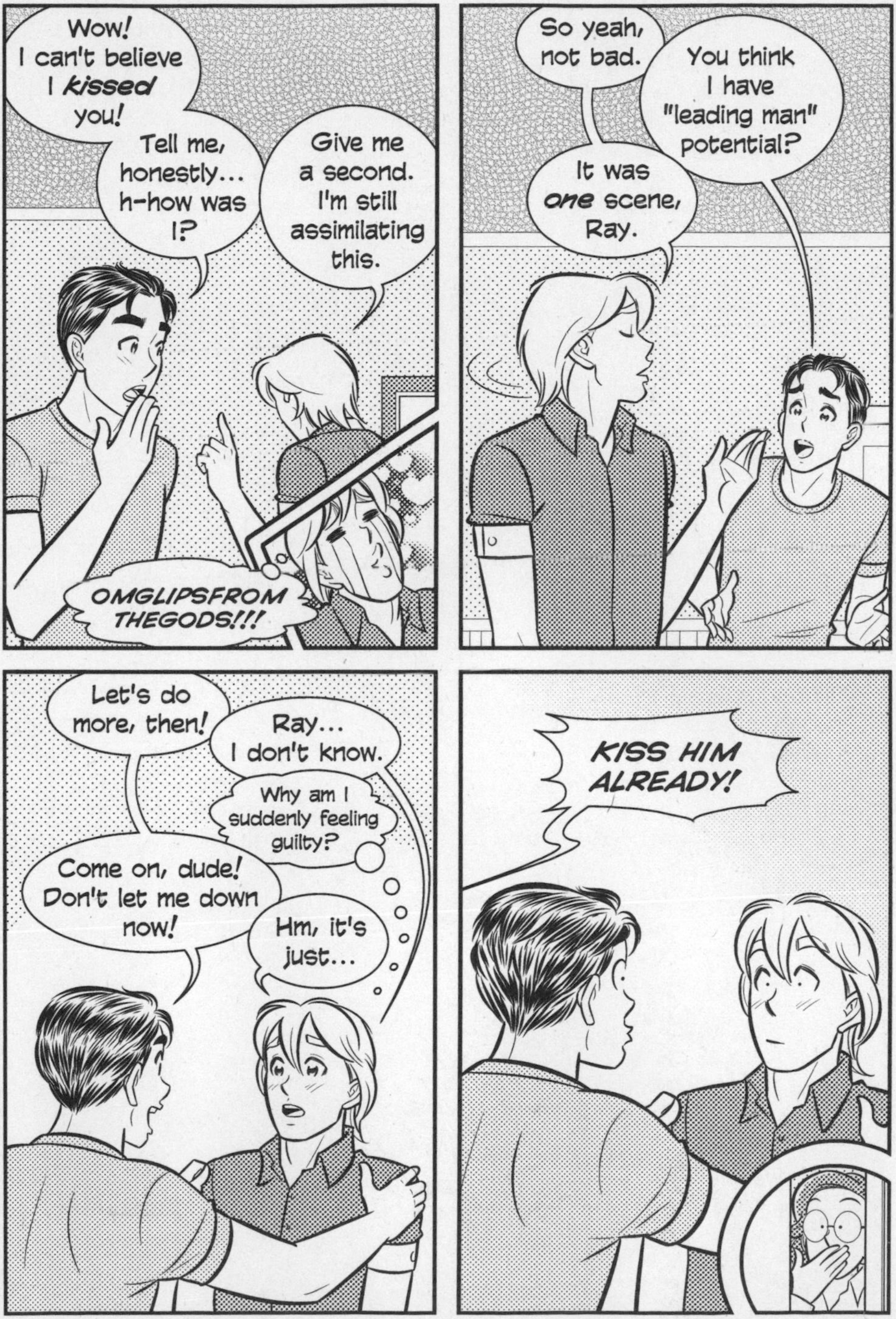

Wow! I can't believe I *kissed* you!
Tell me, honestly... h-how was I?
Give me a second. I'm still assimilating this.
OMGLIPSFROM THEGODS!!!
So yeah, not bad.
It was *one* scene, Ray.
You think I have "leading man" potential?
Let's do more, then!
Ray... I don't know.
Why am I suddenly feeling guilty?
Come on, dude! Don't let me down now!
Hm, it's just...
KISS HIM ALREADY!

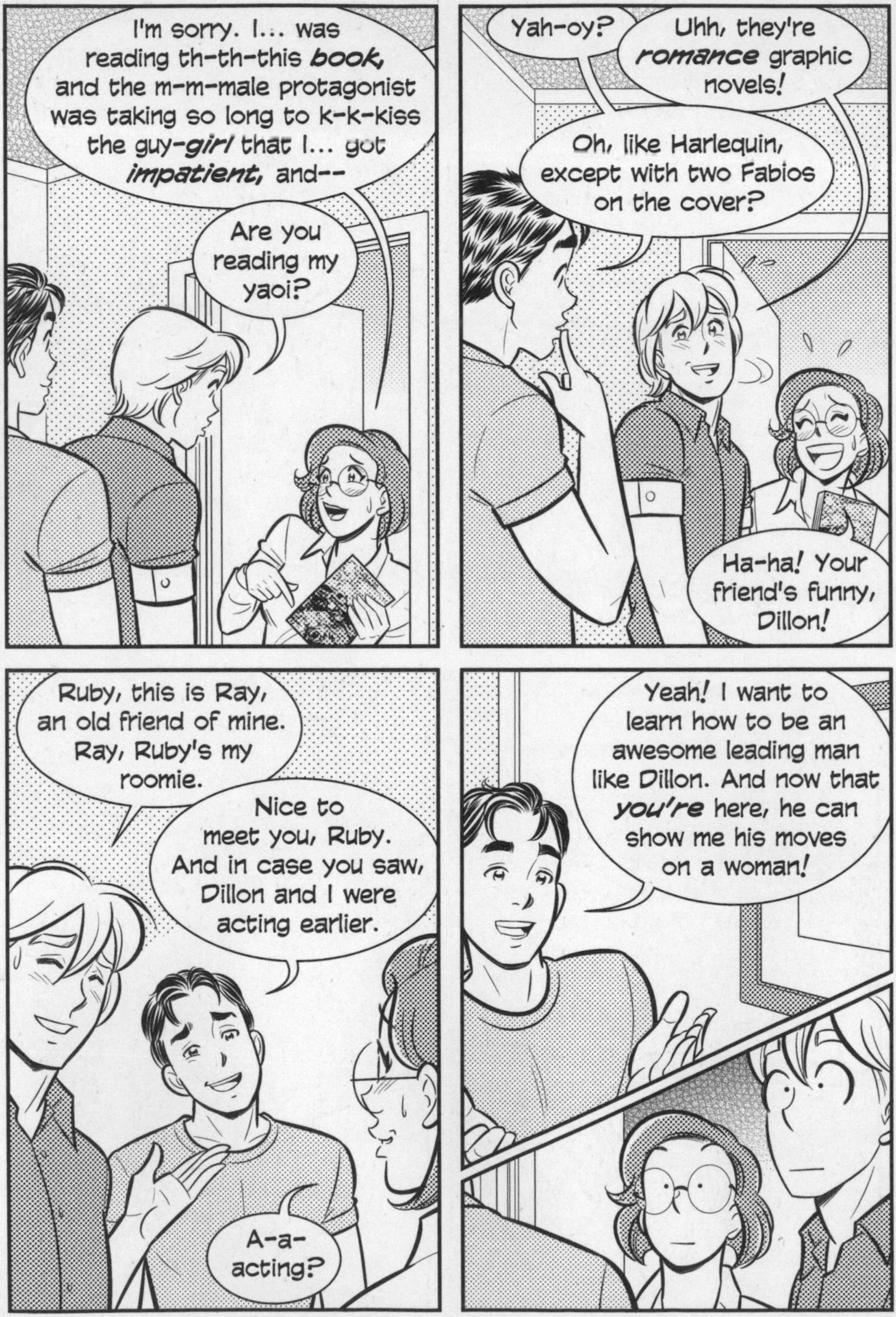
I'm sorry. I... was reading th-th-this *book,* and the m-m-male protagonist was taking so long to k-k-kiss the guy-*girl* that I... got *impatient,* and--
Are you reading my yaoi?
Yah-oy?
Uhh, they're *romance* graphic novels!
Oh, like Harlequin, except with two Fabios on the cover?
Ha-ha! Your friend's funny, Dillon!
Ruby, this is Ray, an old friend of mine. Ray, Ruby's my roomie.
Nice to meet you, Ruby. And in case you saw, Dillon and I were acting earlier.
A-a-acting?
Yeah! I want to learn how to be an awesome leading man like Dillon. And now that *you're* here, he can show me his moves on a woman!

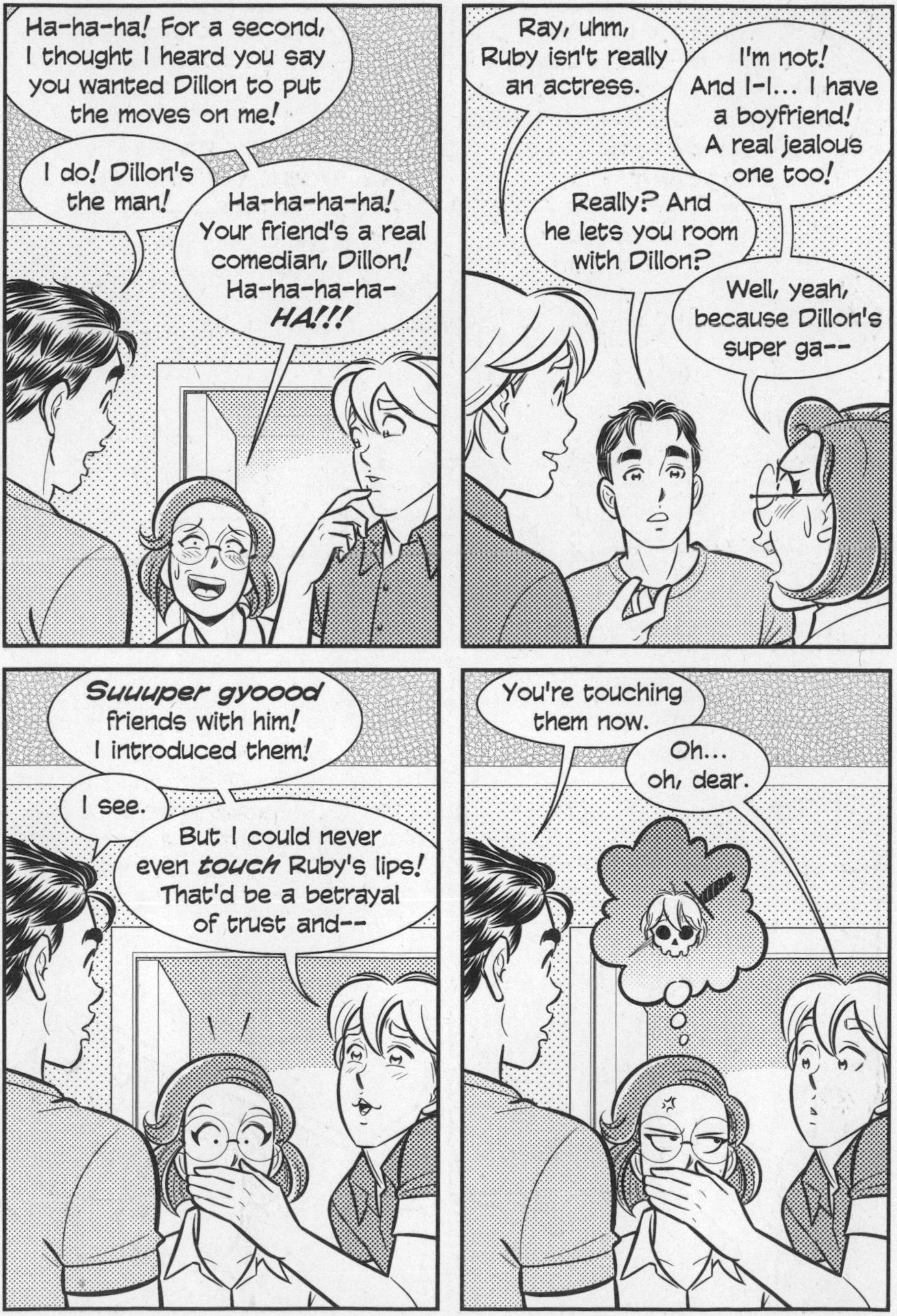
Ha-ha-ha! For a second, I thought I heard you say you wanted Dillon to put the moves on me!
I do! Dillon's the man!
Ha-ha-ha-ha! Your friend's a real comedian, Dillon! Ha-ha-ha-ha-*HA!!!*
Ray, uhm, Ruby isn't really an actress.
I'm not! And I-I... I have a boyfriend! A real jealous one too!
Really? And he lets you room with Dillon?
Well, yeah, because Dillon's super ga--
Suuuper gyoood friends with him! I introduced them!
I see.
But I could never even *touch* Ruby's lips! That'd be a betrayal of trust and--
You're touching them now.
Oh... oh, dear.

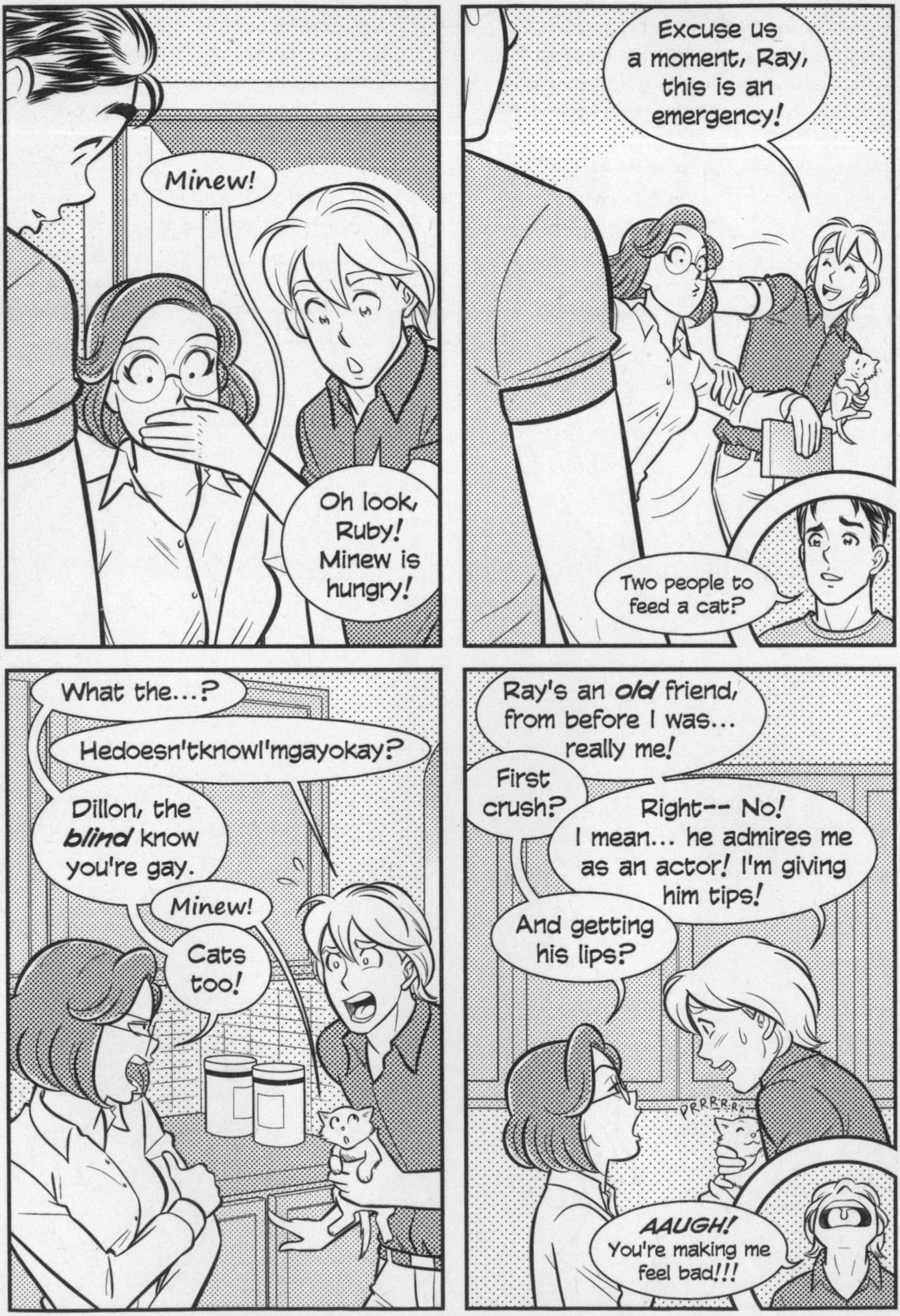
Minew!
Oh look, Ruby! Minew is hungry!
Excuse us a moment, Ray, this is an emergency!
Two people to feed a cat?
What the...?
Hedoesn'tknowI'mgayokay?
Dillon, the *blind* know you're gay.
Minew!
Cats too!
Ray's an *old* friend, from before I was... really me!
First crush?
Right-- No! I mean... he admires me as an actor! I'm giving him tips!
And getting his lips?
PRRRR
AAUGH! You're making me feel bad!!!

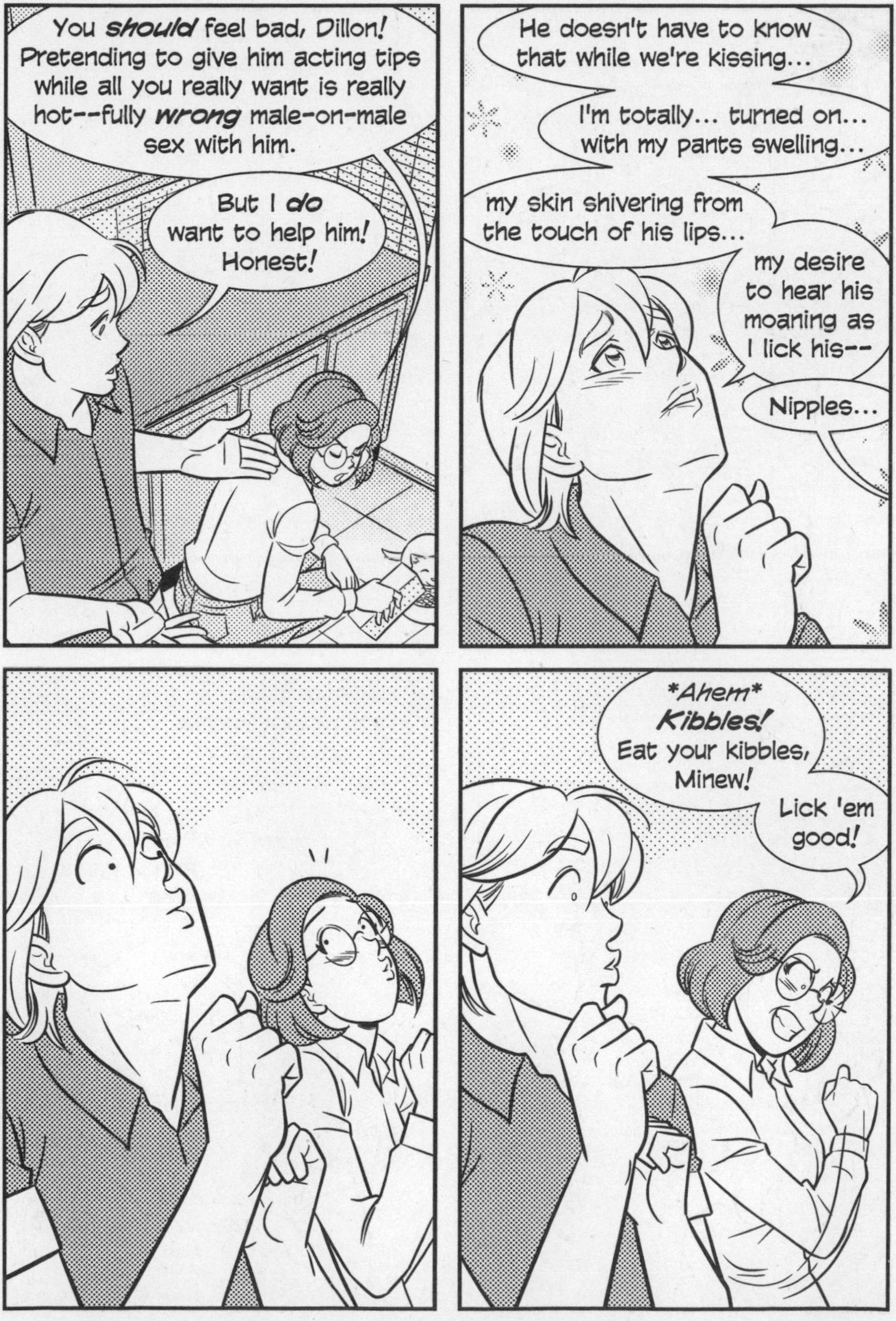
You *should* feel bad, Dillon! Pretending to give him acting tips while all you really want is really hot--fully *wrong* male-on-male sex with him.
But I *do* want to help him! Honest!
He doesn't have to know that while we're kissing...
I'm totally... turned on... with my pants swelling...
my skin shivering from the touch of his lips...
my desire to hear his moaning as I lick his--
Nipples...
Ahem *Kibbles!* Eat your kibbles, Minew!
Lick 'em good!

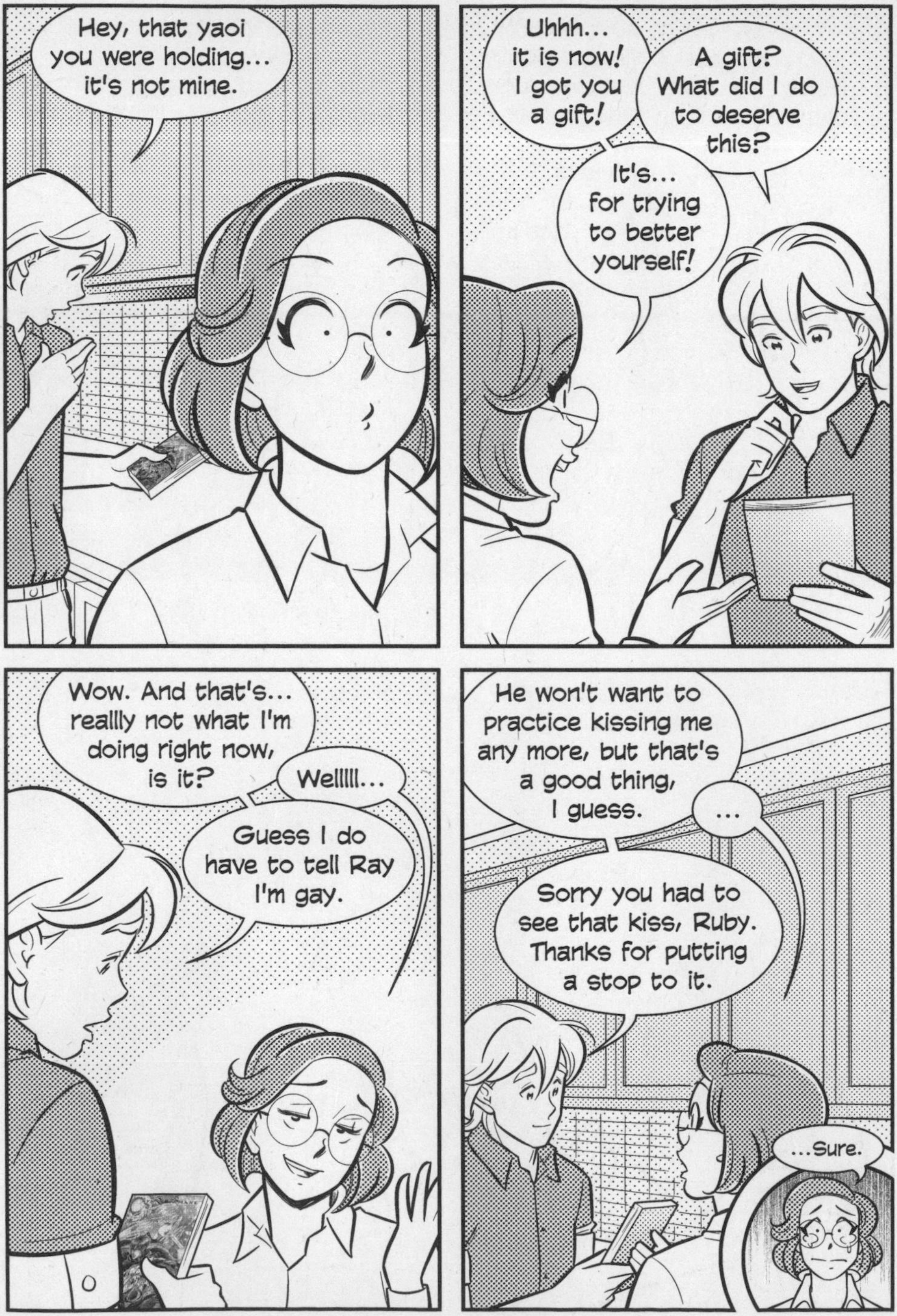
Hey, that yaoi you were holding... it's not mine.
Uhhh... it is now! I got you a gift!
A gift? What did I do to deserve this?
It's... for trying to better yourself!
Wow. And that's... reallly not what I'm doing right now, is it?
Welllll...
Guess I do have to tell Ray I'm gay.
He won't want to practice kissing me any more, but that's a good thing, I guess.
...
Sorry you had to see that kiss, Ruby. Thanks for putting a stop to it.
...Sure.

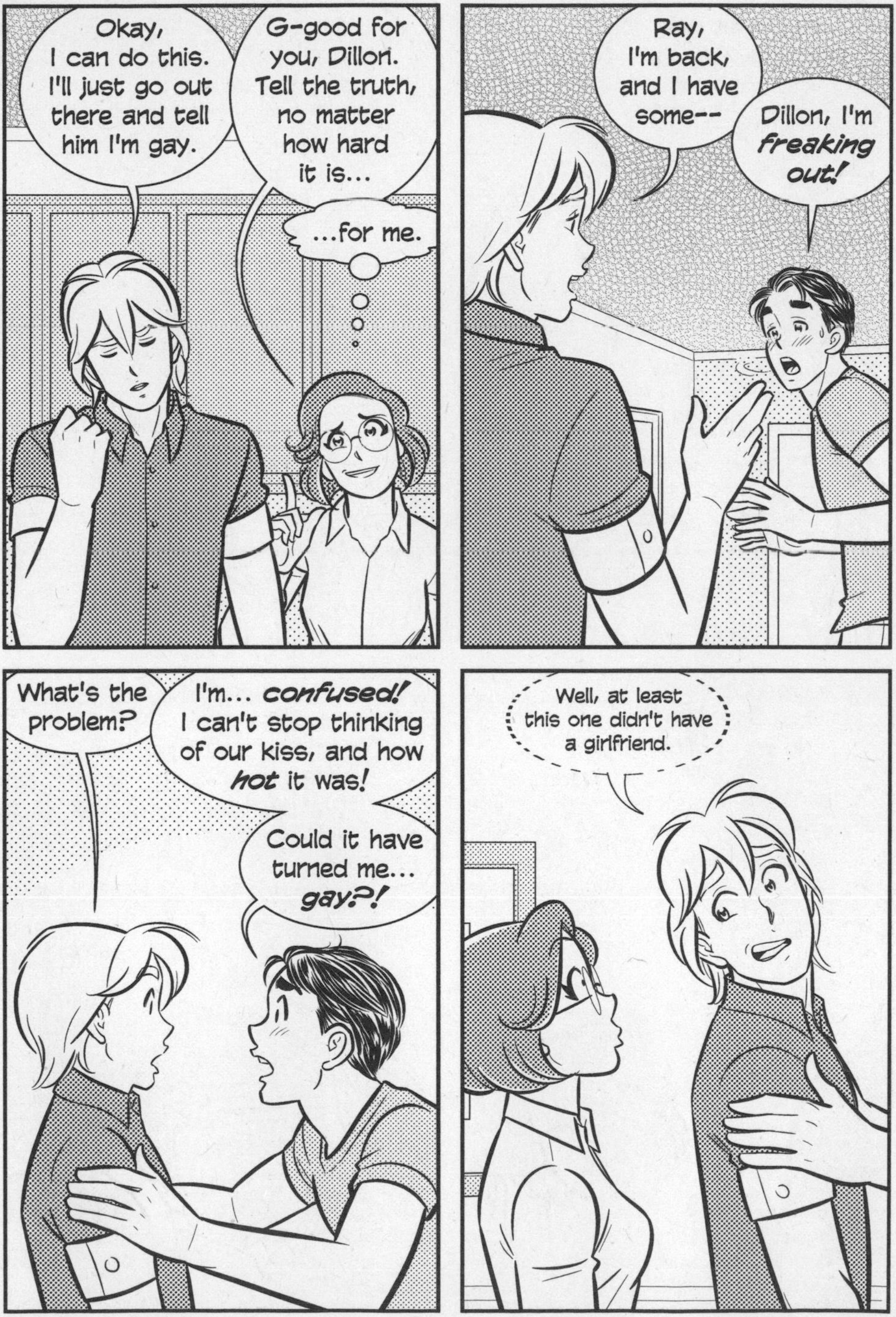

Okay, I can do this. I'll just go out there and tell him I'm gay.
G-good for you, Dillon. Tell the truth, no matter how hard it is...
...for me.
Ray, I'm back, and I have some--
Dillon, I'm *freaking out!*
What's the problem?
I'm... *confused!* I can't stop thinking of our kiss, and how *hot* it was!
Could it have turned me... *gay?!*
Well, at least this one didn't have a girlfriend.

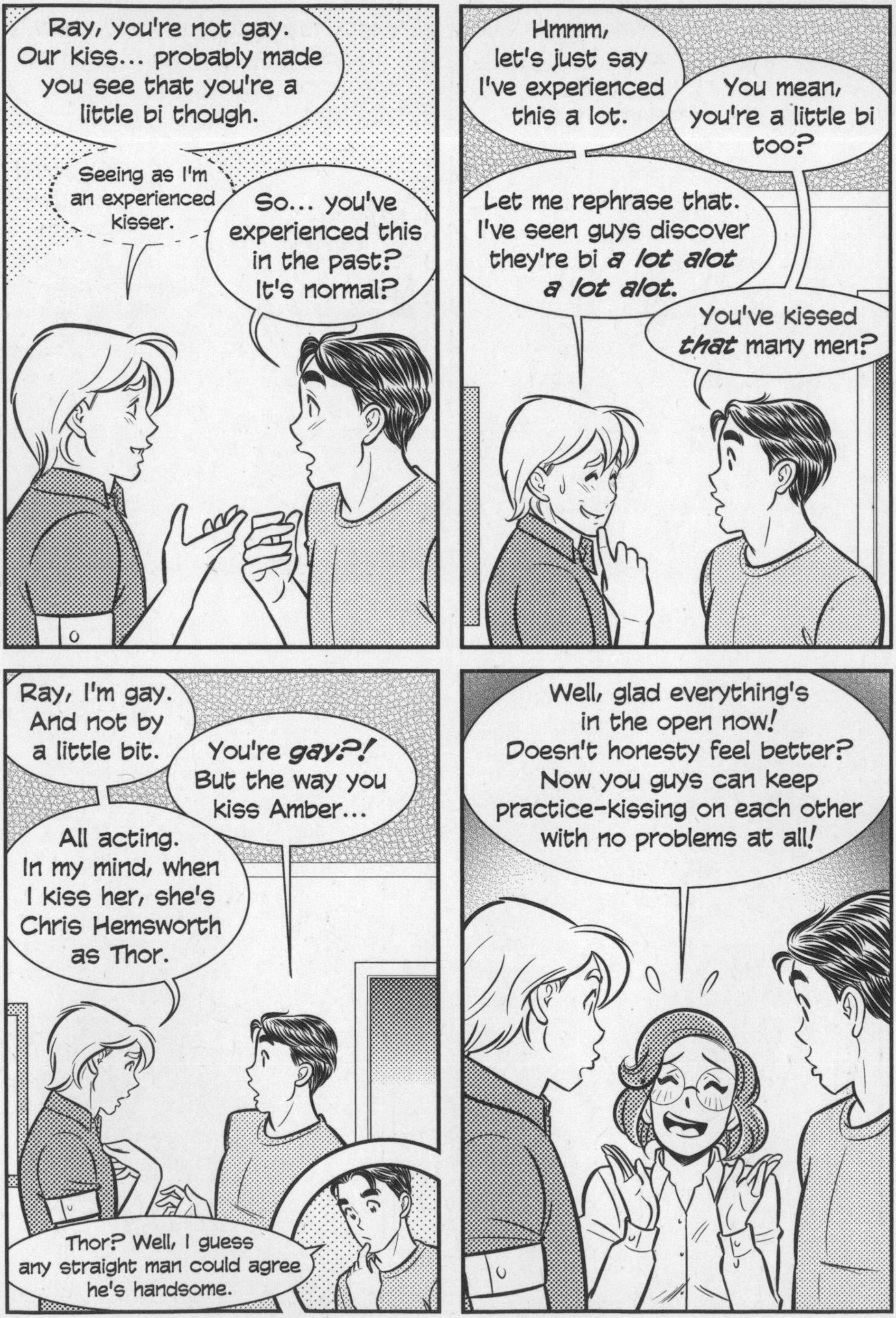
Ray, you're not gay. Our kiss... probably made you see that you're a little bi though.
Seeing as I'm an experienced kisser.
So... you've experienced this in the past? It's normal?
Hmmm, let's just say I've experienced this a lot.
You mean, you're a little bi too?
Let me rephrase that. I've seen guys discover they're bi *a lot alot a lot alot.*
You've kissed *that* many men?
Ray, I'm gay. And not by a little bit.
You're *gay?!* But the way you kiss Amber...
All acting. In my mind, when I kiss her, she's Chris Hemsworth as Thor.
Thor? Well, I guess any straight man could agree he's handsome.
Well, glad everything's in the open now! Doesn't honesty feel better? Now you guys can keep practice-kissing on each other with no problems at all!

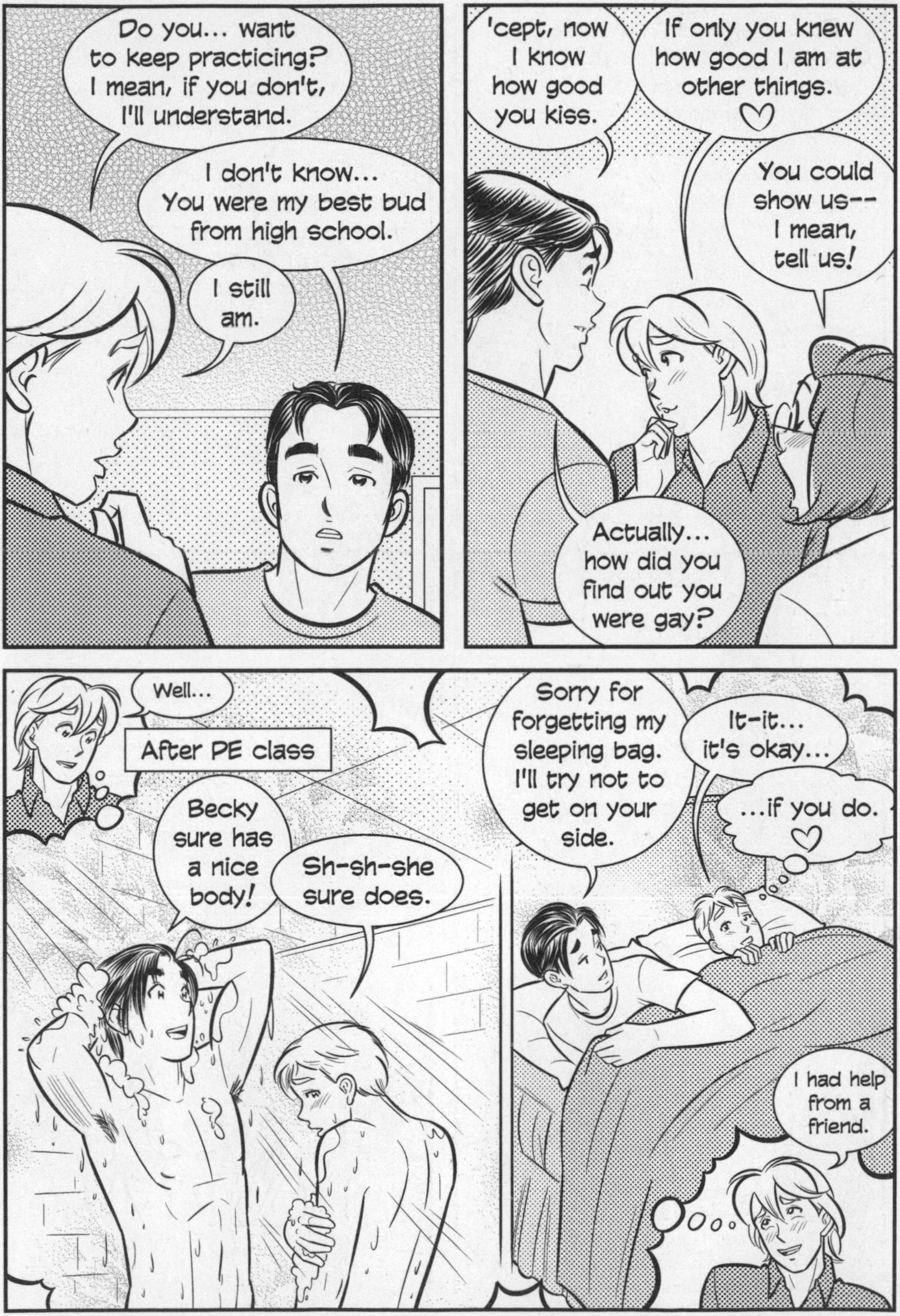
Do you… want to keep practicing? I mean, if you don't, I'll understand.
I don't know… You were my best bud from high school.
I still am.
'cept, now I know how good you kiss.
If only you knew how good I am at other things.
You could show us-- I mean, tell us!
Actually… how did you find out you were gay?
Well…
After PE class
Becky sure has a nice body!
Sh-sh-she sure does.
Sorry for forgetting my sleeping bag. I'll try not to get on your side.
It-it… it's okay…
…if you do.
I had help from a friend.

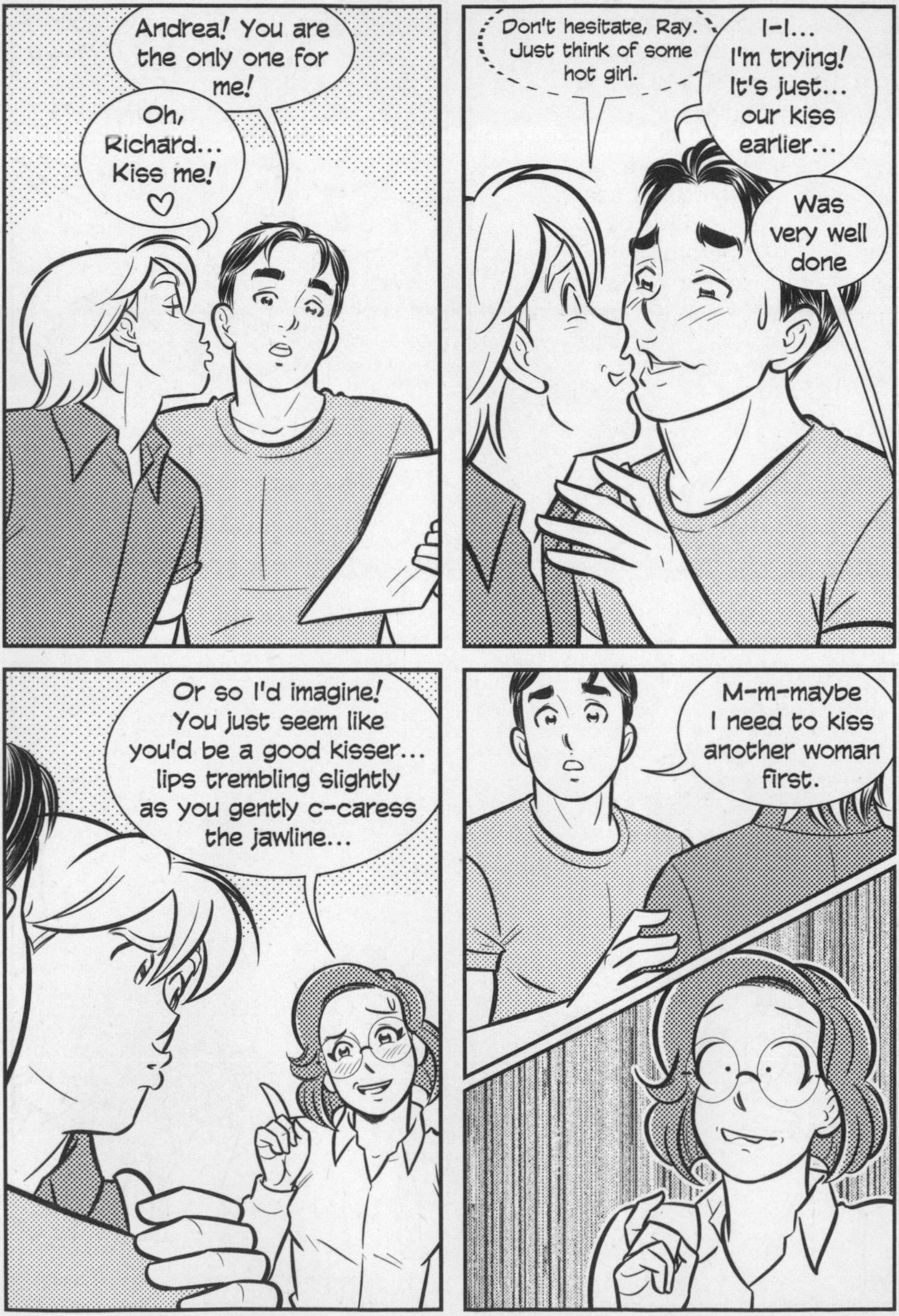
Andrea! You are the only one for me!
Oh, Richard... Kiss me! ♡
Don't hesitate, Ray. Just think of some hot girl.
I-I... I'm trying! It's just... our kiss earlier...
Was very well done
Or so I'd imagine! You just seem like you'd be a good kisser... lips trembling slightly as you gently c-caress the jawline...
M-m-maybe I need to kiss another woman first.

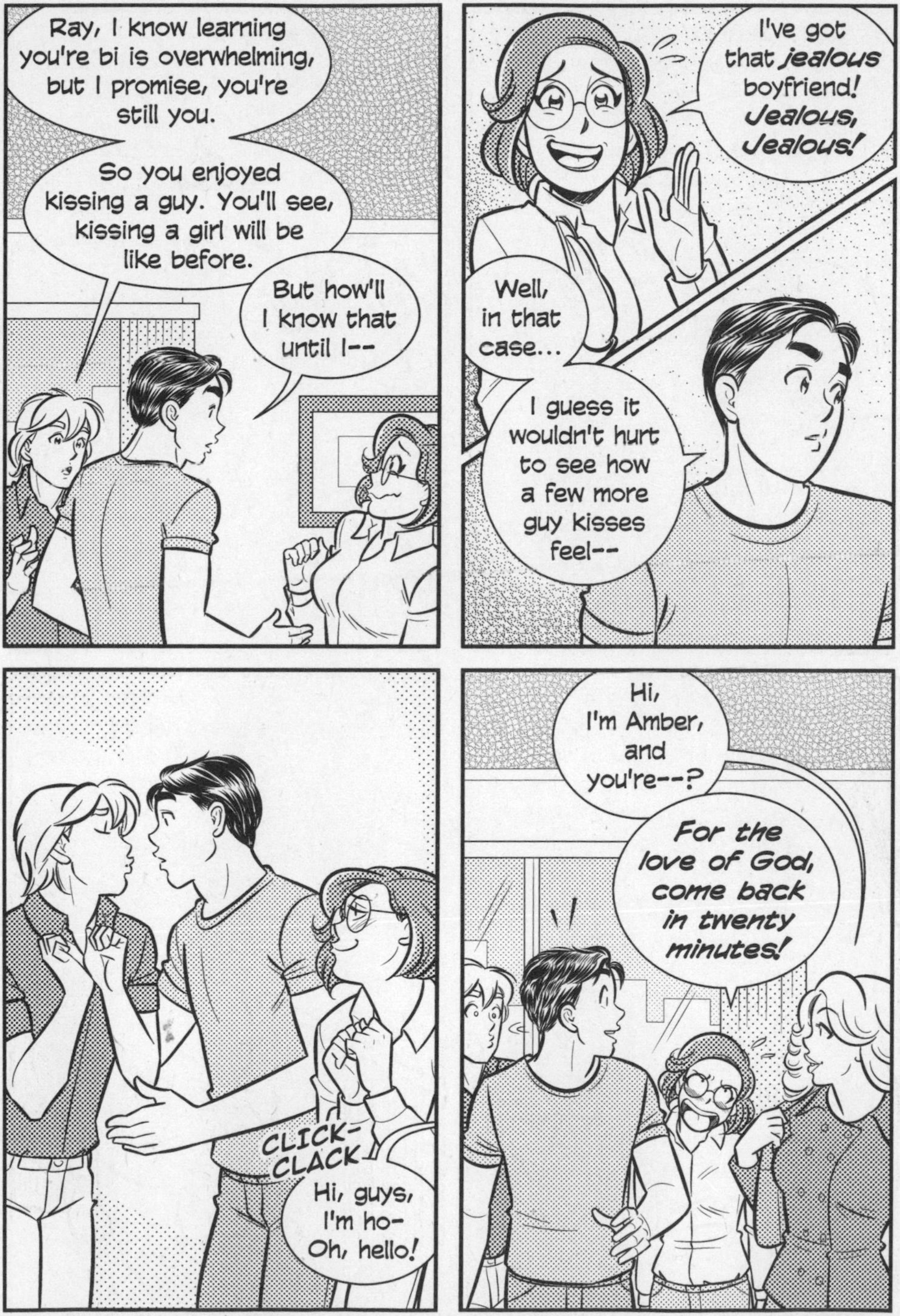
Ray, I know learning you're bi is overwhelming, but I promise, you're still you.
So you enjoyed kissing a guy. You'll see, kissing a girl will be like before.
But how'll I know that until I--
I've got that *jealous* boyfriend! *Jealous, Jealous!*
Well, in that case...
I guess it wouldn't hurt to see how a few more guy kisses feel--
CLICK-CLACK
Hi, guys, I'm ho- Oh, hello!
Hi, I'm Amber, and you're--?
For the love of God, come back in twenty minutes!

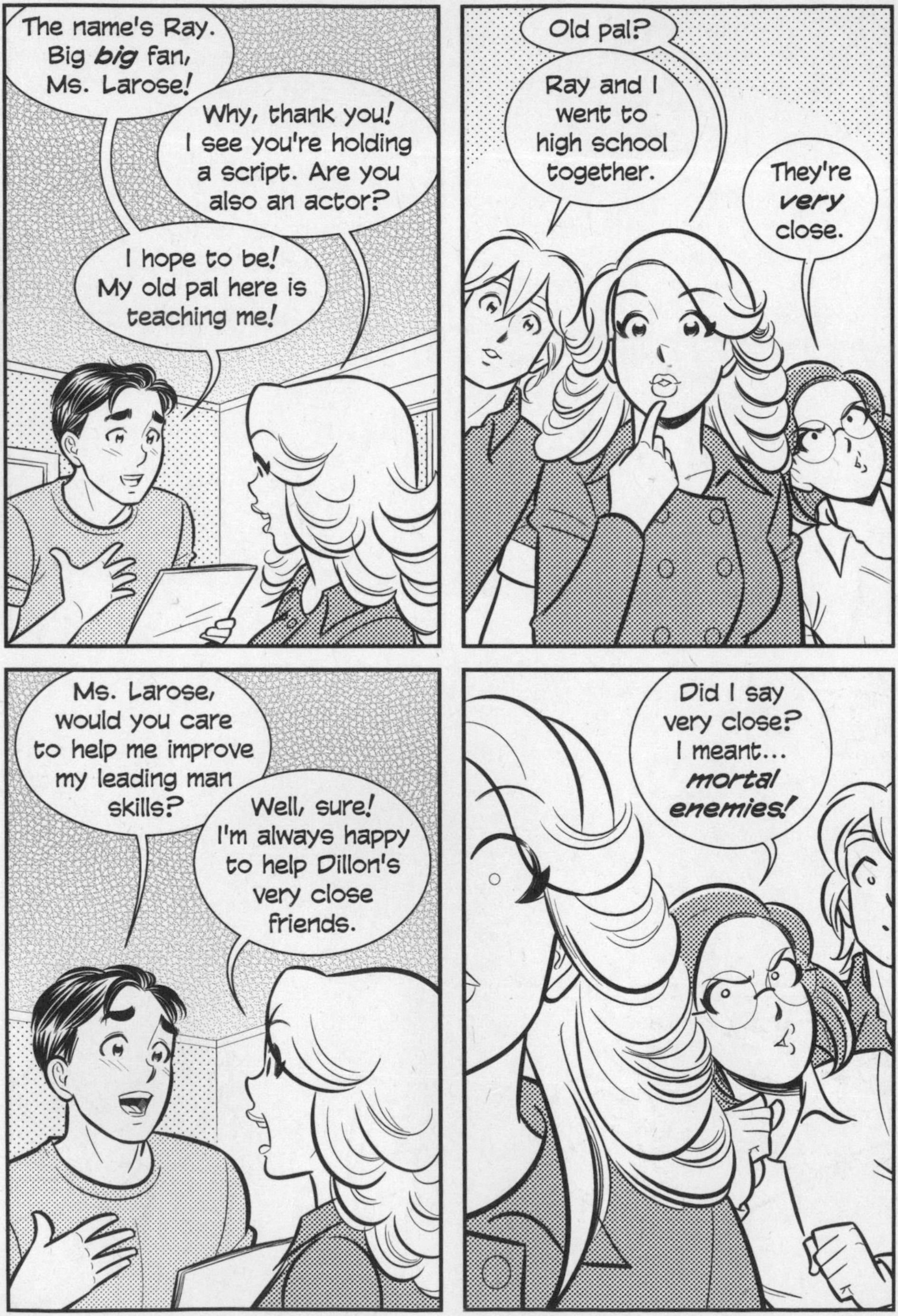
The name's Ray. Big *big* fan, Ms. Larose!
Why, thank you! I see you're holding a script. Are you also an actor?
I hope to be! My old pal here is teaching me!
Old pal?
Ray and I went to high school together.
They're *very* close.
Ms. Larose, would you care to help me improve my leading man skills?
Well, sure! I'm always happy to help Dillon's very close friends.
Did I say very close? I meant... *mortal enemies!*

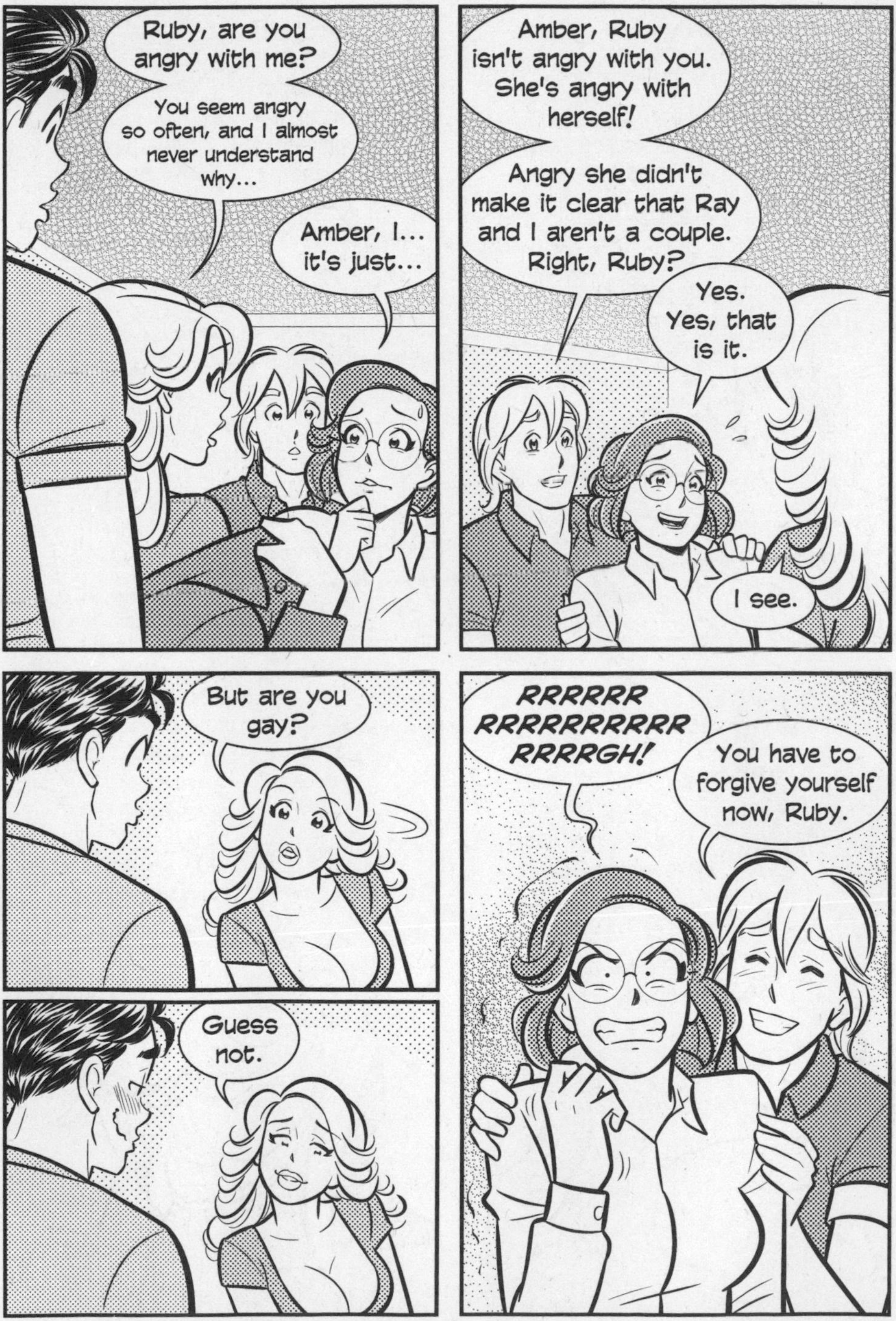

Ruby, are you angry with me?
You seem angry so often, and I almost never understand why...
Amber, I... it's just...
Amber, Ruby isn't angry with you. She's angry with herself!
Angry she didn't make it clear that Ray and I aren't a couple. Right, Ruby?
Yes. Yes, that is it.
I see.
But are you gay?
Guess not.
RRRRRR RRRRRRRRRR RRRRGH!
You have to forgive yourself now, Ruby.

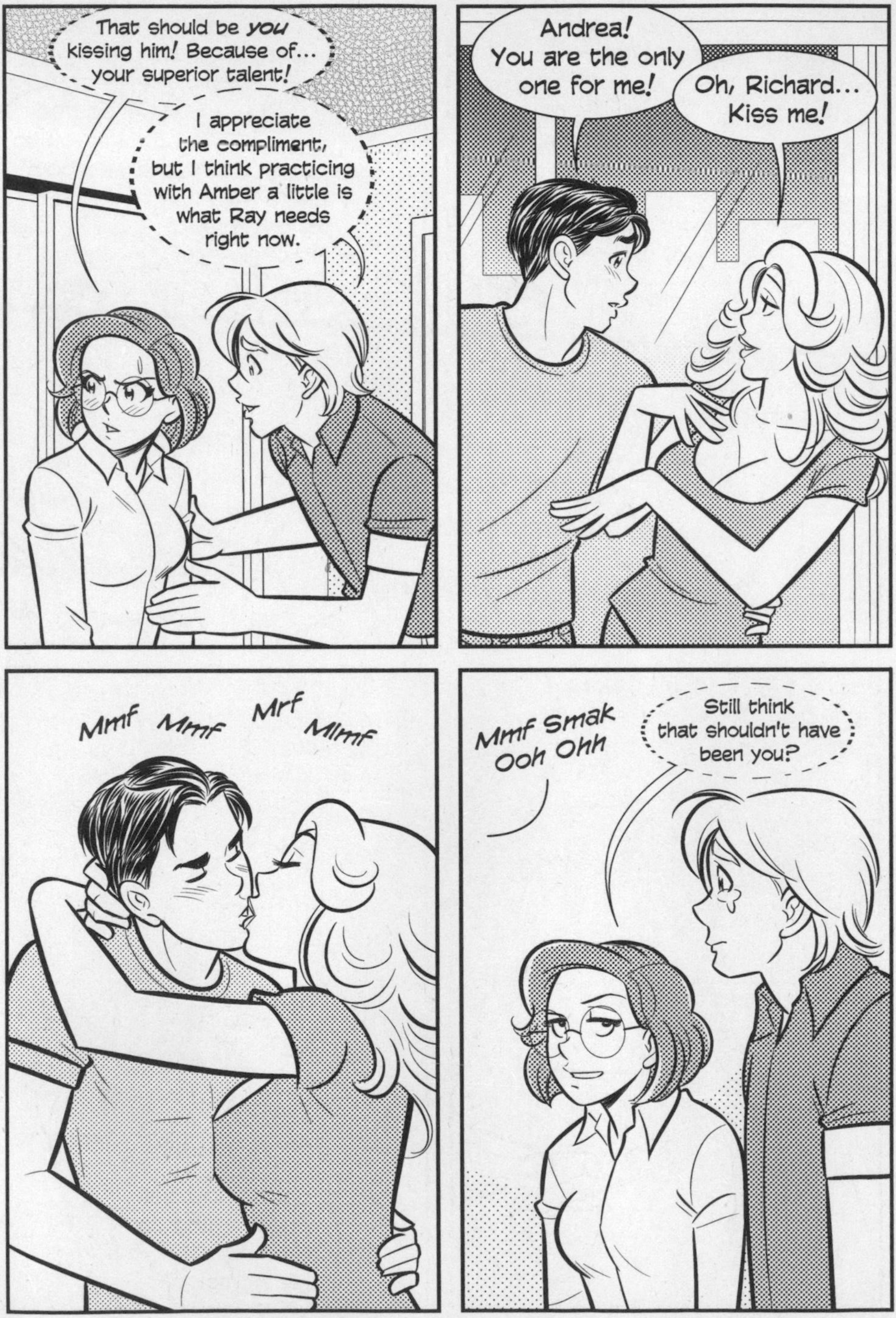
That should be *you* kissing him! Because of... your superior talent!
I appreciate the compliment, but I think practicing with Amber a little is what Ray needs right now.
Andrea! You are the only one for me!
Oh, Richard... Kiss me!
Mmf Mmf Mrf Mlmf
Mmf Smak Ooh Ohh
Still think that shouldn't have been you?

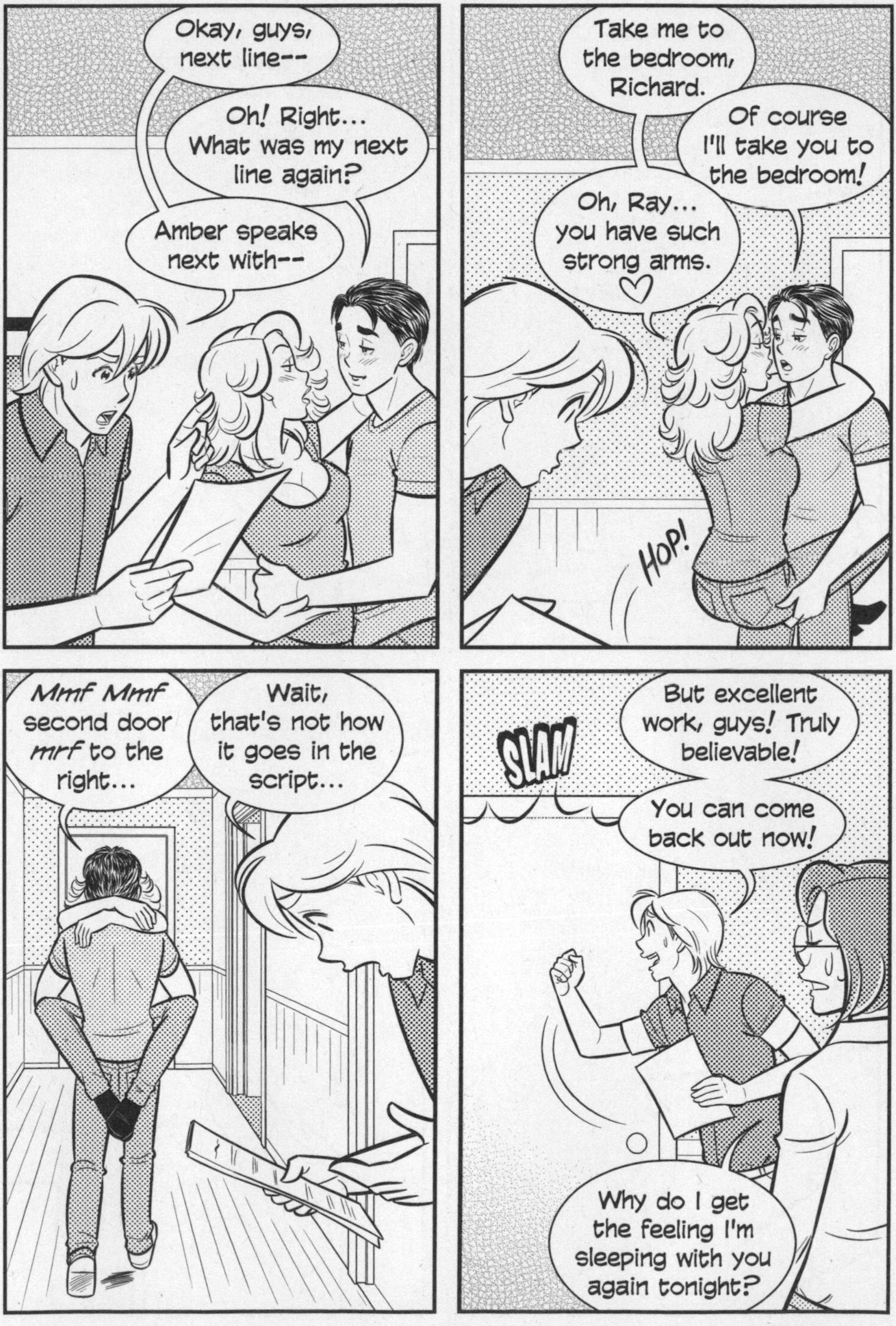
Okay, guys, next line--
Oh! Right... What was my next line again?
Amber speaks next with--
Take me to the bedroom, Richard.
Of course I'll take you to the bedroom!
Oh, Ray... you have such strong arms.
HOP!
Mmf Mmf second door *mrf* to the right...
Wait, that's not how it goes in the script...
SLAM
But excellent work, guys! Truly believable!
You can come back out now!
Why do I get the feeling I'm sleeping with you again tonight?

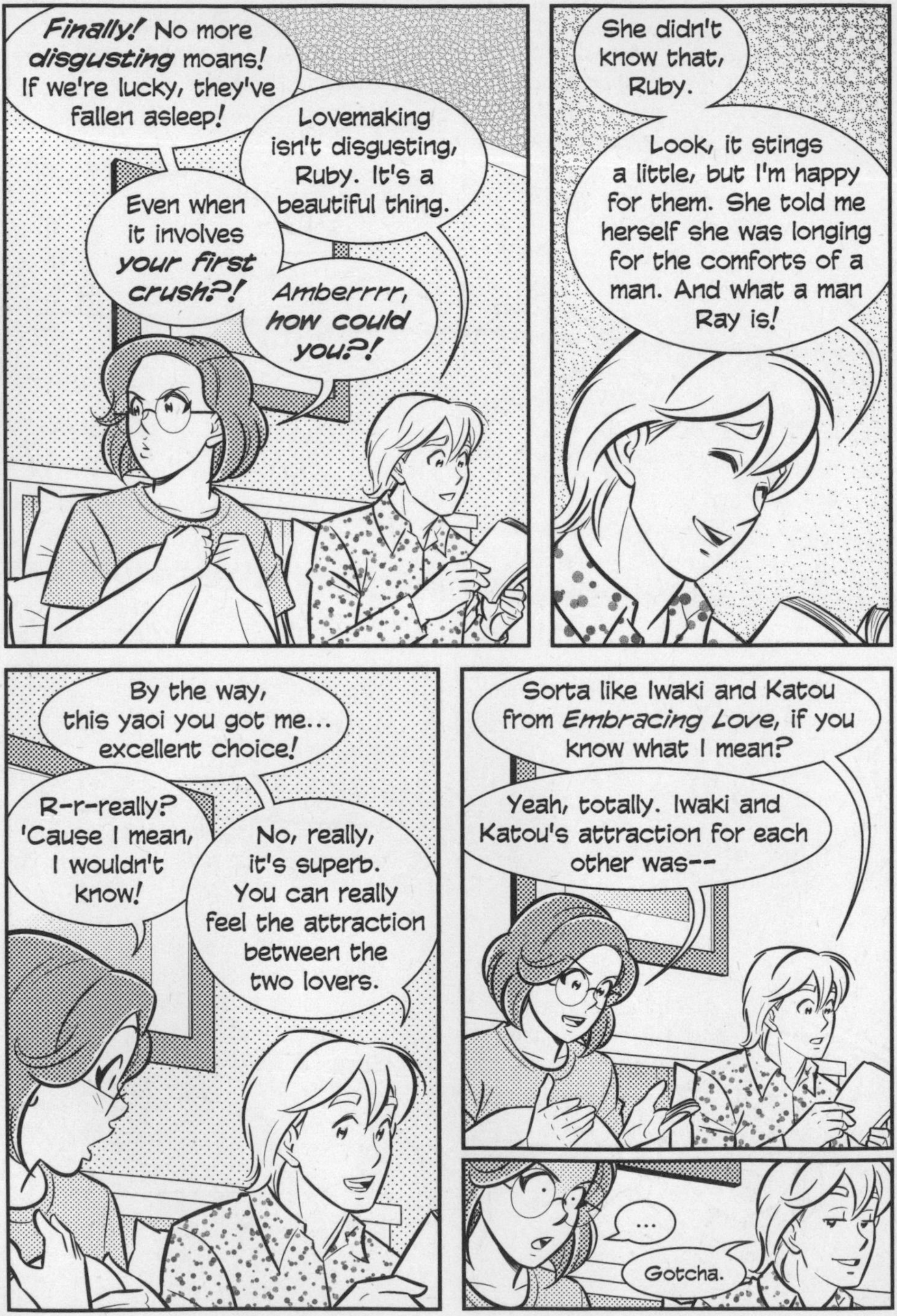
Finally! No more *disgusting* moans! If we're lucky, they've fallen asleep!
Lovemaking isn't disgusting, Ruby. It's a beautiful thing.
Even when it involves *your first crush?!*
Amberrrr, how could you?!
She didn't know that, Ruby.
Look, it stings a little, but I'm happy for them. She told me herself she was longing for the comforts of a man. And what a man Ray is!
By the way, this yaoi you got me... excellent choice!
R-r-really? 'Cause I mean, I wouldn't know!
No, really, it's superb. You can really feel the attraction between the two lovers.
Sorta like Iwaki and Katou from *Embracing Love*, if you know what I mean?
Yeah, totally. Iwaki and Katou's attraction for each other was--
...
Gotcha.

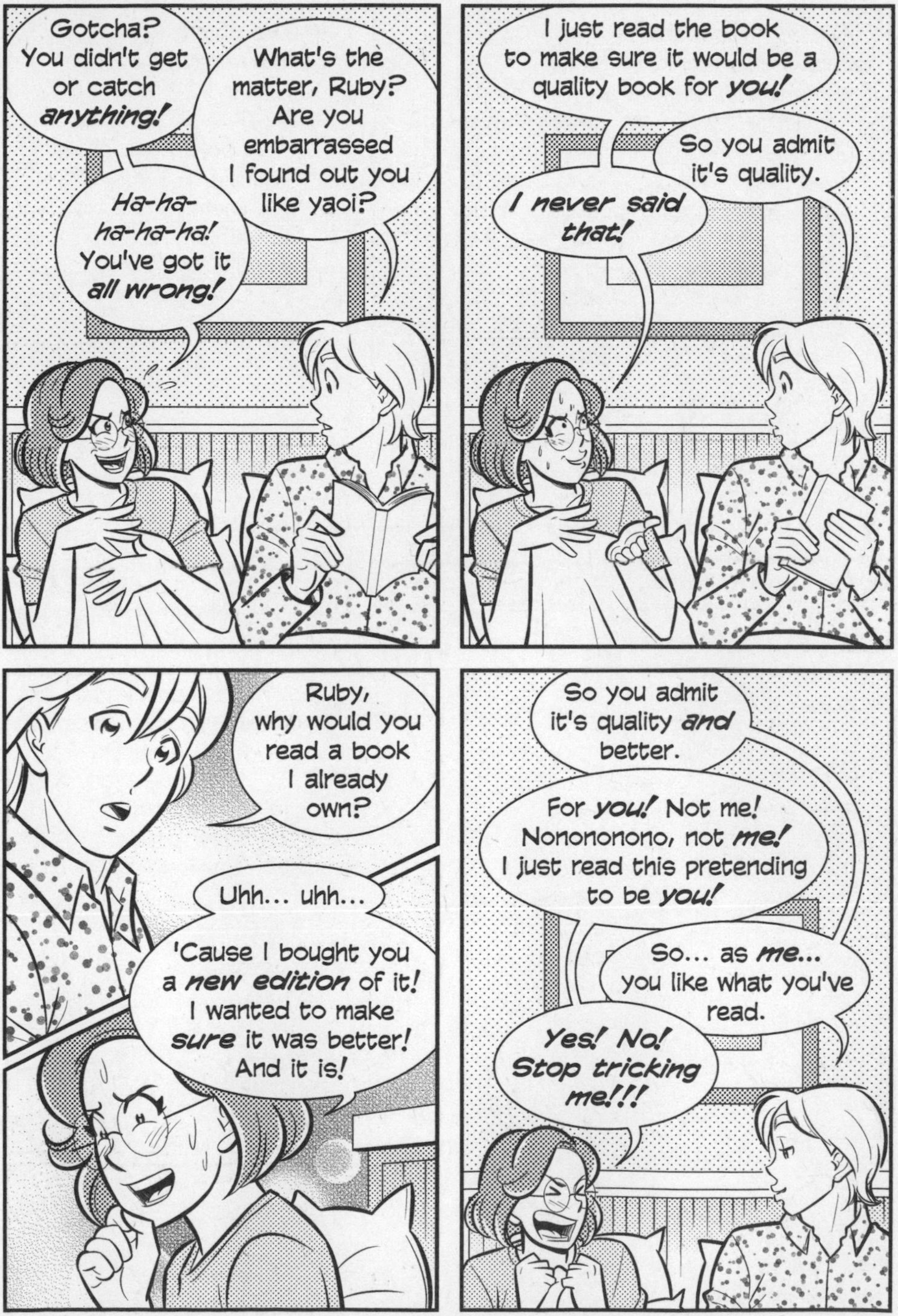
Gotcha? You didn't get or catch *anything!*
What's the matter, Ruby? Are you embarrassed I found out you like yaoi?
Ha-ha-ha-ha-ha! You've got it *all wrong!*
I just read the book to make sure it would be a quality book for *you!*
So you admit it's quality.
I never said that!
Ruby, why would you read a book I already own?
Uhh... uhh...
'Cause I bought you a *new edition* of it! I wanted to make *sure* it was better! And it is!
So you admit it's quality *and* better.
For *you!* Not me! Nononono, not *me!* I just read this pretending to be *you!*
So... as *me*... you like what you've read.
Yes! No! Stop tricking me!!!

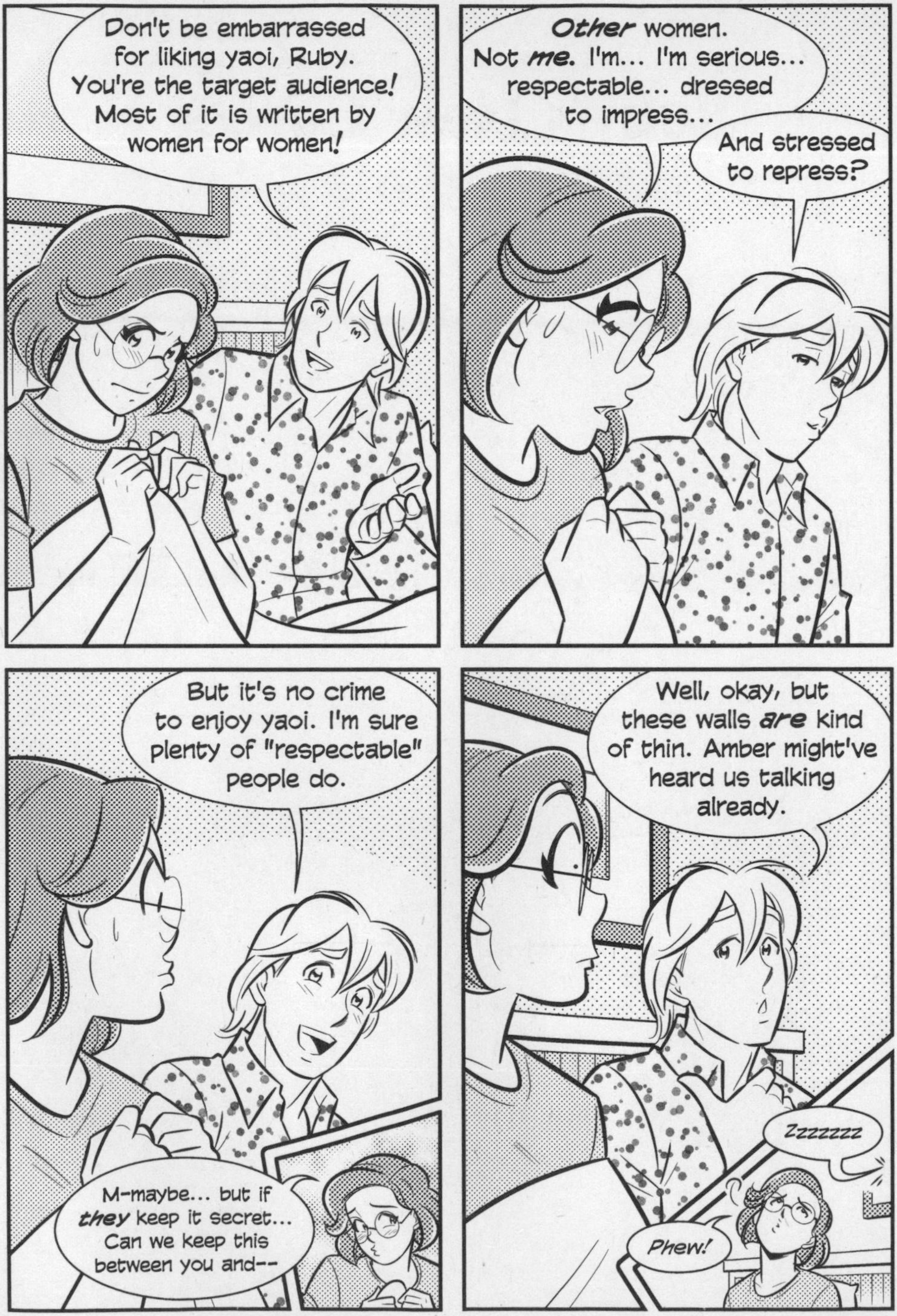
Don't be embarrassed for liking yaoi, Ruby. You're the target audience! Most of it is written by women for women!
Other women. Not *me.* I'm... I'm serious... respectable... dressed to impress...
And stressed to repress?
But it's no crime to enjoy yaoi. I'm sure plenty of "respectable" people do.
M-maybe... but if *they* keep it secret... Can we keep this between you and--
Well, okay, but these walls *are* kind of thin. Amber might've heard us talking already.
Zzzzzzz
Phew!

Ruby's New Career

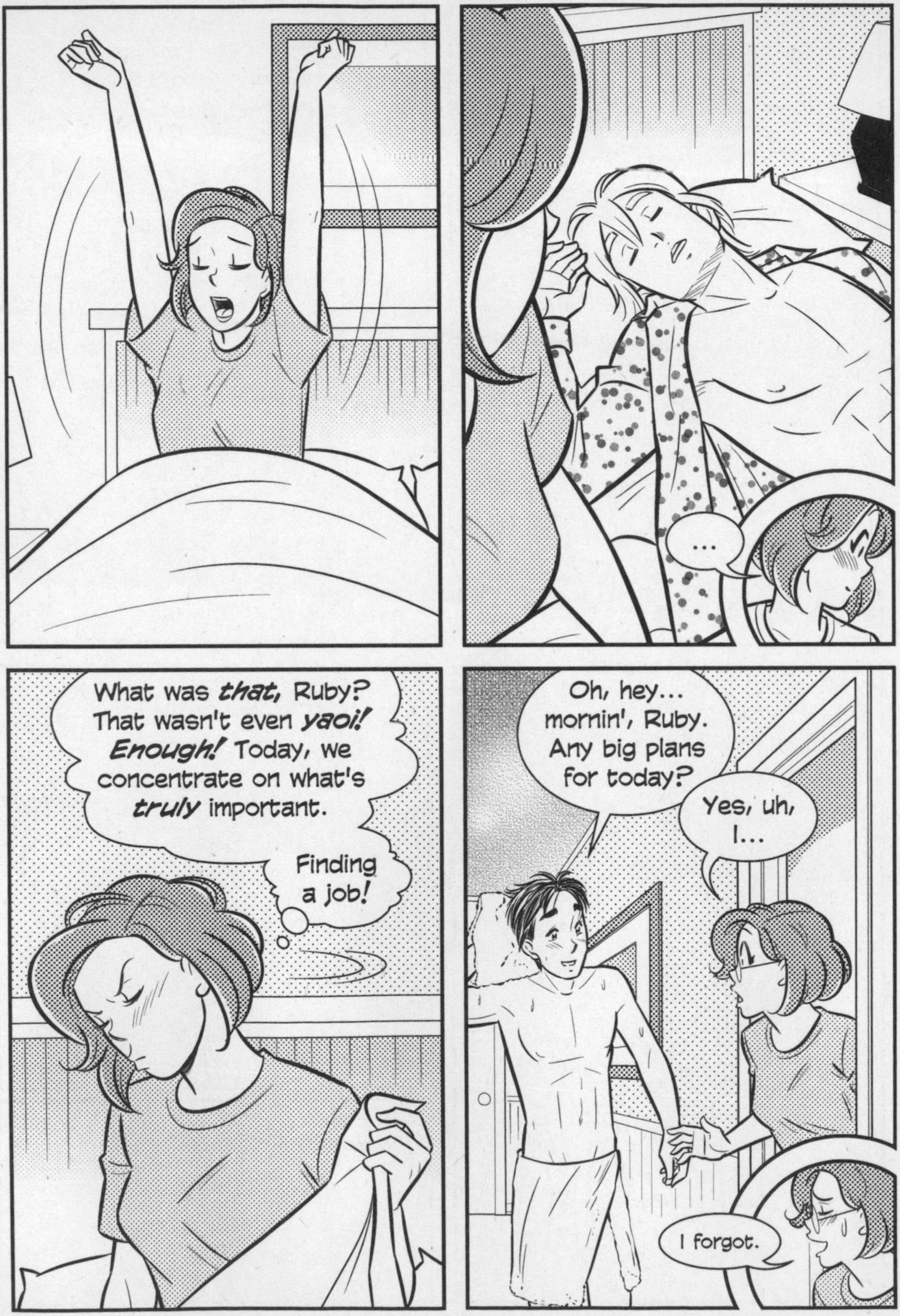
...
What was *that*, Ruby? That wasn't even *yaoi!* *Enough!* Today, we concentrate on what's *truly* important.
Finding a job!
Oh, hey... mornin', Ruby. Any big plans for today?
Yes, uh, I...
I forgot.

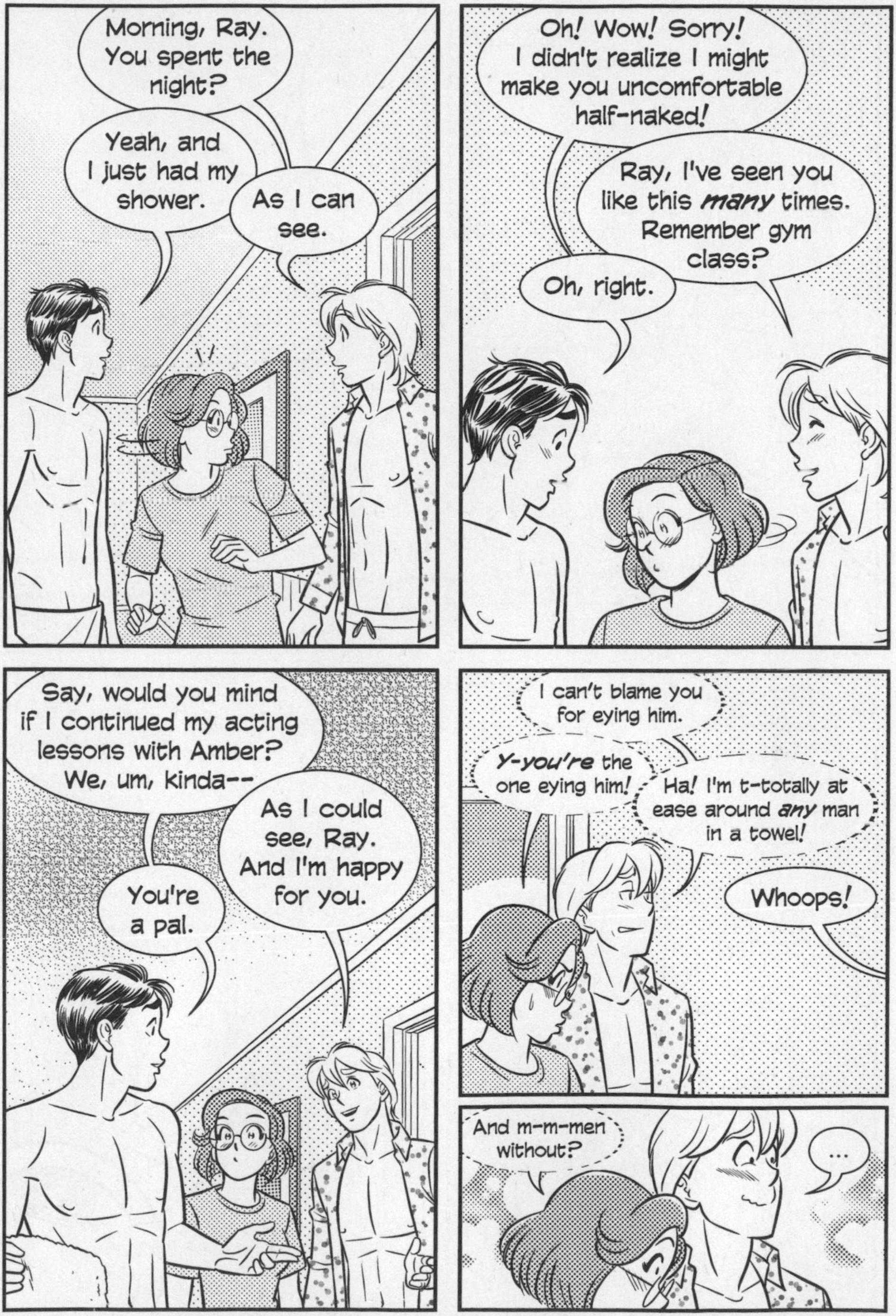
Morning, Ray. You spent the night?
Yeah, and I just had my shower.
As I can see.
Oh! Wow! Sorry! I didn't realize I might make you uncomfortable half-naked!
Ray, I've seen you like this *many* times. Remember gym class?
Oh, right.
Say, would you mind if I continued my acting lessons with Amber? We, um, kinda--
As I could see, Ray. And I'm happy for you.
You're a pal.
I can't blame you for eying him.
Y-you're the one eying him!
Ha! I'm t-totally at ease around *any* man in a towel!
Whoops!
And m-m-men without?
...

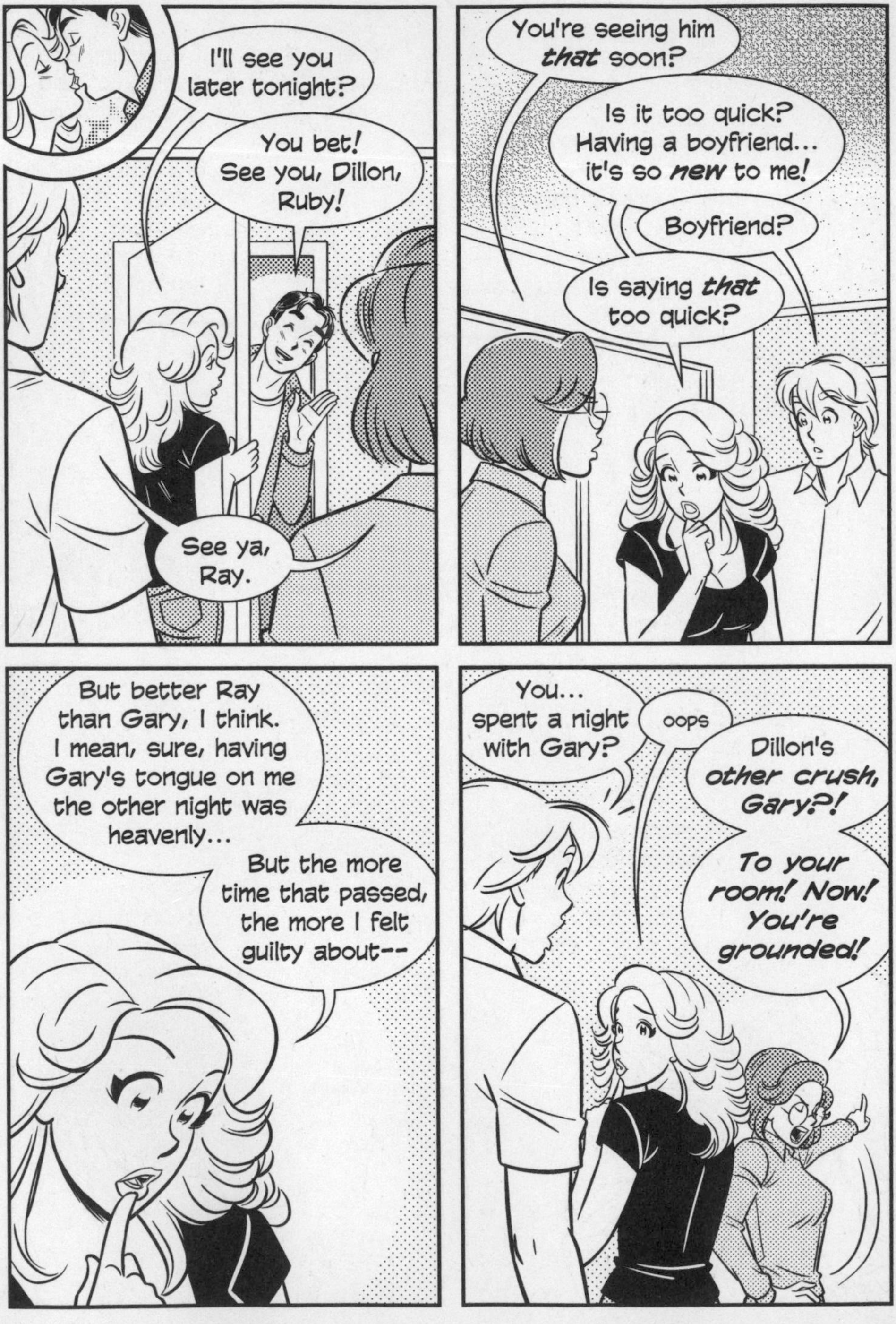
I'll see you later tonight?
You bet! See you, Dillon, Ruby!
See ya, Ray.
You're seeing him *that* soon?
Is it too quick? Having a boyfriend... it's so *new* to me!
Boyfriend?
Is saying *that* too quick?
But better Ray than Gary, I think. I mean, sure, having Gary's tongue on me the other night was heavenly...
But the more time that passed, the more I felt guilty about--
You... spent a night with Gary?
oops
Dillon's *other crush, Gary?!*
To your room! Now! You're grounded!

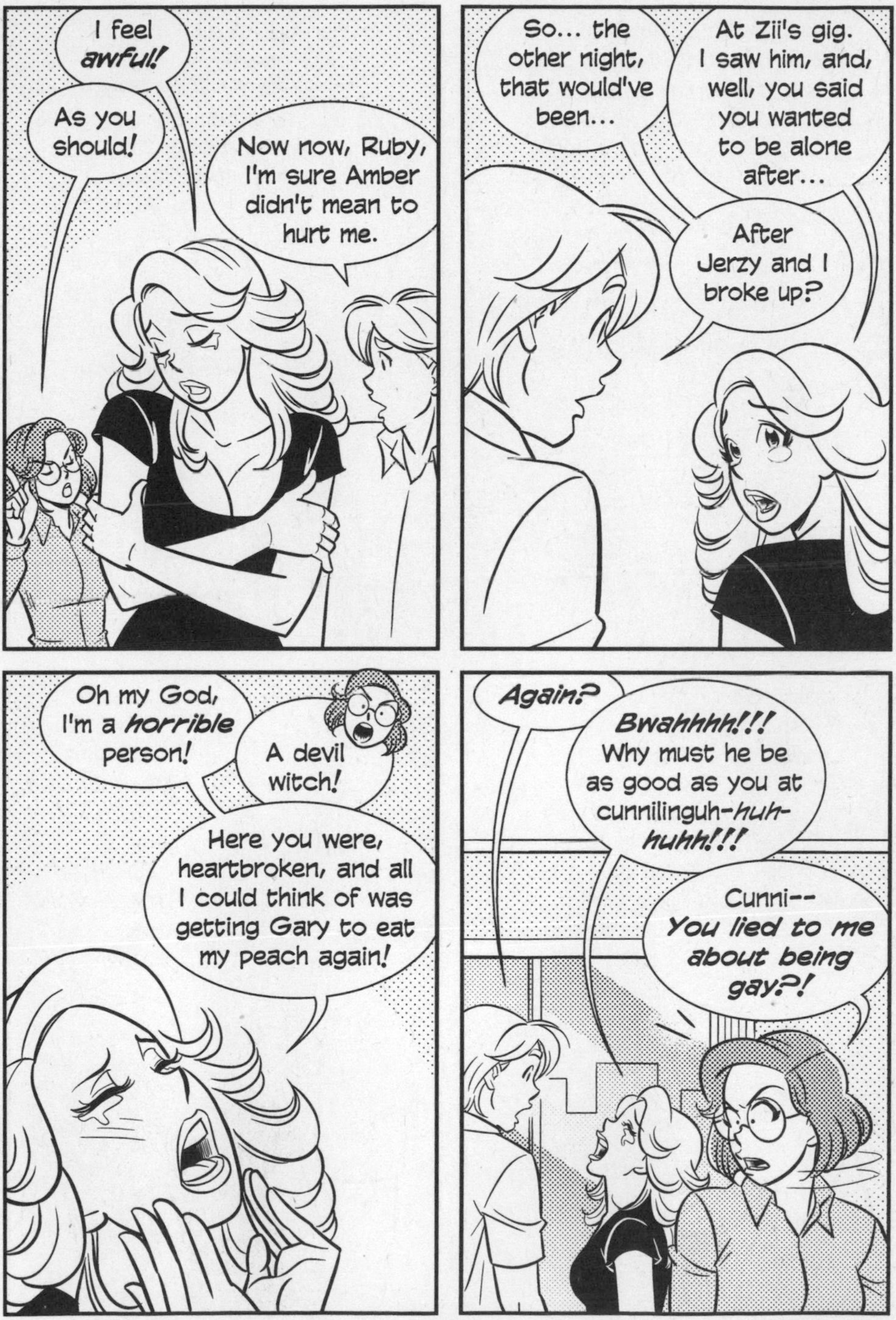
I feel *awful!*
As you should!
Now now, Ruby, I'm sure Amber didn't mean to hurt me.
So... the other night, that would've been...
At Zii's gig. I saw him, and, well, you said you wanted to be alone after...
After Jerzy and I broke up?
Oh my God, I'm a *horrible* person!
A devil witch!
Here you were, heartbroken, and all I could think of was getting Gary to eat my peach again!
Again?
Bwahhhh!!! Why must he be as good as you at cunnilinguh-*huh-huhh!!!*
Cunni-- *You lied to me about being gay?!*

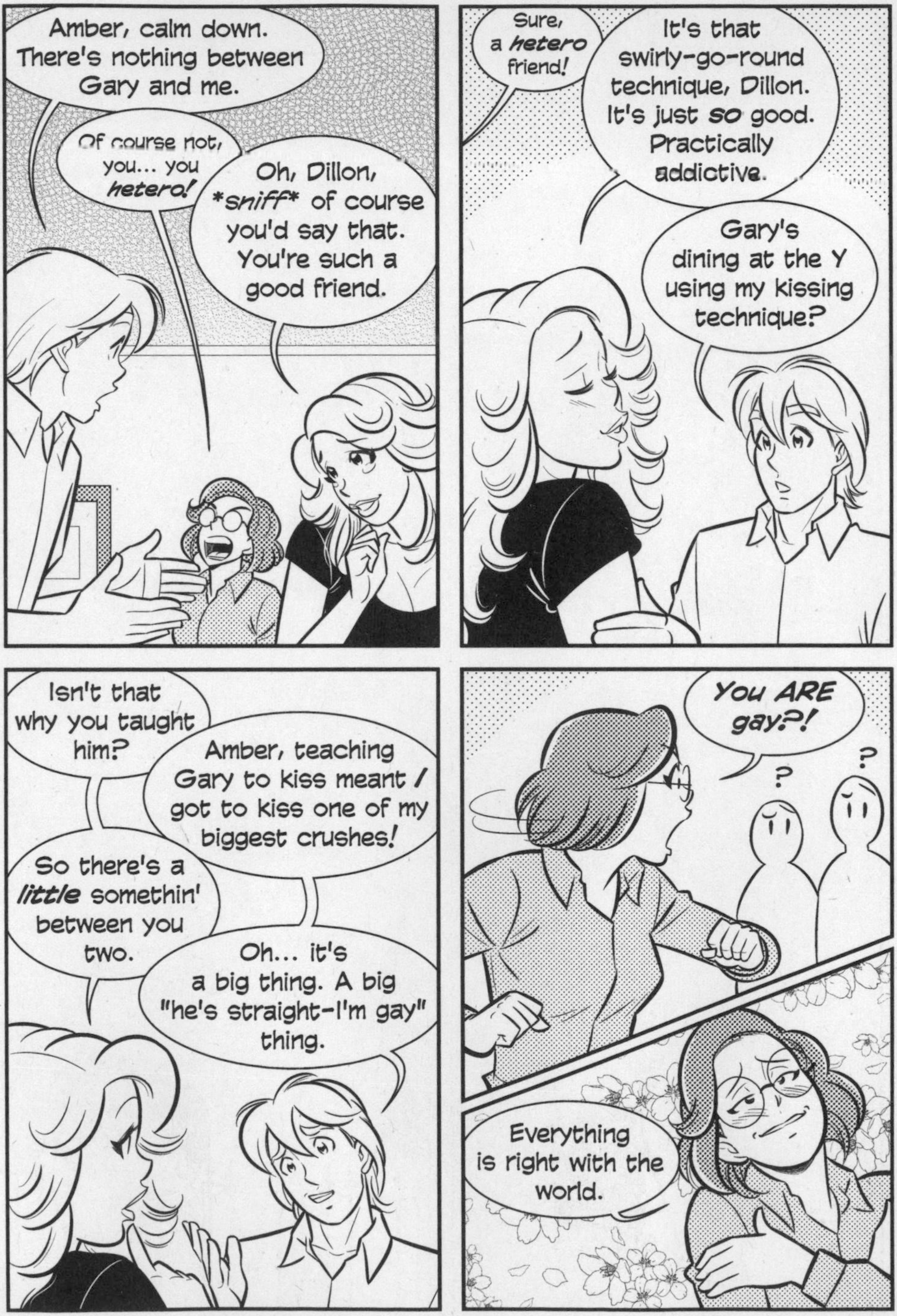
Amber, calm down. There's nothing between Gary and me.
Of course not, you... you hetero!
Oh, Dillon, *sniff* of course you'd say that. You're such a good friend.
Sure, a hetero friend!
It's that swirly-go-round technique, Dillon. It's just so good. Practically addictive.
Gary's dining at the Y using my kissing technique?
Isn't that why you taught him?
Amber, teaching Gary to kiss meant I got to kiss one of my biggest crushes!
So there's a little somethin' between you two.
Oh... it's a big thing. A big "he's straight-I'm gay" thing.
You ARE gay?!
?
?
Everything is right with the world.

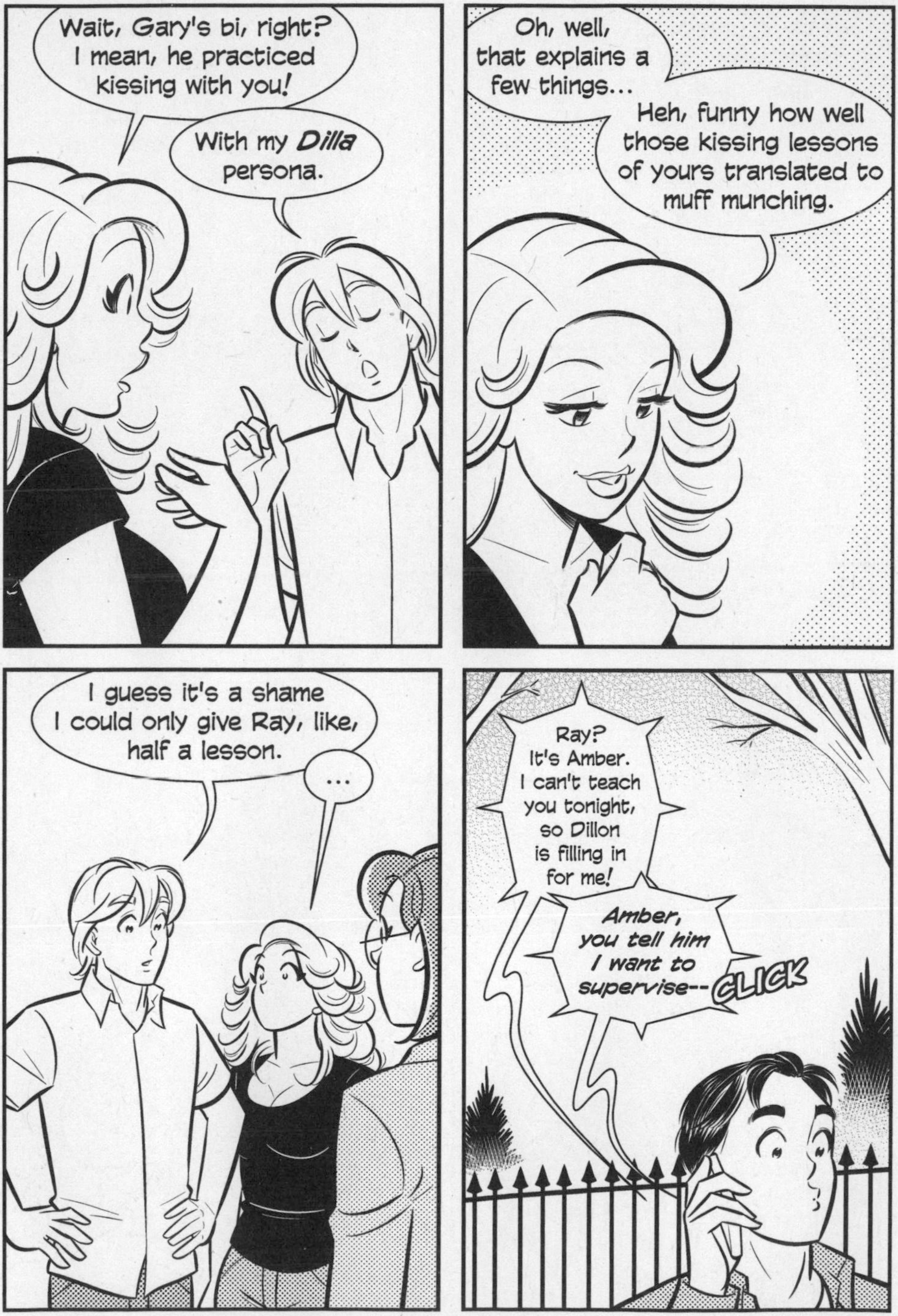
Wait, Gary's bi, right? I mean, he practiced kissing with you!
With my *Dilla* persona.
Oh, well, that explains a few things...
Heh, funny how well those kissing lessons of yours translated to muff munching.
I guess it's a shame I could only give Ray, like, half a lesson.
...
Ray? It's Amber. I can't teach you tonight, so Dillon is filling in for me!
Amber, you tell him I want to supervise--
CLICK

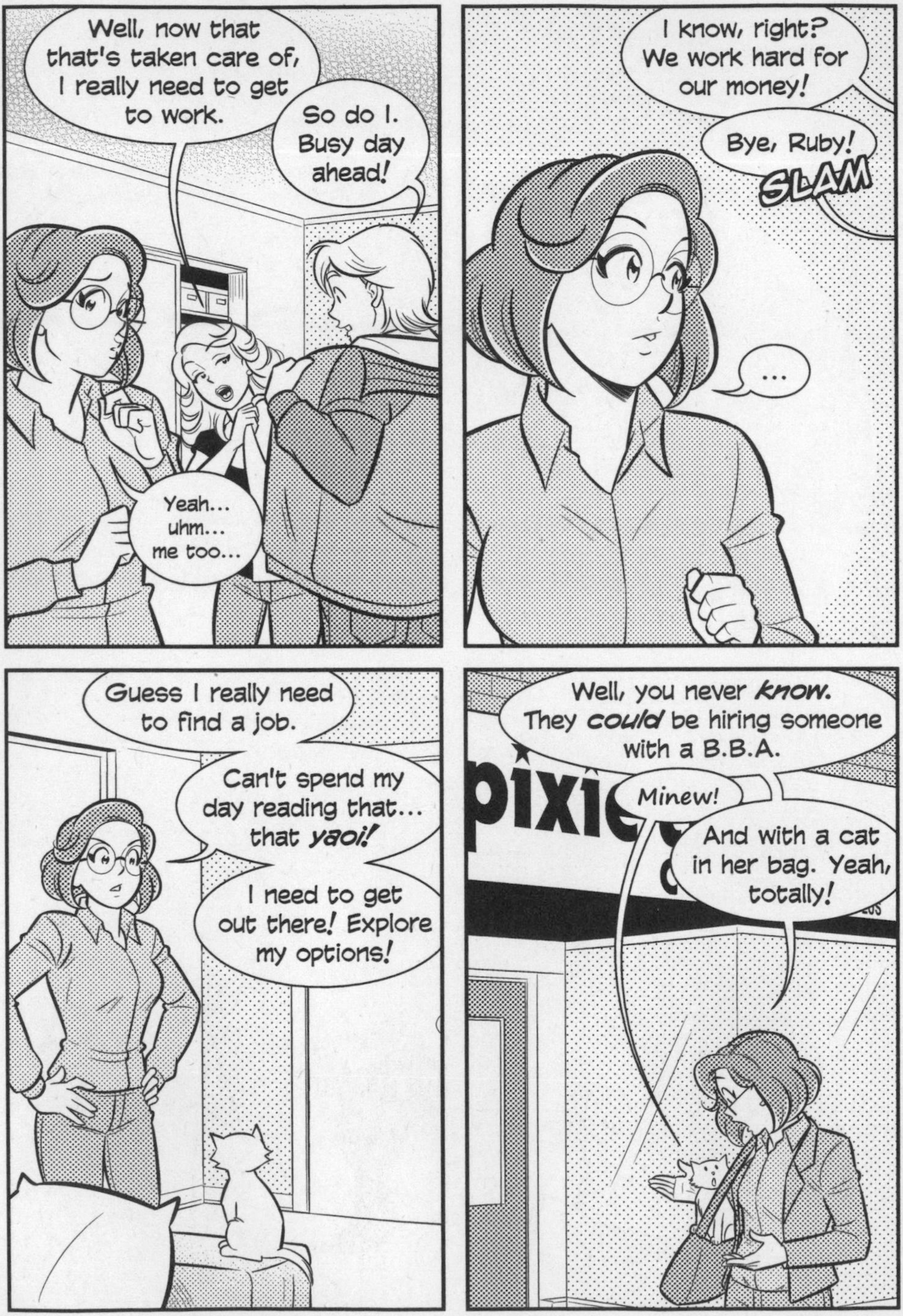
Well, now that that's taken care of, I really need to get to work.
So do I. Busy day ahead!
Yeah... uhm... me too...
I know, right? We work hard for our money!
Bye, Ruby!
SLAM
...
Guess I really need to find a job.
Can't spend my day reading that... that *yaoi!*
I need to get out there! Explore my options!
Well, you never *know.* They *could* be hiring someone with a B.B.A.
Minew!
And with a cat in her bag. Yeah, totally!

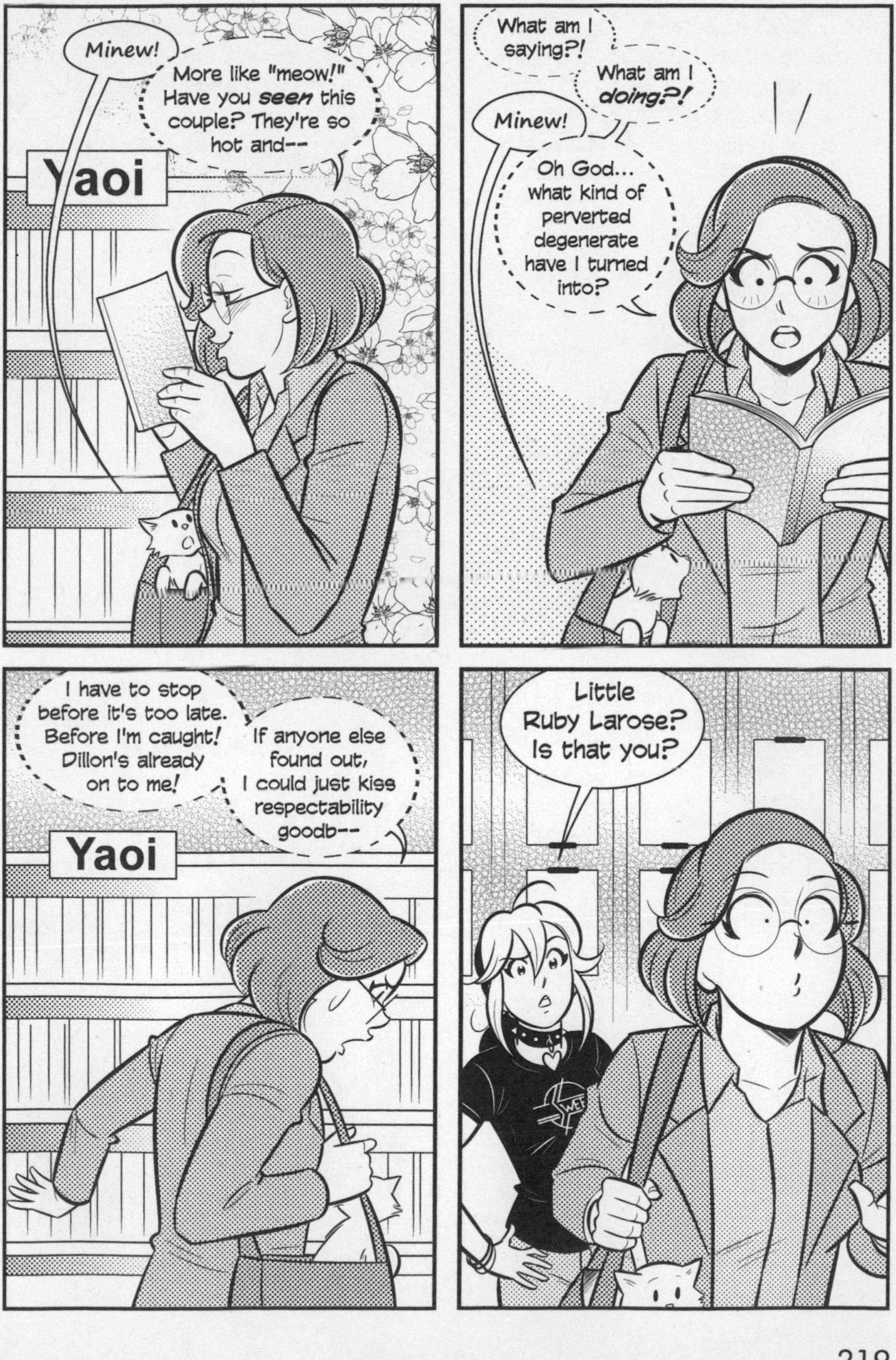
Minew!
More like "meow!" Have you *seen* this couple? They're so hot and--
Yaoi
What am I saying?!
What am I *doing?!*
Minew!
Oh God... what kind of perverted degenerate have I turned into?
I have to stop before it's too late. Before I'm caught! Dillon's already on to me!
If anyone else found out, I could just kiss respectability goodb--
Yaoi
Little Ruby Larose? Is that you?

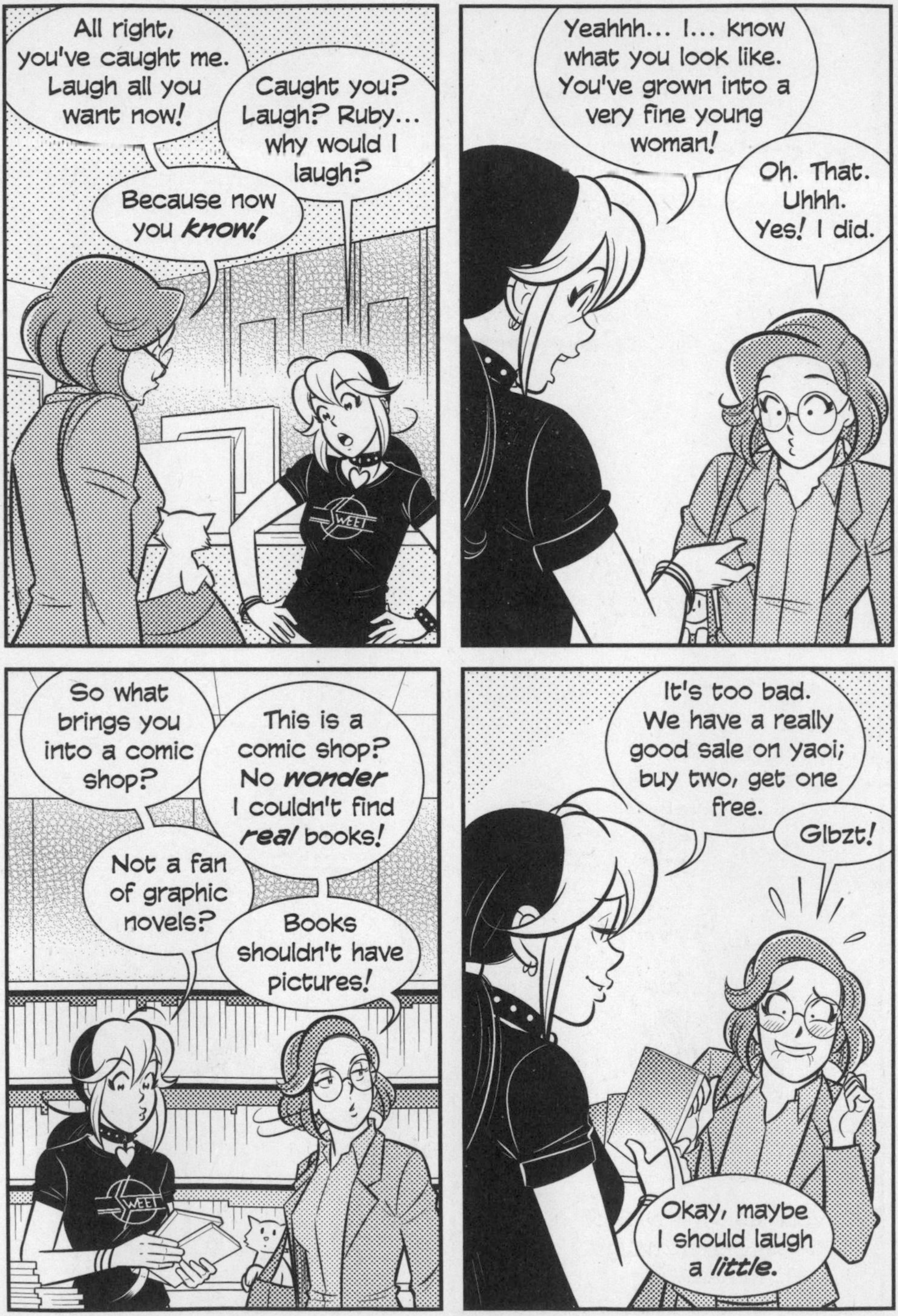
All right, you've caught me. Laugh all you want now!
Caught you? Laugh? Ruby... why would I laugh?
Because now you *know!*
Yeahhh... I... know what you look like. You've grown into a very fine young woman!
Oh. That. Uhhh. Yes! I did.
So what brings you into a comic shop?
This is a comic shop? No *wonder* I couldn't find *real* books!
Not a fan of graphic novels?
Books shouldn't have pictures!
It's too bad. We have a really good sale on yaoi; buy two, get one free.
Glbzt!
Okay, maybe I should laugh a *little.*

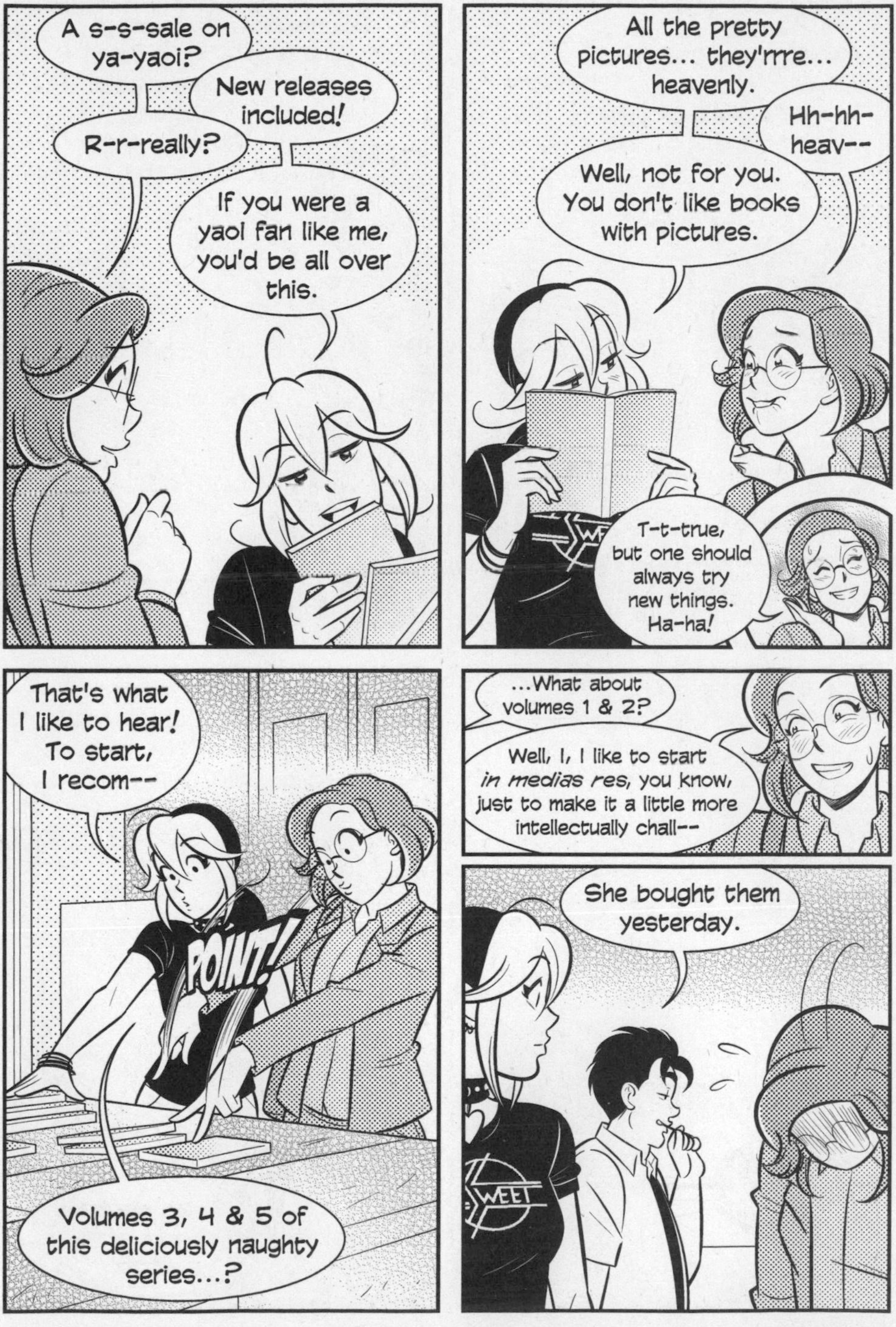
A s-s-sale on ya-yaoi?
New releases included!
R-r-really?
If you were a yaol fan like me, you'd be all over this.
All the pretty pictures... they'rrre... heavenly.
Hh-hh-heav--
Well, not for you. You don't like books with pictures.
T-t-true, but one should always try new things. Ha-ha!
That's what I like to hear! To start, I recom--
POINT!
Volumes 3, 4 & 5 of this deliciously naughty series...?
...What about volumes 1 & 2?
Well, I, I like to start *in medias res*, you know, just to make it a little more intellectually chall--
She bought them yesterday.

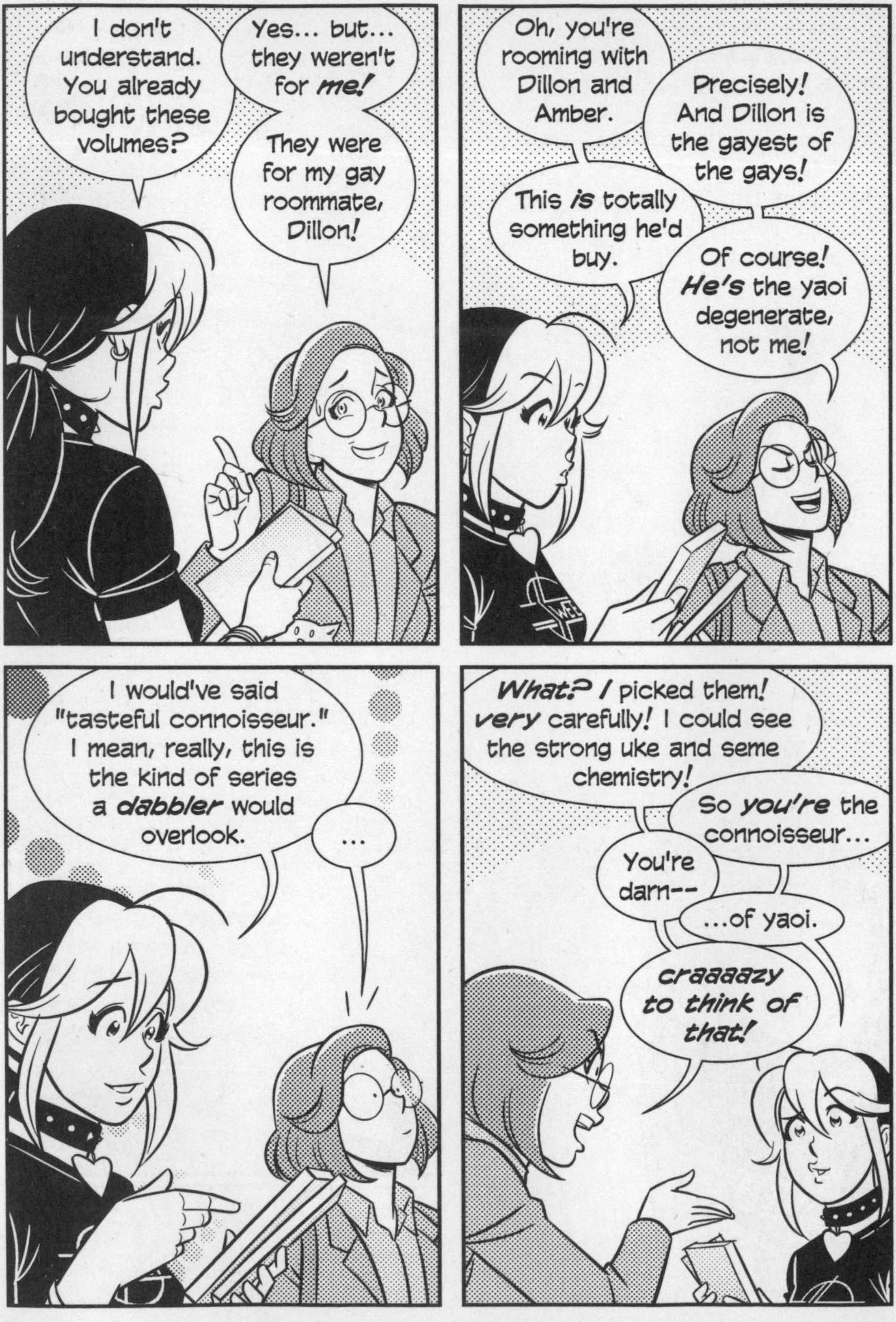
I don't understand. You already bought these volumes?
Yes... but... they weren't for *me!*
They were for my gay roommate, Dillon!
Oh, you're rooming with Dillon and Amber.
This *is* totally something he'd buy.
Precisely! And Dillon is the gayest of the gays!
Of course! *He's* the yaoi degenerate, not me!
I would've said "tasteful connoisseur." I mean, really, this is the kind of series a *dabbler* would overlook.
...
What? I picked them! *very* carefully! I could see the strong uke and seme chemistry!
So *you're* the connoisseur...
You're darn--
...of yaoi.
craaaazy to think of that!

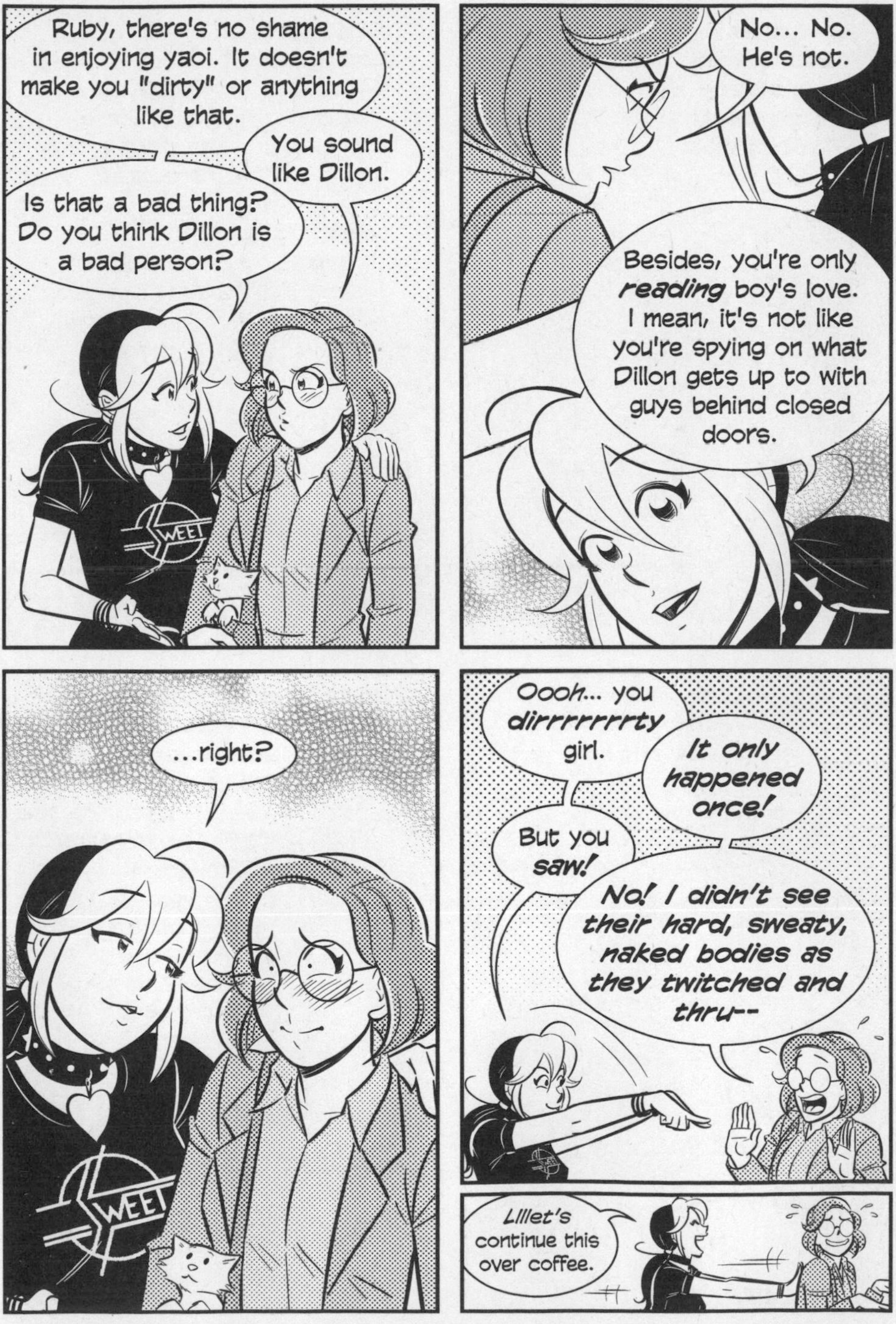
Ruby, there's no shame in enjoying yaoi. It doesn't make you "dirty" or anything like that.
You sound like Dillon.
Is that a bad thing? Do you think Dillon is a bad person?
SWEET
No... No. He's not.
Besides, you're only *reading* boy's love. I mean, it's not like you're spying on what Dillon gets up to with guys behind closed doors.
...right?
SWEET
Oooh... you *dirrrrrrrty* girl.
It only happened once!
But you *saw!*
No! I didn't see their hard, sweaty, naked bodies as they twitched and thru--
Llllet's continue this over coffee.

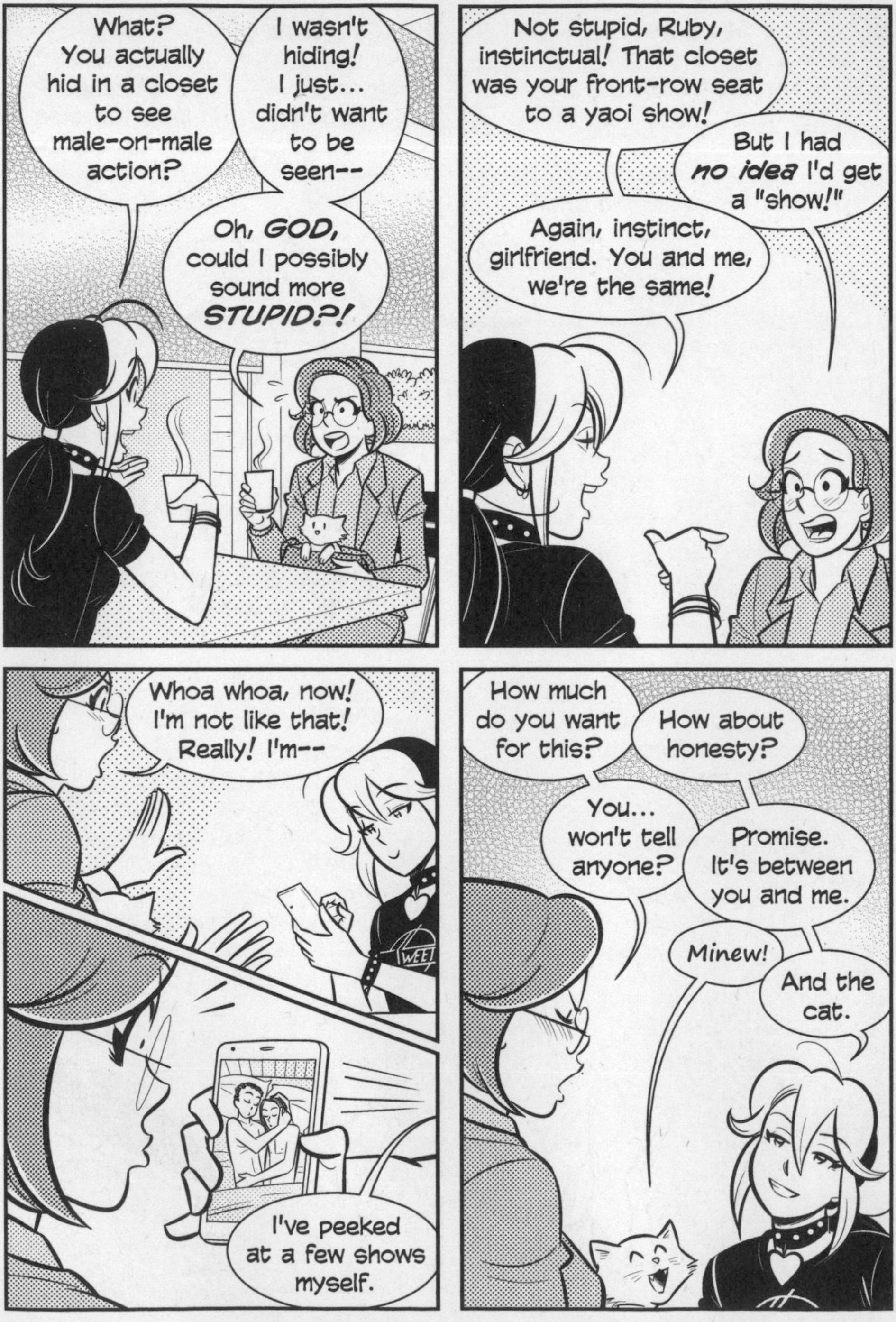
What? You actually hid in a closet to see male-on-male action?
I wasn't hiding! I just... didn't want to be seen--
Oh, GOD, could I possibly sound more STUPID?!
Not stupid, Ruby, instinctual! That closet was your front-row seat to a yaoi show!
But I had no idea I'd get a "show!"
Again, instinct, girlfriend. You and me, we're the same!
Whoa whoa, now! I'm not like that! Really! I'm--
I've peeked at a few shows myself.
How much do you want for this?
How about honesty?
You... won't tell anyone?
Promise. It's between you and me.
Minew!
And the cat.

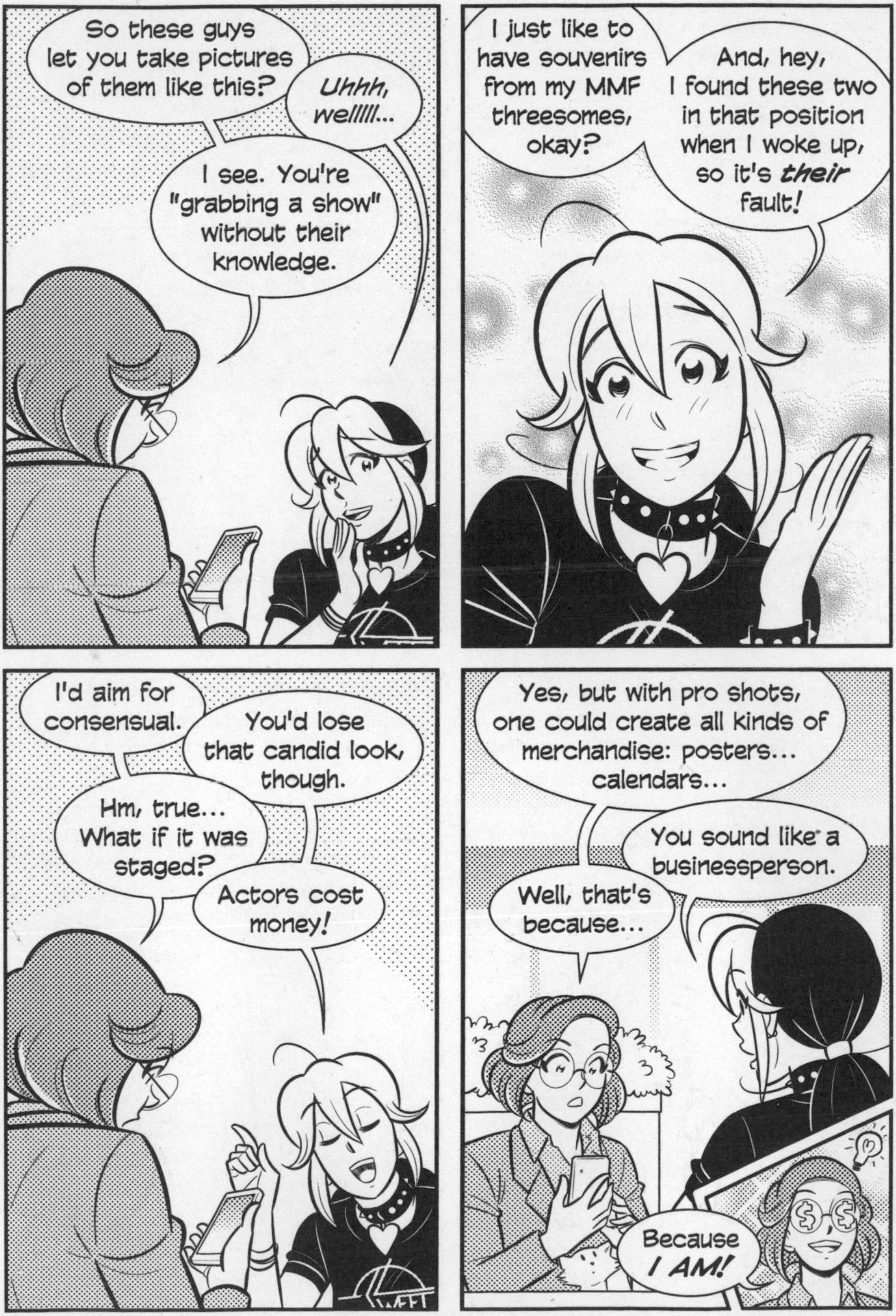
So these guys let you take pictures of them like this?
Uhhh, wellllll...
I see. You're "grabbing a show" without their knowledge.
I just like to have souvenirs from my MMF threesomes, okay?
And, hey, I found these two in that position when I woke up, so it's *their* fault!
I'd aim for consensual.
You'd lose that candid look, though.
Hm, true... What if it was staged?
Actors cost money!
Yes, but with pro shots, one could create all kinds of merchandise: posters... calendars...
You sound like a businessperson.
Well, that's because...
Because *I AM!*

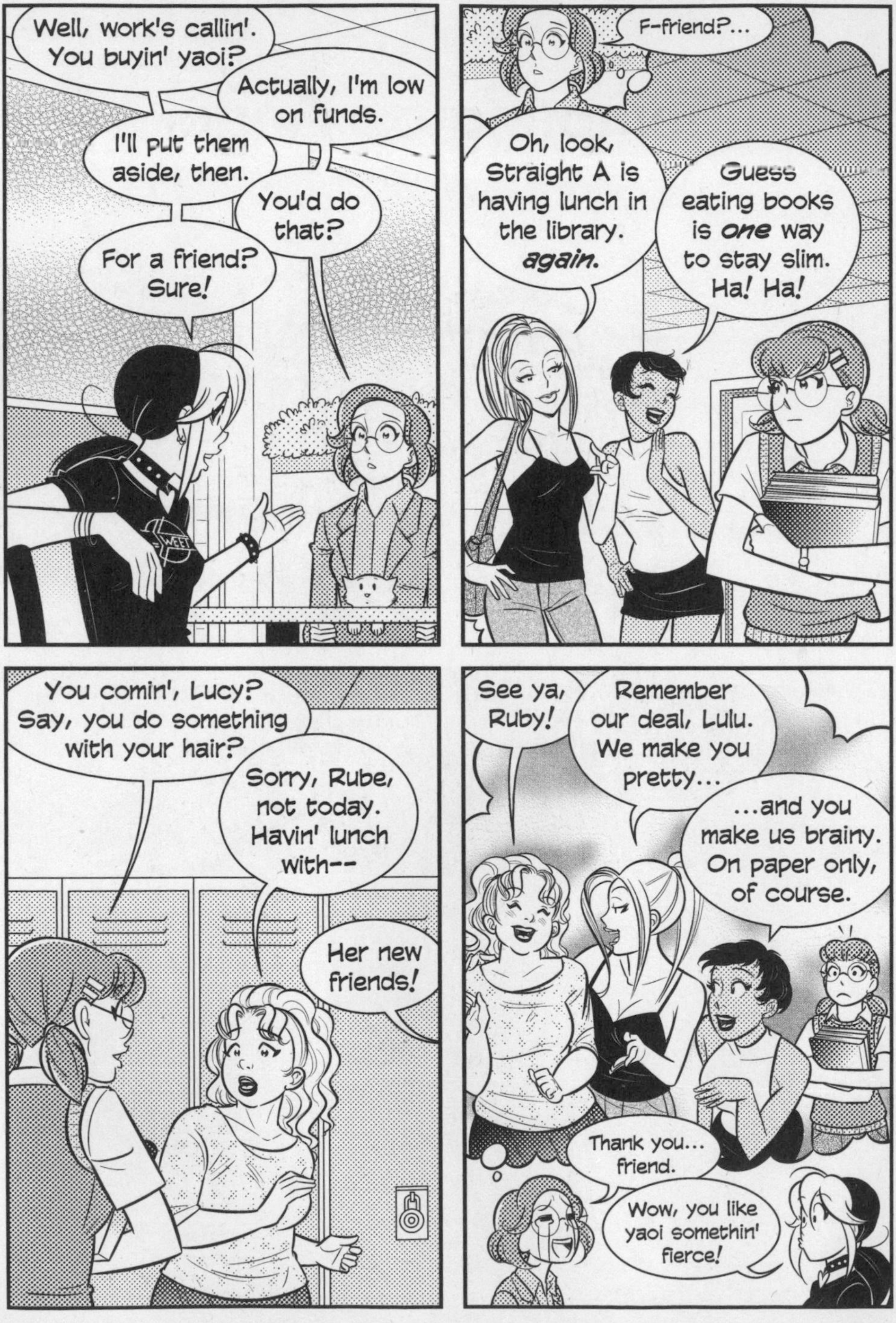
Well, work's callin'. You buyin' yaoi?
Actually, I'm low on funds.
I'll put them aside, then.
You'd do that?
For a friend? Sure!
F-friend?...
Oh, look, Straight A is having lunch in the library. *again*.
Guess eating books is *one* way to stay slim. Ha! Ha!
You comin', Lucy? Say, you do something with your hair?
Sorry, Rube, not today. Havin' lunch with--
Her new friends!
See ya, Ruby!
Remember our deal, Lulu. We make you pretty...
...and you make us brainy. On paper only, of course.
Thank you... friend.
Wow, you like yaoi somethin' fierce!

Tempting an Angel

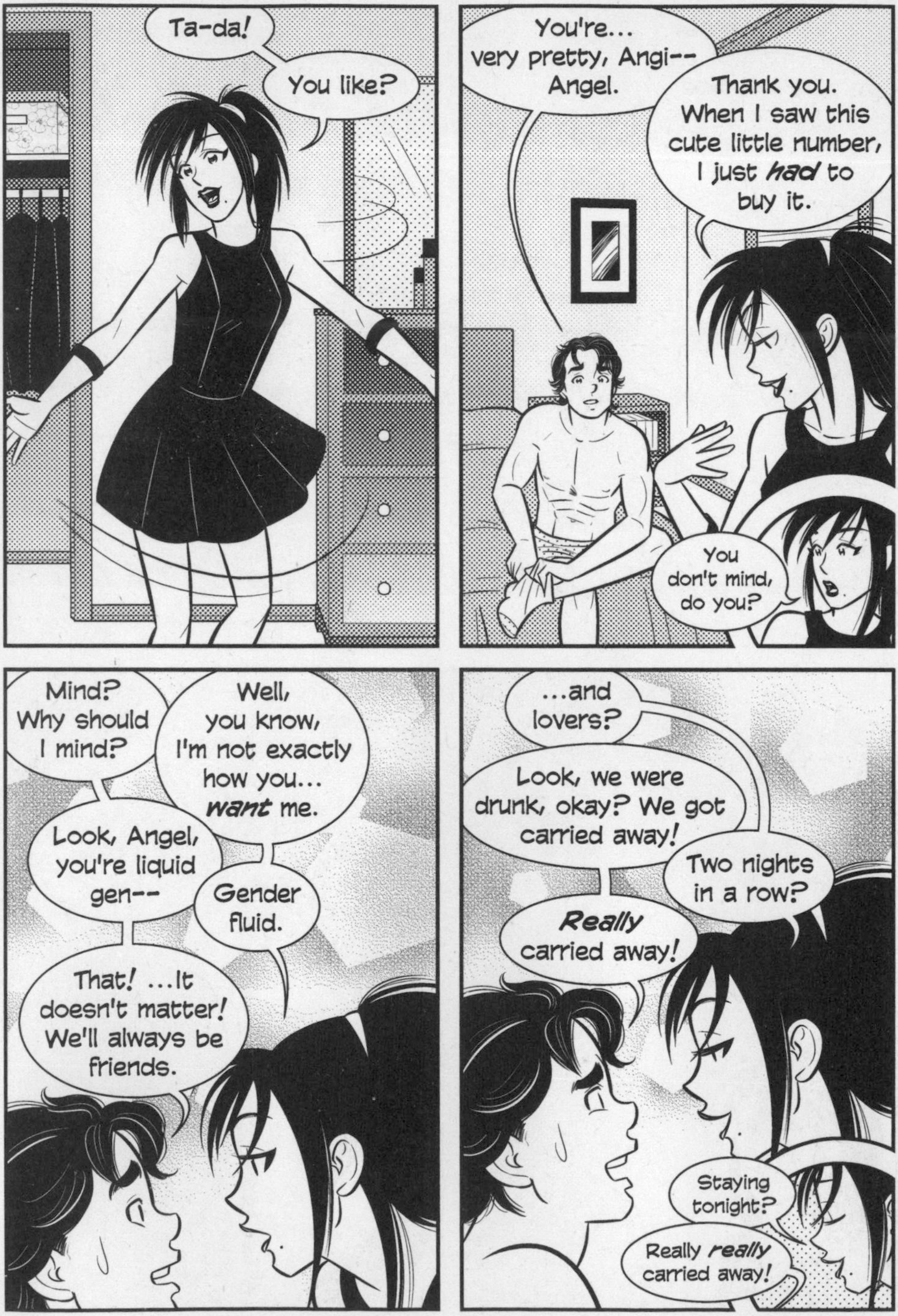
Ta-da!
You like?
You're... very pretty, Angi-- Angel.
Thank you. When I saw this cute little number, I just *had* to buy it.
You don't mind, do you?
Mind? Why should I mind?
Well, you know, I'm not exactly how you... *want* me.
Look, Angel, you're liquid gen--
Gender fluid.
That! ...It doesn't matter! We'll always be friends.
...and lovers?
Look, we were drunk, okay? We got carried away!
Two nights in a row?
Really carried away!
Staying tonight?
Really *really* carried away!

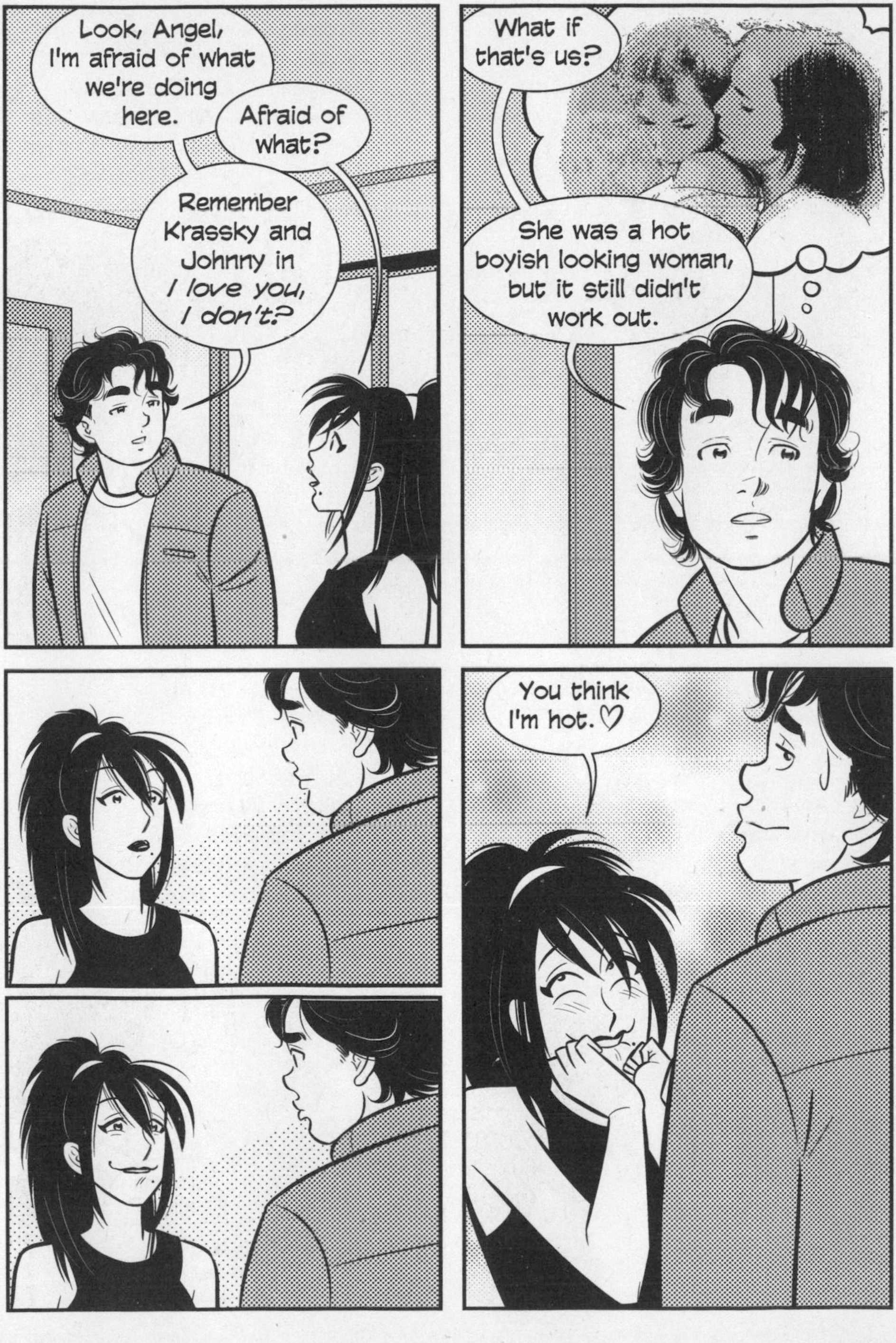
Look, Angel, I'm afraid of what we're doing here.
Afraid of what?
Remember Krassky and Johnny in *I love you, I don't?*
What if that's us?
She was a hot boyish looking woman, but it still didn't work out.
You think I'm hot. ♡

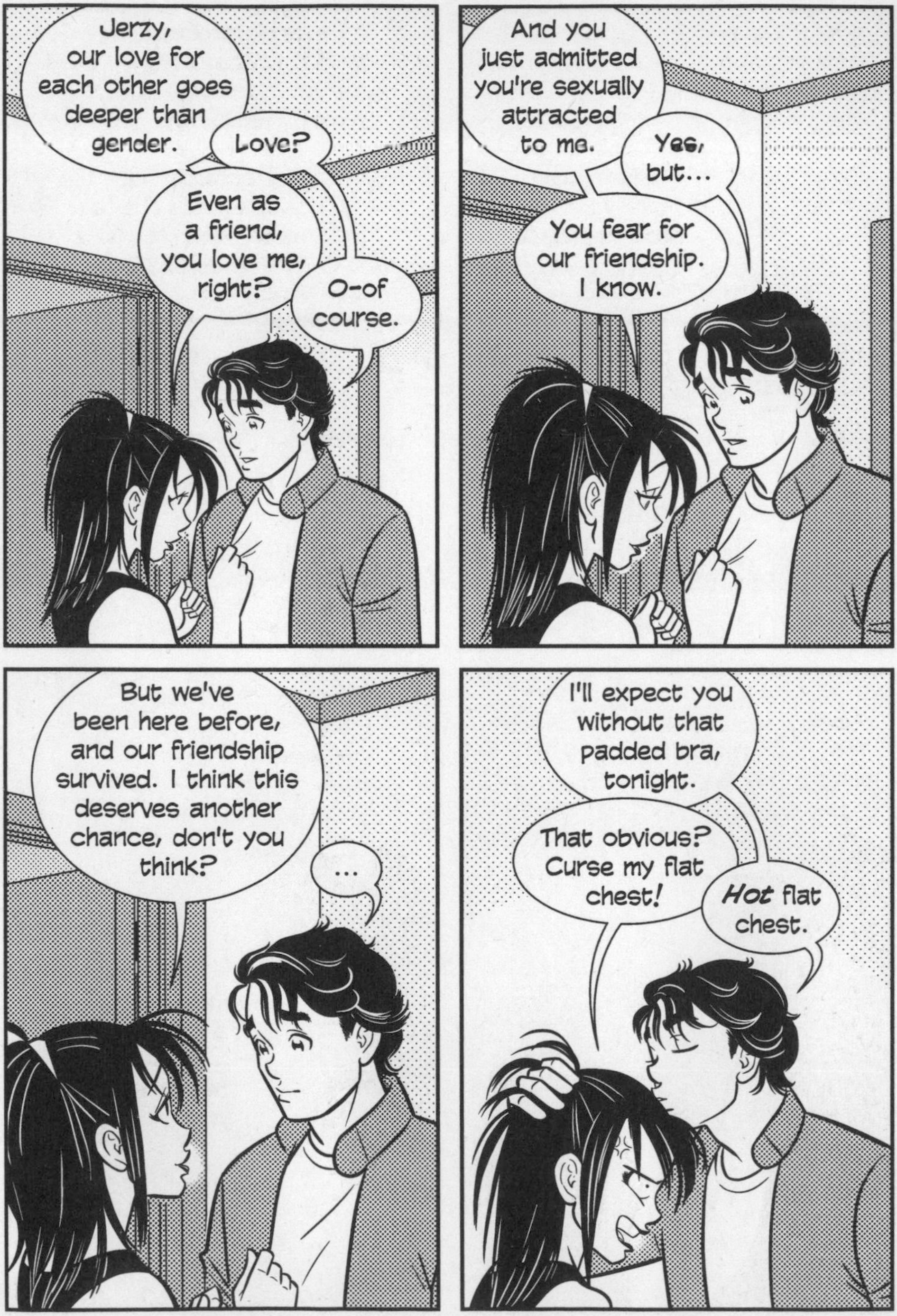

Jerzy, our love for each other goes deeper than gender.
Love?
Even as a friend, you love me, right?
O-of course.
And you just admitted you're sexually attracted to me.
Yes, but...
You fear for our friendship. I know.
But we've been here before, and our friendship survived. I think this deserves another chance, don't you think?
...
I'll expect you without that padded bra, tonight.
That obvious? Curse my flat chest!
Hot flat chest.

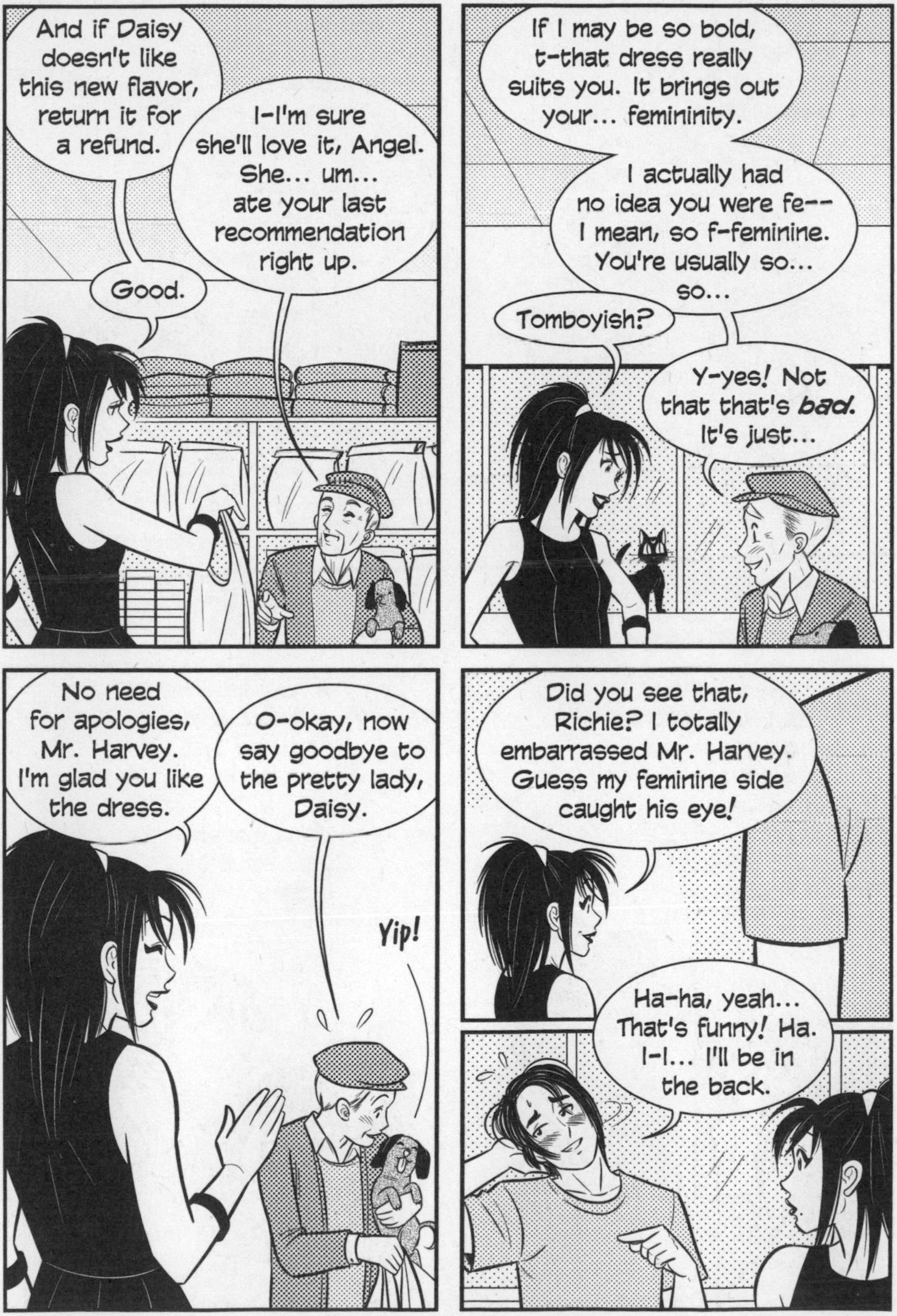
And if Daisy doesn't like this new flavor, return it for a refund.
I-I'm sure she'll love it, Angel. She... um... ate your last recommendation right up.
Good.
If I may be so bold, t-that dress really suits you. It brings out your... femininity.
I actually had no idea you were fe-- I mean, so f-feminine. You're usually so... so...
Tomboyish?
Y-yes! Not that that's *bad*. It's just...
No need for apologies, Mr. Harvey. I'm glad you like the dress.
O-okay, now say goodbye to the pretty lady, Daisy.
Yip!
Did you see that, Richie? I totally embarrassed Mr. Harvey. Guess my feminine side caught his eye!
Ha-ha, yeah... That's funny! Ha. I-I... I'll be in the back.

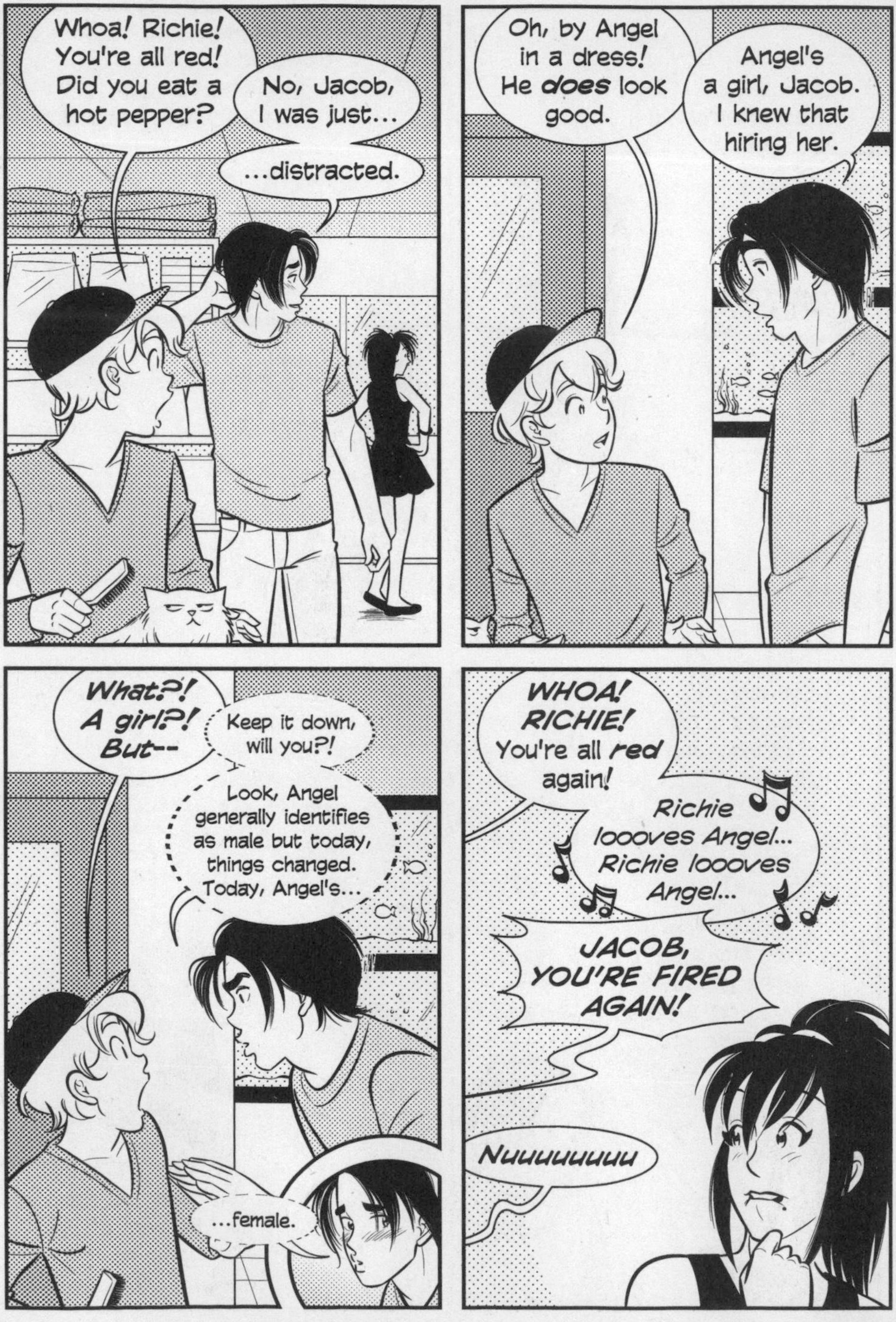
Whoa! Richie! You're all red! Did you eat a hot pepper?
No, Jacob, I was just...
...distracted.
Oh, by Angel in a dress! He *does* look good.
Angel's a girl, Jacob. I knew that hiring her.
What?! A girl?! But--
Keep it down, will you?!
Look, Angel generally identifies as male but today, things changed. Today, Angel's...
...female.
WHOA! RICHIE! You're all *red* again!
Richie loooves Angel... Richie loooves Angel...
JACOB, YOU'RE FIRED AGAIN!
Nuuuuuuuu

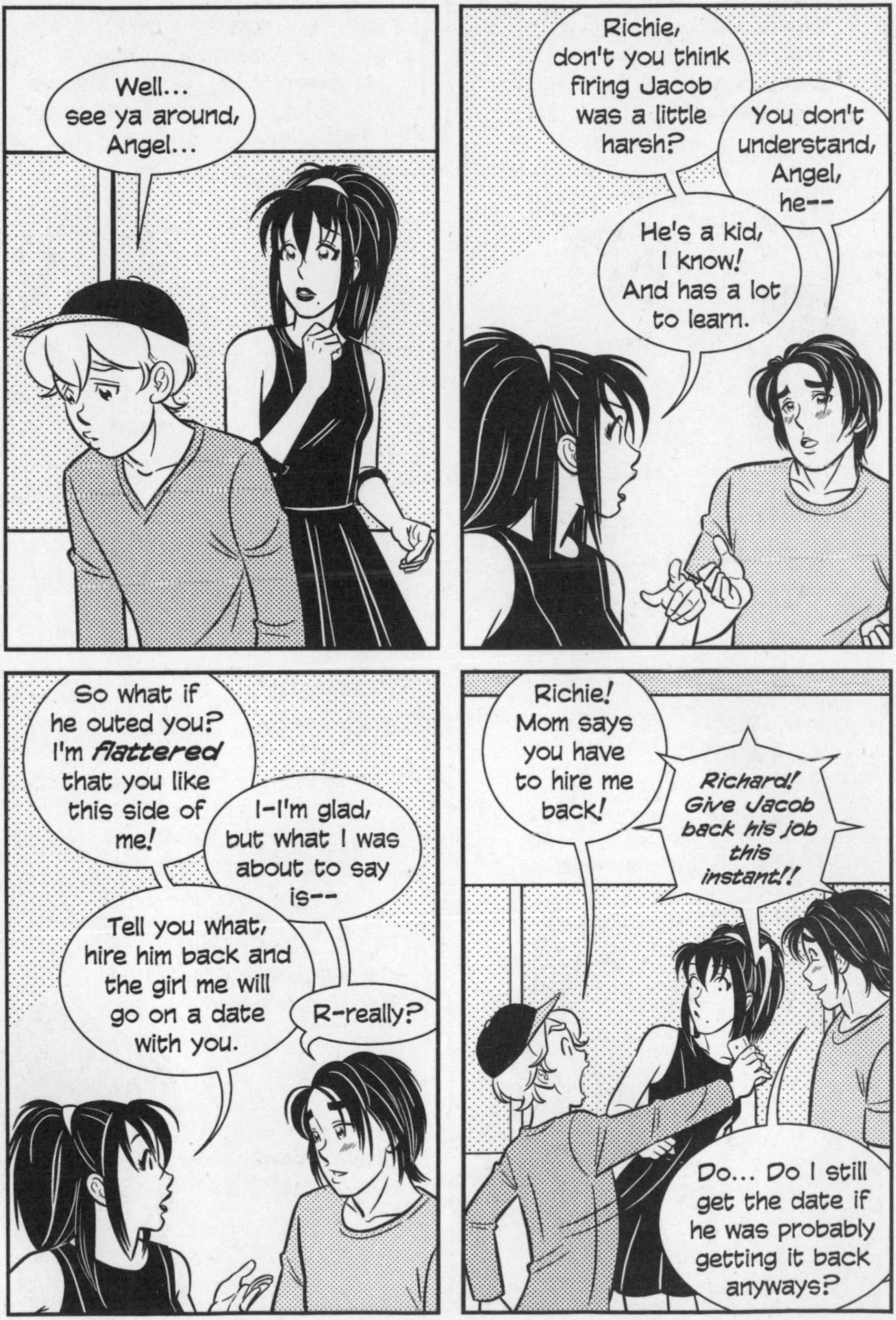
Well... see ya around, Angel...
Richie, don't you think firing Jacob was a little harsh?
You don't understand, Angel, he--
He's a kid, I know! And has a lot to learn.
So what if he outed you? I'm *flattered* that you like this side of me!
I-I'm glad, but what I was about to say is--
Tell you what, hire him back and the girl me will go on a date with you.
R-really?
Richie! Mom says you have to hire me back!
Richard! Give Jacob back his job this instant!!
Do... Do I still get the date if he was probably getting it back anyways?

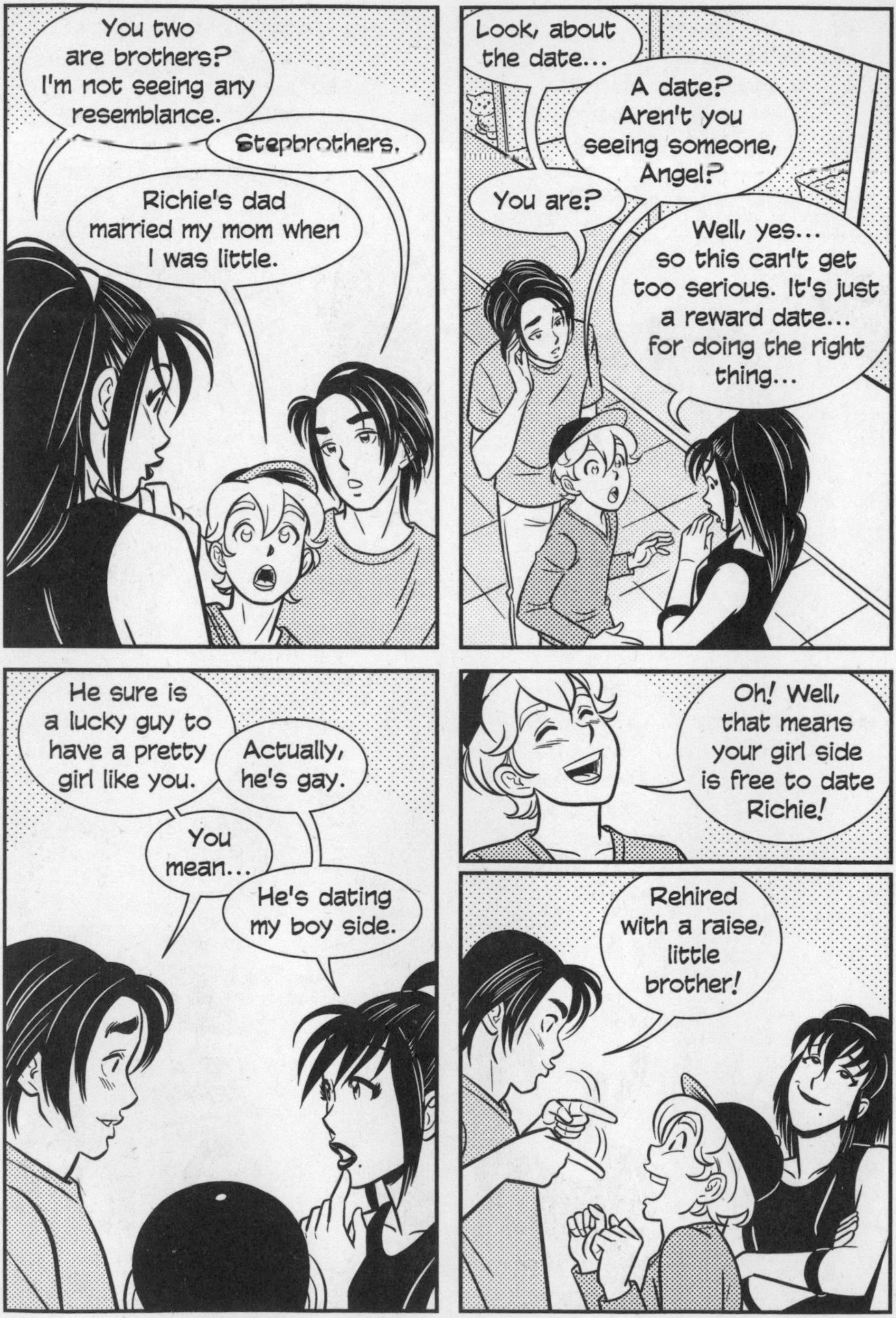
You two are brothers? I'm not seeing any resemblance.
Stepbrothers.
Richie's dad married my mom when I was little.
Look, about the date...
A date? Aren't you seeing someone, Angel?
You are?
Well, yes... so this can't get too serious. It's just a reward date... for doing the right thing...
He sure is a lucky guy to have a pretty girl like you.
Actually, he's gay.
You mean...
He's dating my boy side.
Oh! Well, that means your girl side is free to date Richie!
Rehired with a raise, little brother!

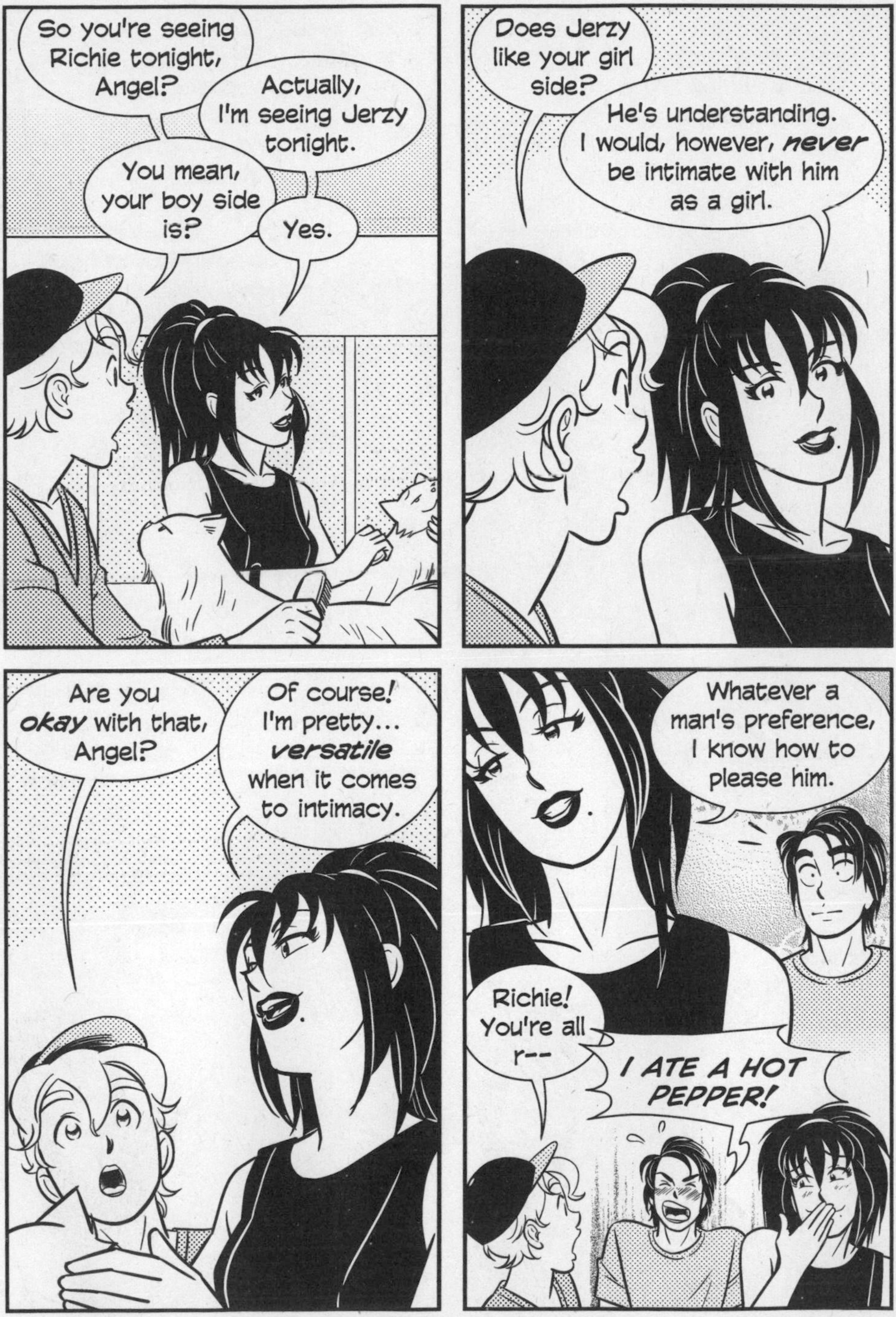

So you're seeing Richie tonight, Angel?
Actually, I'm seeing Jerzy tonight.
You mean, your boy side is?
Yes.
Does Jerzy like your girl side?
He's understanding. I would, however, ***never*** be intimate with him as a girl.
Are you ***okay*** with that, Angel?
Of course! I'm pretty... ***versatile*** when it comes to intimacy.
Whatever a man's preference, I know how to please him.
Richie! You're all r--
I ATE A HOT PEPPER!

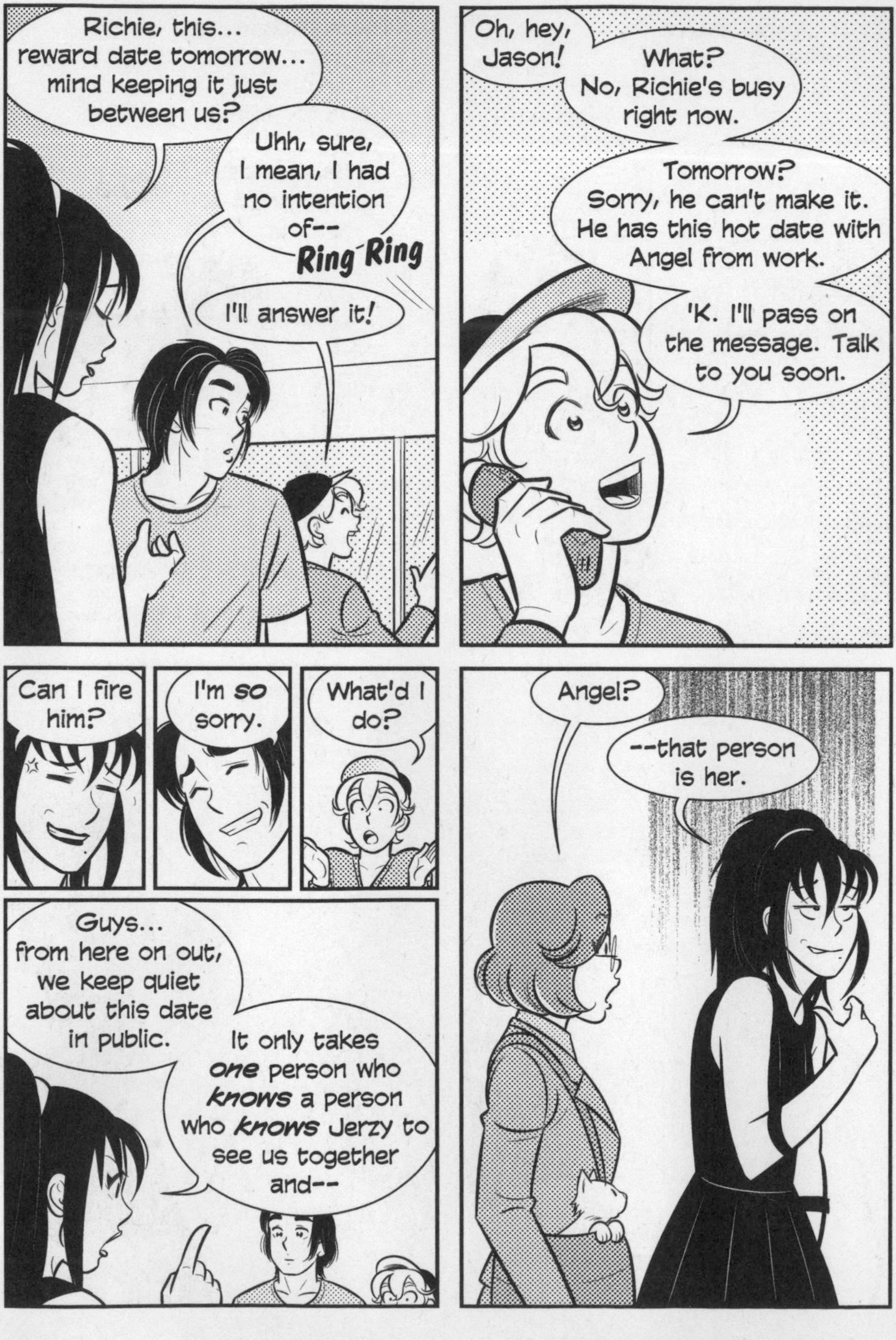
Richie, this... reward date tomorrow... mind keeping it just between us?
Uhh, sure, I mean, I had no intention of--
Ring Ring
I'll answer it!
Oh, hey, Jason!
What? No, Richie's busy right now.
Tomorrow? Sorry, he can't make it. He has this hot date with Angel from work.
'K. I'll pass on the message. Talk to you soon.
Can I fire him?
I'm *so* sorry.
What'd I do?
Angel?
--that person is her.
Guys... from here on out, we keep quiet about this date in public.
It only takes ***one*** person who ***knows*** a person who ***knows*** Jerzy to see us together and--

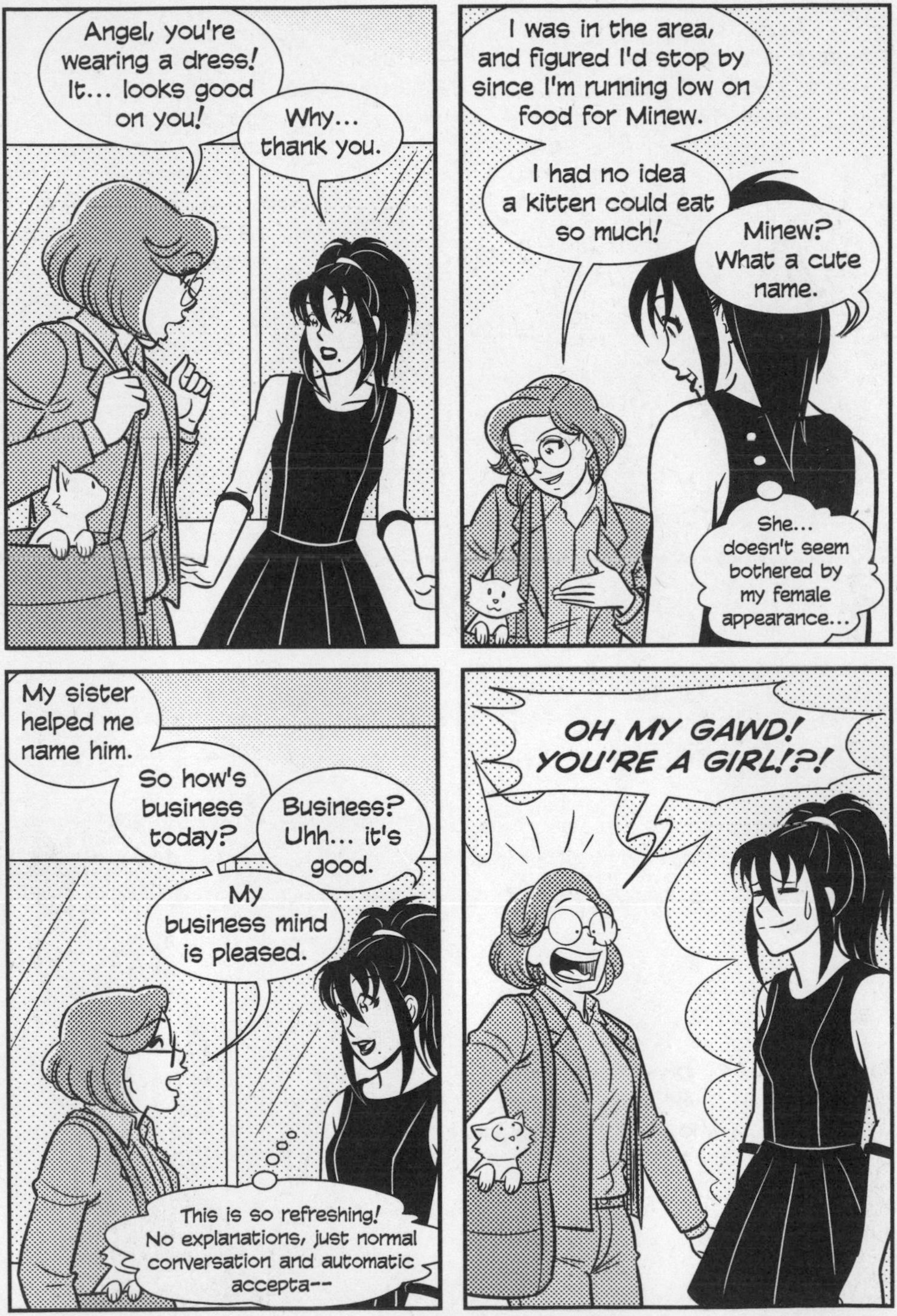
Angel, you're wearing a dress! It... looks good on you!
Why... thank you.
I was in the area, and figured I'd stop by since I'm running low on food for Minew.
I had no idea a kitten could eat so much!
Minew? What a cute name.
She... doesn't seem bothered by my female appearance...
My sister helped me name him.
So how's business today?
Business? Uhh... it's good.
My business mind is pleased.
This is so refreshing! No explanations, just normal conversation and automatic accepta--
OH MY GAWD! YOU'RE A GIRL!?!

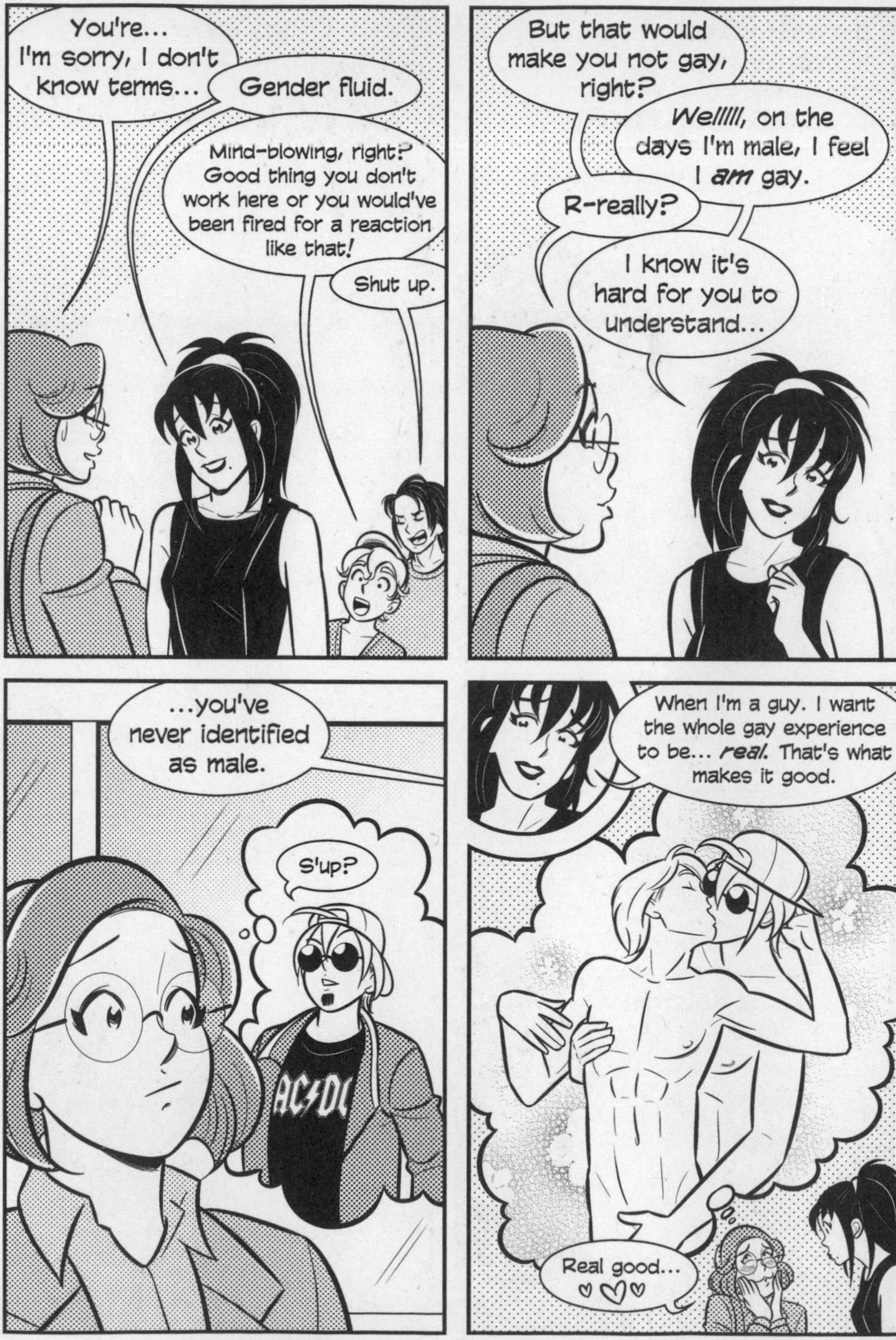
You're...
I'm sorry, I don't know terms...
Gender fluid.
Mind-blowing, right? Good thing you don't work here or you would've been fired for a reaction like that!
Shut up.
But that would make you not gay, right?
Welllll, on the days I'm male, I feel I ***am*** gay.
R-really?
I know it's hard for you to understand...
...you've never identified as male.
S'up?
AC/DC
When I'm a guy. I want the whole gay experience to be... ***real***. That's what makes it good.
Real good...

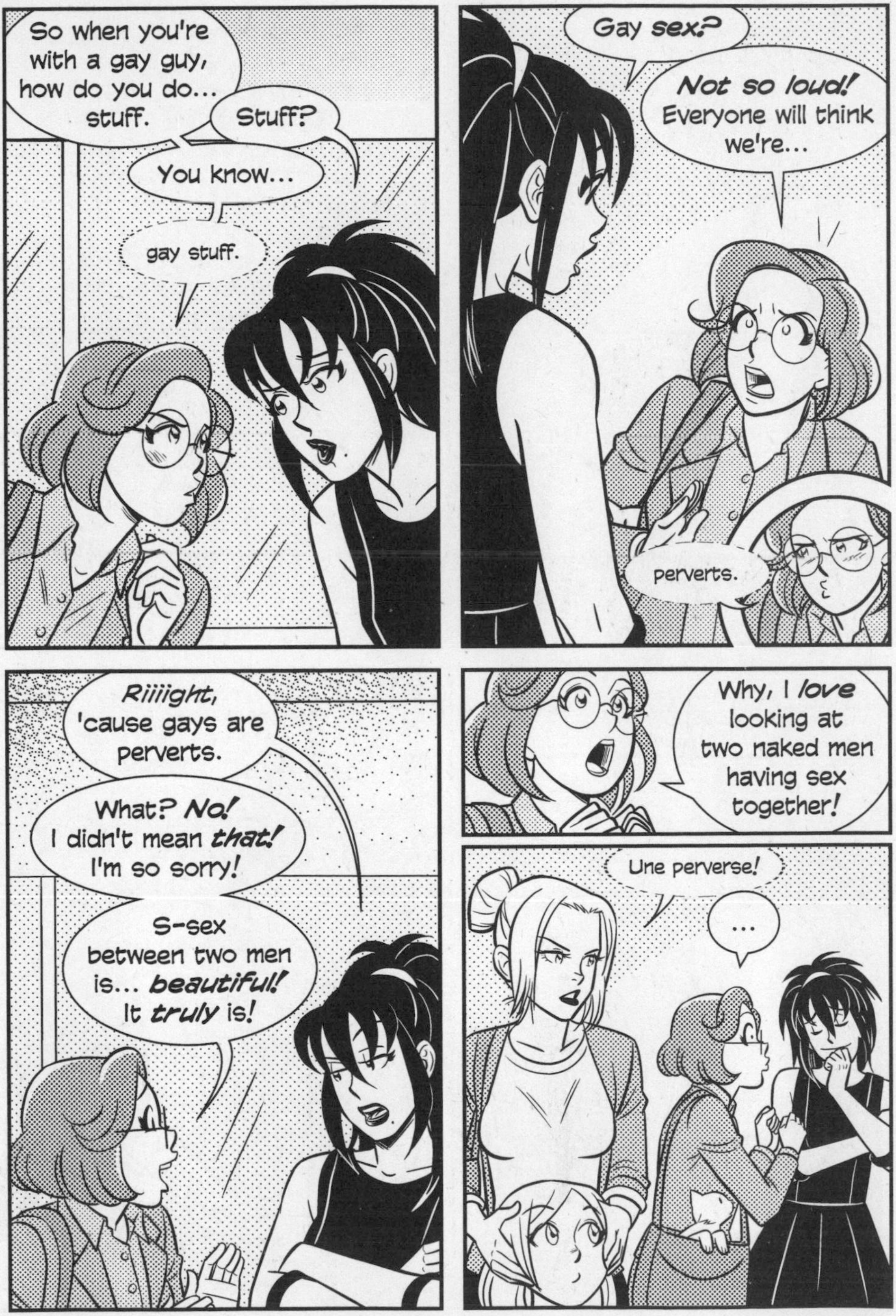

So when you're with a gay guy, how do you do... stuff.
Stuff?
You know...
gay stuff.
Gay *sex?*
Not so loud! Everyone will think we're...
perverts.
Riiiight, 'cause gays are perverts.
What? ***No!*** I didn't mean ***that!*** I'm so sorry!
S-sex between two men is... ***beautiful!*** It ***truly*** is!
Why, I ***love*** looking at two naked men having sex together!
Une perverse!
...

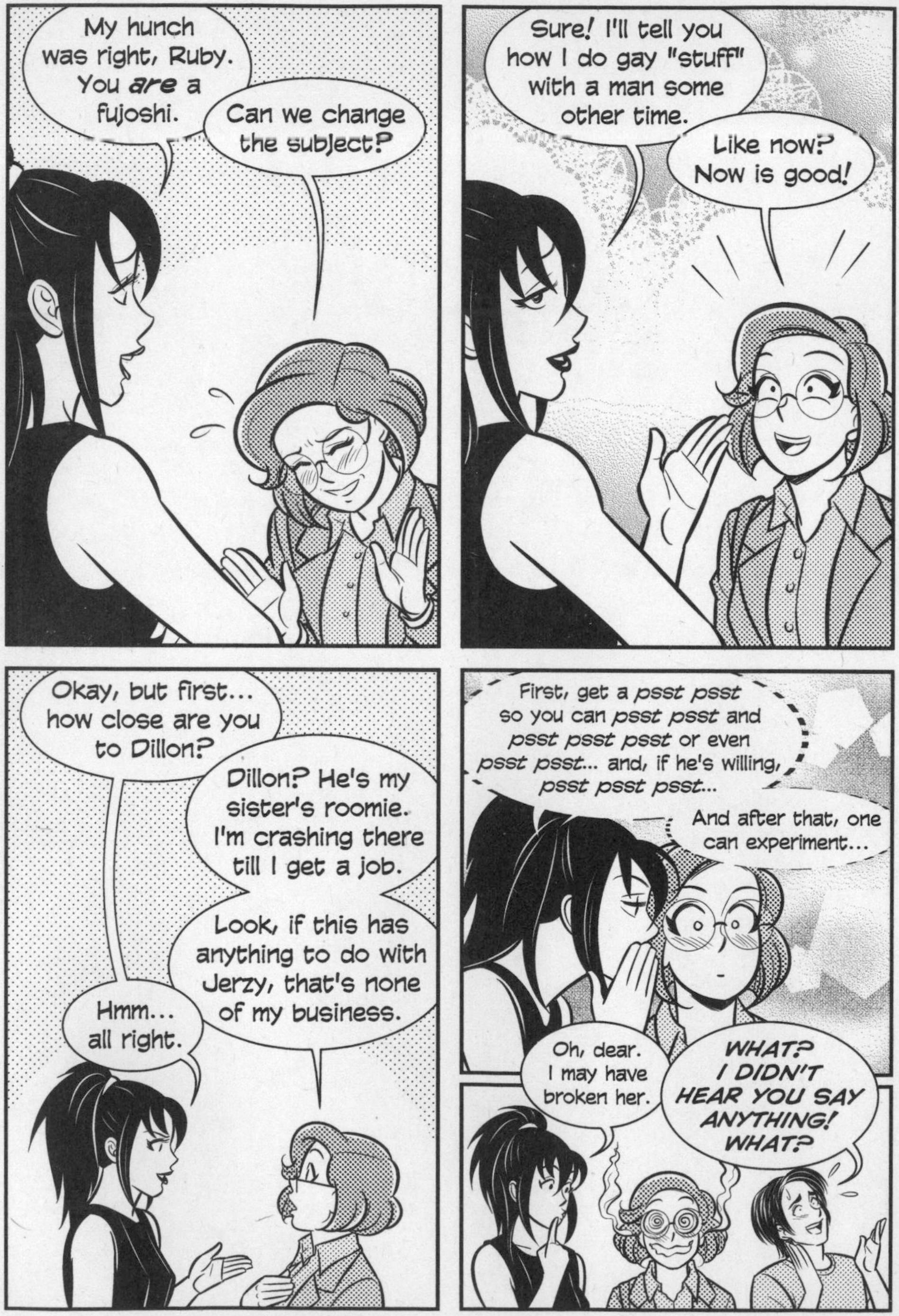

My hunch was right, Ruby. You *are* a fujoshi.
Can we change the subject?
Sure! I'll tell you how I do gay "stuff" with a man some other time.
Like now? Now is good!
Okay, but first... how close are you to Dillon?
Dillon? He's my sister's roomie. I'm crashing there till I get a job.
Look, if this has anything to do with Jerzy, that's none of my business.
Hmm... all right.
First, get a *psst psst* so you can *psst psst* and *psst psst psst* or even *psst psst*... and, if he's willing, *psst psst psst*...
And after that, one can experiment...
Oh, dear. I may have broken her.
WHAT? I DIDN'T HEAR YOU SAY ANYTHING! WHAT?

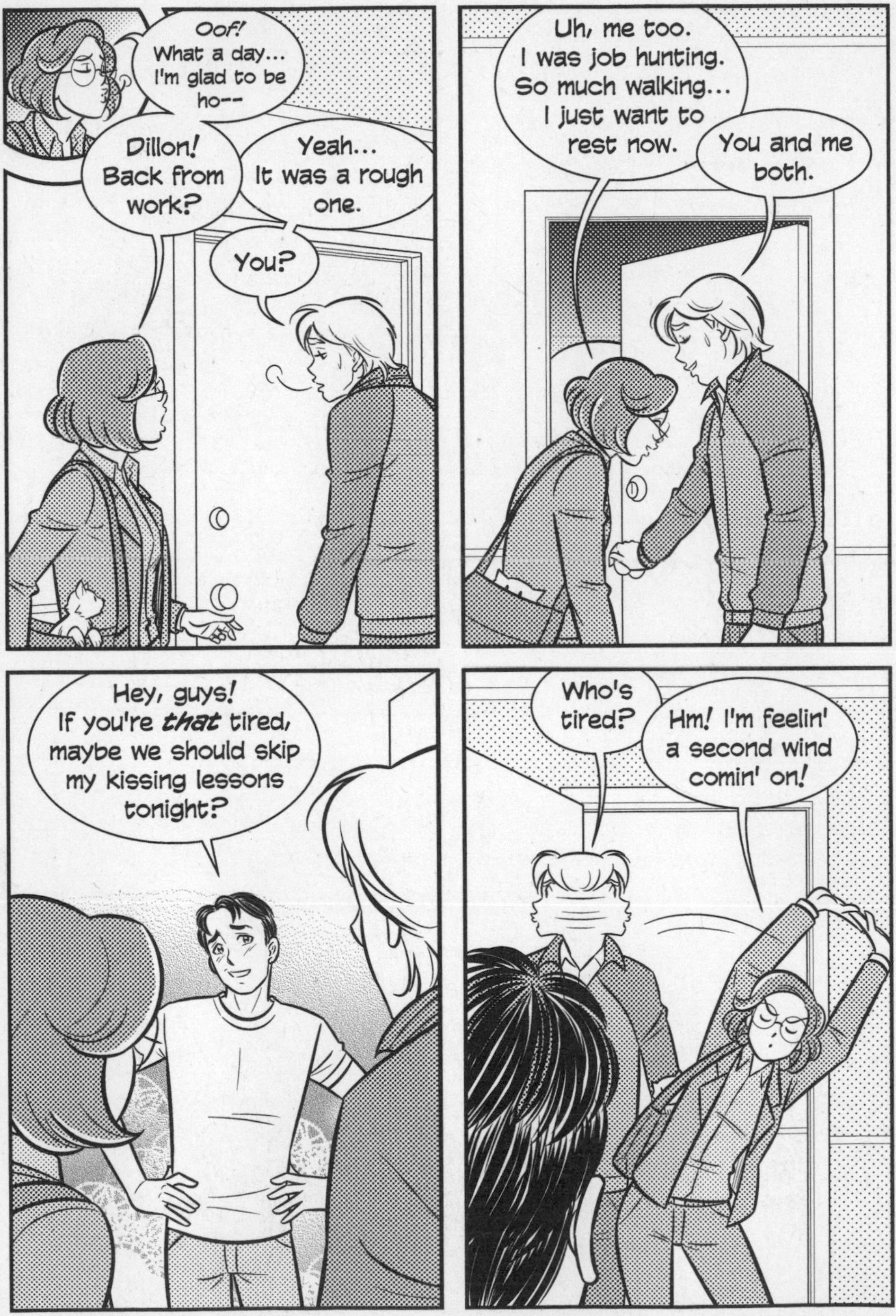
Oof! What a day... I'm glad to be ho--
Dillon! Back from work?
Yeah... It was a rough one.
You?
Uh, me too. I was job hunting. So much walking... I just want to rest now.
You and me both.
Hey, guys! If you're *that* tired, maybe we should skip my kissing lessons tonight?
Who's tired?
Hm! I'm feelin' a second wind comin' on!

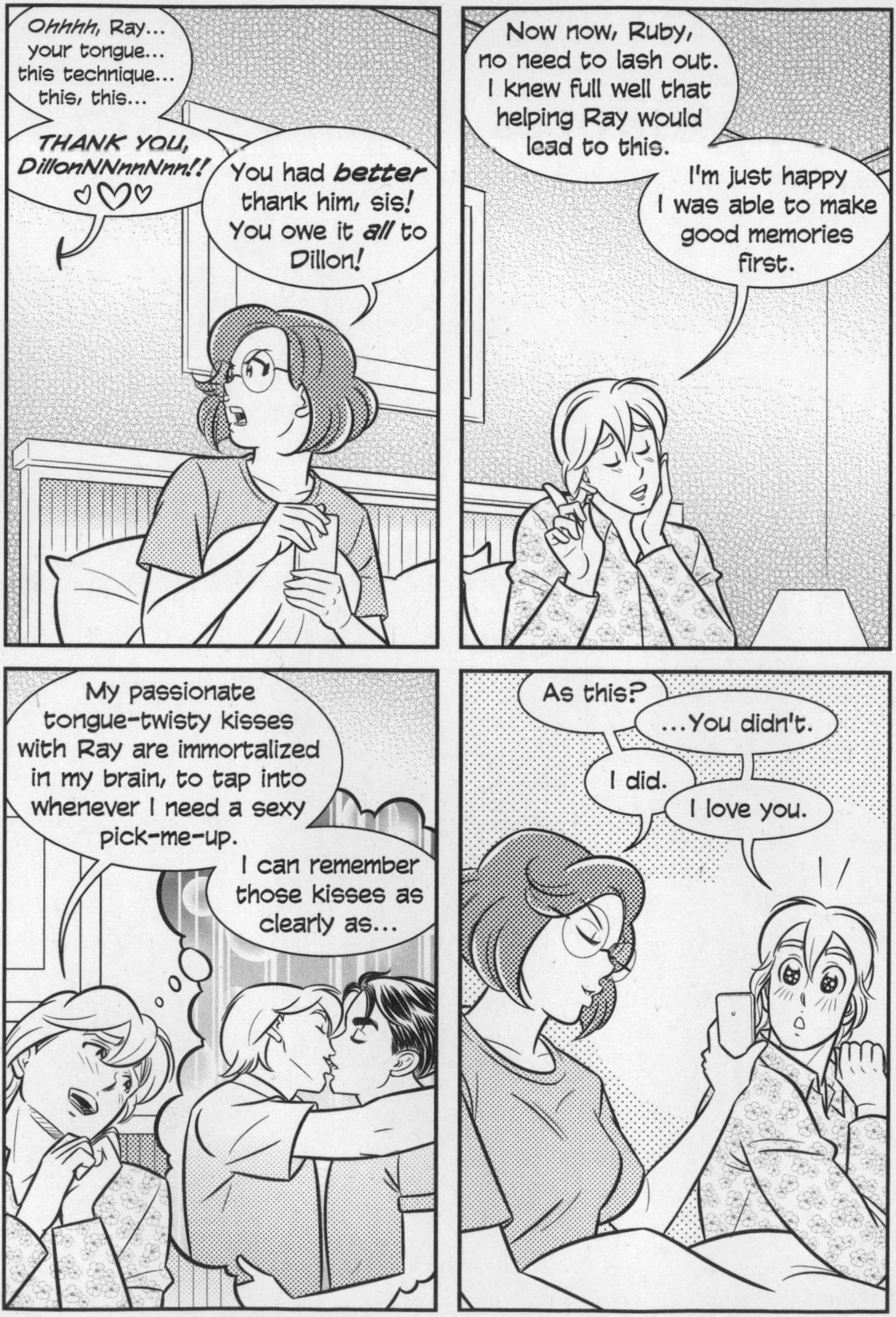

Ohhhh, Ray... your tongue... this technique... this, this...
THANK YOU, DillonNNnnNnn!! ♡♡♡
You had better thank him, sis! You owe it all to Dillon!
Now now, Ruby, no need to lash out. I knew full well that helping Ray would lead to this.
I'm just happy I was able to make good memories first.
My passionate tongue-twisty kisses with Ray are immortalized in my brain, to tap into whenever I need a sexy pick-me-up.
I can remember those kisses as clearly as...
As this?
...You didn't.
I did.
I love you.

Adventures in Babysitting

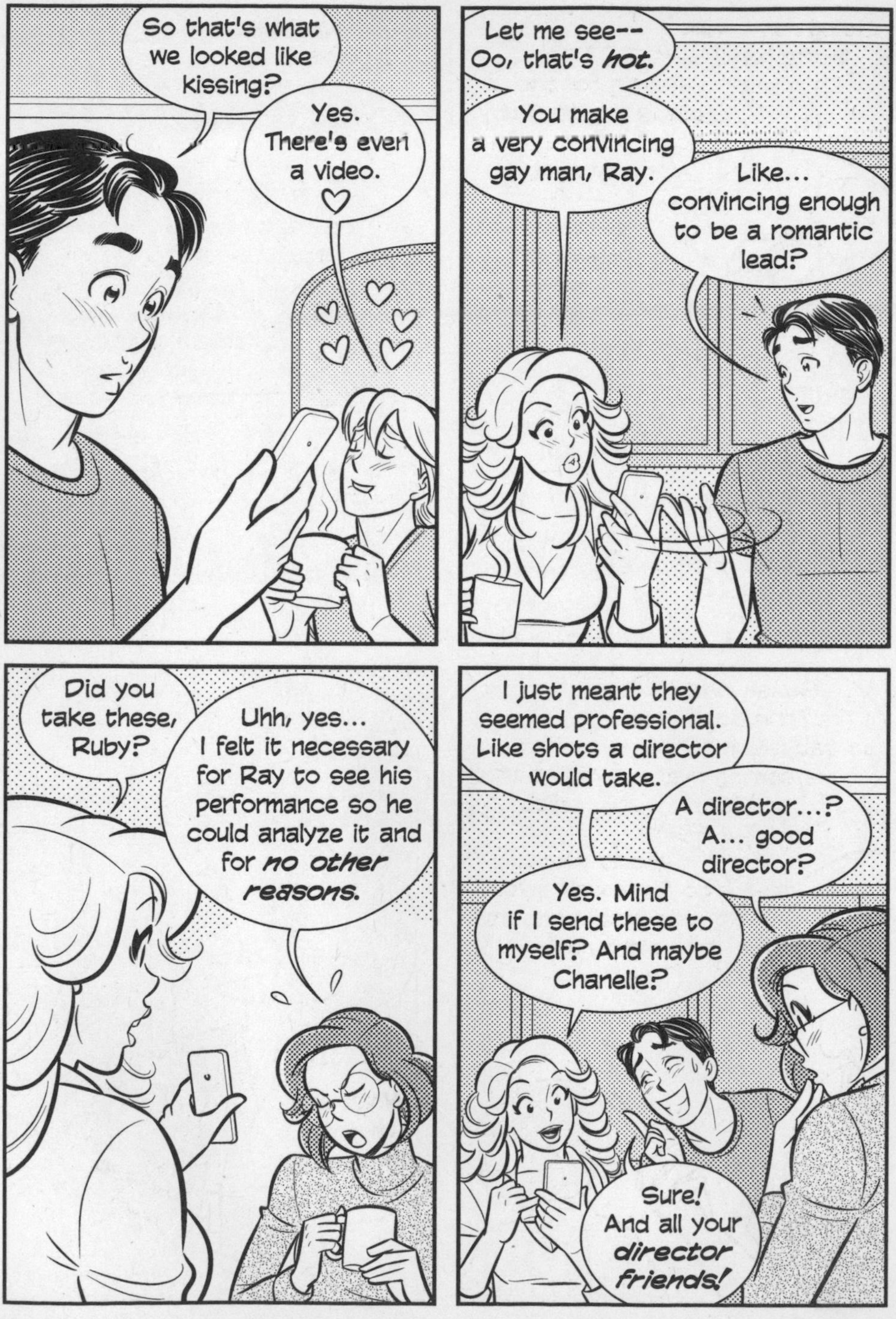
So that's what we looked like kissing?
Yes. There's even a video. ♡
Let me see-- Oo, that's *hot.*
You make a very convincing gay man, Ray.
Like... convincing enough to be a romantic lead?
Did you take these, Ruby?
Uhh, yes... I felt it necessary for Ray to see his performance so he could analyze it and for *no other reasons.*
I just meant they seemed professional. Like shots a director would take.
A director...? A... good director?
Yes. Mind if I send these to myself? And maybe Chanelle?
Sure! And all your *director friends!*

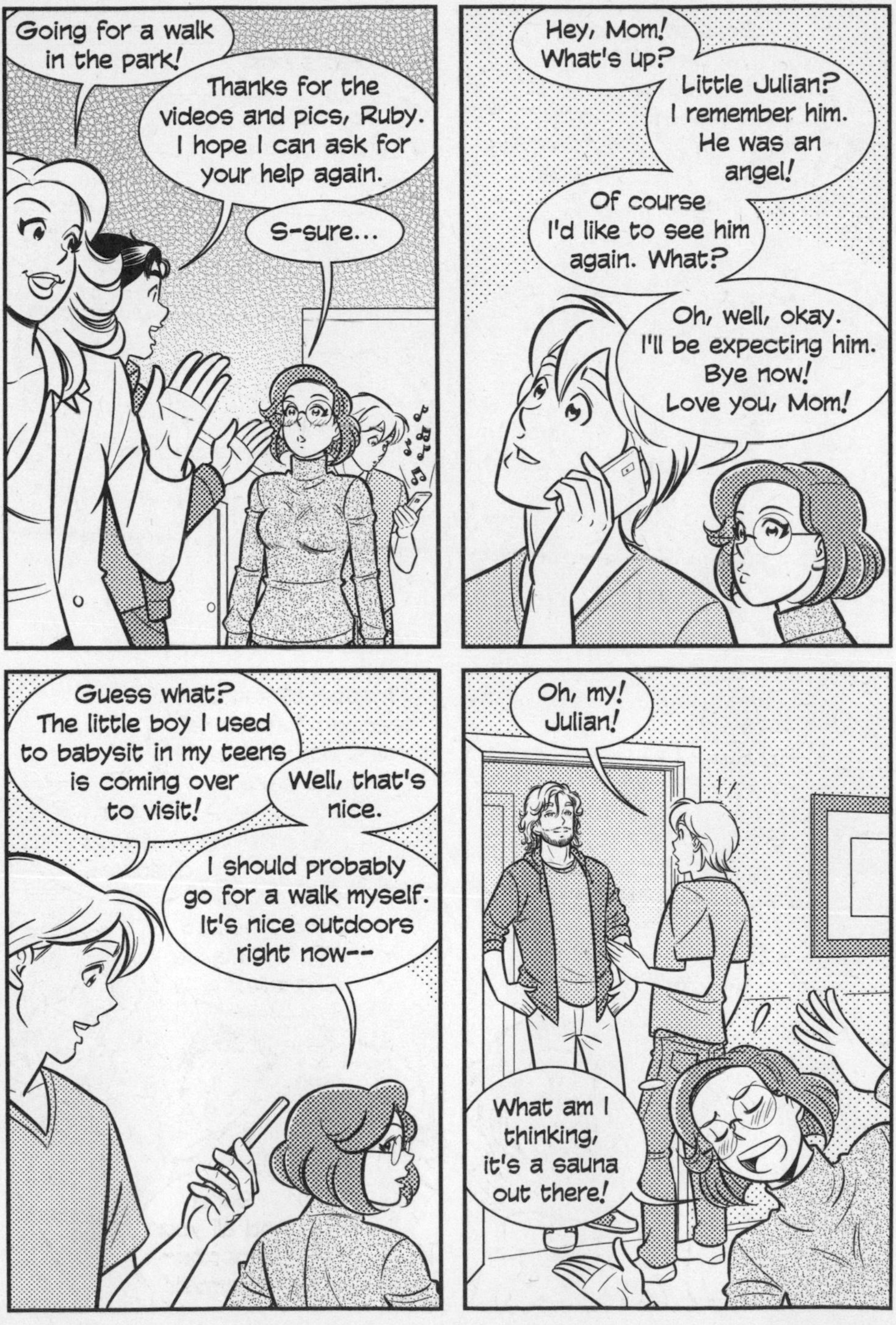

Going for a walk in the park!
Thanks for the videos and pics, Ruby. I hope I can ask for your help again.
S-sure...
Hey, Mom! What's up?
Little Julian? I remember him. He was an angel!
Of course I'd like to see him again. What?
Oh, well, okay. I'll be expecting him. Bye now! Love you, Mom!
Guess what? The little boy I used to babysit in my teens is coming over to visit!
Well, that's nice.
I should probably go for a walk myself. It's nice outdoors right now--
Oh, my! Julian!
What am I thinking, it's a sauna out there!

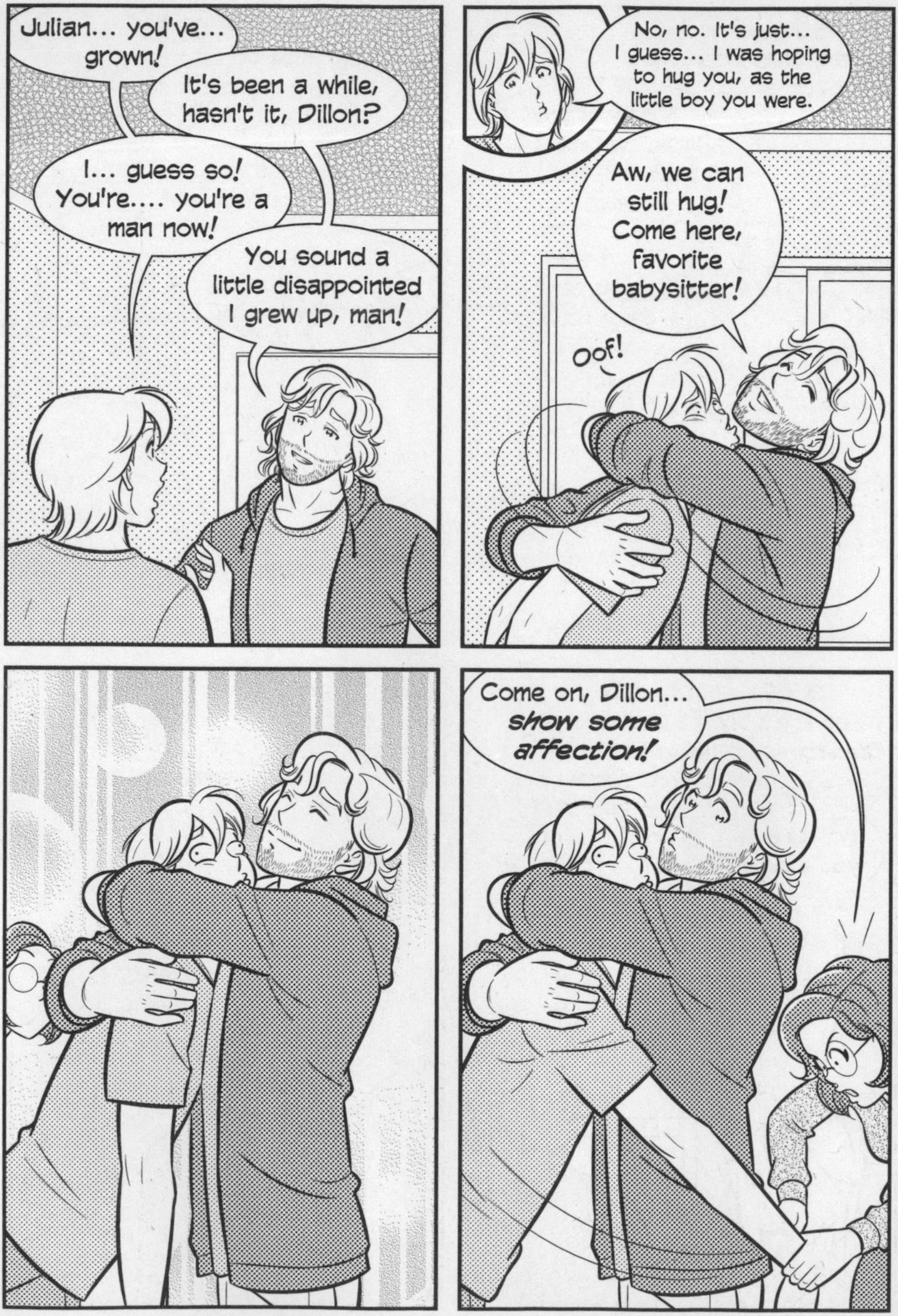
Julian... you've... grown!
It's been a while, hasn't it, Dillon?
I... guess so! You're.... you're a man now!
You sound a little disappointed I grew up, man!
No, no. It's just... I guess... I was hoping to hug you, as the little boy you were.
Aw, we can still hug! Come here, favorite babysitter!
Oof!
Come on, Dillon... *show some affection!*

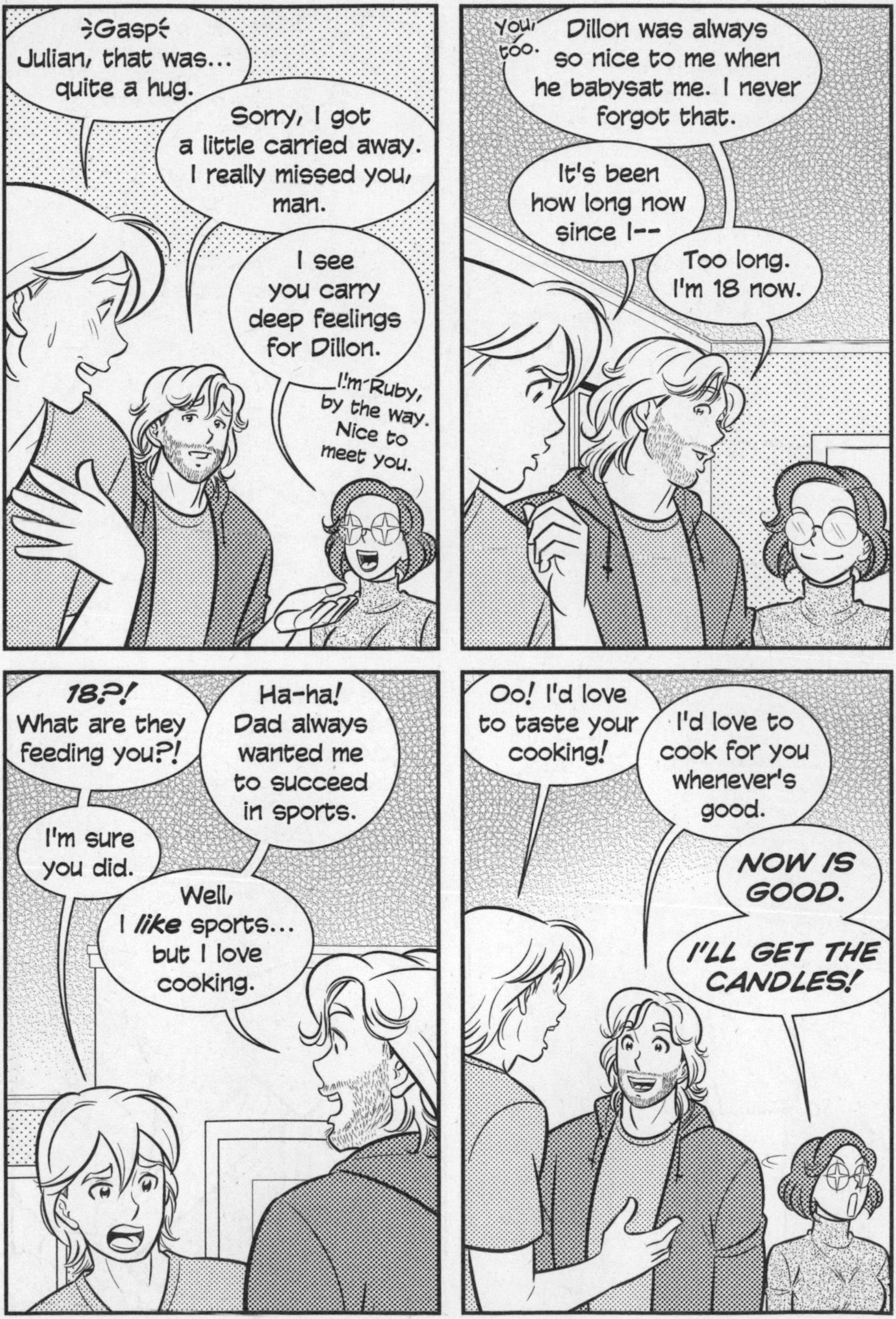

⁐Gasp⁐ Julian, that was... quite a hug.
Sorry, I got a little carried away. I really missed you, man.
I see you carry deep feelings for Dillon.
I'm Ruby, by the way. Nice to meet you.
You, too.
Dillon was always so nice to me when he babysat me. I never forgot that.
It's been how long now since I--
Too long. I'm 18 now.
18?! What are they feeding you?!
Ha-ha! Dad always wanted me to succeed in sports.
I'm sure you did.
Well, I *like* sports... but I love cooking.
Oo! I'd love to taste your cooking!
I'd love to cook for you whenever's good.
NOW IS GOOD.
I'LL GET THE CANDLES!

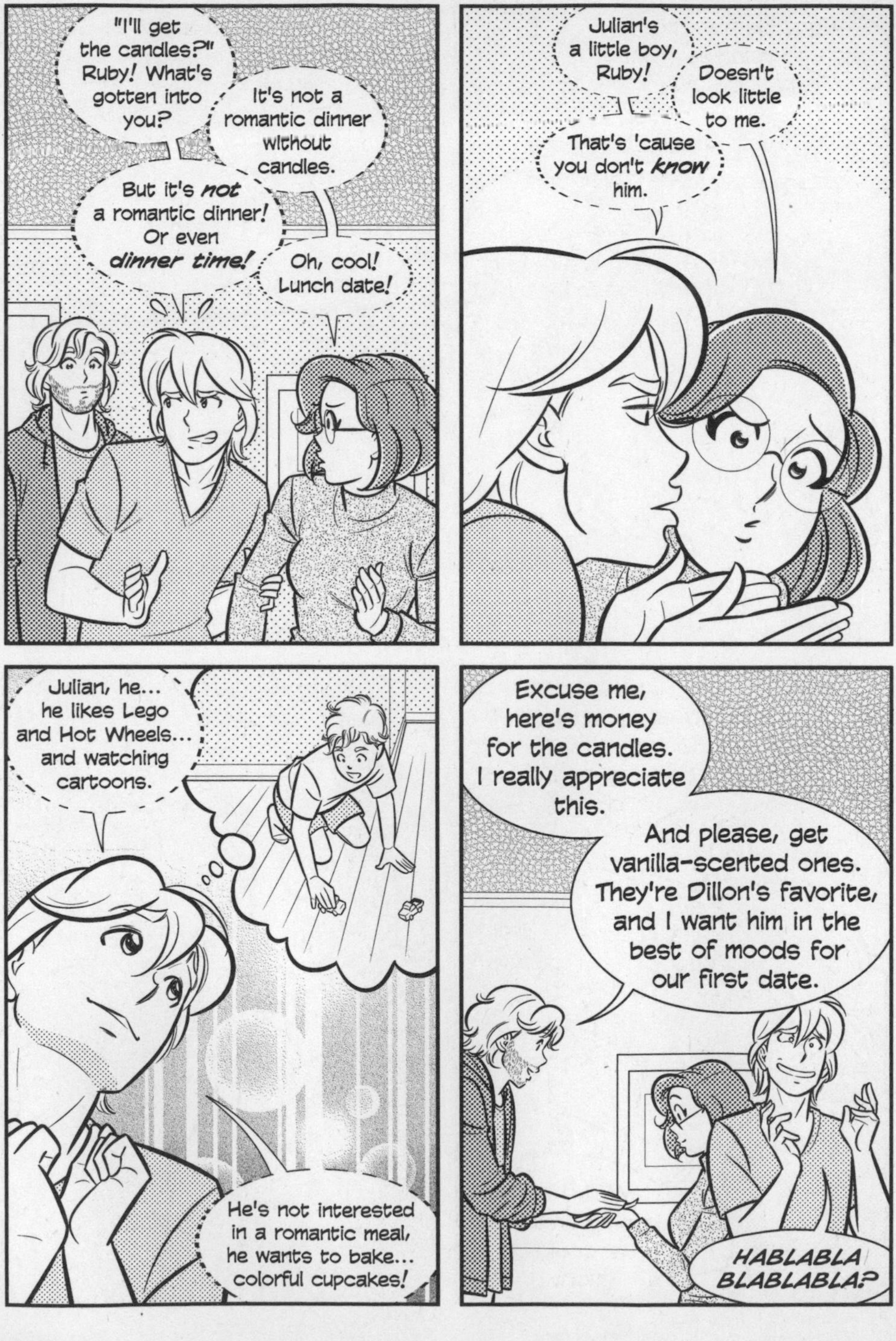
"I'll get the candles?" Ruby! What's gotten into you?
It's not a romantic dinner without candles.
But it's *not* a romantic dinner! Or even *dinner time!*
Oh, cool! Lunch date!
Julian's a little boy, Ruby!
Doesn't look little to me.
That's 'cause you don't *know* him.
Julian, he... he likes Lego and Hot Wheels... and watching cartoons.
He's not interested in a romantic meal, he wants to bake... colorful cupcakes!
Excuse me, here's money for the candles. I really appreciate this.
And please, get vanilla-scented ones. They're Dillon's favorite, and I want him in the best of moods for our first date.
HABLABLA BLABLABLA?

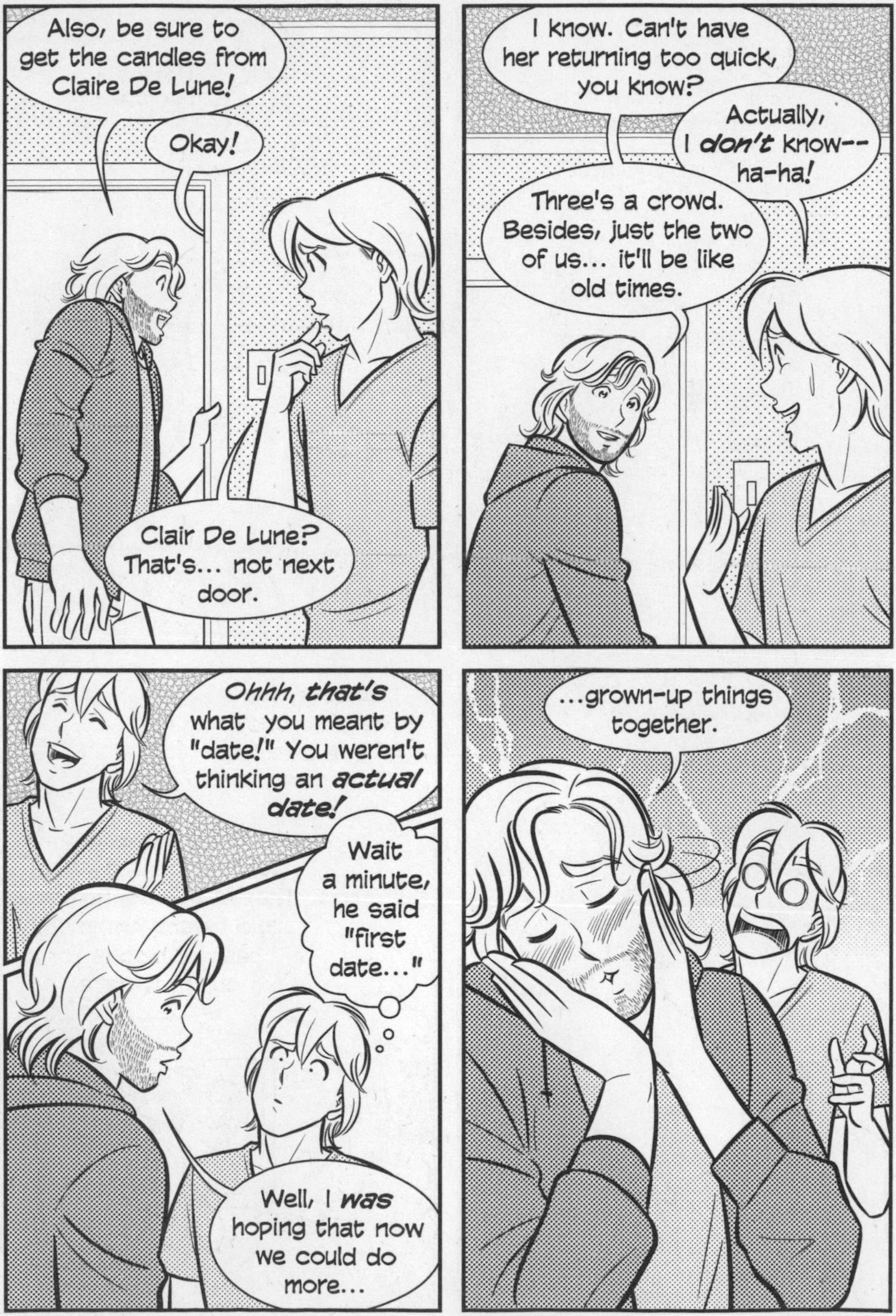
Also, be sure to get the candles from Claire De Lune!
Okay!
Clair De Lune? That's... not next door.
I know. Can't have her returning too quick, you know?
Actually, I *don't* know--ha-ha!
Three's a crowd. Besides, just the two of us... it'll be like old times.
Ohhh, that's what you meant by "date!" You weren't thinking an *actual date!*
Wait a minute, he said "first date..."
Well, I *was* hoping that now we could do more...
...grown-up things together.

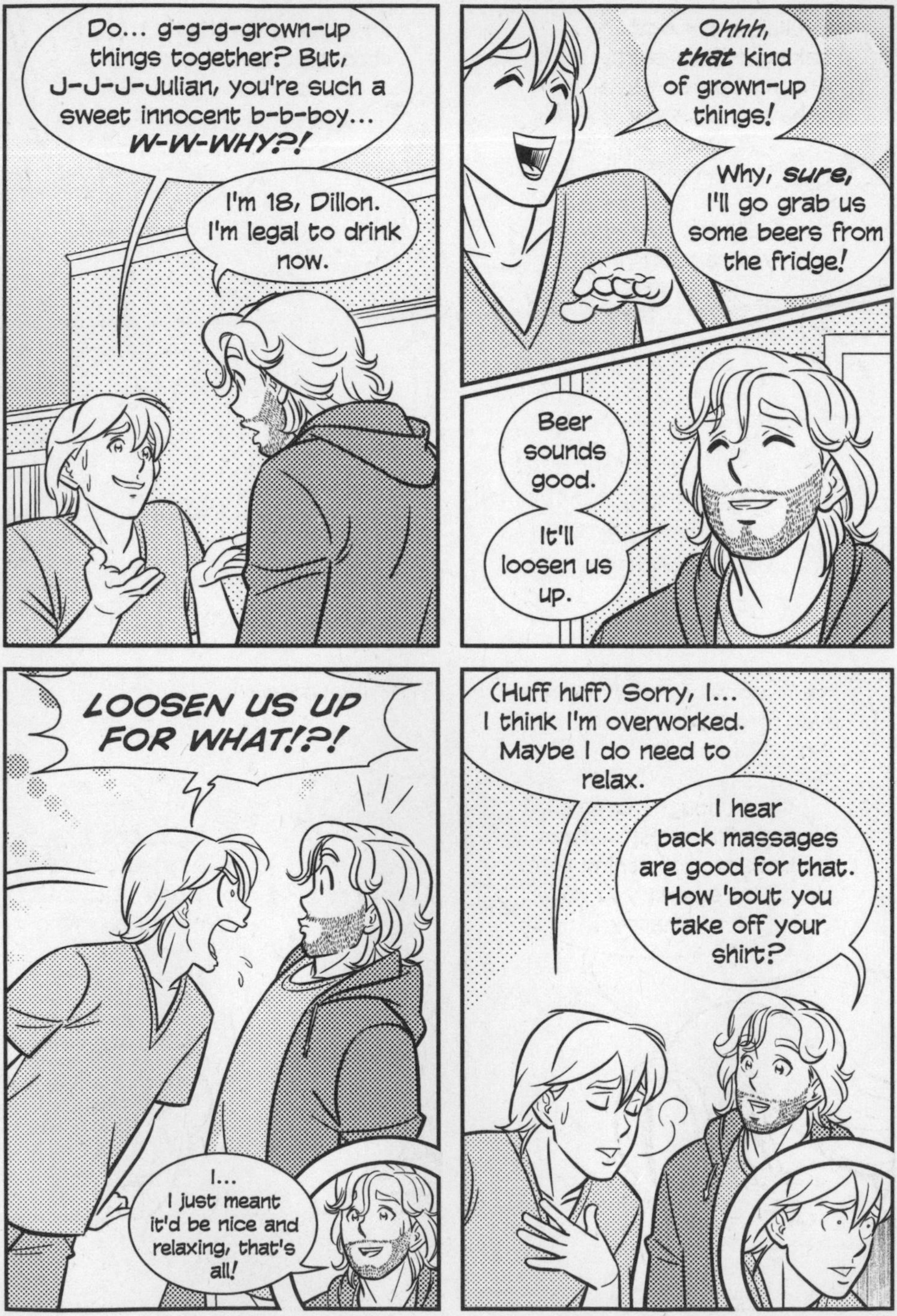
Do... g-g-g-grown-up things together? But, J-J-J-Julian, you're such a sweet innocent b-b-boy... ***W-W-WHY?!***
I'm 18, Dillon. I'm legal to drink now.
Ohhh, ***that*** kind of grown-up things!
Why, ***sure,*** I'll go grab us some beers from the fridge!
Beer sounds good.
It'll loosen us up.
LOOSEN US UP FOR WHAT!?!
I... I just meant it'd be nice and relaxing, that's all!
(Huff huff) Sorry, I... I think I'm overworked. Maybe I do need to relax.
I hear back massages are good for that. How 'bout you take off your shirt?

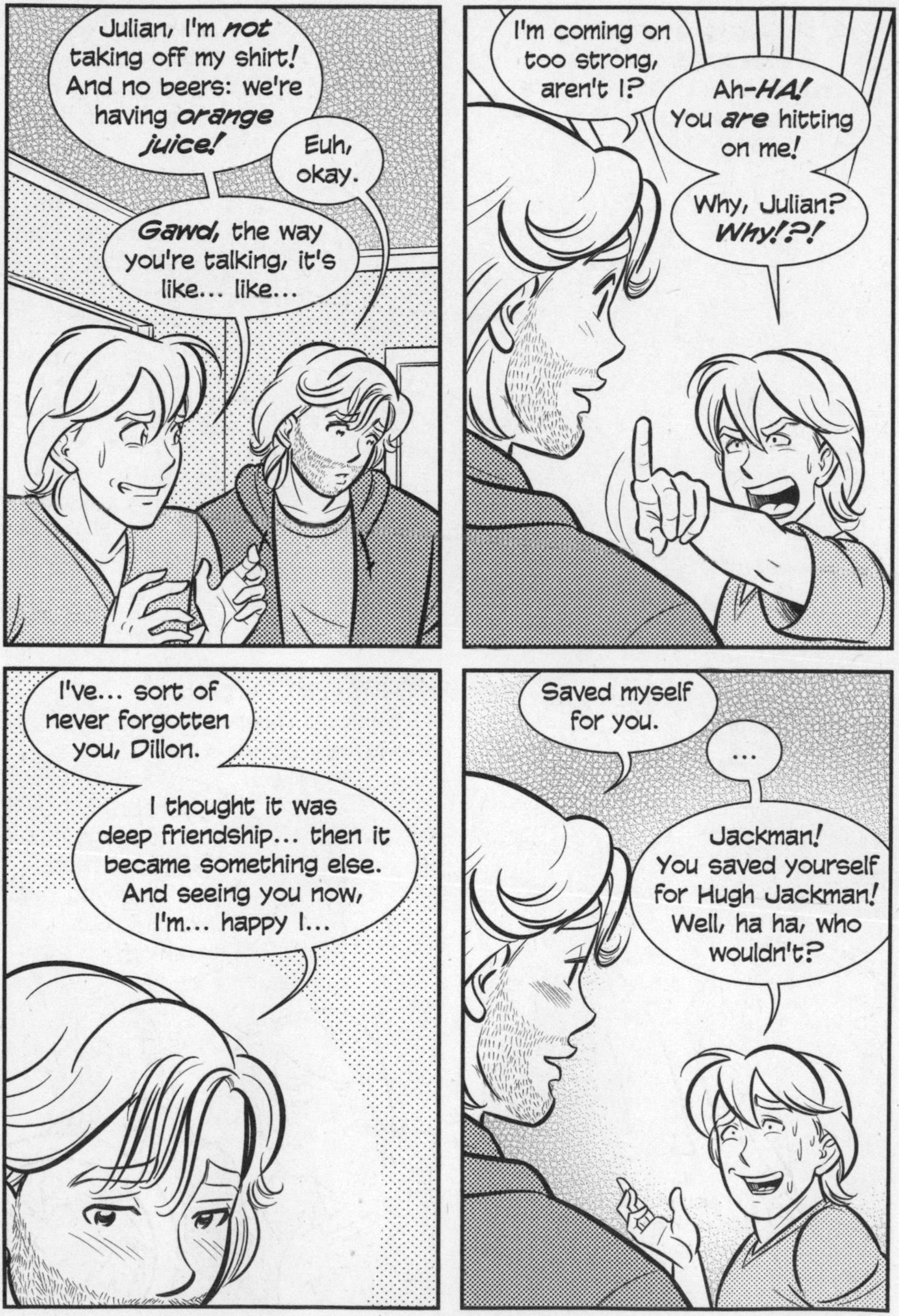
Julian, I'm *not* taking off my shirt! And no beers: we're having *orange juice!*
Euh, okay.
Gawd, the way you're talking, it's like... like...
I'm coming on too strong, aren't I?
Ah-*HA!* You *are* hitting on me!
Why, Julian? *Why!?!*
I've... sort of never forgotten you, Dillon.
I thought it was deep friendship... then it became something else. And seeing you now, I'm... happy I...
Saved myself for you.
...
Jackman! You saved yourself for Hugh Jackman! Well, ha ha, who wouldn't?

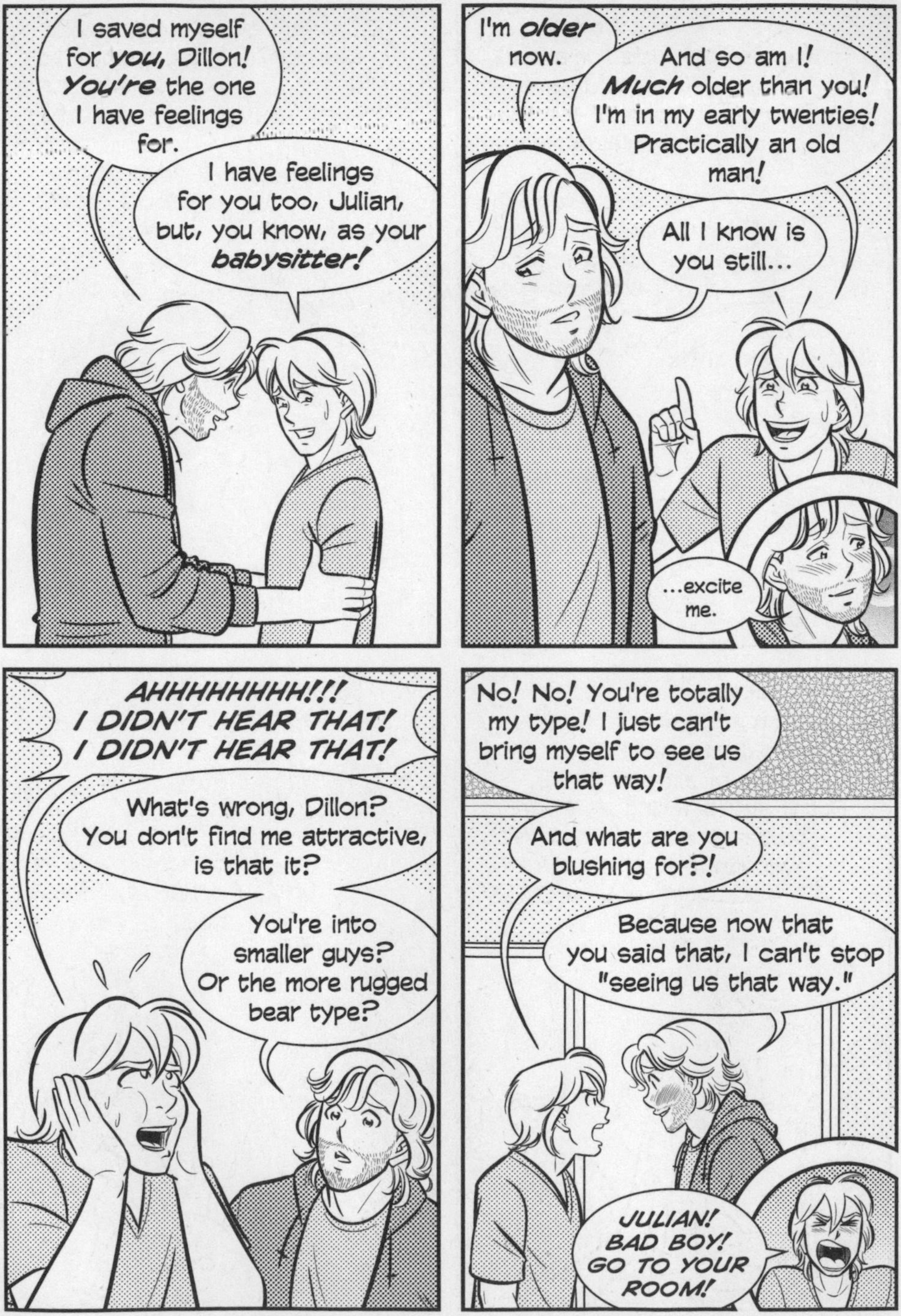

I saved myself for *you*, Dillon! *You're* the one I have feelings for.
I have feelings for you too, Julian, but, you know, as your *babysitter!*
I'm *older* now.
And so am I! *Much* older than you! I'm in my early twenties! Practically an old man!
All I know is you still...
...excite me.
AHHHHHHHH!!! I DIDN'T HEAR THAT! I DIDN'T HEAR THAT!
What's wrong, Dillon? You don't find me attractive, is that it?
You're into smaller guys? Or the more rugged bear type?
No! No! You're totally my type! I just can't bring myself to see us that way!
And what are you blushing for?!
Because now that you said that, I can't stop "seeing us that way."
JULIAN! BAD BOY! GO TO YOUR ROOM!

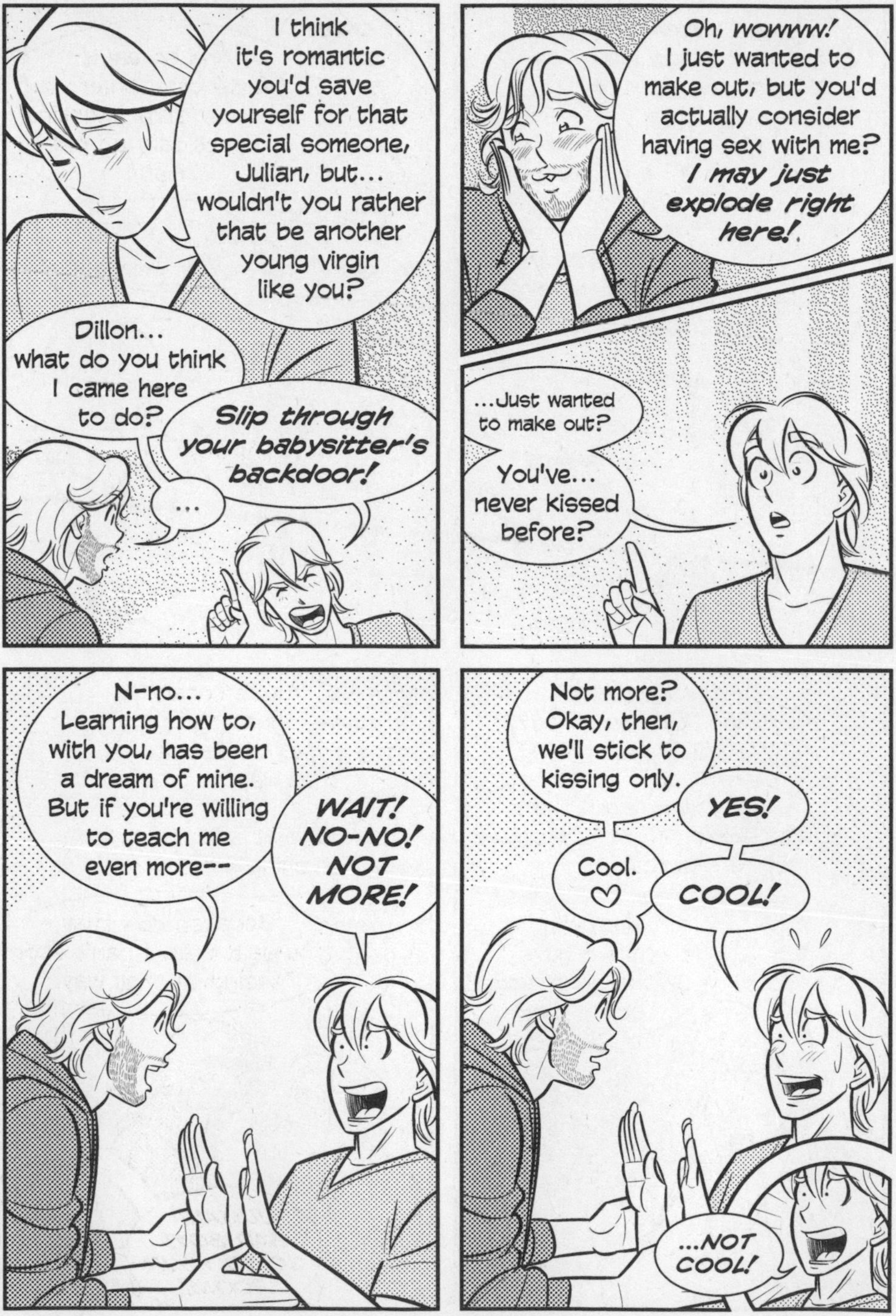
I think it's romantic you'd save yourself for that special someone, Julian, but... wouldn't you rather that be another young virgin like you?
Dillon... what do you think I came here to do?
...
Slip through your babysitter's backdoor!
Oh, wowww! I just wanted to make out, but you'd actually consider having sex with me? I may just explode right here!
...Just wanted to make out?
You've... never kissed before?
N-no... Learning how to, with you, has been a dream of mine. But if you're willing to teach me even more--
WAIT! NO-NO! NOT MORE!
Not more? Okay, then, we'll stick to kissing only.
YES!
Cool. ♡
COOL!
...NOT COOL!

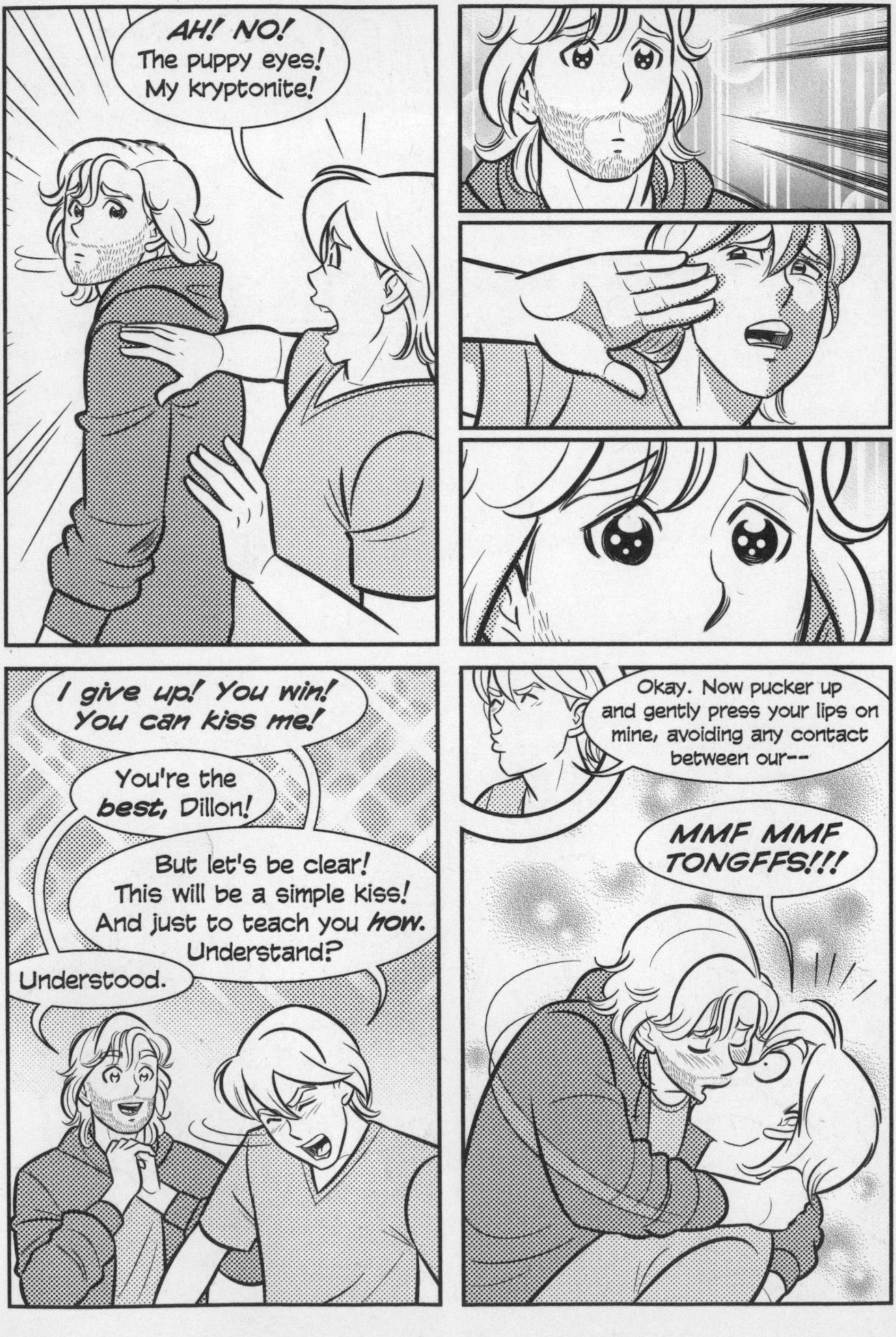
AH! NO!
The puppy eyes!
My kryptonite!
I give up! You win!
You can kiss me!
You're the best, Dillon!
But let's be clear!
This will be a simple kiss!
And just to teach you how.
Understand?
Understood.
Okay. Now pucker up and gently press your lips on mine, avoiding any contact between our--
MMF MMF TONGFFS!!!

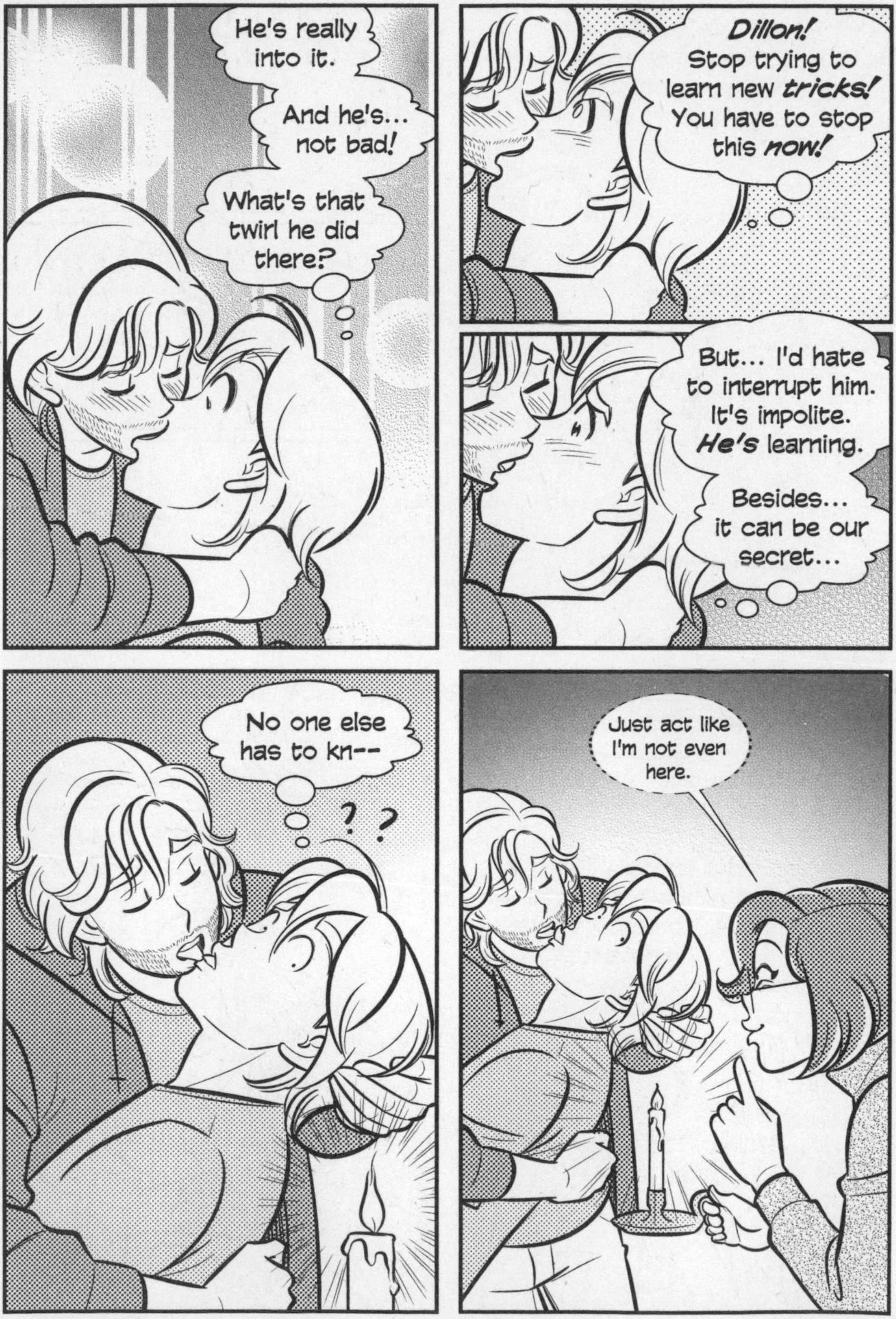
He's really into it.
And he's... not bad!
What's that twirl he did there?
Dillon! Stop trying to learn new tricks! You have to stop this now!
But... I'd hate to interrupt him. It's impolite. He's learning.
Besides... it can be our secret...
No one else has to kn--
? ?
Just act like I'm not even here.

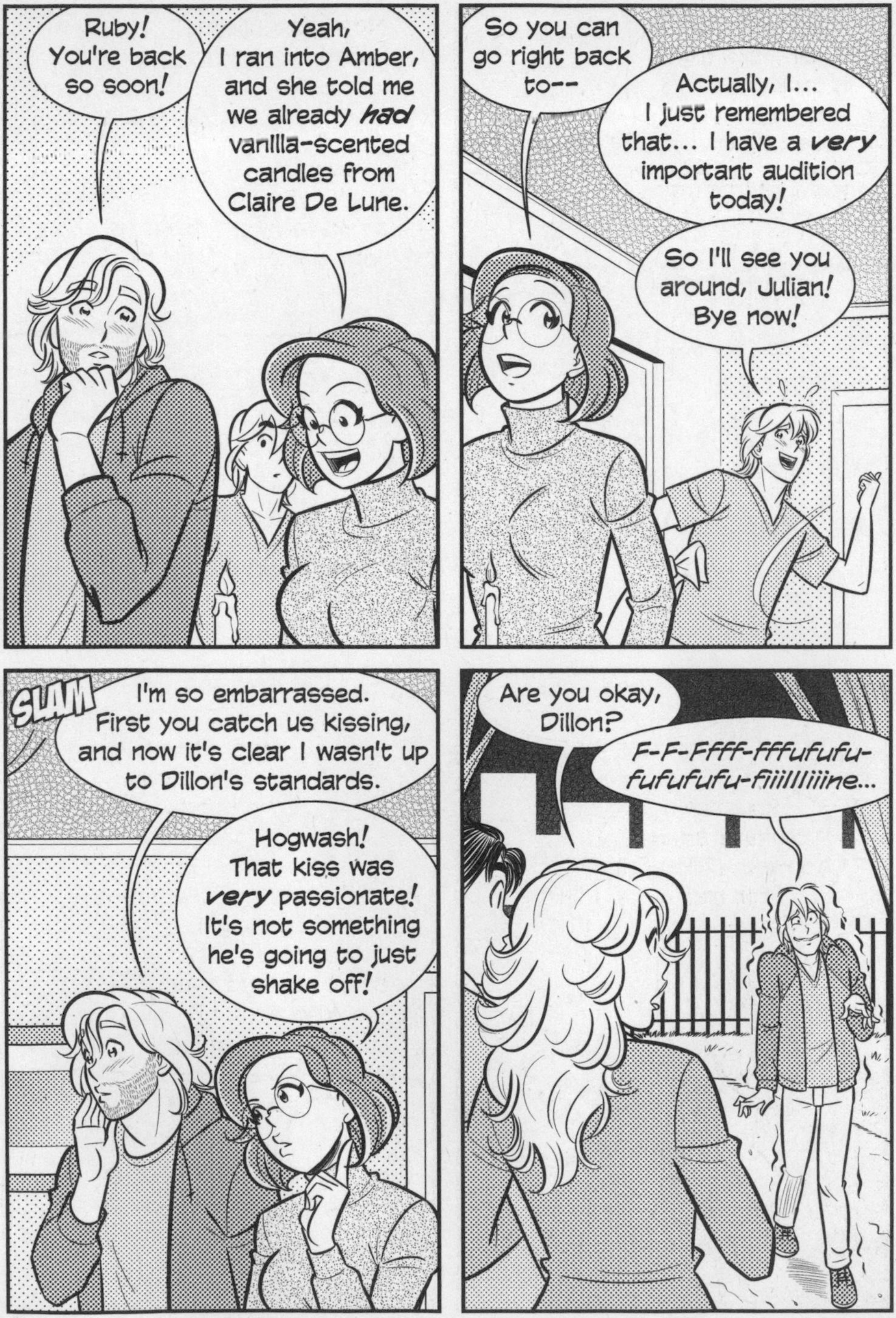
Ruby! You're back so soon!
Yeah, I ran into Amber, and she told me we already *had* vanilla-scented candles from Claire De Lune.
So you can go right back to--
Actually, I... I just remembered that... I have a *very* important audition today!
So I'll see you around, Julian! Bye now!
SLAM
I'm so embarrassed. First you catch us kissing, and now it's clear I wasn't up to Dillon's standards.
Hogwash! That kiss was *very* passionate! It's not something he's going to just shake off!
Are you okay, Dillon?
F-F-Ffff-fffufufu-fufufufu-fiiilllliiine...

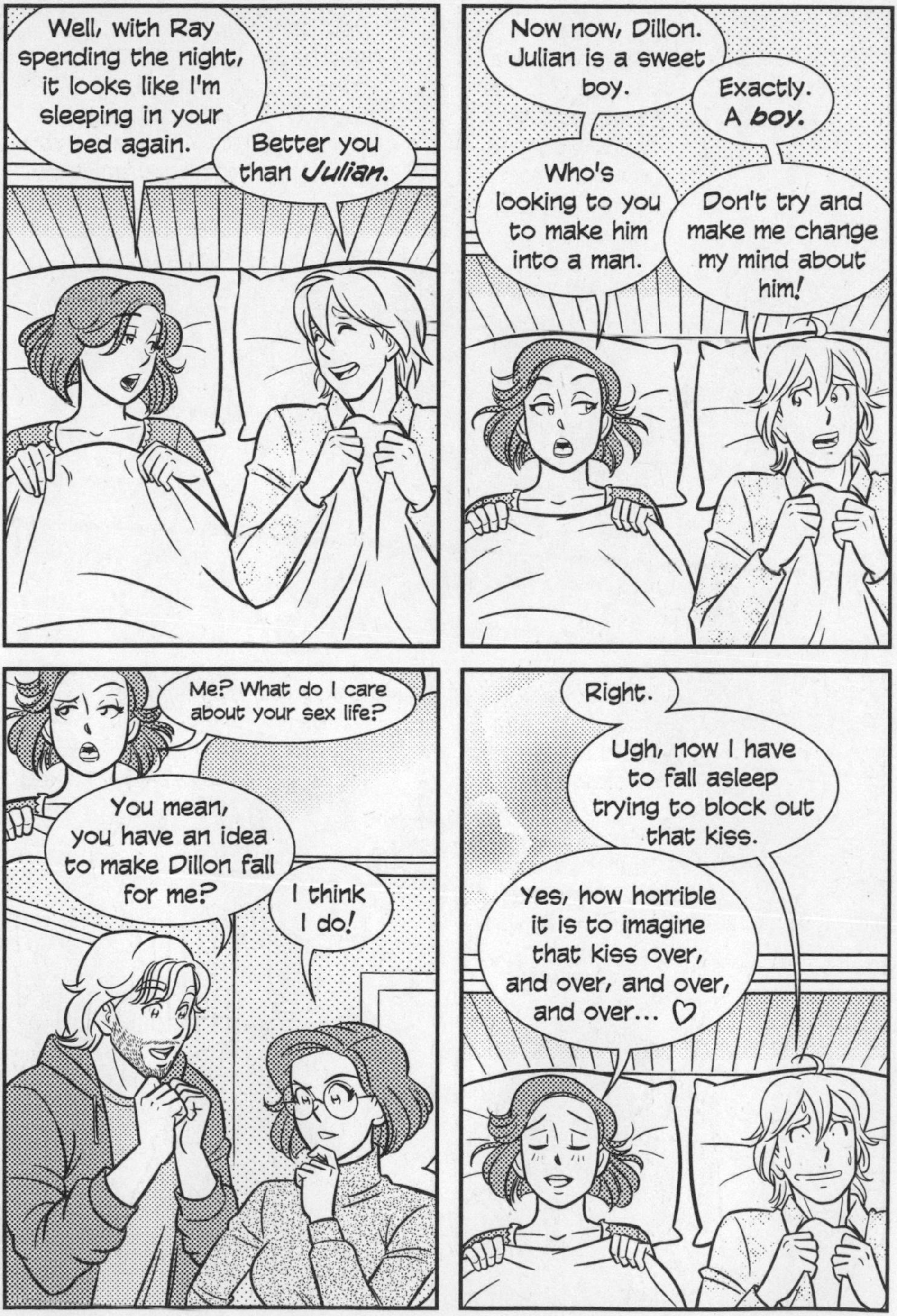
Well, with Ray spending the night, it looks like I'm sleeping in your bed again.
Better you than *Julian.*
Now now, Dillon. Julian is a sweet boy.
Exactly. A ***boy.***
Who's looking to you to make him into a man.
Don't try and make me change my mind about him!
Me? What do I care about your sex life?
You mean, you have an idea to make Dillon fall for me?
I think I do!
Right.
Ugh, now I have to fall asleep trying to block out that kiss.
Yes, how horrible it is to imagine that kiss over, and over, and over, and over... ♡

Ruby's Other New Career

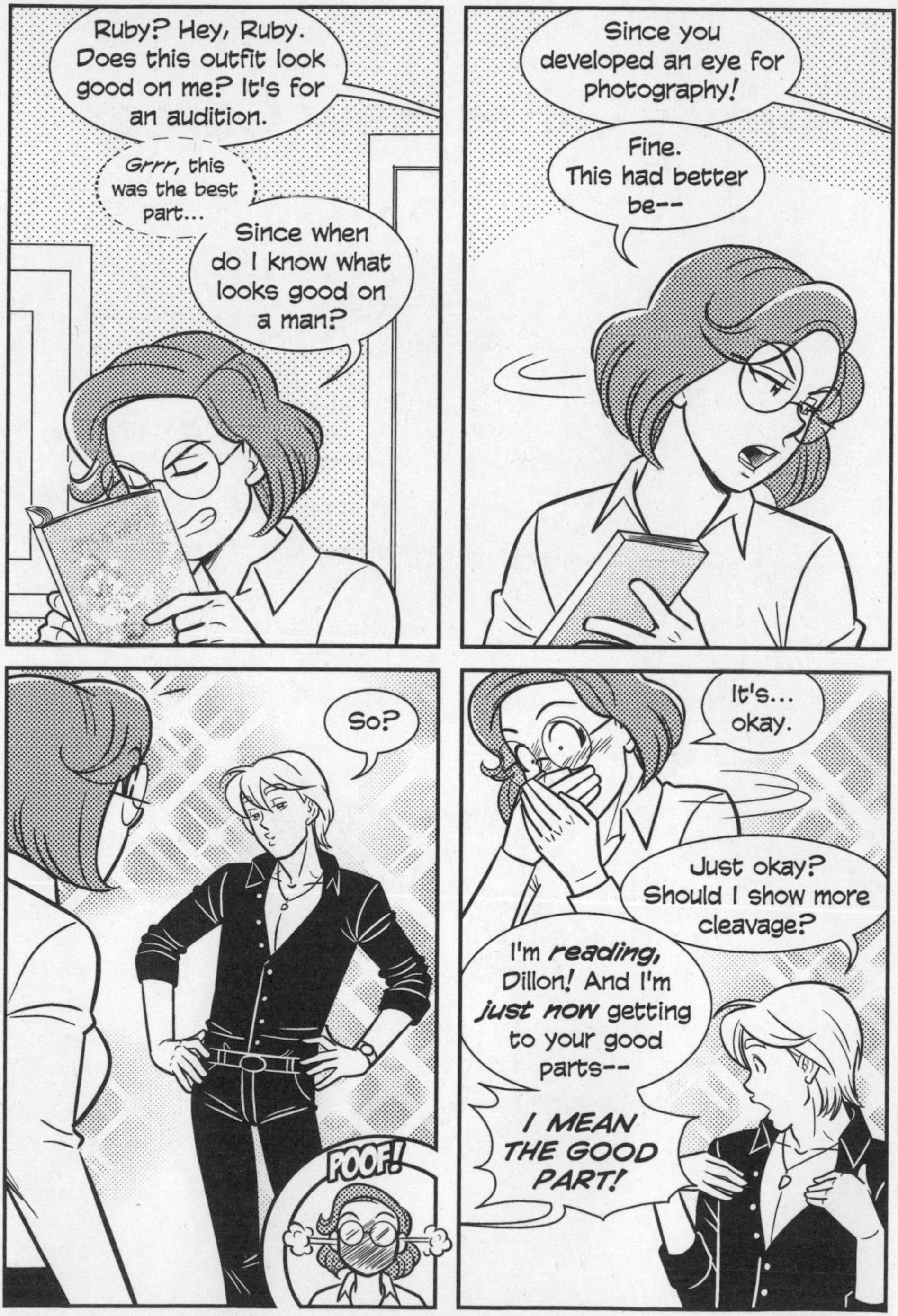
Ruby? Hey, Ruby. Does this outfit look good on me? It's for an audition.
Grrr, this was the best part...
Since when do I know what looks good on a man?
Since you developed an eye for photography!
Fine. This had better be--
So?
POOF!
It's... okay.
Just okay? Should I show more cleavage?
I'm reading, Dillon! And I'm just now getting to your good parts--
I MEAN THE GOOD PART!

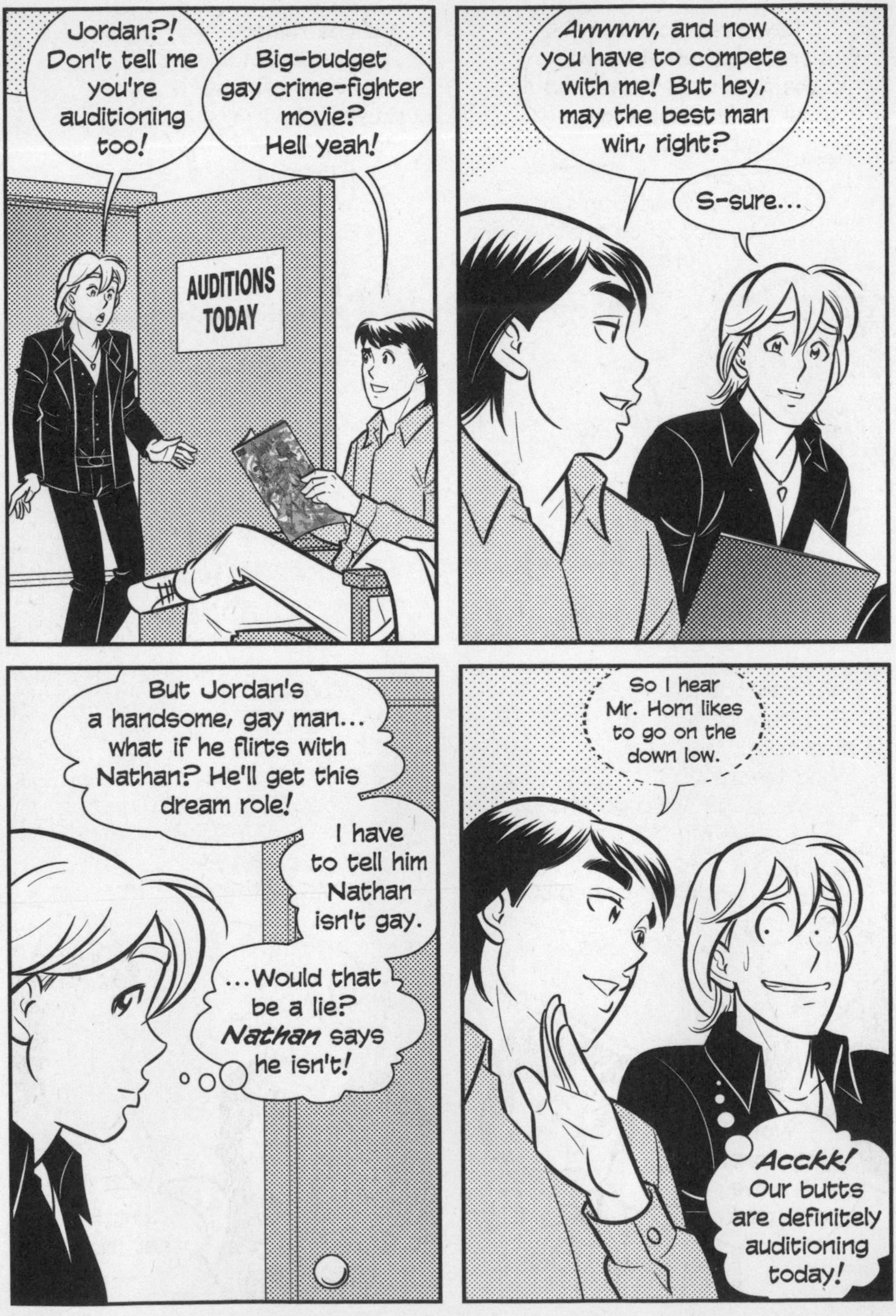
Jordan?! Don't tell me you're auditioning too!
Big-budget gay crime-fighter movie? Hell yeah!
AUDITIONS TODAY
Awwww, and now you have to compete with me! But hey, may the best man win, right?
S-sure...
But Jordan's a handsome, gay man... what if he flirts with Nathan? He'll get this dream role!
I have to tell him Nathan isn't gay.
...Would that be a lie? ***Nathan*** says he isn't!
So I hear Mr. Horn likes to go on the down low.
Acckk! Our butts are definitely auditioning today!

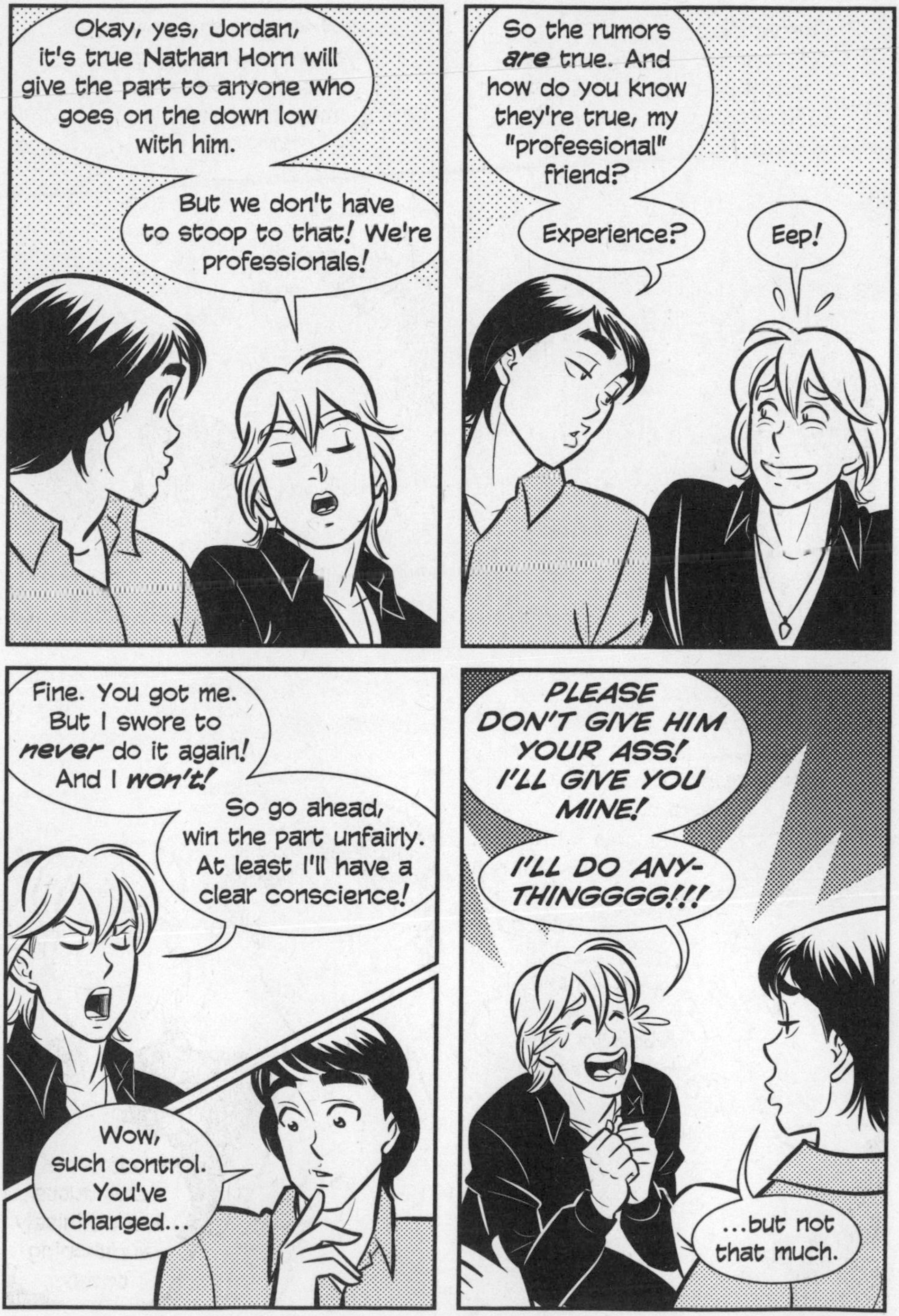
Okay, yes, Jordan, it's true Nathan Horn will give the part to anyone who goes on the down low with him.
But we don't have to stoop to that! We're professionals!
So the rumors *are* true. And how do you know they're true, my "professional" friend?
Experience?
Eep!
Fine. You got me. But I swore to *never* do it again! And I *won't!*
So go ahead, win the part unfairly. At least I'll have a clear conscience!
Wow, such control. You've changed...
PLEASE DON'T GIVE HIM YOUR ASS! I'LL GIVE YOU MINE!
I'LL DO ANY-THINGGGG!!!
...but not that much.

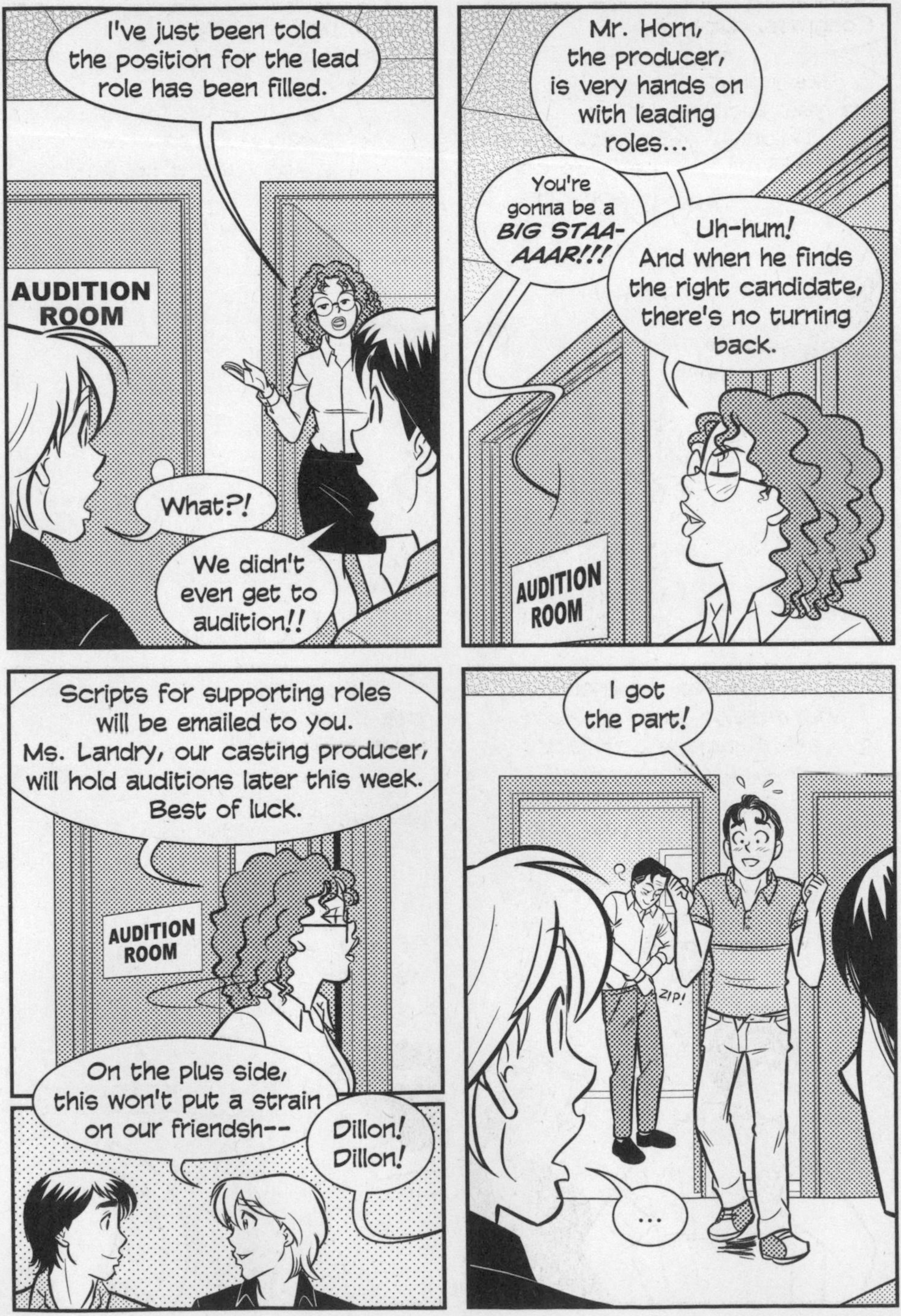
I've just been told the position for the lead role has been filled.
AUDITION ROOM
What?!
We didn't even get to audition!!
Mr. Horn, the producer, is very hands on with leading roles...
You're gonna be a BIG STAA-AAAR!!!
Uh-hum! And when he finds the right candidate, there's no turning back.
AUDITION ROOM
Scripts for supporting roles will be emailed to you. Ms. Landry, our casting producer, will hold auditions later this week. Best of luck.
AUDITION ROOM
On the plus side, this won't put a strain on our friendsh--
Dillon! Dillon!
I got the part!
ZIP!
...

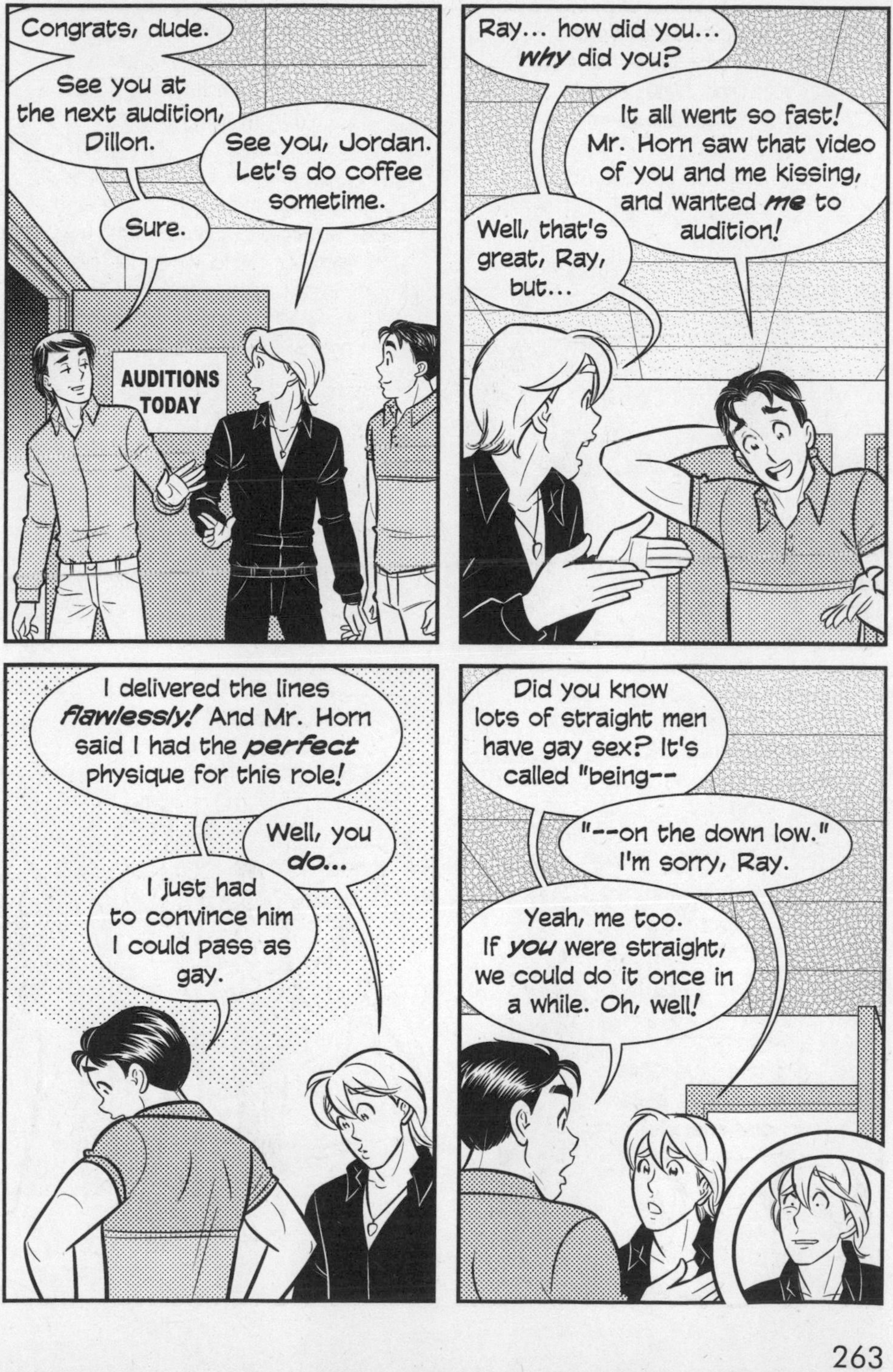
Congrats, dude.
See you at the next audition, Dillon.
Sure.
See you, Jordan. Let's do coffee sometime.
AUDITIONS TODAY
Ray... how did you... *why* did you?
It all went so fast! Mr. Horn saw that video of you and me kissing, and wanted *me* to audition!
Well, that's great, Ray, but...
I delivered the lines *flawlessly!* And Mr. Horn said I had the *perfect* physique for this role!
Well, you *do*...
I just had to convince him I could pass as gay.
Did you know lots of straight men have gay sex? It's called "being--
"--on the down low." I'm sorry, Ray.
Yeah, me too. If *you* were straight, we could do it once in a while. Oh, well!

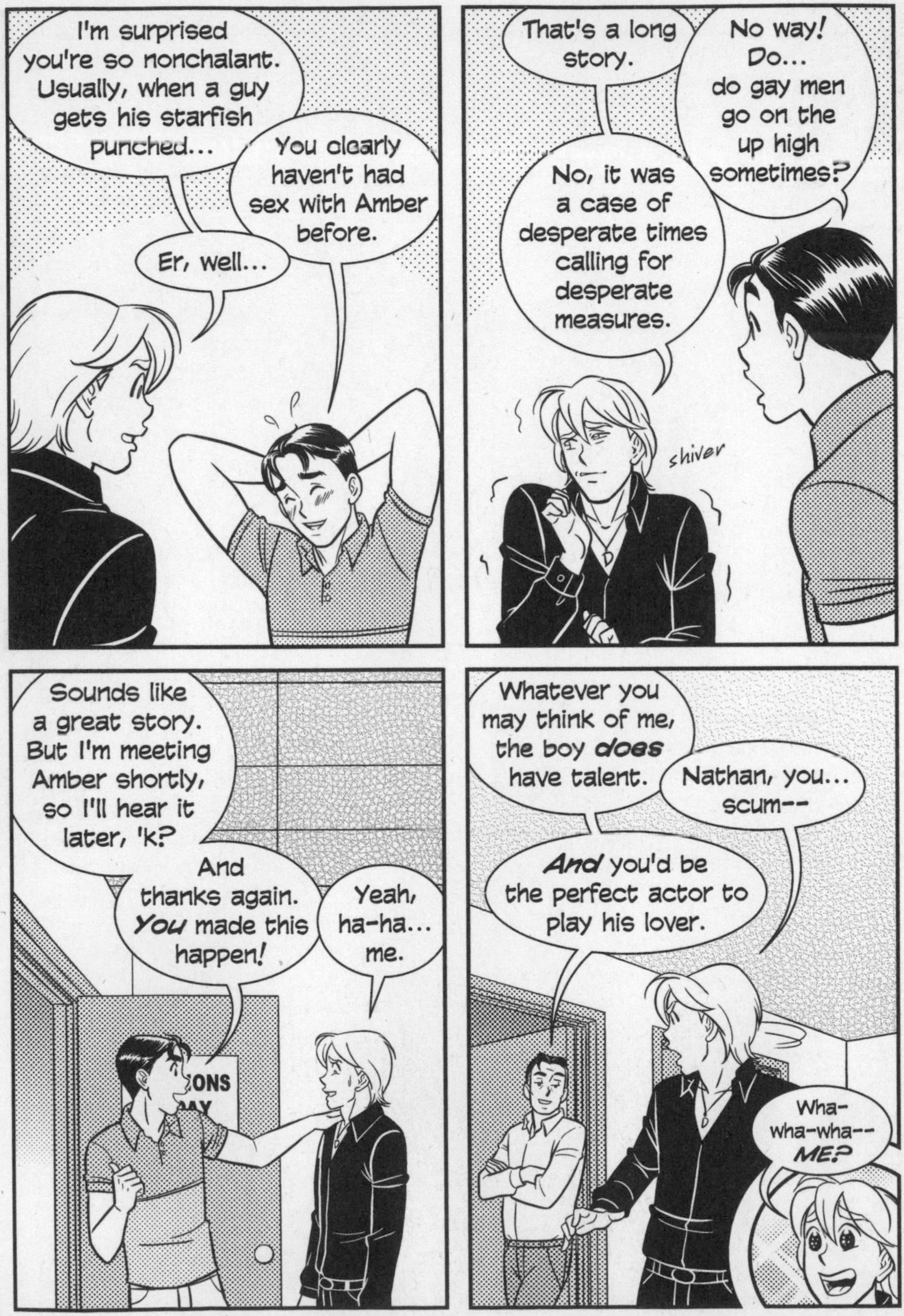
I'm surprised you're so nonchalant. Usually, when a guy gets his starfish punched...
Er, well...
You clearly haven't had sex with Amber before.
That's a long story.
No, it was a case of desperate times calling for desperate measures.
shiver
No way! Do... do gay men go on the up high sometimes?
Sounds like a great story. But I'm meeting Amber shortly, so I'll hear it later, 'k?
And thanks again. *You* made this happen!
Yeah, ha-ha... me.
Whatever you may think of me, the boy *does* have talent.
Nathan, you... scum--
And you'd be the perfect actor to play his lover.
Wha-wha-wha-- *ME?*

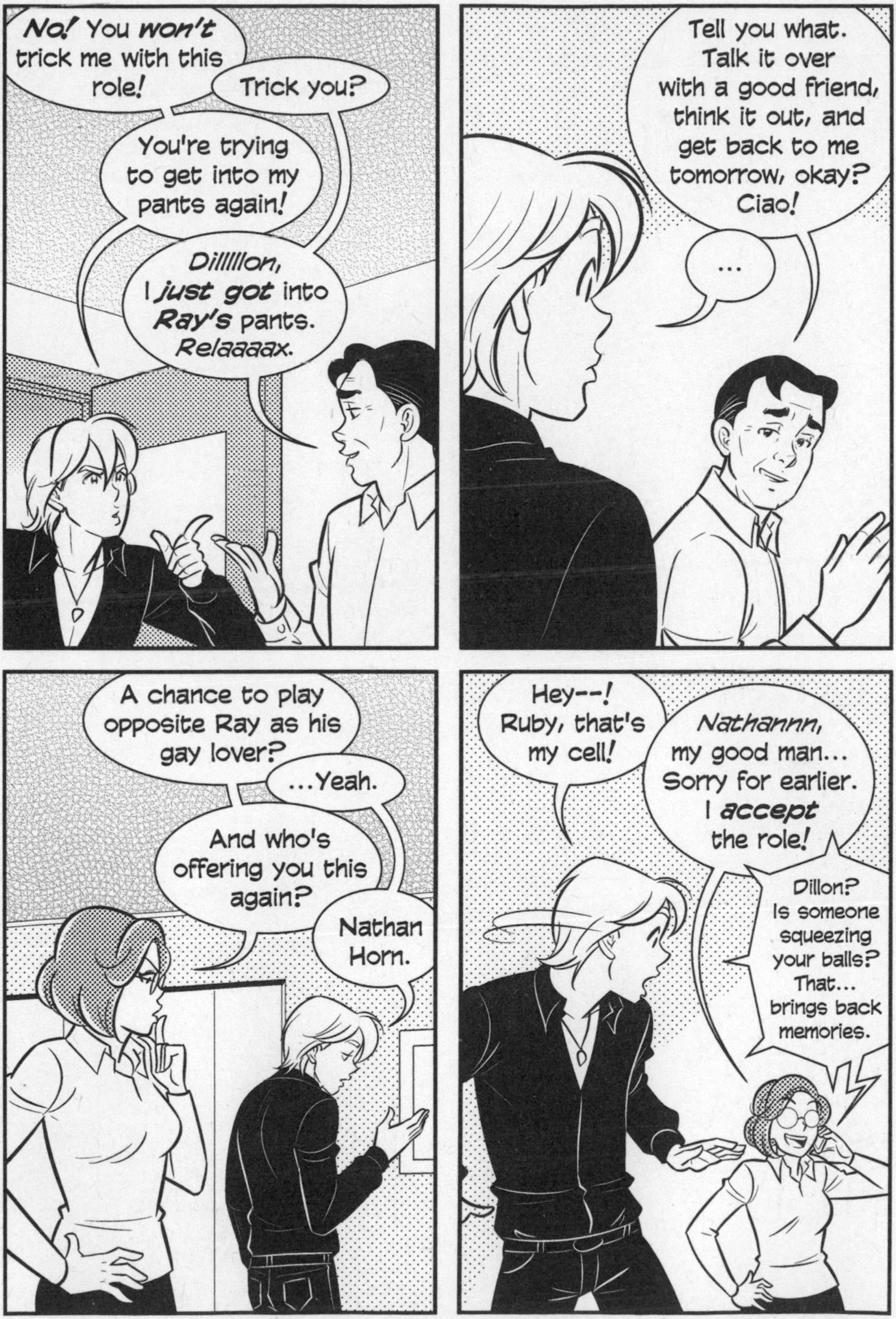
No! You won't trick me with this role!
Trick you?
You're trying to get into my pants again!
Dillllon, I just got into Ray's pants. Relaaaax.
Tell you what. Talk it over with a good friend, think it out, and get back to me tomorrow, okay? Ciao!
...
A chance to play opposite Ray as his gay lover?
...Yeah.
And who's offering you this again?
Nathan Horn.
Hey--! Ruby, that's my cell!
Nathannn, my good man... Sorry for earlier. I accept the role!
Dillon? Is someone squeezing your balls? That... brings back memories.

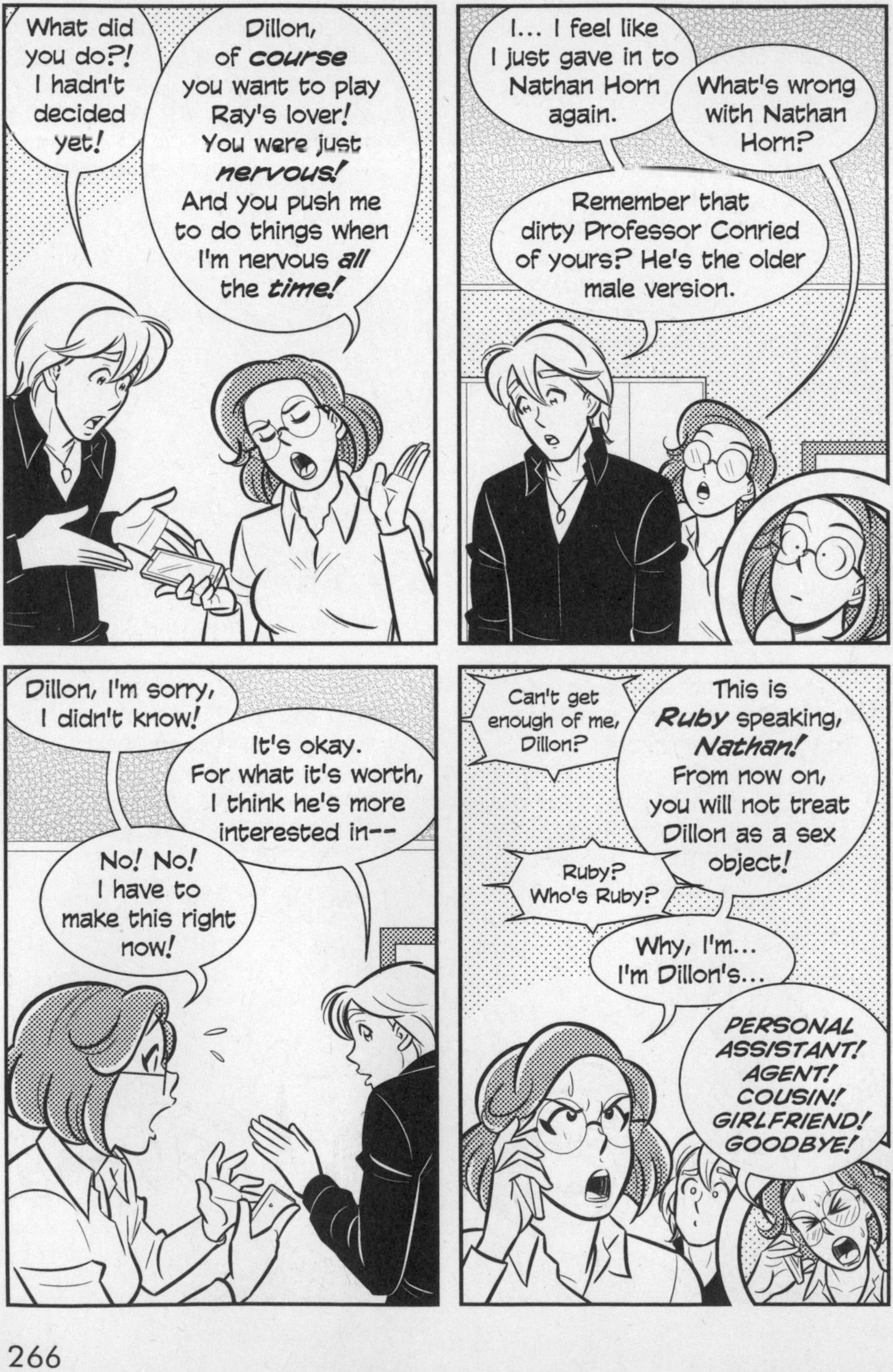
What did you do?! I hadn't decided yet!
Dillon, of course you want to play Ray's lover! You were just nervous! And you push me to do things when I'm nervous all the time!
I... I feel like I just gave in to Nathan Horn again.
What's wrong with Nathan Horn?
Remember that dirty Professor Conried of yours? He's the older male version.
Dillon, I'm sorry, I didn't know!
It's okay. For what it's worth, I think he's more interested in--
No! No! I have to make this right now!
Can't get enough of me, Dillon?
This is Ruby speaking, Nathan! From now on, you will not treat Dillon as a sex object!
Ruby? Who's Ruby?
Why, I'm... I'm Dillon's...
PERSONAL ASSISTANT! AGENT! COUSIN! GIRLFRIEND! GOODBYE!

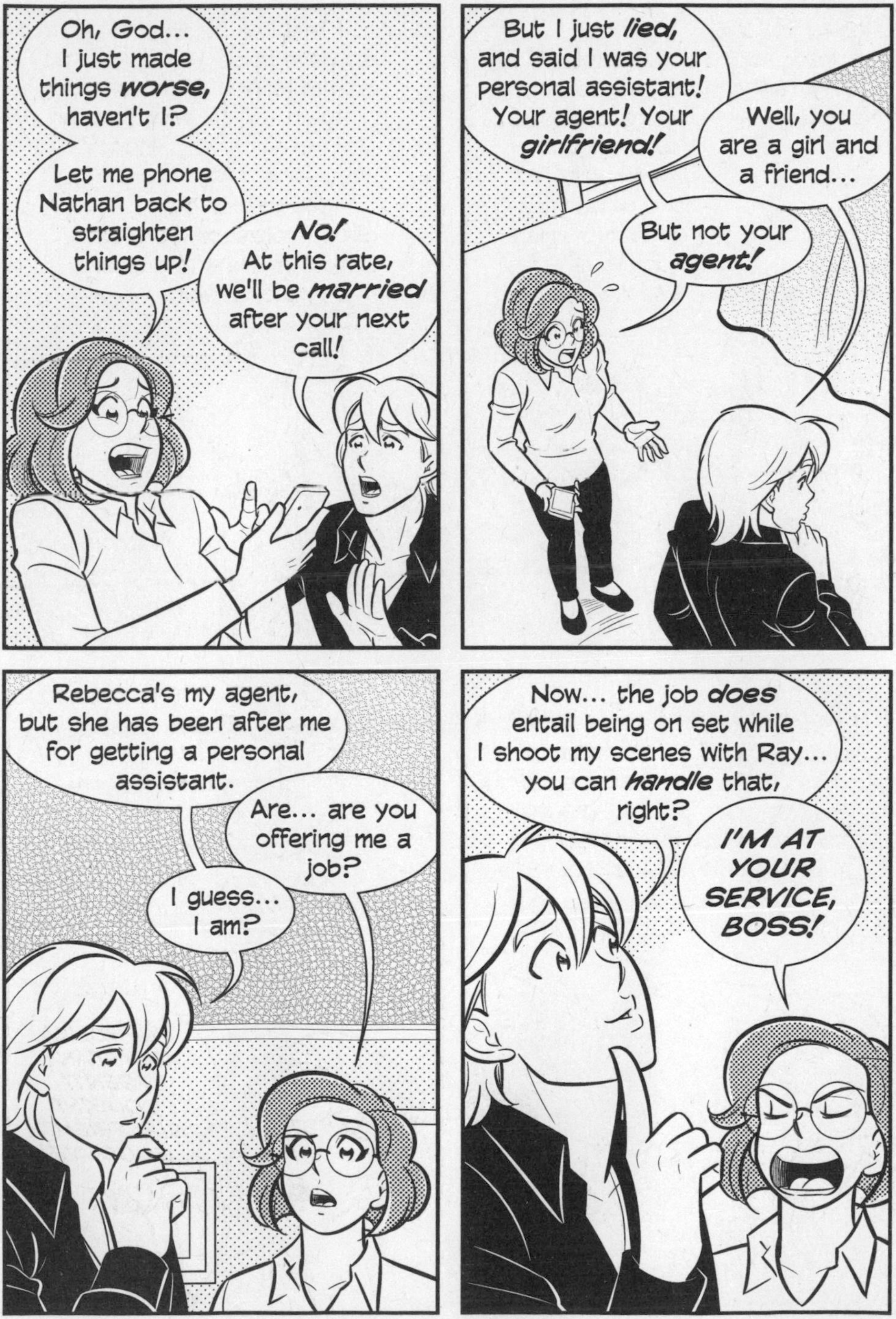
Oh, God... I just made things *worse,* haven't I?
Let me phone Nathan back to straighten things up!
No! At this rate, we'll be *married* after your next call!
But I just *lied,* and said I was your personal assistant! Your agent! Your *girlfriend!*
Well, you are a girl and a friend...
But not your *agent!*
Rebecca's my agent, but she has been after me for getting a personal assistant.
Are... are you offering me a job?
I guess... I am?
Now... the job *does* entail being on set while I shoot my scenes with Ray... you can *handle* that, right?
I'M AT YOUR SERVICE, BOSS!

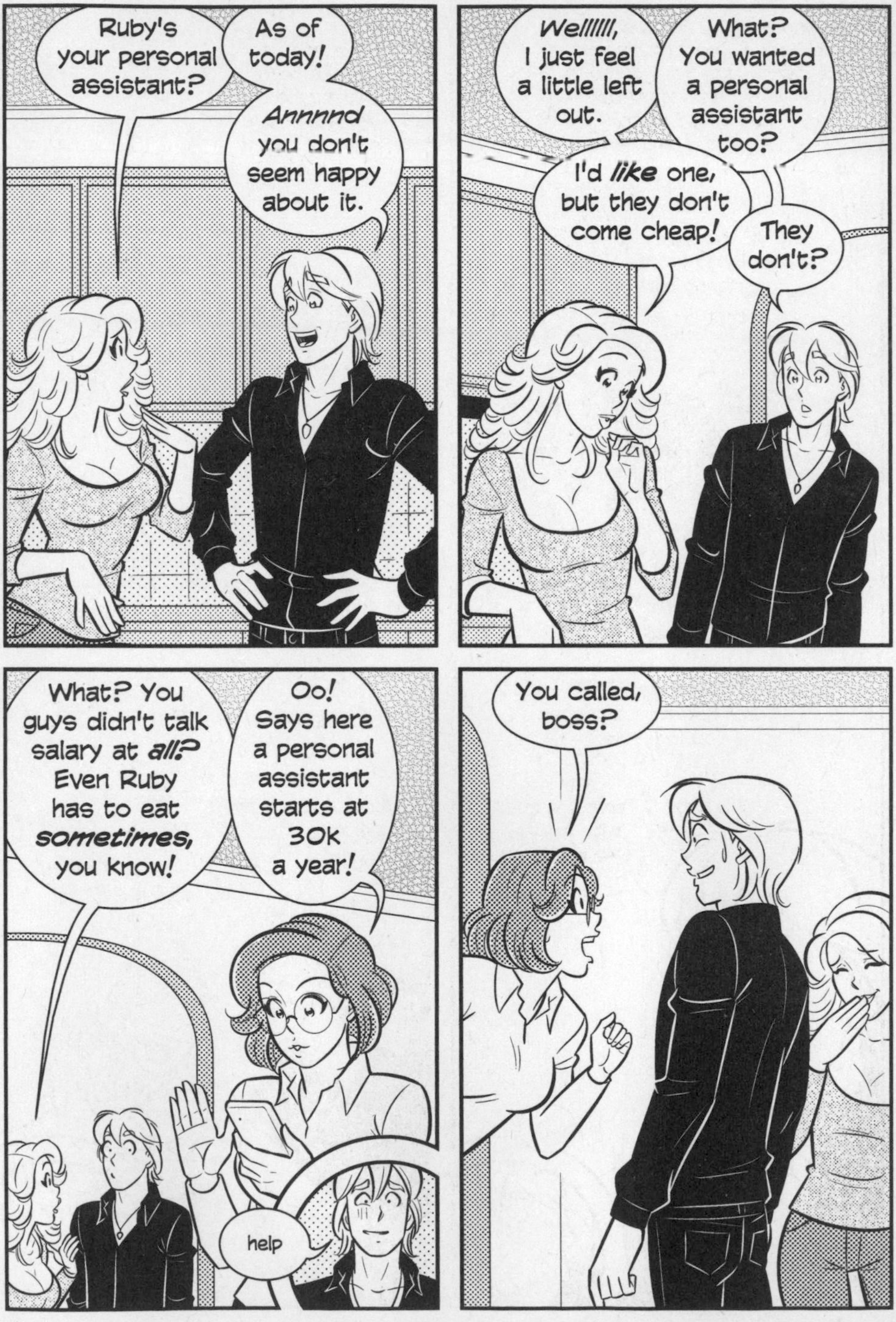

Ruby's your personal assistant?
As of today!
Annnnd you don't seem happy about it.
Wellllll, I just feel a little left out.
What? You wanted a personal assistant too?
I'd ***like*** one, but they don't come cheap!
They don't?
What? You guys didn't talk salary at *all?* Even Ruby has to eat ***sometimes,*** you know!
Oo! Says here a personal assistant starts at 30k a year!
help
You called, boss?

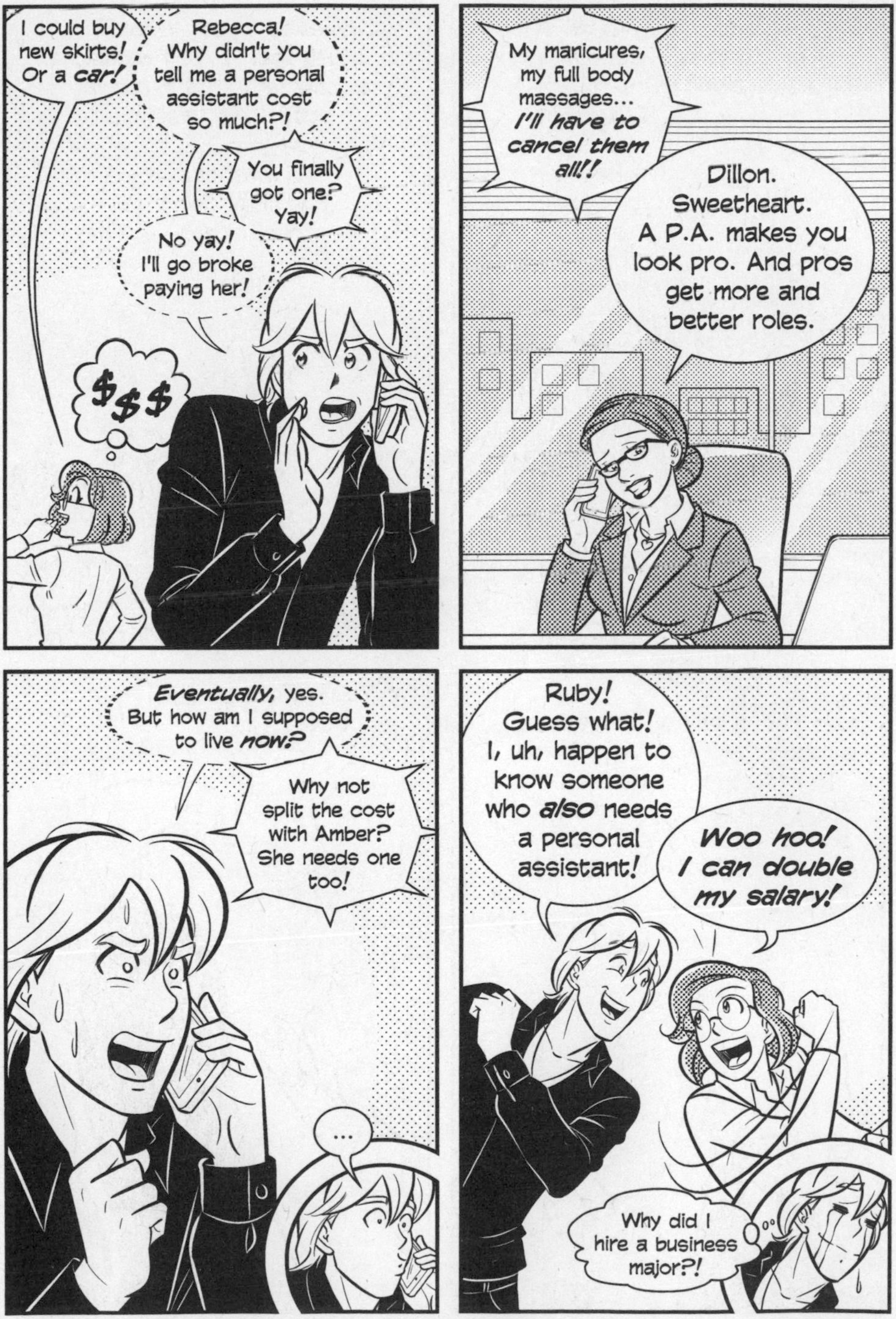

I could buy new skirts! Or a car!
Rebecca! Why didn't you tell me a personal assistant cost so much?!
You finally got one? Yay!
No yay! I'll go broke paying her!
$$$
My manicures, my full body massages... I'll have to cancel them all!!
Dillon. Sweetheart. A P.A. makes you look pro. And pros get more and better roles.
Eventually, yes. But how am I supposed to live now?
Why not split the cost with Amber? She needs one too!
...
Ruby! Guess what! I, uh, happen to know someone who also needs a personal assistant!
Woo hoo! I can double my salary!
Why did I hire a business major?!

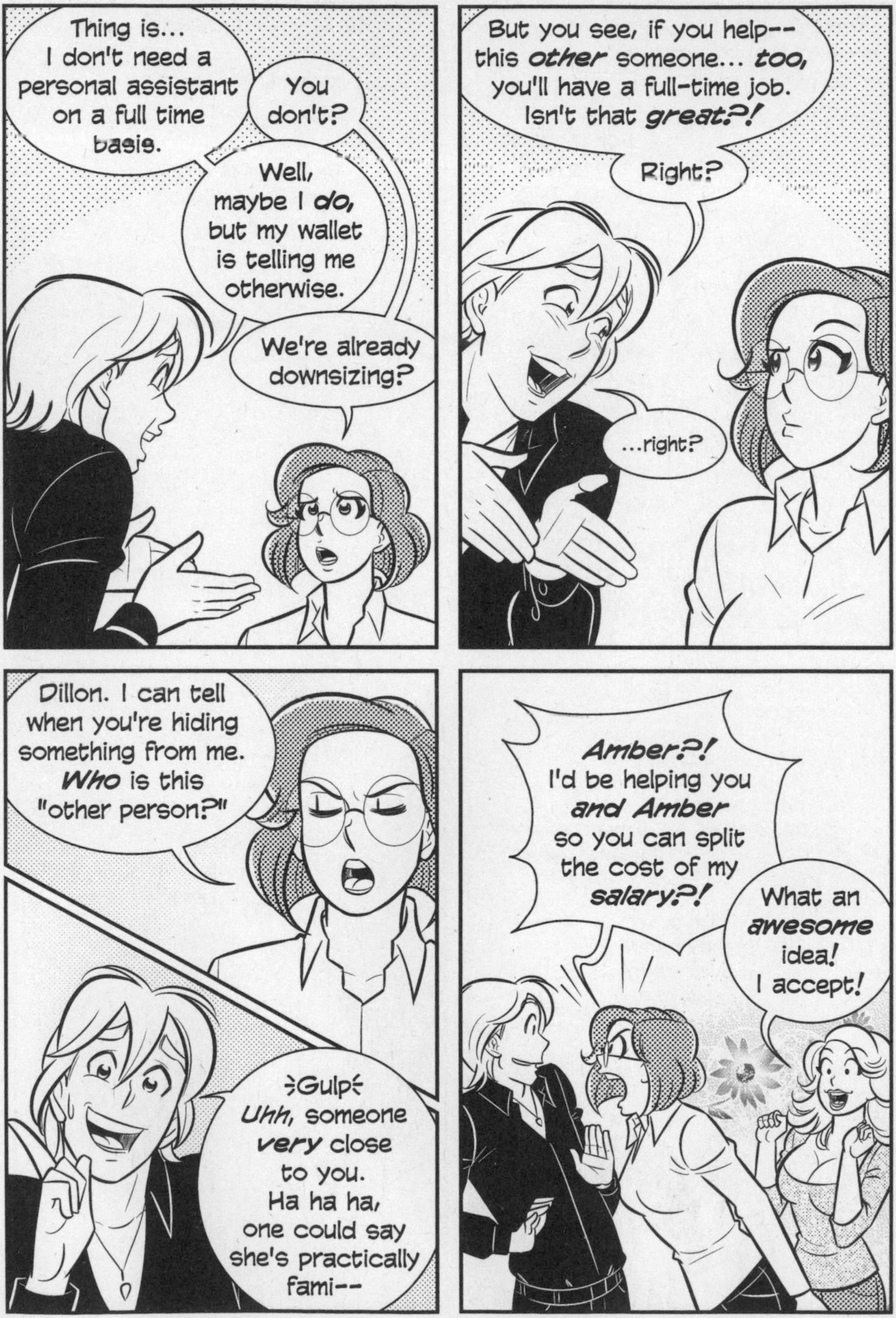
Thing is... I don't need a personal assistant on a full time basis.
You don't?
Well, maybe I do, but my wallet is telling me otherwise.
We're already downsizing?
But you see, if you help-- this other someone... too, you'll have a full-time job. Isn't that great?!
Right?
...right?
Dillon. I can tell when you're hiding something from me. Who is this "other person?"
Gulp
Uhh, someone very close to you. Ha ha ha, one could say she's practically fami--
Amber?! I'd be helping you and Amber so you can split the cost of my salary?!
What an awesome idea! I accept!

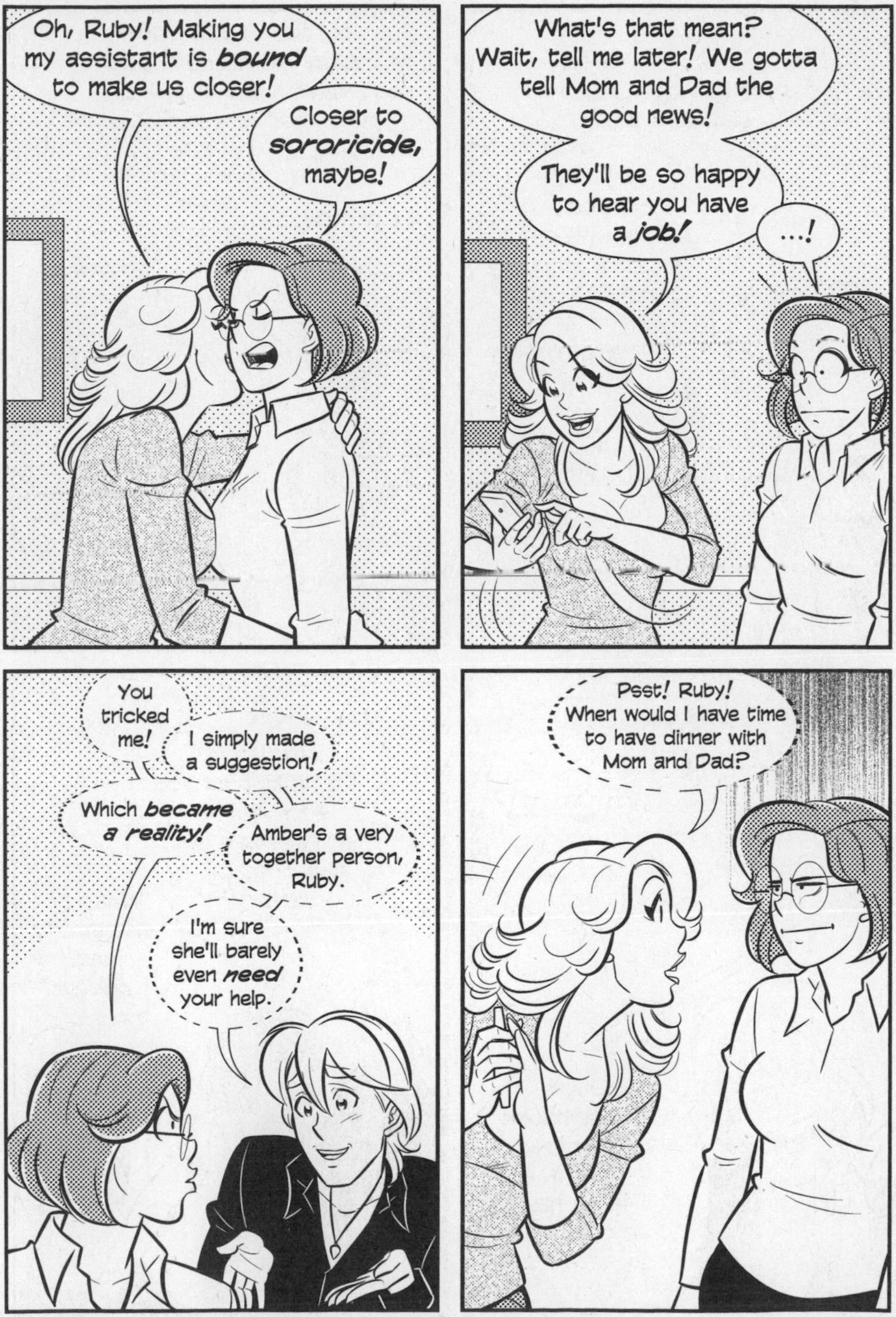
Oh, Ruby! Making you my assistant is *bound* to make us closer!
Closer to *sororicide,* maybe!
What's that mean? Wait, tell me later! We gotta tell Mom and Dad the good news!
They'll be so happy to hear you have a *job!*
...!
You tricked me!
I simply made a suggestion!
Which *became a reality!*
Amber's a very together person, Ruby.
I'm sure she'll barely even *need* your help.
Psst! Ruby! When would I have time to have dinner with Mom and Dad?

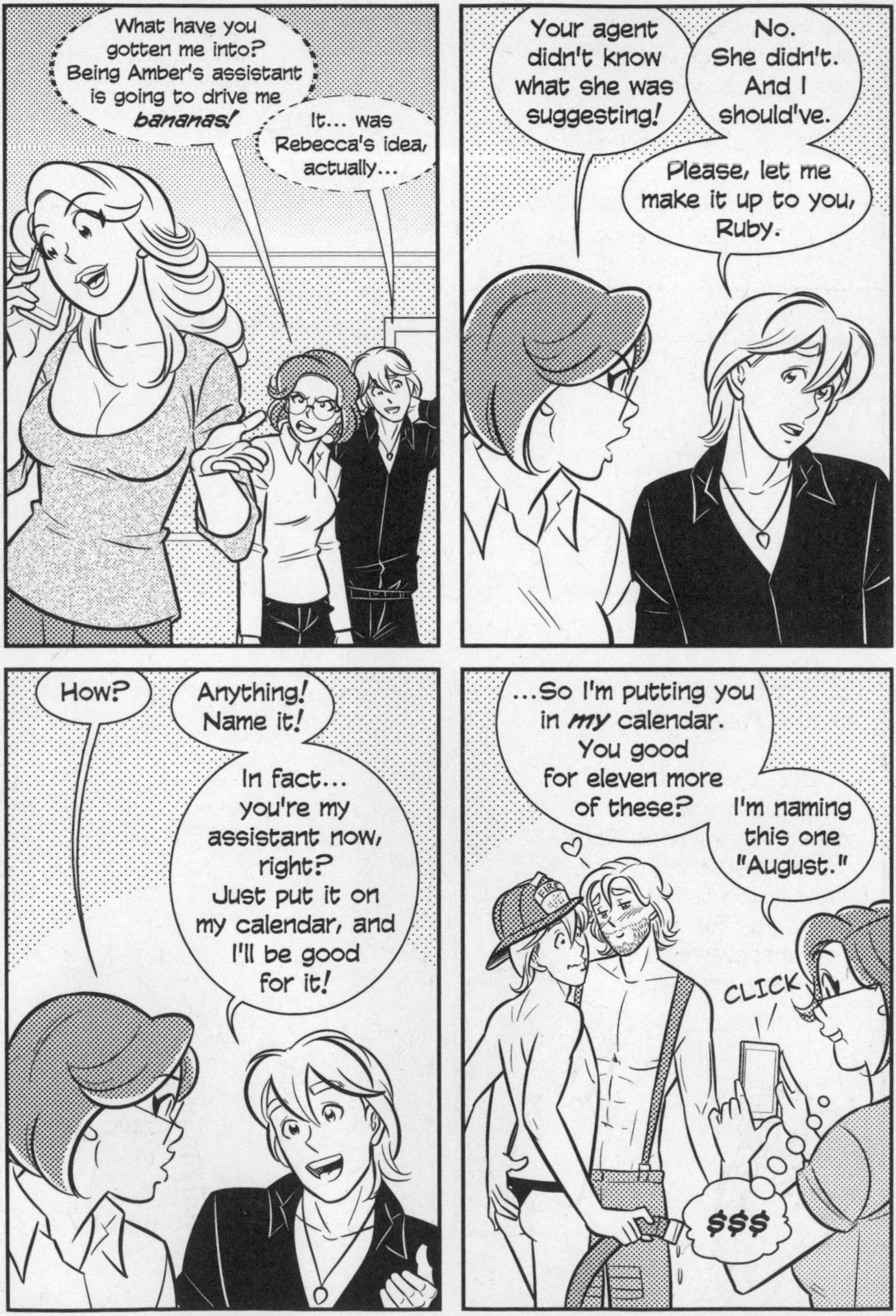
What have you gotten me into? Being Amber's assistant is going to drive me *bananas!*
It... was Rebecca's idea, actually...
Your agent didn't know what she was suggesting!
No. She didn't. And I should've.
Please, let me make it up to you, Ruby.
How?
Anything! Name it!
In fact... you're my assistant now, right? Just put it on my calendar, and I'll be good for it!
...So I'm putting you in *my* calendar. You good for eleven more of these?
I'm naming this one "August."
FIRE
CLICK
$$$

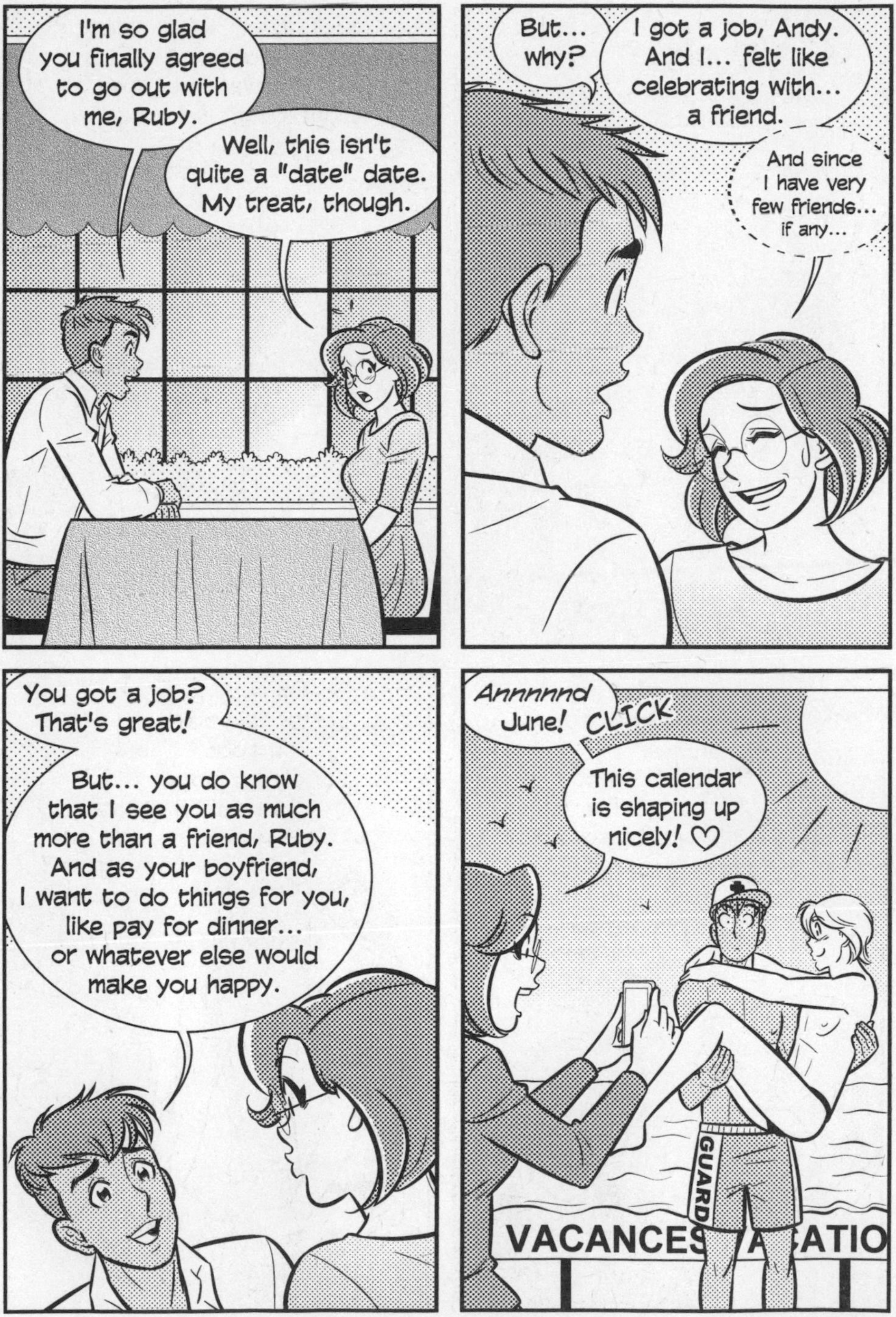
I'm so glad you finally agreed to go out with me, Ruby.
Well, this isn't quite a "date" date. My treat, though.
But... why?
I got a job, Andy. And I... felt like celebrating with... a friend.
And since I have very few friends... if any...
You got a job? That's great!
But... you do know that I see you as much more than a friend, Ruby. And as your boyfriend, I want to do things for you, like pay for dinner... or whatever else would make you happy.
Annnnnd June!
CLICK
This calendar is shaping up nicely! ♡
GUARD
VACANCES VACATIO

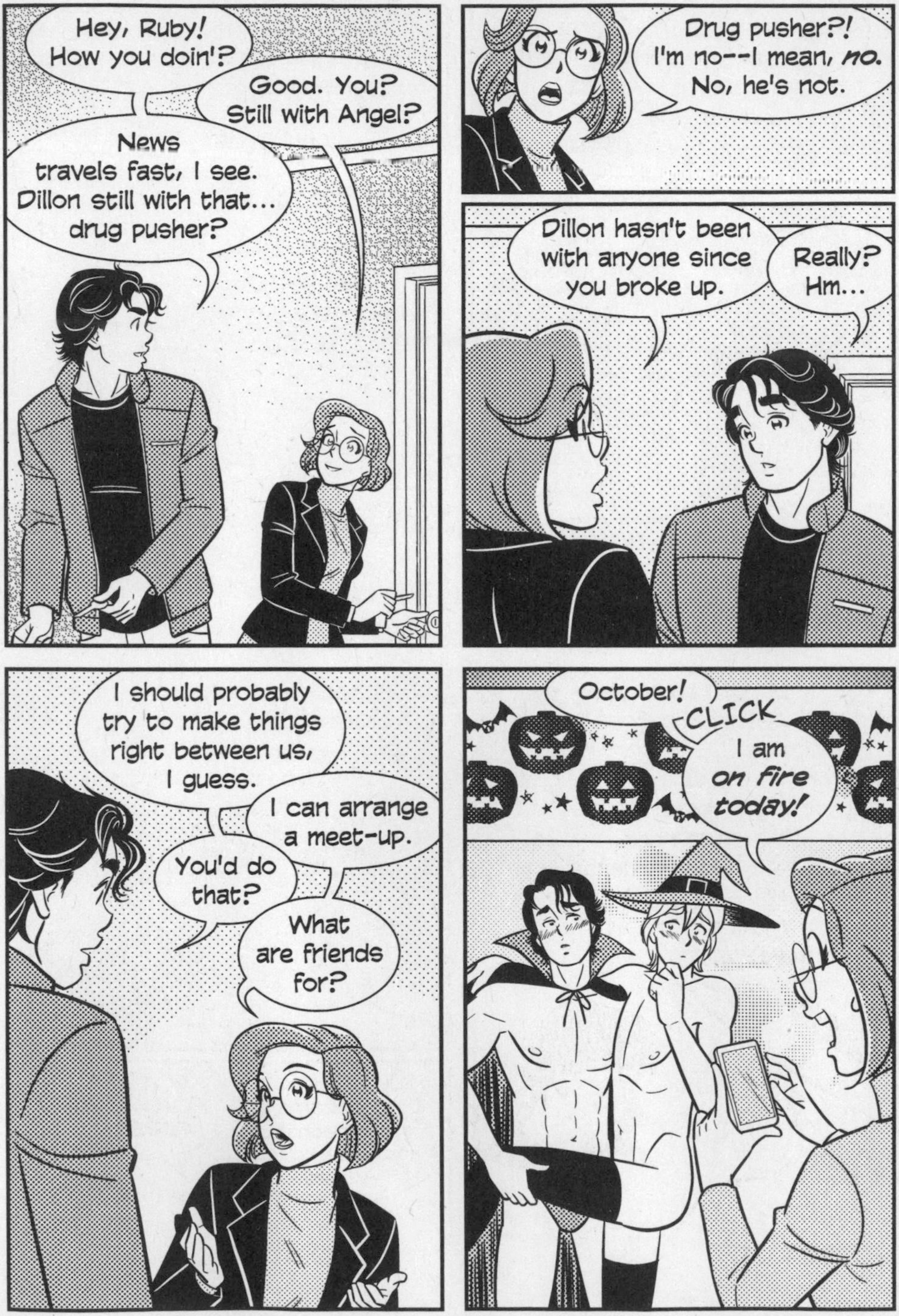
Hey, Ruby!
How you doin'?
Good. You?
Still with Angel?
News
travels fast, I see.
Dillon still with that...
drug pusher?
Drug pusher?!
I'm no--I mean, *no.*
No, he's not.
Dillon hasn't been
with anyone since
you broke up.
Really?
Hm...
I should probably
try to make things
right between us,
I guess.
I can arrange
a meet-up.
You'd do
that?
What
are friends
for?
October!
CLICK
I am
on fire
today!

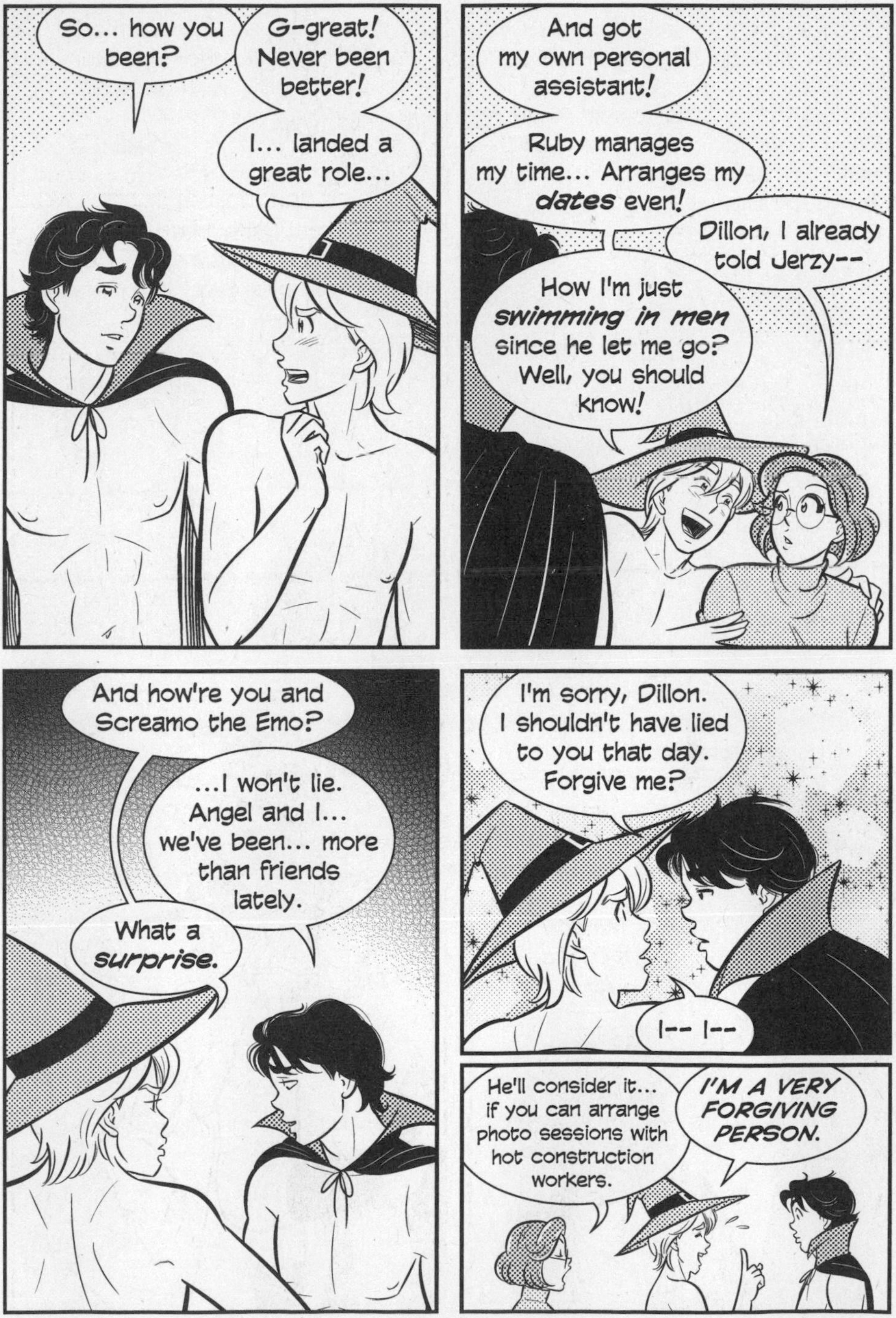
So... how you been?
G-great! Never been better!
I... landed a great role...
And got my own personal assistant!
Ruby manages my time... Arranges my *dates* even!
Dillon, I already told Jerzy--
How I'm just *swimming in men* since he let me go? Well, you should know!
And how're you and Screamo the Emo?
...I won't lie. Angel and I... we've been... more than friends lately.
What a *surprise.*
I'm sorry, Dillon. I shouldn't have lied to you that day. Forgive me?
I-- I--
He'll consider it... if you can arrange photo sessions with hot construction workers.
I'M A VERY FORGIVING PERSON.

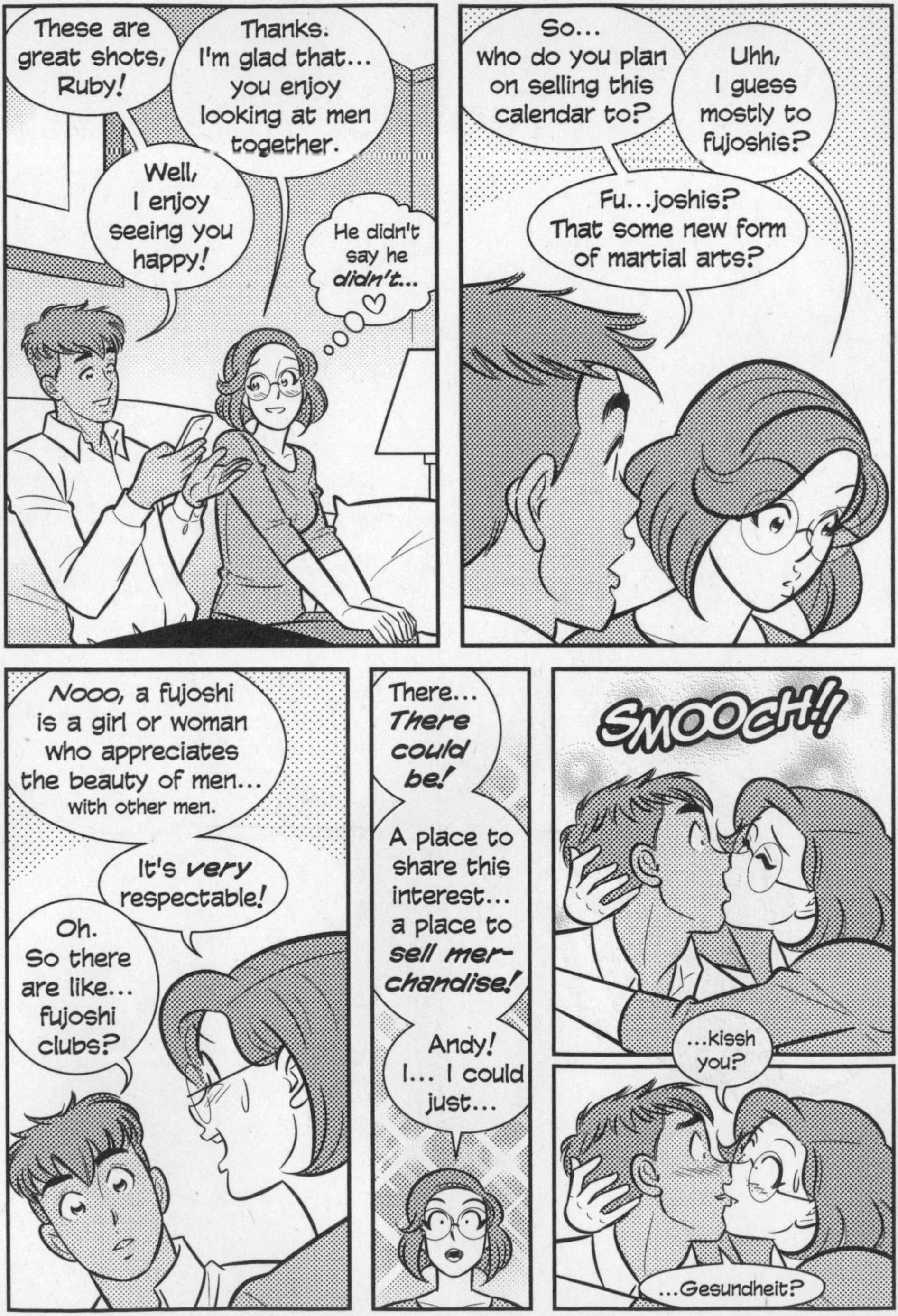
These are great shots, Ruby!
Thanks. I'm glad that... you enjoy looking at men together.
Well, I enjoy seeing you happy!
He didn't say he *didn't*... ♡
So... who do you plan on selling this calendar to?
Uhh, I guess mostly to fujoshis?
Fu...joshis? That some new form of martial arts?
Nooo, a fujoshi is a girl or woman who appreciates the beauty of men... with other men.
It's *very* respectable!
Oh. So there are like... fujoshi clubs?
There... *There could be!*
A place to share this interest... a place to *sell merchandise!*
Andy! I... I could just...
SMOOCH!!
...kissh you?
...Gesundheit?

Yeowie!

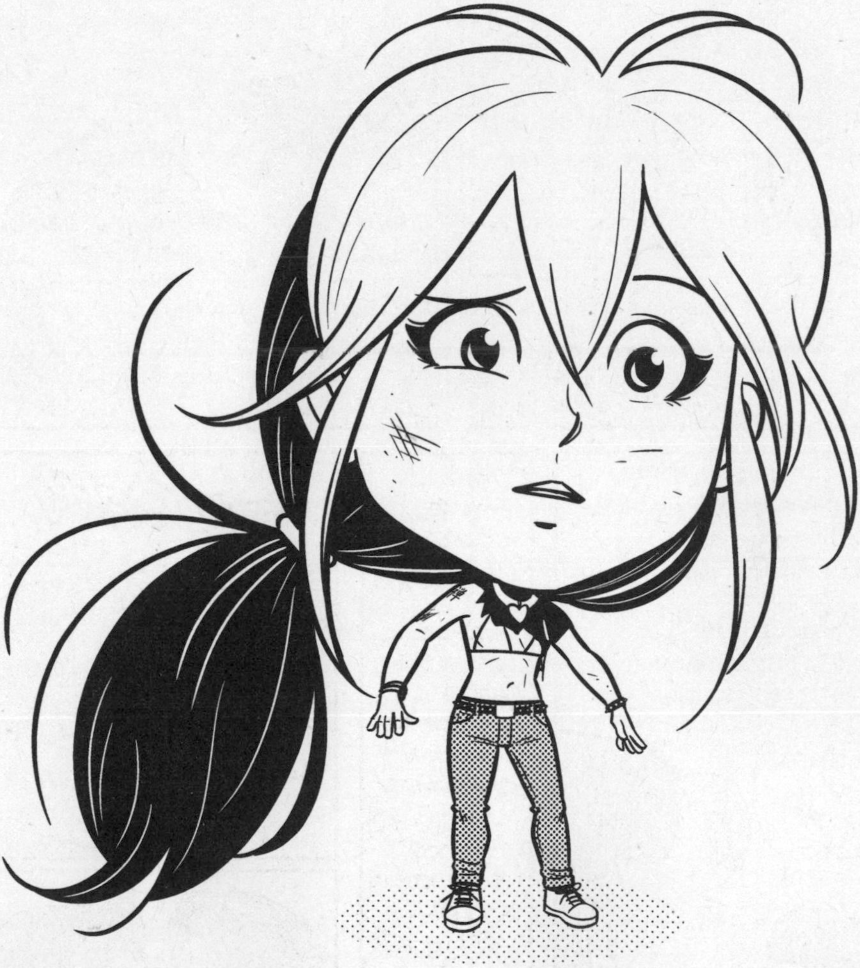

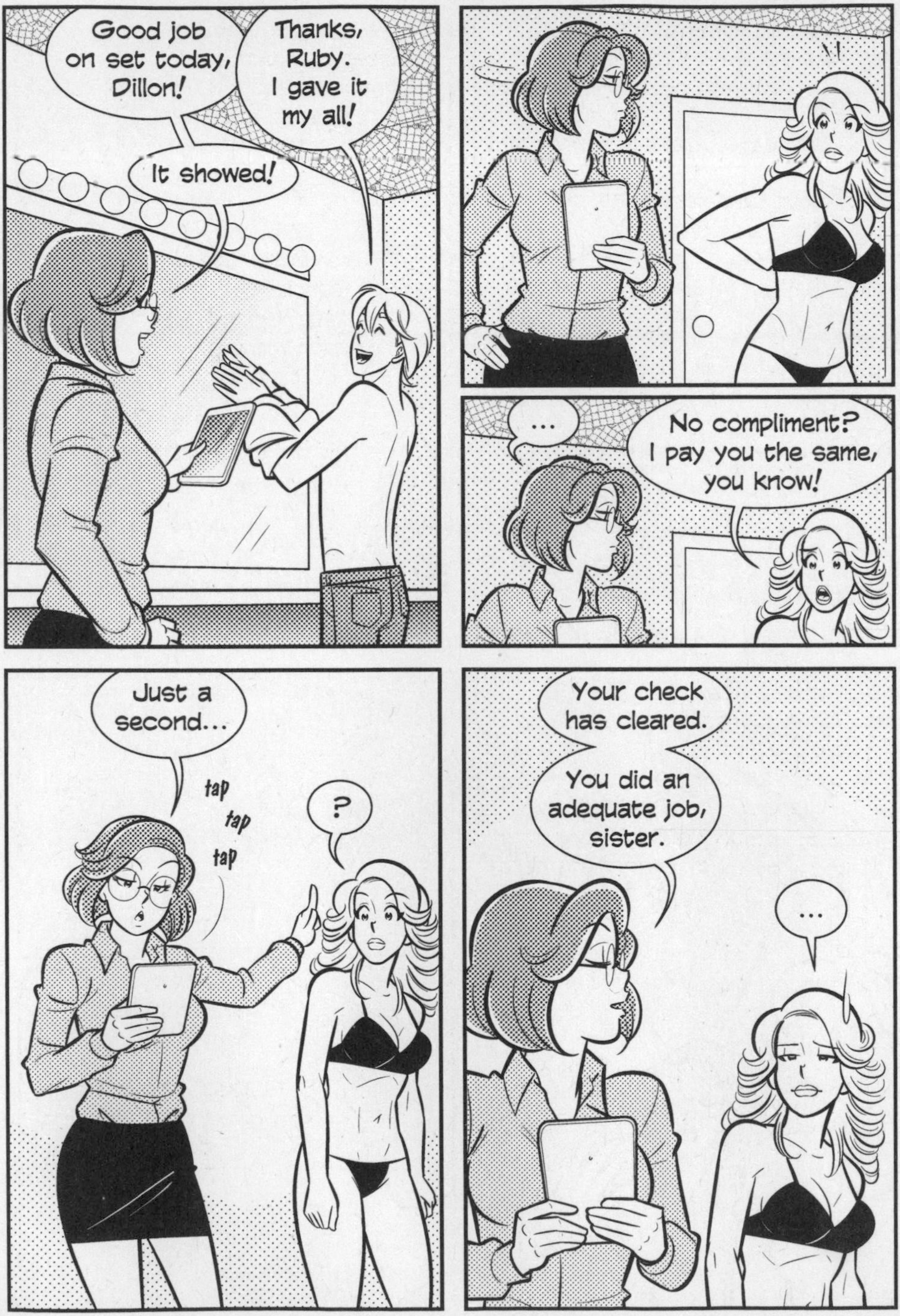
Good job on set today, Dillon!
Thanks, Ruby. I gave it my all!
It showed!
...
No compliment? I pay you the same, you know!
Just a second...
tap
tap
tap
?
Your check has cleared.
You did an adequate job, sister.
...

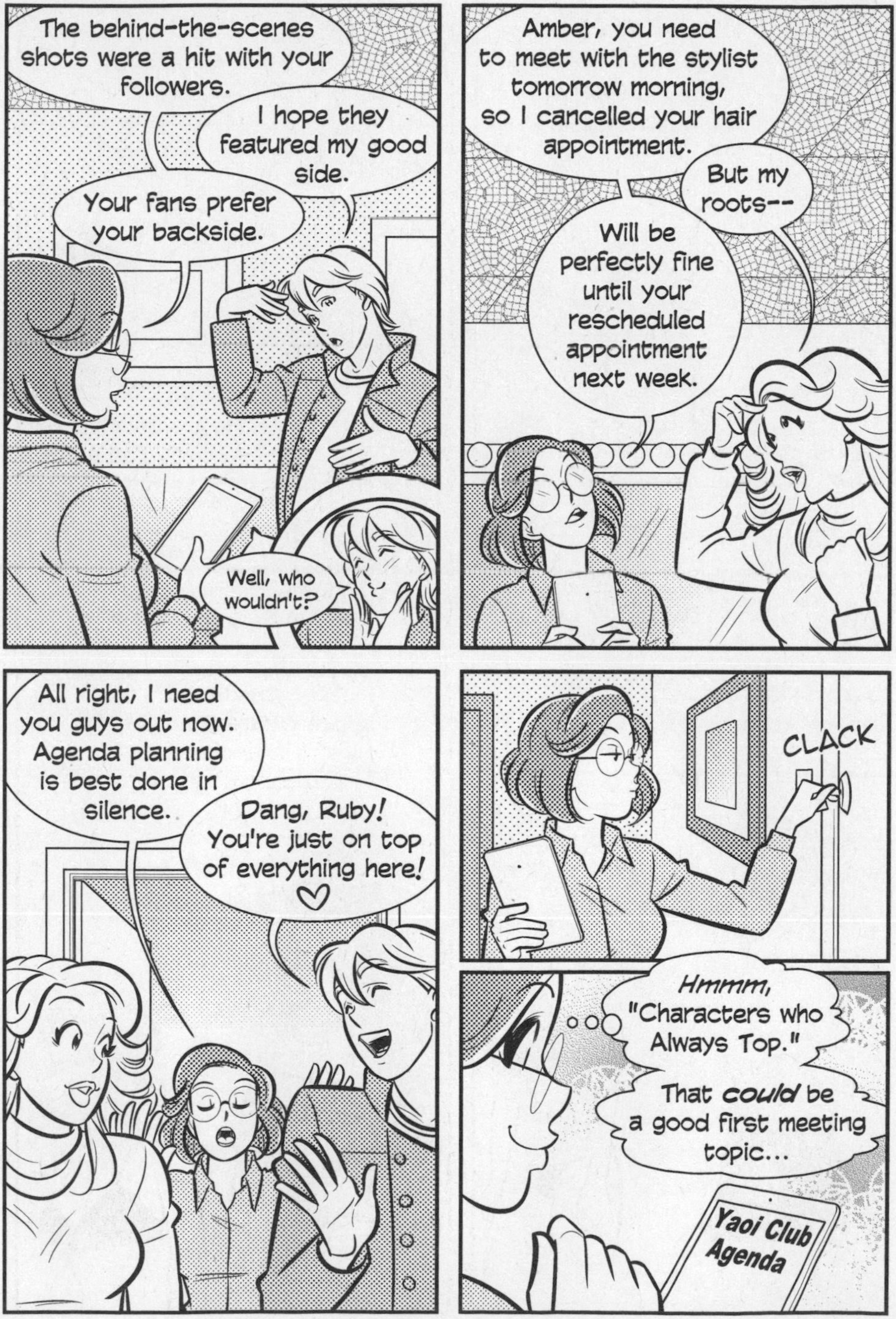
The behind-the-scenes shots were a hit with your followers.
I hope they featured my good side.
Your fans prefer your backside.
Well, who wouldn't?
Amber, you need to meet with the stylist tomorrow morning, so I cancelled your hair appointment.
But my roots--
Will be perfectly fine until your rescheduled appointment next week.
All right, I need you guys out now. Agenda planning is best done in silence.
Dang, Ruby! You're just on top of everything here!
CLACK
Hmmm, "Characters who Always Top."
That *could* be a good first meeting topic...
Yaoi Club Agenda

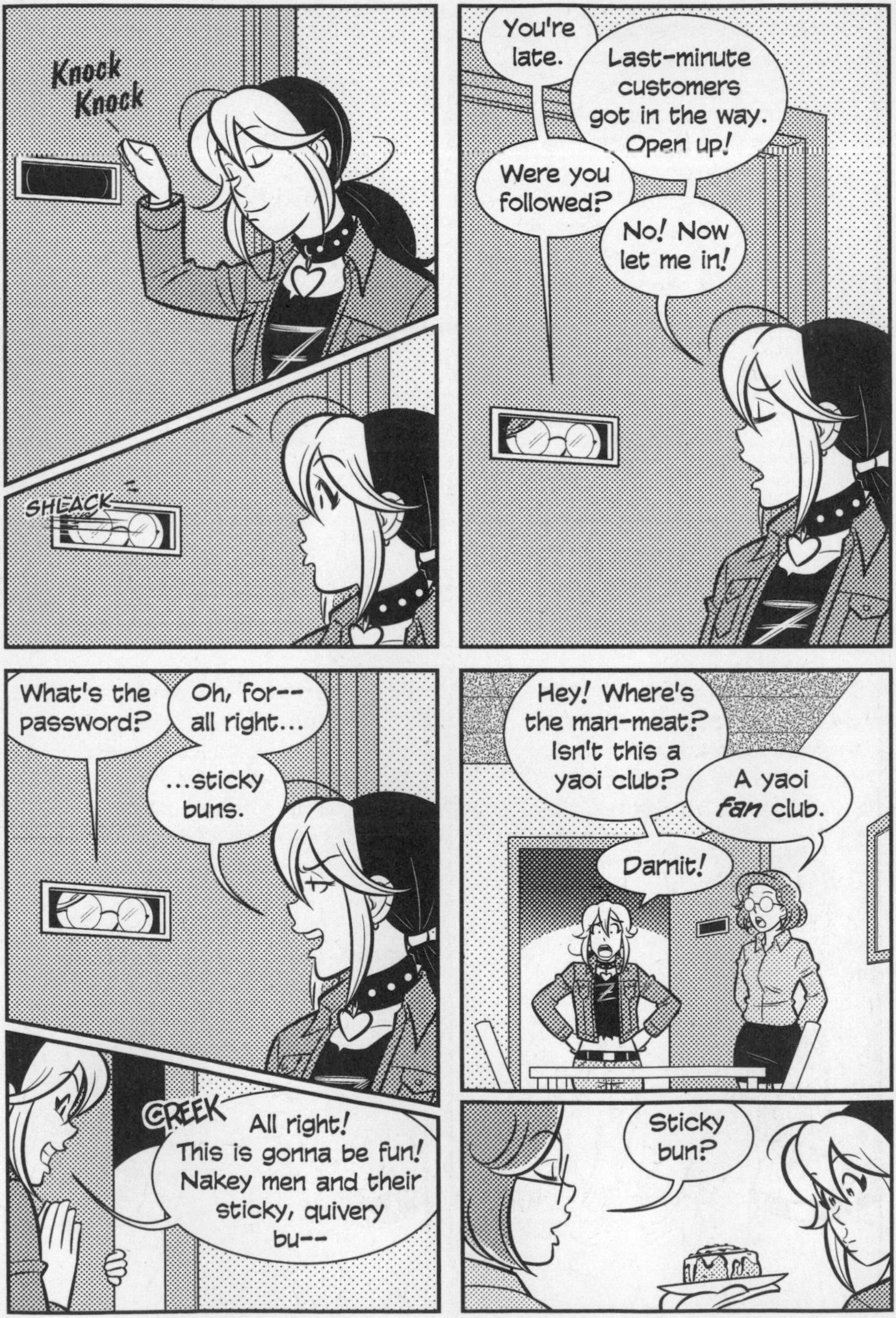
Knock Knock
SHLACK
You're late.
Last-minute customers got in the way. Open up!
Were you followed?
No! Now let me in!
What's the password?
Oh, for-- all right...
...sticky buns.
CREEK
All right! This is gonna be fun! Nakey men and their sticky, quivery bu--
Hey! Where's the man-meat? Isn't this a yaoi club?
A yaoi *fan* club.
Darnit!
Sticky bun?

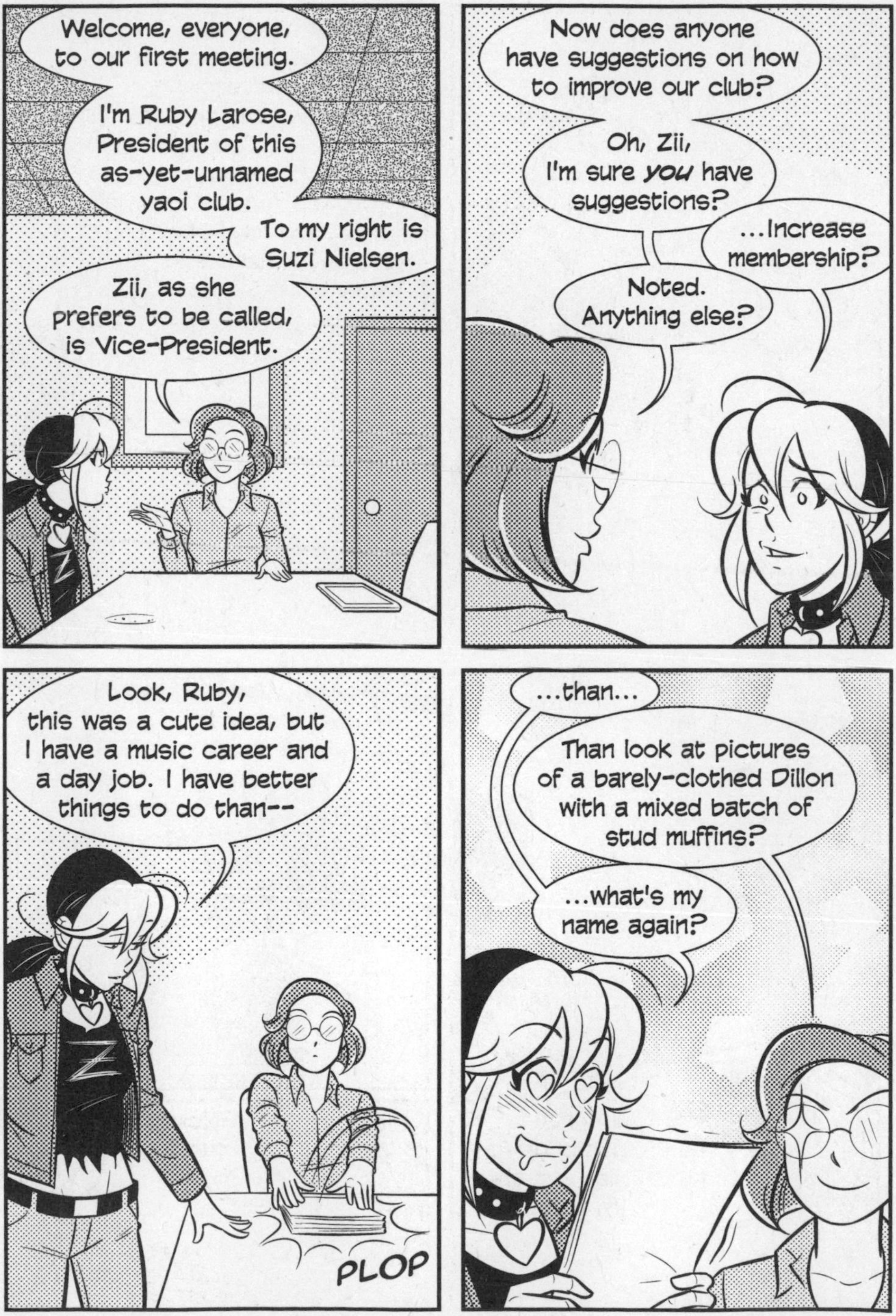
Welcome, everyone, to our first meeting.
I'm Ruby Larose, President of this as-yet-unnamed yaoi club.
To my right is Suzi Nielsen.
Zii, as she prefers to be called, is Vice-President.
Now does anyone have suggestions on how to improve our club?
Oh, Zii, I'm sure *you* have suggestions?
...Increase membership?
Noted. Anything else?
Look, Ruby, this was a cute idea, but I have a music career and a day job. I have better things to do than--
PLOP
...than...
Than look at pictures of a barely-clothed Dillon with a mixed batch of stud muffins?
...what's my name again?

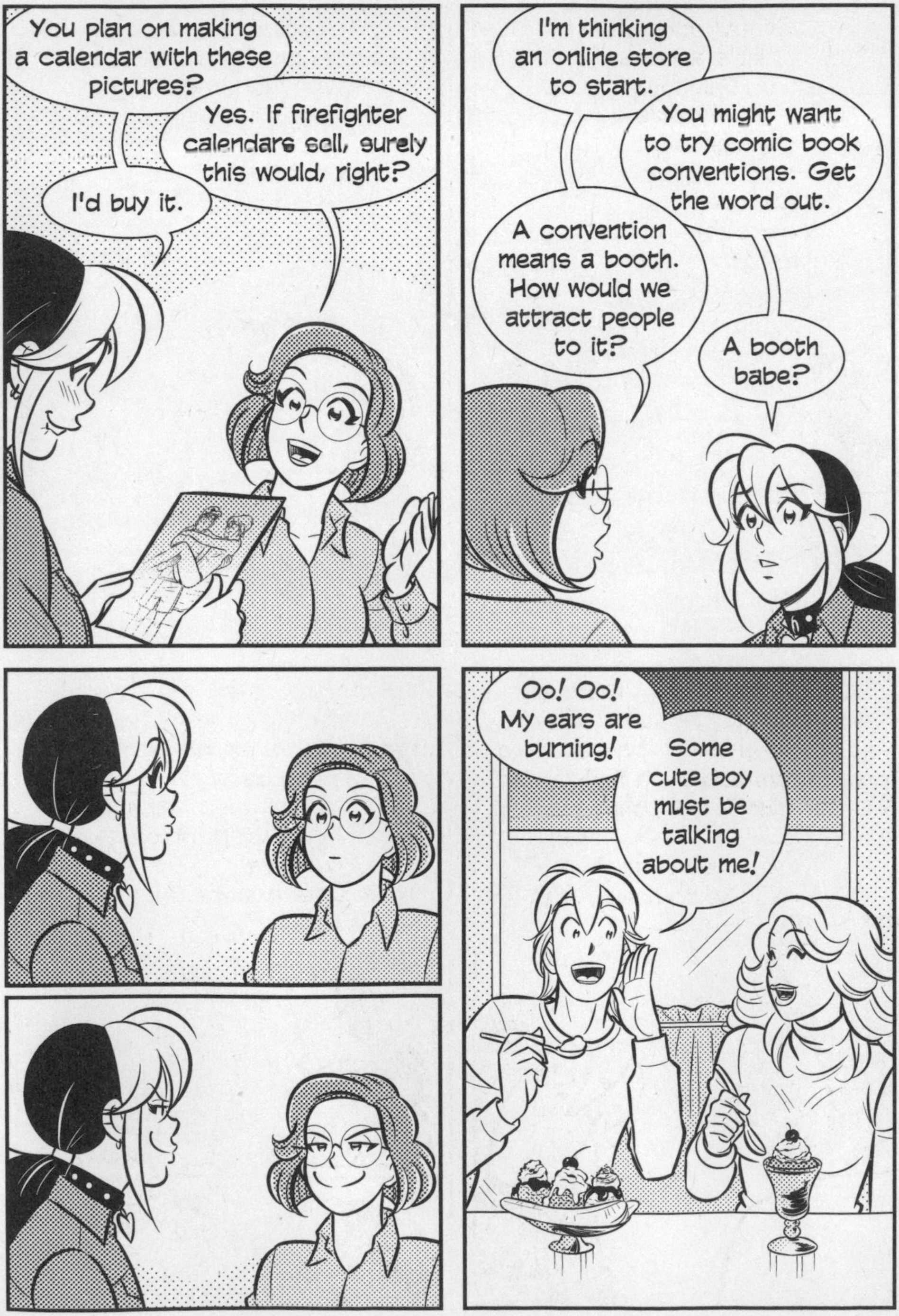
You plan on making a calendar with these pictures?
Yes. If firefighter calendars sell, surely this would, right?
I'd buy it.
I'm thinking an online store to start.
You might want to try comic book conventions. Get the word out.
A convention means a booth. How would we attract people to it?
A booth babe?
Oo! Oo! My ears are burning!
Some cute boy must be talking about me!

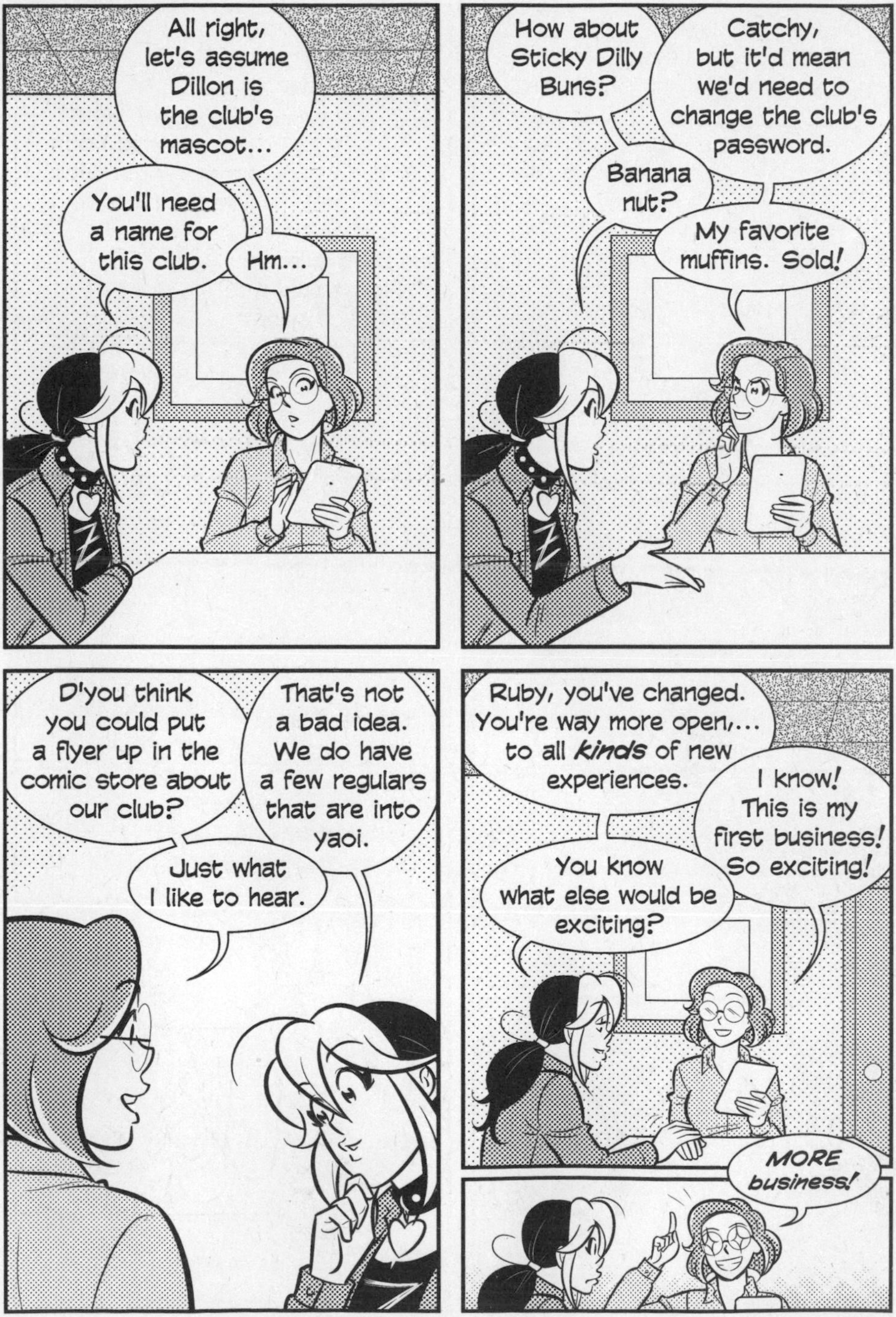
All right, let's assume Dillon is the club's mascot...
You'll need a name for this club.
Hm...
How about Sticky Dilly Buns?
Catchy, but it'd mean we'd need to change the club's password.
Banana nut?
My favorite muffins. Sold!
D'you think you could put a flyer up in the comic store about our club?
That's not a bad idea. We do have a few regulars that are into yaoi.
Just what I like to hear.
Ruby, you've changed. You're way more open,... to all *kinds* of new experiences.
I know! This is my first business! So exciting!
You know what else would be exciting?
MORE business!

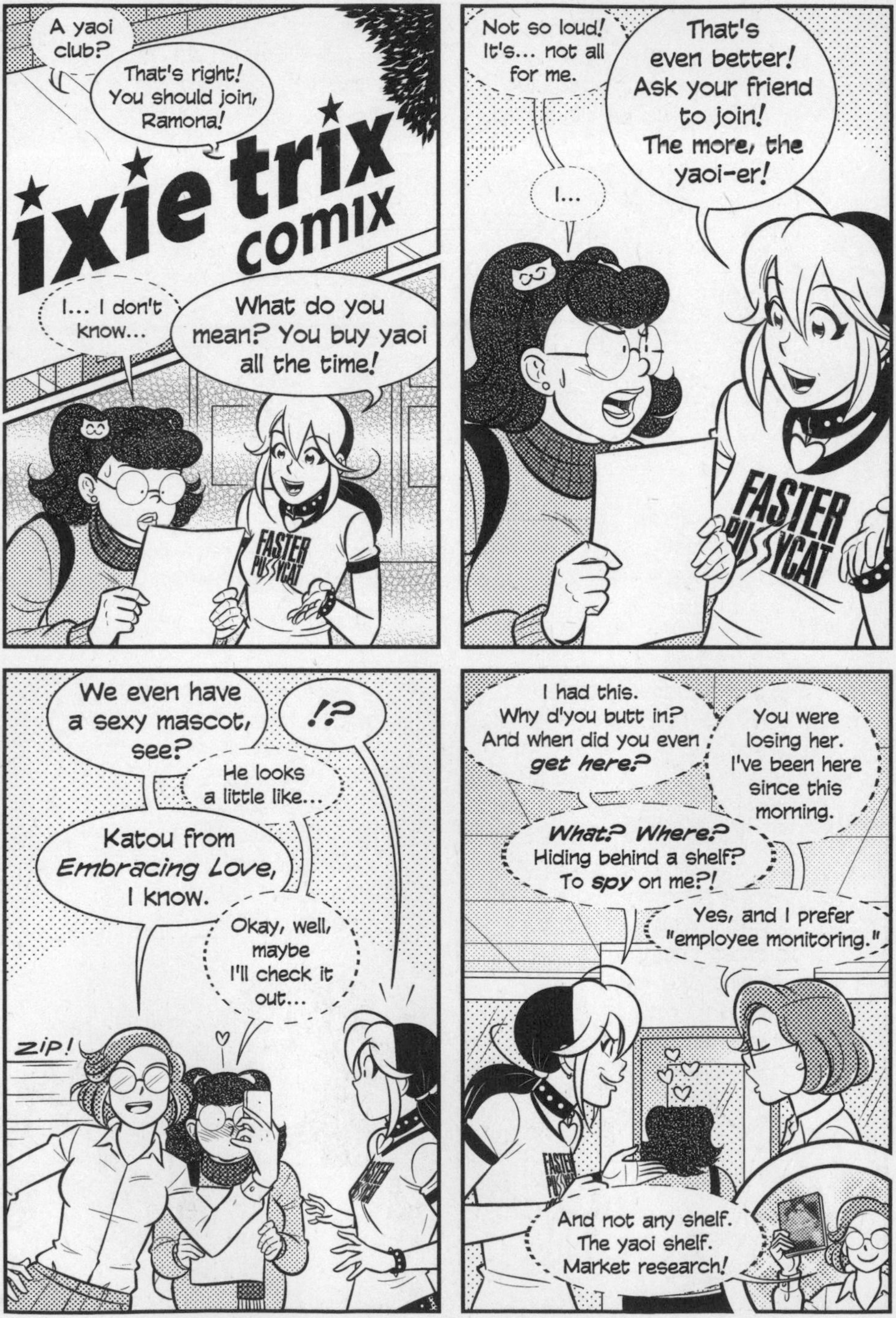
A yaoi club?
That's right! You should join, Ramona!
ixie trix comix
I... I don't know...
What do you mean? You buy yaoi all the time!
FASTER PUSSYCAT
Not so loud! It's... not all for me.
That's even better! Ask your friend to join! The more, the yaoi-er!
I...
FASTER PUSSYCAT
We even have a sexy mascot, see?
!?
He looks a little like...
Katou from *Embracing Love*, I know.
Okay, well, maybe I'll check it out...
ZIP!
I had this. Why d'you butt in? And when did you even *get here?*
You were losing her. I've been here since this morning.
What? Where? Hiding behind a shelf? To *spy* on me?!
Yes, and I prefer "employee monitoring."
And not any shelf. The yaoi shelf. Market research!

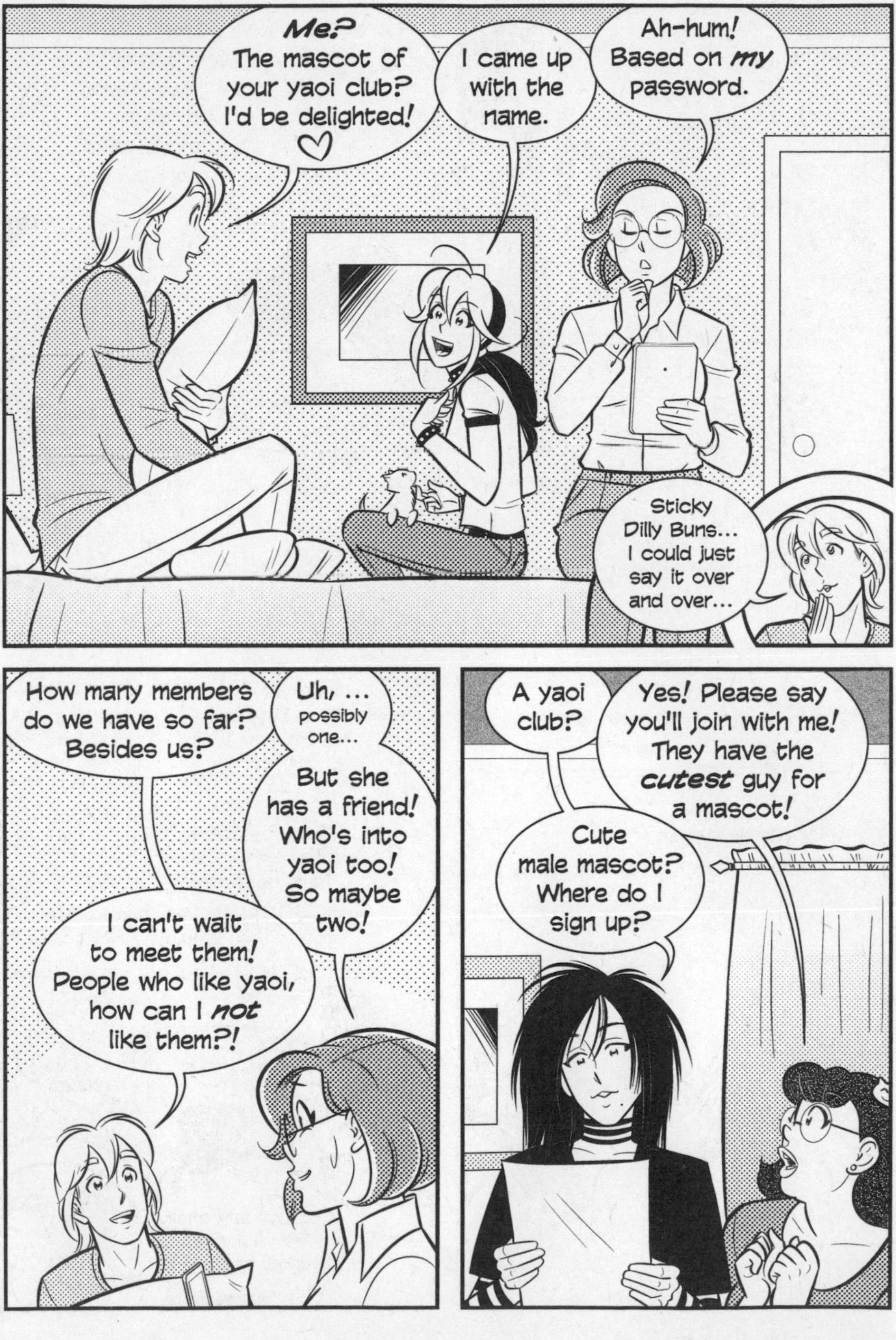
Me? The mascot of your yaoi club? I'd be delighted! ♡
I came up with the name.
Ah-hum! Based on my password.
Sticky Dilly Buns... I could just say it over and over...
How many members do we have so far? Besides us?
Uh, ... possibly one...
But she has a friend! Who's into yaoi too! So maybe two!
I can't wait to meet them! People who like yaoi, how can I not like them?!
A yaoi club?
Yes! Please say you'll join with me! They have the cutest guy for a mascot!
Cute male mascot? Where do I sign up?

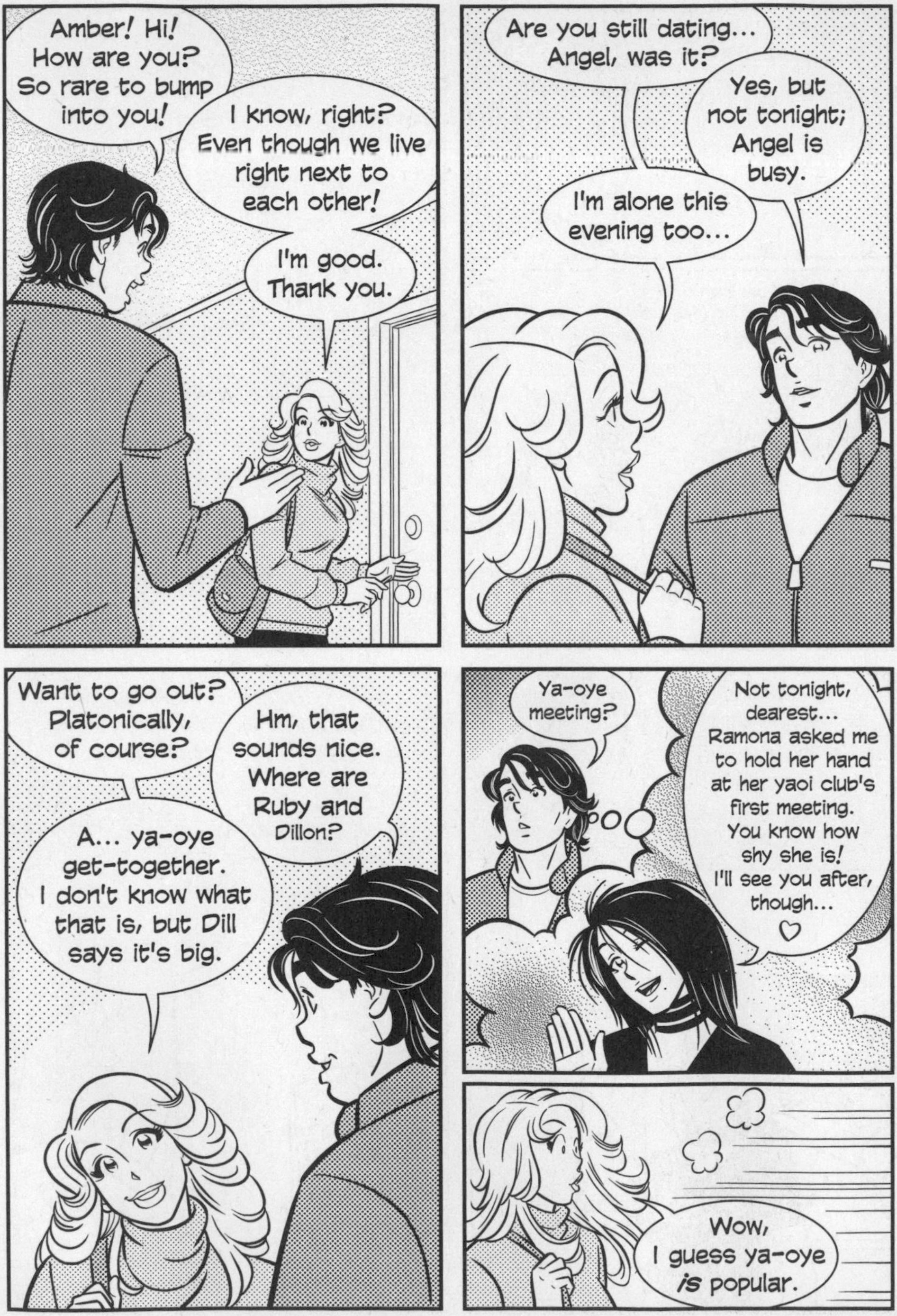
Amber! Hi! How are you? So rare to bump into you!
I know, right? Even though we live right next to each other!
I'm good. Thank you.
Are you still dating... Angel, was it?
Yes, but not tonight; Angel is busy.
I'm alone this evening too...
Want to go out? Platonically, of course?
Hm, that sounds nice. Where are Ruby and Dillon?
A... ya-oye get-together. I don't know what that is, but Dill says it's big.
Ya-oye meeting?
Not tonight, dearest... Ramona asked me to hold her hand at her yaoi club's first meeting. You know how shy she is! I'll see you after, though... ♡
Wow, I guess ya-oye *is* popular.

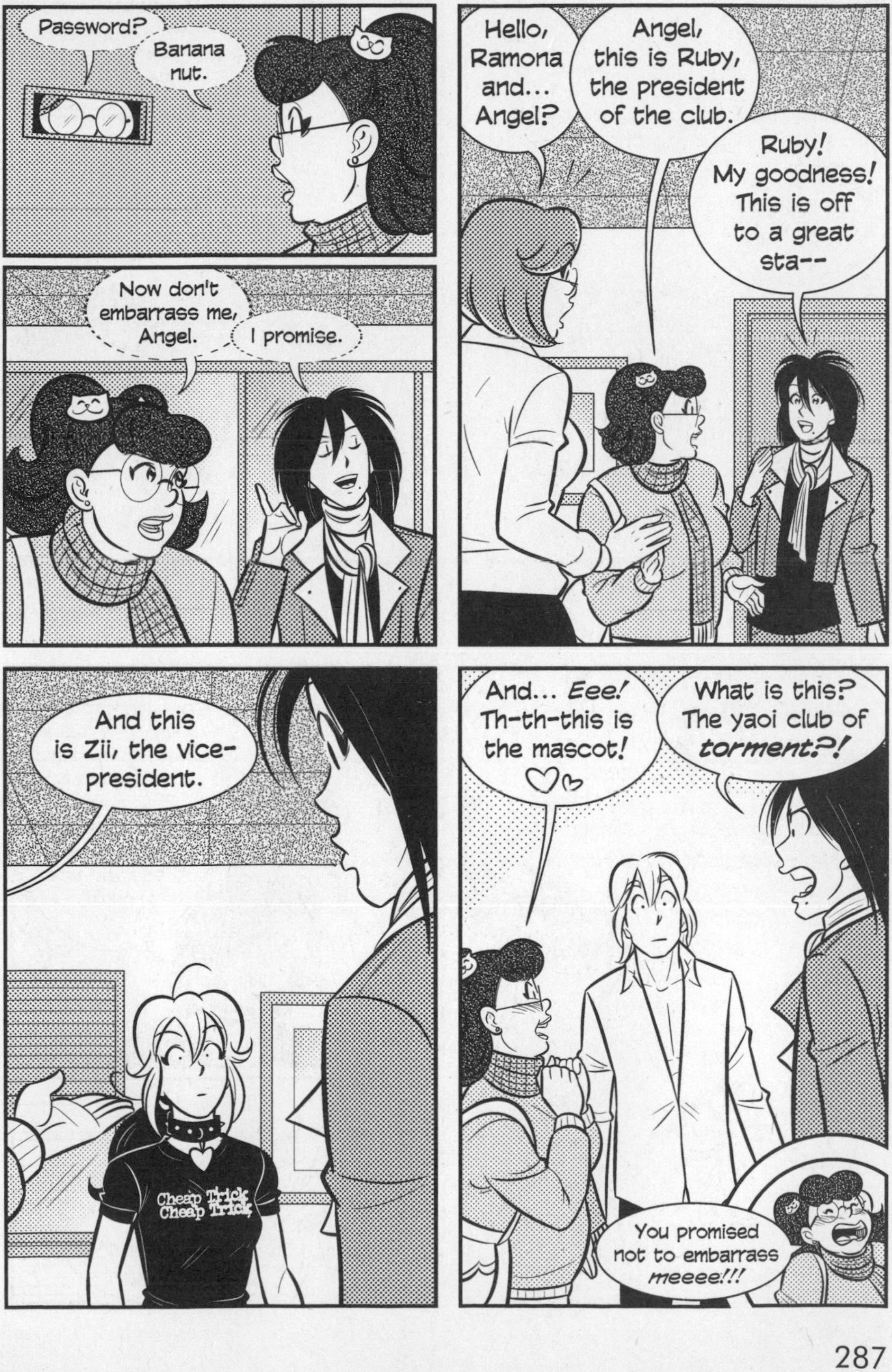

Password?
Banana nut.
Hello, Ramona and... Angel?
Angel, this is Ruby, the president of the club.
Ruby! My goodness! This is off to a great sta--
Now don't embarrass me, Angel.
I promise.
And this is Zii, the vice-president.
Cheap Trick Cheap Trick
And... *Eee!* Th-th-this is the mascot!
What is this? The yaoi club of ***torment?!***
You promised not to embarrass *meeee!!!*

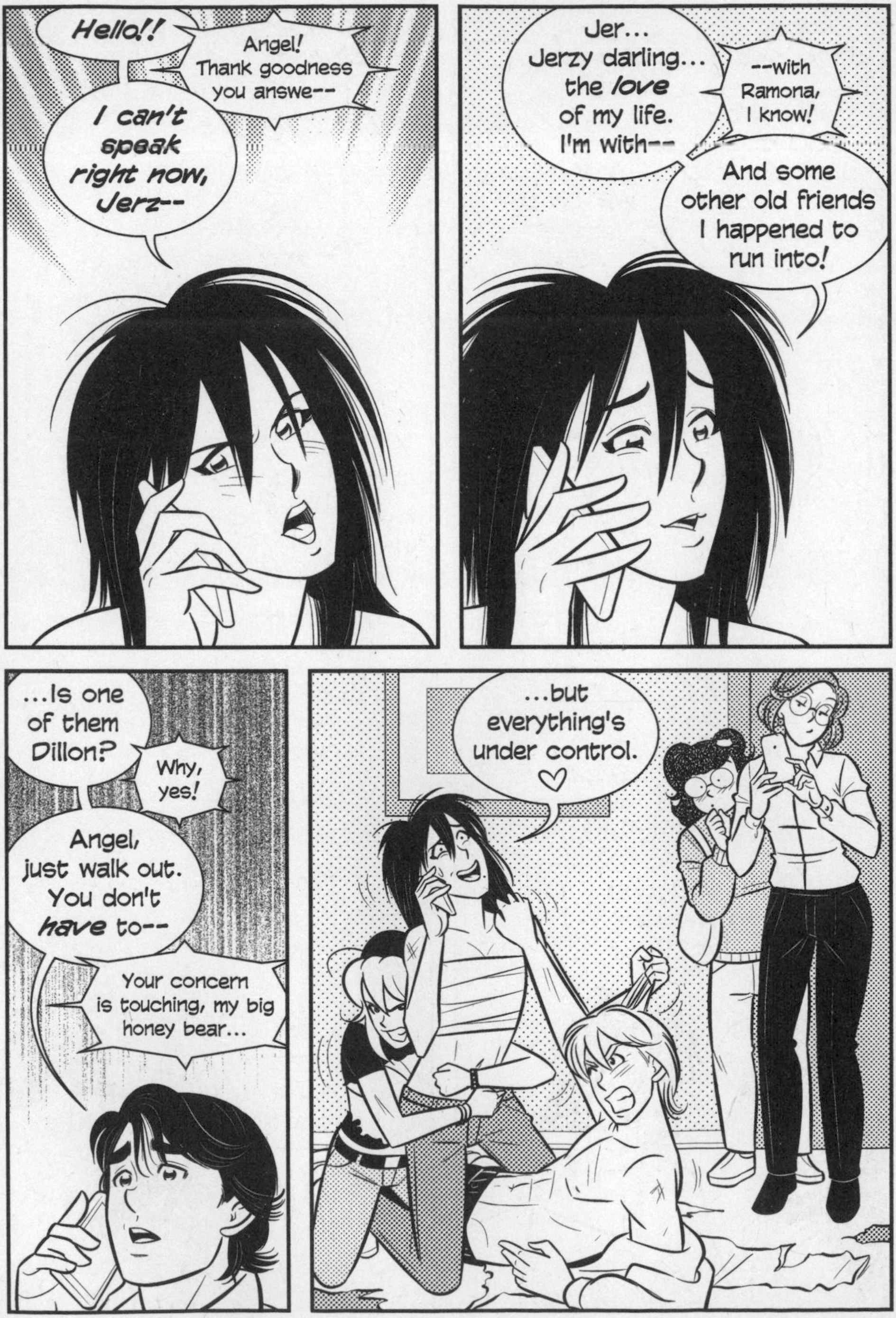
Hello!!
Angel! Thank goodness you answe--
I can't speak right now, Jerz--
Jer... Jerzy darling... the love of my life. I'm with--
--with Ramona, I know!
And some other old friends I happened to run into!
...Is one of them Dillon?
Why, yes!
Angel, just walk out. You don't have to--
Your concern is touching, my big honey bear...
...but everything's under control.

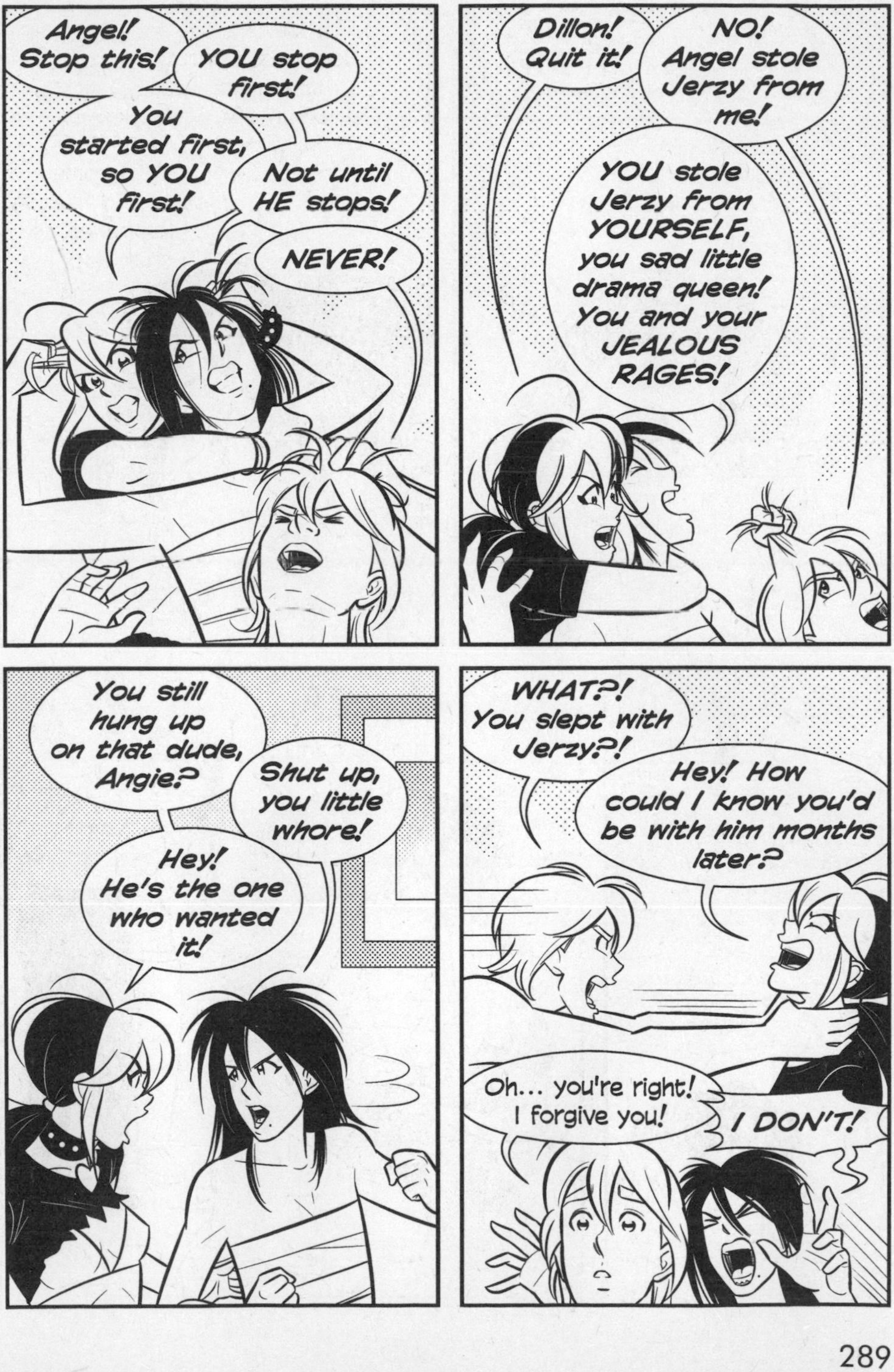
Angel! Stop this!
YOU stop first!
You started first, so YOU first!
Not until HE stops!
NEVER!
Dillon! Quit it!
NO! Angel stole Jerzy from me!
YOU stole Jerzy from YOURSELF, you sad little drama queen! You and your JEALOUS RAGES!
You still hung up on that dude, Angie?
Shut up, you little whore!
Hey! He's the one who wanted it!
WHAT?! You slept with Jerzy?!
Hey! How could I know you'd be with him months later?
Oh... you're right! I forgive you!
I DON'T!

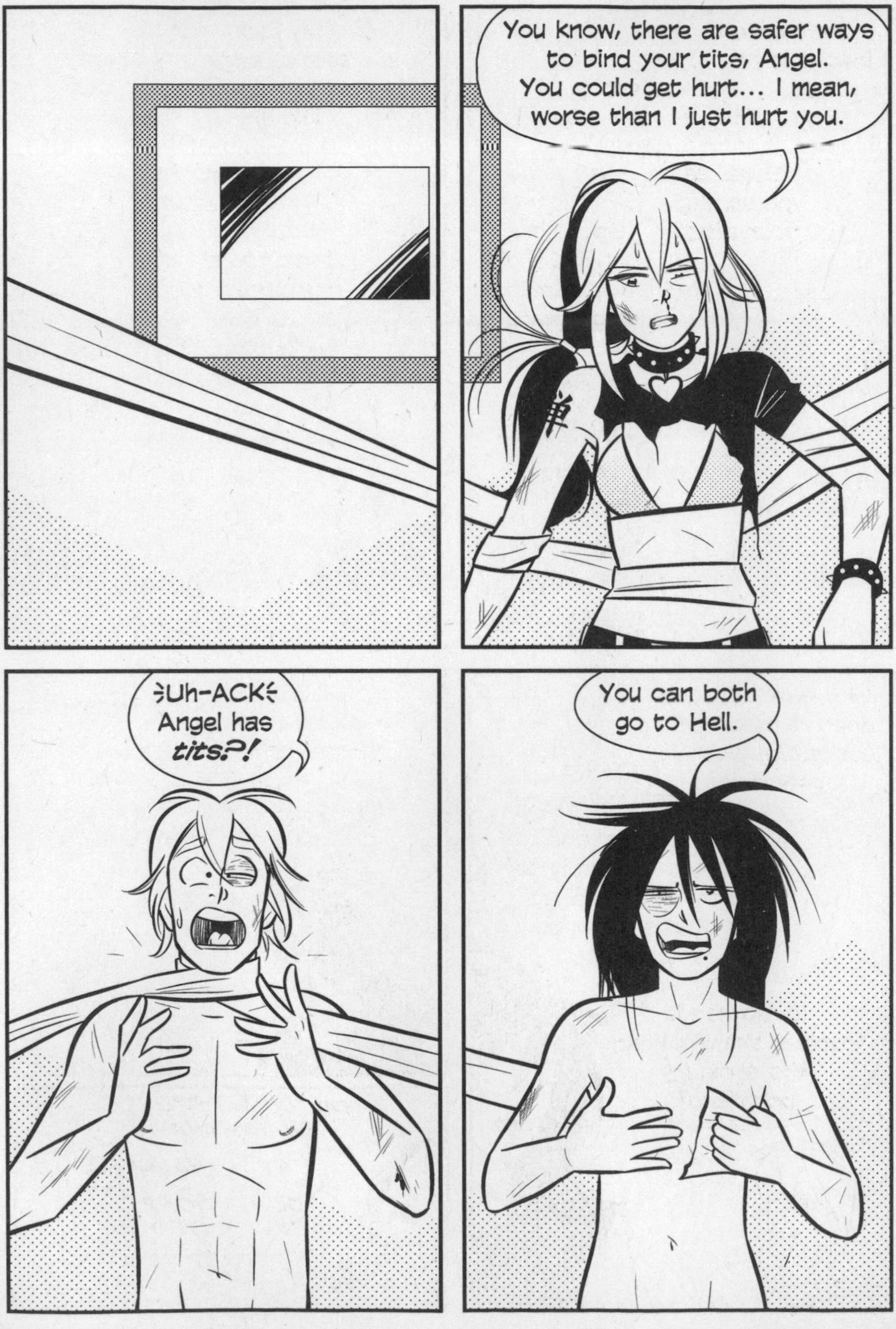
You know, there are safer ways to bind your tits, Angel. You could get hurt... I mean, worse than I just hurt you.
Uh-ACK
Angel has *tits?!*
You can both go to Hell.

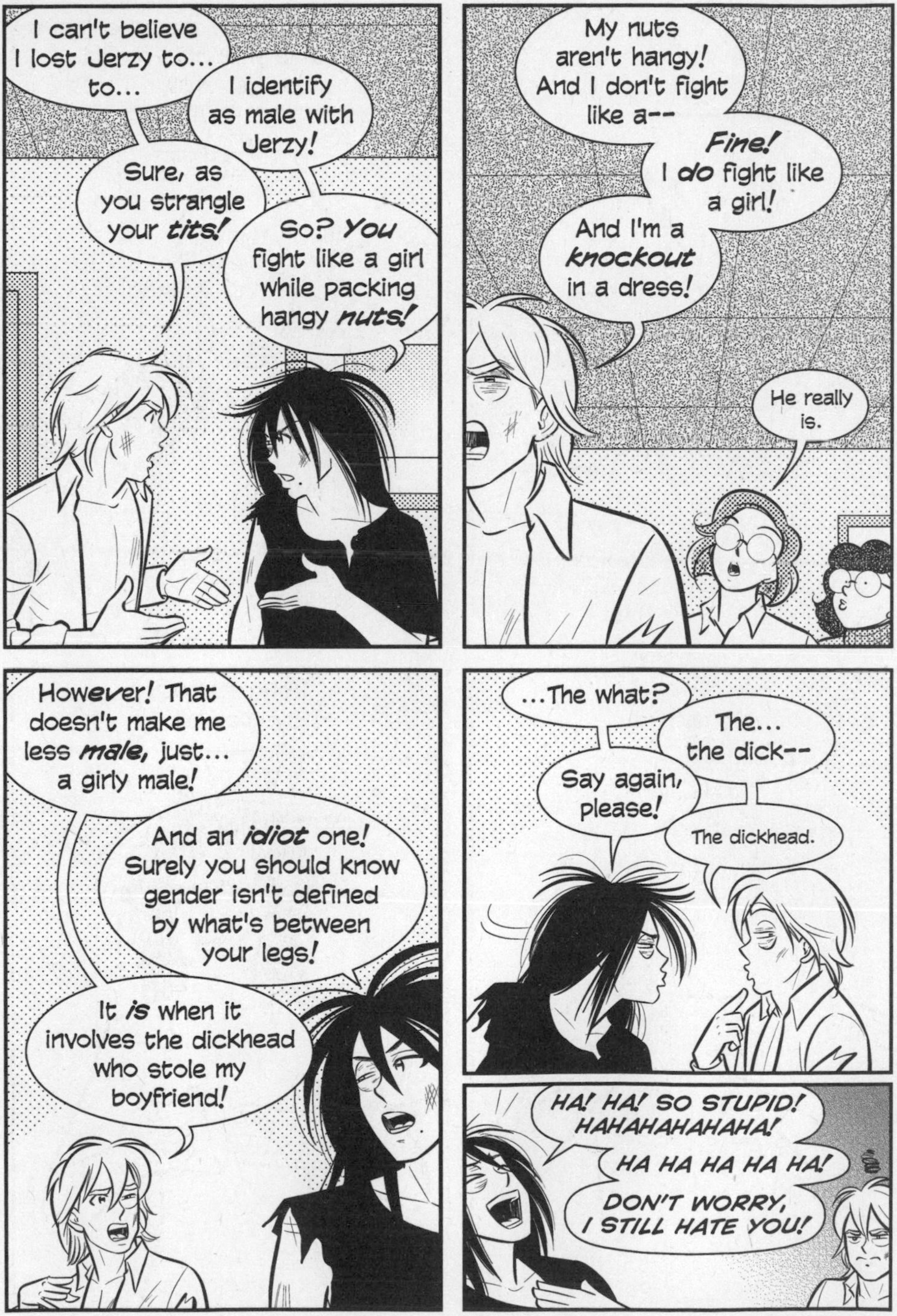
I can't believe I lost Jerzy to... to...
I identify as male with Jerzy!
Sure, as you strangle your *tits!*
So? *You* fight like a girl while packing hangy *nuts!*
My nuts aren't hangy! And I don't fight like a--
Fine! I *do* fight like a girl!
And I'm a *knockout* in a dress!
He really is.
How*ever*! That doesn't make me less *male,* just... a girly male!
And an *idiot* one! Surely you should know gender isn't defined by what's between your legs!
It *is* when it involves the dickhead who stole my boyfriend!
...The what?
The... the dick--
Say again, please!
The dickhead.
HA! HA! SO STUPID! HAHAHAHAHAHA!
HA HA HA HA HA!
DON'T WORRY, I STILL HATE YOU!

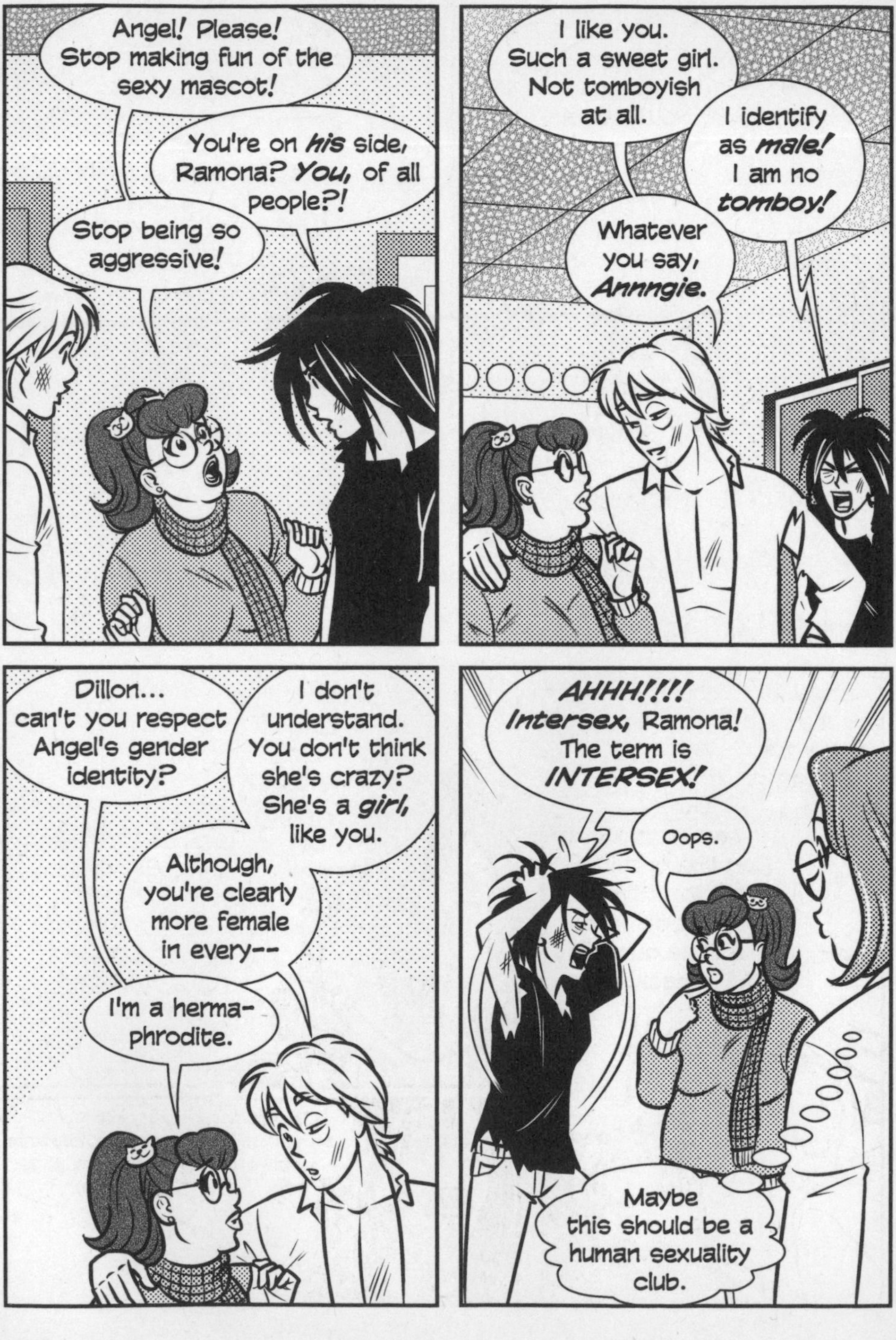
Angel! Please! Stop making fun of the sexy mascot!
You're on *his* side, Ramona? *You,* of all people?!
Stop being so aggressive!
I like you. Such a sweet girl. Not tomboyish at all.
I identify as *male!* I am no *tomboy!*
Whatever you say, *Annngie.*
Dillon... can't you respect Angel's gender identity?
I don't understand. You don't think she's crazy? She's a *girl,* like you.
Although, you're clearly more female in every--
I'm a herma-phrodite.
AHHH!!!! *Intersex,* Ramona! The term is *INTERSEX!*
Oops.
Maybe this should be a human sexuality club.

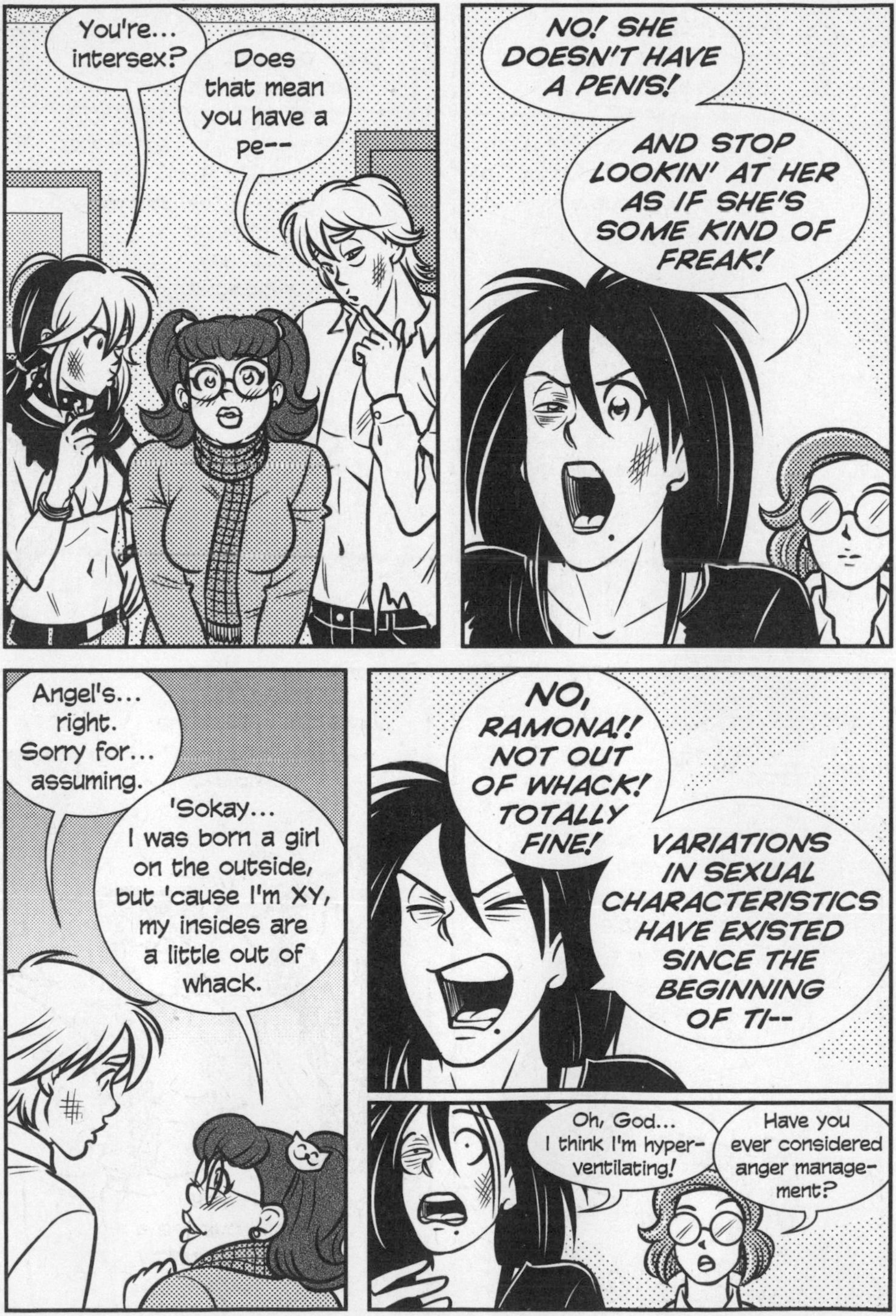

You're... intersex?
Does that mean you have a pe--
NO! SHE DOESN'T HAVE A PENIS!
AND STOP LOOKIN' AT HER AS IF SHE'S SOME KIND OF FREAK!
Angel's... right. Sorry for... assuming.
'Sokay... I was born a girl on the outside, but 'cause I'm XY, my insides are a little out of whack.
NO, RAMONA!! NOT OUT OF WHACK! TOTALLY FINE!
VARIATIONS IN SEXUAL CHARACTERISTICS HAVE EXISTED SINCE THE BEGINNING OF TI--
Oh, God... I think I'm hyper-ventilating!
Have you ever considered anger manage-ment?

Angel, you need to calm down. I'm an adult, and can fend for myself.

But... you're *not* out of whack. And seeing you use that... H-word... it's not even *accurate!*

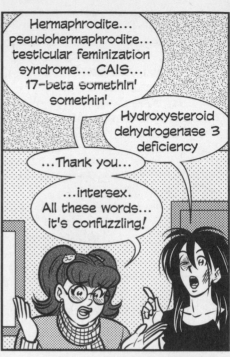

Hermaphrodite... pseudohermaphrodite... testicular feminization syndrome... CAIS... 17-beta somethin' somethin'.

Hydroxysteroid dehydrogenase 3 deficiency

...Thank you...

...intersex. All these words... it's confuzzling!

That's why I'm here for you. Like I've always been.

And I appreciate it, Angel, but you need to learn to control your temper.

I couldn't agr--

You too, sexy mascot!

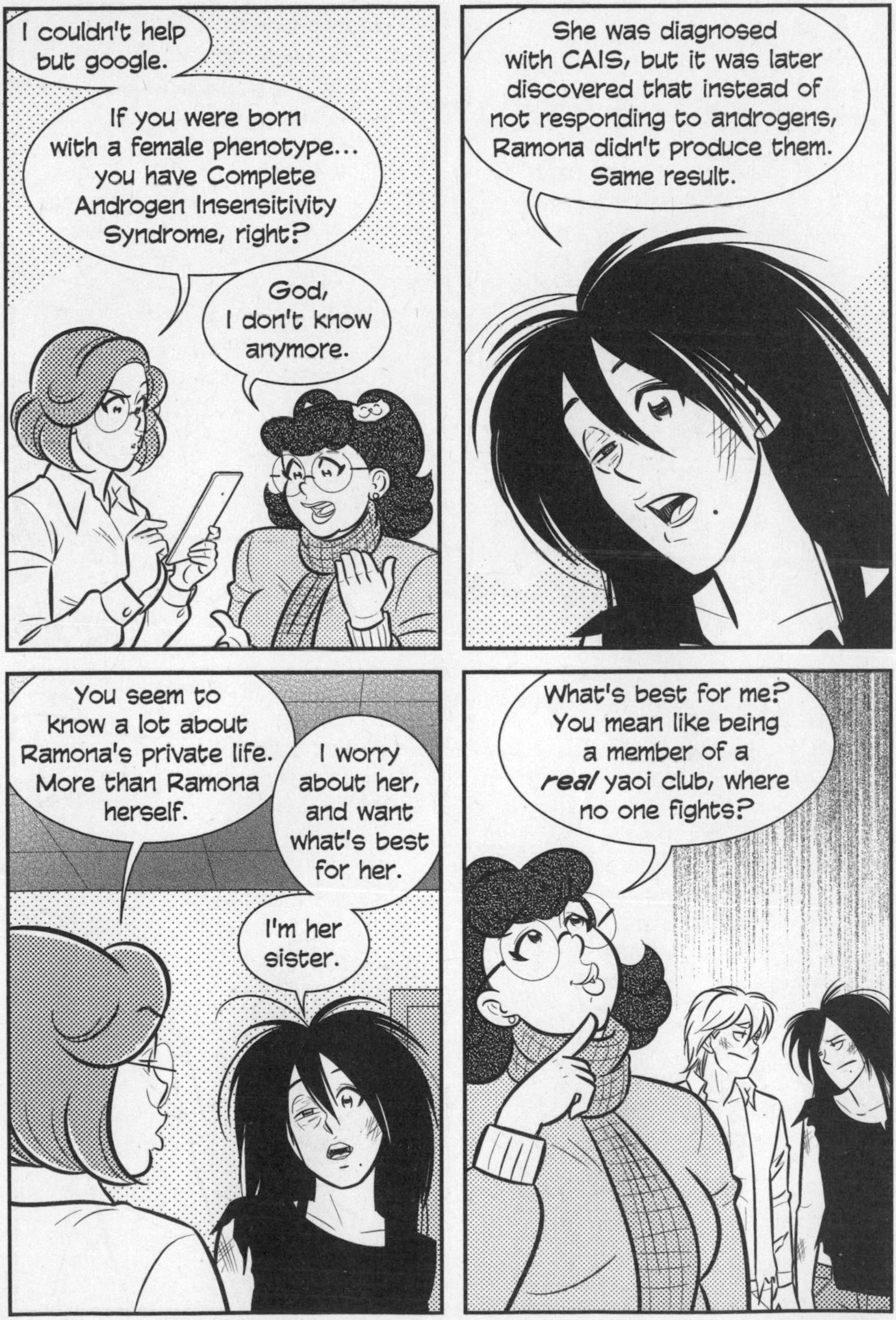
I couldn't help but google.
If you were born with a female phenotype... you have Complete Androgen Insensitivity Syndrome, right?
God, I don't know anymore.
She was diagnosed with CAIS, but it was later discovered that instead of not responding to androgens, Ramona didn't produce them. Same result.
You seem to know a lot about Ramona's private life. More than Ramona herself.
I worry about her, and want what's best for her.
I'm her sister.
What's best for me? You mean like being a member of a *real* yaoi club, where no one fights?

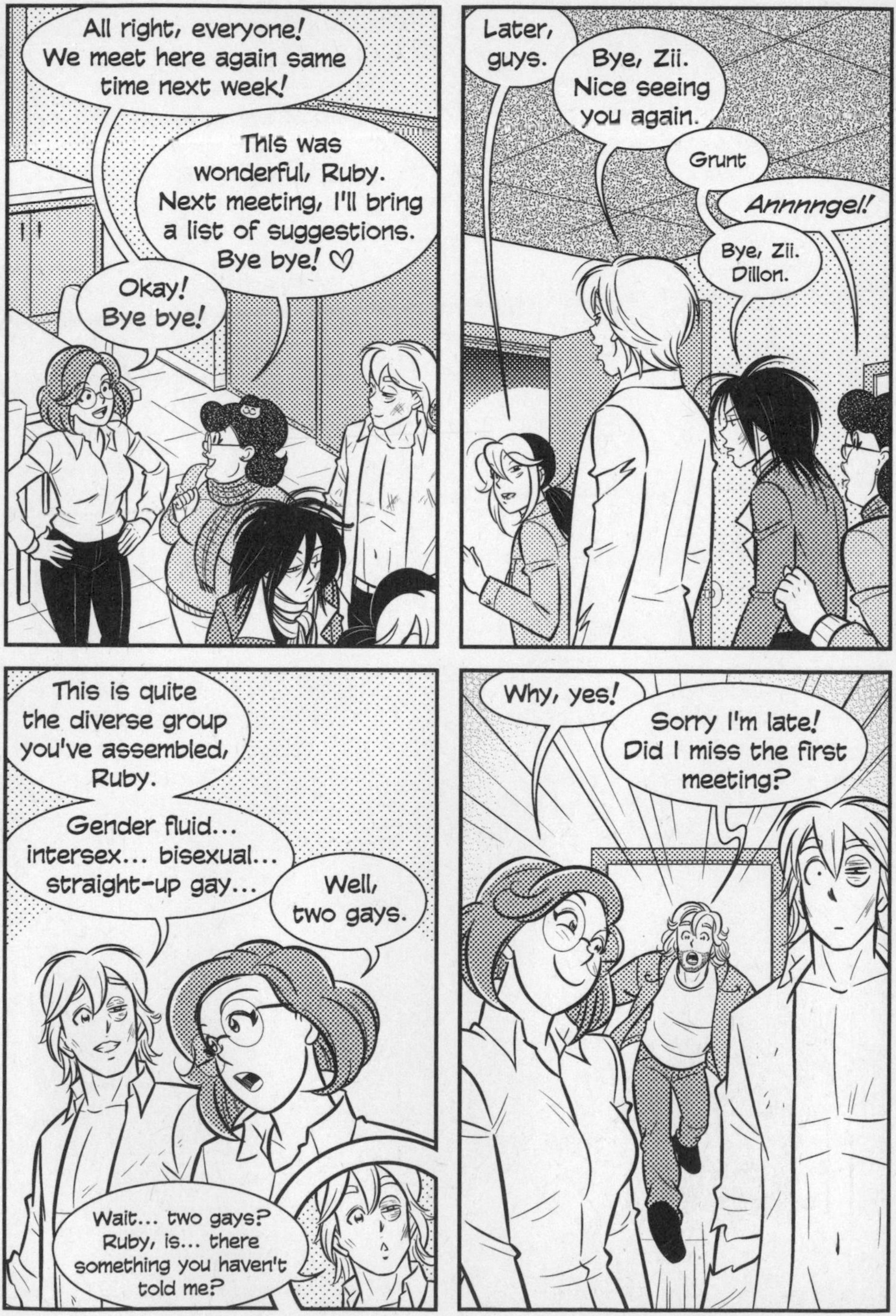
All right, everyone! We meet here again same time next week!
This was wonderful, Ruby. Next meeting, I'll bring a list of suggestions. Bye bye! ♡
Okay! Bye bye!
Later, guys.
Bye, Zii. Nice seeing you again.
Grunt
Annnngel!
Bye, Zii. Dillon.
This is quite the diverse group you've assembled, Ruby.
Gender fluid... intersex... bisexual... straight-up gay...
Well, two gays.
Wait... two gays? Ruby, is... there something you haven't told me?
Why, yes!
Sorry I'm late! Did I miss the first meeting?

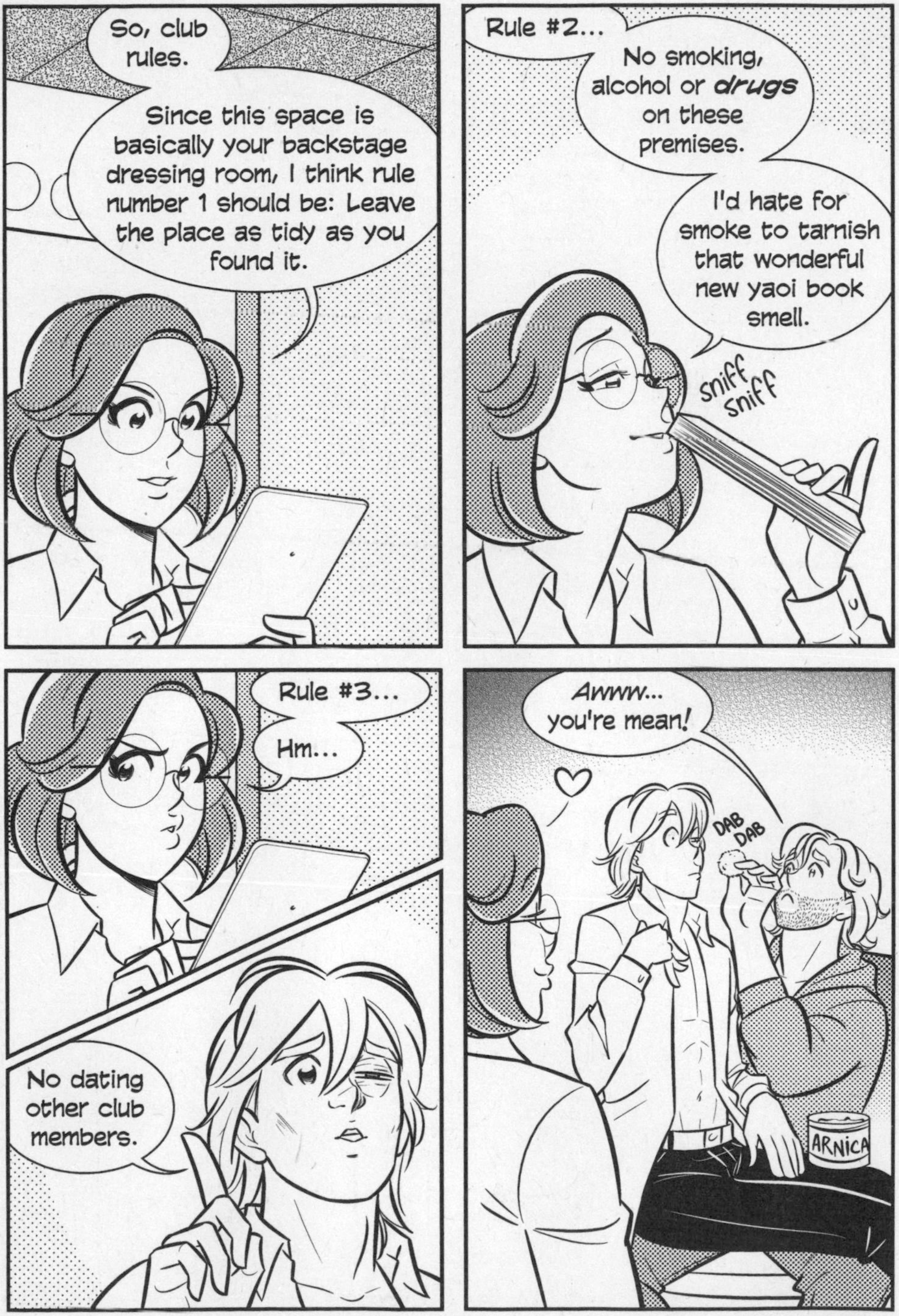
So, club rules.
Since this space is basically your backstage dressing room, I think rule number 1 should be: Leave the place as tidy as you found it.
Rule #2...
No smoking, alcohol or *drugs* on these premises.
I'd hate for smoke to tarnish that wonderful new yaoi book smell.
sniff sniff
Rule #3...
Hm...
No dating other club members.
Awww... you're mean!
DAB DAB
ARNICA

Next Level

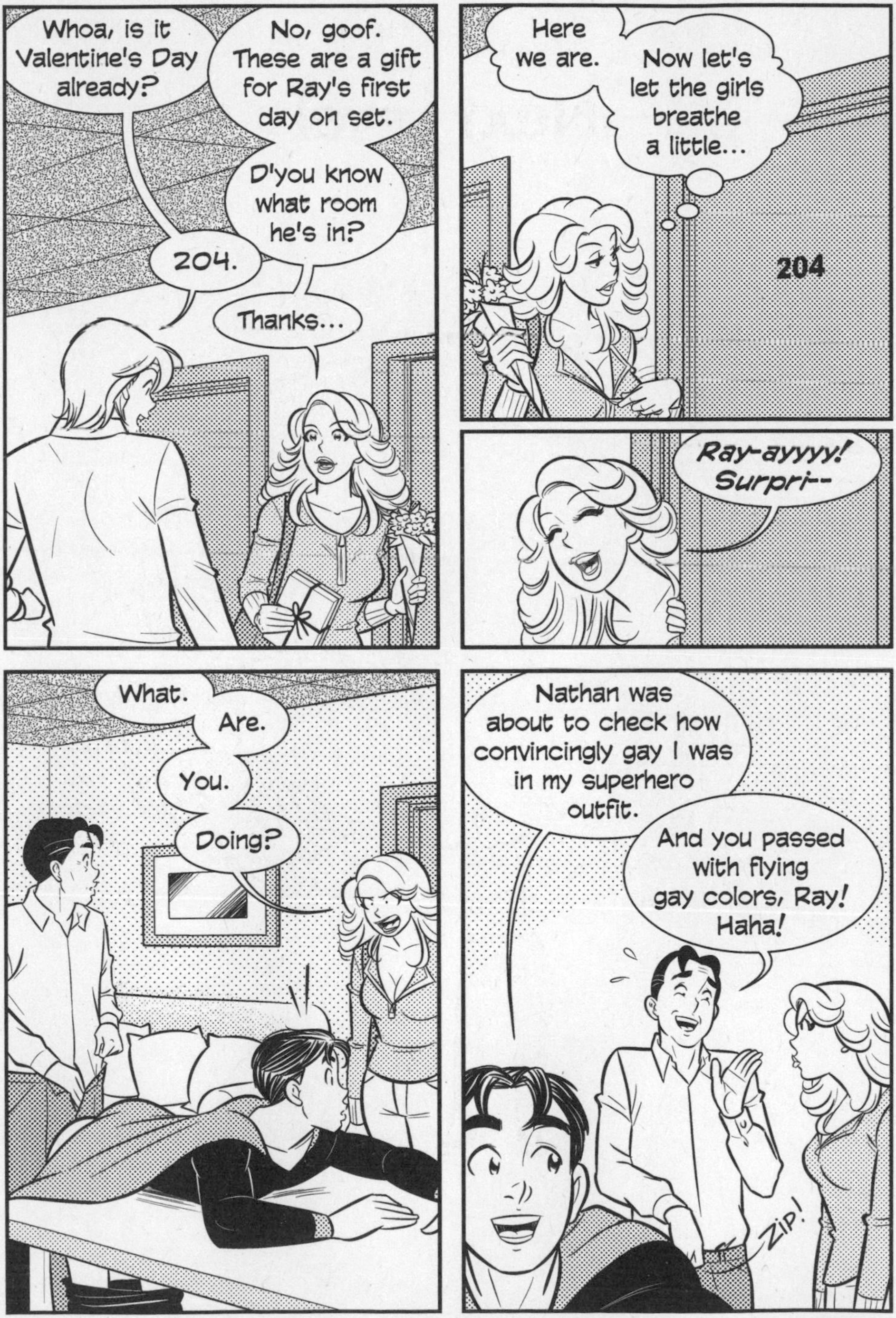
Whoa, is it Valentine's Day already?
No, goof. These are a gift for Ray's first day on set.
D'you know what room he's in?
204.
Thanks...
Here we are.
Now let's let the girls breathe a little...
204
Ray-ayyyy! Surpri--
What.
Are.
You.
Doing?
Nathan was about to check how convincingly gay I was in my superhero outfit.
And you passed with flying gay colors, Ray! Haha!
ZIP!

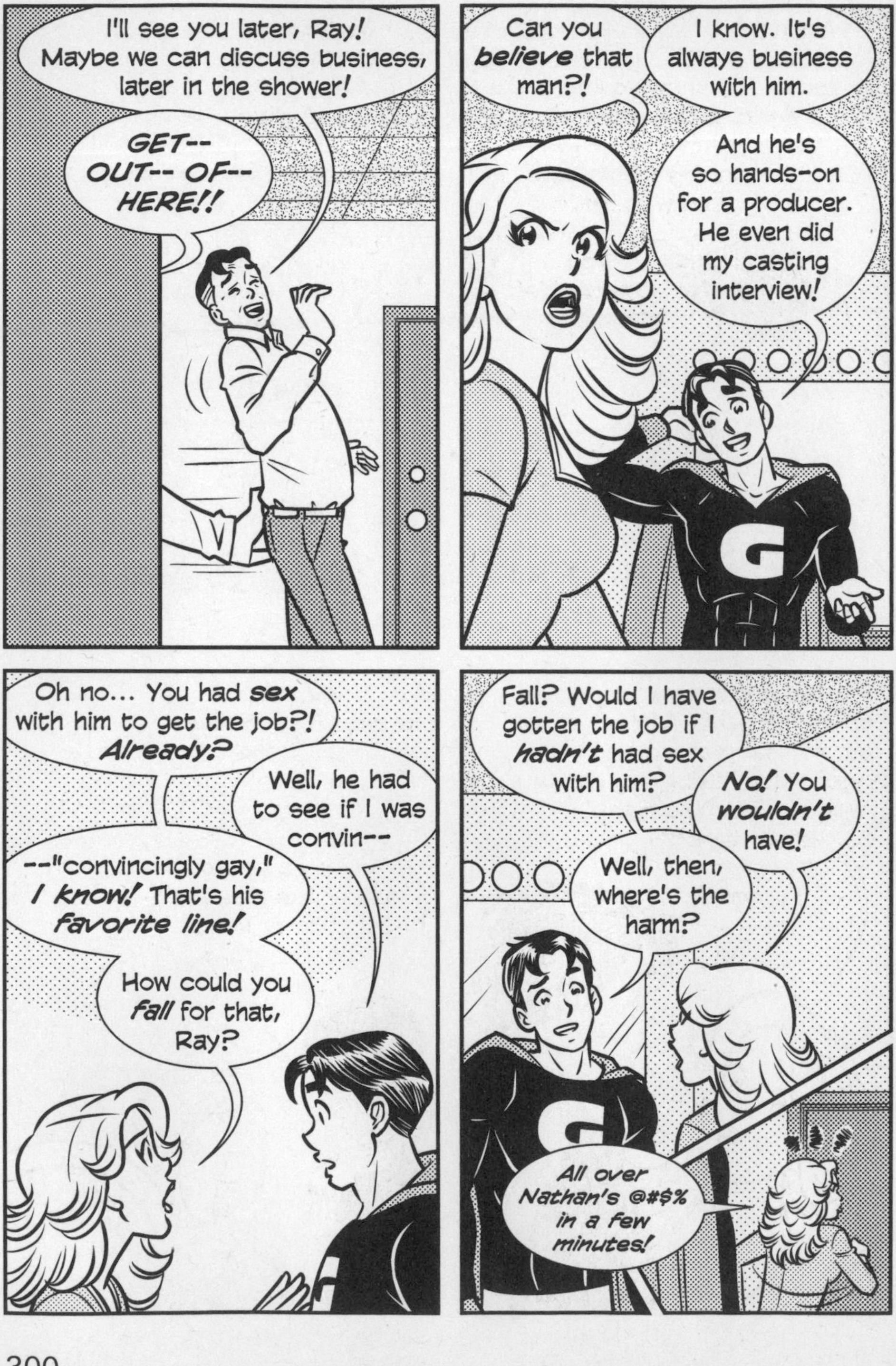
I'll see you later, Ray! Maybe we can discuss business, later in the shower!
GET-- OUT-- OF-- HERE!!
Can you *believe* that man?!
I know. It's always business with him.
And he's so hands-on for a producer. He even did my casting interview!
Oh no... You had *sex* with him to get the job?! *Already?*
Well, he had to see if I was convin--
--"convincingly gay," *I know!* That's his *favorite line!*
How could you *fall* for that, Ray?
Fall? Would I have gotten the job if I *hadn't* had sex with him?
No! You *wouldn't* have!
Well, then, where's the harm?
All over Nathan's @#$% in a few minutes!

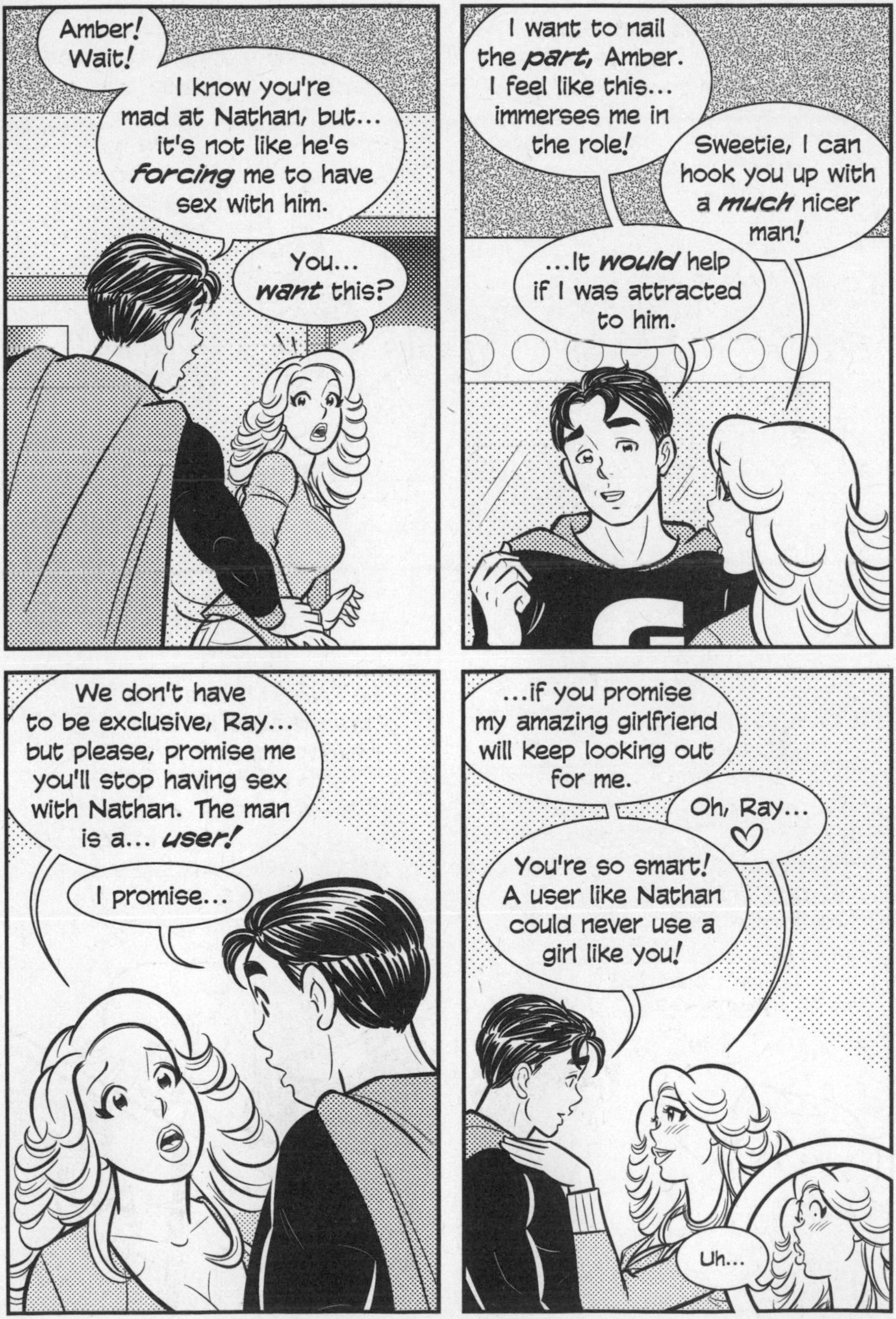
Amber! Wait!
I know you're mad at Nathan, but... it's not like he's *forcing* me to have sex with him.
You... *want* this?
I want to nail the *part,* Amber. I feel like this... immerses me in the role!
Sweetie, I can hook you up with a *much* nicer man!
...It *would* help if I was attracted to him.
We don't have to be exclusive, Ray... but please, promise me you'll stop having sex with Nathan. The man is a... *user!*
I promise...
...if you promise my amazing girlfriend will keep looking out for me.
Oh, Ray... ♡
You're so smart! A user like Nathan could never use a girl like you!
Uh...

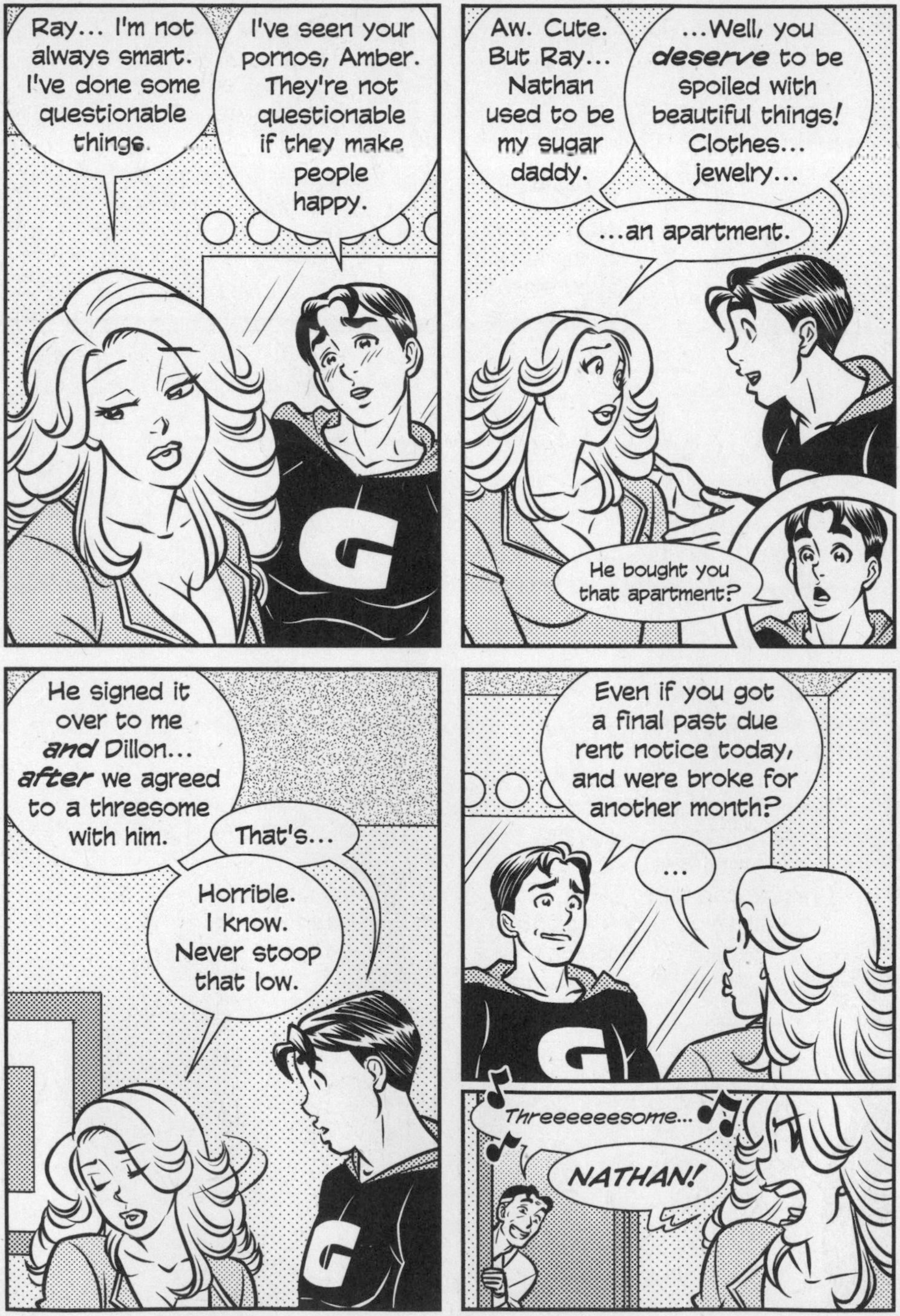
Ray... I'm not always smart. I've done some questionable things.
I've seen your pornos, Amber. They're not questionable if they make people happy.
Aw. Cute. But Ray... Nathan used to be my sugar daddy.
...Well, you *deserve* to be spoiled with beautiful things! Clothes... jewelry...
...an apartment.
He bought you that apartment?
He signed it over to me *and* Dillon... *after* we agreed to a threesome with him.
That's...
Horrible. I know. Never stoop that low.
Even if you got a final past due rent notice today, and were broke for another month?
...
Threeeeeesome...
NATHAN!

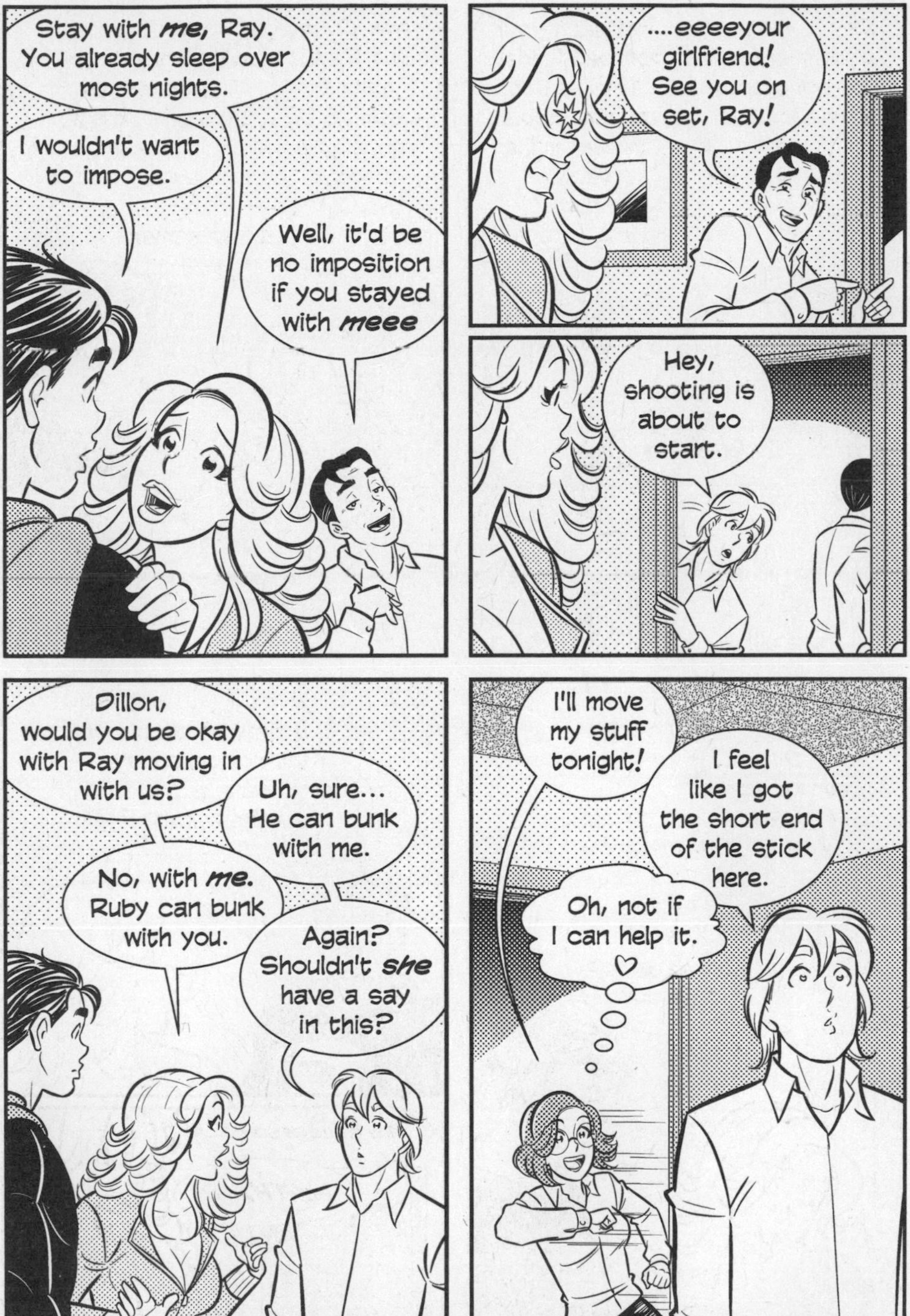
Stay with *me,* Ray. You already sleep over most nights.
I wouldn't want to impose.
Well, it'd be no imposition if you stayed with *meee*
....eeeeyour girlfriend! See you on set, Ray!
Hey, shooting is about to start.
Dillon, would you be okay with Ray moving in with us?
Uh, sure... He can bunk with me.
No, with *me.* Ruby can bunk with you.
Again? Shouldn't *she* have a say in this?
I'll move my stuff tonight!
I feel like I got the short end of the stick here.
Oh, not if I can help it.

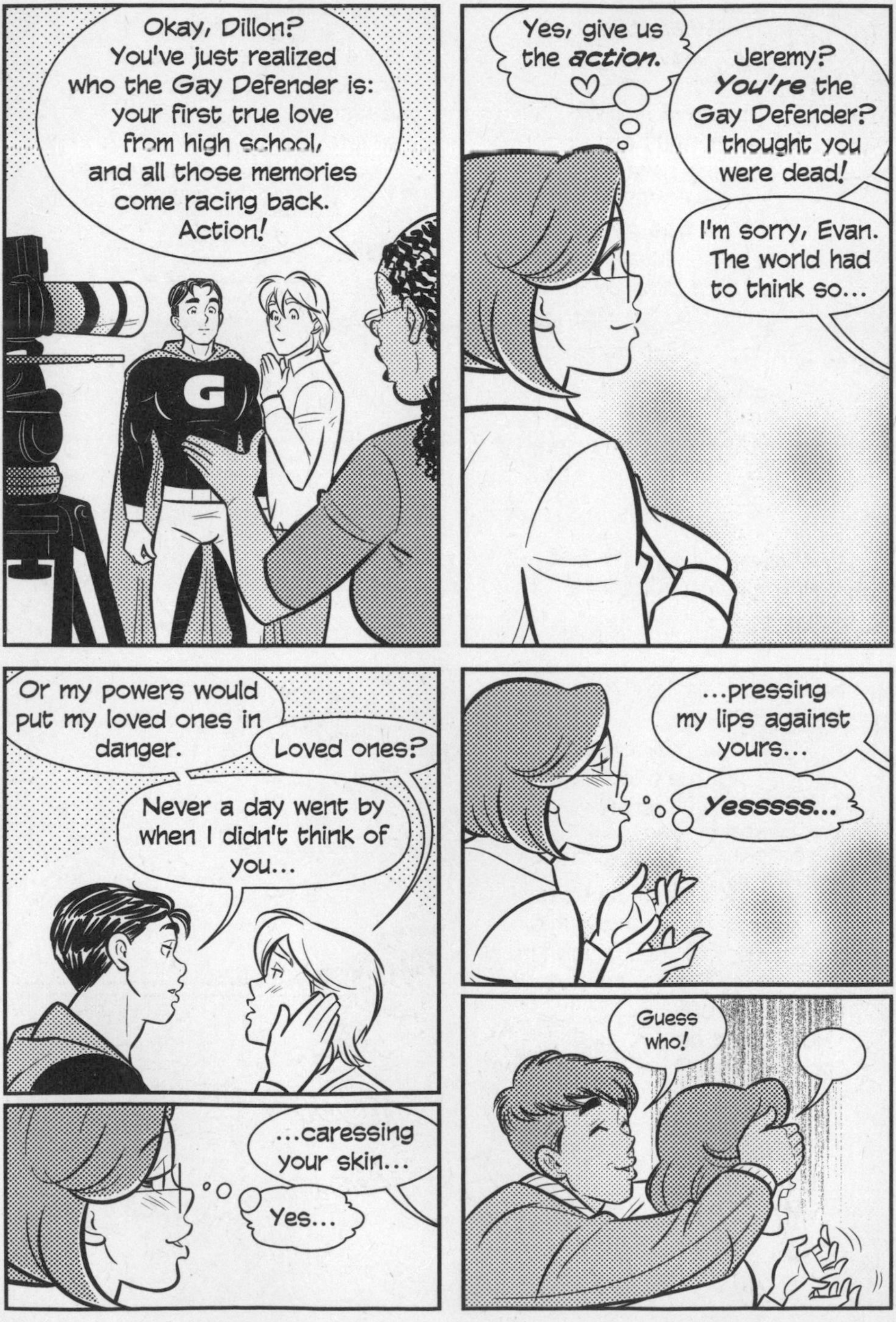
Okay, Dillon? You've just realized who the Gay Defender is: your first true love from high school, and all those memories come racing back. Action!
Yes, give us the *action*.
Jeremy? *You're* the Gay Defender? I thought you were dead!
I'm sorry, Evan. The world had to think so...
Or my powers would put my loved ones in danger.
Loved ones?
Never a day went by when I didn't think of you...
...pressing my lips against yours...
Yesssss...
...caressing your skin...
Yes...
Guess who!

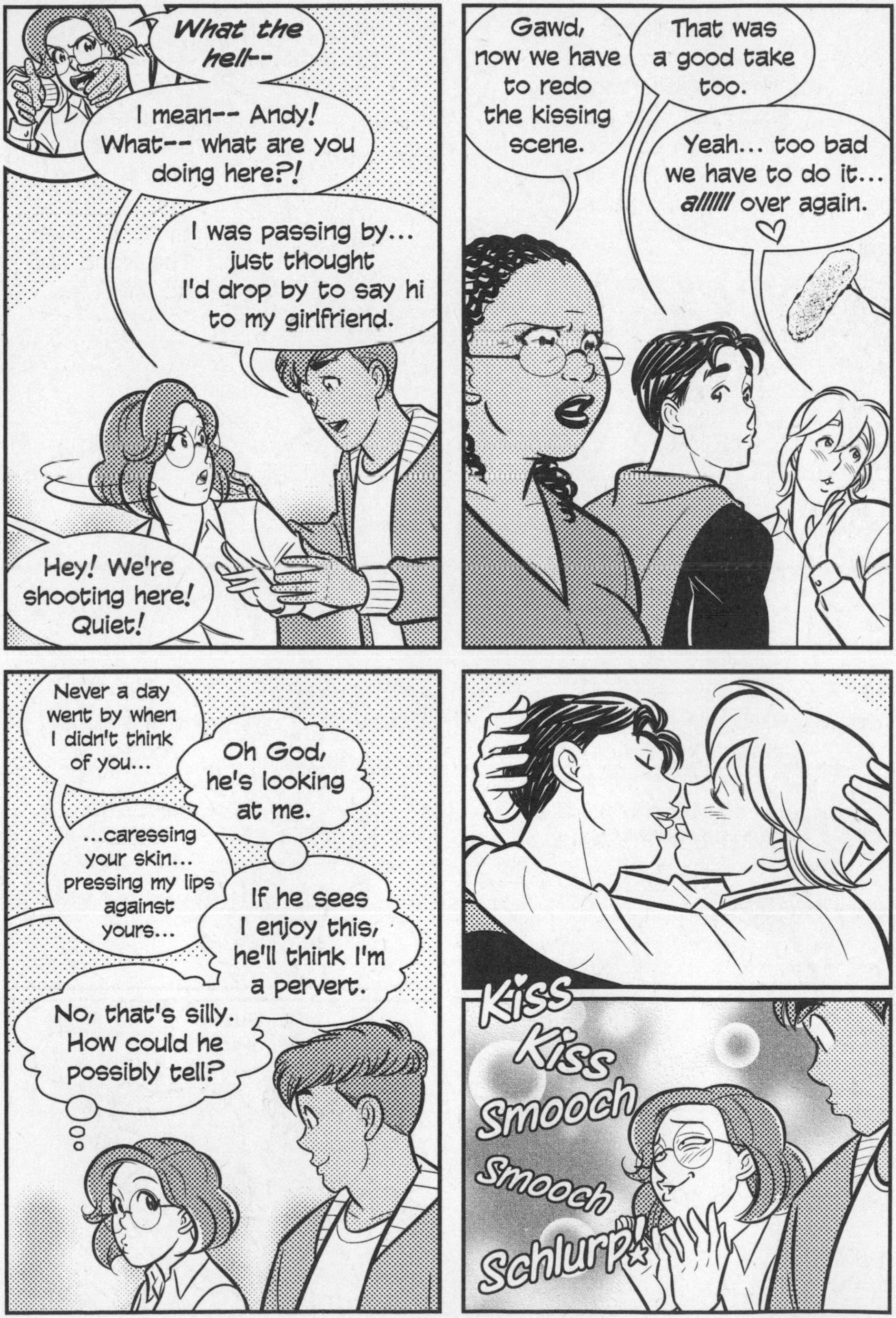
What the hell--
I mean-- Andy! What-- what are you doing here?!
I was passing by... just thought I'd drop by to say hi to my girlfriend.
Hey! We're shooting here! Quiet!
Gawd, now we have to redo the kissing scene.
That was a good take too.
Yeah... too bad we have to do it... allllll over again. ♡
Never a day went by when I didn't think of you...
Oh God, he's looking at me.
...caressing your skin... pressing my lips against yours...
If he sees I enjoy this, he'll think I'm a pervert.
No, that's silly. How could he possibly tell?
Kiss
Kiss
Smooch
Smooch
Schlurp!

And cut! This love scene is a wrap!

Pretty good, weren't they?

Meh!

Passable.

If one likes that sort of thing.

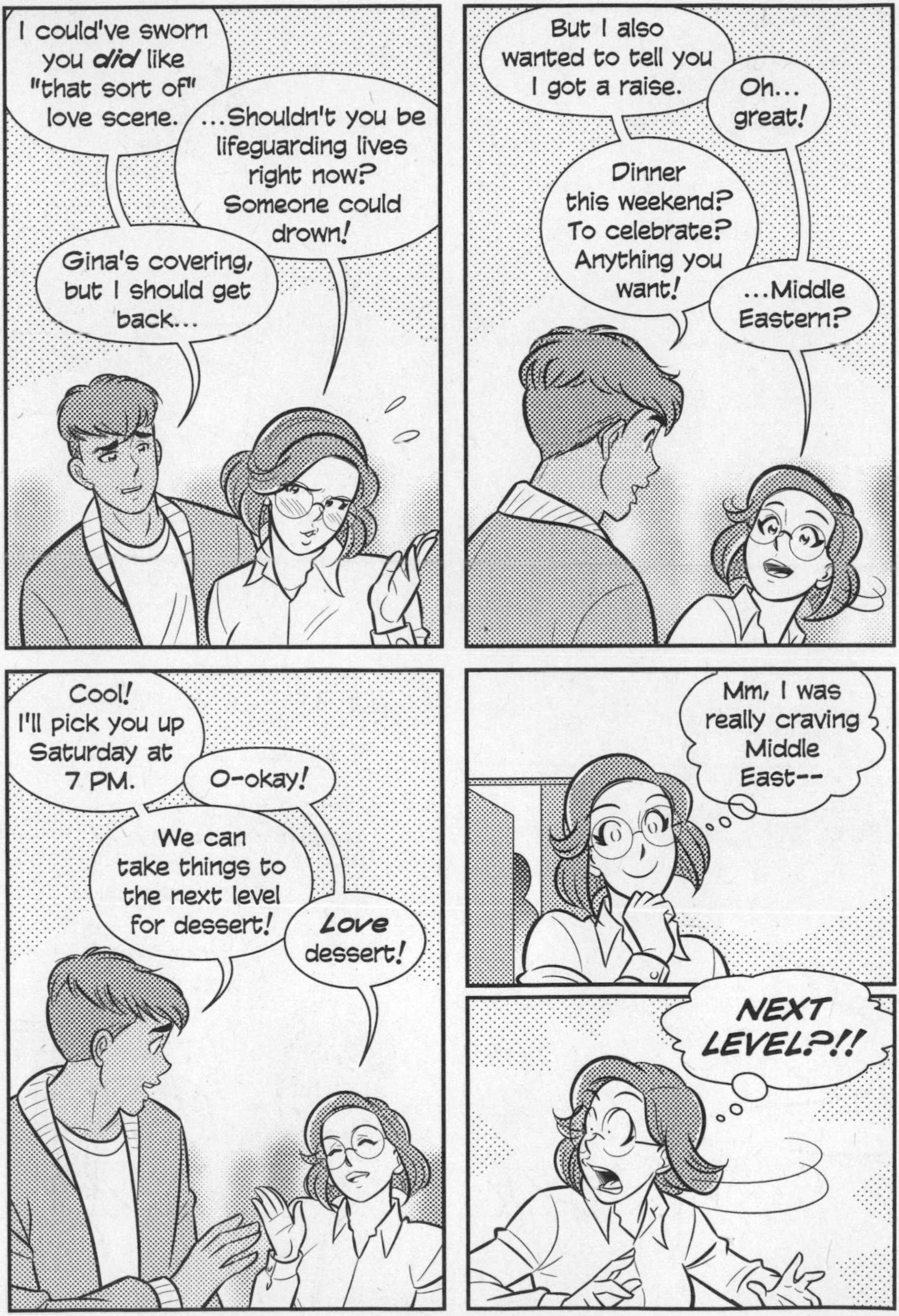

I could've sworn you *did* like "that sort of" love scene.
...Shouldn't you be lifeguarding lives right now? Someone could drown!
Gina's covering, but I should get back...
But I also wanted to tell you I got a raise.
Oh... great!
Dinner this weekend? To celebrate? Anything you want!
...Middle Eastern?
Cool! I'll pick you up Saturday at 7 PM.
O-okay!
We can take things to the next level for dessert!
Love dessert!
Mm, I was really craving Middle East--
NEXT LEVEL?!!

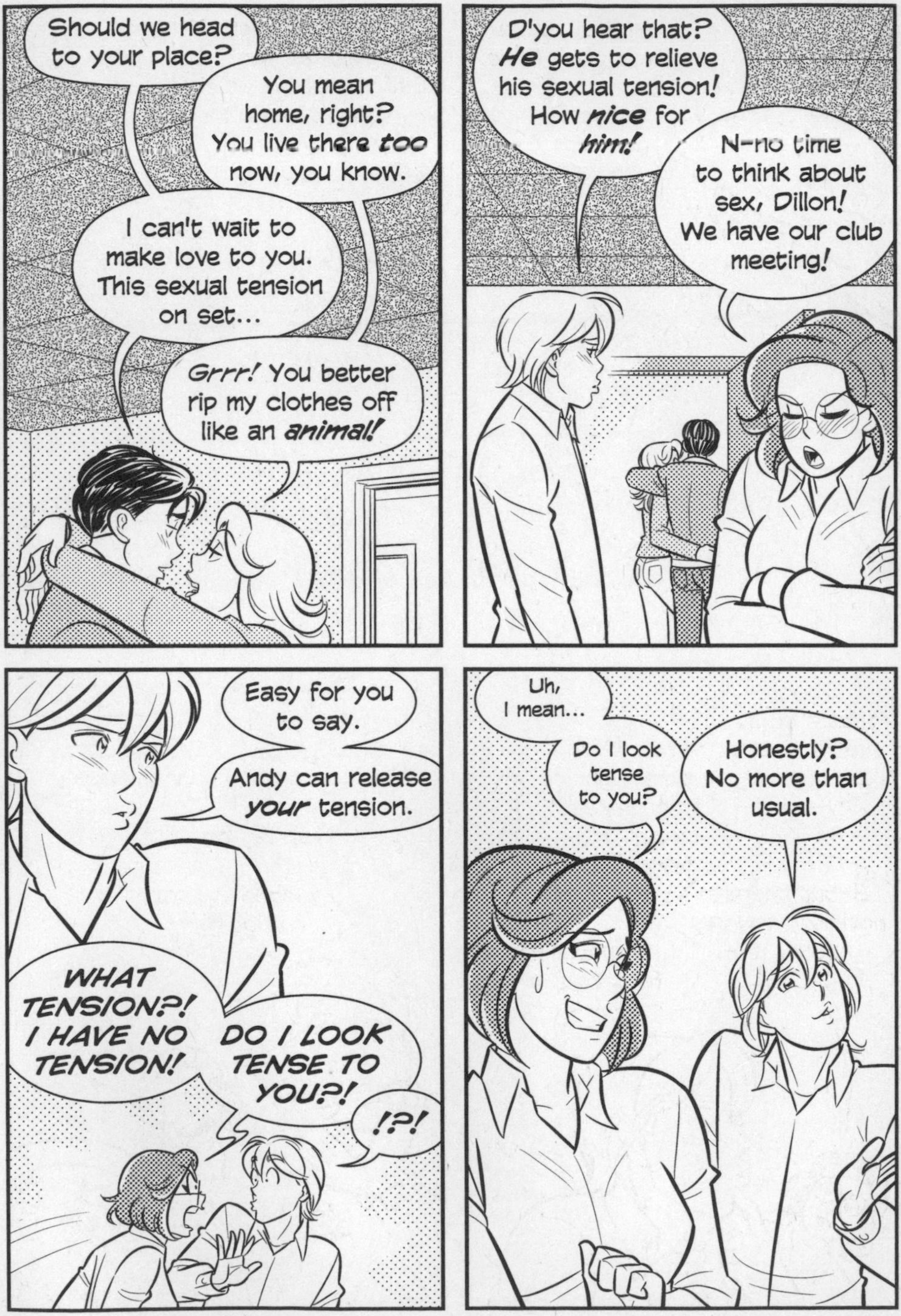

Should we head to your place?
You mean home, right? You live there *too* now, you know.
I can't wait to make love to you. This sexual tension on set...
Grrr! You better rip my clothes off like an *animal!*
D'you hear that? *He* gets to relieve his sexual tension! How *nice* for *him!*
N-no time to think about sex, Dillon! We have our club meeting!
Easy for you to say.
Andy can release *your* tension.
WHAT TENSION?! I HAVE NO TENSION!
DO I LOOK TENSE TO YOU?!
!?!
Uh, I mean...
Do I look tense to you?
Honestly? No more than usual.

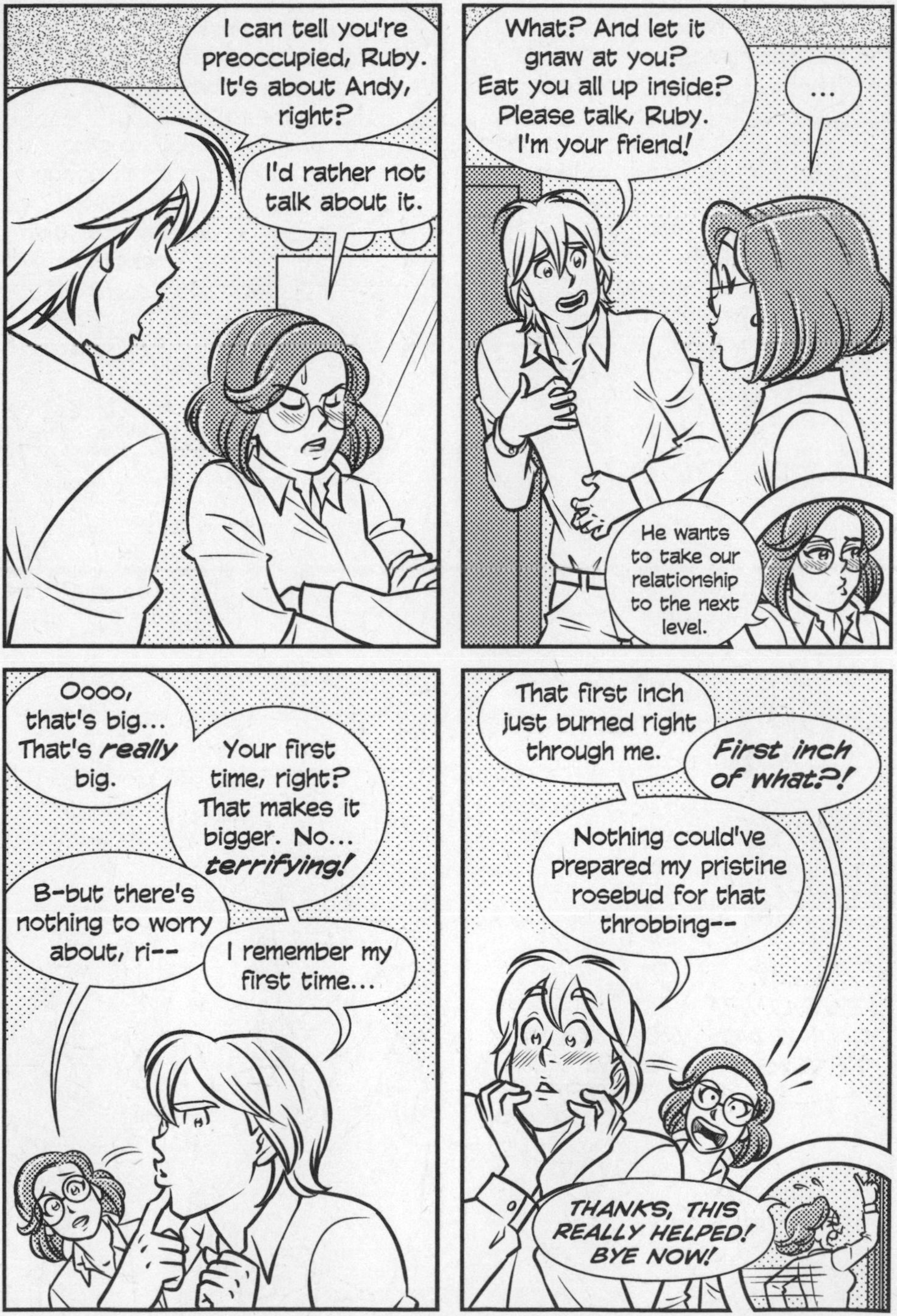
I can tell you're preoccupied, Ruby. It's about Andy, right?
I'd rather not talk about it.
What? And let it gnaw at you? Eat you all up inside? Please talk, Ruby. I'm your friend!
...
He wants to take our relationship to the next level.
Oooo, that's big... That's *really* big.
Your first time, right? That makes it bigger. No... *terrifying!*
B-but there's nothing to worry about, ri--
I remember my first time...
That first inch just burned right through me.
First inch of what?!
Nothing could've prepared my pristine rosebud for that throbbing--
THANKS, THIS REALLY HELPED! BYE NOW!

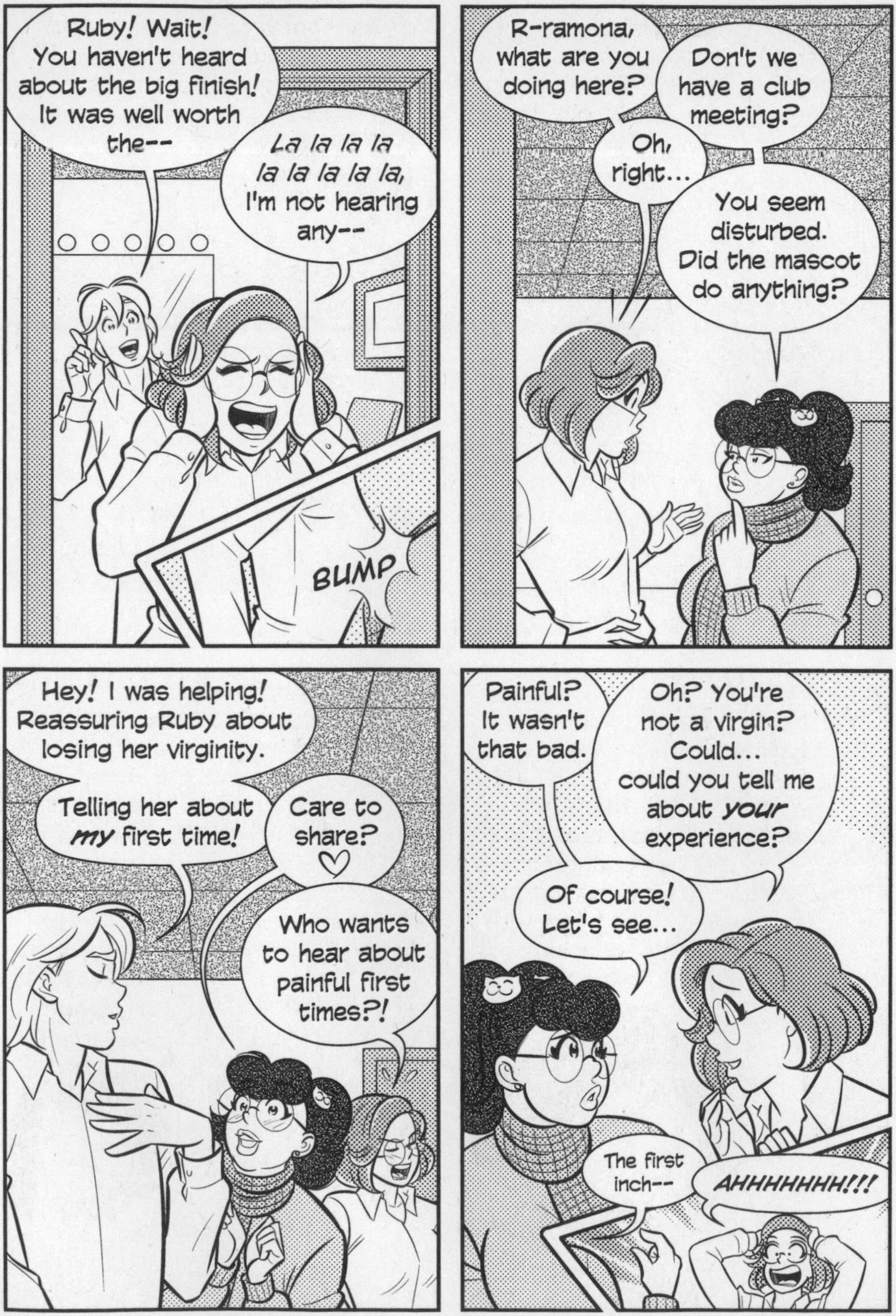

Ruby! Wait! You haven't heard about the big finish! It was well worth the--
La la la la la la la la la, I'm not hearing any--
BUMP
R-ramona, what are you doing here?
Don't we have a club meeting?
Oh, right...
You seem disturbed. Did the mascot do anything?
Hey! I was helping! Reassuring Ruby about losing her virginity.
Telling her about ***my*** first time!
Care to share? ♡
Who wants to hear about painful first times?!
Painful? It wasn't that bad.
Oh? You're not a virgin? Could... could you tell me about ***your*** experience?
Of course! Let's see...
The first inch--
AHHHHHHH!!!

Did I say something wrong?

IgiSTikBkL

Ruby's a bit nervous about *her* first time having sex, Ramona.

Oh, I totally understand! I was frightened too.

Because of your... equipment?

My equipment works just fine, Mascot.

Yay!

It can be frightening, yes! You're vulnerable, you don't know what's expected...

That's why you need to be open and honest with your partner. Like I was with Junghan.

...J-Junghan?

Comic book store guy Junghan?

I couldn't have asked for better.

He started by whispering my yaoi pull list into my ear.

311

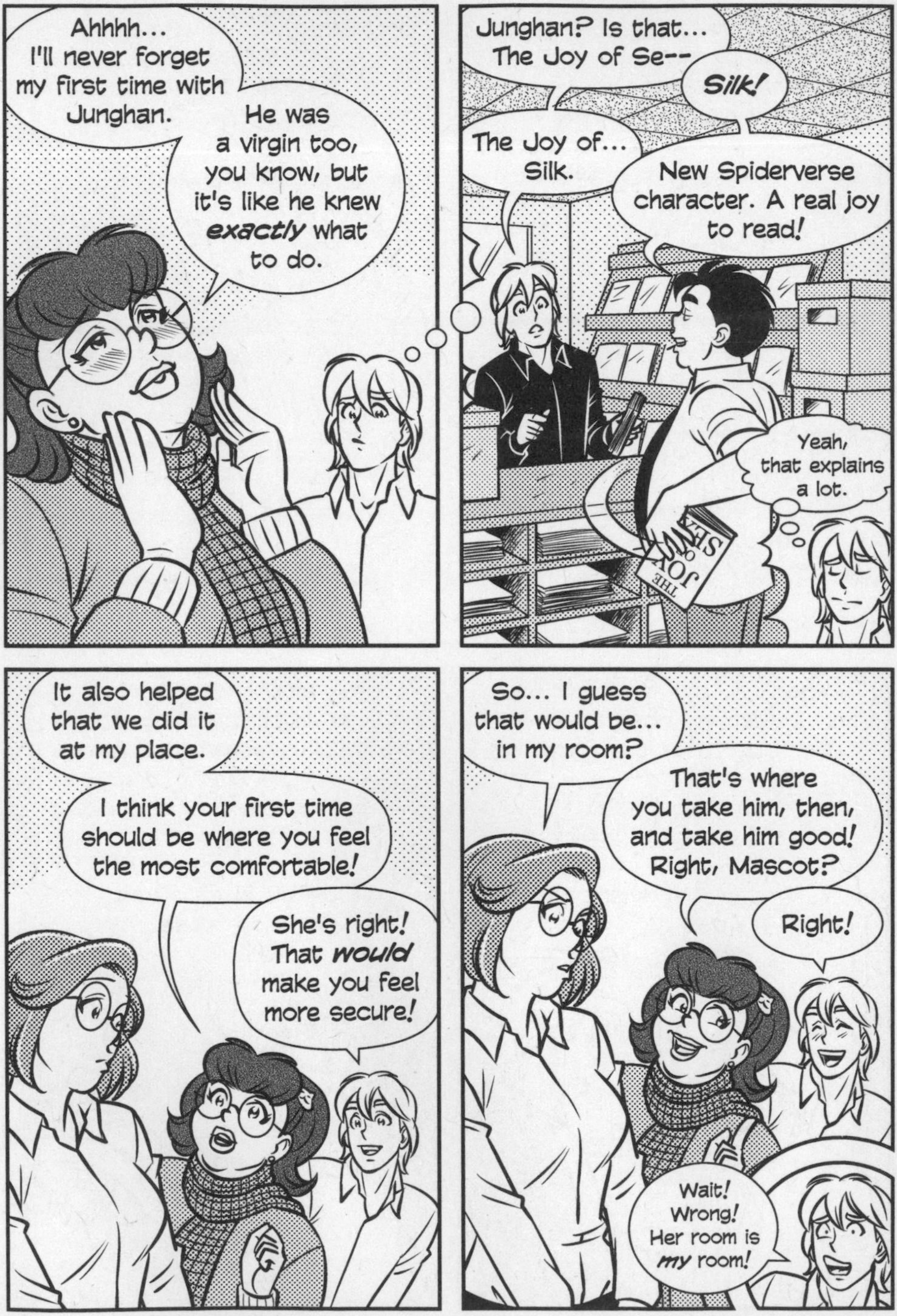
Ahhhh...
I'll never forget my first time with Junghan.
He was a virgin too, you know, but it's like he knew *exactly* what to do.
Junghan? Is that... The Joy of Se--
Silk!
The Joy of... Silk.
New Spiderverse character. A real joy to read!
THE JOY OF SEX
Yeah, that explains a lot.
It also helped that we did it at my place.
I think your first time should be where you feel the most comfortable!
She's right! That *would* make you feel more secure!
So... I guess that would be... in my room?
That's where you take him, then, and take him good! Right, Mascot?
Right!
Wait! Wrong! Her room is *my* room!

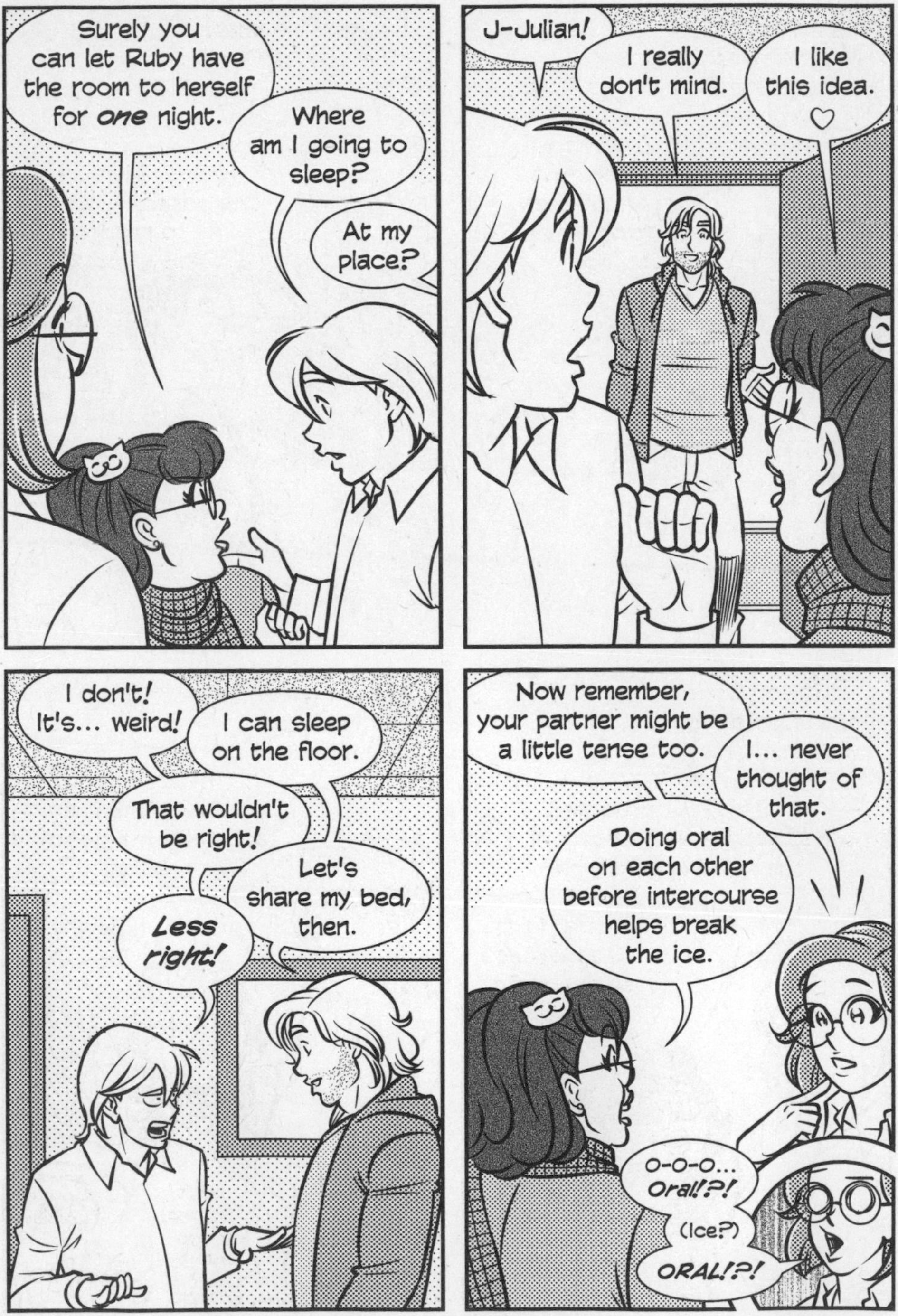
Surely you can let Ruby have the room to herself for *one* night.
Where am I going to sleep?
At my place?
J-Julian!
I really don't mind.
I like this idea. ♡
I don't! It's... weird!
I can sleep on the floor.
That wouldn't be right!
Let's share my bed, then.
Less right!
Now remember, your partner might be a little tense too.
I... never thought of that.
Doing oral on each other before intercourse helps break the ice.
O-O-O... *Oral!?!*
(Ice?)
ORAL!?!

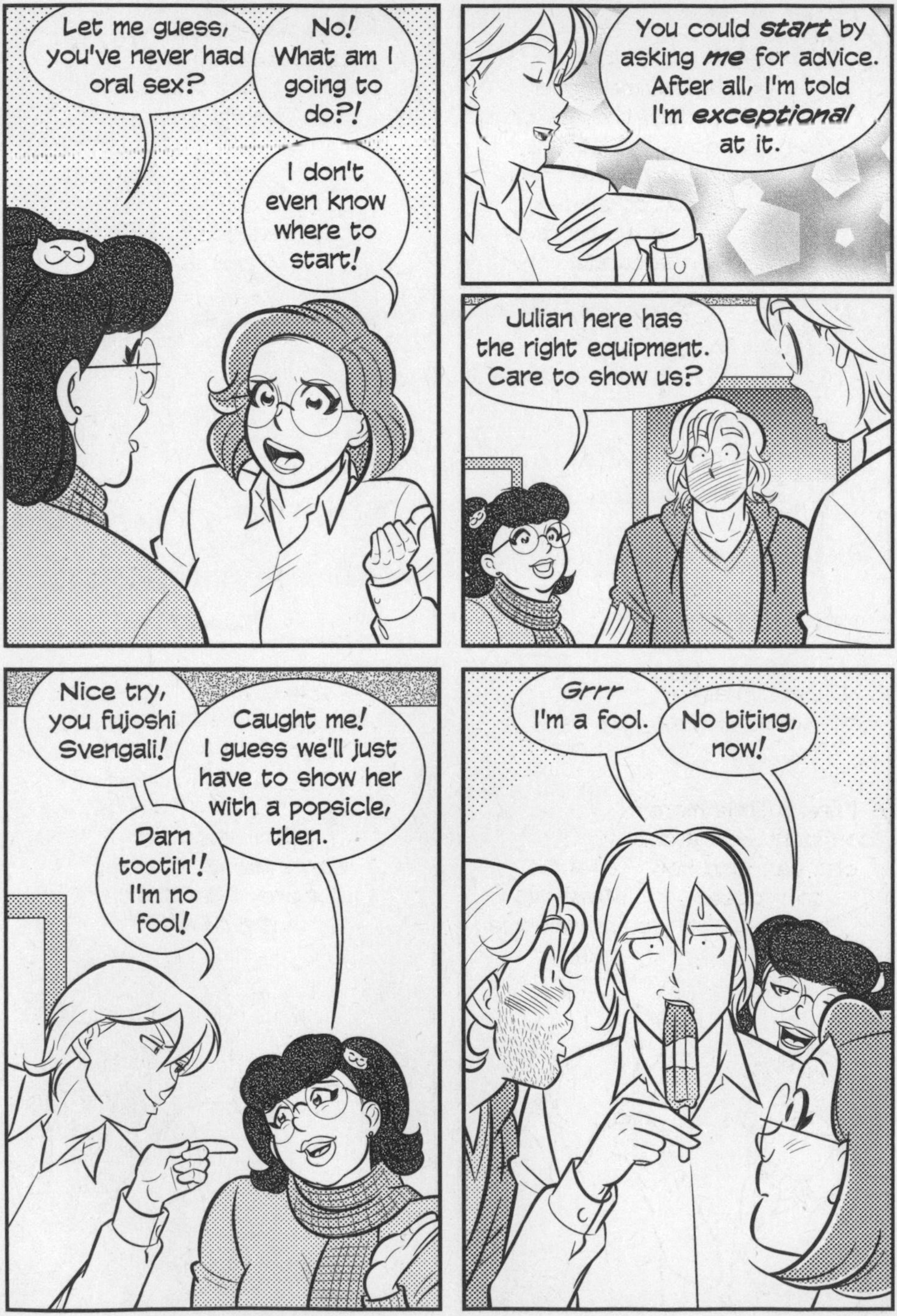
Let me guess, you've never had oral sex?
No! What am I going to do?!
I don't even know where to start!
You could *start* by asking *me* for advice. After all, I'm told I'm *exceptional* at it.
Julian here has the right equipment. Care to show us?
Nice try, you fujoshi Svengali!
Darn tootin'! I'm no fool!
Caught me! I guess we'll just have to show her with a popsicle, then.
Grrr I'm a fool.
No biting, now!

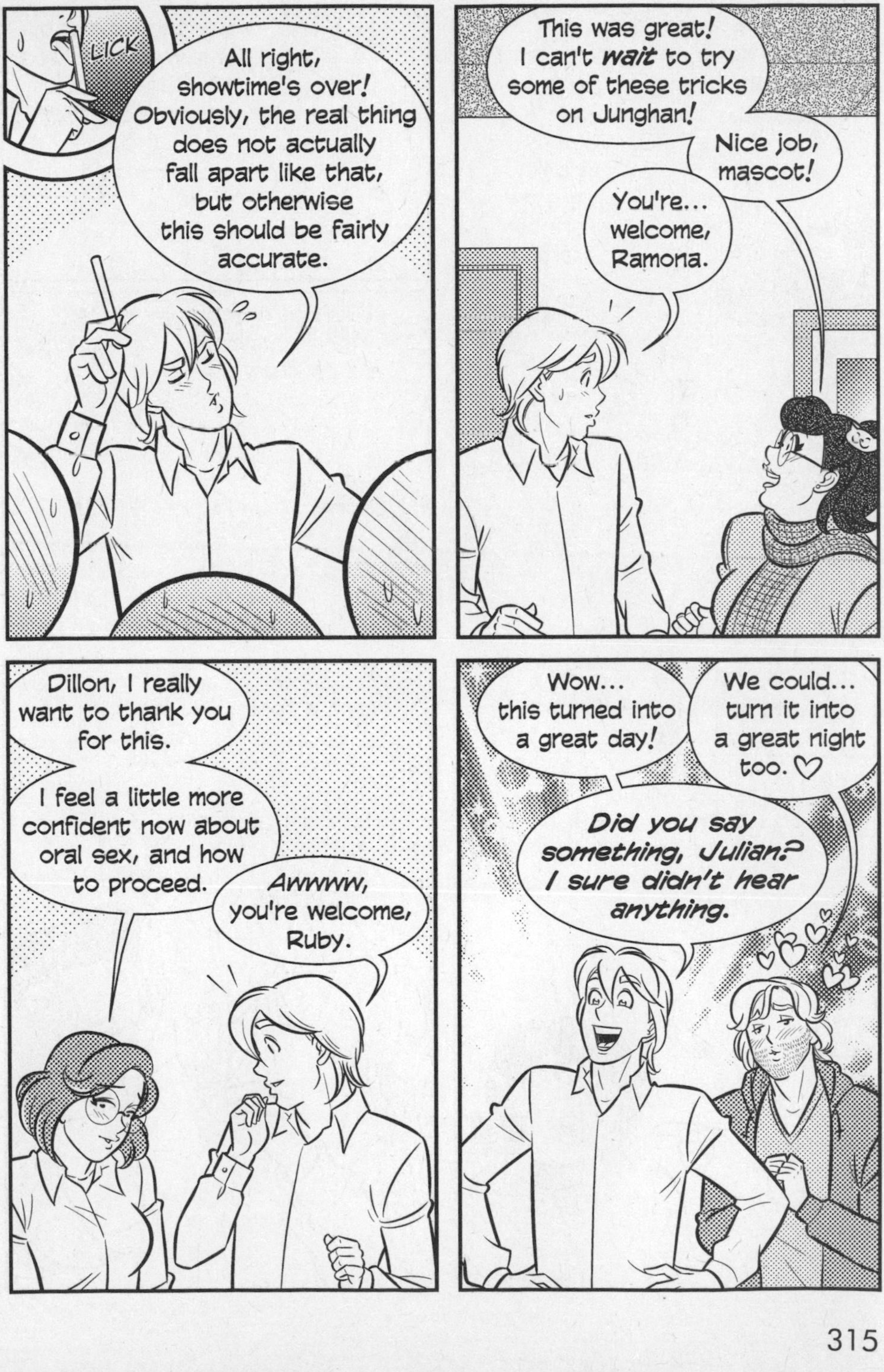
LICK
All right, showtime's over! Obviously, the real thing does not actually fall apart like that, but otherwise this should be fairly accurate.
This was great! I can't *wait* to try some of these tricks on Junghan!
Nice job, mascot!
You're... welcome, Ramona.
Dillon, I really want to thank you for this.
I feel a little more confident now about oral sex, and how to proceed.
Awwww, you're welcome, Ruby.
Wow... this turned into a great day!
We could... turn it into a great night too. ♡
Did you say something, Julian? I sure didn't hear anything.

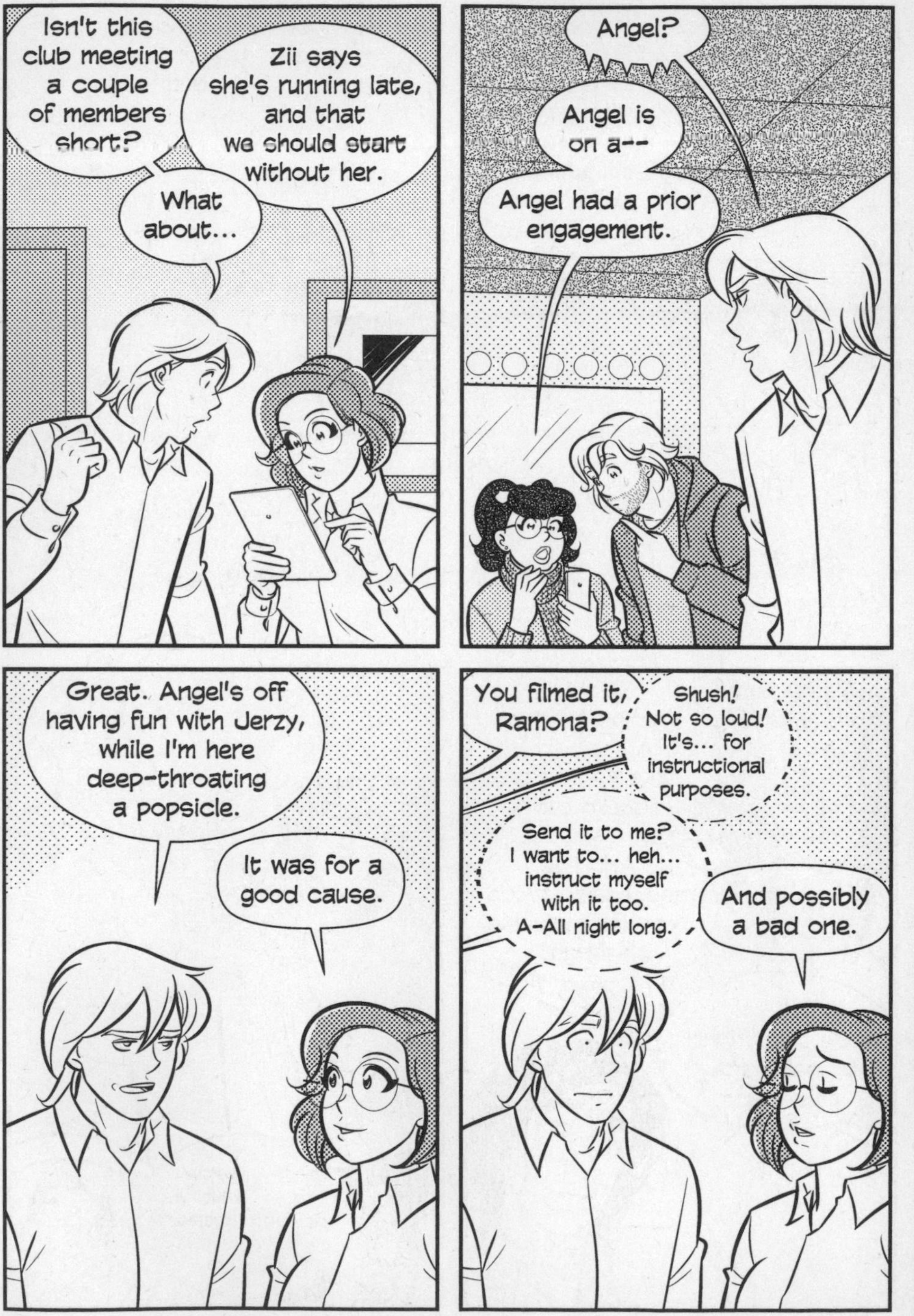
Isn't this club meeting a couple of members short?
Zii says she's running late, and that we should start without her.
What about...
Angel?
Angel is on a--
Angel had a prior engagement.
Great. Angel's off having fun with Jerzy, while I'm here deep-throating a popsicle.
It was for a good cause.
You filmed it, Ramona?
Shush! Not so loud! It's... for instructional purposes.
Send it to me? I want to... heh... instruct myself with it too. A-All night long.
And possibly a bad one.

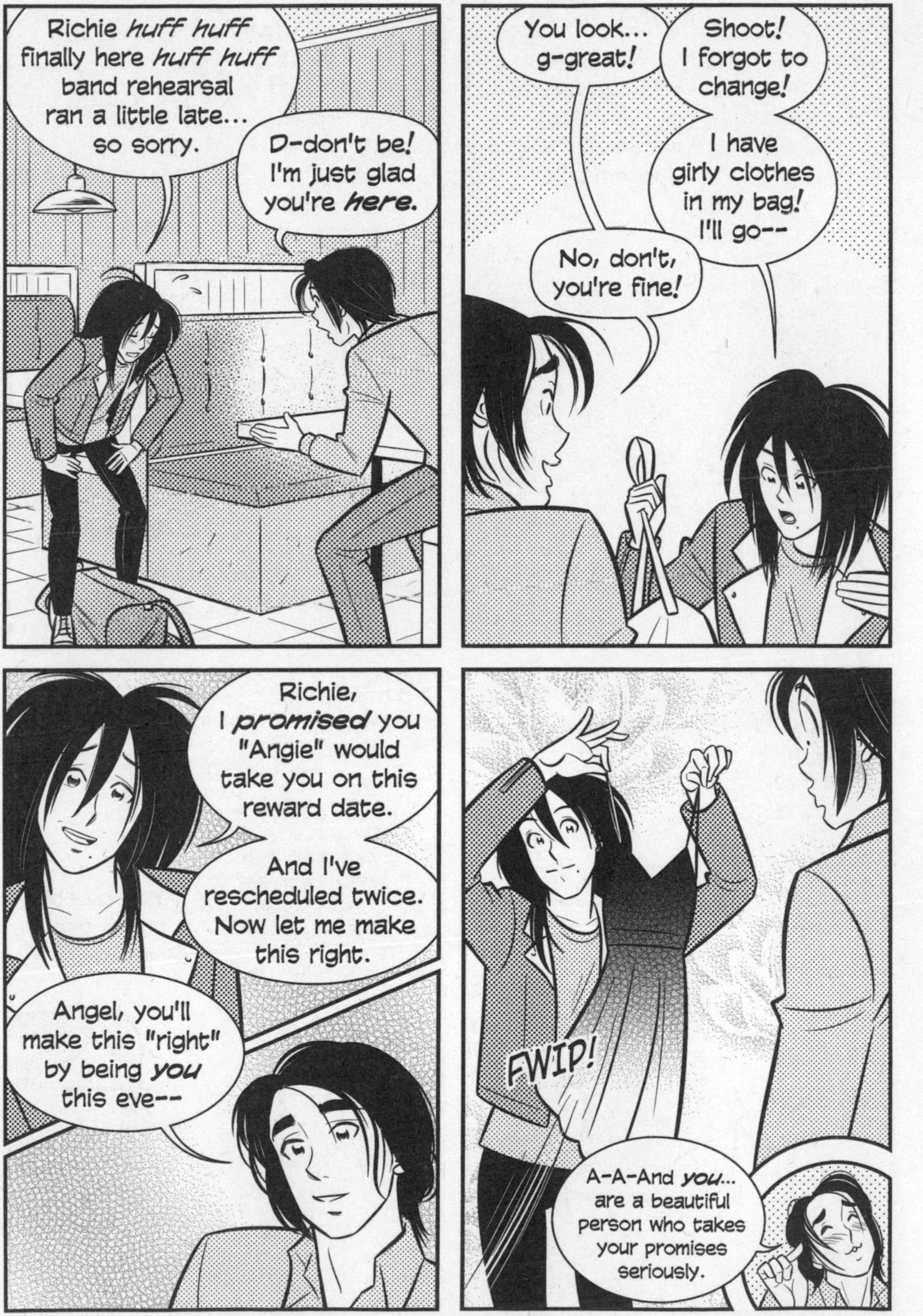
Richie *huff huff* finally here *huff huff* band rehearsal ran a little late... so sorry.
D-don't be! I'm just glad you're ***here.***
You look... g-great!
Shoot! I forgot to change!
I have girly clothes in my bag! I'll go--
No, don't, you're fine!
Richie, I ***promised*** you "Angie" would take you on this reward date.
And I've rescheduled twice. Now let me make this right.
Angel, you'll make this "right" by being ***you*** this eve--
FWIP!
A-A-And ***you***... are a beautiful person who takes your promises seriously.

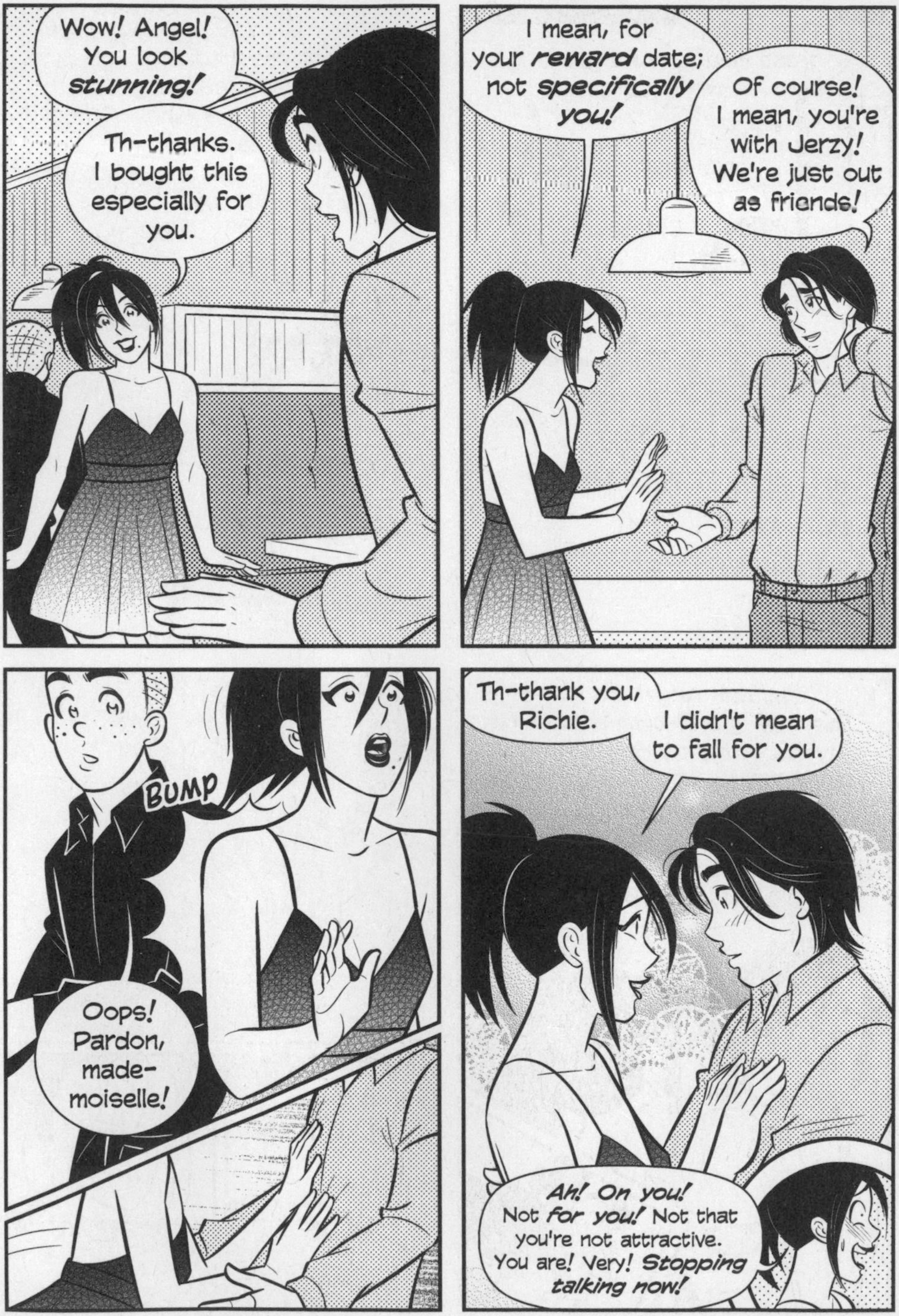
Wow! Angel! You look *stunning!*
Th-thanks. I bought this especially for you.
I mean, for your *reward* date; not *specifically you!*
Of course! I mean, you're with Jerzy! We're just out as friends!
BUMP
Oops! Pardon, made-moiselle!
Th-thank you, Richie.
I didn't mean to fall for you.
Ah! On you! Not *for you!* Not that you're not attractive. You are! Very! *Stopping talking now!*

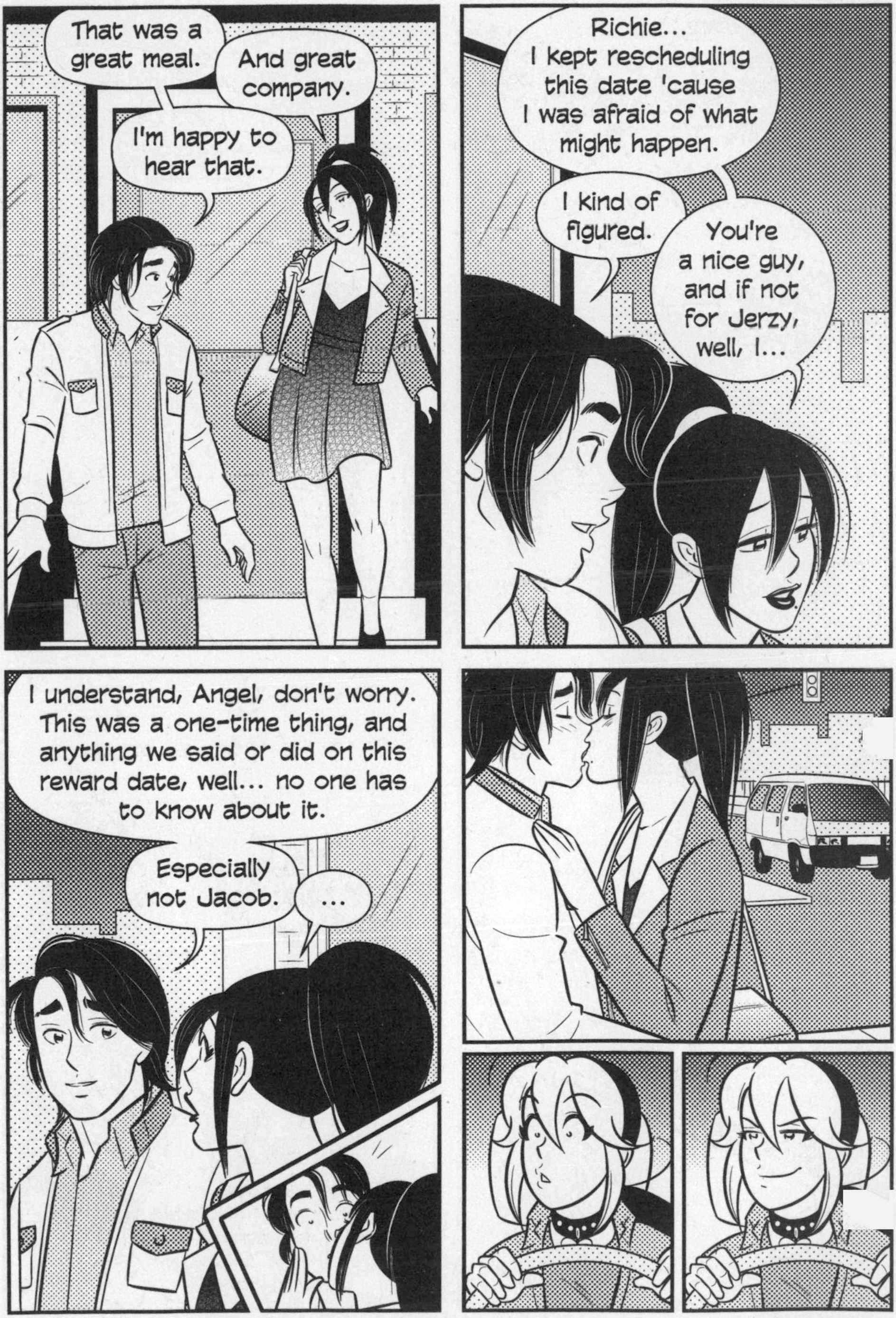
That was a great meal.
And great company.
I'm happy to hear that.
Richie... I kept rescheduling this date 'cause I was afraid of what might happen.
I kind of figured.
You're a nice guy, and if not for Jerzy, well, I...
I understand, Angel, don't worry. This was a one-time thing, and anything we said or did on this reward date, well... no one has to know about it.
Especially not Jacob.
...

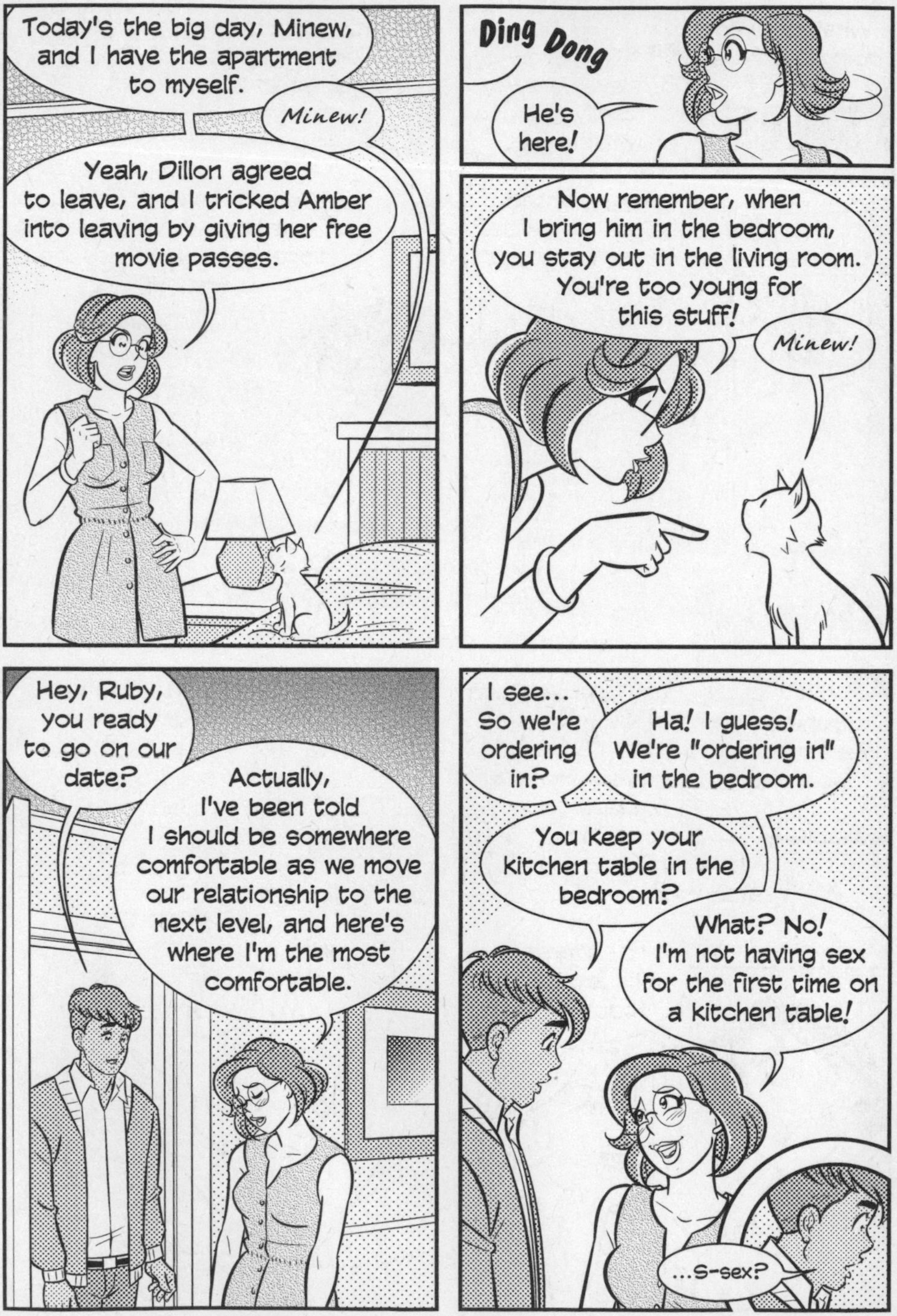
Today's the big day, Minew, and I have the apartment to myself.
Minew!
Yeah, Dillon agreed to leave, and I tricked Amber into leaving by giving her free movie passes.
Ding Dong
He's here!
Now remember, when I bring him in the bedroom, you stay out in the living room. You're too young for this stuff!
Minew!
Hey, Ruby, you ready to go on our date?
Actually, I've been told I should be somewhere comfortable as we move our relationship to the next level, and here's where I'm the most comfortable.
I see... So we're ordering in?
Ha! I guess! We're "ordering in" in the bedroom.
You keep your kitchen table in the bedroom?
What? No! I'm not having sex for the first time on a kitchen table!
...S-sex?

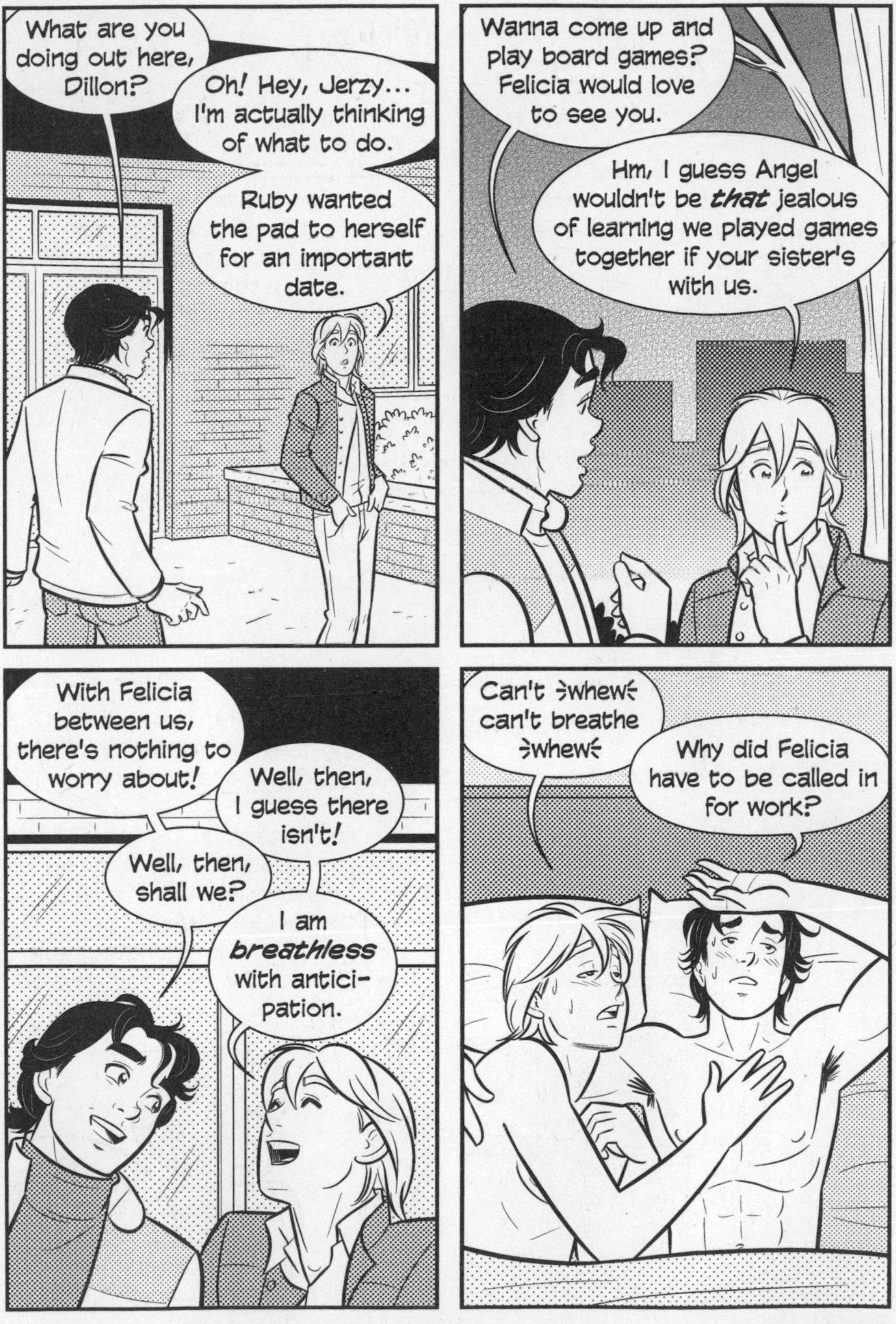
What are you doing out here, Dillon?
Oh! Hey, Jerzy... I'm actually thinking of what to do.
Ruby wanted the pad to herself for an important date.
Wanna come up and play board games? Felicia would love to see you.
Hm, I guess Angel wouldn't be *that* jealous of learning we played games together if your sister's with us.
With Felicia between us, there's nothing to worry about!
Well, then, I guess there isn't!
Well, then, shall we?
I am *breathless* with antici-pation.
Can't ≯whew≮ can't breathe ≯whew≮
Why did Felicia have to be called in for work?

Advice for the Lovelorn

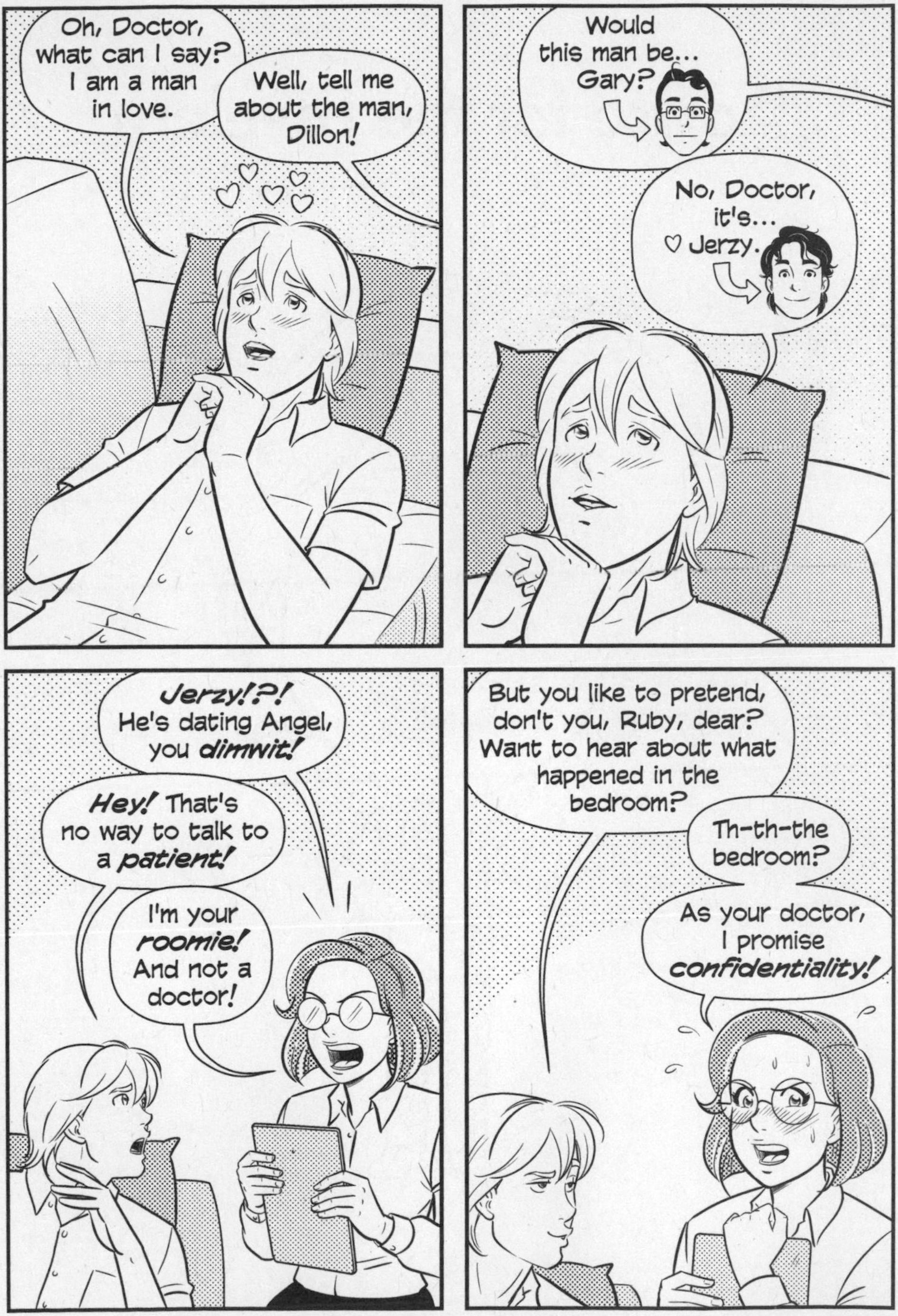
Oh, Doctor, what can I say? I am a man in love.
Well, tell me about the man, Dillon!
Would this man be... Gary?
No, Doctor, it's... ♡ Jerzy.
Jerzy!?! He's dating Angel, you dimwit!
Hey! That's no way to talk to a patient!
I'm your roomie! And not a doctor!
But you like to pretend, don't you, Ruby, dear? Want to hear about what happened in the bedroom?
Th-th-the bedroom?
As your doctor, I promise confidentiality!

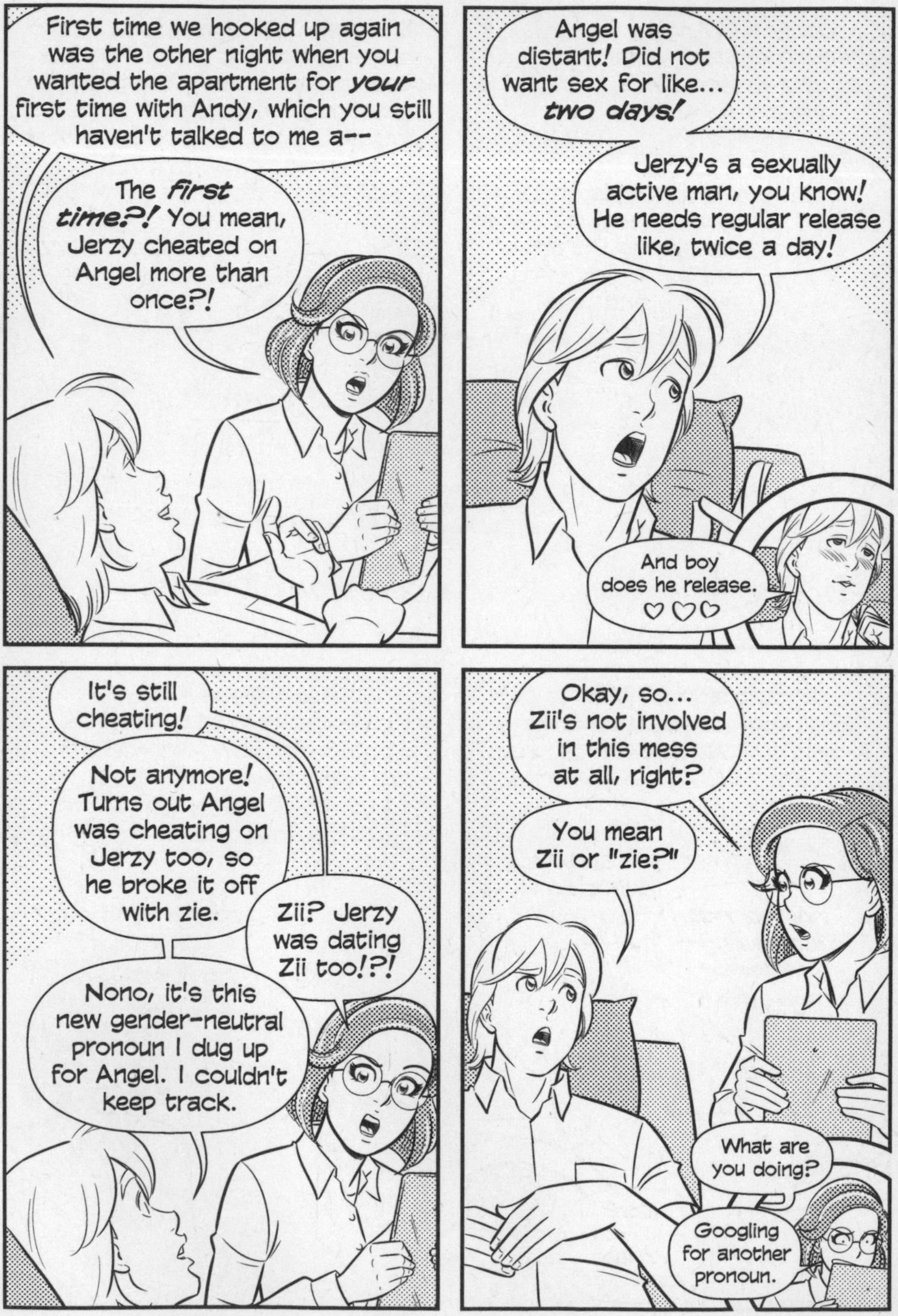
First time we hooked up again was the other night when you wanted the apartment for *your* first time with Andy, which you still haven't talked to me a--
The *first time?!* You mean, Jerzy cheated on Angel more than once?!
Angel was distant! Did not want sex for like... *two days!*
Jerzy's a sexually active man, you know! He needs regular release like, twice a day!
And boy does he release. ♡♡♡
It's still cheating!
Not anymore! Turns out Angel was cheating on Jerzy too, so he broke it off with zie.
Zii? Jerzy was dating Zii too!?!
Nono, it's this new gender-neutral pronoun I dug up for Angel. I couldn't keep track.
Okay, so... Zii's not involved in this mess at all, right?
You mean Zii or "zie?"
What are you doing?
Googling for another pronoun.

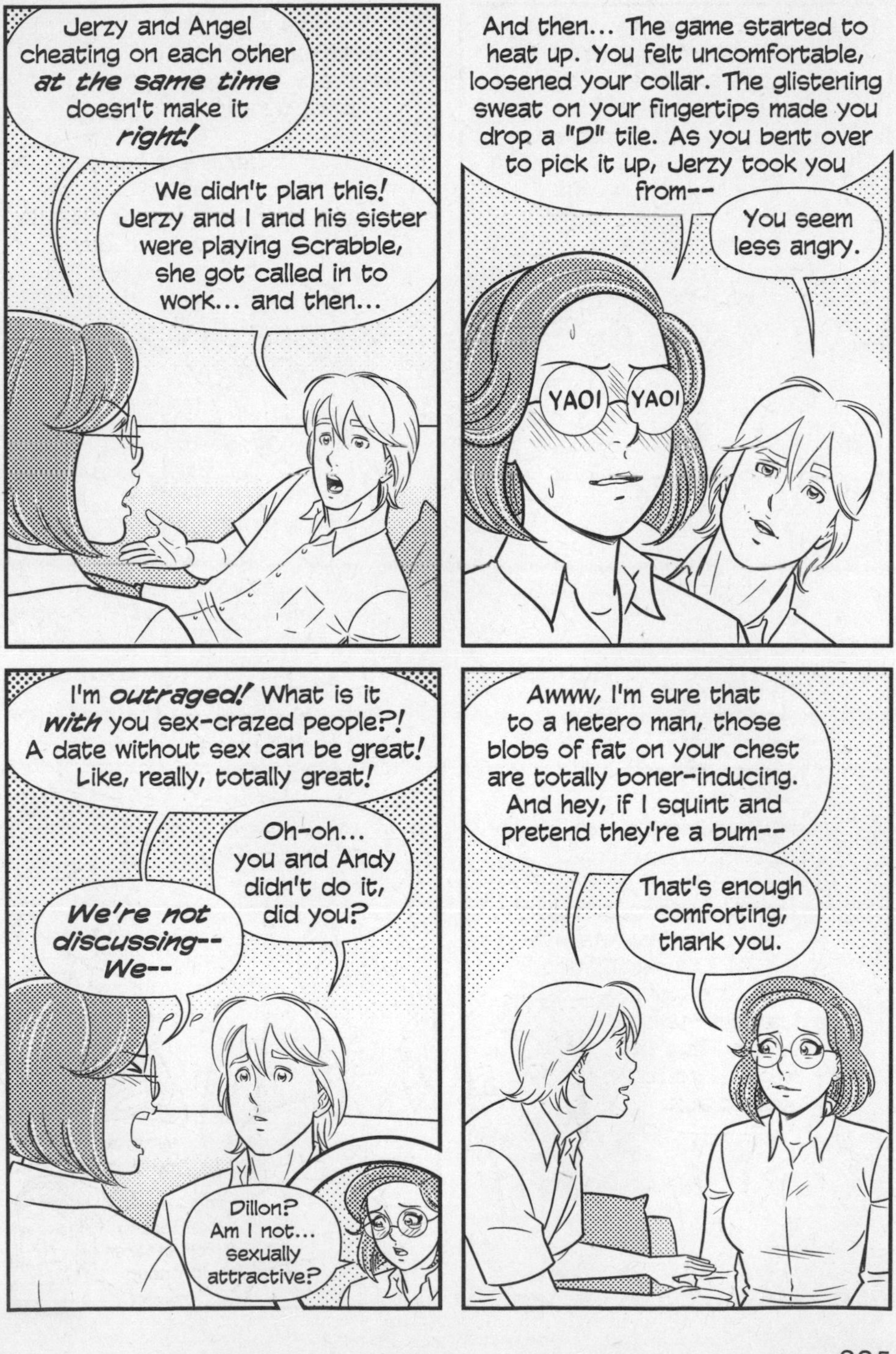
Jerzy and Angel cheating on each other *at the same time* doesn't make it *right!*
We didn't plan this! Jerzy and I and his sister were playing Scrabble, she got called in to work... and then...
And then... The game started to heat up. You felt uncomfortable, loosened your collar. The glistening sweat on your fingertips made you drop a "D" tile. As you bent over to pick it up, Jerzy took you from--
YAOI
YAOI
You seem less angry.
I'm *outraged!* What is it *with* you sex-crazed people?! A date without sex can be great! Like, really, totally great!
Oh-oh... you and Andy didn't do it, did you?
We're not discussing-- We--
Dillon? Am I not... sexually attractive?
Awww, I'm sure that to a hetero man, those blobs of fat on your chest are totally boner-inducing. And hey, if I squint and pretend they're a bum--
That's enough comforting, thank you.

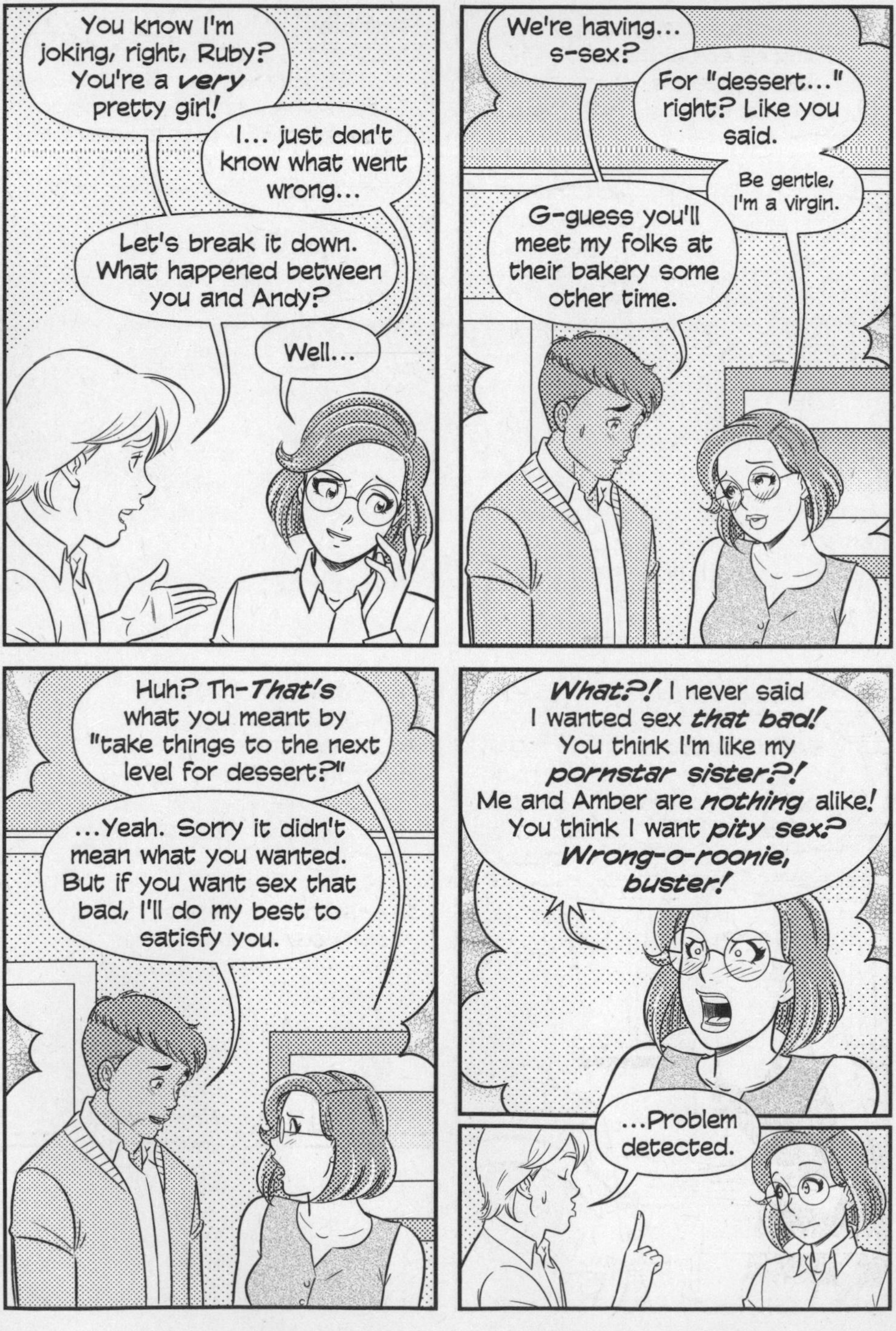
You know I'm joking, right, Ruby? You're a *very* pretty girl!
I... just don't know what went wrong...
Let's break it down. What happened between you and Andy?
Well...
We're having... s-sex?
For "dessert..." right? Like you said.
Be gentle, I'm a virgin.
G-guess you'll meet my folks at their bakery some other time.
Huh? Th-*That's* what you meant by "take things to the next level for dessert?"
...Yeah. Sorry it didn't mean what you wanted. But if you want sex that bad, I'll do my best to satisfy you.
What?! I never said I wanted sex *that bad!* You think I'm like my *pornstar sister?!* Me and Amber are *nothing* alike! You think I want *pity sex?* *Wrong-o-roonie, buster!*
...Problem detected.

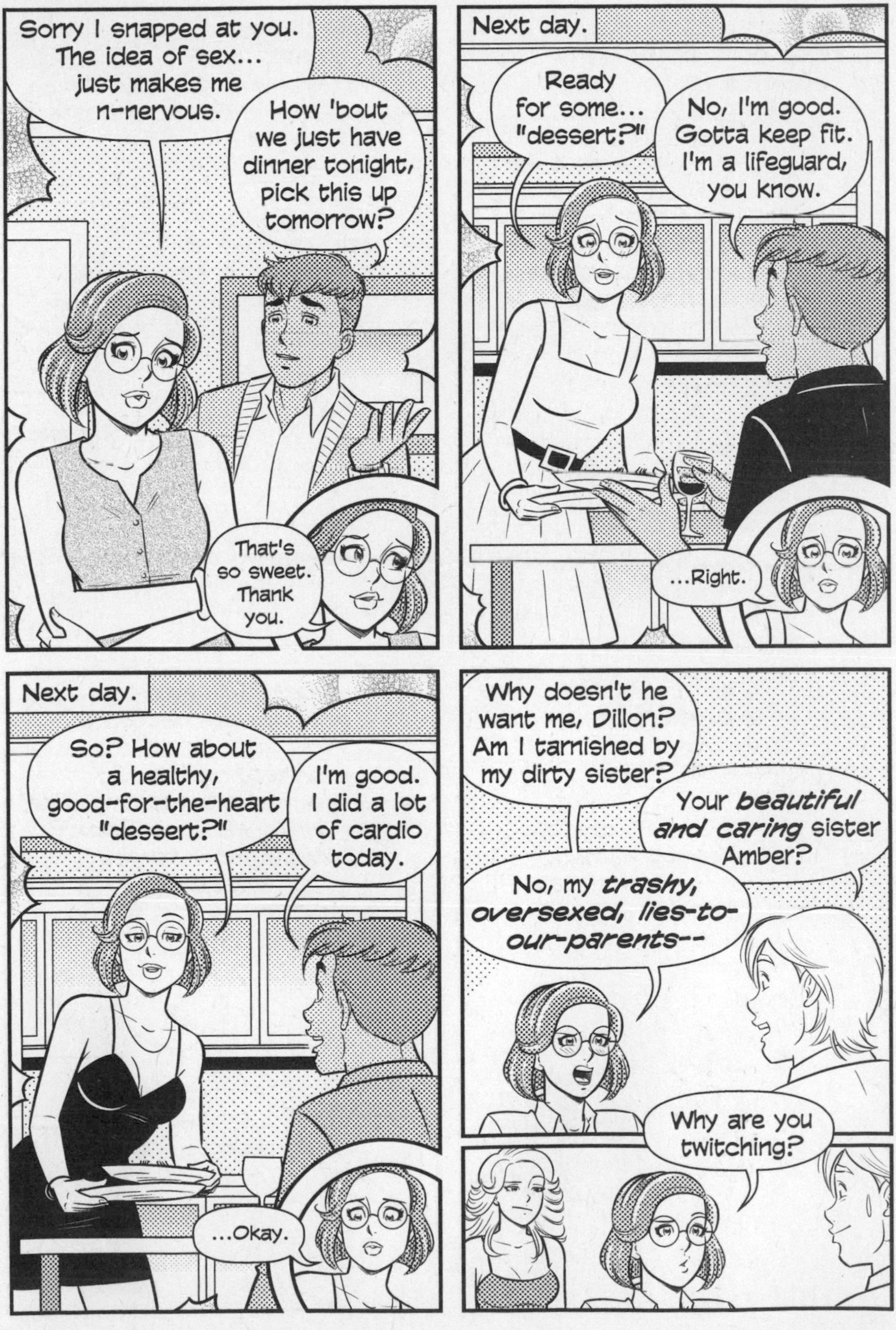

Sorry I snapped at you. The idea of sex... just makes me n-nervous.
How 'bout we just have dinner tonight, pick this up tomorrow?
That's so sweet. Thank you.
Next day.
Ready for some... "dessert?"
No, I'm good. Gotta keep fit. I'm a lifeguard, you know.
...Right.
Next day.
So? How about a healthy, good-for-the-heart "dessert?"
I'm good. I did a lot of cardio today.
...Okay.
Why doesn't he want me, Dillon? Am I tarnished by my dirty sister?
Your *beautiful and caring* sister Amber?
No, my *trashy, oversexed, lies-to-our-parents--*
Why are you twitching?

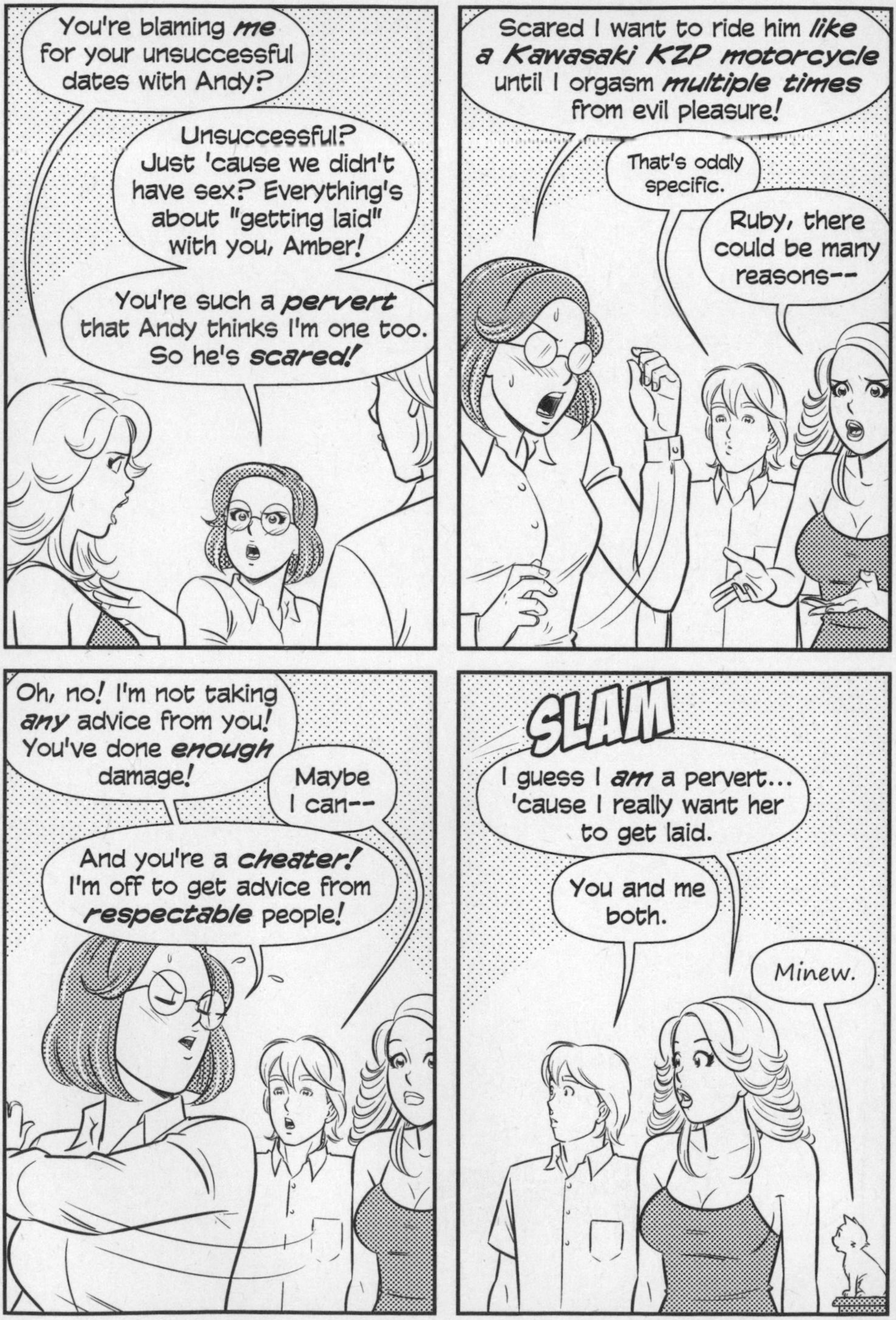
You're blaming *me* for your unsuccessful dates with Andy?
Unsuccessful? Just 'cause we didn't have sex? Everything's about "getting laid" with you, Amber!
You're such a *pervert* that Andy thinks I'm one too. So he's *scared!*
Scared I want to ride him *like a Kawasaki KZP motorcycle* until I orgasm *multiple times* from evil pleasure!
That's oddly specific.
Ruby, there could be many reasons--
Oh, no! I'm not taking *any* advice from you! You've done *enough* damage!
Maybe I can--
And you're a *cheater!* I'm off to get advice from *respectable* people!
SLAM
I guess I *am* a pervert... 'cause I really want her to get laid.
You and me both.
Minew.

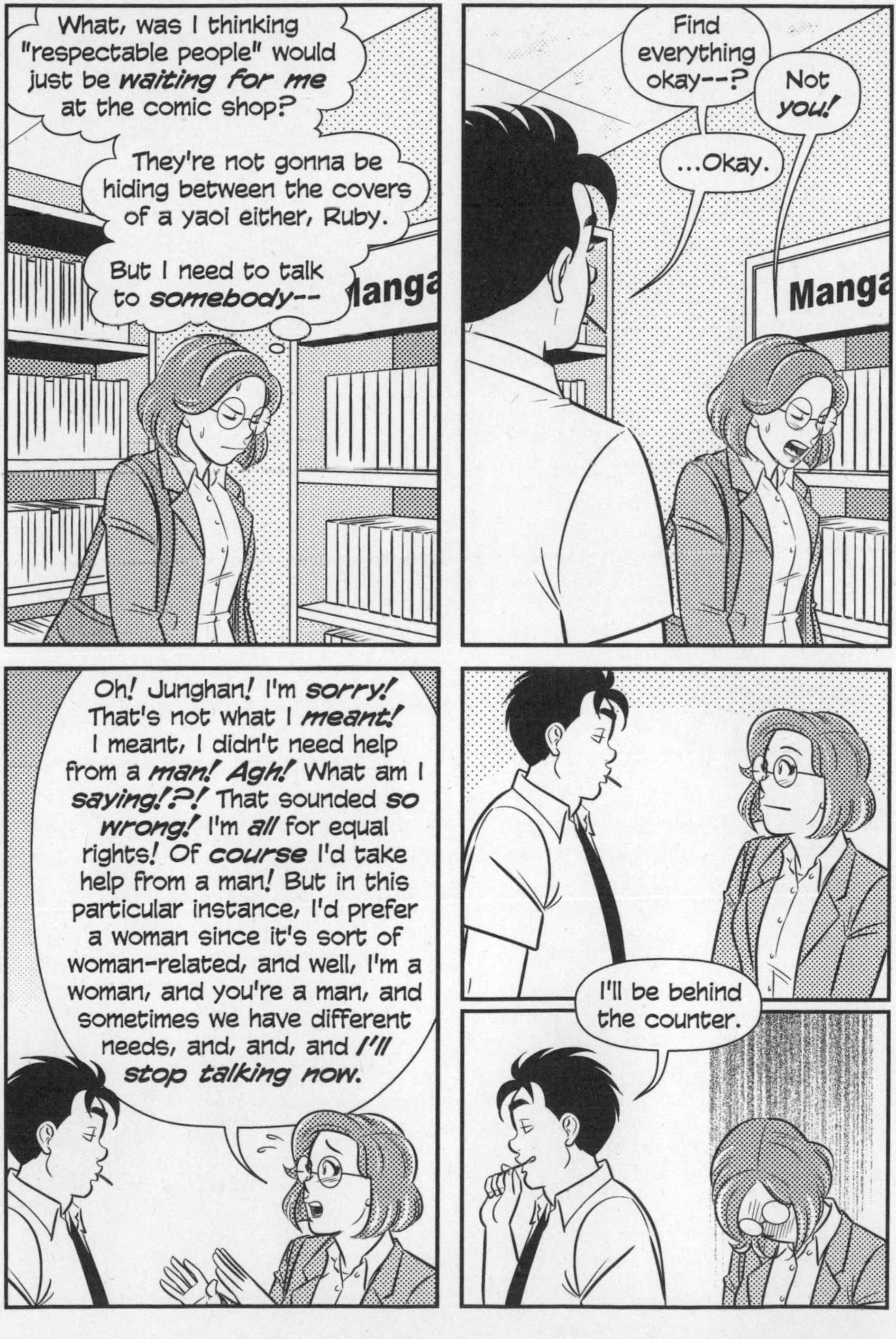
What, was I thinking "respectable people" would just be *waiting for me* at the comic shop?
They're not gonna be hiding between the covers of a yaoi either, Ruby.
But I need to talk to *somebody*--
Manga
Find everything okay--?
Not *you!*
...Okay.
Manga
Oh! Junghan! I'm *sorry!* That's not what I *meant!* I meant, I didn't need help from a *man! Agh!* What am I *saying!?!* That sounded *so wrong!* I'm *all* for equal rights! Of *course* I'd take help from a man! But in this particular instance, I'd prefer a woman since it's sort of woman-related, and well, I'm a woman, and you're a man, and sometimes we have different needs, and, and, and *I'll stop talking now.*
I'll be behind the counter.

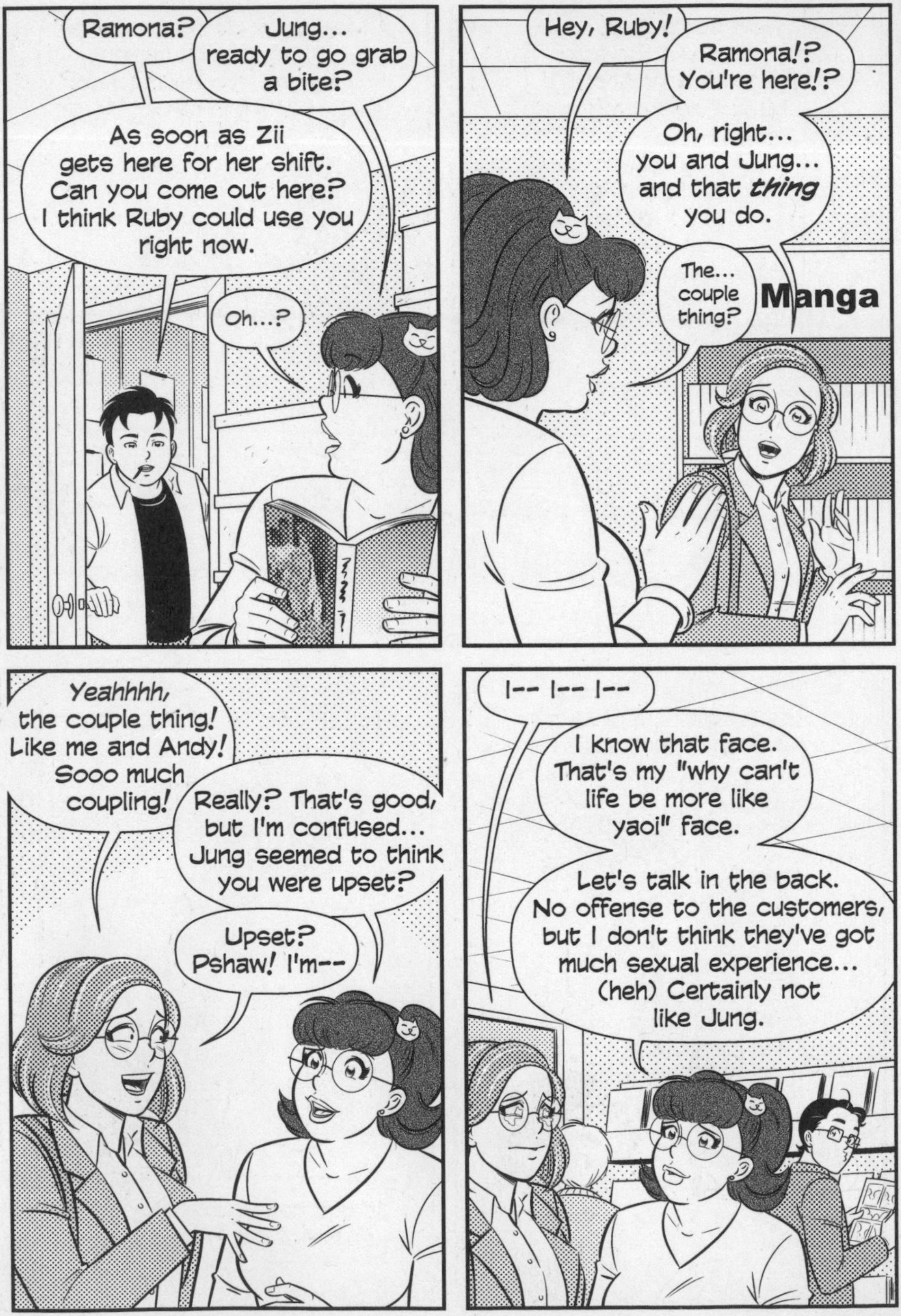
Ramona?
Jung... ready to go grab a bite?
As soon as Zii gets here for her shift. Can you come out here? I think Ruby could use you right now.
Oh...?
Hey, Ruby!
Ramona!? You're here!?
Oh, right... you and Jung... and that *thing* you do.
The... couple thing?
Manga
Yeahhhh, the couple thing! Like me and Andy! Sooo much coupling!
Really? That's good, but I'm confused... Jung seemed to think you were upset?
Upset? Pshaw! I'm--
I-- I-- I--
I know that face. That's my "why can't life be more like yaoi" face.
Let's talk in the back. No offense to the customers, but I don't think they've got much sexual experience... (heh) Certainly not like Jung.

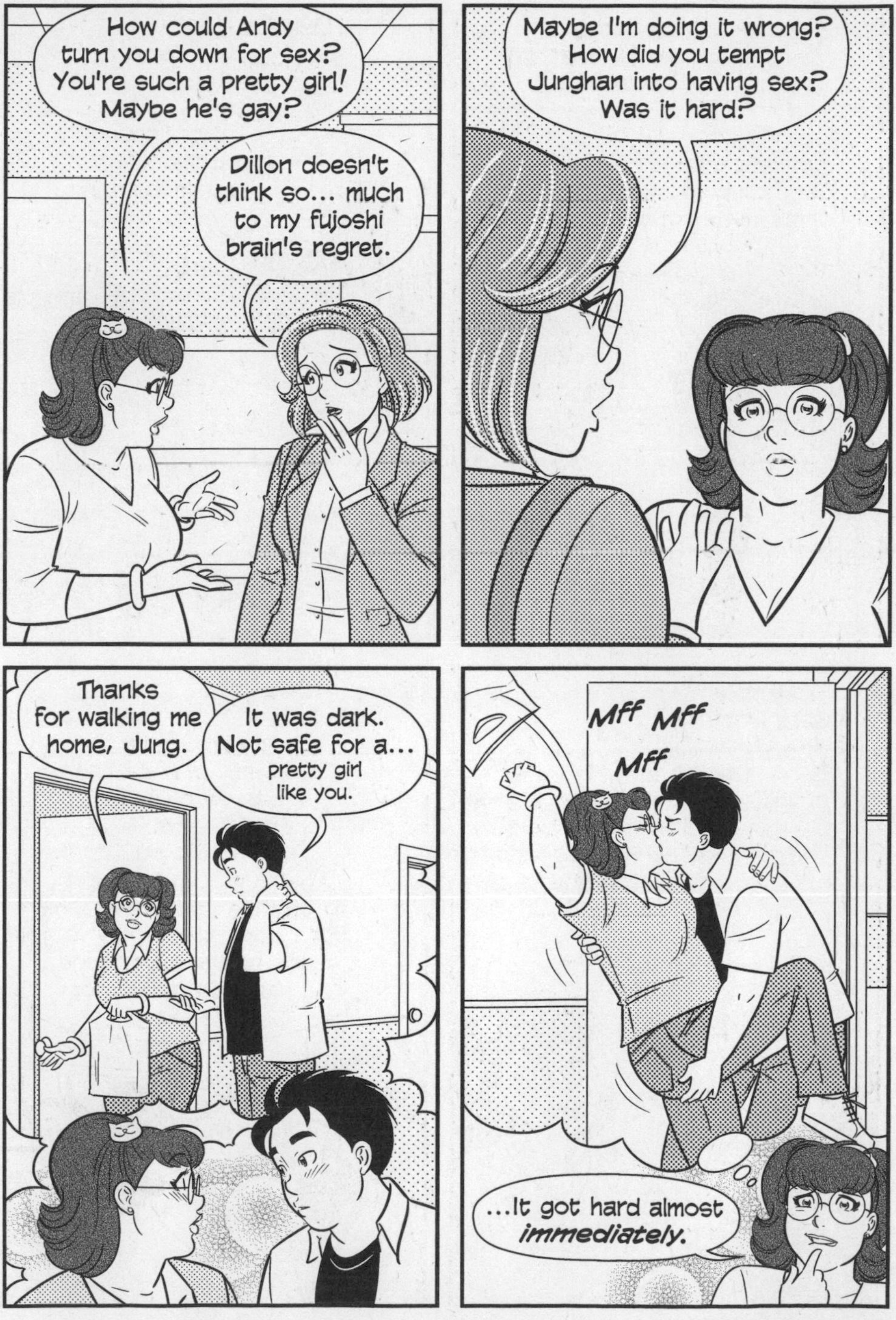
How could Andy turn you down for sex? You're such a pretty girl! Maybe he's gay?
Dillon doesn't think so... much to my fujoshi brain's regret.
Maybe I'm doing it wrong? How did you tempt Junghan into having sex? Was it hard?
Thanks for walking me home, Jung.
It was dark. Not safe for a... pretty girl like you.
Mff Mff
Mff
...It got hard almost *immediately*.

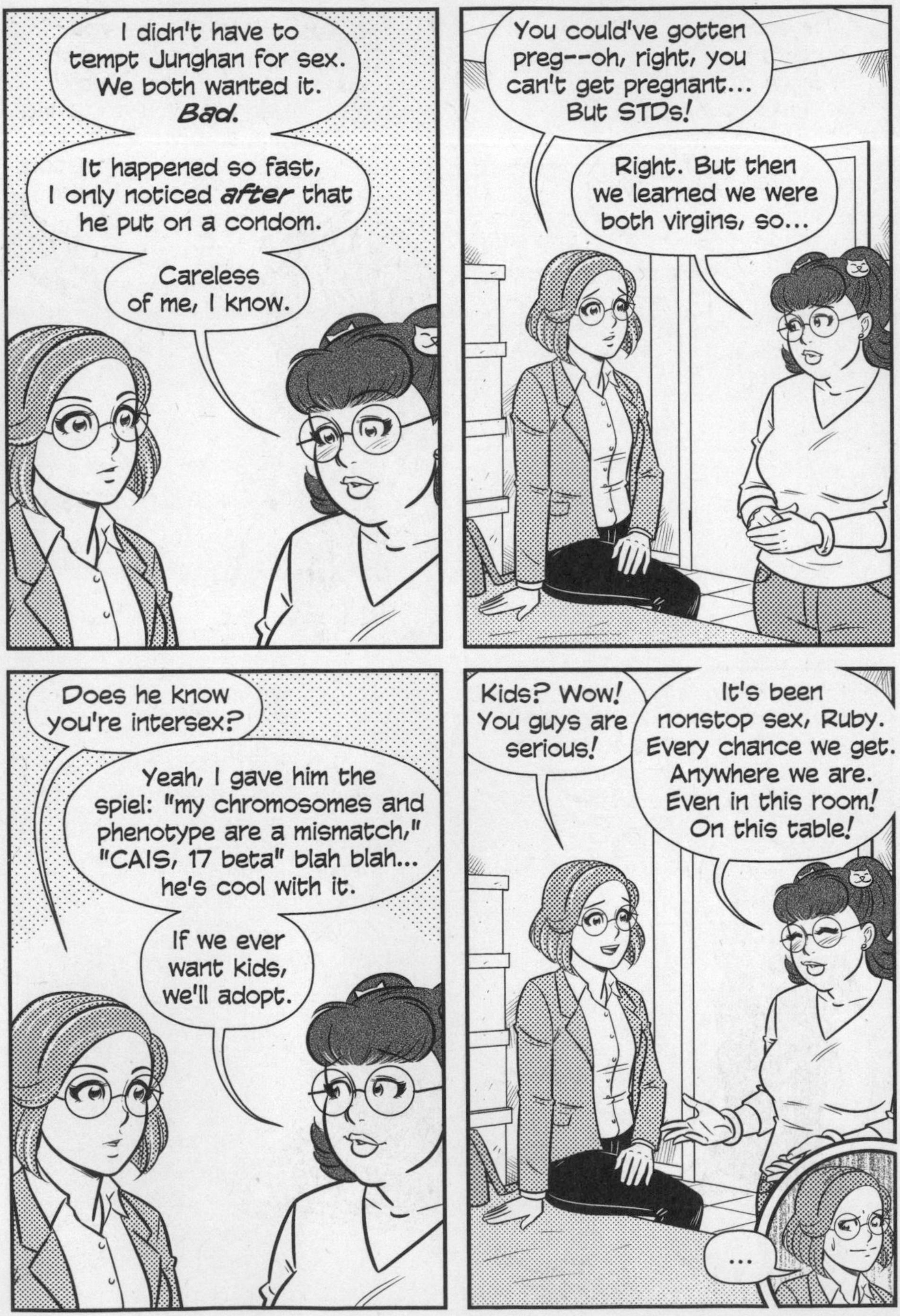
I didn't have to tempt Junghan for sex. We both wanted it. *Bad.*
It happened so fast, I only noticed *after* that he put on a condom.
Careless of me, I know.
You could've gotten preg--oh, right, you can't get pregnant... But STDs!
Right. But then we learned we were both virgins, so...
Does he know you're intersex?
Yeah, I gave him the spiel: "my chromosomes and phenotype are a mismatch," "CAIS, 17 beta" blah blah... he's cool with it.
If we ever want kids, we'll adopt.
Kids? Wow! You guys are serious!
It's been nonstop sex, Ruby. Every chance we get. Anywhere we are. Even in this room! On this table!
...

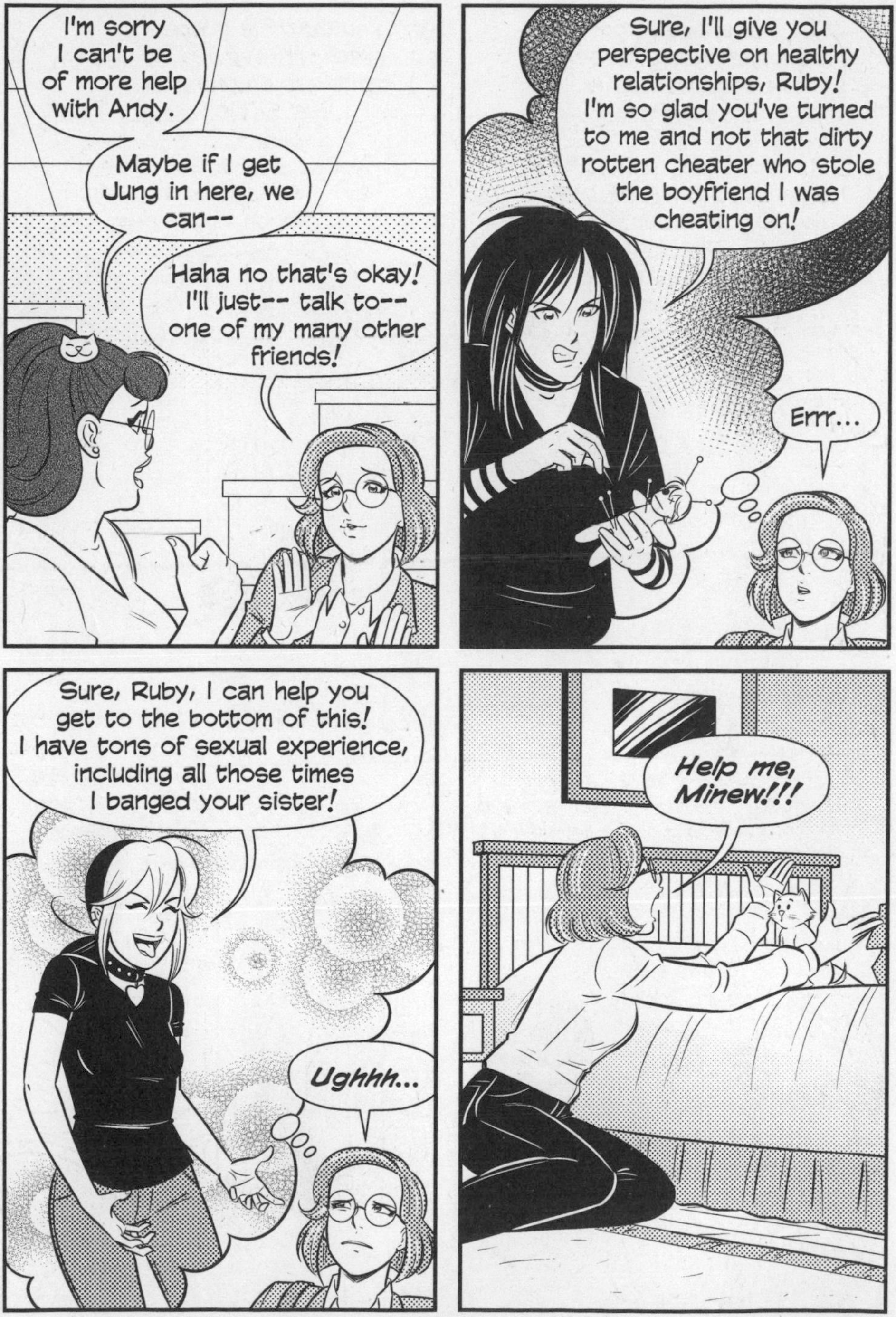
I'm sorry I can't be of more help with Andy.
Maybe if I get Jung in here, we can--
Haha no that's okay! I'll just-- talk to-- one of my many other friends!
Sure, I'll give you perspective on healthy relationships, Ruby! I'm so glad you've turned to me and not that dirty rotten cheater who stole the boyfriend I was cheating on!
Errr...
Sure, Ruby, I can help you get to the bottom of this! I have tons of sexual experience, including all those times I banged your sister!
Ughhh...
Help me, Minew!!!

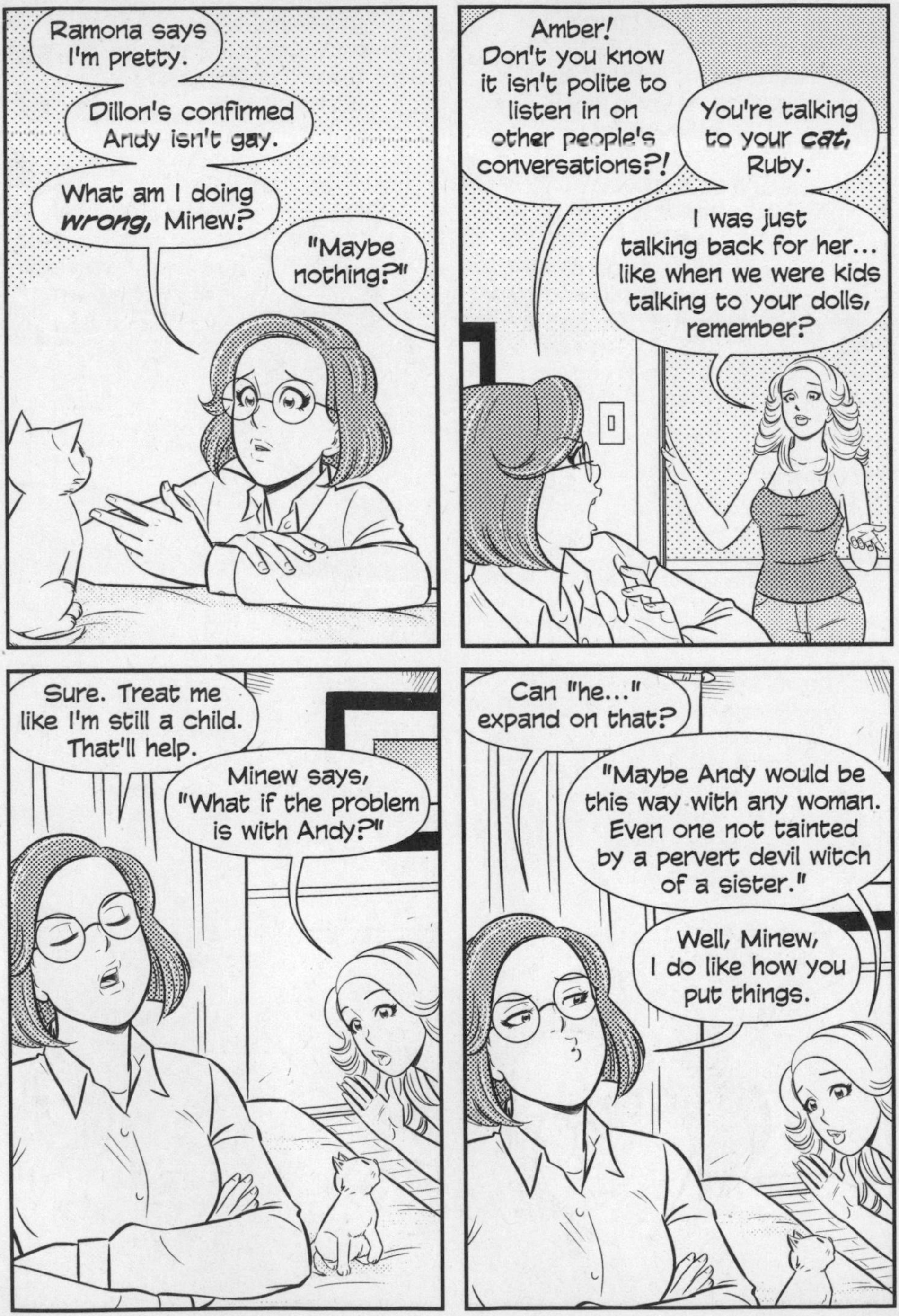
Ramona says I'm pretty.
Dillon's confirmed Andy isn't gay.
What am I doing *wrong,* Minew?
"Maybe nothing?"
Amber! Don't you know it isn't polite to listen in on other people's conversations?!
You're talking to your *cat,* Ruby.
I was just talking back for her... like when we were kids talking to your dolls, remember?
Sure. Treat me like I'm still a child. That'll help.
Minew says, "What if the problem is with Andy?"
Can "he..." expand on that?
"Maybe Andy would be this way with any woman. Even one not tainted by a pervert devil witch of a sister."
Well, Minew, I do like how you put things.

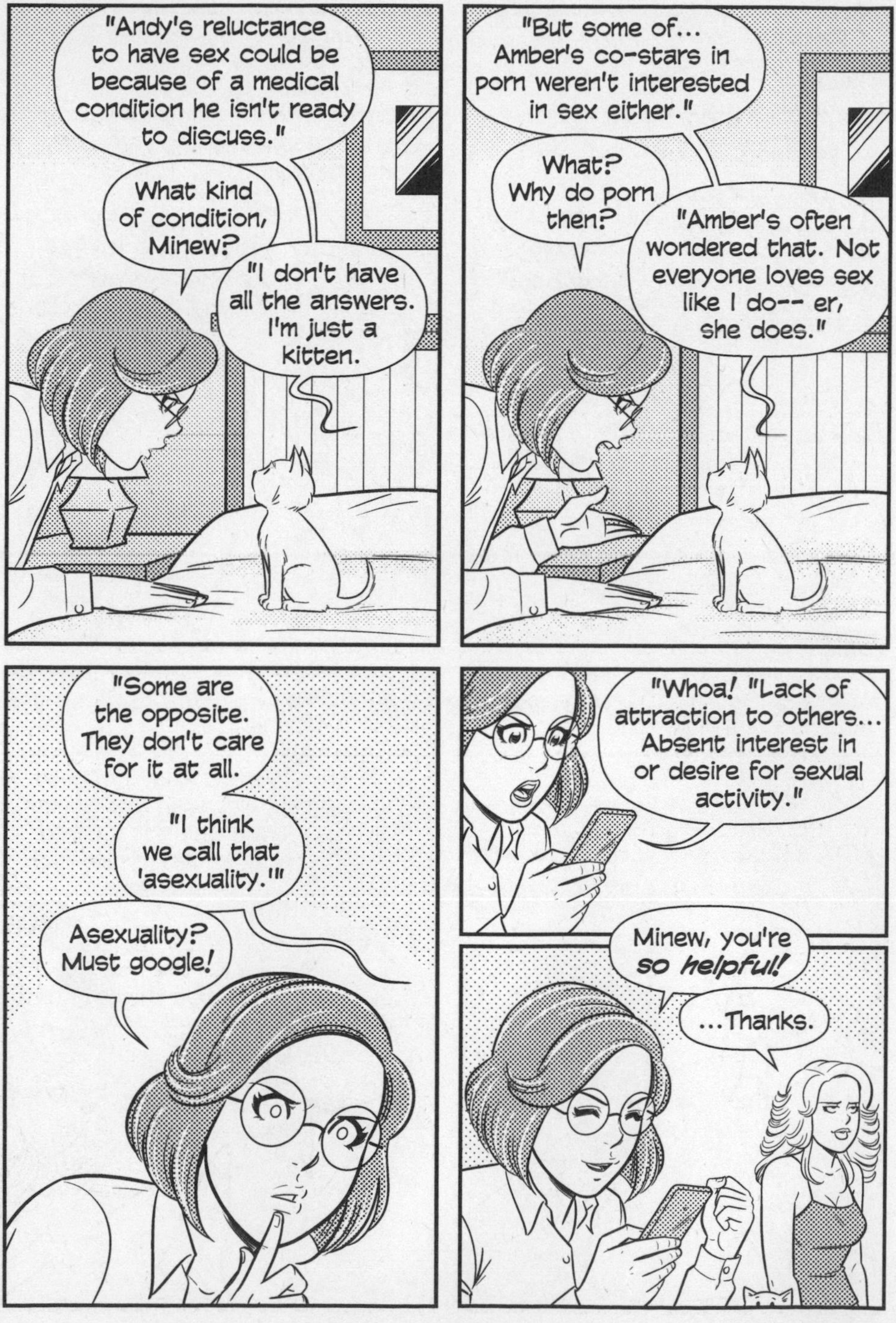
"Andy's reluctance to have sex could be because of a medical condition he isn't ready to discuss."
What kind of condition, Minew?
"I don't have all the answers. I'm just a kitten.
"But some of... Amber's co-stars in porn weren't interested in sex either."
What? Why do porn then?
"Amber's often wondered that. Not everyone loves sex like I do-- er, she does."
"Some are the opposite. They don't care for it at all.
"I think we call that 'asexuality.'"
Asexuality? Must google!
"Whoa! "Lack of attraction to others... Absent interest in or desire for sexual activity."
Minew, you're *so helpful!*
...Thanks.

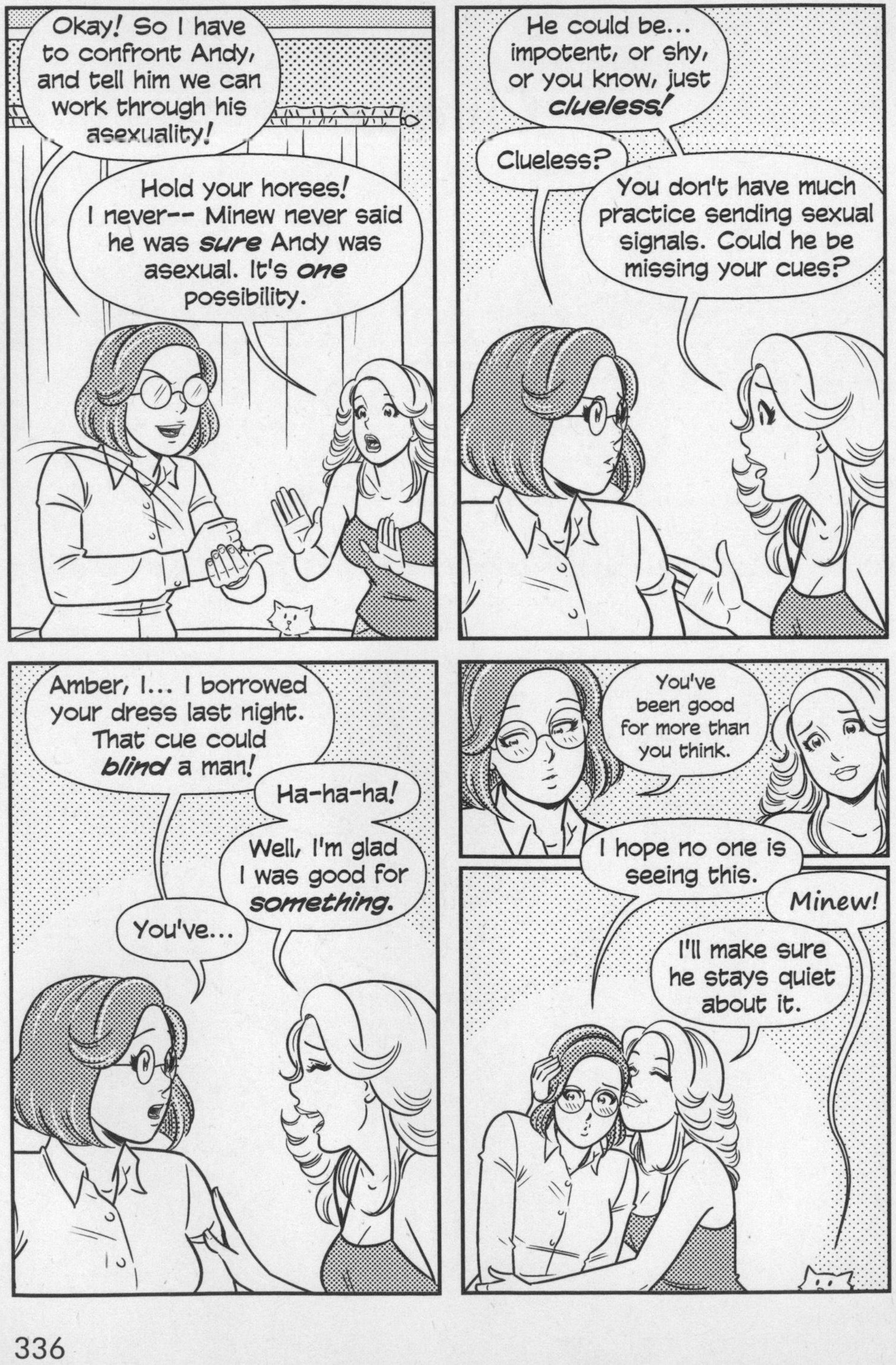
Okay! So I have to confront Andy, and tell him we can work through his asexuality!
Hold your horses! I never-- Minew never said he was *sure* Andy was asexual. It's *one* possibility.
He could be... impotent, or shy, or you know, just *clueless!*
Clueless?
You don't have much practice sending sexual signals. Could he be missing your cues?
Amber, I... I borrowed your dress last night. That cue could *blind* a man!
Ha-ha-ha!
Well, I'm glad I was good for *something*.
You've...
You've been good for more than you think.
I hope no one is seeing this.
Minew!
I'll make sure he stays quiet about it.

Climax

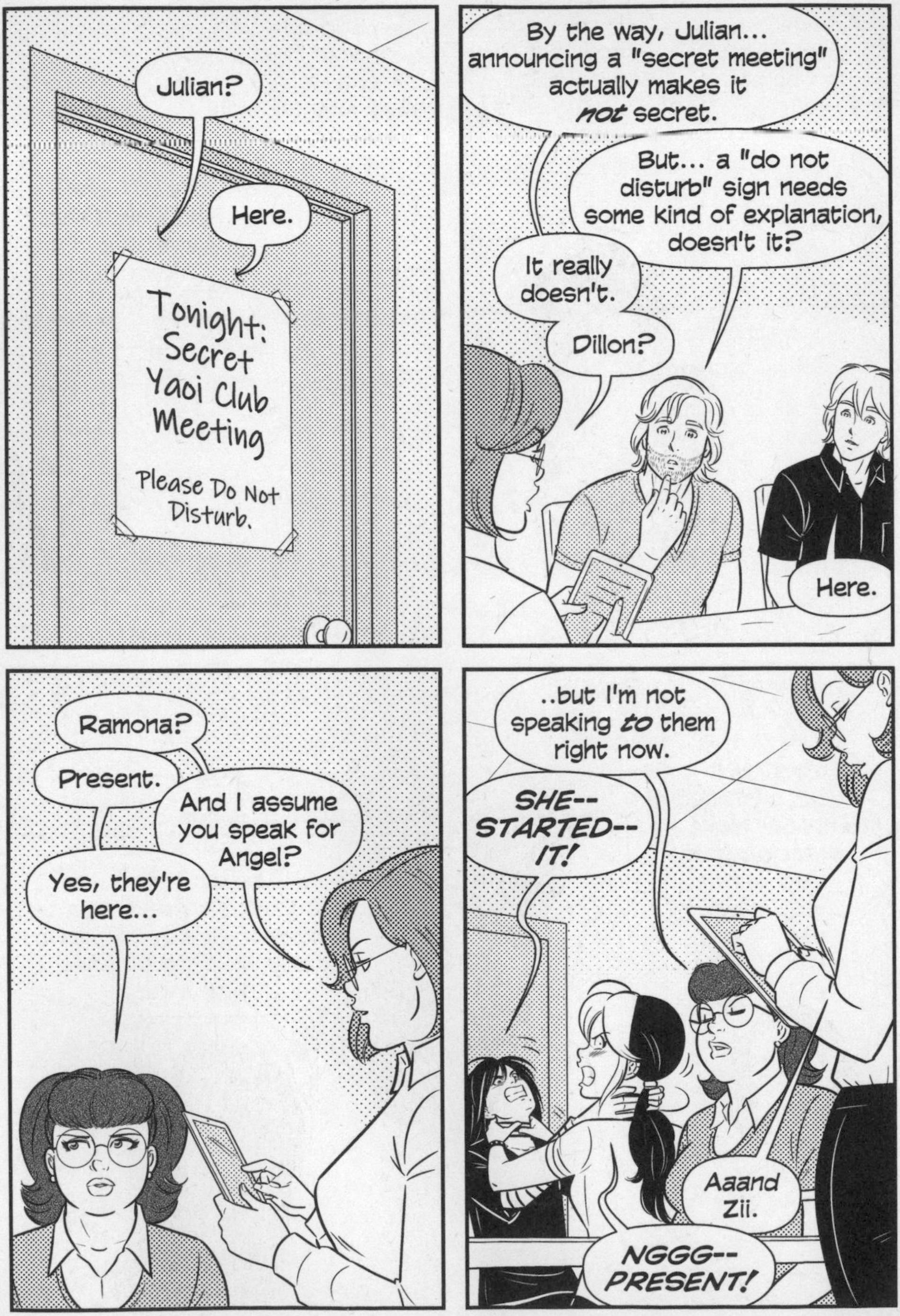
Julian?
Here.
Tonight: Secret Yaoi Club Meeting
Please Do Not Disturb.
By the way, Julian... announcing a "secret meeting" actually makes it *not* secret.
But... a "do not disturb" sign needs some kind of explanation, doesn't it?
It really doesn't.
Dillon?
Here.
Ramona?
Present.
And I assume you speak for Angel?
Yes, they're here...
..but I'm not speaking *to* them right now.
SHE-- STARTED-- IT!
Aaand Zii.
NGGG-- PRESENT!

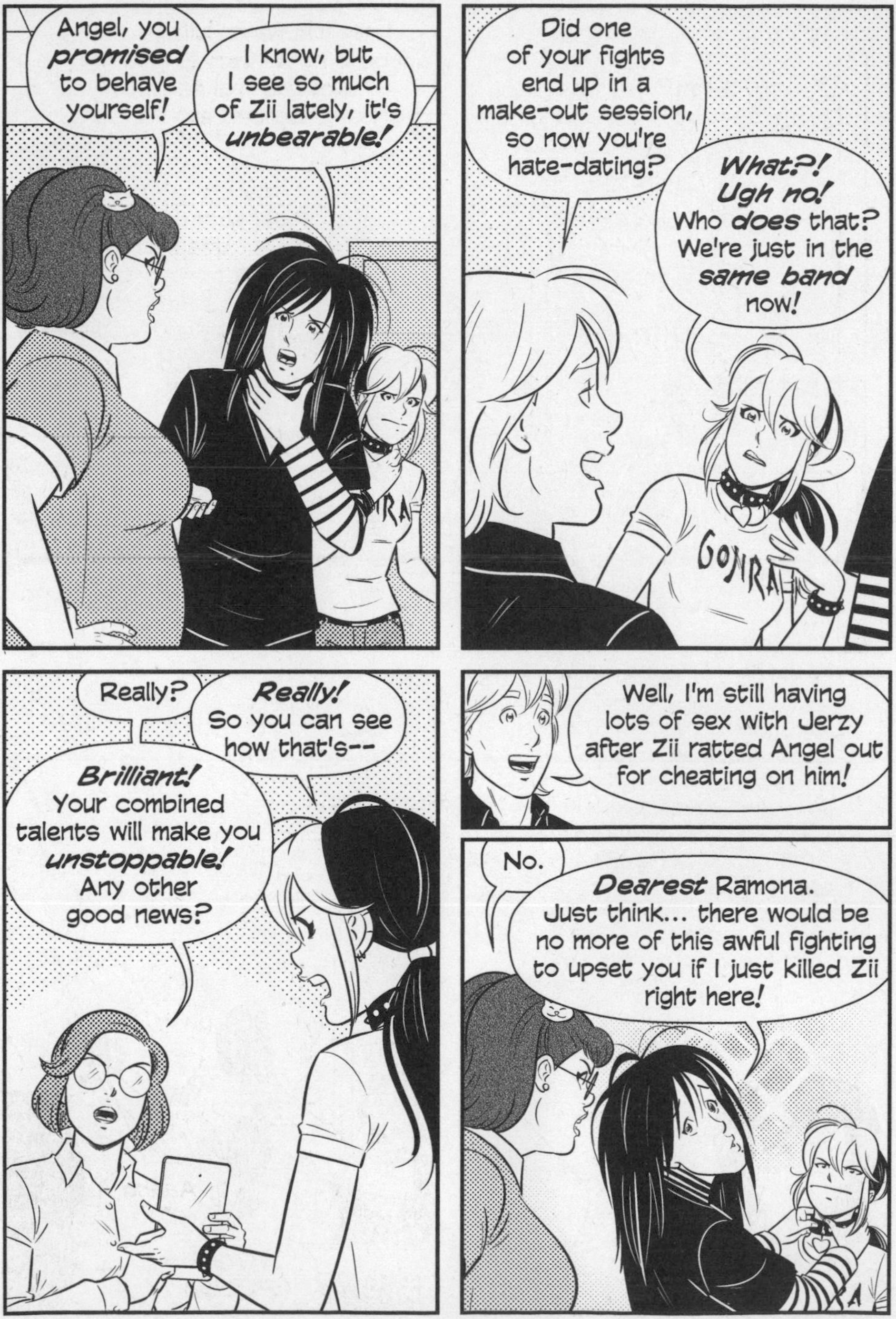
Angel, you promised to behave yourself!
I know, but I see so much of Zii lately, it's unbearable!
Did one of your fights end up in a make-out session, so now you're hate-dating?
What?! Ugh no! Who does that? We're just in the same band now!
GONRA
Really?
Really! So you can see how that's--
Brilliant! Your combined talents will make you unstoppable! Any other good news?
Well, I'm still having lots of sex with Jerzy after Zii ratted Angel out for cheating on him!
No.
Dearest Ramona. Just think... there would be no more of this awful fighting to upset you if I just killed Zii right here!

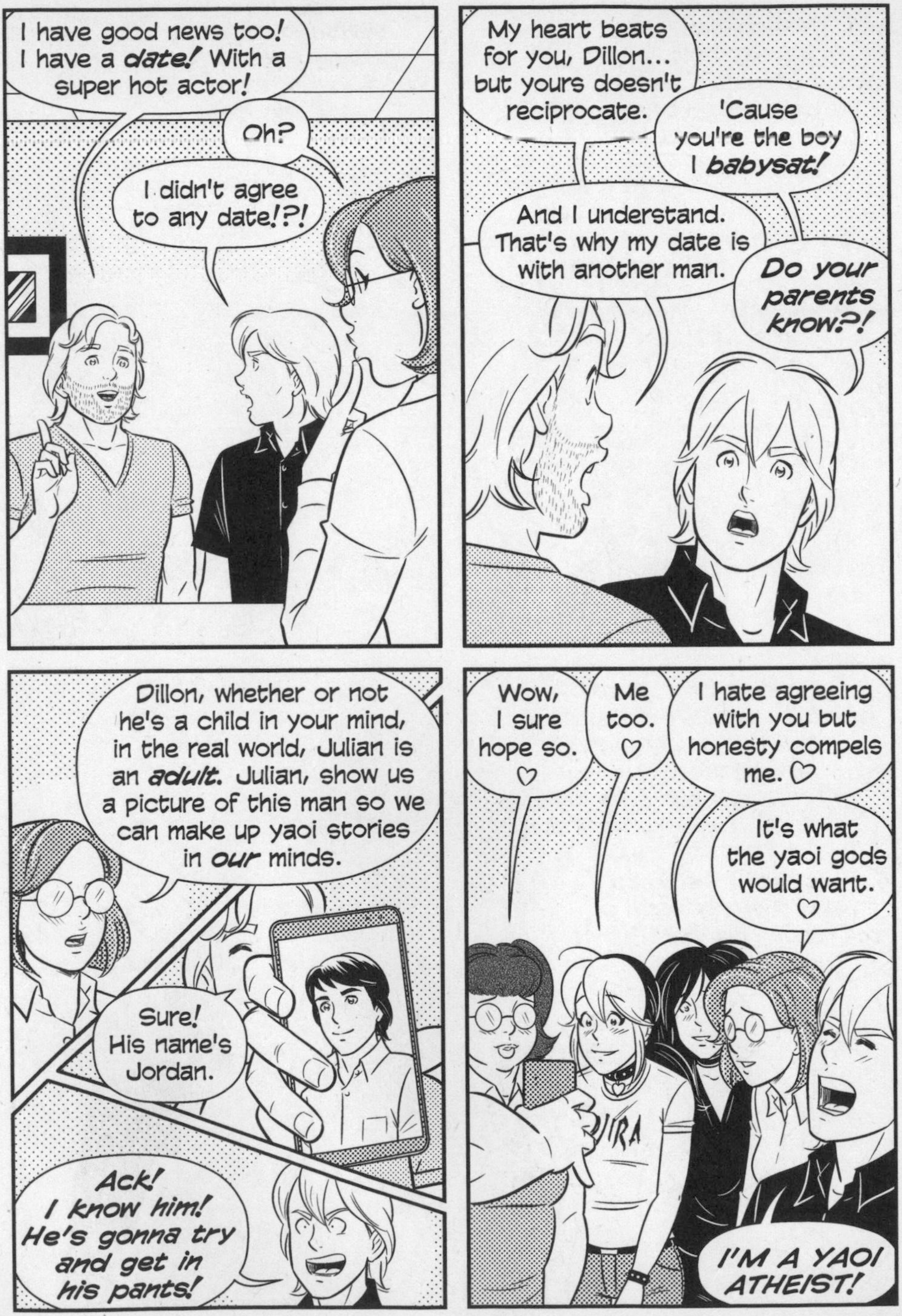
I have good news too! I have a date! With a super hot actor!
Oh?
I didn't agree to any date!?!
My heart beats for you, Dillon... but yours doesn't reciprocate.
'Cause you're the boy I babysat!
And I understand. That's why my date is with another man.
Do your parents know?!
Dillon, whether or not he's a child in your mind, in the real world, Julian is an adult. Julian, show us a picture of this man so we can make up yaoi stories in our minds.
Sure! His name's Jordan.
Ack! I know him! He's gonna try and get in his pants!
Wow, I sure hope so. ♡
Me too. ♡
I hate agreeing with you but honesty compels me. ♡
It's what the yaoi gods would want. ♡
I'M A YAOI ATHEIST!

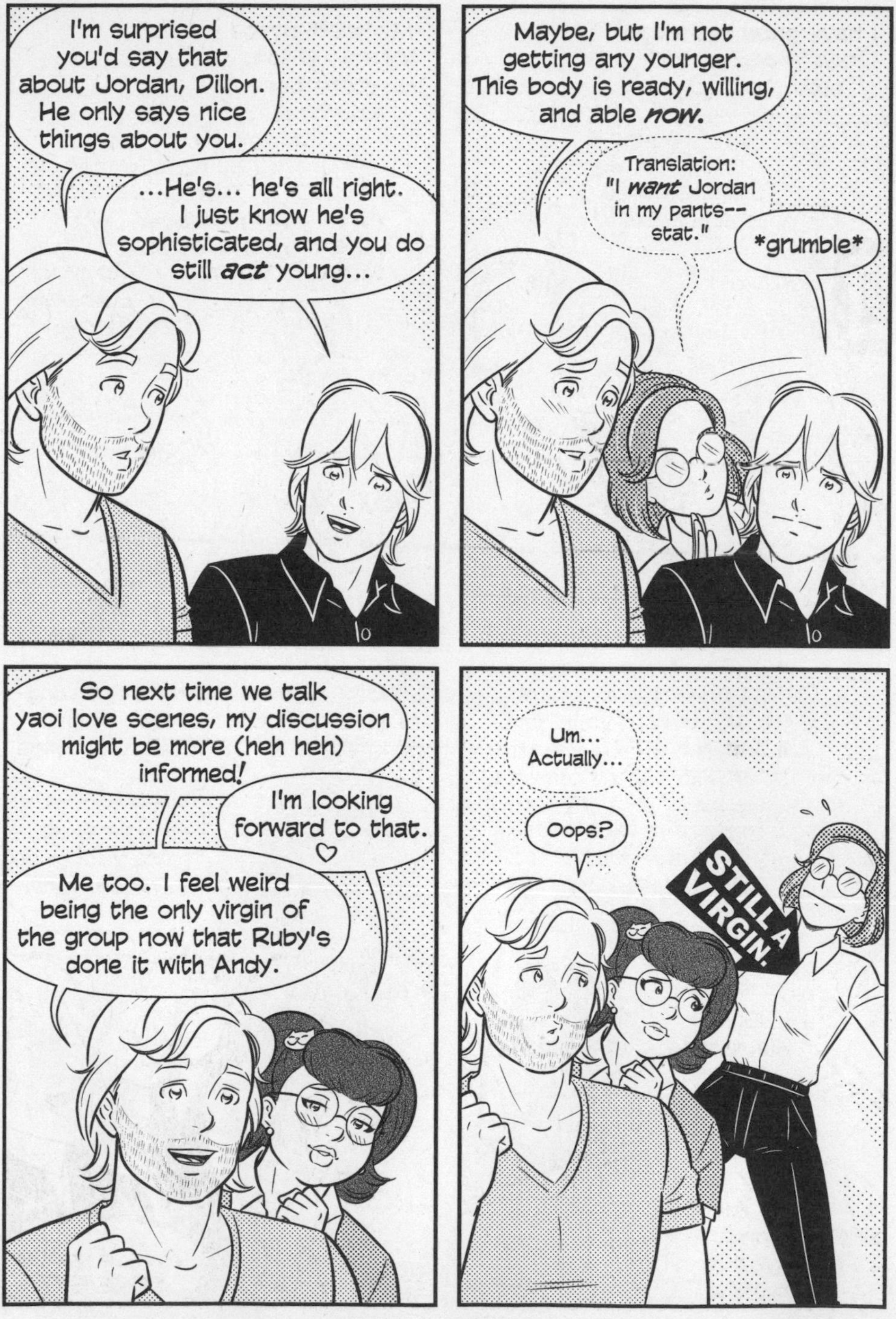
I'm surprised you'd say that about Jordan, Dillon. He only says nice things about you.
...He's... he's all right. I just know he's sophisticated, and you do still *act* young...
Maybe, but I'm not getting any younger. This body is ready, willing, and able ***now.***
Translation: "I *want* Jordan in my pants--stat."
grumble
So next time we talk yaoi love scenes, my discussion might be more (heh heh) informed!
I'm looking forward to that.
Me too. I feel weird being the only virgin of the group now that Ruby's done it with Andy.
Um... Actually...
Oops?
STILL A VIRGIN.

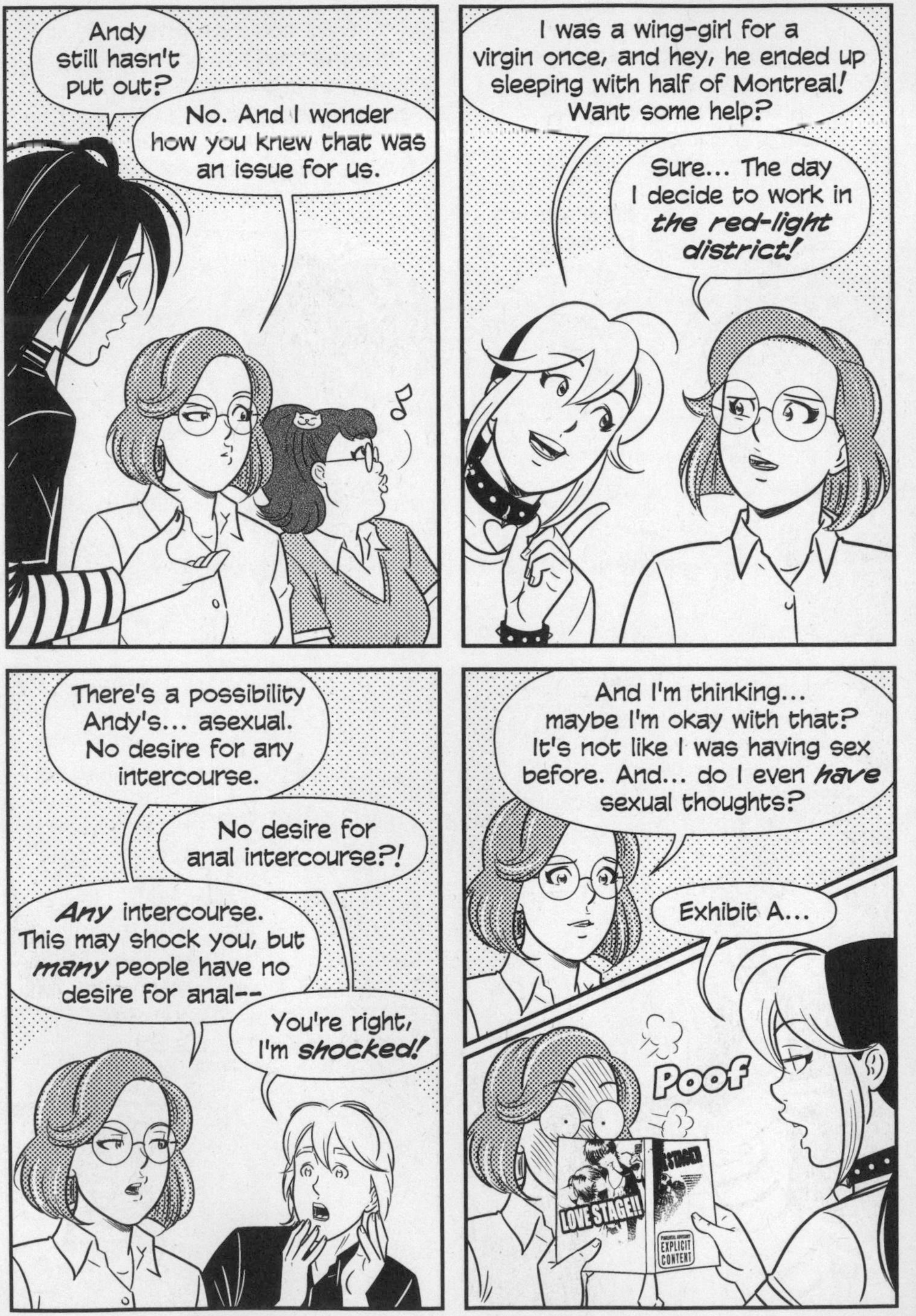

Andy still hasn't put out?
No. And I wonder how you knew that was an issue for us.
I was a wing-girl for a virgin once, and hey, he ended up sleeping with half of Montreal! Want some help?
Sure... The day I decide to work in *the red-light district!*
There's a possibility Andy's... asexual. No desire for any intercourse.
No desire for anal intercourse?!
Any intercourse. This may shock you, but *many* people have no desire for anal--
You're right, I'm *shocked!*
And I'm thinking... maybe I'm okay with that? It's not like I was having sex before. And... do I even *have* sexual thoughts?
Exhibit A...
Poof
LOVE STAGE!!
EXPLICIT CONTENT

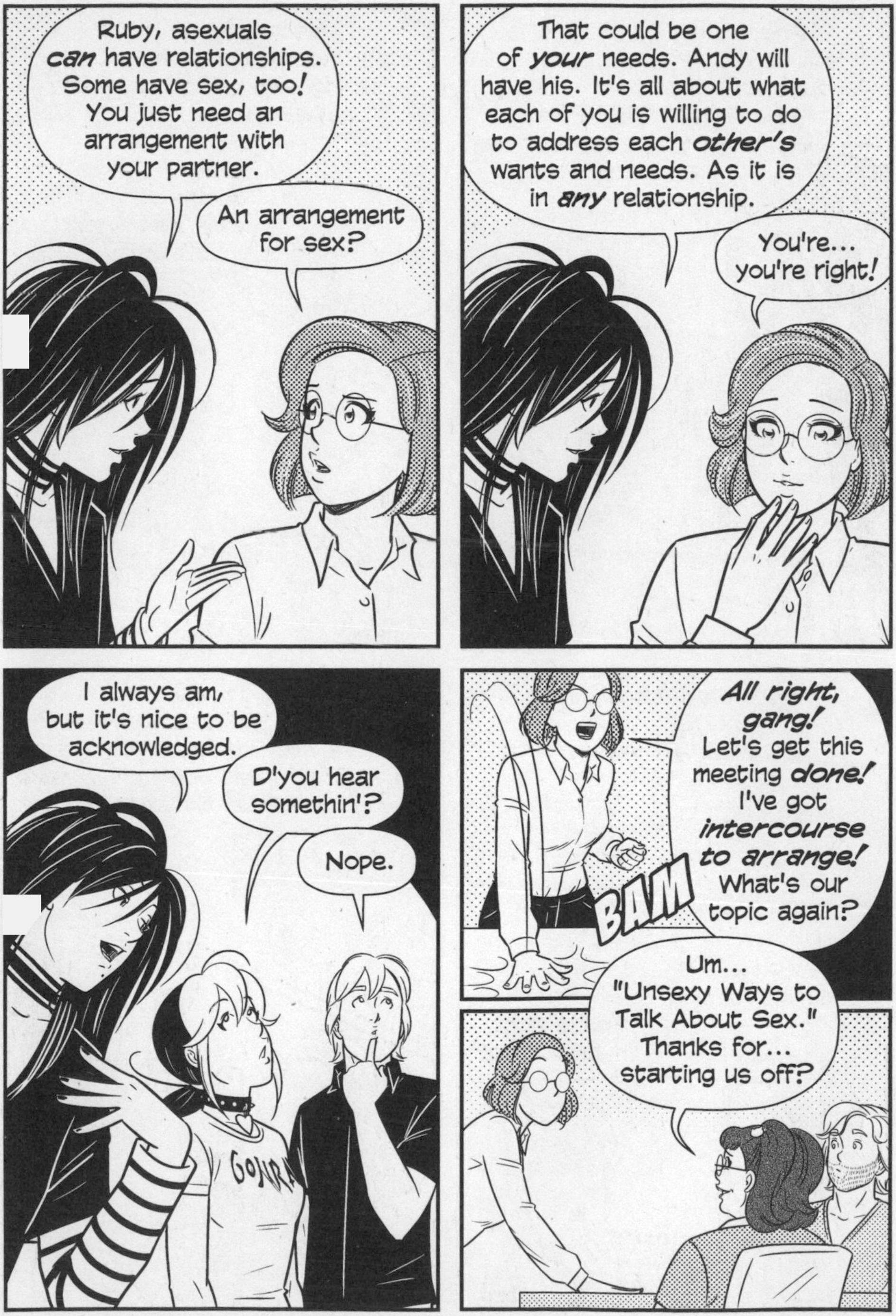

Ruby, asexuals *can* have relationships. Some have sex, too! You just need an arrangement with your partner.
An arrangement for sex?
That could be one of *your* needs. Andy will have his. It's all about what each of you is willing to do to address each *other's* wants and needs. As it is in *any* relationship.
You're... you're right!
I always am, but it's nice to be acknowledged.
D'you hear somethin'?
Nope.
GONR
All right, gang! Let's get this meeting *done!* I've got *intercourse to arrange!* What's our topic again?
BAM
Um... "Unsexy Ways to Talk About Sex." Thanks for... starting us off?

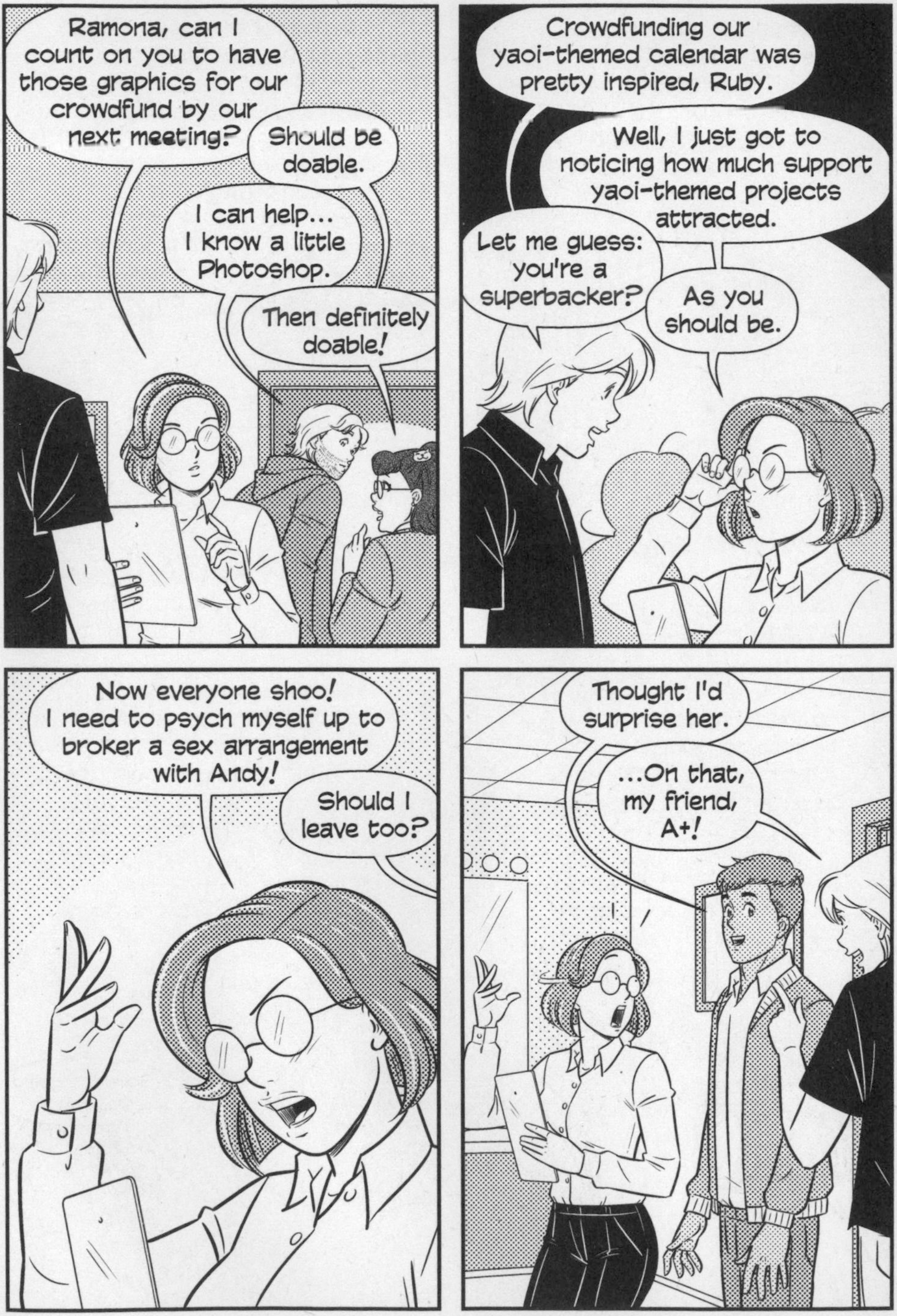
Ramona, can I count on you to have those graphics for our crowdfund by our next meeting?
Should be doable.
I can help... I know a little Photoshop.
Then definitely doable!
Crowdfunding our yaoi-themed calendar was pretty inspired, Ruby.
Well, I just got to noticing how much support yaoi-themed projects attracted.
Let me guess: you're a superbacker?
As you should be.
Now everyone shoo! I need to psych myself up to broker a sex arrangement with Andy!
Should I leave too?
Thought I'd surprise her.
...On that, my friend, A+!

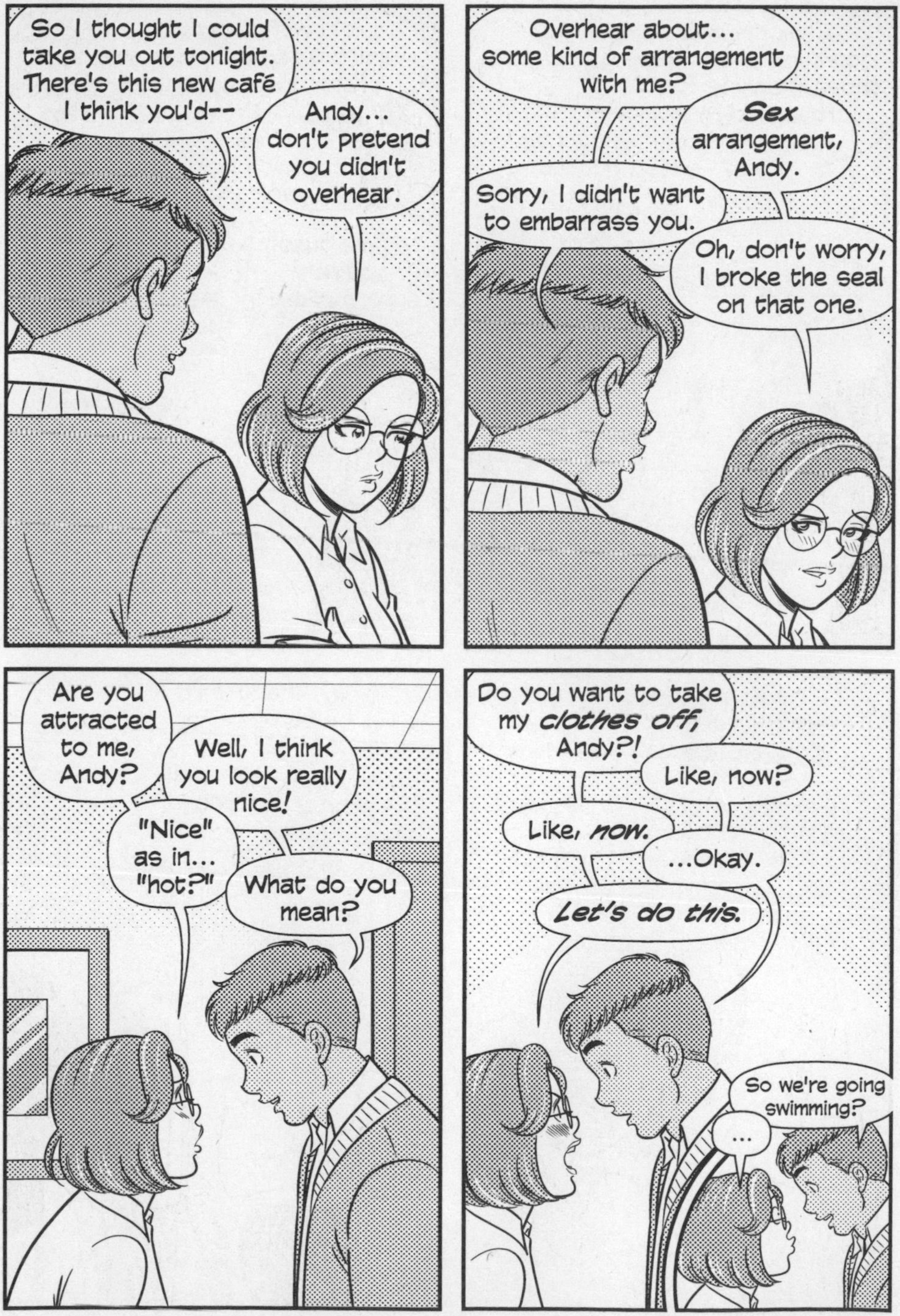
So I thought I could take you out tonight. There's this new café I think you'd--
Andy... don't pretend you didn't overhear.
Overhear about... some kind of arrangement with me?
Sex arrangement, Andy.
Sorry, I didn't want to embarrass you.
Oh, don't worry, I broke the seal on that one.
Are you attracted to me, Andy?
Well, I think you look really nice!
"Nice" as in... "hot?"
What do you mean?
Do you want to take my clothes off, Andy?!
Like, now?
Like, now.
...Okay.
Let's do this.
So we're going swimming?
...

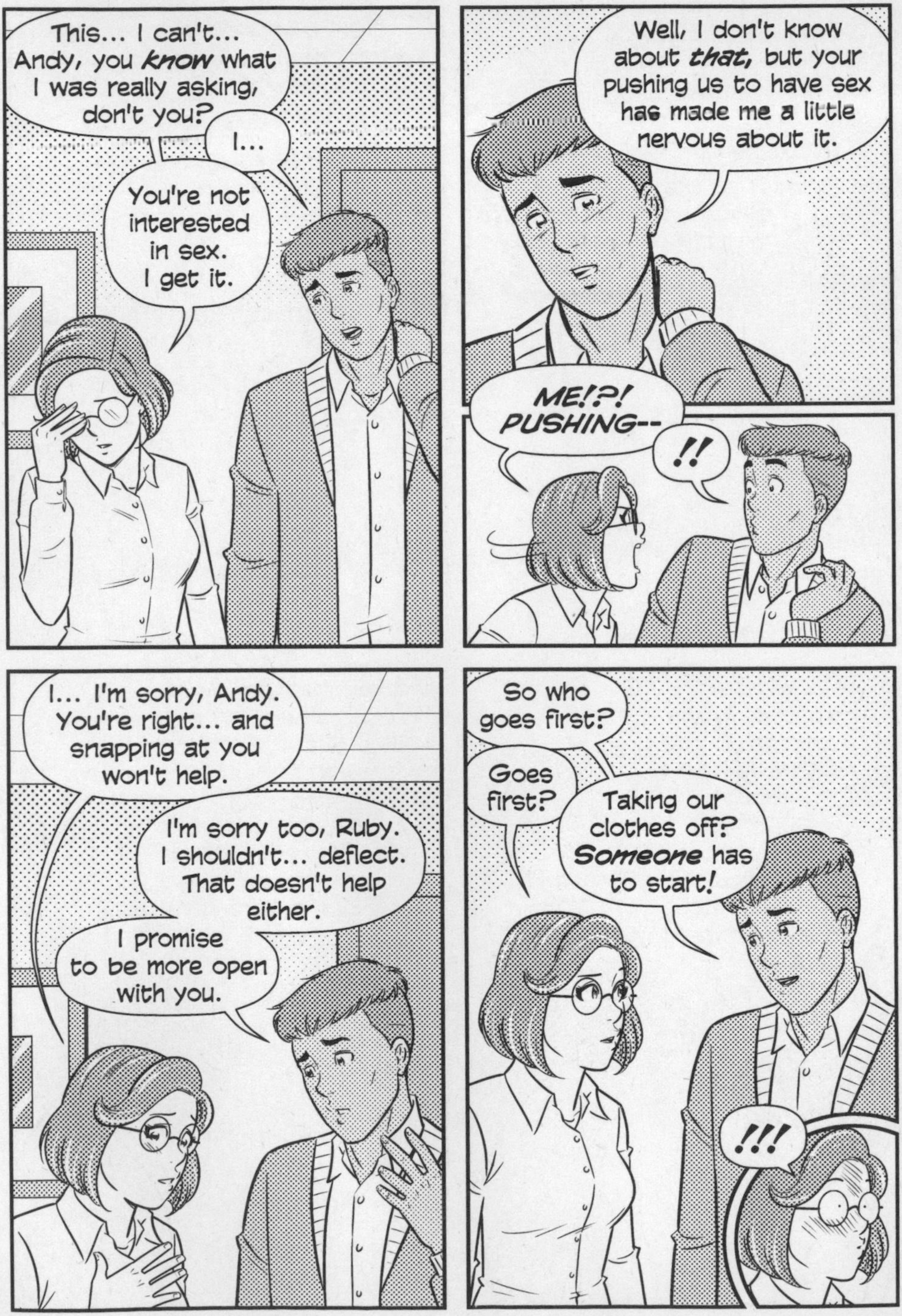
This... I can't... Andy, you *know* what I was really asking, don't you?
I...
You're not interested in sex. I get it.
Well, I don't know about *that,* but your pushing us to have sex has made me a little nervous about it.
ME!?! PUSHING--
!!
I... I'm sorry, Andy. You're right... and snapping at you won't help.
I'm sorry too, Ruby. I shouldn't... deflect. That doesn't help either.
I promise to be more open with you.
So who goes first?
Goes first?
Taking our clothes off? *Someone* has to start!
!!!

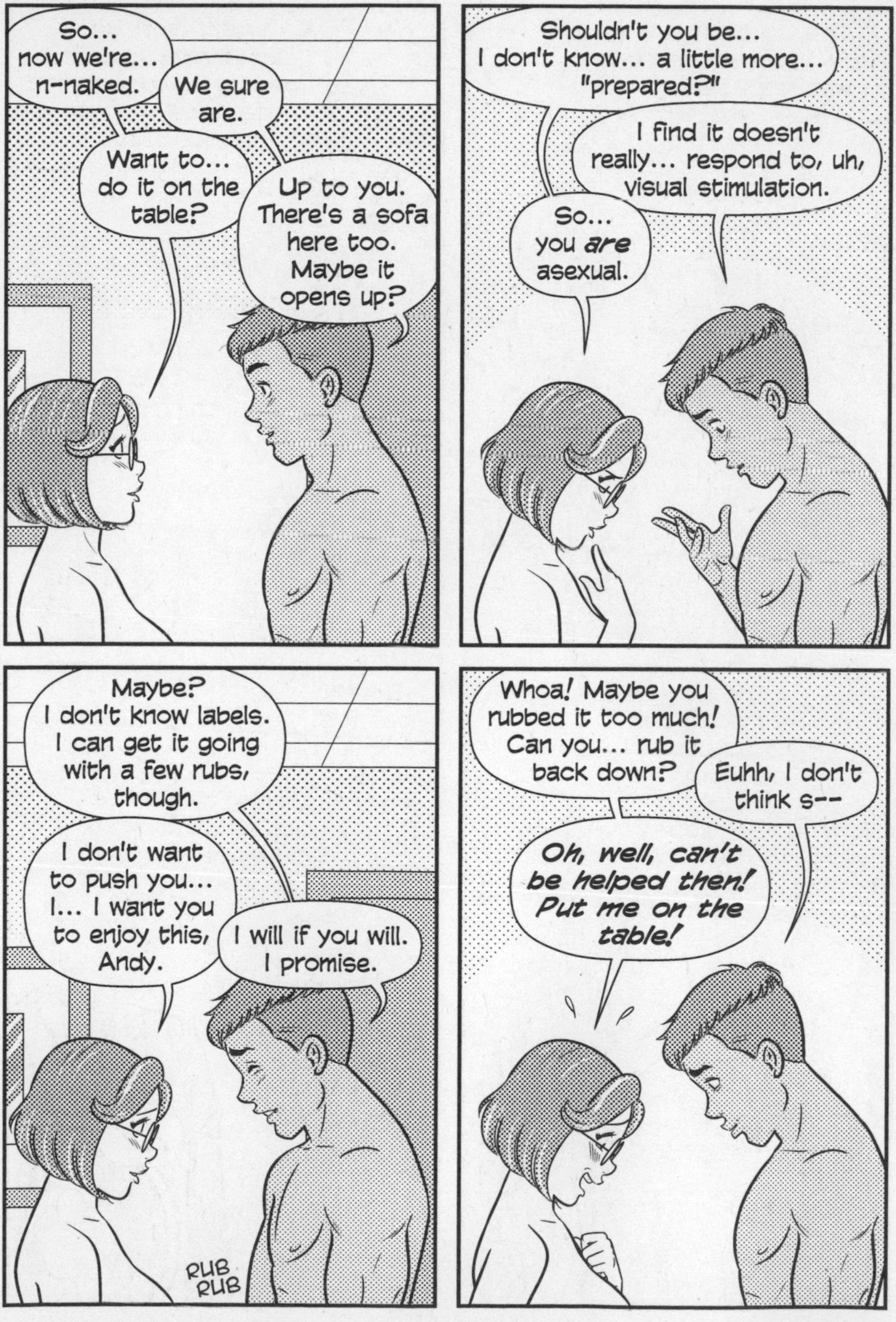

So... now we're... n-naked.
We sure are.
Want to... do it on the table?
Up to you. There's a sofa here too. Maybe it opens up?
Shouldn't you be... I don't know... a little more... "prepared?"
I find it doesn't really... respond to, uh, visual stimulation.
So... you *are* asexual.
Maybe? I don't know labels. I can get it going with a few rubs, though.
I don't want to push you... I... I want you to enjoy this, Andy.
I will if you will. I promise.
RUB RUB
Whoa! Maybe you rubbed it too much! Can you... rub it back down?
Euhh, I don't think s--
Oh, well, can't be helped then! Put me on the table!

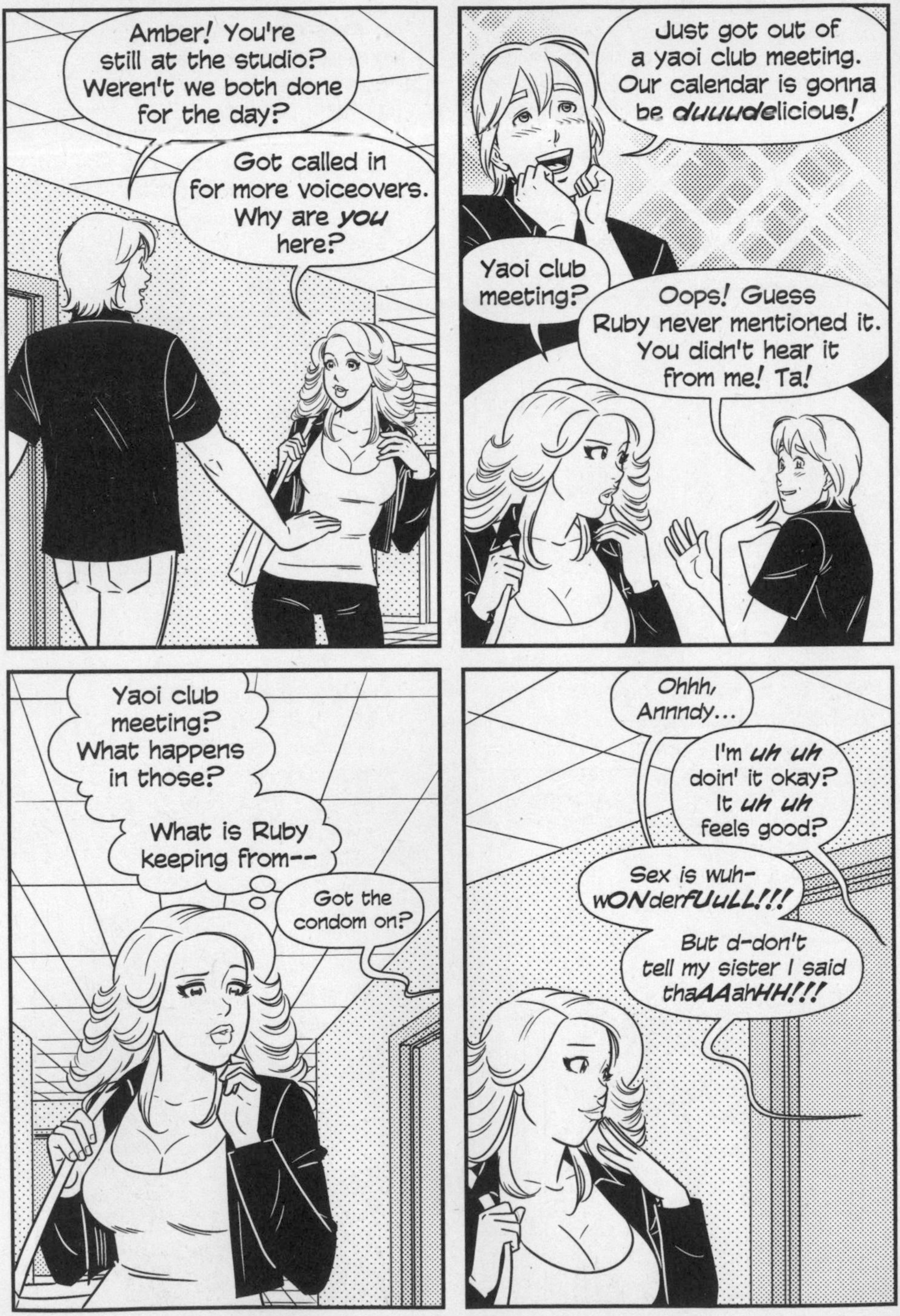
Amber! You're still at the studio? Weren't we both done for the day?
Got called in for more voiceovers. Why are *you* here?
Just got out of a yaoi club meeting. Our calendar is gonna be *duuude*licious!
Yaoi club meeting?
Oops! Guess Ruby never mentioned it. You didn't hear it from me! Ta!
Yaoi club meeting? What happens in those?
What is Ruby keeping from--
Got the condom on?
Ohhh, Annndy...
I'm *uh uh* doin' it okay? It *uh uh* feels good?
Sex is wuh-wONderfUuLL!!!
But d-don't tell my sister I said thaAAahHH!!!

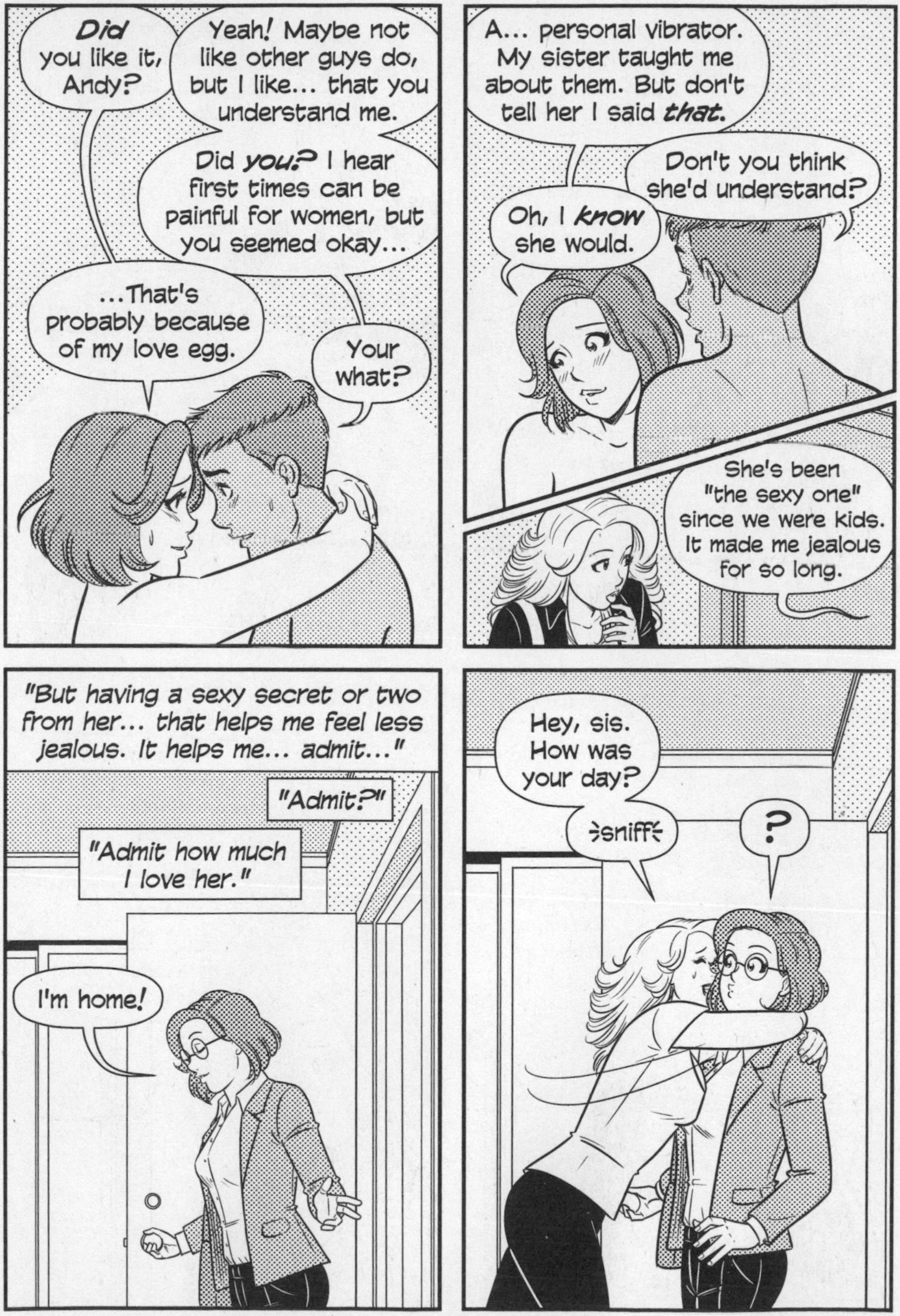
Did you like it, Andy?
Yeah! Maybe not like other guys do, but I like... that you understand me.
Did you? I hear first times can be painful for women, but you seemed okay...
...That's probably because of my love egg.
Your what?
A... personal vibrator. My sister taught me about them. But don't tell her I said that.
Don't you think she'd understand?
Oh, I know she would.
She's been "the sexy one" since we were kids. It made me jealous for so long.
"But having a sexy secret or two from her... that helps me feel less jealous. It helps me... admit..."
"Admit?"
"Admit how much I love her."
I'm home!
Hey, sis. How was your day?
sniff
?

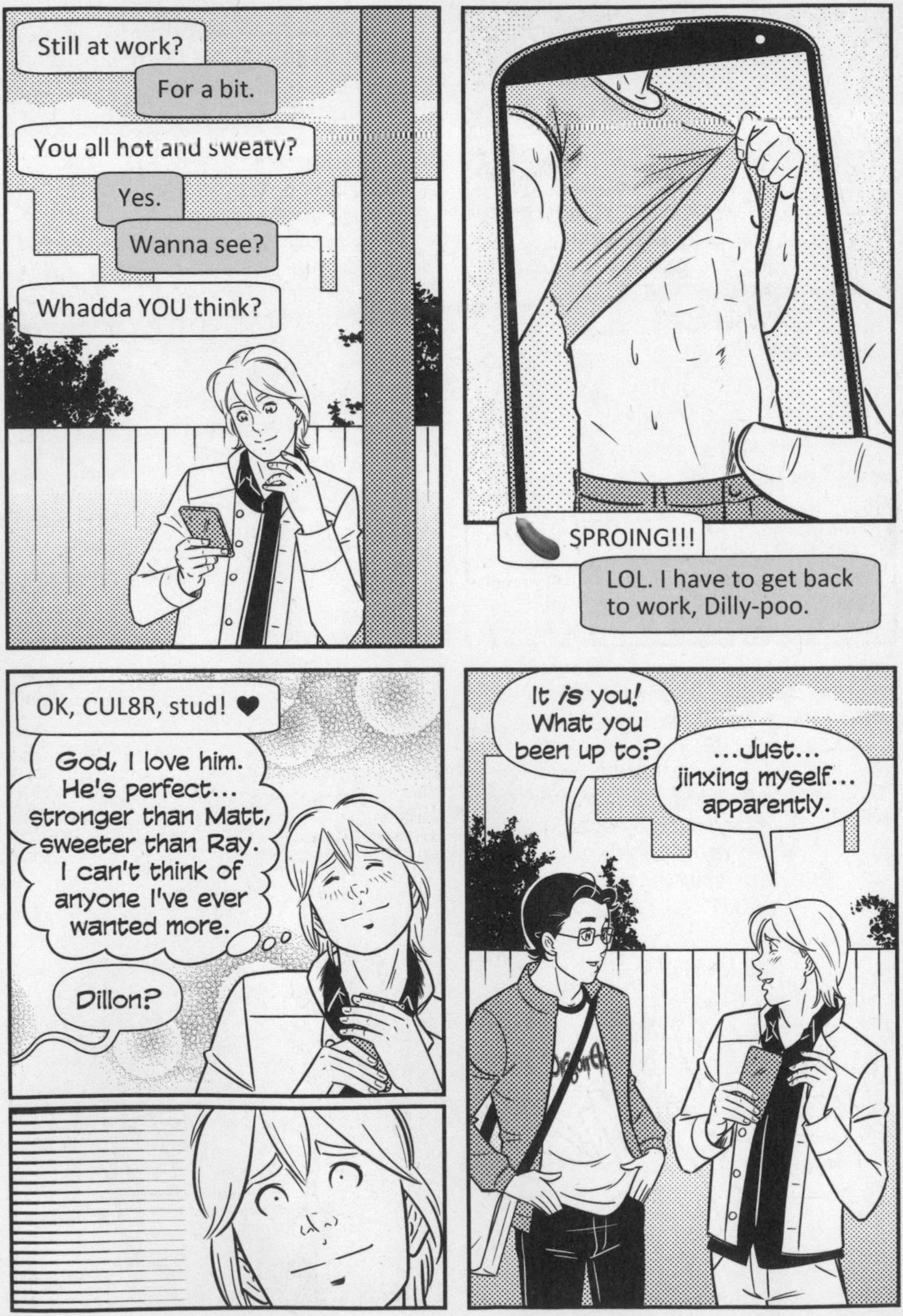

Still at work?
For a bit.
You all hot and sweaty?
Yes.
Wanna see?
Whadda YOU think?
SPROING!!!
LOL. I have to get back to work, Dilly-poo.
OK, CUL8R, stud! ♥
God, I love him. He's perfect... stronger than Matt, sweeter than Ray. I can't think of anyone I've ever wanted more.
Dillon?
It *is* you! What you been up to?
...Just... jinxing myself... apparently.

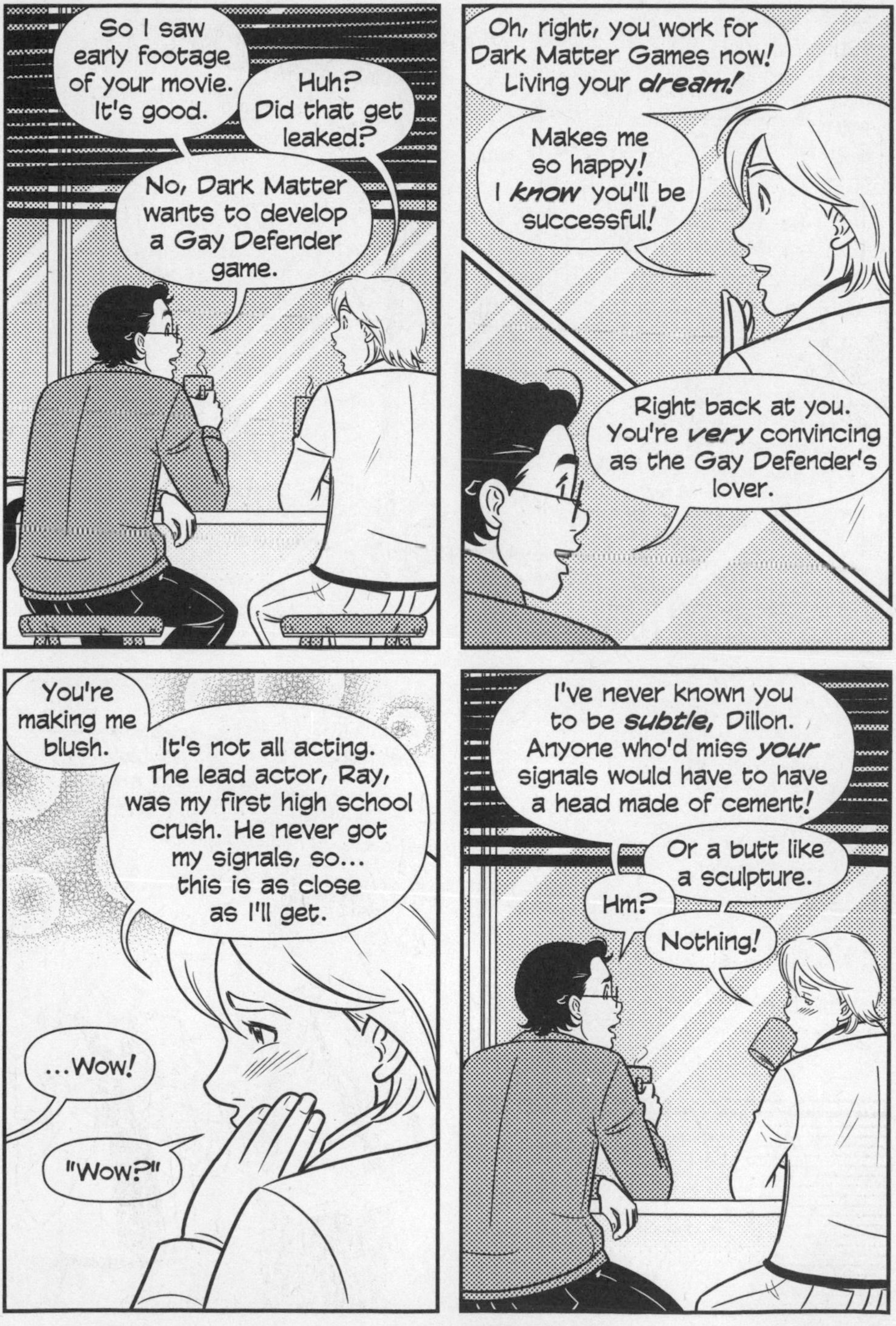
So I saw early footage of your movie. It's good.
Huh? Did that get leaked?
No, Dark Matter wants to develop a Gay Defender game.
Oh, right, you work for Dark Matter Games now! Living your *dream!*
Makes me so happy! I *know* you'll be successful!
Right back at you. You're *very* convincing as the Gay Defender's lover.
You're making me blush.
It's not all acting. The lead actor, Ray, was my first high school crush. He never got my signals, so... this is as close as I'll get.
...Wow!
"Wow?"
I've never known you to be *subtle,* Dillon. Anyone who'd miss *your* signals would have to have a head made of cement!
Or a butt like a sculpture.
Hm?
Nothing!

Tell Ray how you feel, Dillon. Be direct. My love life's a lot better since I started doing that.

Right. How is Yuki?

Euhhh, dating Matt now.

Matt?! *My* Matt?

Yup.

He gets around!

He does. But... so have I, lately. And taking your advice... helped me a lot, there.

So I hope you'll take mine.

Not long ago, I told a casual partner I was ready to be... less casual. It felt great getting that off my chest. Even if she and I end up just friends... you should be honest with friends, right?

In that case...

Gary, I love you!

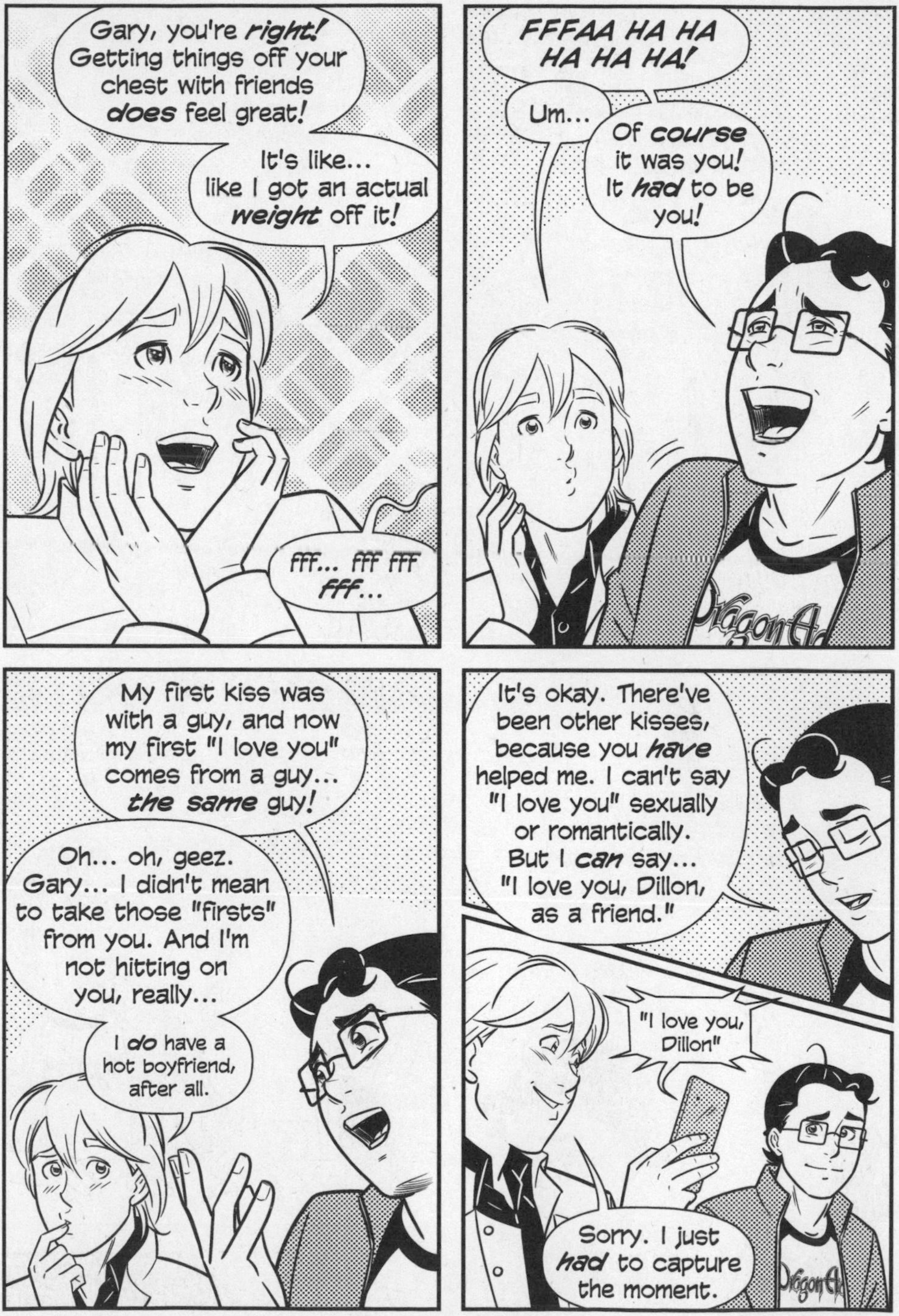
Gary, you're right! Getting things off your chest with friends does feel great!
It's like... like I got an actual weight off it!
fff... fff fff fff...
FFFAA HA HA HA HA HA!
Um...
Of course it was you! It had to be you!
DragonAc
My first kiss was with a guy, and now my first "I love you" comes from a guy... the same guy!
Oh... oh, geez. Gary... I didn't mean to take those "firsts" from you. And I'm not hitting on you, really...
I do have a hot boyfriend, after all.
It's okay. There've been other kisses, because you have helped me. I can't say "I love you" sexually or romantically. But I can say... "I love you, Dillon, as a friend."
"I love you, Dillon"
Sorry. I just had to capture the moment.
DragonAc

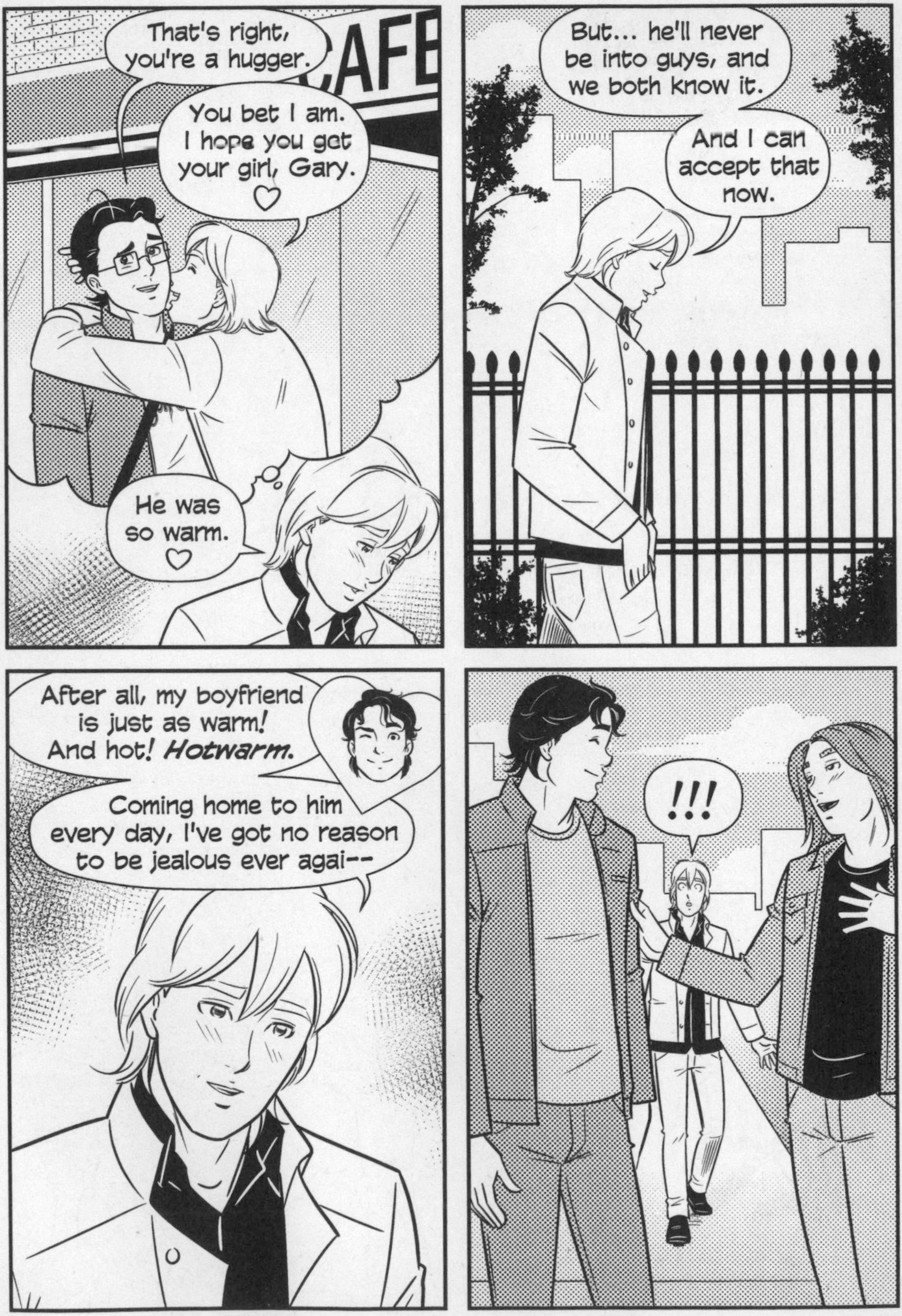
That's right, you're a hugger.
CAFE
You bet I am. I hope you get your girl, Gary.
He was so warm.
But... he'll never be into guys, and we both know it.
And I can accept that now.
After all, my boyfriend is just as warm! And hot! *Hotwarm.*
Coming home to him every day, I've got no reason to be jealous ever agai--
!!!

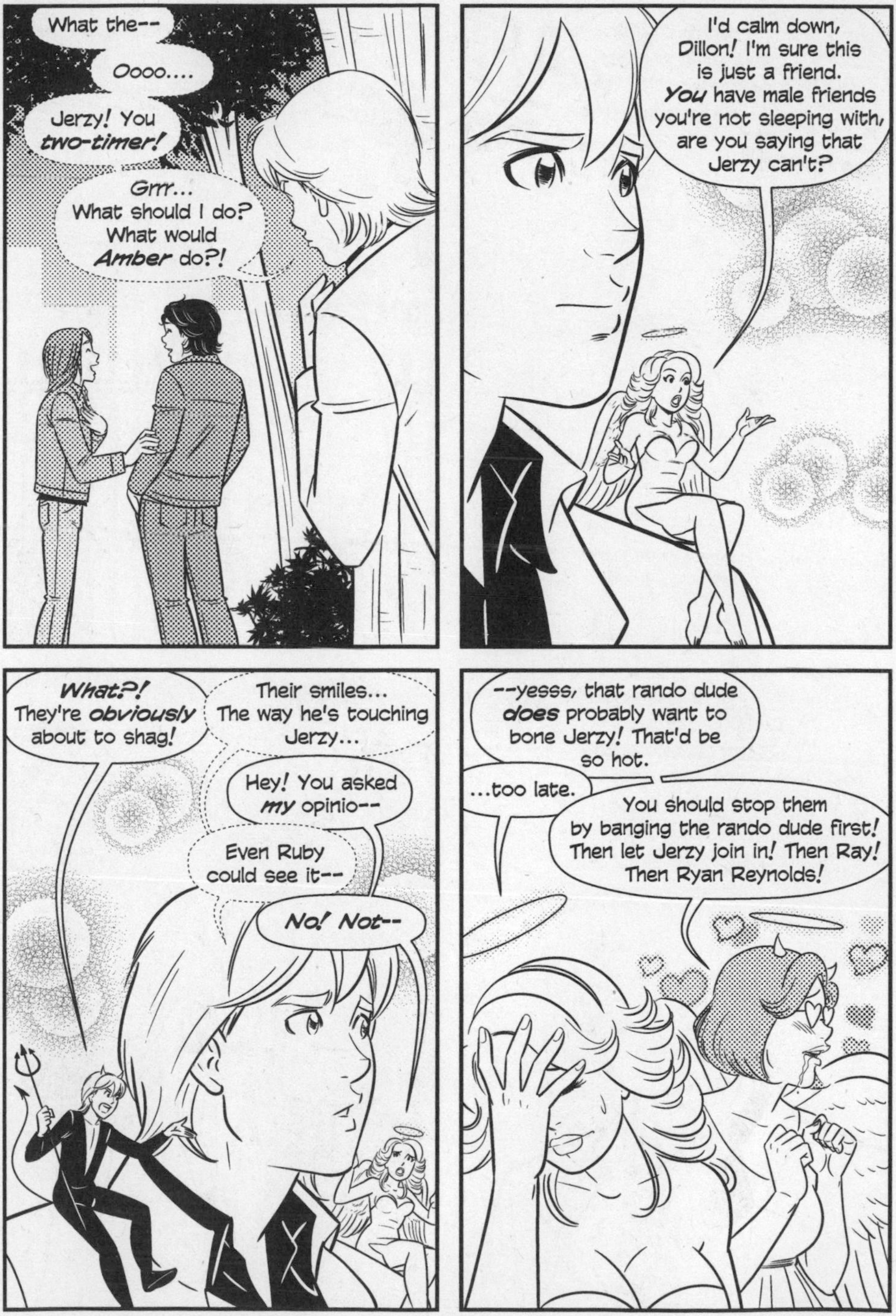
What the--
Oooo....
Jerzy! You *two-timer!*
Grrr... What should I do? What would *Amber* do?!
I'd calm down, Dillon! I'm sure this is just a friend. *You* have male friends you're not sleeping with, are you saying that Jerzy can't?
What?! They're *obviously* about to shag!
Their smiles... The way he's touching Jerzy...
Hey! You asked *my* opinio--
Even Ruby could see it--
No! Not--
--yesss, that rando dude *does* probably want to bone Jerzy! That'd be so hot.
...too late.
You should stop them by banging the rando dude first! Then let Jerzy join in! Then Ray! Then Ryan Reynolds!

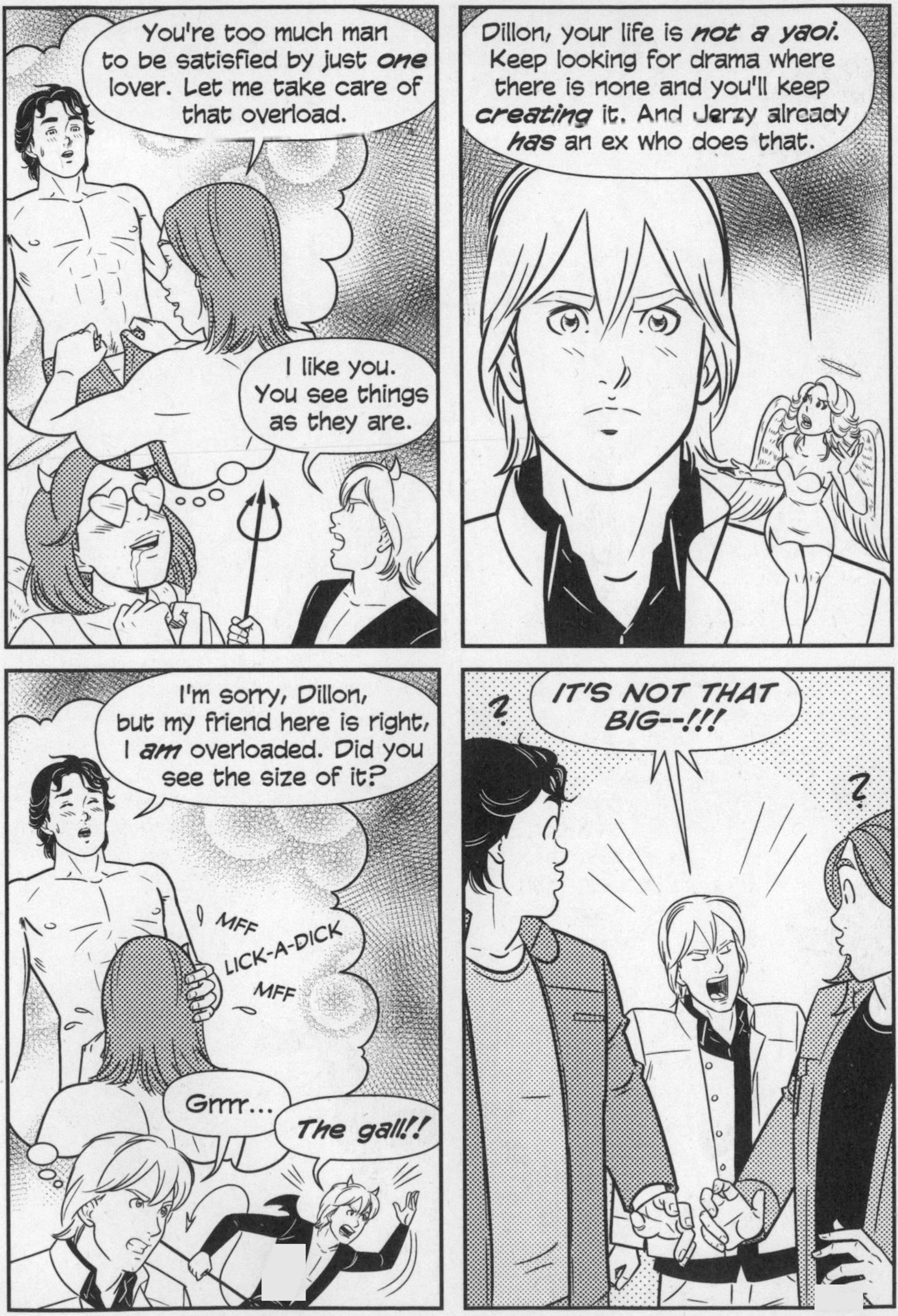

You're too much man to be satisfied by just *one* lover. Let me take care of that overload.
I like you. You see things as they are.
Dillon, your life is *not a yaoi.* Keep looking for drama where there is none and you'll keep *creating* it. And Jerzy already *has* an ex who does that.
I'm sorry, Dillon, but my friend here is right, I *am* overloaded. Did you see the size of it?
MFF
LICK-A-DICK
MFF
Grrr...
The gall!!
?
IT'S NOT THAT BIG--!!!
?

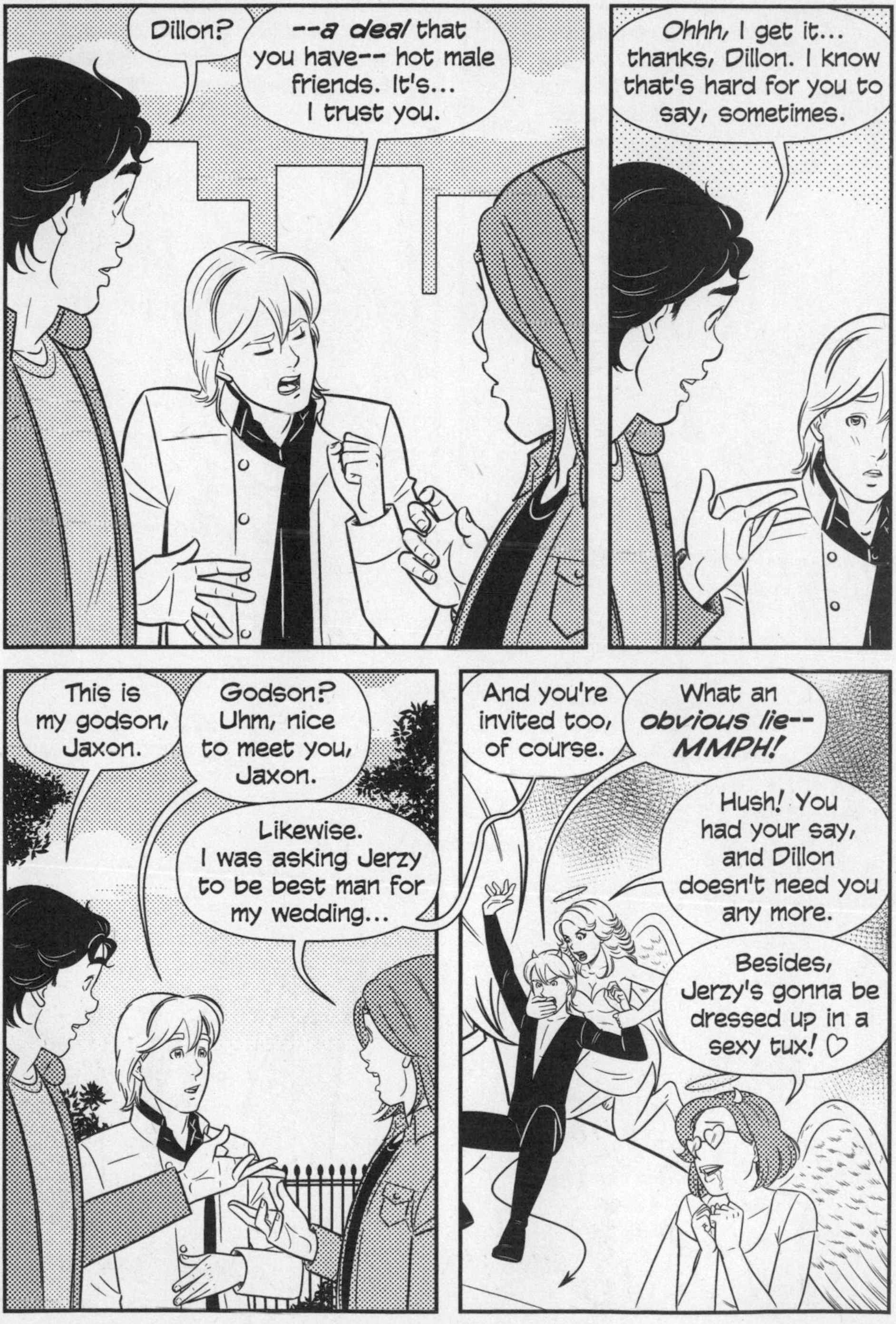
Dillon?
--a deal that you have-- hot male friends. It's... I trust you.
Ohhh, I get it... thanks, Dillon. I know that's hard for you to say, sometimes.
This is my godson, Jaxon.
Godson? Uhm, nice to meet you, Jaxon.
Likewise. I was asking Jerzy to be best man for my wedding...
And you're invited too, of course.
What an obvious lie-- MMPH!
Hush! You had your say, and Dillon doesn't need you any more.
Besides, Jerzy's gonna be dressed up in a sexy tux! ♡

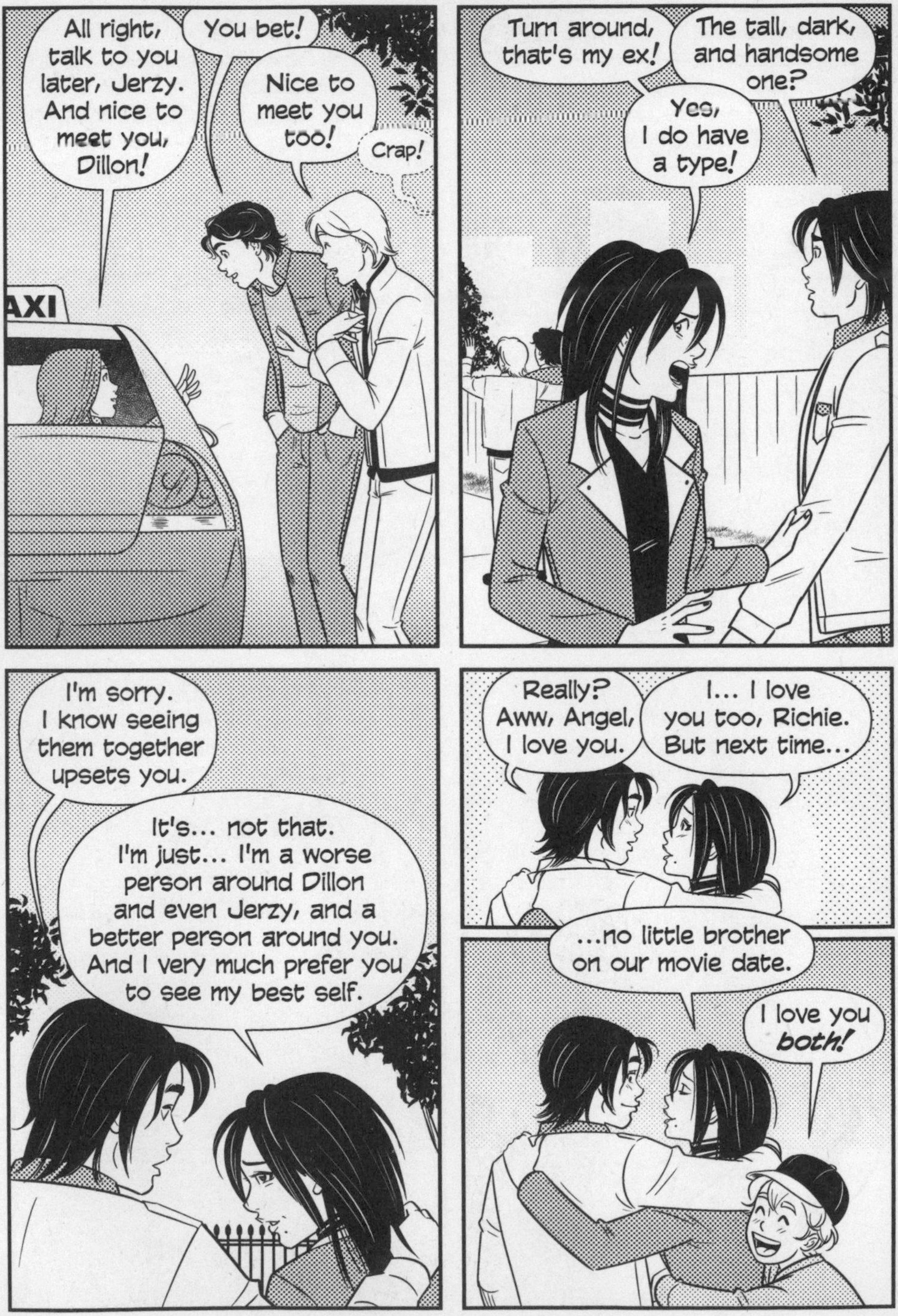
All right, talk to you later, Jerzy. And nice to meet you, Dillon!
You bet!
Nice to meet you too!
Crap!
Turn around, that's my ex!
The tall, dark, and handsome one?
Yes, I do have a type!
I'm sorry. I know seeing them together upsets you.
It's... not that. I'm just... I'm a worse person around Dillon and even Jerzy, and a better person around you. And I very much prefer you to see my best self.
Really? Aww, Angel, I love you.
I... I love you too, Richie. But next time...
...no little brother on our movie date.
I love you *both!*

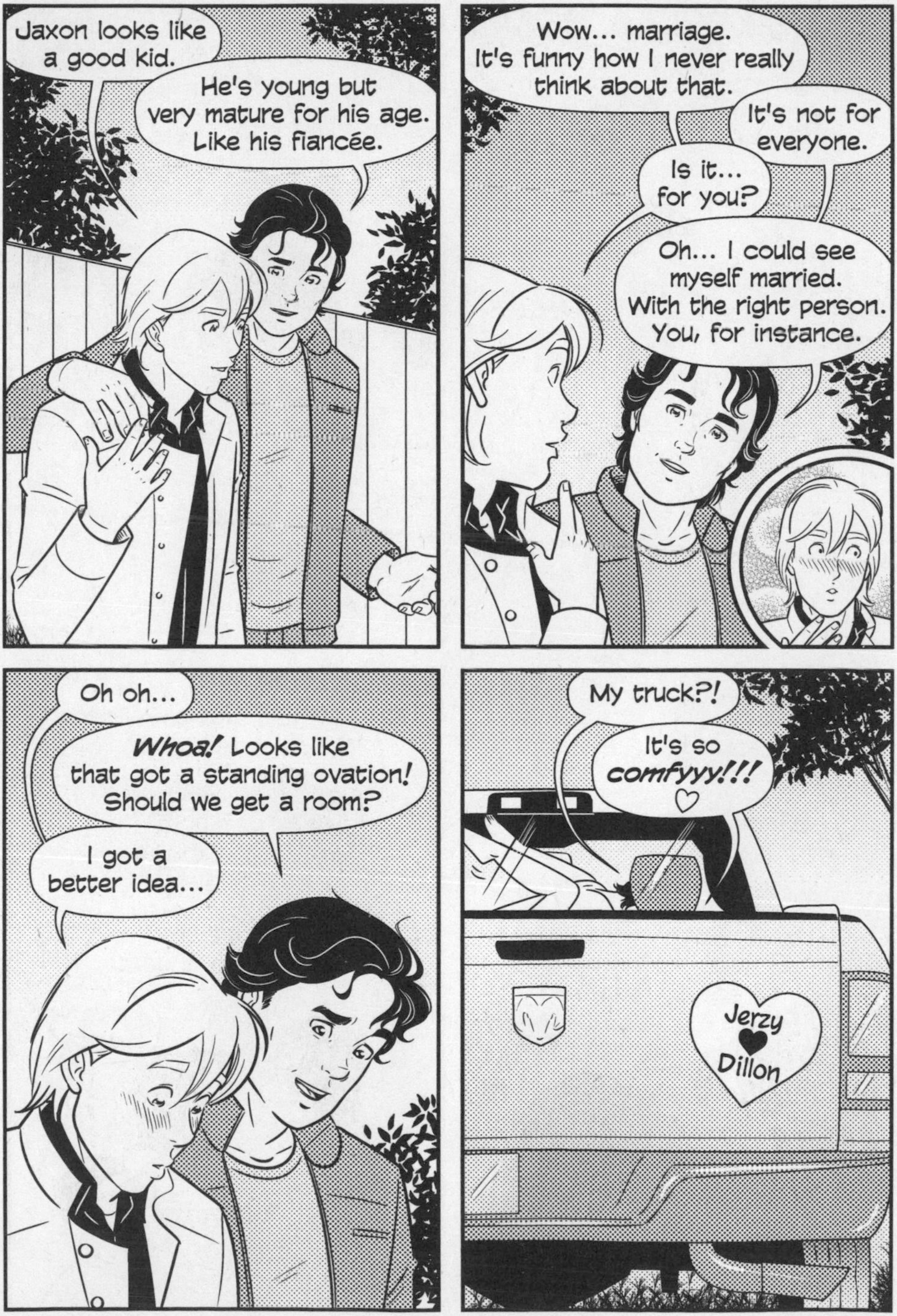
Jaxon looks like a good kid.
He's young but very mature for his age. Like his fiancée.
Wow... marriage. It's funny how I never really think about that.
It's not for everyone.
Is it... for you?
Oh... I could see myself married. With the right person. You, for instance.
Oh oh...
Whoa! Looks like that got a standing ovation! Should we get a room?
I got a better idea...
My truck?!
It's so *comfyyy!!!*
Jerzy Dillon

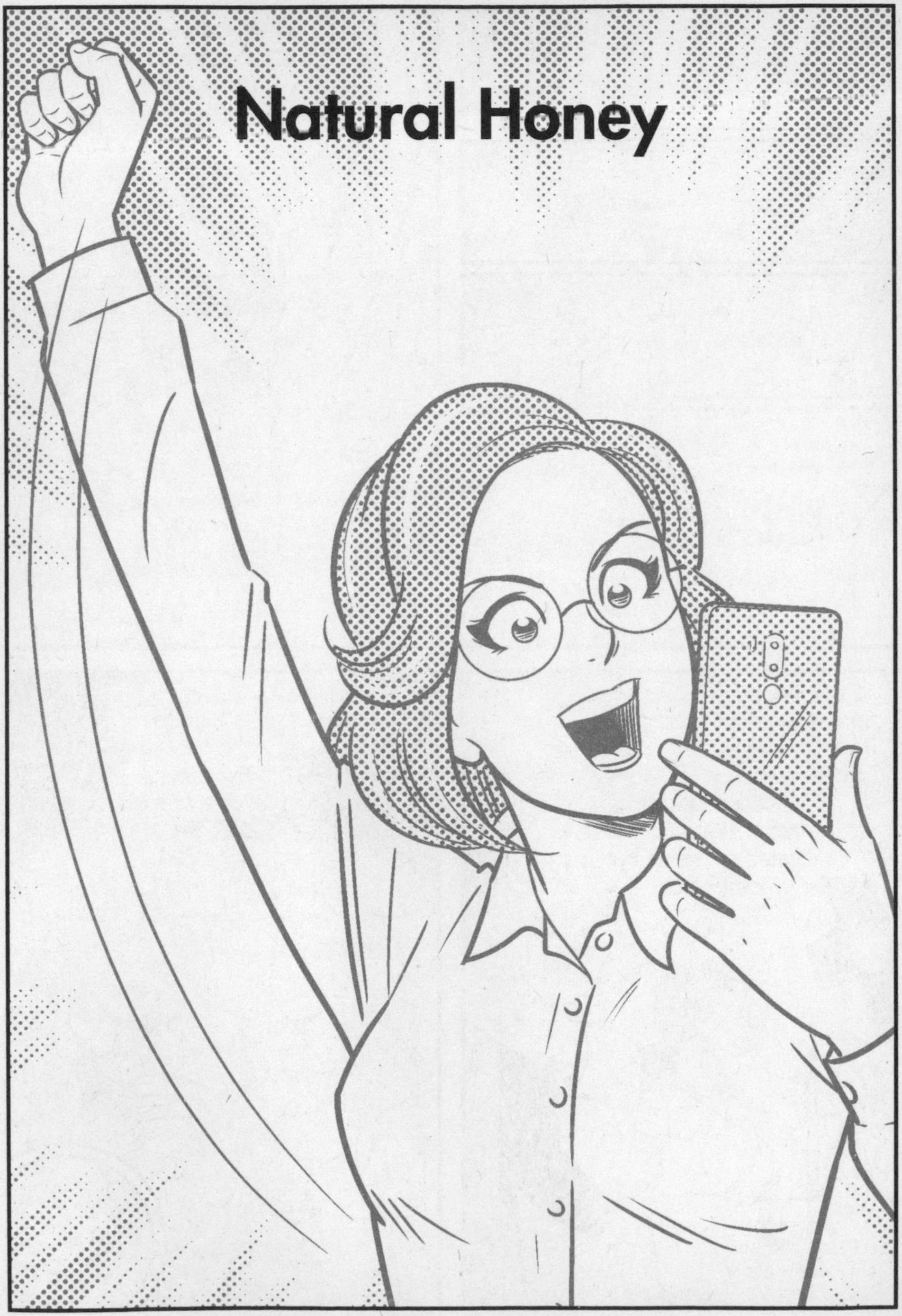
Natural Honey

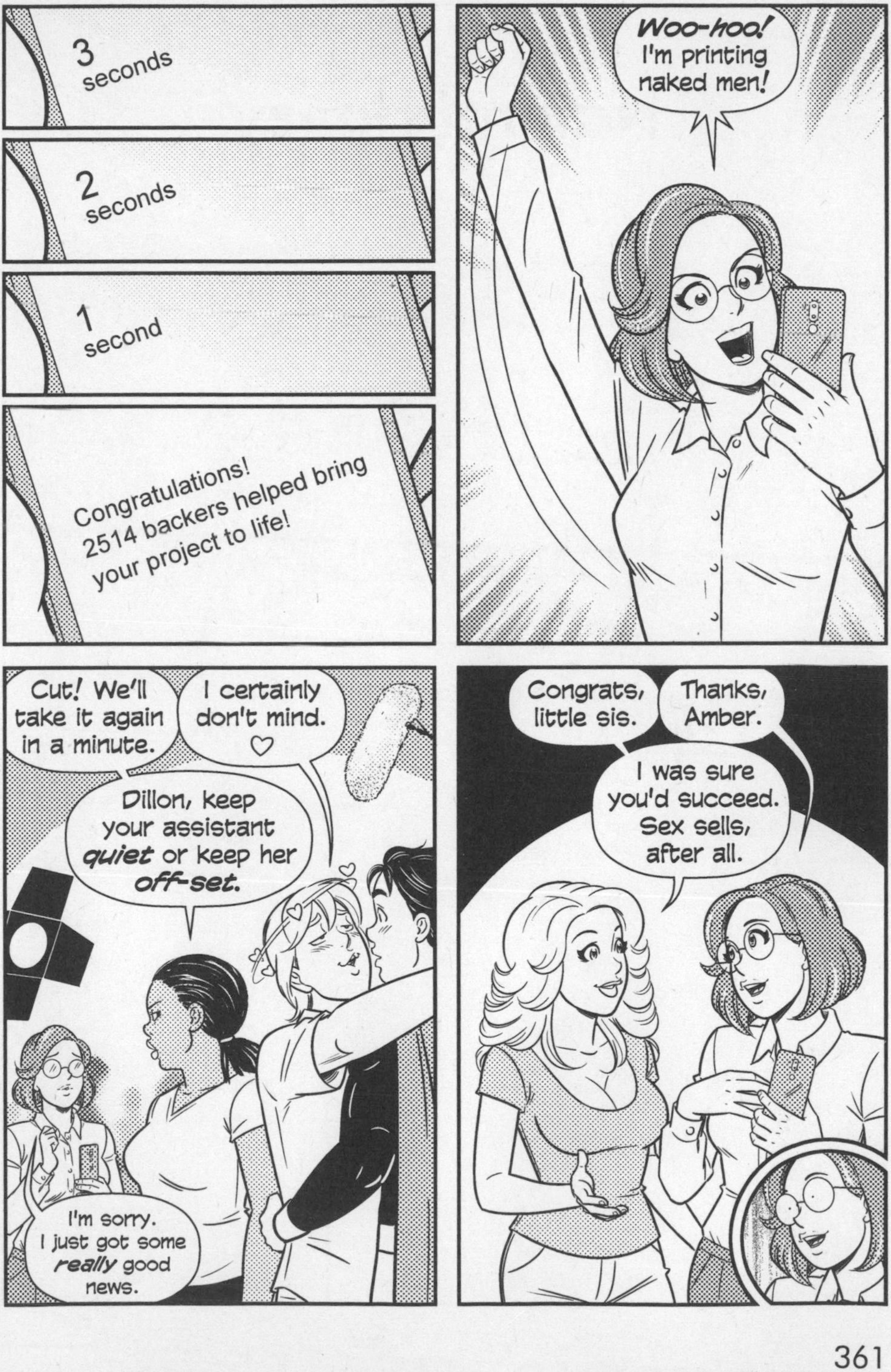
3 seconds
2 seconds
1 second
Congratulations! 2514 backers helped bring your project to life!
Woo-hoo! I'm printing naked men!
Cut! We'll take it again in a minute.
I certainly don't mind. ♡
Dillon, keep your assistant quiet or keep her off-set.
I'm sorry. I just got some really good news.
Congrats, little sis.
Thanks, Amber.
I was sure you'd succeed. Sex sells, after all.

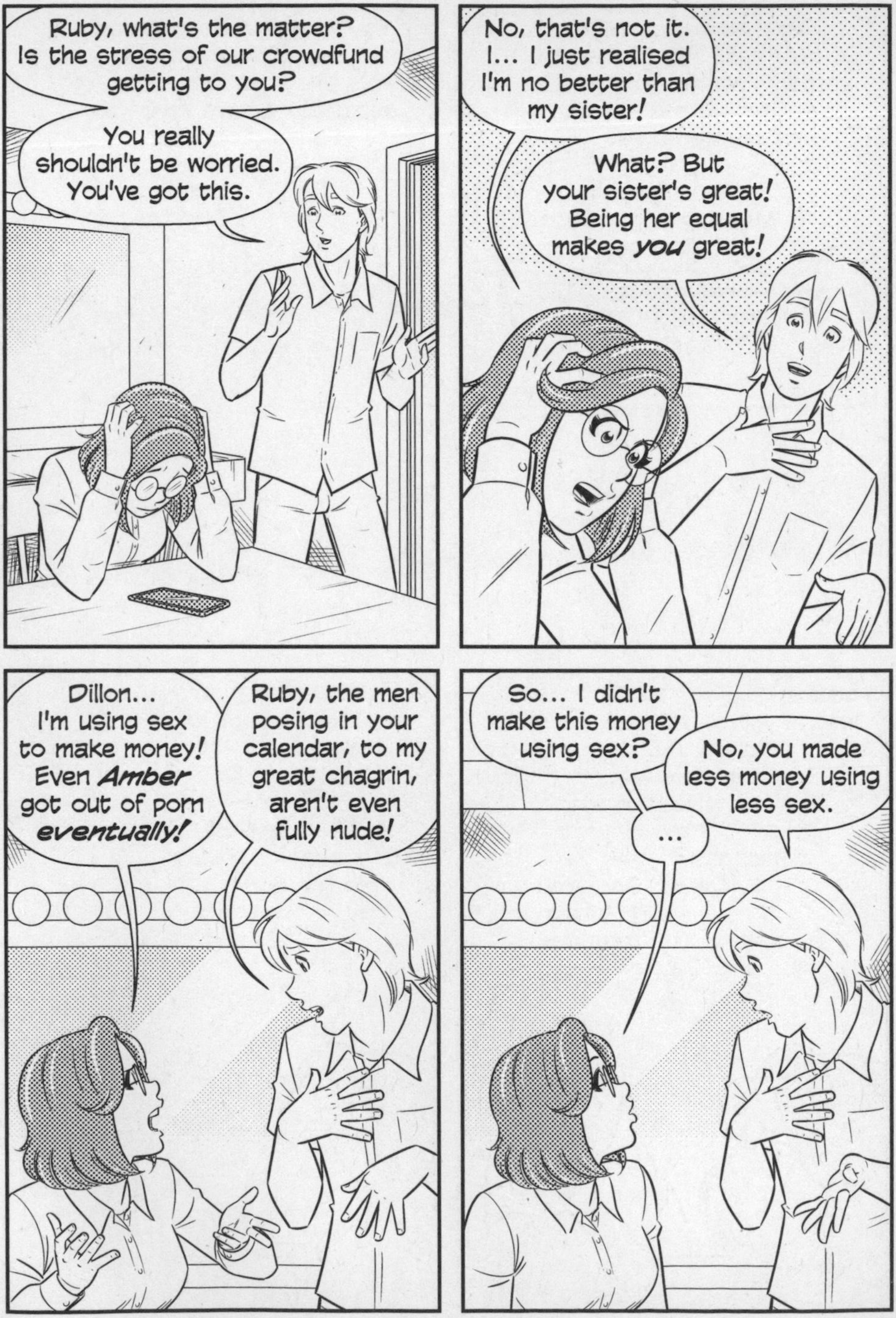
Ruby, what's the matter? Is the stress of our crowdfund getting to you?
You really shouldn't be worried. You've got this.
No, that's not it. I... I just realised I'm no better than my sister!
What? But your sister's great! Being her equal makes *you* great!
Dillon... I'm using sex to make money! Even *Amber* got out of porn *eventually!*
Ruby, the men posing in your calendar, to my great chagrin, aren't even fully nude!
So... I didn't make this money using sex?
No, you made less money using less sex.
...

Ruby, I couldn't help but overhear. If it makes you feel any better, your yaoi calendar will make a lot of people happy.

Yeah, "people." Meaning degenerates like me.

Shouldn't Andy be enough for me?

You're *not* a degenerate! You're just someone who enjoys the male form. And who especially enjoys *two* male forms. Together.

Just say it: "I like gay porn."

I like gay porn!

I meant *me*.

Not as much as me! I have a whole treasure box of gay porn secretly hidden under my bed.

"Secretly?"

Shh! You didn't hear it from me.

And I'll be away *allllll* weekend with that secret kept *allllll* to myself.

You just secretly told a bear where you hid the honey.

Allllll natural honey. ♡

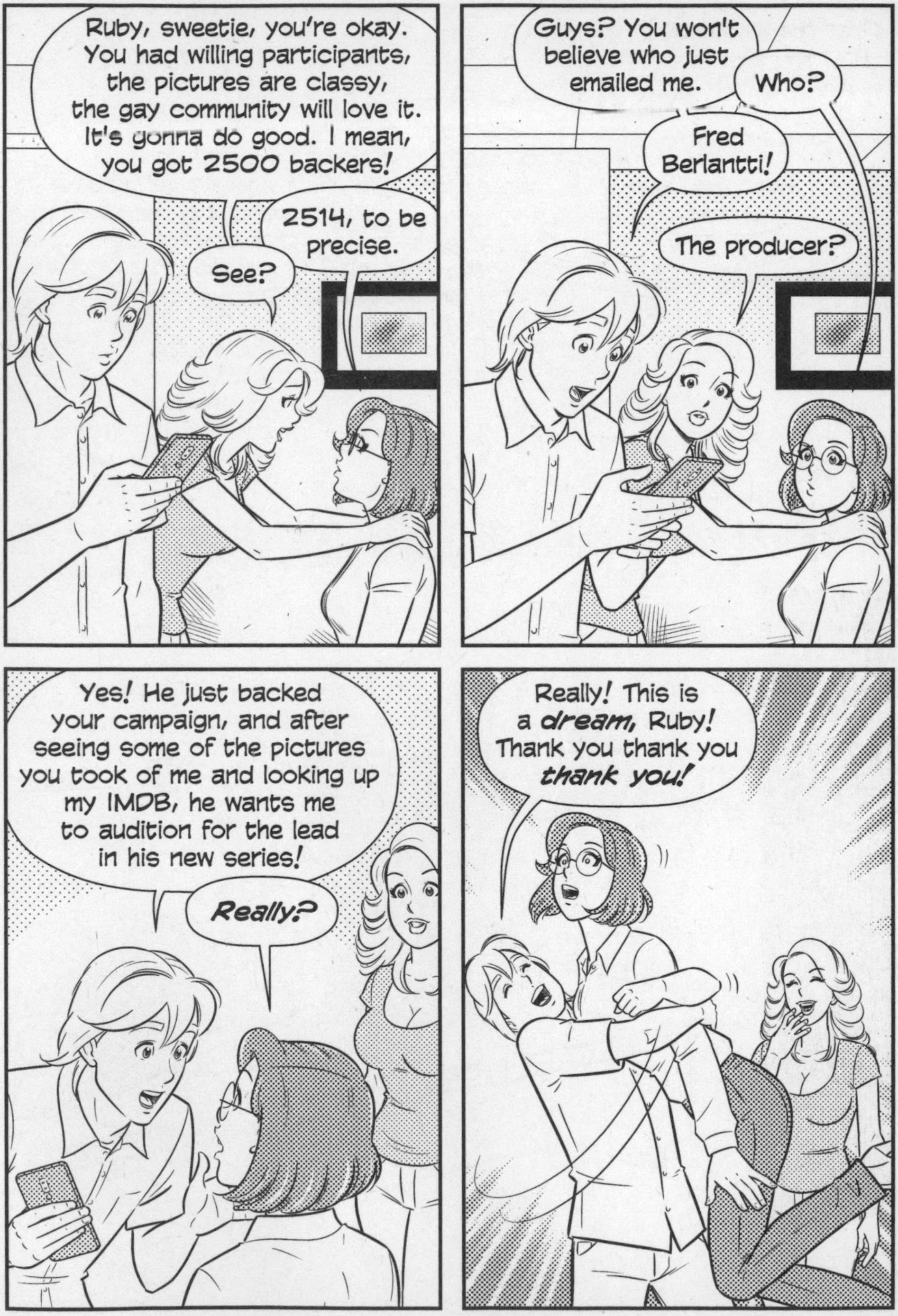
Ruby, sweetie, you're okay. You had willing participants, the pictures are classy, the gay community will love it. It's gonna do good. I mean, you got 2500 backers!
See?
2514, to be precise.
Guys? You won't believe who just emailed me.
Who?
Fred Berlantti!
The producer?
Yes! He just backed your campaign, and after seeing some of the pictures you took of me and looking up my IMDB, he wants me to audition for the lead in his new series!
Really?
Really! This is a dream, Ruby! Thank you thank you thank you!

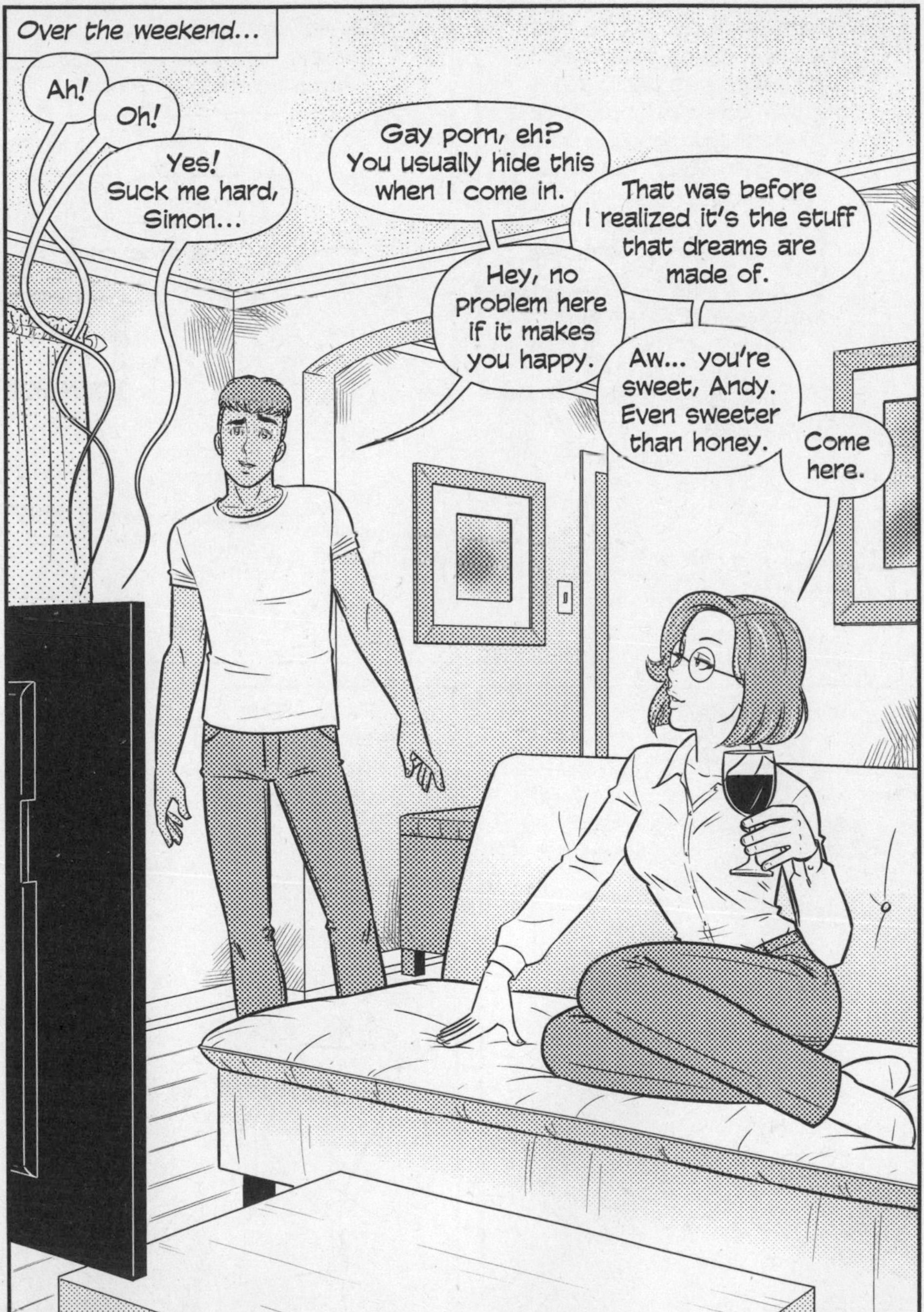
Over the weekend...
Ah!
Oh!
Yes! Suck me hard, Simon...
Gay porn, eh? You usually hide this when I come in.
That was before I realized it's the stuff that dreams are made of.
Hey, no problem here if it makes you happy.
Aw... you're sweet, Andy. Even sweeter than honey.
Come here.

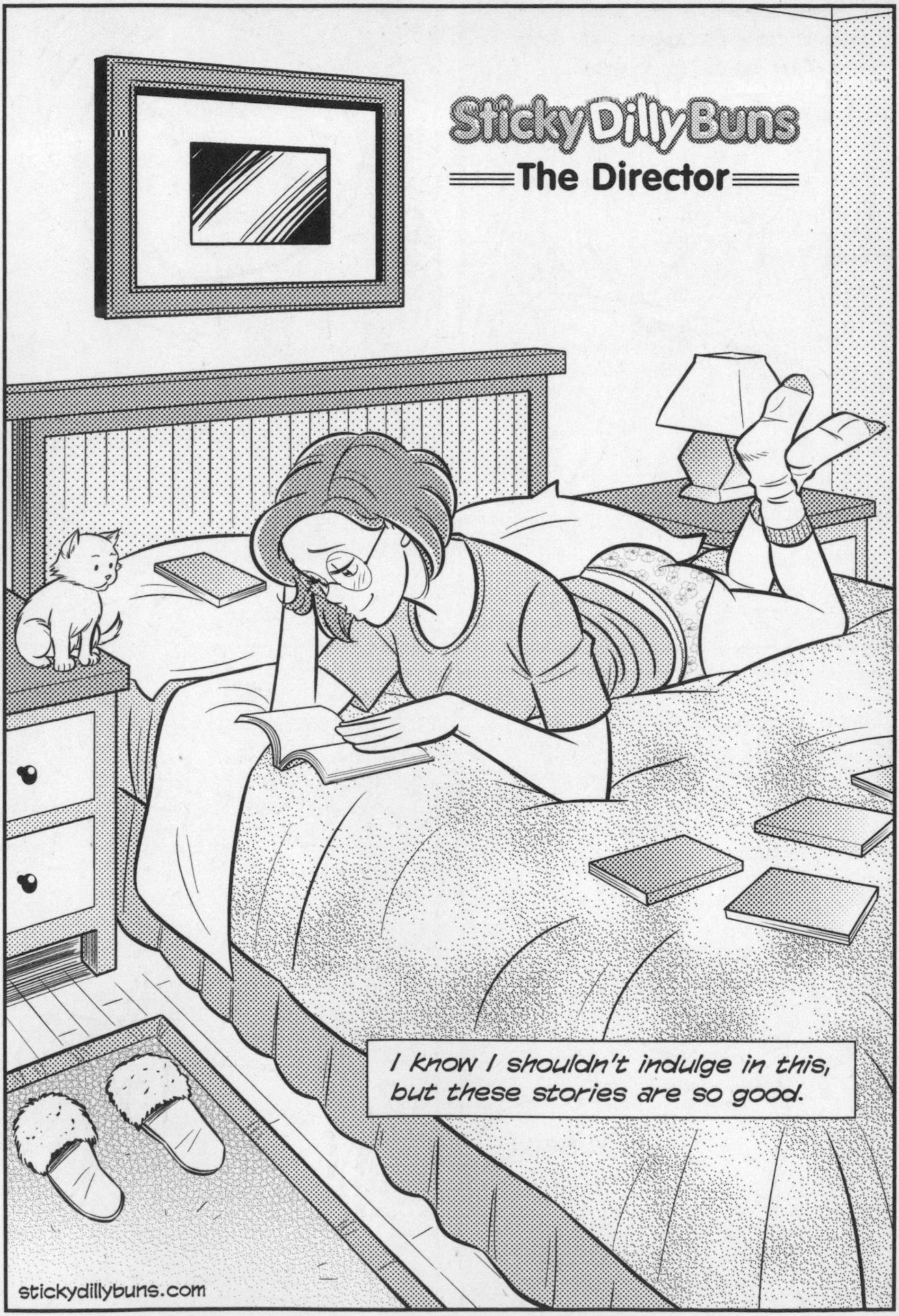
Sticky Dilly Buns
The Director
I know I shouldn't indulge in this, but these stories are so good.
stickydillybuns.com

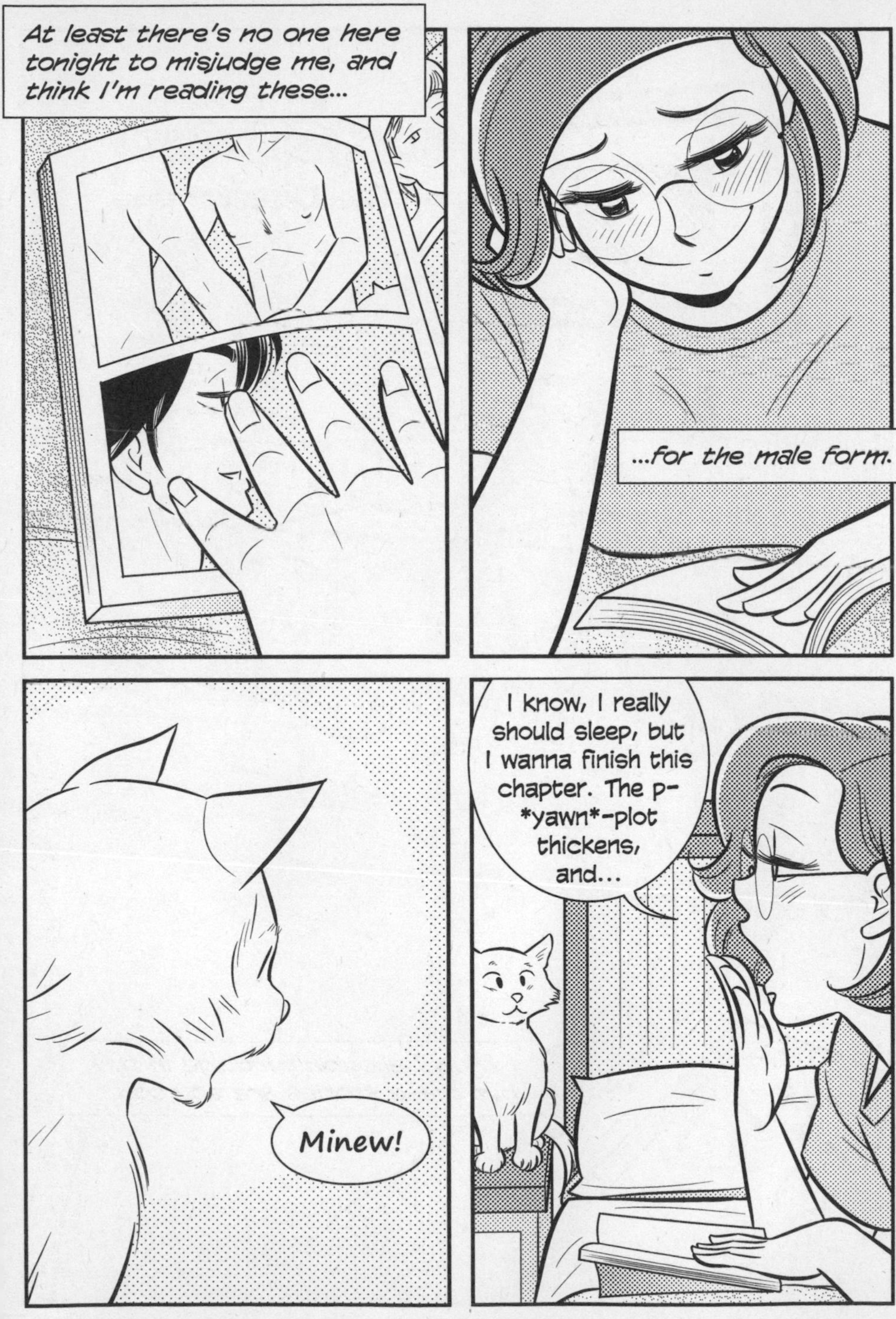
At least there's no one here tonight to misjudge me, and think I'm reading these...
...for the male form.
Minew!
I know, I really should sleep, but I wanna finish this chapter. The p-*yawn*-plot thickens, and...

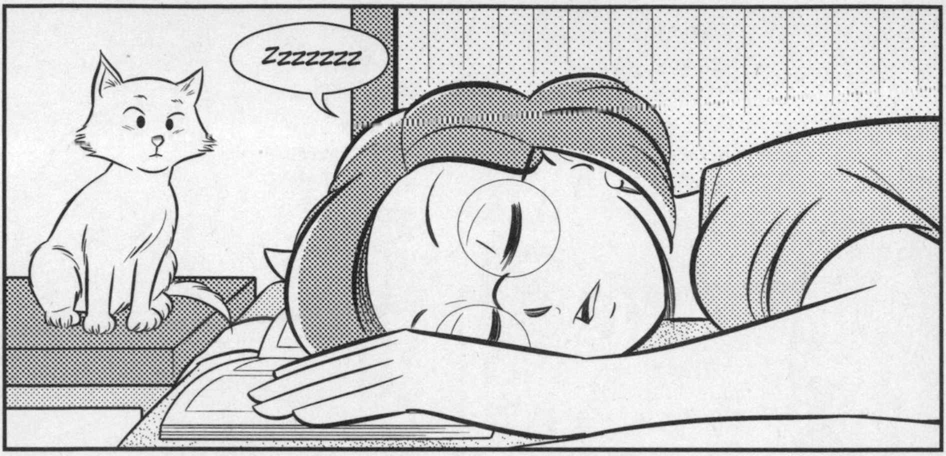
Zzzzzzz

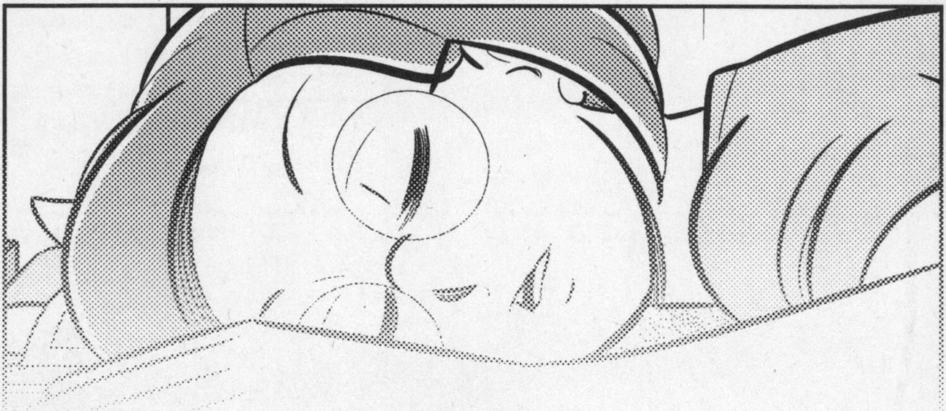

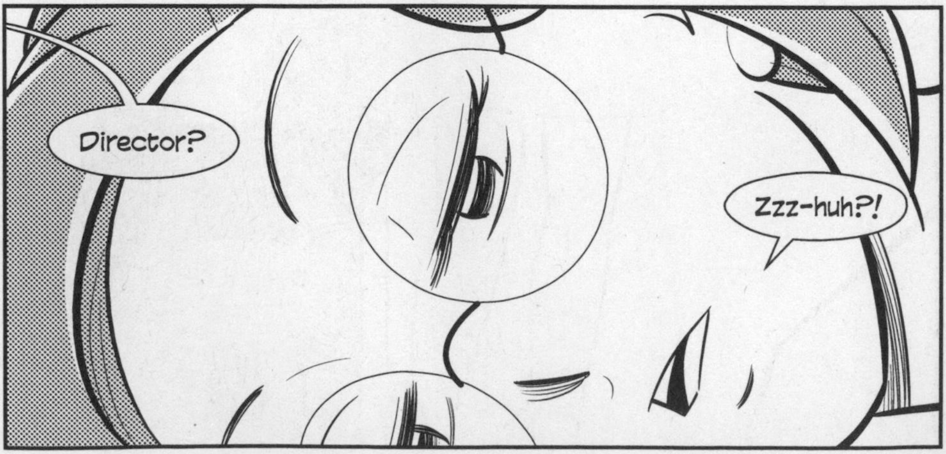
Director?
Zzz-huh?!

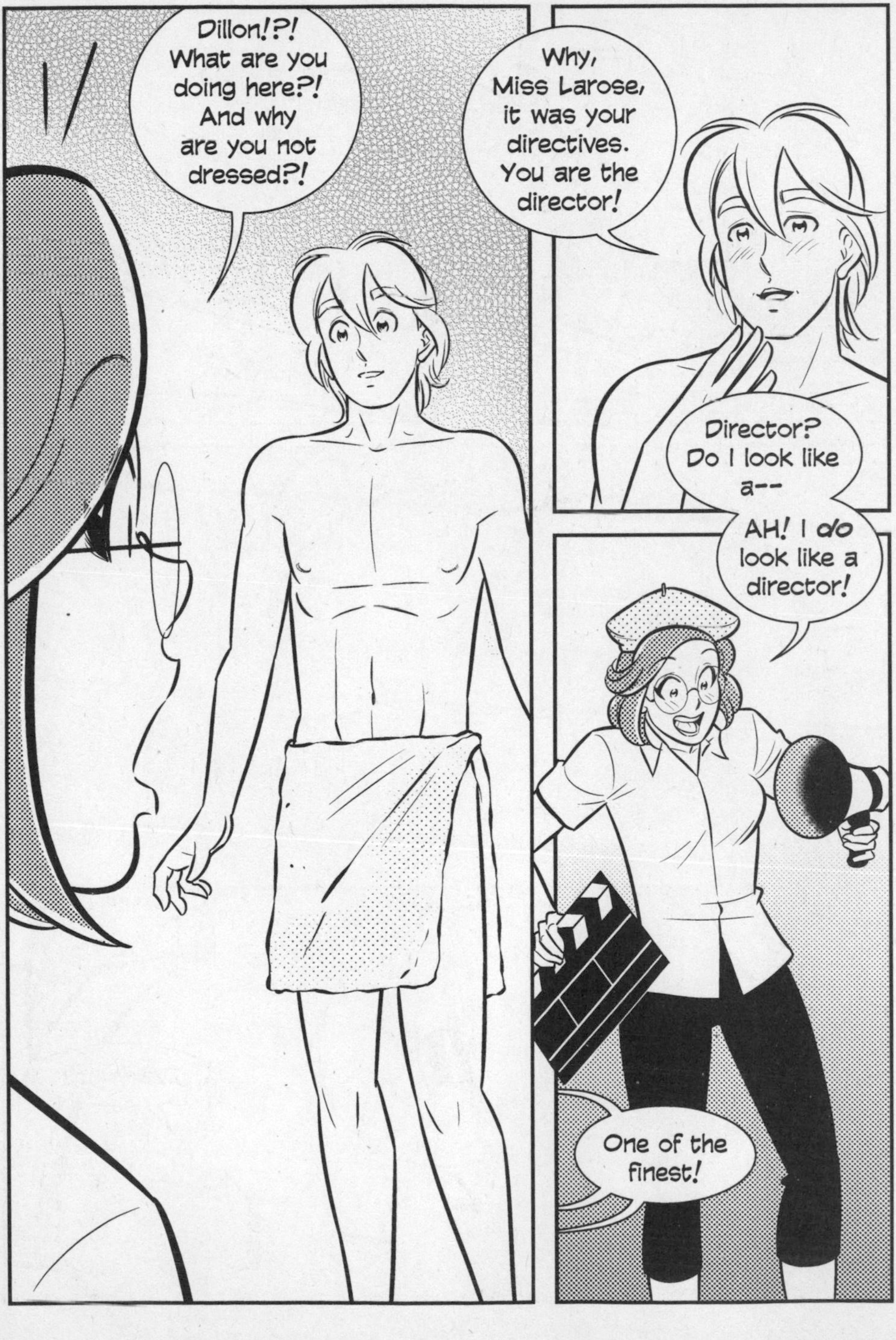

Dillon!?! What are you doing here?! And why are you not dressed?!
Why, Miss Larose, it was your directives. You are the director!
Director? Do I look like a--
AH! I *do* look like a director!
One of the finest!

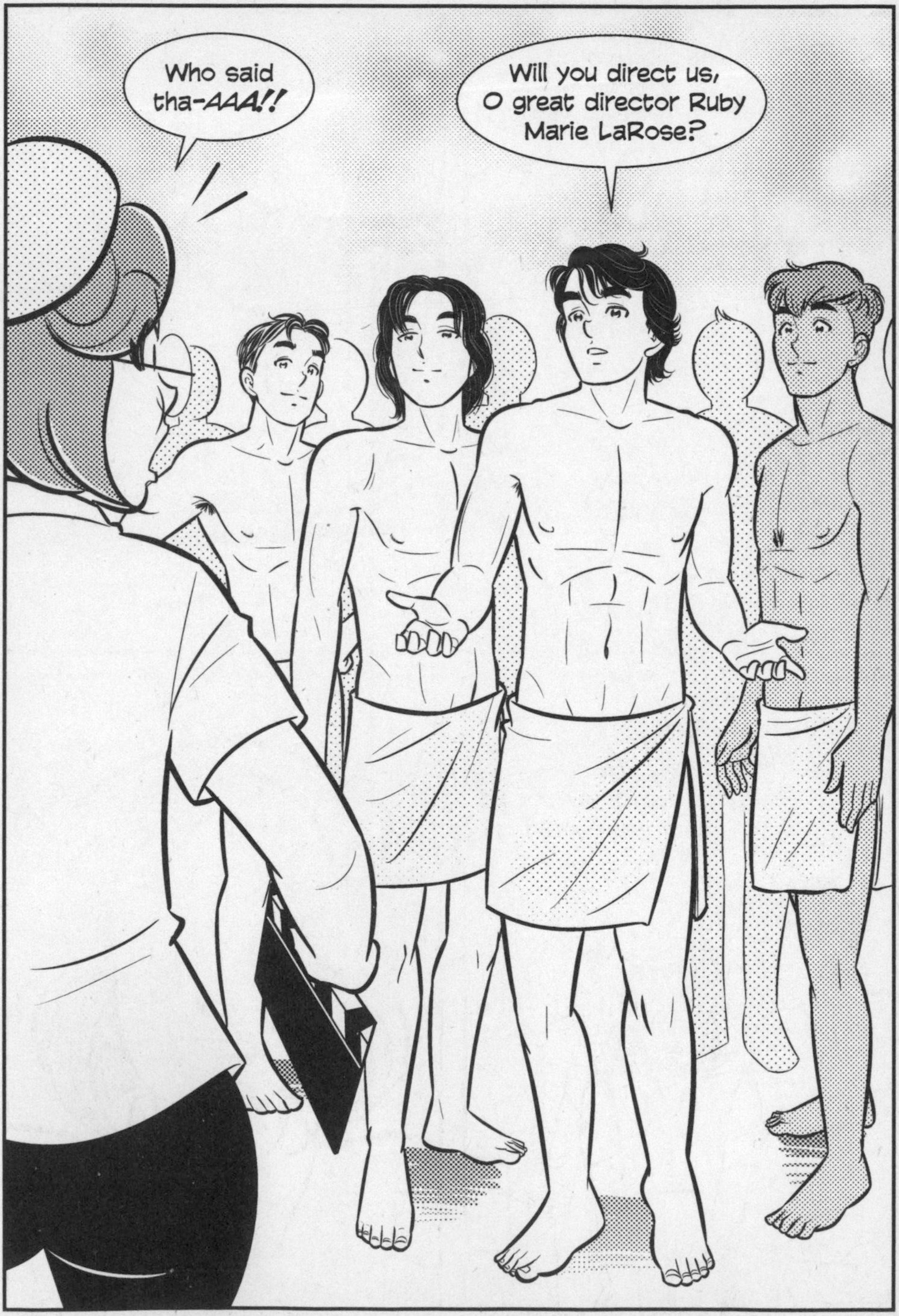
Who said tha-AAA!!
Will you direct us, O great director Ruby Marie LaRose?

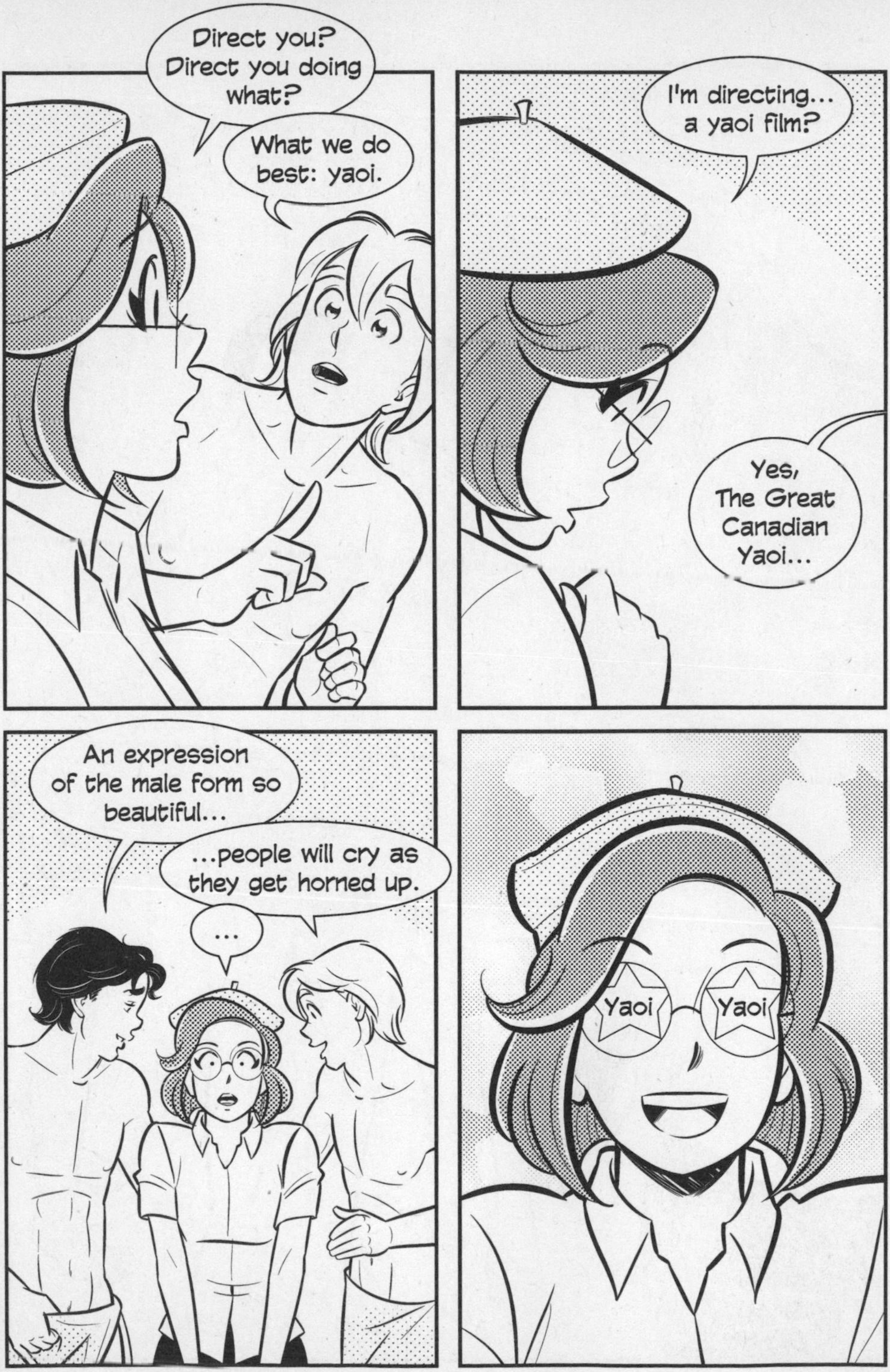
Direct you? Direct you doing what?
What we do best: yaoi.
I'm directing... a yaoi film?
Yes, The Great Canadian Yaoi...
An expression of the male form so beautiful...
...people will cry as they get horned up.
...
Yaoi
Yaoi

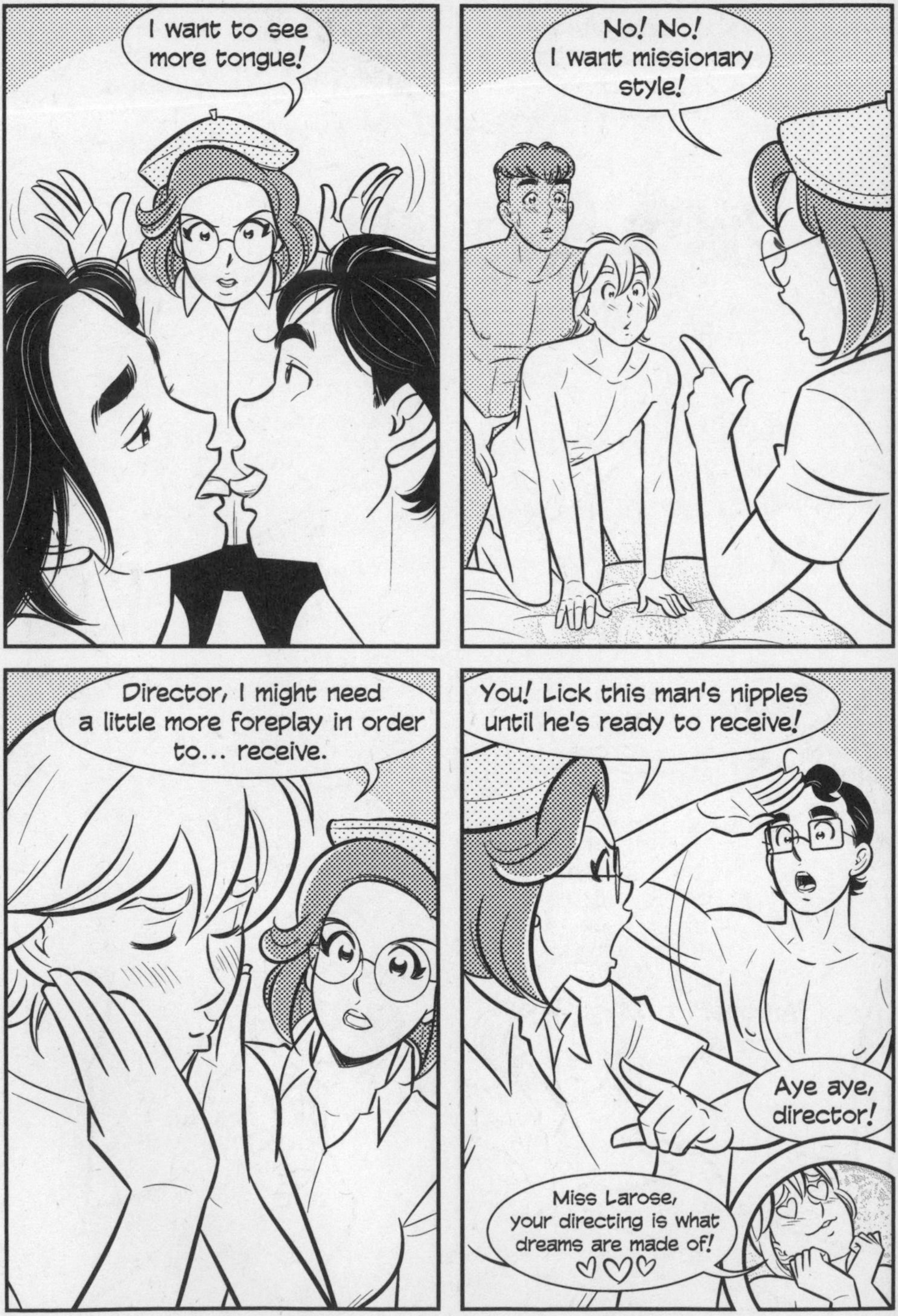
I want to see more tongue!
No! No! I want missionary style!
Director, I might need a little more foreplay in order to... receive.
You! Lick this man's nipples until he's ready to receive!
Aye aye, director!
Miss Larose, your directing is what dreams are made of! ♡♡♡

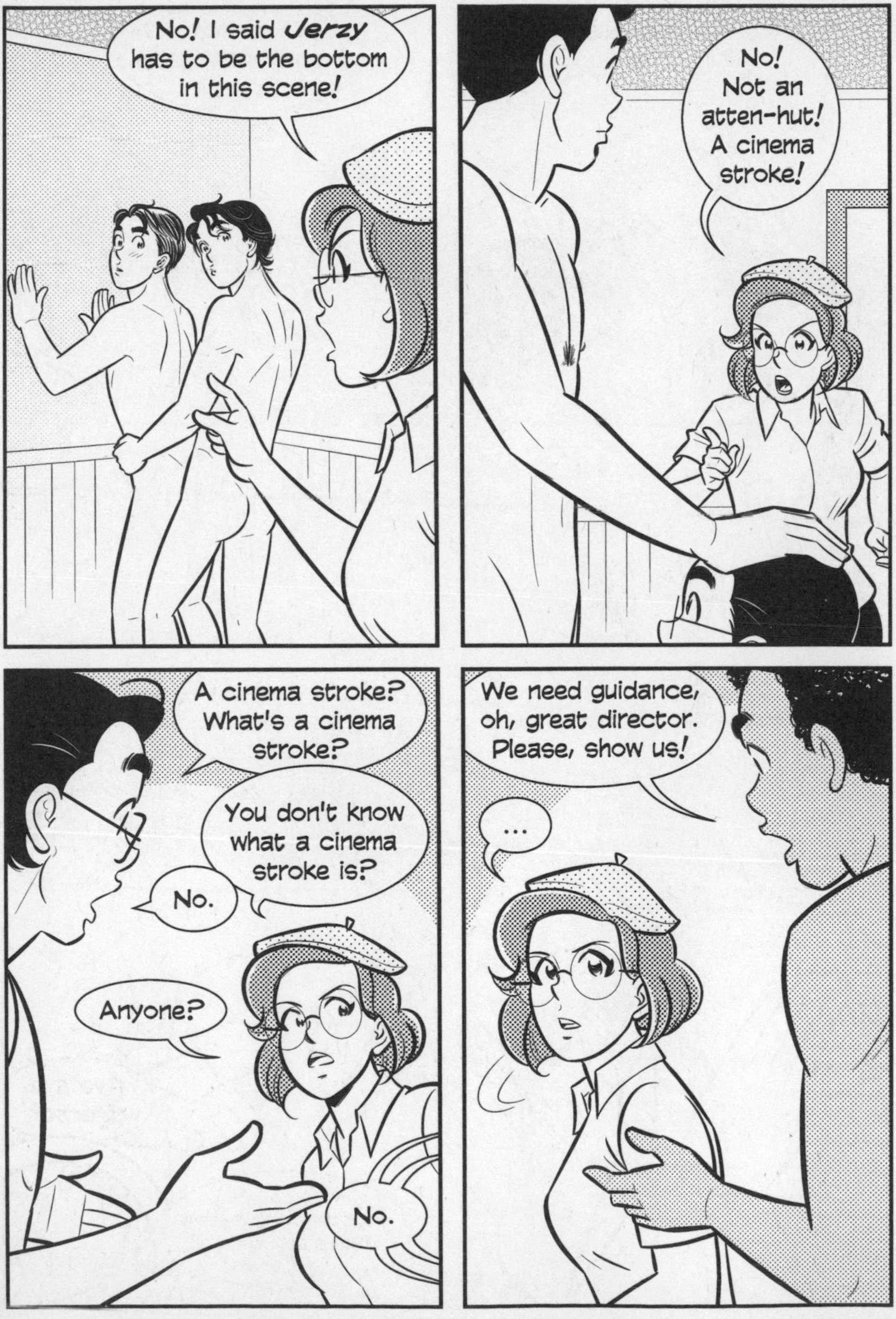
No! I said Jerzy has to be the bottom in this scene!
No! Not an atten-hut! A cinema stroke!
A cinema stroke? What's a cinema stroke?
You don't know what a cinema stroke is?
No.
Anyone?
No.
We need guidance, oh, great director. Please, show us!
...

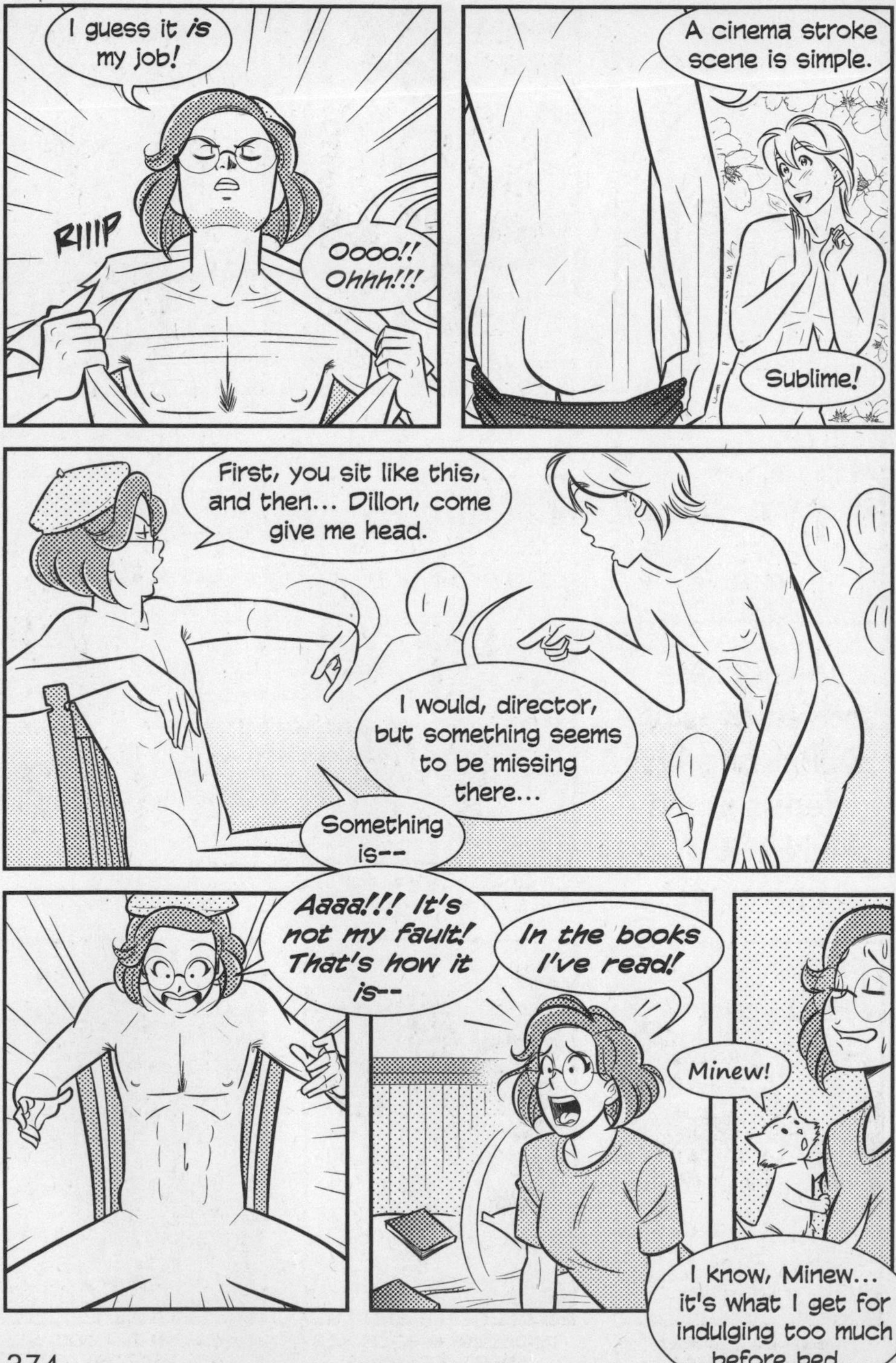
I guess it *is* my job!
RIIIP
Oooo!! Ohhh!!!
A cinema stroke scene is simple.
Sublime!
First, you sit like this, and then... Dillon, come give me head.
I would, director, but something seems to be missing there...
Something is--
Aaaa!!! It's not my fault! That's how it is--
In the books I've read!
Minew!
I know, Minew... it's what I get for indulging too much before bed.

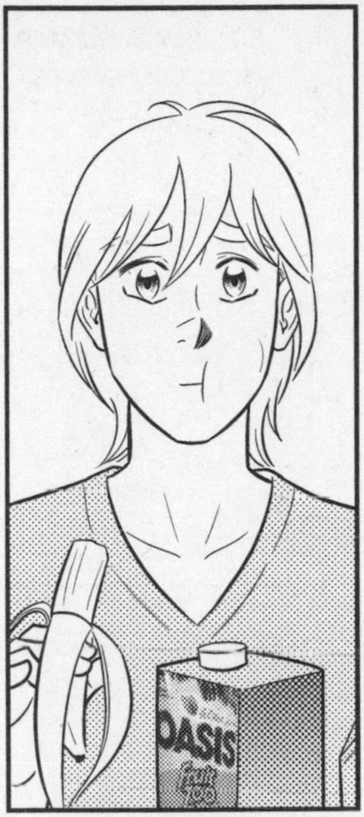
OASIS

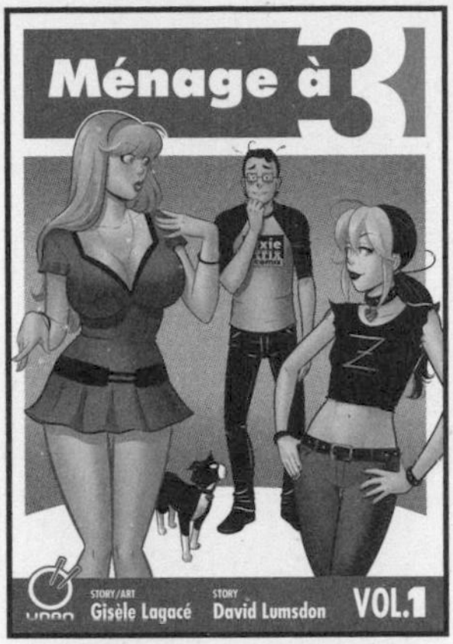
Ménage à 3
STORY/ART Gisèle Lagacé
STORY David Lumsdon
VOL.1

MÉNAGE À 3 Volume 1
ISBN: 978-1-77294-059-6

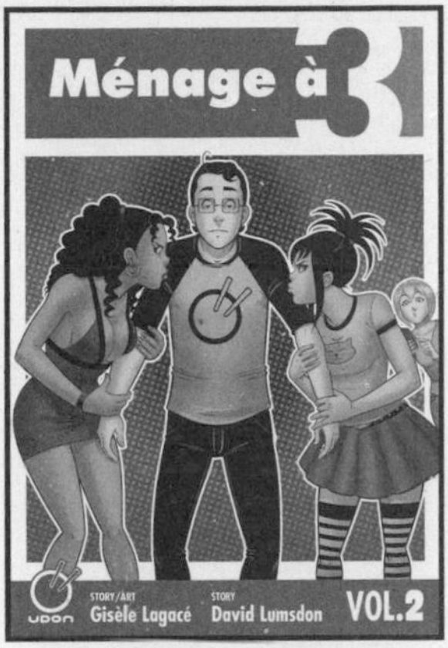
Ménage à 3
STORY/ART Gisèle Lagacé
STORY David Lumsdon
VOL.2

MÉNAGE À 3 Volume 2
ISBN: 978-1-77294-066-4

Enjoy more adventures of Dillon and his friends in the MÉNAGE À 3 universe!

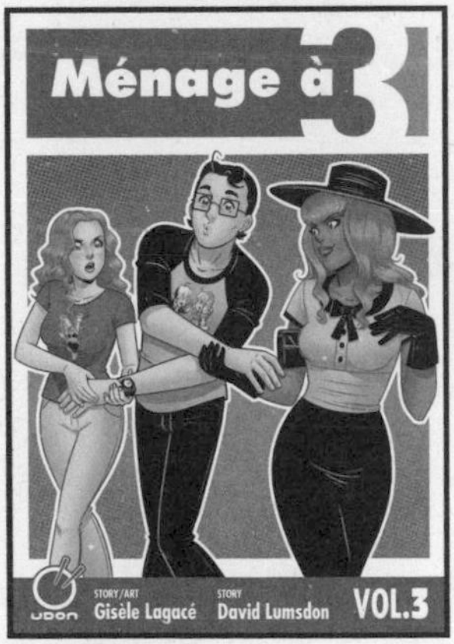
Ménage à 3
STORY/ART Gisèle Lagacé
STORY David Lumsdon
VOL.3

MÉNAGE À 3 Volume 3
ISBN: 978-1-77294-090-9

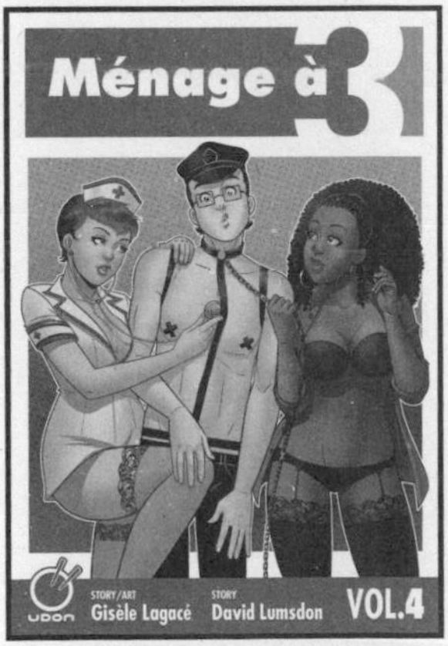
Ménage à 3
STORY/ART Gisèle Lagacé
STORY David Lumsdon
VOL.4

MÉNAGE À 3 Volume 4
ISBN: 978-1-77294-106-7

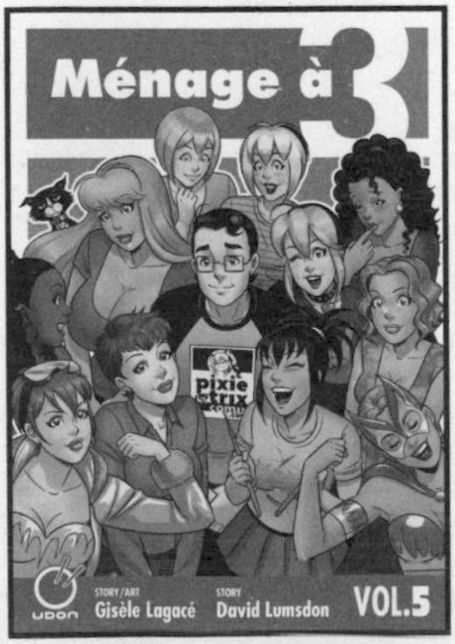
Ménage à 3
STORY/ART Gisèle Lagacé
STORY David Lumsdon
VOL.5

MÉNAGE À 3 Volume 5
ISBN: 978-1-77294-123-4

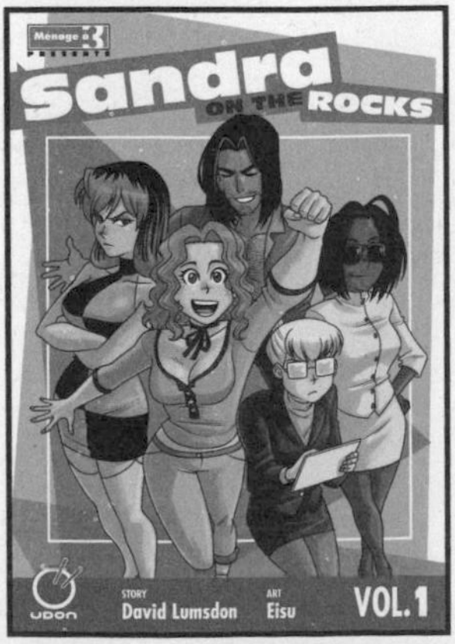
Ménage à 3
Sandra ON THE ROCKS
STORY David Lumsdon
ART Eisu
VOL.1

SANDRA ON THE ROCKS Vol.1
ISBN: 978-1-77294-113-5

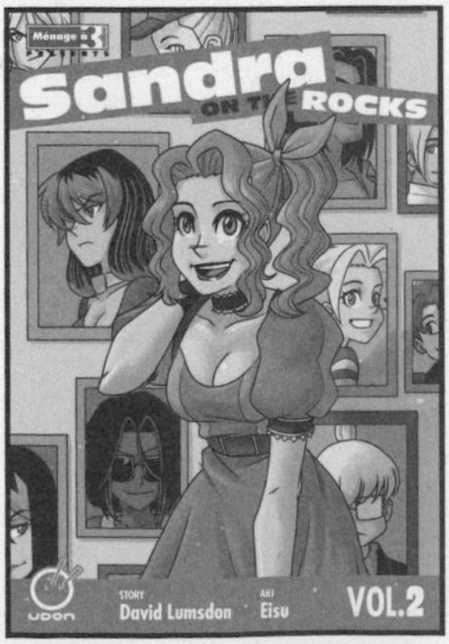
Ménage à 3
Sandra ON THE ROCKS
STORY David Lumsdon
ART Eisu
VOL.2

SANDRA ON THE ROCKS Vol.2
ISBN: 978-1-77294-124-1

VOLUME 1
OMNIBUS

Story/Pencils/Letters: GISÈLE LAGACÉ
Inks: M. VICTORIA ROBADO (SHOURI), GISÈLE LAGACÉ
CASSANDRA WEDEKING, SAIFUL REMY "EISU" MOKHTAR
Chapter Break Illustrations: CH.1-4 M. VICTORIA ROBADO (SHOURI)
CH.5-13 GISÈLE LAGACÉ
Series Editor: T CAMPBELL
Front/Back Cover Colors: PETE PANTAZIS

UDON STAFF
Chief of Operations: ERIK KO
Director of Publishing: MATT MOYLAN
VP of Business Development: CORY CASONI
Director of Marketing: MEGAN MAIDEN
Japanese Liaisons: STEVEN CUMMINGS
ANNA KAWASHIMA

STICKY DILLY BUNS: VOLUME 1 OMNIBUS

Created by Gisèle Lagacé
All content © Gisèle Lagacé

Published by UDON Entertainment Inc.
118 Tower Hill Road, C1, PO Box 20008
Richmond Hill, Ontario, L4K 0K0 CANADA

www.UDONentertainment.com

First Printing: January 2020
ISBN-13: 978-1772941210
ISBN-10: 1772941212

Printed in Canada